Lecture Notes in Computer Science 16458

The series Lecture Notes in Computer Science (LNCS), including its subseries Lecture Notes in Artificial Intelligence (LNAI) and Lecture Notes in Bioinformatics (LNBI), has established itself as a medium for the publication of new developments in computer science and information technology research, teaching, and education.

LNCS enjoys close cooperation with the computer science R & D community, the series counts many renowned academics among its volume editors and paper authors, and collaborates with prestigious societies. Its mission is to serve this international community by providing an invaluable service, mainly focused on the publication of conference and workshop proceedings and postproceedings. LNCS commenced publication in 1973.

Amir Goharshady · Christoph Haase
Editors

Dependable Software Engineering

Theories, Tools, and Applications

11th International Symposium on Dependable Software Engineering: Theories, Tools, and Applications, SETTA 2025
Oxford, UK, December 1–3, 2025
Proceedings

Editors
Amir Goharshady
University of Oxford
Oxford, UK

Christoph Haase
University of Oxford
Oxford, UK

ISSN 0302-9743 ISSN 1611-3349 (electronic)
Lecture Notes in Computer Science
ISBN 978-981-95-7825-2 ISBN 978-981-95-7826-9 (eBook)
https://doi.org/10.1007/978-981-95-7826-9

This Springer imprint is published by the registered company Springer Nature Singapore Pte Ltd.
The registered company address is: 152 Beach Road, #21-01/04 Gateway East, Singapore 189721, Singapore

Preface

This volume contains the peer-reviewed Proceedings of the 11th International Symposium on Dependable Software Engineering: Theories, Tools and Applications (SETTA 2025), which was held at St Catherine's College, University of Oxford, on December 1–3, 2025.

SETTA is a well-established international symposium in Formal Methods, Program Verification and Software Engineering. It traces its roots back to China. Previous editions of SETTA took place in Nanjing (2015, 2023), Beijing (2016, 2018, 2021, 2022), Changsha (2017), Shanghai (2019), Guangzhou (2020), and Hong Kong (2024). In 2025, SETTA was organized outside of China for the first time. The primary goal of the SETTA symposium series is to bring international researchers together to exchange research results and ideas on bridging the gap between formal methods and software engineering.

SETTA 2025 was highly international. We received 46 submissions from authors in 71 different institutions in 14 countries. All submissions went through a rigorous double-blind peer-review process by an international panel of experts on the program committee, as well as external reviewers. Each article was reviewed by three to five referees. This was followed by an online discussion among the reviewers, overseen by the PC chairs. In the end, consensus was reached to accept 18 high-quality papers with novel contributions for presentation at SETTA 2025 and inclusion in the present volume.

The symposium also featured well-received invited talks by three distinguished researchers in our field:

- Cristina David, University of Bristol
- Tobias Grosser, University of Cambridge
- David Parker, University of Oxford

We are grateful to the invited speakers for their support and contribution to SETTA.

We thank Springer for sponsoring the SETTA 2025 *Best Paper Award*. Based on the nominations and votes cast by the program committee, the following article was chosen for this award:

"Synchronous System Design with Quantitative Types" by Rui Chen and Ingo Sander, School of EECS, KTH Royal Institute of Technology, Sweden

Additionally, the following PC members were selected for the *Distinguished Reviewer Award*, also based on votes cast by other PC members:

- Alessio Mansutti
- Christian Schilling
- Liqian Chen
- R Govind

We extend our sincere thanks to the program committee members and external reviewers for their invaluable voluntary efforts in providing thorough, high-quality reviews, which allowed us to select the strongest submissions for inclusion in SETTA 2025. Above all, SETTA is made possible by the excellent research contributions of its authors, and we appreciate their choice to publish their work in this symposium. We hope you find their results enjoyable and inspiring to read.

St Catherine's College, University of Oxford

December 2025

Amir Goharshady
Christoph Haase

Organization

Technical Program Committee Chairs

Amir Goharshady	University of Oxford, UK
Christoph Haase	University of Oxford, UK

General Chair

Naijun Zhan	Peking University, China

Publicity Chairs

Jie An	Institute of Software Chinese Academy of Sciences, China
Jonathan Bowen	Museophile/London South Bank University, UK

Local Organization Team

Jonathan Bowen	Museophile/London South Bank University, UK
Xuran Cai	University of Oxford, UK/Max Planck Institute for Software Systems, Germany
Amir Goharshady	University of Oxford, UK
Christoph Haase	University of Oxford, UK

Technical Program Committee

S Akshay	Indian Institute of Technology Bombay, India
Guy Amir	Cornell University, USA
Jie An	Institute of Software Chinese Academy of Sciences, China
Luca Arnaboldi	University of Birmingham, UK
Martin Berger	University of Sussex, UK
Dariusz Biernacki	University of Wrocław, Poland
Michael Blondin	Université de Sherbrooke, Canada

Benedikt Bollig	ENS Paris-Saclay/CNRS, France
Timothy Bourke	Inria/ENS, France
Qinxiang Cao	Shanghai Jiao Tong University, China
Supratik Chakraborty	Indian Institute of Technology Bombay, India
Liqian Chen	National University of Defense Technology, China
Guillaume Dupont	Institut de Recherche en Informatique de Toulouse, France
Pascal Fontaine	Université de Liège, Belgium
Hongfei Fu	Shanghai Jiao Tong University, China
Luca Geatti	University of Udine, Italy
Mirco Giacobbe	University of Birmingham, UK
R Govind	Uppsala University, Sweden
Ashutosh Gupta	Indian Institute of Technology Bombay, India
Hossein Hojjat	Tehran Institute for Advanced Studies, Iran
Lukáš Holík	Brno University of Technology, Czechia
Minghao Liu	University of Oxford, UK
Andreas Lööw	Imperial College London, UK
Kaushik Mallik	IMDEA Software Institute, Spain
Alessio Mansutti	IMDEA Software Institute, Spain
Umang Mathur	National University of Singapore, Singapore
Harshit Motwani	Max Planck Institute for Software Systems, Germany
Muhammad Syifa'ul Mufid	Institut Teknologi Sepuluh Nopember, Indonesia
Amy Nejati	Newcastle University, UK
Andreas Pavlogiannis	Aarhus University, Denmark
Guillermo Perez	University of Antwerp, Belgium
Basile Pesin	École nationale de l'aviation civile, France
Rajarshi Roy	University of Oxford, UK
Andrew Ryzhikov	University of Warsaw, Poland
Christian Schilling	Aalborg University, Denmark
Taro Sekiyama	National Institute of Informatics, Japan
Mikhail Starchak	St Petersburg University, Russia
Chenglin Wang	Hong Kong University of Science and Technology, China
Guannan Wei	INRIA / ENS, France
Georg Weissenbacher	TU Wien, Austria
Nisansala Yatapanage	Australian National University, Australia
Bohua Zhan	Institute of Software Chinese Academy of Sciences, China
Đorđe Žikelić	Singapore Management University, Singapore

External Reviewers

Mikael Bisgaard Dahlsen-Jensen	Aarhus University, Denmark
Soroush Farokhnia	Hong Kong University of Science and Technology, China
Shenghua Feng	Institute of Software Chinese Academy of Sciences, China
Ehsan Goharshady	Institute of Science and Technology Austria, Austria
S Hitarth	Hong Kong University of Science and Technology, China
Harshal Kaushik	University of Texas at Dallas, USA
Sergei Novozhilov	Hong Kong University of Science and Technology, China
Radoslaw Piórkowski	University of Oxford, UK
Tian Shu	Hong Kong University of Science and Technology, China
Han Su	Institute of Software Chinese Academy of Sciences, China
Zeyu Sun	Institute of Software Chinese Academy of Sciences, China

Steering Committee

Zhenhua Duan	Xidian University, China
Martin Fränzle	University of Oldenburg, Germany
Kim Larsen	Aalborg University, Denmark
Xuandong Li	Nanjing University, China
Zhiming Liu	Southwest University, China
Sriram Rajamani	Microsoft Research, USA
Ji Wang	National University of Defense Technology, China
Kwangkeun Yi	Seoul National University, South Korea
Naijun Zhan	Peking University, China

Advisory Board

Zhou Chaochen	Institute of Software Chinese Academy of Sciences, China
He Jifeng	East China Normal University, China

Contents

Automata

Monitoring

Formal Verification

Neural Networks and Large Language Models

Invited Contribution

Automated Translation of Real-World Codebases: How Far Are We?

Cristina David[1](✉), Hanliang Zhang[1,2], and Meng Wang[1]

[1] University of Bristol, Bristol, UK
cristina.david@bristol.ac.uk
[2] Amazon, Seattle, WA, USA

Abstract. Automated translation of legacy software into modern languages is essential for adopting safer programming practices at scale. We review current rule-based, neural and neurosymbolic approaches and show why none fully address the needs of real-world repositories. Rule-based tools scale but mirror the source language, producing unidiomatic target code. LLM-based methods capture idioms but lack correctness guarantees. Hybrid systems partially bridge the gap but remain brittle when faced with complex features such as concurrency or third-party dependencies.

Keywords: Code translation · Large Language Models · Rust

1 Introduction

Software is at the heart of modern life, from banking systems and medical devices to critical infrastructure. Yet ensuring software reliability remains a major challenge, especially as systems grow in size and complexity. A long-standing and pervasive source of reliability issues is memory-safety bugs. Languages such as C and C++, which permit unchecked pointer manipulation, have been responsible for such bugs for decades, with reports from Microsoft and Google revealing that approximately 70% of their security vulnerabilities are rooted in memory errors [7,25].

Traditional approaches—manual code review, testing and formal verification tools—help identify bugs but struggle to keep pace with the size and evolution of modern software systems. As a result, the software engineering community is increasingly embracing modern, safety-focused programming languages that proactively prevent many classes of vulnerabilities from arising in the first place. For instance, languages like Java, Go, C# and Kotlin ensure memory safety through garbage collection, balancing safety with performance. Newer languages such as Swift and Rust take a different approach, using ownership

This work was done prior to joining Amazon.

A. Goharshady and C. Haase (Eds.): SETTA 2025, LNCS 16458, pp. 3–10, 2026.
https://doi.org/10.1007/978-981-95-7826-9_1

models and compile-time checks to achieve memory safety without incurring a runtime overhead.

While adopting modern languages for new development is relatively straightforward, modernising the enormous legacy codebases written in older, unsafe languages remains the major barrier to practical migration. Translation in today's industrial settings is still predominantly manual, requiring deep domain knowledge, considerable engineering resources, and months, if not years, of sustained effort [24,30]. This paper examines whether automated code translation can realistically meet the demands of real-world repositories.

Trade-off Between Scalability, Correctness and Idiomaticity. While automated code translation has received sustained attention across a wide range of language pairs, substantial challenges remain—particularly when the goal is to produce idiomatic, readable and scalable translations suitable for integration into real-world repositories. Traditional rule-based systems offer stability and semantic rigor, but their translations tend to closely mirror the structure and idioms of the source language, yielding code that is syntactically correct yet hard to understand, modify or extend in the target ecosystem. At the other extreme, data-driven or LLM-based approaches can generate high-quality, human-like translations that capture idioms, conventions and design patterns, but lack formal guarantees of semantic preservation and struggle to scale to large, real-world, projects. Consequently, *current techniques are effectively constrained by a three-way trade-off between idiomaticity, scalability and correctness*: improvements along one axis often degrade performance along the others, and different approaches choose different compromises. Breaking this trade-off and achieving translations that are both high quality and applicable to large, evolving software systems remains a core challenge for automated code translation research.

The remainder of this paper examines different translation directions and outlines the unresolved research problems that must be addressed. For concreteness, we focus our discussion on tools that translate other languages into Rust—a language whose growing industrial adoption is driven by its strong guarantees of memory safety and high performance. In recent years, Rust has emerged as a popular target for automated code translation, making it a particularly relevant setting for understanding the strengths and limitations of current approaches.

2 Rule-Based Code Translation

Automated code translation has been a topic of extensive research for decades [6, 20]. In programming languages research, this process is often referred to as "transpilation". Unlike traditional compilers, which convert code from a high-level programming language to a lower-level one, transpilers bridge programming languages that operate at a similar level of abstraction. Throughout this paper, we use the term "translation" to refer to this form of transpilation.

Traditionally, code translation techniques were *rule-based*, which work by applying handcrafted rewrite rules to the source code or some representation of it such as the Abstract Syntax Tree in order to transform elements of the source language into the target language [5,13,22,29]. One advantage of this approach is its predictability and stability, as identical inputs always yield the same results, as well as the strong correctness guarantees when the rules are rigorously defined and verified. The most significant drawback of rule-based translation is that it generally produces code that is unreadable and unidiomatic, making it challenging to maintain [11,24]. This approach often mirrors the structure of the original code too closely, failing to fully leverage the features and idiomatic patterns of the target language.

While rule-based techniques can effectively scale to entire projects—with notable examples targeting C to Rust [2,9,38], C to Go [1], and Java to C# [3]—developing these rules is a highly labor-intensive process and may fall short of being exhaustive. The sheer number of translation rules required to handle all cases across all involved codebases, including libraries, makes comprehensive coverage a significant challenge [31]. Moreover, rule-based translation systems typically operate with a local view of the code: individual rewrite rules are triggered by syntactic patterns or local AST fragments. However, high-quality translations often require global semantic information—how data flows through the program, how pointers relate, or how abstractions are used across modules. Without such context, these systems tend to replicate low-level constructs from the source language rather than recovering appropriate abstractions in the target language.

A prime example of a rule-based translator is C2Rust [2], an industrial-strength tool that rewrites C programs into Rust syntax while preserving semantics. Because its translation rules operate locally and do not synthesise an ownership model, C pointers are mapped directly to raw Rust pointers. This in turn produces large regions of code that must be marked with unsafe, , signalling that the compiler cannot enforce Rust's safety guarantees and shifting the burden of correctness back onto the programmer. Although the resulting Rust compiles, it preserves C's pointer-centric design rather than Rust's ownership-oriented patterns. The generated code is therefore harder to read, reason about and maintain, and fails to leverage Rust's idiomatic abstractions such as Box, Option, borrowing or pattern matching—ultimately undermining many of the benefits motivating migration to Rust in the first place.

Subsequent work attempts to post-process such translations to recover safer idioms. Laertes [10] explores the space of candidate rewrites, guided by Rust compiler error messages, in order to eliminate unnecessary unsafe blocks. While effective in targeted cases, its search remains brittle and leaves many unsafe constructs unresolved. CROWN [38] addresses this limitation by placing ownership at the core of the translation process. Starting from the C2Rust output, it performs static analyses over Rust MIR to infer a pointer ownership model compatible with Rust's semantics, and then rewrites pointers using safe abstractions (Box<T>, &mut T, etc.). This ownership-guided pipeline enables the translation of real-world C codebases (up to hundreds of thousands of lines of code) into significantly safer and more idiomatic Rust. However, CROWN still struggles when encountering patterns not covered by its predefined rewrite rules, often producing code that still fails to provide meaningful safety improvements over the original C.

Beyond these approaches that target unsafe pointers, Hong and Ryu examine other specific pain points in the C2Rust translation and redesign them using Rust-appropriate abstractions. They propose automated rewrites for C lock APIs [15], translation of tagged unions [18], and the elimination of output-parameter patterns in favour of algebraic data types [17]. These studies highlight the benefits of domain-specific refactorings, but each targets a narrow class of features, leaving many others untreated. As a result, the overall translation still diverges significantly from what an expert Rust developer would naturally write.

3 Neural-Based Code Translation

Neural-based code translation offers substantial advantages over rule-based methods in terms of idiomaticity. Neural models can produce code that better reflects human-written idioms and, unlike handcrafted rewrite systems, are typically not bound to a single language pair [11,27]. A seminal line of work by Rozière et al. demonstrated that unsupervised neural models can translate functions across C++, Java, and Python without paired training data [30,31], showing that neural representations capture cross-language structure and patterns often invisible to purely syntactic rewriting.

However, these early approaches were largely evaluated on small, self-contained snippets—typically from GeeksforGeeks [14], competitive programming datasets [23,28], or educational corpora [4,34]. Such settings privilege short, isolated problems and fail to reflect the architectural dependencies, implicit invariants and cross-module interactions characteristic of real software systems. Although subsequent works introduce improved training objectives, prompt strategies or post-generation repair [21,33,36], they largely remain confined to this small-program paradigm.

As a result, recent progress has been driven by large language models (LLMs), which have become the de-facto foundation for neural translation [8,21,33,35,36]. A prominent line of work combines LLMs with static program analysis [12,21,35,36]. In C to Rust pipelines [26,39], scalability is typically achieved by first invoking C2Rust [2] and then using LLMs to "idiomatise" the output. Because these approaches inherit C2Rust's pointer-centric structure, they operate on syntactically translated, largely unsafe Rust. While the LLM is able to correct some of the unidiomatic parts, a large proportion is still present in the result.

For end-to-end LLM approaches without a rule-based front-end, Ibrahimzada et al. [19] propose a compositional pipeline for translating Java to Python, generating code module by module and validating local invariants. Shiraishi and Shinagawa [32] instead target C to Rust, using a context-aware segmentation strategy to partition repositories prior to translation. While both approaches scale to entire projects, their translations largely fail to preserve the behaviour of the original code, highlighting the difficulty of full-project translation with LLMs alone. For translating Go to Rust, Zhang et al. introduce a neurosymbolic pipeline implemented in Oxidizer [37]. Oxidizer couples LLM-based generation with static mapping of constructs between the source and target languages, type-compatibility checks, and input–output semantic validation, demonstrating that repository-scale translation becomes practical when neural generation is grounded in domain-specific program analysis.

4 Current Limitations

Despite progress in rule-based, neural and neurosymbolic pipelines, current systems still fall short of the requirements for real-world translation. The remainder of this section examines several of the most persistent barriers.

Concurrency. Translating concurrent code remains highly challenging. Programming languages often embody fundamentally different concurrency paradigms—e.g. shared-memory threads, message passing, async/await—which makes rule-based translation unfeasible in the general case. Existing work has so far only tackled narrow subproblems; for instance, Hong and Ryu's Concrat system automatically rewrites C lock APIs to Rust equivalents, but is restricted to lock-based synchronization and requires accurate static summaries of lock behaviour to succeed [16]. LLM-based approaches do not solve this: concurrency invariants are hard to specify and even harder to verify, and neural-based translation may introduce subtle race conditions or deadlocks. Meaningful progress likely depends on advances in scalable program verification for concurrent systems.

Third-Party Dependencies. Automated translation also struggles when source code depends on rich ecosystems of libraries. Rule-based systems can only cover APIs they explicitly know how to rewrite, while neural approaches often hallucinate import paths and APIs, or generate syntactically correct but semantically incompatible replacements. Moreover, target languages may lack direct equivalents for libraries used in the source project. Bridging this gap requires explicit modeling of dependency ecosystems, for example through API mapping databases or retrieval-augmented approaches to API translation.

Lack of Formal Verification in Neural-Based Translation. Most current neural or neurosymbolic translation pipelines ultimately validate the correctness of the generated code using input–output examples. These checks provide only partial assurance: they can detect obvious regressions, but cannot guarantee preservation of behaviour across the (potentially infinite) input space or through complex execution paths. This limitation is particularly acute for repository-level translation, where small errors in data structures or pointer manipulation can remain latent until deployment. Formal verification offers a more principled alternative, but so far has only seen early adoption. One notable example is VERT [35], which combines LLM-generated Rust with an oracle Rust program compiled from WebAssembly, and then performs property-based testing and bounded model checking to verify semantic equivalence. While VERT demonstrates that formal guarantees are feasible, it remains constrained: verification must be performed function-by-function, requires bounds on loops, and faces scalability limits for real-world codebases. Meaningful progress will likely require advances in scalable software verification, including automated invariant inference and robust verification techniques that operate across language boundaries.

5 Conclusions

Automated translation of real-world codebases remains challenging. Rule-based approaches scale and preserve semantics, but typically produce unidiomatic code that is hard to read and maintain. Neural approaches generate idiomatic code, yet remain brittle and opaque. Neurosymbolic pipelines offer a pragmatic middle ground, combining analysis-driven guidance with validation, but still struggle with external dependencies, concurrency abstractions and the absence of formal guarantees. Addressing these challenges will require hybrid methods that integrate language-specific reasoning, richer specification mechanisms and verification that goes beyond input–output testing to provide trustworthy translations at repository scale.

References

1. C to Go translator. https://github.com/gotranspile/cxgo. Accessed 16 Dec 2024
2. C2Rust transpiler. https://c2rust.com/. Accessed 16 Dec 2024
3. Sharpen - automated Java-C# coversion. https://github.com/mono/sharpen. Accessed 16 Dec 2024
4. Ahmad, W.U., Tushar, M.G.R., Chakraborty, S., Chang, K.: AVATAR: a parallel corpus for java-python program translation. In: Rogers, A., Boyd-Graber, J.L., Okazaki, N. (eds.) Findings of the Association for Computational Linguistics: ACL 2023, Toronto, Canada, July 9–14, 2023, pp. 2268–2281. Association for Computational Linguistics (2023). https://doi.org/10.18653/V1/2023.FINDINGS-ACL.143
5. Babel is a javascript compiler. https://babeljs.io/. Accessed 09 Dec 2024
6. Bastidas Fuertes, A., Pérez, M., Meza Hormaza, J.: Transpilers: a systematic mapping review of their usage in research and industry. Appl. Sci. **13**(6) (2023). https://doi.org/10.3390/app13063667, https://www.mdpi.com/2076-3417/13/6/3667
7. Chromium: Chromium security - memory safety. https://www.chromium.org/Home/chromium-security/memory-safety/. Accessed 20 Nov 2024
8. Di, P., et al.: CodeFuse-13B: a pretrained multi-lingual code large language model. In: International Conference on Software Engineering: Software Engineering in Practice, p. 418–429. ICSE-SEIP '24, ACM (2024). https://doi.org/10.1145/3639477.3639719
9. Emre, M., Schroeder, R., Dewey, K., Hardekopf, B.: Translating C to safer rust. Proc. ACM Program. Lang. **5**(OOPSLA), 1–29 (2021)
10. Emre, M., Schroeder, R., Dewey, K., Hardekopf, B.: Translating c to safer rust. Proc. ACM Program. Lang. 5(OOPSLA) (2021). https://doi.org/10.1145/3485498
11. Eniser, H.F., et al.: Towards translating real-world code with LLMs: a study of translating to Rust (2024). https://arxiv.org/abs/2405.11514
12. Farrukh, M., Shah, S., Coskun, B., Polychronakis, M.: Safetrans: LLM-assisted transpilation from C to rust (2025). https://arxiv.org/abs/2505.10708

13. Foundation, T.P.S.: 2 to 3 – automated python 2 to 3 code translation. https://docs.python.org/3.12/library/2to3.html. Accessed 09 Dec 2024
14. GeeksforGeeks: a computer science portal for geeks. https://www.geeksforgeeks.org/. Accessed 10 Dec 2024
15. Hong, J., Ryu, S.: Concrat: An automatic C-to-rust lock API translator for concurrent programs. In: Proceedings of the 45th International Conference on Software Engineering (ICSE), pp. 716–728. IEEE (2023). https://doi.org/10.1109/ICSE48619.2023.00069
16. Hong, J., Ryu, S.: Concrat: an automatic C-to-rust lock API translator for concurrent programs. In: 45th IEEE/ACM International Conference on Software Engineering, ICSE 2023, Melbourne, Australia, pp. 716–728. IEEE (2023). https://doi.org/10.1109/ICSE48619.2023.00069
17. Hong, J., Ryu, S.: Don't write, but return: replacing output parameters with algebraic data types in C-to-rust translation. Proc. ACM Program. Lang. **8**(PLDI) (2024). https://doi.org/10.1145/3656406
18. Hong, J., Ryu, S.: To tag, or not to tag: translating C's unions to rust's tagged unions. In: Proceedings of the 39th IEEE/ACM International Conference on Automated Software Engineering (ASE), pp. 40–52. ACM (2024). https://doi.org/10.1145/3691620.3694985
19. Ibrahimzada, A.R., et al.: Repository-level compositional code translation and validation (2024). https://arxiv.org/abs/2410.24117
20. Intel: MCS-86 Assembly Language Converter Operating Instructions for ISIS-II Users. Technical report, Intel (1978). Accessed 11 Dec 2024
21. Jana, P., Jha, P., Ju, H., Kishore, G., Mahajan, A., Ganesh, V.: Attention, compilation, and solver-based symbolic analysis are all you need (2023). arXiv preprint arXiv:2306.06755
22. Kimura, K., Sekiguchi, A., Choudhary, S., Uehara, T.: A javascript transpiler for escaping from complicated usage of cloud services and APIs. In: 25th Asia-Pacific Software Engineering Conference, APSEC 2018, Nara, Japan, pp. 69–78. IEEE (2018). https://doi.org/10.1109/APSEC.2018.00021
23. Lu, S., et al.: CodeXGLUE: a machine learning benchmark dataset for code understanding and generation. In: Proceedings of the Neural Information Processing Systems Track on Datasets and Benchmarks. vol. 1 (2021). https://datasets-benchmarks-proceedings.neurips.cc/paper_files/paper/2021/file/c16a5320fa475530d9583c34fd356ef5-Paper-round1.pdf
24. Malyala, A., Zhou, K., Ray, B., Chakraborty, S.: On ML-based program translation: perils and promises. In: 45th IEEE/ACM International Conference on Software Engineering: New Ideas and Emerging Results, NIER@ICSE, Melbourne, Australia, pp. 60–65. IEEE (2023). https://doi.org/10.1109/ICSE-NIER58687.2023.00017
25. Microsoft: a proactive approach to more secure code. https://msrc.microsoft.com/blog/2019/07/a-proactive-approach-to-more-secure-code/ (2019). Accessed 20 Nov 2024
26. Nitin, V., Krishna, R., do Valle, L.L., Ray, B.: C2saferrust: transforming C projects into safer rust with neurosymbolic techniques (2025). https://arxiv.org/abs/2501.14257
27. Pan, R., et al.: Lost in translation: a study of bugs introduced by large language models while translating code. In: Proceedings of the 46th IEEE/ACM International Conference on Software Engineering, ICSE 2024, Lisbon, Portugal, April 14–20, 2024, pp. 82:1–82:13. ACM (2024). https://doi.org/10.1145/3597503.3639226

28. Puri, R., et al.: CodeNet: a large-scale AI for code dataset for learning a diversity of coding tasks (2021). arXiv preprint arXiv:2105.12655
29. Radoi, C., Fink, S.J., Rabbah, R.M., Sridharan, M.: Translating imperative code to mapreduce. In: Black, A.P., Millstein, T.D. (eds.) Proceedings of the 2014 ACM International Conference on Object Oriented Programming Systems Languages nd Applications, OOPSLA 2014, part of SPLASH 2014, Portland, OR, USA, October 20–24, 2014, pp. 909–927. ACM (2014). https://doi.org/10.1145/2660193.2660228
30. Rozière, B., Lachaux, M., Chanussot, L., Lample, G.: Unsupervised translation of programming languages. In: Larochelle, H., Ranzato, M., Hadsell, R., Balcan, M., Lin, H. (eds.) Advances in Neural Information Processing Systems 33: Annual Conference on Neural Information Processing Systems 2020, NeurIPS 2020, December 6–12, 2020, virtual (2020). https://proceedings.neurips.cc/paper/2020/hash/ed23fbf18c2cd35f8c7f8de44f85c08d-Abstract.html
31. Rozière, B., Zhang, J., Charton, F., Harman, M., Synnaeve, G., Lample, G.: Leveraging automated unit tests for unsupervised code translation. In: The Tenth International Conference on Learning Representations, ICLR 2022, Virtual Event, April 25–29, 2022. OpenReview.net (2022). https://openreview.net/forum?id=cmt-6KtR4c4
32. Shiraishi, M., Shinagawa, T.: Context-aware code segmentation for C-to-rust translation using large language models (2024). https://arxiv.org/abs/2409.10506
33. Tang, Z., et al.: Explain-then-translate: an analysis on improving program translation with self-generated explanations. In: Findings of the Association for Computational Linguistics: EMNLP 2023. pp. 1741–1788. Association for Computational Linguistics (2023). https://doi.org/10.18653/v1/2023.findings-emnlp.119
34. Yan, W., Tian, Y., Li, Y., Chen, Q., Wang, W.: CodeTransOcean: a comprehensive multilingual benchmark for code translation (2023). arXiv preprint arXiv:2310.04951
35. Yang, A.Z.H., Takashima, Y., Paulsen, B., Dodds, J., Kroening, D.: VERT: verified equivalent Rust transpilation with large language models as few-shot learners (2024). https://arxiv.org/abs/2404.18852
36. Yin, X., Ni, C., Nguyen, T.N., Wang, S., Yang, X.: Rectifier: code translation with corrector via LLMs. CoRR abs/2407.07472 (2024). https://doi.org/10.48550/ARXIV.2407.07472
37. Zhang, H., David, C., Wang, M., Paulsen, B., Kroening, D.: Scalable, validated code translation of entire projects using large language models (under submission) (2024). https://arxiv.org/abs/2412.08035
38. Zhang, H., David, C., Yu, Y., Wang, M.: Ownership guided C to rust translation. In: Enea, C., Lal, A. (eds) Computer Aided Verification (CAV). LNCS, vol. 13966, pp. 459–482. Springer (2023). https://doi.org/10.1007/978-3-031-37709-9_22
39. Zhou, T., Lin, H., Jha, S., Christodorescu, M., Levchenko, K., Chandrasekaran, V.: LLM-driven multi-step translation from C to rust using static analysis (2025). https://arxiv.org/abs/2503.12511

Software Quality and System Design

Synchronous System Design with Quantitative Types

Rui Chen[(✉)] and Ingo Sander

School of EECS, KTH Royal Institute of Technology, Stockholm, Sweden
{ruich,ingo}@kth.se

Abstract. Modern type-theory-based proof assistants/languages are increasingly supporting general-purpose programming, making them both practical and formally rigorous. This dual nature aligns well with the needs of safety-critical embedded system design. It is hence promising that such a language can be employed as a proper meta-language for building an embedded system design framework that integrates reasoning and programming. In this paper, we demonstrate a unified framework for synchronous embedded system design, which leverages both aspects of the quantitatively typed language Idris2, with a focus on an embedded domain-specific language (EDSL), named SynQ, in the framework. Specifically, we show that the leveraging of the expressiveness of quantitative type theory and the tagless final embedding allows synchronous systems to be properly modelled by SynQ. This then enables a systematic usage of Idris2 for facilitating both design and verification of synchronous systems, demonstrating an initial step towards a correct-by-construction embedded system design process.

Keywords: Embedded System Design · Interactive Theorem Prover · Quantitative Type Theory · Functional Programming

1 Introduction

A framework for safety-critical embedded system design requires both *practicality* and *formality* (or rigorousness according to Sifakis [39]). The former enables both *executable* models and *applicative* design steps in the design process, which can be used for virtual prototyping and design automation, respectively. The latter makes it possible to conduct formal specification and reasoning so that the *correctness* of the designed and implemented systems can be assured. With both achieved, a correct-by-construction design methodology can be expected.

The recent development of type-theory-based proof assistants/languages has created new possibilities to create a unified framework in which both requirements can be satisfied. In type theory, *computations* and *formal logic*, which respectively correspond to the two needs of a system design framework, are harmoniously combined through the Curry-Howard correspondence. It makes a type theory a proper meta-theory above what system design frameworks can be built. Furthermore, many type-theory-based proof assistants, e.g. Agda

A. Goharshady and C. Haase (Eds.): SETTA 2025, LNCS 16458, pp. 13–32, 2026.
https://doi.org/10.1007/978-981-95-7826-9_2

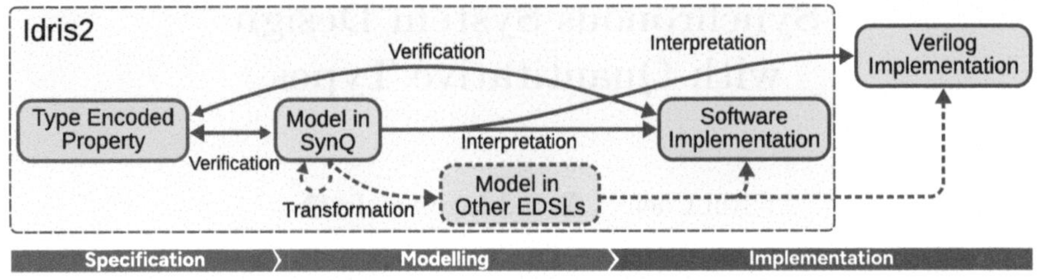

Fig. 1. An overview of the framework considered in this paper. The dashed part will not be discussed in detail as it is out of the focus of this paper.

[32], Lean4 [30], and Rocq (formerly Coq) [40], are increasingly accommodating general-purpose programming. This trend, together with the emergence of general-purpose programming languages with advanced type systems, e.g. Idris and Idris2 [9,10], suggests that type-theory-based proof assistants/languages, beyond their conventional use in formal specification and verification, may also be effectively employed for modelling and implementing systems, which, hence, can facilitate a unified framework in type theory that integrates reasoning and programming.

In this paper, we consider a framework for synchronous system [4,35] design, which leverages the quantitative-type-theory (QTT, a combination of linear [1] and dependent types) [2,28] based language Idris2 [10], with a focus on how the framework is enabled by a *systematic* usage of QTT and the *tagless final embedding* [11]. An overview of the framework, aligned with the three-phase system design model proposed by Sifakis [38], is illustrated in Fig. 1. At the centre of the framework is the embedded domain-specific language (EDSL) SynQ (**Syn**chronous system design with **Q**uantitative types) which employs QTT to precisely model synchronous systems, in a component-based manner [39], as Idris2 terms. Based on SynQ, well-defined *interpretations* and *transformations* are implemented as functions in Idris2, which correspond to implementation and optimisation steps, respectively. By having both design steps and (most of the) artefacts produced during a design process in Idris2, the *logic aspect* of QTT, which enables formal specification and verification, is leveraged to facilitate a transparent, correct-by-construction design process.

To have a system design framework built upon, instead of being verified in, QTT, SynQ is embedded relatively *shallower* (cf. [17]) than other works in which languages are formalised and verified, such as in [31]. That is, synchronous systems are modelled in Idris2 with their behaviour denoted by Idris2 programs/terms in QTT. For instance, a conditional expression, namely `if_`, in SynQ is a *function* with the following type signature

```
if_: ... -> comb () Bool -> comb () a -> comb () a -> comb () a
```

In which `comb () t` denotes signals (values) of type `t` in SynQ. Such a shallower embedding of SynQ enables: (1) an intuitive modelling approach with systems modelled by programs instead of data; (2) an extensible framework in which new *components* (sub-systems) can be easily introduced; and (3) an easier and straightforward decoupling between a system's model and its implementation(s). Combining the last two points allows black-box components implemented outside of the "Idris2 world" to be easily introduced into the framework.

SynQ leverages QTT and the tagless final embedding to address *two specific challenges* so that it can be properly embedded at Idris2's term level and enables the rest of Idris2 to be leveraged for a system design framework. *Firstly*, from the language point of view, there is no easy way to distinguish EDSL terms from Idris2 terms. Hence, we can have models that are typed as EDSL terms, yet internally dependent on general Idris2 terms. Such terms challenge interpretations that implement models in the EDSL because an interpreter has to cover all features Idris2 has, such as pattern matching and computation on types, instead of covering primitives that are in the EDSL only. *Secondly*, language embedding at the term level could inherit unexpected implementation details from Idris2. For example, the evaluation of `if_` must obey the call-by-value strategy implemented in Idris2 because it is a function in Idris2. However, in the framework presented in Fig. 1, the implementation of a model may not be an Idris2 term and, hence, may require a distinct strategy, e.g., the behaviour of synchronous circuits (Verilog HDL implementation) requires the call-by-need evaluation strategy.

We summarise the contributions as follows:

- this paper presents SynQ, an EDSL for modelling synchronous systems with a focus on how QTT, combined with the tagless final approach, is leveraged so that the two challenges above are addressed; and
- this paper showcases that, with SynQ as the enabler, QTT can be leveraged to facilitate a framework in which both design (modelling and implementation) and formal specification/verification can be conducted.

With these contributions, the authors believe this paper forms an initial step towards a correct-by-construction embedded system design methodology that leverages QTT as its meta-theory.

The rest of the paper is organised as follows. Section 2 provides a brief introduction to the quantitative type theory and synchronous systems. In Sect. 3, a simple example is presented to provide an overview of SynQ and the system design framework. After that, a detailed discussion about the embedding of SynQ and how the two challenges discussed above are addressed is given in Sects. 4 and 5. Then we wrap up our discussion in Sect. 6 with a larger example in which a FIFO with a handshake protocol is designed and verified. Finally, related work and conclusion are given in Sects. 7 and 8, respectively.

2 Preliminary

2.1 Quantitative Types

The quantitative type theory (QTT) [2,28] is a combination of dependent types and linear types [1]. We now briefly introduce QTT. The interested reader is referred to [1,2,19,28] for further details.

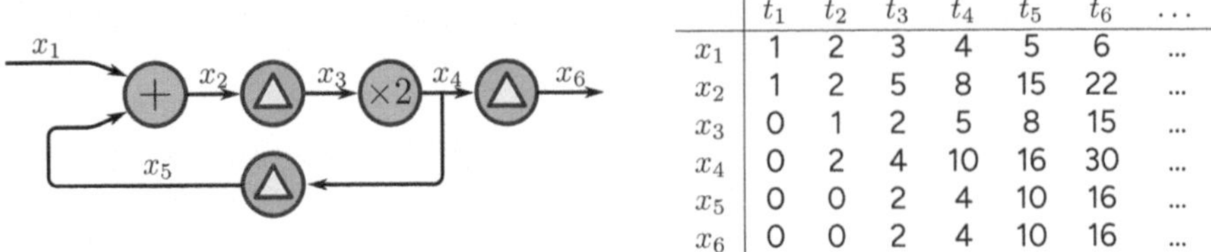

	t_1	t_2	t_3	t_4	t_5	t_6	...
x_1	1	2	3	4	5	6	...
x_2	1	2	5	8	15	22	...
x_3	0	1	2	5	8	15	...
x_4	0	2	4	10	16	30	...
x_5	0	0	2	4	10	16	...
x_6	0	0	2	4	10	16	...

Fig. 2. An exemplified synchronous system (left) illustrated as a network consists of combinational operators (blue) and unit delays (red); and streams' value at each clock event by assuming all unit delays have initial value 0. (Color figure online)

Dependent types allow types to be constructed from terms and vice versa. It then enables extra information to be specified in types. For instance, we can define the type `Vect n a` for all vectors of length `n` whose elements are of type `a`.

The expressiveness of dependent types allows the Curry-Howard correspondence to be leveraged to reason about programs' behaviour. Intuitively, the Curry-Howard correspondence refers to the fact that type checking a term t of type T in a type system corresponds to proving a proposition P_T in a corresponding proof calculus, which makes the type-checked term t the witness of the fact that P_T *can be proved.* With dependent types, propositions over terms (programs) can be encoded in types and formally proved.

The *linear type system* restricts the terms to be used *exactly once (linearity).* The combination of dependent and linear types is a non-trivial task because terms may be referred to in types in dependent types. QTT addresses this issue by associating terms with *multiplicities* on their type bindings to specify the usage of terms. These multiplicities are expected to form a semiring so that they are closed under addition and multiplication, which are used to sum up multiple uses of a term and account for nested uses of terms, respectively. Associating terms with the multiplicity corresponding to the absorbing element of multiplication (0) removes restrictions on term usage, thus permitting the combination of linear and dependent types. Specifically, Idris2 implements QTT with the $\{0, 1, \omega\}$ semiring, with regular terms bound with multiplicity ω, terms that can be used only in types bound with multiplicity 0, and linear terms bound with multiplicity 1.

2.2 Synchronous Systems

Synchronous systems are reactive systems obeying the *perfect synchrony hypothesis* that "reactions are instantaneous so that activations and productions of output are synchronous, as if programs were executed on an infinitely fast machine" [8]. In other words, a synchronous model of a system eliminates (physical) time consumed by computations, yet preserves the order between a system's input events, and hence between its output events/firings, which implies the existence of a *global clock* in a system that synchronises the entire system.

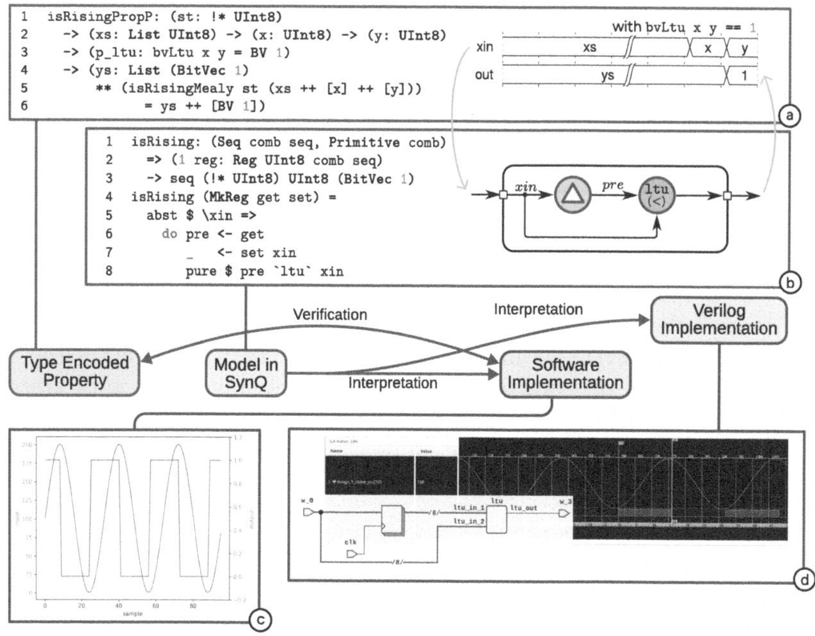

Fig. 3. An illustration of the design of a rising pattern detecting system: (a) the specification of the functional behaviour of the system's software implementation in QTT; (b) the SynQ model of the system; (c) and (d) the illustration of the input-output behaviour of the software and hardware implemented system.

Synchronous systems' behaviour can be specified by the dataflow model as a set of equations over *synchronous isomorphic* (cf. Section 3 of [16]) streams (sequences of events, dataflow) [18,35] that are mutually recursive. For instance, the following set of equations defines a synchronous system:

$$x_2 = x_1 + x_5 \qquad x_4 = x_3 \times 2 \qquad x_6 = D\, x_4$$
$$x_3 = D\, x_2 \qquad x_5 = D\, x_4$$

which can be directly interpreted as a netlist and visualised as a network illustrated in Fig. 2. In this set of equations, x_{1-6} are streams such that $x_1[k]$ refers to the value of x_1 at the k-th clock event, and the constant 2 represents a constant stream of value 2. Operators $(+)$ and $(\times)$ indicate *point-wise* (combinational) operations over streams and D is the primitive of unit delay such that $x[k-1] = (D\, x)[k]$ with a pre-defined $(D\, x)[0]$.

3 An Illustrative Example

We now demonstrate SynQ and the framework it enables with an example. In this example, the system to be designed detects the *rising pattern* in its input and outputs "1" when the pattern is detected. The design process of this system and the artefacts/results involved in each step of the design process are presented in Fig. 3. Note that this example aims to provide an overview; details will be elaborated in successive sections.

For rising pattern detection, one of the expected functional behaviours of the system in the dataflow model is the following, which corresponds to the type of `isRisingPropP` presented in Fig. 3a.

$$\forall\, \texttt{st}, \texttt{xs}, \texttt{x}, \texttt{y}.\ \exists\, \texttt{ys}.\ (\texttt{x} \mathrel{\bar{<}} \texttt{y}) \equiv \texttt{1} \implies [\![\texttt{isRising}]\!]_{\texttt{st}}\,(\texttt{xs} \prec \texttt{x} \prec \texttt{y}) \equiv \texttt{ys} \prec \texttt{1}$$

Here $\bar{<}$ denotes the *less-than-comparison* implemented *externally* (out of Idris2) that corresponds to `bvLtu` at line 3 of Fig. 3a; $[\![\texttt{isRising}]\!]_{\texttt{st}}$ denotes the software implementation of `isRising` (the SynQ model) initialised with state `st` (`isRisingMealy st` at line 5); and $\prec$ is the *followed-by* operator that combines two sequences (`(++)`). The corresponding proof in Idris2 is conducted by pattern matching on the prefix of the input (`xs`), i.e.:

```
1  isRisingPropP (MkBang st) [] x y p_ltu =
2    rewrite p_ltu in ([bvLtu st x] ** Refl)
3  isRisingPropP (MkBang st) (st' :: xs) x y p_ltu =
4    let (ys ** prf) = isRisingPropP (MkBang st') xs x y p_ltu
5    in rewrite prf in (bvLtu st st' :: ys ** Refl)
```

In which, line 1 and 2 verifies the case where the input is just `x` followed by `y` (the base case). Meanwhile, the rest inductively proves that the property hold for arbitrary non-empty `xs`.

Figure 3b illustrate the system model in SynQ and its visualisation as a network. The type signature of the model (line 1–3 of Fig. 3b) is twofold. Lines 1 and 2 specify in which context, i.e. *with what components*, the system is built. In Line 2, by associating `reg` with multiplicity 1, it is explicitly specified that the system should use exactly one register (delay element) for data of type `UInt8`. Line 3 specifies the type of the system, indicating that the system is a sequential system with its internal state (introduced by the register), input and output of type `!* UInt8`, `UInt8` and `BitVec 1`, respectively, with `!*` referring to the unrestricted modality in linear types. With this type, the system can be safely composed with others for constructing larger systems.

From line 4, the model is given. Following the intuition that parameters (line 1 and 2) of `isRising` specify the context in which the system is constructed, the `(MkReg get set)` appearing on the lhs of `(=)` unpacks the register declared in the type signature and exposes two primitives of the register (`get` and `set`, which correspond to the output and input of the delay element, respectively) for constructing the system. Then, at line 5, the `abst` expression binds the input of the system with the variable `xin`. The rest of the model (inside the `do`-block) gives a structural description of the system. Which corresponds to the network presented on the right-hand side of Fig. 3b.

Two interpretations are made for the model, which gives us the software and hardware implementation, respectively. The software implementation is an

Idris2 program in which C-implemented components are invoked (in, e.g., `bvLtu`), which allows platform primitives to be employed to increase efficiency. The result program can be verified or tested against the type-encoded property. Figure 3c illustrates the input/output behaviour, in red and blue, respectively, of this implementation. The hardware implementation of the system is a synthesizable Verilog HDL file, which can be synthesised and deployed as a digital circuit. The visualisation of the generated HDL file and the input/output waveform of the FPGA-deployed system captured by a logic analyser is presented in Fig. 3d.

4 The Embedding of SynQ and Multiplicity 0

SynQ implements a component-based design framework (based on the idea from Sifakis [39]) with the tagless final approach [11]. In this section, we discuss component-based design in SynQ, its implementation, and how multiplicity 0 from QTT is used in the implementation of SynQ.

4.1 Component-Based Design in SynQ

In general, a component-based design framework abstracts both *basic building blocks* and their *coordination/interaction* involved in a system as *components*. They are respectively recognised as atomic and glue components. By enforcing systems to be built upon only these components, both productivity and correctness are enhanced. Meanwhile, with this abstraction, a system design process can be formalised by operations over components. For instance, implementing a system can be conducted by substituting all components with their implementation and design refinement can be conducted by substituting the set of components involved with another set.

SynQ implements a two-layer component-based framework. The first layer is the *combinational layer*, in which side-effect-free systems are modelled. This layer employs a subset of *simply typed lambda calculus (STLC) with product* as glue components and *pure-functional constants* as atomic components. In this way, the compositional layer leverages well-established equivalence relations defined on lambda terms, such as β/η-reduction, for obtaining a sound design space of a system. Meanwhile, the Church-Rosser theorem entailed in STLC also facilitates the modelling of systems with inherent parallelism/concurrency.

The second layer is the *sequential layer*, in which the register (delay element) is introduced as an atomic component for modelling stateful systems. Glue components in this layer are *combinators*, which are similar to combinators for arrows [22] but are constrained with linearity (multiplicity 1). As will be discussed in detail in Sect. 5, by constraining these components with linearity, models constructed from these components directly correspond to synchronous systems.

```
interface Comb (0 comb: Type -> Type -> Type) where
  lam: {auto aIsSig: Sig a} -> {auto bIsSig: Sig b}
    -> (comb () a -> comb () b) -> comb a b
  app: {auto aIsSig: Sig a} -> {auto bIsSig: Sig b}
    -> comb a b -> comb () a -> comb () b
  ...
```

(a)

```
interface Comb comb
  => Seq (0 comb: Type -> Type -> Type)
         (0 seq: Type -> Type -> Type -> Type) | seq where
  abst : {auto aIsSig: Sig a} -> {auto bIsSig: Sig b}
      -> {auto sIsState: St s}
      -> (1 _: comb () a -> seq s () b) -> seq s a b
  (=<<): ... -> (1 _: seq s b c) -> (1 _: seq s a b)
      -> seq s a c
  (<<<): ... -> (1 _: seq s2 b c) -> (1 _: seq s1 a b)
      -> seq (LPair s1 s2) a c
  ...
```

(b)

Listing 1: The *symantics* of the combinational and sequential glue components in SynQ: (a) the interface that defines the *symantics* of combinational glue components of SynQ; (b) the interface that defines the *symantics* of combinational glue components of SynQ. Note that some implicit parameters are omitted here.

4.2 The Tagless Final Embedding of SynQ

In the tagless final approach, a language is introduced by declaring interface(s), better known as *type classes* in Haskell [21,23,24], parametrised by type constructors that specify terms in the language. Such interface(s) are recognised as the **symantics** (**syn**tax + se**mantics**) of the language as it constrains both aspects of the language. As a two-layer component-based design framework, SynQ is embedded with four interfaces, namely `Comb`, `Primitive`, `Seq`, and `Reg`, which correspond to atomic and glue components in the combinational and sequential layer, respectively. Here, we discuss the embedding of SynQ based on a subset of the glue components in the combinational and sequential layer, as shown in Listing 1. The full definition of SynQ can be found in the git repository[1].

As shown in Listing 1, glue components are defined in the interfaces `Comb` and `Seq`, with sequential glues dependent on combinational glues. Terms in SynQ are type constructors (`comb` and `seq`) that are parametrising these interfaces. These constructors represent abstract systems that are parametrised by the types of their input, output, and internal state (if any). That is, a term in SynQ that is typed with `comb a b` is a model of a side-effect-free system with input of type

[1] https://github.com/ruich95/SynQ.

a and output of type b. Similarly, a term typed with seq s a b corresponds to a system with its internal state, input and output typed of types s, a and b, respectively. And 950422 is used to represent the absence of an input, output, or state, making a type of the form comb () a representing a constant value in SynQ (a constant sequence in the dataflow model).

Methods in this interface are glue components that specify how a system can be constructed from other subsystems (components). Implicit parameters wrapped in curly brackets in each method are *predicates on types* constructed from generalised algebraic data types (GADTs) [14], with what SynQ terms can only be parametrised by a limited subset of types in QTT. For instance, the Sig is defined as follows.

```
data Sig: Type -> Type where
  U : Sig Unit
  BV: {n:_} -> Sig $ BitVec n
  P : Sig a -> Sig b -> Sig (a, b)
```

A term of type Sig a hence restricts the type variable a to range over only the *subset of types* that consist of:

- the unit type (Unit/());
- bit-vectors with arbitrary length (Sig $ BitVec n); and
- product of types that belongs to the subset (Sig (a, b)).

Terms in the combinational layer are then restricted to a subset of terms in STLC. It ensures that SynQ models are all well-behaved synchronous systems.

Components lam and abst are the key enablers that allow SynQ terms to be embedded at the term level of Idris2. Intuitively, these components send functions in Idris2 to components in SynQ, allowing terms, such as if_ in Sect. 1, to be used as components. Formally, with these components, SynQ is embedded in Idris2 with the higher-order abstract syntax (HOAS) [34]. That is, SynQ borrows binders in Idris2 as its own binders, which has been shown in line 5 of Fig. 3b, in which xin, a variable in Idris2, is employed to represent the input of the system model in SynQ.

With these components, the *second challenge* mentioned in Sect. 1 is *partially addressed.* Even though binders in Idris2 are borrowed, the interface-based abstraction enforces the behaviour of these bindings, and their applications remain abstract. It enables different evaluation orders, which may not align with Idris2's implementation of QTT, to be introduced when these interfaces are implemented.

A Component-Based Design Perspective. We may directly regard SynQ embedded with the tagless final approach as a component-based design framework. From this point of view, the type signature of isRising in Fig. 3b that

```
isRising: (Seq comb seq, Primitive comb)
  => (1 reg: Reg UInt8 comb seq)
  -> seq (!* UInt8) UInt8 (BitVec 1)
```

is interpreted as that the final system model of the type seq ... is built upon

- sequential glues for terms of type `seq s a b`, as specified by `Seq _ seq`;
- combinational glues and atomics of type `comb a b` with combinational glues being the dependency of sequential glues (cf. Listing 1b) and atoms being specified by `Primitive comb`; and
- a register of type `seq s a b`, specifying by `Reg UInt8 _ seq`.

with `seq` and `comb` consistently representing the same *kind* of implementation, e.g., software, Verilog HDL, etc., of glues and atoms.

Note that `reg: Reg ...` specifies a *term* `reg` in the context, instead of being used as a declaration of an interface before `(=>)`. Indeed, we may use the *dictionary passing* technique [33] to make other component sets be explicitly modelled as Idris2 terms, as well. With this approach, an interface is replaced by a tagged product (record in Idris2), which is, in essence, a dictionary with names of components as indices. For instance, the interface `Comb` can be defined in the following form:

```
record Comb (comb: Type -> Type -> Type) where
  constructor MkComb
  lam : ... -> (comb () a -> comb () b) -> comb a b
  ...
```

We can then rewrite `isRising` so that it has the following type signature:

```
isRising: (Seq comb seq) -> (Primitive comb)
  -> (1 reg: Reg UInt8 comb seq)
  -> seq (!* UInt8) UInt8 (BitVec 1)
```

which can be interpreted as a "recipe" telling how the system is built based on component sets passed to it. Explicitly specifying component sets as terms allows transformations between them to be specified explicitly. Such a transformation is often a *vertical transformation* that lowers the abstraction level in a design process, e.g., implementing a high-level language with LLVM IR. These transformations will be functions of the following form:

```
trans: ... -> (Comb comb1  -> comb1 a b) --before
  -> (Comb' comb2 -> comb2 a b)          --after
```

This signature indicates that an arbitrary component (`comb1`) with its input and output of type `a` and `b`, respectively, constructed with components `Comb` *can* be transformed to a component (`comb2`) of the same input/output types constructed with `Comb'`. Hence, `trans` is a function that encodes operations entailed in a transformation.

Two Interpretations of SynQ Terms. An interpretation of SynQ is a *concrete type* on which all the interfaces/records defining the language are implemented. With the implementation of these interfaces passing to SynQ terms, abstract components in these terms are then substituted with the implemented component, which yields the implemented systems.

Two interpretations demonstrated in Sect. 3 map SynQ terms into Idris2 functions (software implementations) and typed netlists, which are then translated to Verilog HDL code (hardware implementations), respectively. The software implementation, for the *combinational layer*, employs the following type

```
data Eval: Type -> Type -> Type where
  MkEval: (eval: a -> b) -> Eval a b
```

together with `Comb Eval` and `Primitive Eval` implemented. With this type and implementation, a SynQ model of type `comb a b` is interpreted as a term of type `Eval a b` that consists of a function `eval` of type `a -> b`. For the *sequential layer*, the following type is employed

```
data EvalS: Type -> Type -> Type -> Type where
  MkEvalS: (1 evalS: a -> (1 _: s) -> LC s b) -> EvalS s a b
```

in which `LC s b` is a product of `s` and `b` that preserves the linearity on `s` during pattern matching. With this type, stateful systems are interpreted as *Mealy machines* because `evalS` is, in essence, the function characterising Mealy machines. For *hardware implementation*, the following two types are employed.

```
record CombinationalNL a b where
  constructor MkComb
  genComb: Nat -> (Nat, CombNL a b)
```

```
record SequentialNL a b where
  constructor MkSeq
  1 genSeq: Nat
      -> LC (SeqNL s a b) Nat
```

In these types, `CombNL` and `SeqNL` are the types of netlists, and the parameter of type `Nat` is used to generate unique names.

4.3 The Necessity of Multiplicity 0

Multiplicity 0 in QTT is used in two places in the embedding of SynQ. The first is in the definition of the *symantics* of SynQ, as illustrated in Listing 1. It is also associated by default with *free* type variables in a type signature. That is, the complete type signature of `isRising` is of the following form:

```
isRising: {0 comb: _} -> {0 seq: _} -> ...
```

This usage of multiplicity 0 ensures that *a SynQ model like `isRising` employs only components defined in the symantics of SynQ*. It, hence, addresses the *first challenge* in the embedding of SynQ identified in Sect. 1 and allows us to treat SynQ embedded in QTT as a component-based design framework.

Originally in Haskell and OCaml, the tagless final approach with HOAS follows "enforcing term parametricity with type parametricity" in [43] so that a term is constructed from only the *symantics* of the embedded language. It is a similar idea to that, in the System F, the type $\forall \texttt{a}.\, \texttt{a} \rightarrow \texttt{a}$ uniquely characterises the identity function because this type does not consist of any information about which primitives can be applied to terms of type `a`.

This property, however, does not naturally hold in Idris2, in which types can be referred to as terms. A counterexample is the following, in which the type variable `a` is pattern matched.

```
notId: {a:_} -> a -> a
notId {a=Int} x = x + 1
notId {a} x = x
```

The utilisation of multiplicity 0, e.g., binding the type variable a with multiplicity 0, prevents us from such a situation and guarantees that there are no other primitives, except those defined in the *symantics*, that are invoked for models in SynQ. Note that, in Agda or Rocq, the example above is prohibited by implementation. Compared to them, quantitative types provide an implementation-agnostic solution, which also allows types to be used, e.g., for code generation, on demand.

5 Synchronous Models in SynQ and Multiplicity 1

SynQ aims at a syntactically restricted subset of synchronous dataflow models. This subset is chosen so that the usage of delay elements (registers) is explicitly specified in the type signature of SynQ terms and feedback loops can be correctly handled. In this section, we discuss the restricted subset of synchronous models and how, with the usage of multiplicity 1 (linearity), these models are related to SynQ terms and their implementations.

5.1 Synchronous Models in SynQ

Generally, in a synchronous dataflow model, delay elements can be placed anywhere. It guarantees the expressiveness but also allows ill-behaved models, e.g., models that consist of zero-delay feedback loops, to be specified. To correctly handle delay elements and feedback loops, SynQ considers synchronous models in a form that: (1) the occurrences of combinational components and delay elements are strictly limited to the forward (from a system's input to its output) and backwards paths, respectively; and (2) there exists *exactly one* unit delay per backwards path. In this way, the *existence* of feedback loops is associated with the usage of delay elements (registers), which, as shown in Fig. 3b, can be explicitly specified in the signature of SynQ models. Combining with the carefully selected glue components in the sequential layer, we can, by type checking, reject all zero-delay feedbacks.

Under these restrictions, forward delays, such as the one in Fig. 3b, can be transformed and introduced as a component as follows:

Meanwhile, even though each backwards path is restricted to have exactly one unit delay, SynQ still has an expressiveness that is similar to Lustre, in which only zero-delay loops are forbidden [35]. This can be illustrated by the following example of how a feedback loop with two delays is specified in the desired form.

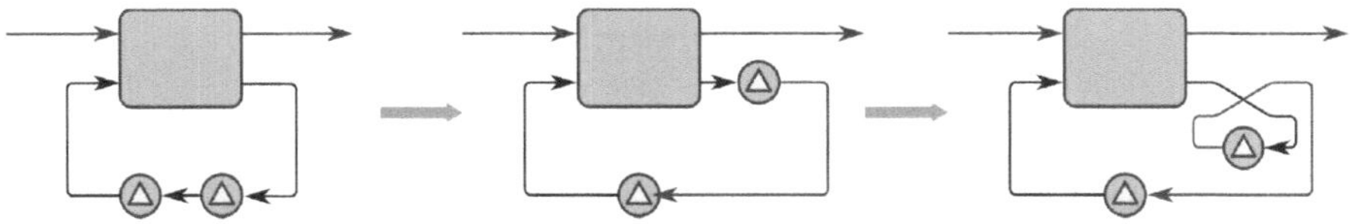

5.2 The Usage of Multiplicity 1

The multiplicity 1 is used in SynQ for two intertwined purposes: (1) it is associated with components in the context of SynQ models so that a model specified with the symantics of SynQ always corresponds to a restricted synchronous dataflow model discussed earlier; and (2) it is employed in the symantics of sequential components to restrict their implementation space. The *first* usage is demonstrated in the `isRising` example illustrated in Fig. 3b, in which the register is bound with multiplicity 1. Recall that we are targeting models in which there is a one-to-one correspondence between feedback loops and delay elements (registers). The multiplicity 1 in `isRising` guarantees that there will be exactly one usage of the register[2] and, hence, one feedback loop in the SynQ model. In this way, the type signature of SynQ models and the synchronous models specified in SynQ always agree with each other.

The *second* usage can be observed in the symantics and interpretations of sequential components, which are illustrated in Listing 1b and the last part of Sect. 4.2, respectively. The multiplicity 1 in this case ensures that all implementations of the same component share some common behaviour. For instance, an implementation of glue components `(=<<)` and `(<<<)` in Listing 1b should implement the following two compositions of sequential components, in which the components to be composed are represented in grey boxes.

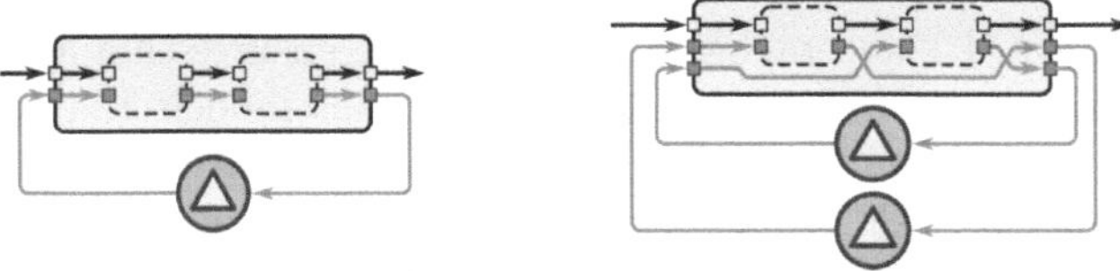

The muliplicity 1 ensures that the *software implementation* of `(=<<)` and `(<<<)` with the type `EvalS`, which is presented in the last part of Sect. 4.2, is *unique* in Idris2. Following the discussion in Sect. 4.2, this usage of multiplicity 1 further addresses the *second challenge* identified in Sect. 1 by restricting possible evaluation orders with linearity.

6 A Larger Example: FIFO with Handshake

We now use the design of a FIFO with a simple handshake protocol (Fig. 4) to demonstrate how, with the embedding of SynQ, modelling, testing and verifying synchronous systems are facilitated. This example is of interest because a

[2] In practice, only the `set` primitive (the input of the delay element) is restricted.

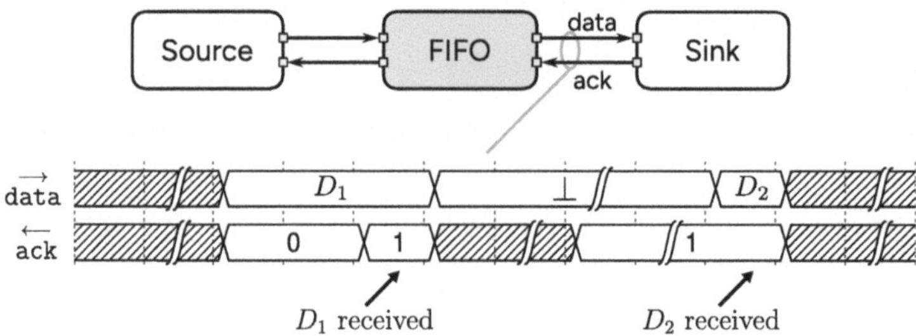

Fig. 4. An illustration of the handshake protocol implemented in Sect. 6.

FIFO, implemented as both hardware and software, is a fundamental component used for signal processing applications, which is an important target application domain of synchronous systems.

The protocol to be implemented is illustrated in Fig. 4. In this protocol, we have a forwarded data signal, from sender to receiver, whose elements may have the absent value denoted by $\perp$, and a backwards acknowledgement (ack) signal, with which the receiver acknowledges to the sender that the data has been received and new data can be produced. A valid datum is held by the sender until the `ack` signal is received. The receiver may also acknowledge to the sender that it is ready for new data when the current data is absent. In such cases, the `ack` signal is held until a valid datum is received. Note that, in this protocol, data receiving and `ack` signal producing happen simultaneously at the same clock event, which results in the zero-delay feedback, as shown in Fig. 4, in high-level models.

6.1 Modelling the FIFO in SynQ

The leveraging of QTT and tagless final embedding ensures that all closed terms typed with `comb a b` and `seq s a b` are synchronous models that can be interpreted into software or hardware implementation. It means that we can leverage the full expressiveness of Idris2 as a programming language for system modelling. For instance, even though the current primitive types of SynQ illustrated in Sect. 4.2 are relatively restricted, the state of a FIFO with arbitrary depth can be modelled by a vector-like type `Repeat n a` that is introduced by the following function.

```
Repeat: Nat -> Type -> Type
Repeat 0 t = ()
Repeat 1 t = t
Repeat (S $ S k) t = (t, Repeat (S k) t)
```

It is easy to verify that `Repeat n a` satisfies the predicate `Sig` (c.f. Section 4.2) if the type `a` satisfies `Sig` and, hence, it is a type that can be handled by SynQ models. Based on this type, we can have a universal component inductively defined for updating the state of an arbitrary FIFO, its core is the follows.

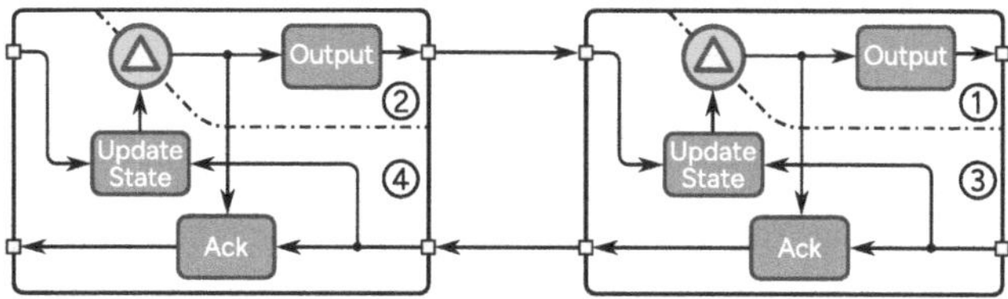

Fig. 5. An illustration of the composition of two FIFOs. The dashed lines indicate where a FIFO is partitioned, and numbers indicate the order of invocation.

```
dropLast: ... -> {n: _}
  -> comb () (Repeat (n+1) a) -> comb () (Repeat n a)
dropLast {n = 0} x = unit
dropLast {n = (S 0)} x = proj1 x
dropLast {n = (S (S k))} x = prod (proj1 x) (dropLast $ proj2 x)
```

With this component built, the rest of the FIFO is relatively straightforward.

The feedback loop entailed in the handshake protocol is eliminated by partitioning models implementing this protocol into two parts, which correspond to the forward (data) and backwards (ack) paths, respectively. This partitioning is enabled by Idris2's capability of specifying higher-order functions and the fact that the delay elements are modelled in SynQ with two separated primitives `get` and `set` that are for delay elements' output and input, respectively. Partitioned models can then be composed by invoking each part of the model in an order that obeys data dependency. Figure 5 illustrates how two FIFOs are partitioned and composed, with numbers indicating the order of invocation.

6.2 Property-Based Testing and Formal Verification

Interpreting SynQ models as Idris2 functions allows Idris2 to be leveraged for property-based testing and formal verification. For example, consider a desired property of a FIFO that: *all valid data consumed by a FIFO will eventually be produced in the consumption order.* We can easily define the following Idris2 function, in which the software implementation of a FIFO (`fifoMealy`) is tested against the property under the dataflow semantic model.

```
fifoProp input =
  let (dataIn , ackIn)  = unzip input
      (dataOut, ackOut) = unzip $ fifoMealy input
  in (squeeze $ dataOut `zip` ackIn) <: (squeeze $ dataIn `zip` ackOut)
```

In this function, `zip` and `unzip` send lists of products to products of lists and vice versa; `squeeze` drops events, which consist of an invalid datum or a false `ack` signal, in a given list; and `(<:)` is the *prefix-of* predicate that asserts whether a list on its lhs is a prefix of the list on its rhs. Note that functions invoked in `fifoProp`, except `fifoMealy`, are normal Idris2 functions that may not even be implementable as synchronous systems.

Instead of directly verifying the property that is being tested, in QTT we specify and verify the implemented FIFO's stepwise behaviour, meaning that the verification concerns the system's output and state transition for each input event. For instance, the following proposition is specified and verified:

Proposition. *For arbitrary valid input data and* `ack` *signal from the successor stage, if the* `ack` *signal 1 is produced, then, at the next clock event, the current input data is at the end of the FIFO (data is consumed if* `ack` *is set).*

The verification follows the conventional theorem-proving process. In this way, the performance limitation of Idris2's implementation of QTT is minimised.

What is of interest is that, by treating atomic components of SynQ as black boxes whose behaviour is not exposed to the type checker, proving a proposition, like the one above, of an implemented SynQ model enables properties that these black boxes must have to be identified. These identified properties can then be used as *proof obligations* and be verified against the external implementation (C-implementation in our case) of these components. For instance, one identified property about the *bitwise-and component* is that:

$$\forall x : \mathtt{BV_n}.\ \mathtt{bvAnd}\, x\, 0 \equiv 0$$

In which `bvAnd` internally calls the corresponding C function introduced by FFI. This property suggests the following contract specified in ACSL (ANSI/ISO C Specification Language) [3] for the C function:

```
/*@ assigns \nothing;
  @ ensures (val_2 == 0) ==> (\result == 0);
  @ */
uint64_t bv_and(uint8_t len, uint64_t val_1, uint64_t val_2);
```

The verification of this contract then ensures the correctness of the verification of the FIFO.

7 Related Work

Theorem proving has been proven to be a realistic approach for building high-assurance software through many projects, such as seL4 [25], CompCert [27], and Vélus [7]. In these projects, a microkernel (seL4) and compilers for C (CompCert) and Lustre (Vélus) are built and verified. The latter two involve programs directly written in Rocq (formerly Coq), which shares a similar usage of a proof assistant to the usage of Idris2 in this paper. While these projects focus on the verified final products, this paper aims to demonstrate that an expressive type theory can be employed for the separation of concerns. This, then, enables a proof assistant to be systematically used as a framework for designing safety-critical embedded systems.

Being less formal, functional programming languages have been employed for modelling both synchronous systems and digital circuits. Lucid-Synchrone [13] is a synchronous language built upon OCaml that extends Lustre with higher-level mechanisms provided by OCaml, such as types and higher-order functions. Besides the original work, there is also a shallow embedding of Lucid-Synchrone in Rocq [6] relying on the *clocks as types* paradigm [12]. Compared to them, the design and implementation of SynQ follows the idea of the *hierarchy of languages* proposed by Turner [41]. Specifically, with QTT and the tagless final embedding, we intend to employ Idris2 as the more expressive language inside which terms in SynQ, the less expressive language that is easier for reasoning, are designed. ForSyDe [37,42] is a framework that allows models of computation [26], including the synchronous model of computation, to be modelled in Haskell. Lava [5] is an EDSL in Haskell for digital circuit design, which, similar to SynQ, allows circuits to be simulated as Haskell programs and also to be formally verified based on a symbolic interpretation. Limited by Haskell, verification of Lava terms has to be conducted externally. In [29], the κ-calculus is employed to build a DSL for digital circuit design in Haskell. It allows recursive structures in circuits to be specified by higher-order functions in Haskell while ensuring that the results remain only in the κ-calculus, and hence are all well-formed digital circuits.

Finally, the *first challenge* mentioned in Sect. 1 is often referred to as the problem about *exotic terms*, and there have been some investigations. Besides the methodology employed here, this challenge may also be addressed by introducing the *necessity modality*. The interested reader is referred to [15,20,43] for detailed discussions.

8 Conclusion

This paper demonstrated how the challenges of the embedding of SynQ can be addressed by the usage of QTT's multiplicity 0 (Sect. 4.3), multicity 1 (Sect. 5.2), combined with the tagless final embedding (Sect. 4.2). Successfully addressing these challenges makes SynQ a well-typed EDSL, which not only enables synchronous systems to be modelled and implemented, but also allows the rest of Idris2 and its QTT implementation to be leveraged for synchronous system design and verification (Sects. 3 and 6). It is worth mentioning here that, even though Idris2 is chosen for its off-the-shelf support of QTT and well-implemented compilation infrastructure, the method discussed can also fit into other type-theory-based proof assistants because linear type theory is a substructural type theory that can be embedded in others [36]. As future work, we plan to investigate domain-specific methodologies, e.g., tactics, tailored for testing and verifying SynQ terms against the dataflow semantic model. Since SynQ considers only a subset of Idris2 terms, these methodologies are expected to be more efficient than simply verifying SynQ terms as Idris2 terms.

Acknowledgments. This research was partially funded by the Sweden's Innovation Agency via the NFFP7 project 2019-02743: TRANSFORM – Design transformation for correct-by-construction design methodology, and the Advanced and innovative digitalization project 2021-02484: EARLY BIRD – Seamless System Design from Concept Phase to Implementation.

References

1. Abramsky, S.: Computational interpretations of linear logic. Theor. Comput. Sci. **111**(1–2), 3–57 (1993)
2. Atkey, R.: Syntax and semantics of quantitative type theory. In: Proceedings of the 33rd Annual ACM/IEEE Symposium on Logic in Computer Science, pp. 56–65 (2018)
3. Baudin, P., Filliâtre, J.C., Marché, C., Monate, B., Moy, Y., Prevosto, V.: ACSL: ANSI/ISO C specification (2021). https://frama-c.com/html/acsl.html
4. Benveniste, A., Le Guernic, P., Jacquemot, C.: Synchronous programming with events and relations: the SIGNAL language and its semantics. Sci. Comput. Program. **16**(2), 103–149 (1991)
5. Bjesse, P., Claessen, K., Sheeran, M., Singh, S.: Lava: hardware design in Haskell. ACM SIGPLAN Not. **34**(1), 174–184 (1998)
6. Boulmé, S., Hamon, G.: A clocked denotational semantics for lucid-synchrone in coq. Rap. tech., LIP6 (2001)
7. Bourke, T., Pesin, B., Pouzet, M.: Verified compilation of synchronous dataflow with state machines. ACM Trans. Embed. Comput. Syst. **22**(5s), 1–26 (2023)
8. Boussinot, F., De Simone, R.: The ESTEREL language. Proc. IEEE **79**(9), 1293–1304 (1991)
9. Brady, E.: Idris, a general-purpose dependently typed programming language: design and implementation. J. Funct. Program. **23**(5), 552–593 (2013)
10. Brady, E.: Idris 2: Quantitative type theory in practice. In: 35th European Conference on Object-Oriented Programming (ECOOP 2021). Schloss Dagstuhl-Leibniz-Zentrum für Informatik (2021)
11. Carette, J., Kiselyov, O., Shan, C.C.: Finally tagless, partially evaluated: tagless staged interpreters for simpler typed languages. J. Funct. Program. **19**(5), 509–543 (2009)
12. Caspi, P.: Clocks in dataflow languages. Theor. Comput. Sci. **94**(1), 125–140 (1992)
13. Caspi, P., Hamon, G., Pouzet, M.: Synchronous functional programming: the lucid synchrone experiment. In: Real-Time Systems: Description and Verification Techniques: Theory and Tools. Hermes, pp. 28–41 (2008)
14. Cheney, J., Hinze, R.: First-class phantom types. Technical report, Cornell University (2003)
15. Despeyroux, J., Pfenning, F., Schürmann, C.: Primitive recursion for higher-order abstract syntax. In: de Groote, P., Roger Hindley, J. (eds.) TLCA 1997. LNCS, vol. 1210, pp. 147–163. Springer, Heidelberg (1997). https://doi.org/10.1007/3-540-62688-3_34
16. Gammie, P.: Synchronous digital circuits as functional programs. ACM Comput. Surv. (CSUR) **46**(2), 1–27 (2013)
17. Gibbons, J., Wu, N.: Folding domain-specific languages: deep and shallow embeddings (functional pearl). In: Proceedings of the 19th ACM SIGPLAN International Conference on Functional Programming, pp. 339–347 (2014)
18. Gilles, K.: The semantics of a simple language for parallel programming. Inf. Process. **74**(471–475), 15–28 (1974)

19. Girard, J.Y.: Linear logic. Theor. Comput. Sci. **50**(1), 1–101 (1987)
20. Hofmann, M.: Semantical analysis of higher-order abstract syntax. In: Proceedings. 14th Symposium on Logic in Computer Science (Cat. No. PR00158), pp. 204–213. IEEE (1999)
21. Hudak, P., Hughes, J., Peyton Jones, S., Wadler, P.: A history of Haskell: being lazy with class. In: Proceedings of the third ACM SIGPLAN Conference on History of Programming Languages, pp. 12–1 (2007)
22. Hughes, J.: Generalising monads to arrows. Sci. Comput. Program. **37**(1–3), 67–111 (2000)
23. Jones, M.P.: A system of constructor classes: overloading and implicit higher-order polymorphism. In: Proceedings of the Conference on Functional Programming Languages and Computer Architecture, pp. 52–61 (1993)
24. Jones, S.P., Jones, M., Meijer, E.: Type classes: an exploration of the design space. In: Haskell Workshop, pp. 1–16 (1997)
25. Klein, G., et al.: seL4: formal verification of an os kernel. In: Proceedings of the ACM SIGOPS 22nd Symposium on Operating Systems Principles, pp. 207–220 (2009)
26. Lee, E.A., Sangiovanni-Vincentelli, A.: A framework for comparing models of computation. IEEE Trans. Comput. Aided Des. Integr. Circuits Syst. **17**(12), 1217–1229 (1998)
27. Leroy, X.: Formal verification of a realistic compiler. Commun. ACM **52**(7), 107–115 (2009). http://xavierleroy.org/publi/compcert-CACM.pdf
28. McBride, C.: I got plenty o'nuttin'. iN: A List of Successes That Can Change the World: Essays Dedicated to Philip Wadler on the Occasion of His 60th Birthday, pp. 207–233 (2016)
29. Megacz, A.: Hardware design with generalized arrows. In: Gill, A., Hage, J. (eds.) IFL 2011. LNCS, vol. 7257, pp. 164–180. Springer, Heidelberg (2012). https://doi.org/10.1007/978-3-642-34407-7_11
30. Moura, L., Ullrich, S.: The Lean 4 theorem prover and programming language. In: Platzer, A., Sutcliffe, G. (eds.) CADE 2021. LNCS (LNAI), vol. 12699, pp. 625–635. Springer, Cham (2021). https://doi.org/10.1007/978-3-030-79876-5_37
31. de Muijnck-Hughes, J., Allais, G., Brady, E.: Type theory as a language workbench. In: Eelco Visser Commemorative Symposium (2023)
32. Norell, U.: Towards a practical programming language based on dependent type theory. Ph.D. thesis (2007)
33. Peterson, J., Jones, M.: Implementing type classes. ACM SIGPLAN Not. **28**(6), 227–236 (1993)
34. Pfenning, F., Elliott, C.: Higher-order abstract syntax. ACM SIGPLAN Not. **23**(7), 199–208 (1988)
35. Pilaud, D., Halbwachs, N., Plaice, J.: Lustre: a declarative language for programming synchronous systems. In: Proceedings of the 14th Annual ACM Symposium on Principles of Programming Languages (14th POPL 1987), vol. 178, p. 188. ACM, New York. Citeseer (1987)
36. Polakow, J.: Embedding a full linear lambda calculus in haskell. ACM SIGPLAN Not. **50**(12), 177–188 (2015)
37. Sander, I., Jantsch, A.: System modeling and transformational design refinement in ForSyDe. IEEE Trans. Comput. Aided Des. Integr. Circuits Syst. **23**(1), 17–32 (2004)
38. Sifakis, J.: Toward a system design science. In: Bensalem, S., Lakhneck, Y., Legay, A. (eds.) ETAPS 2014. LNCS, vol. 8415, pp. 225–234. Springer, Heidelberg (2014). https://doi.org/10.1007/978-3-642-54848-2_15

39. Sifakis, J.: System design automation: challenges and limitations. Proc. IEEE **103**(11), 2093–2103 (2015)
40. Team, T.C.D.: The Coq Proof Assistant (2024). https://doi.org/10.5281/zenodo.14542673
41. Turner, D.A.: Total functional programming. J. Univ. Comput. Sci. **10**(7), 751–768 (2004)
42. Ungureanu, G., Medeiros, J.E.G.D., Sundström, T., Söderquist, I., Åhlander, A., Sander, I.: ForSyDe-atom: taming complexity in cyber physical system design with layers. ACM Trans. Embed. Comput. Syst. (TECS) **20**(2), 1–27 (2021)
43. Washburn, G., Weirich, S.: Boxes go bananas: encoding higher-order abstract syntax with parametric polymorphism. ACM SIGPLAN Not. **38**(9), 249–262 (2003)

Modular Data Refinement

David Faitelson[1(✉)], Leonid Shepetovsky[2], and Shmuel Tyszberowicz[1,3]

[1] Afeka Tel Aviv Academic College of Engineering, Mivtza Kadesh 38, Tel Aviv, Israel
davidf@afeka.ac.il, tyshbe@tau.ac.il
[2] The Open University of Israel, 1 University Road, Ra'anana, Israel
[3] Southwest University, Chongqing, China
https://www.afeka.ac.il/en/faculty-en/david-faitelson

Abstract. Modularity and refinement are two important software engineering concepts. Modularity is essential for maintaining intellectual control over complex systems by breaking them into loosely coupled subsystems. Refinement is a systematic approach that gradually transforms a specification into a working system while ensuring correctness at each step. Unfortunately, modularity and refinement have an uneasy relationship with each other, as the operators used to describe a system model in a modular way are generally nonmonotonic with respect to refinement. In this work we present a useful technique and the necessary conditions to ensure that data refinement is monotonic with respect to conjunction. The essential idea is to represent all system operations using a smaller set of operations (kernel) that do not interfere with each other. It is then possible to refine the entire system by refining just the kernel. We demonstrate this technique with a simple example and refer to a larger case study in which this technique was applied to a model of a real-world application.

Keywords: Data Refinement · Modular Refinement · State-Based Specification · Z · Alloy

1 Introduction

Modularity is essential for our ability to design complex software systems. This is true for both traditional (non-formal) and formal development, whether we employ proof-based methods or model checking [12]. By decomposing a large system description into more or less independent modules, we can develop each module independently with the confidence that when the modules are assembled, the entire assembly will conform to its intended behavior.

In formal development, the high-level system description is an abstract model, and its design constitutes a more detailed and concrete model. The relationship between these models is captured by *data refinement*. Data refinement is a standard formal development technique (e.g., [1,11]) in which we begin with an abstract description of a system and gradually make it more concrete by adding details and removing nondeterminism, until we end with a concrete and

A. Goharshady and C. Haase (Eds.): SETTA 2025, LNCS 16458, pp. 33–56, 2026.
https://doi.org/10.1007/978-981-95-7826-9_3

deterministic model that can be easily translated into executable code. At each step, we must prove that the concrete level correctly refines the preceding, more abstract level. However, this task can be tedious because, as the model becomes more concrete, we often have to add new state variables and operations, which increases the burden of refinement in all subsequent levels.

In the context of formal development, modularity is our ability to break the abstract system model into separate smaller models, such that we can refine the entire system by refining each model. However, creating an effective modular structure is often difficult because interdependencies between the system's parts may prevent us from reasoning about them in isolation.

We showed in [6] that systems with many state variables can be partitioned into separate subsystems, where the operations in each subsystem access and manipulate mostly their state variables. It is then possible to refine the entire system by refining each subsystem individually. However, while attempting to apply this technique to our case study (see Sect. 5), we found that its high-level specification consists of many operations that manipulate a few state variables. As a result, this technique cannot be used.

This kind of model is not unique to our particular case study. It arises whenever the high-level specification is simple, but the implementation is challenging due to demanding nonfunctional requirements. In this work we propose a technique we call *modular refinement* that could be used to create a modular structure for systems of this kind. We show that in such cases, it is possible to encapsulate the variables within a small set of system operations (which we refer to as *kernel operations*), with which we can describe all other system operations. We then demonstrate that under appropriate conditions, we can refine the entire system by refining only its kernel operations.

The remainder of this paper is organized as follows. Section 2 introduces the formal foundations in which we represent state-based systems, their operations, and the precise notion of data refinement. This is followed by a section introducing a simple system to illustrate the modular refinement technique (Sect. 3). Section 4 defines and analyses the conditions under which modular refinement holds. Then we briefly outline a larger case study that applies this technique to analyze the structure of a real-world application (Sect. 5). A related work review is given in Sect. 6. We finish the paper with a discussion that expands the meaning of our results beyond the domain of formal specification (Sect. 7), and a conclusion section that reviews the limitations of the approach and suggests directions for future work (Sect. 8).

We provide a GitHub repository[1] to accompany this paper. The repository includes the entire development of the case study, as well as the full development of the resource manager example in both Z and Alloy notations. The Z model includes manual proofs, and the Alloy models contain automatically checked assertions that demonstrate that data refinement holds between the abstract and concrete models.

---

[1] https://github.com/drdavidf/modular-refinement.

2 Background

In this section we briefly describe the semantic domain in which we formalize the concepts of software systems and how we represent them in Z, the notation we use to illustrate the ideas with concrete examples.

2.1 State-Based Specifications

A state-based specification describes a system as a collection of state variables, each of which may hold values constrained by type and invariants (e.g., numbers, sets, relations). A system state is determined by an assignment of values to the state variables. System operations are described as predicates over pairs of states: the current state and the state after the operation has been applied. These predicates define the meaning of operations as relations between system states. Because operation specifications are predicates, we can use logical operators such as conjunction or disjunction to combine them. For example, a conjunction of two operation specifications indicates that the system's implementation should satisfy both. There are many notations for specifying state-based models. The more familiar ones are *Z* [11], *B* [1], *EventB* [2], and *Alloy* [8]. In this work, we use the *Z* notation to present our ideas; however, they can be readily translated to any other state-based modeling language. Indeed, the underlying work on which this paper is based [10] was originally developed in the *Alloy* notation.

2.2 The Z Notation

To help readers unfamiliar with the Z notation, we provide a concise overview of the notation's syntax and major specification constructs. For a proper introduction, we recommend the excellent textbook Using Z, which is freely available online [11].

As a brief overview of the Z notation, consider, for example, a simple resource manager that keeps track of resources that are either free or currently used. The manager provides the following operations: *init*, which initializes the system; *acquire*, which provides a free resource and marks it as used; *release*, which returns a used resource to the pool of free resources; *purchase*, which adds a new resource to the pool of free resources; and *discard*, which removes a resource from the system.

Figure 1 shows how the system's state space may be represented in the Z notation. The first definition is *ID*—a finite set of integers. This represents the total set of resource identifiers available to the system.

The next definition is a Z schema. A Z schema is a versatile tool that is used to describe the system's state space and its operations. In addition, it can be used as a predicate or a data type.

| $ID : \mathbb{F}\,\mathbb{N}$

System

$used : \mathbb{P}\,ID$
$free : \mathbb{P}\,ID$

$used \cap free = \emptyset$

Fig. 1. An abstract model of a simple resource manager. The set of identifiers must be finite. A resource may be either in use or free, but not both simultaneously.

A Z schema consists of two parts: the top section defines the variables, and the bottom specifies a predicate that constrains their values. In the resource manager example, the top part describes the state variables and their types, and the bottom part determines the system's invariant. We can see that the manager has two sets of identifiers that are always disjoint.

Z schemas can include other schemas. When a schema S includes another schema T, all the definitions in T are added to S and T's predicate is conjoined to S's predicate. The example in Fig. 2 is a common pattern that introduces two sets of variables based on the same schema that is used extensively to model operations. In general, when S is a schema of a system structure, then ΔS is the schema that includes S and S'.

Fig. 2. This schema includes two *System* schemas. The prime operator applied to the second occurrence of *System* adds a prime symbol to every variable in that schema. Thus, the variables in this schema are: $used$, $free$, $used'$, $free'$. Unprimed variables denote initial states, primed variables indicate final states. The predicate of this schema is the conjunction of the predicates in *System* and $System'$.

A schema that models an operation includes two instances of a state schema: one representing the system's state just before the operation is applied (the operation's initial state), and the other representing the state just after the operation is completed (the operation's final state). When used in this role, the bottom part is a predicate that defines the relation between the initial and final states of the operation. Thus, a Z schema operation defines a relation between system states (and the operation's precondition corresponds to the relation's domain). For example, Fig. 3 shows a model of the *release* operation. We can see that the operation is applied to the state of the entire resource manager. In addition, it takes an identifier as input, and its specification indicates that the identifier must be a used resource; the operation removes the identifier from the *used* set and adds it to the *free* set.

```
┌─ Release ─────────────────────────────
│ ΔSystem
│ id : ID
├──────────
│ id ∈ used
│ used' = used \ {id}
│ free' = free ∪ {id}
└───────────────────────────────────────
```

Fig. 3. A Z specification of the resource manager's release operation.

Quantifiers in the Z notation have the following meaning:

Quantifier	Meaning
$\forall x : X \bullet P$	For each x in X, predicate P holds.
$\exists x : X \bullet P$	There exists an x in X such that P holds.
$\forall x : X \mid P \bullet Q$	For each x in X, if P holds, then Q holds.

We may also quantify over schemas. In this case, we quantify over their definitions and restrict them according to their constraint. For example,

$$\exists\, System \bullet 7 \in used$$

Intuitively, this says that there exists a system in which the identifier 7 is one of the used identifiers. Formally, we substitute *System* with its equivalent meaning to get,

$$\exists\, used, free : \mathbb{P}\, ID \mid used \cap free = \emptyset \bullet 7 \in used$$

Note that the system's invariant appears in the implication's antecedent to ensure that we always refer to sound systems.

One common case of quantifying over a schema is when we calculate an operation's precondition—the predicate that defines the initial states from which the operation is guaranteed to meet its specification. These states are exactly those for which a final state exists. Formally, pre $Operation = \exists\, System' \bullet Operation$. For more details, see [11] and the Z model that we provide in the accompanying website [9].

Finally, here is the meaning of several relational operators that we use throughout the paper (in all cases $r \in A \leftrightarrow B$ is a relation between sets A and B:

Operator	Meaning
$\text{dom} r$	the first members of each pair in r
$\text{ran} r$	the second members of each pair in r
$X \lhd r$	all pairs in r whose first member is in X
$r \fatsemi u$	the relational composition of r with u

We use Z in this work to illustrate our ideas with concrete examples. However, we will conduct the mathematical analysis in terms of the underlying relational semantics of state-based specifications. Thus, the mathematical analysis is language-independent, and its conclusions can be applied to any state-based modeling language, provided the results are appropriately translated into the specific notation.

2.3 Data Refinement

Data refinement links two descriptions of the same system at two abstraction levels. The difference in the abstraction levels manifests itself in the difference between the states of each level. States at the concrete level are more detailed than those at the abstract level. For data refinement to hold between two system descriptions, every operation described at a concrete level must be simulated by the corresponding operation at the abstract level. Because each level is described in a different state space, we must use a linking relation, called *retrieve*, that associates abstract states with their concrete representations.

There are several ways to specify the conditions under which data refinement holds. Here we use the condition called *forwards simulation* [11]:

$$\text{dom} op_A \subseteq \text{dom}(r \fatsemi op_c) \tag{1}$$

$$\text{dom} op_A \lhd (r \fatsemi op_C) \subseteq op_A \fatsemi r \tag{2}$$

The first condition (1) states that every concrete operation op_C[2] must be defined anywhere the corresponding abstract operation op_A is defined. The second condition (2) states that within the abstract operation's domain, every possible effect of the concrete operation must correspond to some possible effect of the abstract operation. The retrieve relation r translates between corresponding abstract and concrete states. See Fig. 4.

If these two equations hold for two operations and a relation r, we will say that op_A simulates op_C under the relation r and write

$$op_A \leq_r op_C.$$

[2] Unless otherwise mentioned, we conduct the analysis using the relational meaning of operations.

Note that for data refinement to hold between an abstract and a concrete model, there must be a single retrieve relation that can be used for all the system operations.

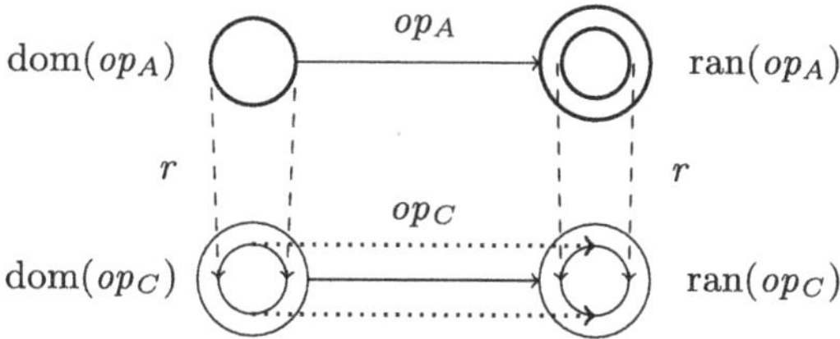

Fig. 4. The relationship in a simulation of a concrete operation op_C by an abstract operation op_A. The retrieve relation r maps every state in op_A's domain to some concrete state in op_C's domain. Op_A can simulate op_C on these states, because r^-1 maps each concrete final state to a possible final abstract state.

When translated to the Z notation, the rules for forwards simulation look like this (R is the retrieve relation) [11]:

$$\forall A;\ C \bullet \text{pre } Op_A \wedge R \Rightarrow \text{pre } Op_C$$

$$\forall A;\ C;\ C' \bullet \text{pre } Op_A \wedge R \wedge Op_C \Rightarrow \exists A' \bullet Op_A \wedge R'$$

2.4 Functional Refinement

In many cases, the concrete representation encodes a single abstract representation. For example, when a set is represented by a linked list, many different linked lists may represent the same set, but a single linked list always represents a single set. In such cases, the inverse of the retrieve relation is a function that maps each concrete state to the abstract state it represents; thus, the refinement is called *functional refinement*. Functional refinement is very useful because it is common and simplifies the proofs of simulation. We will see that it plays an essential role in enabling modular refinement.

3 Illustrative Example

To illustrate our technique, we describe a simple example building on the previously introduced specification of a simple resource manager.[3] See Fig. 5. We have made this example as simple as possible to avoid unnecessary technical details

[3] This example was inspired by the operating system scheduler model given in [11]. The complete development is available in the accompanying GitHub repository.

that will distract from the essential ideas of the technique. We describe a more realistic application in Sect. 5.

We have added the prefix *A_* to indicate that this is the abstract version of the resource manager and marked 0 as an illegal identifier. But, otherwise, it is identical to the previous model. The concrete manager represents the *used* and *free* sets with chains (models of linked lists).

$$ID : \mathbb{F}\,\mathbb{N}$$
$$0 \in ID$$

A_System

$$used : \mathbb{P}\,ID$$
$$free : \mathbb{P}\,ID$$
$$0 \notin used$$
$$0 \notin free$$
$$used \cap free = \emptyset$$

Fig. 5. An abstract model of a simple resource manager. A non-zero natural number identifies a resource. It may be either in use or free.

In Fig. 6 we illustrate how one operation (release) is modeled at the two abstraction levels. Notice that while the abstract *release* operation accesses the state variables directly, the concrete version is defined in terms of operations that manipulate the chain data structure.

In a traditional refinement step, we must prove that the concrete model refines the abstract model by proving for each operation that the abstract model of that operation simulates the corresponding concrete model. However, most of what happens in the operations involves using a linked list to implement a set. If we can exploit this fact to reduce the proof load to just showing that the chain refines the set, we will significantly simplify and speed up the development process. To achieve this reduction, we first transform the abstract model into a form that is similar to the concrete model; see Fig. 7. The operations *X_AddToFree*, *X_RemoveFromUsed* encapsulate the state space of the data structure in each version of the model (X stands for A or C). We will call them *kernel operations*. We can describe all the other manager operations using such kernel operations. Because the abstract and concrete versions have the same structure, we do not need to explicitly write the concrete manager operations. It is enough to write only the abstract operations. Indeed, with proper tool support, the concrete version can be automatically generated from the abstract version.

As we will see in the next section, to prove that the concrete manager refines the abstract manager, it is enough to prove that the abstract kernel operations simulate their corresponding concrete versions. Once we have proved that the abstract version of each kernel operation simulates its concrete version, we have automatically proven that the concrete system refines the abstract system.

This is easier to do than to prove the simulation between all the concrete and abstract manager operations, because it requires fewer proofs, and the proofs are easier because the kernel operations are defined on fewer state variables and are simpler than the manager operations. Whereas for a small example like the resource manager, this may not be apparent, for a larger model (as we demonstrate later in the case study (Sect. 5), the difference becomes significant.

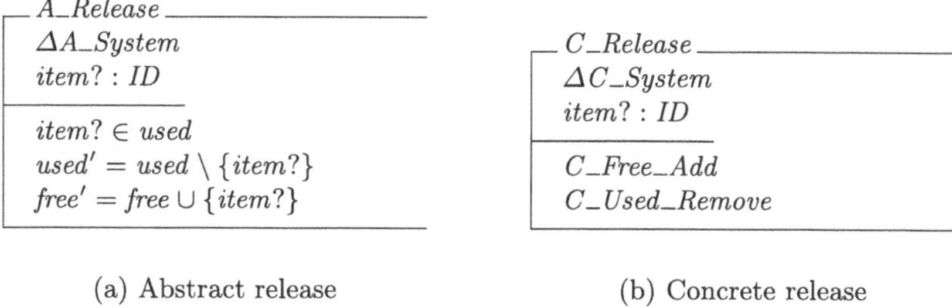

Fig. 6. The abstract and concrete versions representing a traditional modeling approach.

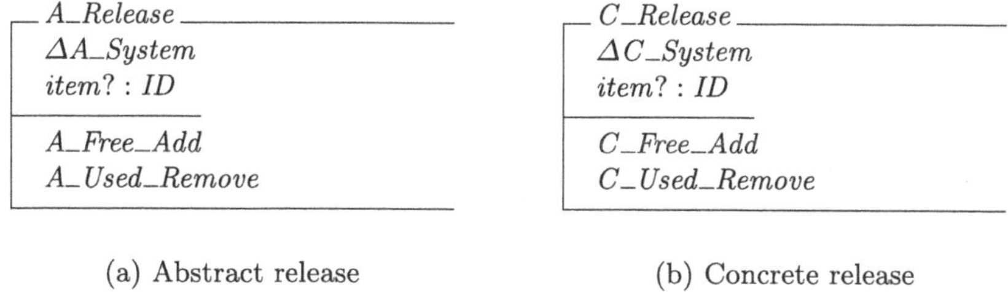

Fig. 7. A modular representation of the *release* operation. The kernel operations are compatible because they constrain different state variables.

4 Modular Refinement

When we have a system description that involves a large set of operations $OP_A = op_A^1, \ldots, op_A^n$, all accessing the same set of state variables, we can sometimes find a simpler set of operations $\widehat{OP}_A = \hat{op}_A^1, \ldots, \hat{op}_A^k$ $(k \leq n)$ with which we can construct all the system operations in OP_A. Only the operations in $\widehat{OP}_A$ access the state variables directly, hiding them from the larger set of operations. Under appropriate conditions, which we describe later in this section, it is possible to refine the entire system by refining only the operations in $\widehat{OP}_A$. We call this technique *modular refinement*.

Modular refinement significantly reduces the time and effort invested in refining the system compared to a standard refinement, where we have to refine all the operations in OP_A. It becomes more useful the more refinement levels we have, because each refinement step adds yet another set of operations and complexity, making further refinements of the original operations more difficult and tedious to perform.

For modular refinement to succeed, we must find a set of k kernel operations such that every system operation op_A can be expressed as a conjunction of some subset of the kernel operations.

$$op_A = \bigcap_{i \in ix} \hat{op}^i_A \qquad \text{where } ix \subseteq \{1..k\}$$

We can start by looking at the conditions necessary for an operation that is expressed using just a pair of kernel operations u_A and v_A:

$$op_A = u_A \cap v_A$$

Assume that we simulate u_A with u_C and separately v_A with v_C, when can we say that op_A simulates $u_C \cap v_C$?

It turns out (see Sect. 9.2 for the proofs) that we must require two things:

1. The inverse of the retrieve relation must be *functional*,
2. The two operations must be *compatible*—they must be able to achieve their goals without interfering with each other.

The first requirement means that we must use functional refinement, but this is not a severe restriction. In most cases, concrete models represent a single abstraction; thus, the mapping from concrete to abstract states will be functional. The second requirement is novel; let us spend some time discussing it.

4.1 Compatible Operations

In the following sections, when we talk about operations, we always mean operation specifications, not their implementation. An implementation is, in most cases, deterministic. But a specification can be non-deterministic. That is, we may specify the desired effect of an operation without determining the exact value of the state variables. For example, we may specify that an acquire operation provides a free resource without determining which resource to provide.

When the specifications of two system operations op_1 and op_2 are compatible, it is possible to implement the system in such a way that it will satisfy both operation specifications at once. In other words, $op_1 \cap op_2$ could be simulated separately by op_1 and by op_2. See Fig. 8.

Formally, we define compatibility between relations as follows:

Definition 41. *Two binary relations $X : A \leftrightarrow B$ and $Y : A \leftrightarrow B$ are compatible if* $\mathrm{dom}(X) = \mathrm{dom}(Y)$ *and* $\forall\, a \in \mathrm{dom}(X) \bullet \exists\, b \in B \bullet a \mapsto b \in (X \cap Y)$.

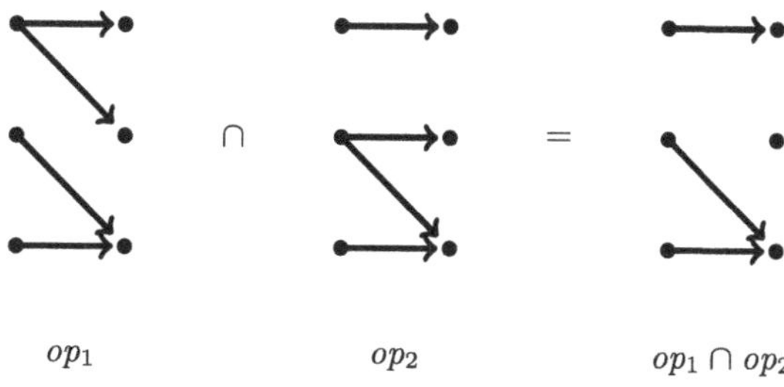

Fig. 8. A relational representation of compatible operations. The two operations op_1 and op_2 are compatible because they have the same precondition (domain) and for each initial state, there is a final state that is mutually acceptable by both.

Note that these two conditions are necessary. Two relations can be *consistent*, i.e., have the same domain [4], but not compatible. The reason is that they can have the same domain yet not agree on the final state of a given initial state.

In a Z model, we can adapt the schema refinement rules to check for compatibility. The original rules for a functional forwards simulation are [11]

$$\forall A;\ A';\ C;\ C' \bullet \text{pre}\ Op_A \wedge R \wedge Op_C \wedge R' \Rightarrow Op_A$$

$$\forall A;\ C \bullet \text{pre}\ Op_A \wedge R \Rightarrow \text{pre}\ Op_C$$

However, because we are checking for simulation in the same space S, we have $A = C = S$ and the retrieve relation is the identity relation. This simplifies the rules, which become:

$$\forall S;\ S' \bullet (\text{pre}\ Op_A) \wedge Op_C \Rightarrow Op_A$$

$$\forall S \bullet \text{pre}\ Op_A \Rightarrow \text{pre}\ Op_C$$

Therefore, given two operation schemas Op_1 and Op_2, the operation $Op_1 \wedge Op_2$ is simulated by each one exactly when

$$\forall S;\ S' \bullet Op_1 \wedge Op_2 \Rightarrow Op_1$$

$$\forall S \bullet \text{pre}\ Op_1 \Leftrightarrow \text{pre}\,(Op_1 \wedge Op_2)$$

$$\forall S;\ S' \bullet Op_1 \wedge Op_2 \Rightarrow Op_2$$

$$\forall S \bullet \text{pre}\ Op_2 \Leftrightarrow \text{pre}\,(Op_1 \wedge Op_2)$$

Note that the implication in the simplified rule became an equivalence. This is because the conjunction can only strengthen the precondition.

The following is a concrete example that demonstrates the idea of compatible operations. Op_1 and Op_2 are two operations that constrain the value of the same state variable x:

Op_1
$x : \mathbb{N}$ $x' : \mathbb{N}$
$x' > x$

Op_2
$x : \mathbb{N}$ $x' : \mathbb{N}$
$x' \in \{2x, x\}$

It is easy to see that the precondition of each operation is *true*. Thus, they are consistent, both have the same precondition. Yet their conjunction fails to refine Op_1 because,

$$
\begin{aligned}
& Op_1 \wedge Op_2 \\
& \quad \Rightarrow x' > x \wedge x' \in \{2x, x\} \\
& \quad \Rightarrow x' = 2x
\end{aligned}
$$

The last predicate $x' = 2x$ does not imply Op_1 because for $x = 0$ we have $x' = 2x = 0$ thus $\neg(x' > 0)$. Therefore, Op_1 and Op_2 are not compatible. They conflict on the initial state $x = 0$.

We can modify them slightly to achieve a pair of compatible operations by strengthening their precondition to require that $x > 0$.

$$
\begin{aligned}
Op_3 &= Op_1 \wedge x > 0 \\
Op_4 &= Op_2 \wedge x > 0
\end{aligned}
$$

With this stronger precondition, we have

$$
\begin{aligned}
& Op_3 \wedge Op_4 \\
& \quad \Rightarrow x > 0 \wedge x' > x \wedge x' \in \{2x, x\} \\
& \quad \Rightarrow x > 0 \wedge x' = 2x \\
& \quad \Rightarrow x > 0 \wedge x' > x \\
& \quad \Rightarrow Op_3
\end{aligned}
$$

$$
\begin{aligned}
& Op_3 \wedge Op_4 \\
& \quad \Rightarrow x > 0 \wedge x' = 2x \\
& \quad \Rightarrow Op_4
\end{aligned}
$$

Thus, Op_3 and Op_4 are compatible.

Compatibility is not only sufficient but in fact a necessary condition for compositional refinement of conjunctions. We demonstrate why this is the case in the appendix.

A common and important case where operations are compatible is when they operate on different variables in the system's state [7].

For example, the operations in the resource manager's *acquire* schema in both the abstract and the concrete versions are compatible.

5 Case Study

To evaluate the approach on a realistic system, we have created a model of the core structure of the Audacity software application.[4] Audacity is an open-source desktop software application for editing and recording audio files. It is well documented, in particular, its major design decisions are documented in [3].

We will now briefly discuss the case study and its conclusions. As we have mentioned in the introduction, the models for the case study are available in a git repository, and a fully detailed presentation of the approach, the models, and the case study is available in the master thesis [10].

Initially, we have tried to break Audacity's functionality into separate modules, following the ideas suggested in [6]. However, we soon found that this is not possible because all the functionality is focused on editing the audio samples. As a result, the system operations are all strongly coupled to the same set of state variables. This has prompted us to find a different way to modularize the system, which eventually resulted in the work presented in this paper.

Audacity's core functionality focuses on the ability to efficiently edit tracks, very large sequences of integers representing audio samples. At an abstract level, a track is just a sequence of integers. However, due to its large size (when sampling at 96 kbps, even a short 3-minute song contains more than 17 million samples), being able to quickly edit the track is a non-trivial challenge. Audacity's solution to this problem is to divide the track into smaller blocks that can be edited, loaded, and stored into files, without having to load the entire track into memory. Each track is associated with a window that determines the area of the track that is currently visible. In addition, Audacity has an undo mechanism that we have modeled in the case study, but will not discuss here.
In the case study, we modeled the following operations:

import: load new tracks into the system
cut: remove a subsequence from a track and put it into the clipboard
paste: copy the content of the clipboard to a position in the track
copy: copy a subsequence from a track and put it into the clipboard
zoomIn: increase the size of the visible window for a particular track
zoomOut: decrease the size of the visible window for a particular track
undo: cancel the effects of the previous operation
redo: reapply a previously cancelled operation

Even though the Audacity model is much more complicated than the resource manager example, they share a similar structure. Just like in the resource manager example, the Audacity model at an abstract level is manipulating a simple data structure (a set in the resource manager, a sequence of samples in Audacity) that becomes more complicated in the concrete model (a linked list in the resource manager, a sequence of references to blocks in Audacity) (Fig. 9). Accordingly, as in the resource manager, we can isolate the operations that manipulate the abstract data structure into a small kernel and describe the

[4] https://www.audacityteam.org/.

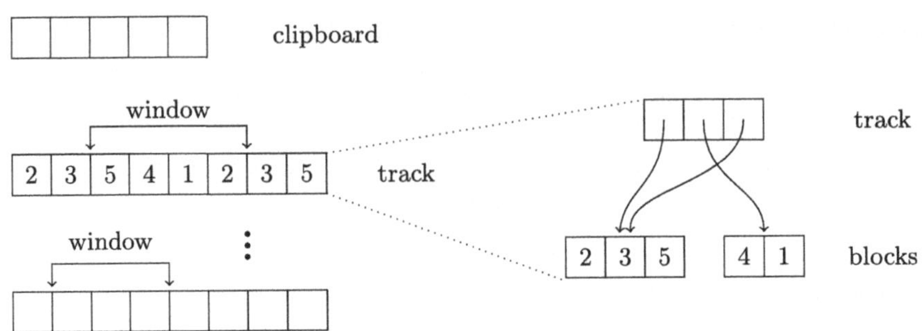

Fig. 9. Audacity's core functionality at two abstraction levels. Audacity manages multiple tracks, each with its own window, and a single clipboard. At the concrete level, a track is represented as a sequence of references to blocks. Each block holds a sequence of samples. Blocks can be shared multiple times in the same track.

Audacity operations using this kernel. Specifically, all the operations that edit the tracks can be modeled using a kernel with two operations: *ExtractSamples*, which reads a subsequence of samples from a track, and *InsertSamples*, which adds a subsequence at a given position in a track. For example, we can model the *cut* operation by requiring that by adding (*InsertSamples*) the part that we have cut to the final state of the track we get back the initial state of the track, and that the final state of the clipboard is equal (*ExtractSamples*) to the part that we cut. The full implementation of the entire Audacity model is provided in the accompanying git repository.[5]

The amount of work that we save by having to prove the simulation only for the kernel operations becomes apparent when studying the abstract and concrete models in the case study. In particular, it is evident that the system operations are much more complicated than the kernel operations. As a result, proving the simulation between all the abstract and concrete system operations will be significantly more tedious and time-consuming than proving the simulation only for the kernel.

6 Related Work

Previous work on the semantics of Z has already recognized that refinement is not monotonic with respect to Z schema operators [5,7]. However, these works focus on how to refine a single Z operation schema into a programming language construct and do not address the problem of refining an entire system. Therefore, they do not address the problem in the wider context of data refinement.

The approach suggested by [5] suggests that the problem is in the semantics of the Z operators and offers a different semantics for Z schema operators. In contrast, we believe that nonmonotonicity of refinement with respect to conjunction is inherent in the fact that when two operation specifications have conflicting

[5] https://github.com/drdavidf/modular-refinement.

goals, it is impossible to satisfy both. Therefore, our approach is to look for conditions under which different operations do not conflict with one another.

Our approach is also shared by [7], albeit only in the more restricted context of operational refinement. Indeed, they define two operations as *consistent* exactly when their preconditions are equivalent. This is one half of our definition of *compatibility*, the other half being the requirement that the conjunction of both operations refines each one.

It is well known that data refinement is monotonic for schema conjunction in the particular case of a *free promotion* [11]. Promotion is a technique for specifying an operation that modifies a system that consists of many identical components indexed by a unique identifier. It is common in such systems that an operation changes a single component. We may describe such operations as achieving two goals: selecting a specific component given an index (*Promote*), and (separately) changing the local component's state (*LocalOp*). Thus, we may write $SystemOp = Promote \wedge LocalOp$. If the *Promote* and *LocalOp* do not restrict each other, then we say that the promotion is free, and in that case, refining *SystemOp* can be achieved by the conjunction of the refinements of *Promote* and *LocalOp*.

7 Discussion

In [6], the authors have described a technique for breaking a system model into separate subsystems by representing the system's state space as a collection of relations rather than as a collection of objects. This representation offers additional opportunities for dividing a system into independent parts because it enables grouping relations that represent information from different classes, which in a traditional object-oriented style would have to appear together. However, as we have seen in this work, there are system models where all the operations are tightly coupled to a small set of state variables. In such cases, there are no opportunities for partitioning the state variables into separate components without incurring so many dependencies between them as to render the partition useless. Our current work offers an additional modularity technique that may be successfully applied in such cases.

This analysis reveals that there are two different sources of system complexity, and accordingly, there are two different ways to combat them. We may label the first one *functional complexity*, as it is often the result of systems that provide a rich functionality and therefore require many state variables. We may label the other *nonfunctional complexity* because often when the source of complexity is due to nonfunctional requirements (e.g., very fast, very large data sets), the abstract description is simple, but the concrete representation could become very complicated.

In general, this means that to overcome functional complexity, we should partition the system into separate functional subsystems. But to overcome nonfunctional complexity, we should organize the system in layers, with the kernel of one layer being the lower layer's interface.

8 Conclusion

Of course, modular refinement is not a silver bullet. There is no apriori guarantee that it is possible to find a small enough kernel of compatible operations (in the worst case, the kernel will be the entire set of system operations). And even when there is such a kernel, there is overhead in having to prove that the kernel operations are compatible. If a system operation is constructed from n kernel operations, we have to provide $2n(n-1)/2 = n(n-1)$ compatibility proofs (both the abstract and the concrete kernel operations require proofs). However, this burden can be mitigated in the common case where the kernel operations are applied to separate state variables, since in this case the compatibility can be ascertained syntactically. But an even greater obstacle is that a structure that can be effectively exploited for modular refinement will not materialize by itself, but must be explicitly designed and, in many cases, requires the adjustment of both the abstract and the concrete models. Despite these limitations, we believe that modular refinement adds a valuable tool to the toolkit of the formal modeler.

An obvious avenue for future work is to discover conditions under which additional specification combinators (e.g., disjunction and sequential composition) can become monotonic with respect to data refinement. In addition, it will be useful to develop similar rules for backwards simulation. Finally, one could imagine a high-level modeling language where notions of modular system descriptions will have explicit language support and the appropriate refinement checks will be automatically generated and checked using, for example, the Alloy analyzer.

9 Appendix

9.1 Resource Manager Schemas

The purpose of this section is to provide just enough details to understand the modular composition of the abstract and concrete resource managers. We have removed most parts of the model to keep the presentation short. The full details, including the proofs, can be found in the online repository.

A *Set* schema represents a simple set subsystem:

Set

$items : \mathbb{F}\, ID$

$0 \notin items$

We provide operations to add and remove (not shown here) items to the set.

```
┌─ Set_Add ──────────────────────────
│ ΔSet
│ item? : ID
├──────────
│ items' = items ∪ {item?}
└────────────────────────────────────
```

The abstract resource manager uses two sets.

```
┌─ A_System ─────────────────────────
│ used : Set
│ free : Set
├──────────
│ Set_items used ∩ Set_items free = ∅
└────────────────────────────────────
```

We use the following schema to specify which set we wish to operate on (this is very similar to promotion; see also Sect. 6).

```
┌─ A_Select_Used ────────────────────
│ ΔA_RM
│ ΔSet
├──────────
│ used = θSet
│ used' = θSet'
└────────────────────────────────────
```

$$A\_Used\_Add \mathrel{\widehat=} \exists \Delta Set \bullet A\_Select\_Used \land Set\_Add$$

$$A\_Free\_Remove \mathrel{\widehat=} \exists \Delta Set \bullet A\_Select\_Free \land Set\_Remove$$

We express the abstract resource manager operations using the abstract *Add* and *Remove* kernel operations.

```
┌─ A_Release ────────────────────────
│ ΔA_RM
│ item? : ID
├──────────
│ A_Used_Remove
│ A_Free_Add
└────────────────────────────────────
```

The concrete manager has the exact same structure, but it uses *Chains* instead of *Sets*.

$$\begin{array}{|l} \textit{C\_System} \\ \hline \textit{used} : \textit{Chain} \\ \textit{free} : \textit{Chain} \\ \hline \textit{Chain\_items}\ \textit{used} \cap \textit{Chain\_items}\ \textit{free} = \emptyset \\ \hline \end{array}$$

$$\begin{array}{|l} \textit{C\_Select\_Used} \\ \hline \Delta \textit{C\_RM} \\ \Delta \textit{Chain} \\ \hline \textit{used} = \theta \textit{Chain} \\ \textit{used}' = \theta \textit{Chain}' \\ \hline \end{array}$$

$$\begin{array}{|l} \textit{C\_Select\_Free} \\ \hline \Delta \textit{C\_RM} \\ \Delta \textit{Chain} \\ \hline \textit{free} = \theta \textit{Chain} \\ \textit{free}' = \theta \textit{Chain}' \\ \hline \end{array}$$

$$\textit{C\_Used\_Add} \mathrel{\widehat{=}} \exists \Delta \textit{Chain} \bullet \textit{C\_Select\_Used} \land \textit{Chain\_Add}$$

$$\textit{C\_Free\_Remove} \mathrel{\widehat{=}} \exists \Delta \textit{Chain} \bullet \textit{C\_Select\_Free} \land \textit{Chain\_Remove}$$

$$\begin{array}{|l} \textit{C\_Release} \\ \hline \Delta \textit{C\_RM} \\ \textit{item?} : \textit{ID} \\ \hline \textit{C\_Used\_Remove} \\ \textit{C\_Free\_Add} \\ \hline \end{array}$$

As we can see, the concrete model has the same structure as the abstract model. With proper tool support, it can be generated automatically from the abstract model. Thus, the proof effort can focus on *Chain*. In principle, we can continue this process until we have a refined *Chain* model that can be translated into executable code. At this point, we can generate the entire system implementation by plugging the executable code into the abstract structure defined by the initial specification.

9.2 Compatible Relations

Theorem 1. *Let u_A and v_A be two compatible relations on an abstract state space A, and u_C and v_C be two compatible relations on a concrete state space C such that $u_A \leq_r u_C$ and $v_A \leq_r v_C$, and assume that the relation r^{-1} is a function. Then,*

$$u_A \cap v_A \leq_r u_C \cap v_C$$

Proof. We argue as follows,

$$\begin{aligned}
& u_A \cap v_A \leq_r u_C \cap v_C \\
& \quad \Leftrightarrow \mathrm{dom}(u_A \cap v_A) \subseteq \mathrm{dom}(r \mathbin{⨾} (u_C \cap v_C))) \wedge \\
& \qquad \mathrm{dom}(u_A \cap v_A) \lhd (r \mathbin{⨾} (u_C \cap v_C)) \subseteq (u_A \cap v_A) \mathbin{⨾} r && \text{[simulation]}
\end{aligned}$$

We will prove the first conjunct.

$$\begin{aligned}
\mathrm{dom}(u_A \cap v_A) & \subseteq \mathrm{dom}(u_A) && \text{[intersection]} \\
& \subseteq \mathrm{dom}(r \mathbin{⨾} u_C) && [u_A \leq_r u_C \wedge v_A \leq_r v_C] \\
& \subseteq \mathrm{dom}(r \mathbin{⨾} (u_C \cap v_C)) && \text{[lemma 1]}
\end{aligned}$$

The last step requires that the concrete operations u_C and v_C are compatible. Next, we will prove the second conjunct.

$$\begin{aligned}
& \mathrm{dom}(u_A \cap v_A) \lhd (r \mathbin{⨾} (u_C \cap v_C)) \\
& \quad \subseteq \mathrm{dom}(u_A \cap v_A) \lhd (r \mathbin{⨾} u_C) \cap (r \mathbin{⨾} v_C) && \text{[lemma 3]} \\
& \quad = \mathrm{dom}(u_A \cap v_A) \lhd (r \mathbin{⨾} u_C) \cap \mathrm{dom}(u_A \cap v_A) \lhd (r \mathbin{⨾} v_C) && \text{[domain restrict]} \\
& \quad = \mathrm{dom}(u_A) \lhd (r \mathbin{⨾} u_C) \cap \mathrm{dom}(v_A) \lhd (r \mathbin{⨾} v_C) && [u_A \text{ and } v_A \text{ compatible}] \\
& \quad \subseteq (u_A \mathbin{⨾} r) \cap (v_A \mathbin{⨾} r) && [u_A \leq_r u_c \wedge v_A \leq_r v_C] \\
& \quad = (u_A \cap v_A) \mathbin{⨾} r && \text{[lemma 2]}
\end{aligned}$$

The last step requires that r^{-1} is a function.

Lemma 1. *If X and Y are compatible relations, then*

$$\mathrm{dom}(R \mathbin{⨾} X) \subseteq \mathrm{dom}(R \mathbin{⨾} (X \cap Y)) \wedge \mathrm{dom}(R \mathbin{⨾} Y) \subseteq \mathrm{dom}(R \mathbin{⨾} (X \cap Y))$$

Proof. Let $a \in \text{dom}(R \,{}_{9}^{\circ}\, X)$. We argue as follows:

$$
\begin{array}{ll}
a \in \text{dom}(R \,{}_{9}^{\circ}\, X) & \\
\quad \Rightarrow \exists\, b' \in B \bullet a \mapsto b \in (R \,{}_{9}^{\circ}\, X) & \text{[definition of dom]} \\
\quad \Rightarrow \exists\, c \in A \bullet a \mapsto c \in R \wedge c \mapsto b \in X & \text{[relational composition]} \\
\quad \Rightarrow \exists\, b' \in B \bullet c \mapsto b' \in X \cap Y & \text{[compatibility]} \\
\quad \Rightarrow a \mapsto b' \in R \,{}_{9}^{\circ}\, (X \cap Y) & \text{[relational composition]} \\
\quad \Rightarrow a \in \text{dom}(R \,{}_{9}^{\circ}\, X \cap Y) & \text{[definition of dom]}
\end{array}
$$

The proof that $\text{dom}(R \,{}_{9}^{\circ}\, Y) \subseteq \text{dom}(R \,{}_{9}^{\circ}\, (X \cap Y)$ is symmetric. □

Lemma 2. *If $u \in A \leftrightarrow A$ and $v \in A \leftrightarrow A$ and $r \in A \leftrightarrow B$ such that r^{-1} is a function, then*

$$(u \,{}_{9}^{\circ}\, r) \cap (v \,{}_{9}^{\circ}\, r) = (u \cap v) \,{}_{9}^{\circ}\, r$$

We prove the lemma by showing that the left-hand side is a subset of the right-hand side, and vice versa. Let $a \mapsto c \in (u \,{}_{9}^{\circ}\, r) \cap (v \,{}_{9}^{\circ}\, r)$. Then,

$$
\begin{array}{ll}
a \mapsto c \in (u \,{}_{9}^{\circ}\, r) \wedge a \mapsto c \in (v \,{}_{9}^{\circ}\, r) & \text{[intersection]} \\
\quad \Rightarrow \exists\, b \bullet a \mapsto b \in u \wedge b \mapsto c \in r \wedge & \\
\qquad \exists\, b' \bullet a \mapsto b' \in v \wedge b' \mapsto c \in r & \text{[composition]} \\
\quad \Rightarrow b' = b & [r^{-1} \text{ is a function}] \\
\quad \Rightarrow a \mapsto b \in u \cap v & \text{[intersection]} \\
\quad \Rightarrow a \mapsto c \in (u \cap v) \,{}_{9}^{\circ}\, r & \text{[composition]}
\end{array}
$$

Arguing in the other direction is even easier. Let $a \mapsto c \in (u \cap v) \,{}_{9}^{\circ}\, r$,

$$
\begin{array}{ll}
a \mapsto c \in (u \cap v) \,{}_{9}^{\circ}\, r & \\
\quad \Leftrightarrow \exists\, b \bullet a \mapsto b \in u \cap v \wedge b \mapsto c \in r & \text{[composition]} \\
\quad \Leftrightarrow a \mapsto b \in u \wedge a \mapsto b \in v \wedge b \mapsto c \in r & \text{[intersection]} \\
\quad \Rightarrow a \mapsto c \in u \,{}_{9}^{\circ}\, r \wedge a \mapsto c \in v \,{}_{9}^{\circ}\, r & \text{[composition]} \\
\quad \Leftrightarrow a \mapsto c \in (u \,{}_{9}^{\circ}\, r) \cap (v \,{}_{9}^{\circ}\, r) & \text{[intersection]}
\end{array}
$$

□

Lemma 3. *For every $r \in A \leftrightarrow B$, $u \in B \leftrightarrow B$, and $v \in B \leftrightarrow B$,*

$$r \,{}_{9}^{\circ}\, (u \cap v) \subseteq (r \,{}_{9}^{\circ}\, u) \cap (r \,{}_{9}^{\circ}\, v).$$

Proof. Let $x \mapsto z \in r \mathbin{;} (u \cap v)$. We argue,

$$
\begin{aligned}
& x \mapsto z \in r \mathbin{;} (u \cap v) && \\
& \quad \Rightarrow \exists\, y \in B \bullet x \mapsto z \in r \land y \mapsto z \in (u \cap v) && \text{[relational composition]} \\
& \quad \Rightarrow x \mapsto z \in r \land y \mapsto z \in u \land y \mapsto z \in v && \text{[intersection]} \\
& \quad \Rightarrow x \mapsto z \in r \mathbin{;} u \land x \mapsto z \in r \mathbin{;} v && \text{[relational composition]} \\
& \quad \Rightarrow x \mapsto z \in (r \mathbin{;} u) \cap (r \mathbin{;} v) && \text{[intersection]}
\end{aligned}
$$

□

9.3 Necessity of the Compatibility Relation

The compatibility of both the abstract and the concrete operation specifications is essential for the compositional refinement of operation conjunction. In Figs. 10, 11, 12 we demonstrate that if either the abstract or the concrete operation specifications are not compatible, then it is possible to find refinements whose conjunction does not refine the abstract conjunction.

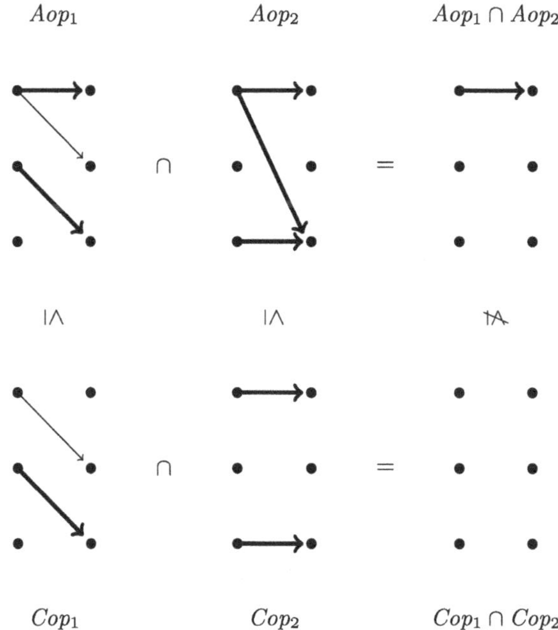

Fig. 10. Two abstract operation specifications with different domains, and two concrete refinements whose conjunction does not refine the abstract specification's conjunction.

Two operation specifications are not compatible if either their domains are not equal or they do not agree on a common mapping for an element in their domain. Accordingly, there are four possible cases of non-compatibility, two for the abstract specifications and two for the concrete specifications. However, when the abstract operations are compatible and the concrete operations that refine them are only incompatible in their domains we still get a compositional refinement, because in this case the concrete operations only differ in the parts of the domain that are not specified by their abstraction specifications and thus do not affect the specified behavior. In simple terms it means that if two concrete operations are in agreement in their specified domains then we can weaken their preconditions without affecting the correctness of the conjoined specification.

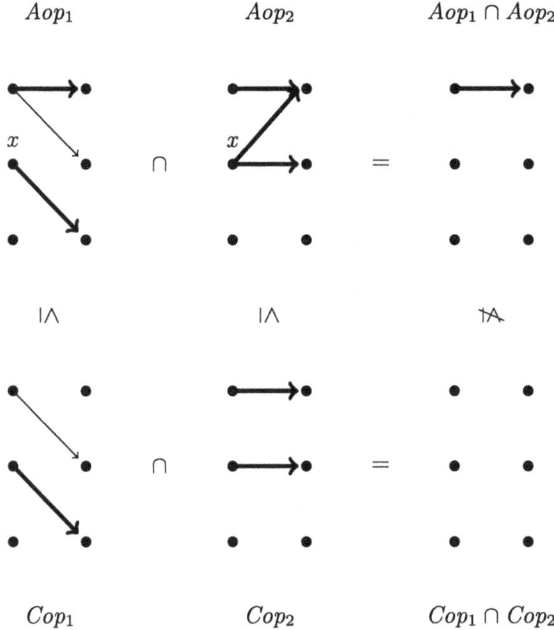

Fig. 11. Two abstract operation specifications that do not agree on the effect of an initial state (x), and two concrete refinements whose conjunction does not refine the abstract specification's conjunction.

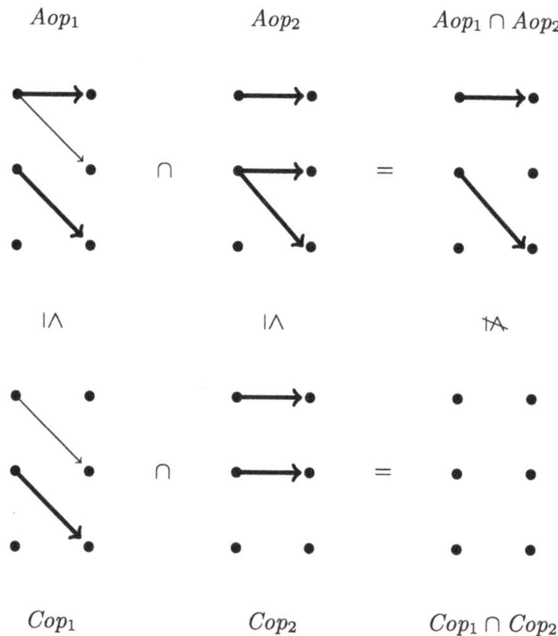

Fig. 12. Two compatible abstract operation specifications and two concrete refinements that do not agree on a common initial state, and thus their conjunction does not refine the abstract specification's conjunction.

References

1. Abrial, J.: The B-Book - Assigning Programs to Meanings. Cambridge University Press (1996). https://doi.org/10.1017/CBO9780511624162
2. Abrial, J.: Modeling in Event-B - System and Software Engineering. Cambridge University Press (2010)
3. Crook, J.: The Architecture of Open Source Applications. San Val (2016)
4. Dave, N., Ng, M.C., Pellauer, M., Arvind: A design flow based on modular refinement. In: 8th ACM/IEEE International Conference on Formal Methods and Models for Codesign (MEMOCODE 2010), Grenoble, France, 26–28 July 2010, pp. 11–20. IEEE Computer Society (2010)
5. Deutsch, M., Henson, M.C., Kajtazi, B.: Modular refinement in novel schema calculi. In: 10th Asia-Pacific Software Engineering Conference (APSEC 2003), 10–12 December 2003, Chiang Mai, Thailand, p. 197. IEEE Computer Society (2003)
6. Faitelson, D., Tyszberowicz, S.: Improving design decomposition (Extended Version). Formal Aspects Comput. **29**(4), 601–627 (2017)
7. Groves, L.: Refinement and the Z schema calculus. Electron. Notes Theoret. Comput. Sci. **70**(3), 70–93 (2002)
8. Jackson, D.: Software Abstractions: Logic, Language, and Analysis. The MIT Press (2016)

9. Shepetovsky, L.: Complete code of audacity alloy model: the source-code for an M.Sc in CS degree project and thesis at Open University of Israel. https://github.com/leonidsh119/audacity-alloy-model/tree/master/AudacityLayers, visited on 07 Apr 2020
10. Shepetovsky, L.: Intellectually Manageable Formal Models. Master's thesis, Department of Computer Science, The Open University of Israel (2025), submitted
11. Woodcock, J., Davies, J.: Using Z: Specification, Refinement, and Proof. Prentice-Hall International Series in Computer Science, Prentice Hall (1996)
12. Zheng, H., Yao, H., Yoneda, T.: Modular model checking of large asynchronous designs with efficient abstraction refinement. IEEE Trans. Comput. **59**(4), 561–573 (2010)

Keep it Simple, or Teach Them Logics: Attack-Defense Tree Perception by Laypeople

Florian Dorfhuber[1,2(✉)], Marisol Barrientos[2], Julia Eisentraut[2,3], and Jan Křetínský[1,2]

[1] Masaryk University, Brno, Czech Republic
jan.kretinsky@fi.muni.cz
[2] Technical University of Munich, Munich, Germany
florian.dorfhuber@in.tum.de, marisol.barrientos@tum.de, julia.eisentraut@posteo.de
[3] State Parliament of Northrhine-Westfalia, Düsseldorf, Germany

Abstract. Threat modelling is crucial for analysing how attacks may affect security-critical systems, detecting present vulnerabilities, and managing risk. System designers use attack trees and their extensions during an application's design and implementation phase for these tasks. However, it is equally essential that end-users know how to use the final system securely. The competence profiles of end-users highly differ from the profiles of system designers. Therefore, we aim to reflect these different levels of competences in our proposition to enhance the models. Our research examines the perception of attack trees and their extensions among laypeople. We conducted a task-oriented survey (n=133), where non-experts in cyber-security had to interpret three attack-defense tree representations of two different attack scenarios. Additionally, we use the technology acceptance model (TAM) to investigate how participants perceived these representations. Our survey demonstrates that standard attack-defense tree visualisations are on average as effective as running text for risk communication to laypeople. However, they may currently not evolve their full potential as laypeople usually lack logical skills. Basic logic is a crucial element for teaching laypeople about security. Motivated by the results, we suggest ways the models could be simplified for the users, to ease the access through simpler perspectives on the logical relationships described by the models.

Keywords: Attack-Defense Tree · Attack Model Techniques · Technology Acceptance Model · Cyber-attack

1 Introduction

Many economic, social, and institutional activities are taking place online. Ensuring the security of those transactions has become a worldwide priority for governments and companies. 2023 had the highest average costs caused by data breaches since the pandemic [16]. By 2025, the dollar value of cyber-attacks may

A. Goharshady and C. Haase (Eds.): SETTA 2025, LNCS 16458, pp. 57–77, 2026.
https://doi.org/10.1007/978-981-95-7826-9_4

globally amount to 10.5 trillion dollars [33]. Hence, ensuring system security is crucial.

Understanding the nature of attacks is essential in improving a system's security. It allows for recognizing threats affecting a particular system, highlighting vulnerabilities, and designing appropriate risk management.

Techniques dedicated to modelling and then analyzing attacks are known as *attack modelling techniques* (AMTs) [19,34]. Among all techniques, we focus on attack-trees and their extensions attack-defense-trees ADT, which originated in industrial applications [29] and are now widespread in research [35], too. There is a longstanding line of research debating whether such graphical attack modelling techniques effectively communicate security risks. Prior research claims that the representation as Graph-Tree (see Sect. 2) has an inefficient design since it does not have a standardized version [22].

While, ADT are designed for the use by security professionals, there will be always laypeople that need to use them. For instance managers at software-companies need to be able to understand potential risks and their mitigation strategies to decide on a course of action. [31] This can be extended beyond Threat-modelling in software, to all areas that can be potential users of ADT. Therefore, extending the range of ADT-readers to workers in critical processes.

Additionally, there is a lack of empirical evaluation of the effectiveness of Graph-Trees in helping laypeople understand cyber-attacks [20]. Therefore, our study investigates whether our representations of ADT facilitate communicating security risks to laypeople compared to running text descriptions.

To this end, we devised four hypothesis and tested them in our survey. The focus is on evaluating how different representations facilitate the participants' understanding and solving capabilities. We added pre-task tutorials of different depths to analyze how they affect performance and how they change the participants' perceptions.

Based on the results, we sketch several future lines of research, suggesting to improve the usability of such models. The key aspect is to offer simplifying views on the models, which can in a well-defined sense simplify the complete information contained in the model, and do so in a way tailored to users with different backgrounds.

Organisation. First, we summarise the results of related studies in the following subsection. A short introduction to attack-defense trees is given in Sect. 2. We discuss our methodology in Sect. 3. The results are introduced in Sect. 4. Section 5 discusses potential implications. Finally, we discuss different interpretations and possible future work in Sect. 6.

1.1 Related Studies

In [15,22], the authors extensively overview different ways to represent attack trees and user experience studies. This section focuses on quantitative studies similar to the later introduced study design. First, this comprises studies analysing how the visualisation of AMTs supports the cognitive process of understanding security risks. Second, we thus focus on results investigating how different people interact with each other when they have to model an attack scenario.

Based on the study aim and design, our survey is closest to [27]. In this paper, the authors compare misuse cases and ADT concerning the number of threats found, the type of threats discovered and the user's perception of the techniques based on the Technology Acceptance Model. In the objective number of discovered threats the ADT was superior to the description as misuse case. However, both representations were subjectively perceived similarly. Additionally, the objective performance did not correlate with the subjective perception of the model. This study was designed to aid security practitioners in model selection. Therefore, laypeople were not included in the analysis.

In the recent work of Broccia et al. [5] the authors investigated attack-defense trees on a method evaluation model. They included 25 participants, but only among computer science students and faculty. Additionally, almost 70% of their participants already knew about ADT. Their results showed a high level of understanding and ease of use among the participants. However, the paper does not compare the results to the performance of other model representations. Furthermore, the small sample size and the specific background of participants in this study raise concerns about whether the results are transferable to a more general audience, which we consider here.

There is concurrent work to be published by Schiele & Gadyatskaya [28], which investigates the performance on ADT-related tasks of students with either high or limited technical background. All participants were given a lecture with interactive parts by experts in advance. The research suggests that such more extensive training may suffice to equalize the level of intuition about the models across the differences in their technical background. However, there is no comparison to using other representations than ADT.

In [21], the authors compare two different AMTs: attack graphs and fault trees. While their study included participants with and without a computer science background, they did not consider non-visual representations of attacks. Their main conclusion is that attack graphs better aid cyber-attack perception than fault trees. However, none of their representations fit our attack-tree model. We allow for a richer set of operators and include actions governed by the attacking and defending parties. Hence, our attack scenarios can be more complex.

Furthermore, in [20], researchers compared participants' interpretation of an attack graph when modifying the arrangement of various elements, such as arrows, boxes, colour, or line width. Additionally, they pointed out that future work should consider non-experts' perspectives because experts may already be familiar with these representations.

In [15], scientists summarised past research on assessing AMTs in generation, representation, evaluation, and modification. Then, experts reviewed several AMTs in various application domains. Users seem to struggle in understanding the capabilities of all investigated AMTs. Accordingly, they have difficulties with the selection of the AMT that would suit their needs best.

In [8], the authors investigate the collaboration between a security expert, an API designer, and a developer. They emphasised that the key is communication, i.e. cyber-security experts should ensure that the team understands both the AMT they are proposing and the usability of their security model. Furthermore, security experts should not expect the rest of the team members to have general cyber-security knowledge. Finally, in [26], they argued that security thinking requires cognitive resources. Therefore, developers tend to reduce their cognitive load by not prioritising security.

2 Attack-Defense Trees and Their Representations

This section briefly presents the notion of *attack-defense trees*, e.g., [14,18]. Attack-defense trees are labelled trees, where the root represents the overall goal to attack a system. To refine the goal into smaller sub-goals, inner nodes are equipped with operators determining how the child nodes' success or failure contributes to the superior goal's success or failure. This recursive refinement ends at leaves, called *basic events*, i.e. unique observable happenings in the real world, which cannot be further split. We allow both *basic attack steps* and *basic defense steps.*

Definition 1. *An* attack-defense tree *(over a set of basic events* BE*) is a tuple* $\mathsf{ADT} = (\mathsf{V}, \mathsf{E}, \mathsf{t})$ *where:*

- (V, E) *is a directed acyclic graph (DAG), with a designated goal sink vertex* g *for the attacker.*
- *The source vertices* $\mathsf{BE} \subseteq \mathsf{V}$ *are called* basic events. *All other vertices are called* gates *and* $\mathsf{G} \subseteq \mathsf{V}$ *denotes the set of all gates; each gate's direct predecessors (with respect to* E*) are called its* inputs.
- *We additionally require that gates labeled with* AND *or* OR *have at least two inputs, whereas other gates must have exactly one input.*
- $\mathsf{t} : \mathsf{G} \to \{\mathtt{AND}, \mathtt{OR}, \mathtt{NOT}\}$ *is the* type function *assigning an operator to each gate.*

Example 1. In Fig. 1, we present our first attack-defense tree used in our survey. It depicts an attacker who maliciously wants to break into a building by opening a door. The goal node (with a blue border) represents the overall attack goal. All tree leaves are basic attack steps (coloured red) or basic defense steps (coloured green).

In the following, we use an intuitive semantics of attack-defense trees to demonstrate how graphical representations of attacks correspond to real-world scenarios. This semantics works as follows: Players may *attempt* their basic events *successfully* or *unsuccessfully* (or not at all). Operators define how the successful attempt of a basic event is propagated (bottom-up) through the tree. For instance, the operators AND and OR propagate successful attempts like their logical equivalents: AND propagates successful attempts if all its children are successfully attempted (independently of the order). OR propagates a successful attempt if at least one child is successfully attempted.

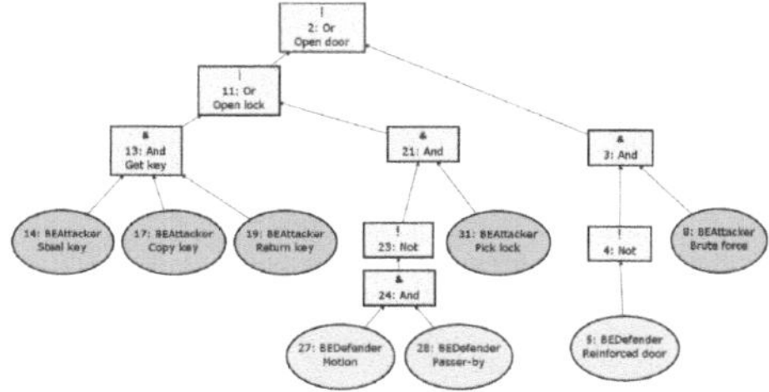

Fig. 1. Attack scenario 1 of the study represented as Graph-Tree.

Example 2 (Continued Example 1). The goal is refined into different subtrees using the operator `OR`, i.e., only one of the subtrees needs to be successfully attempted for the overall attack to be successful. The overall attack is successful if, for instance, the attacker can open the door's lock (event (11)[1]). This can be again refined, by a subtree rooted in event (11) which represents opening the door with a key. This goal consists of the basic attack events steal key (event (14)), copy key (event (17)), return key (event (19)). All of these have to be successfully attempted due to the `AND` refinement of event (13). The second subtree of opening the lock (event (11)) represents picking the lock (event (31)) which only works if the subtree in event (23) is not attempted by the defender. This subtree involves the defender noticing the attack. However, this only happens if a guard is passing by the door (event (28)) and they are recognising the motion of the lock (event (27)). The second subtree of the root (event (3)) is refined using the operator `AND` (events (4) and (8)). To successfully attempt this subtree, the attacker needs to open the door by brute force, and the defender must not have installed a reinforced door (event (4) and event (5)).

The Running-Text description of the attack scenario underlying the Graph-Tree in Fig. 1 can be found in Appendix A.

The third and final representation of this attack scenario, depicted in Fig. 2, uses bullet points as an alternative way to illustrate the refinement of attack goals.

For clarity, we refer to the graphical representation of the attack-defense tree by Graph-Tree*, to the running text by* Running-Text *and to the tree-structured text by* Text-Tree.

[1] The IDs were generated by the used tool [10] in order of node creation.

```
2 Or: Open door
  11 Or: Open lock
    13 And: Get key
      14 Attacker: Steal key
      17 Attacker: Copy key
      19 Attacker: Return key
    21 And:
      23 Not:
        24 And:
          27 Defender: Motion
          28 Defender: Passer-by
      31 Attacker: Pick lock
  3 And:
    4 Not:
      5 Defender: Reinforced door
    8 Attacker: Brute force
```

Fig. 2. Attack scenario 1 represented as Text-Tree.

3 Study Design

Our study focuses on understanding how participants, mostly laypeople in cybersecurity, perceive the three different attack scenario representations introduced in Sect. 2. We designed a task-oriented survey structured in three steps: pre-task, main task, and post-task, visually illustrated in Fig. 3. Therefore, we devised four hypotheses:

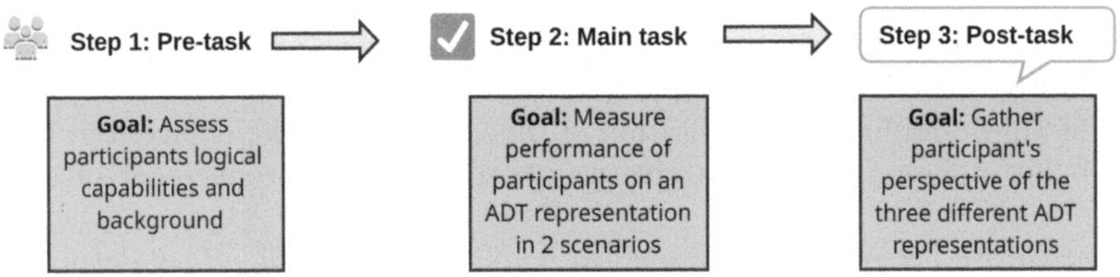

Fig. 3. Three steps of our task-oriented survey.

Hypothesis 1. *A graphical representation of an attack scenario enhances the understanding.*

Hypothesis 2. *The tutorial length positively influences the overall performance.*

Hypothesis 3. *A better result in the main-task positively influences the given representation's perception.*

Hypothesis 4. *A graphical representation of an attack scenario is positively perceived, as measured by the Technology Acceptance Model.*

In [4,30], and [6], the authors showed that logical reasoning impacts formal reasoning and everyday reasoning tasks. Hence, we created a pre-task to determine the sampling w.r.t. the logic competence profile of participants. We did not aim to distinguish between computer scientists and non-computer scientists. But the call for participation clearly excluded people working in cyber security.

For the main task, participants had to answer questions testing their understanding of two different attack scenarios. We split participants according to two criteria into groups: 1. being supported by one of the three different attack scenario representations and 2. receiving a tutorial or not. Objective performance was measured by the number of correctly answered questions.

To measure how participants perceived the given representations, we introduced a post-task based on the Technology Acceptance Model (TAM) [9], which is a widely used psychological theory to evaluate the acceptance of new technology. [23] The TAM-model consists of three main items: the Perceived Usefulness (PU), the Perceived Ease of Use (PEU), and the Intention to Use (IU) [9]. We aim to apply the model to the proposed representations, to measure the impression the users developed for the assigned representation. We want to emphasise that measuring the perception of the participants' for the ADT representation is as essential as measuring the correctness of their performance. Even the best representation objectively enhancing the understanding of the attack scenario is not helpful if users refuse it because they do not perceive it as applicable or it costs them a lot of cognitive resources to use it [25].

In this chapter, we discuss data collection and analysis in detail.

3.1 Data Collection and Groups

The survey was distributed via general online forums and mailing lists to non-experts in cyber-security from 12th November 2021 until 12th March 2022. We stopped enrollment after the planned study time frame was reached, with the minimum enrollment of 100 participants met. The study was translated into English, German and Spanish to feature many potential participants. People did the translations with at least a C1 level proficiency in the corresponding language. To ensure proper anonymisation and reduce privacy concerns of the participants, we have not collected data that allows for participant identification. There was no financial compensation for participation.

We randomly assigned the participants to one of eight groups divided by the attack scenario representation and tutorial type. Randomization was done with the first access of the survey webpage. Model representations ranged over *Running-Text*, *Text-Tree* and *Graph-Tree* (see Sect. 2). For tutorials, one cohort got no tutorial, one got a short tutorial, and others an extended version. The *Running-Text* group did not receive an extended tutorial to avoid over-complicated explanations. To ensure equal sample sizes for each representation, the tutorial sub-group in the *Running-Text*-group was twice as big as in other groups, as there were no participants in the extended tutorial group (see Table 2).

3.2 Pre-task

Our pre-task follows the idea of [4]. Participants had to answer three questions covering verbal, spatial, and numerical reasoning of participants. Additionally, the survey asked if participants had taken any logic lectures. In this way, we can detect participants from STEM fields and avoid introducing an unknown sampling bias in the analysis. However, randomisation happened independently of the answers the users gave in this section.

3.3 Main Task

Assigned to different attack scenario representations, participants had to answer questions about system security in two cases. We present the first attack scenario in Sect. 2.

We posed eleven questions for each scenario, comprising yes-no-questions to answer and questions where an event from the model, suitable to fulfil a statement, had to be picked. Our performance measure was the amount of correctly answered questions.

3.4 Post-task

The last section of the survey measures the participants' perception using TAM. Table 1 summarises the parameters collected during the post-task. As this study targets mainly laypeople, without regular use of security models, the category "Intention to Use" can hardly be assessed correctly. Thus, we restrict the analysis to the other two components. We measure the "Perceived Ease of Use" by asking participants about their frustration and familiarity with the representation while solving the tasks. Additionally, we assess the "Perceived Usefulness" with items about the understandability and how participants perceive the correctness of their answers. All post-task questions were on a ten-point Likert-scale.

Table 1. Post-task parameters. The questions of the post task. Answers were collected on 10 item Likert-Scales. The labels on the lower and upper bound of the scale are displayed in square brackets.

Category	Item	Question/Description
Perceived Ease of Use	Frustration	The tasks were ... [frustrating - encouraging]
Perceived Ease of Use	Familiarity	Working with the representation felt ... [unfamiliar - familiar]
Perceived Usefulness	Understandability	How understandable were the representations? [incomprehensible - comprehensible]
Perceived Usefulness	Correctness	How many questions do you think you answered correctly? [10%–100%]

4 Results

In this section, we present the results of our survey. First, we summarise the outcomes of the pre-task to illustrate the participants' preknowledge. Second, we discuss the perception of different representations of the attack scenarios w.r.t. participants' skills measured in the pre-task. We examine hypotheses **H** 1 and **H** 2 in this subsection. Third, we analyse the perception of the different attack scenario representations using the technology acceptance model (TAM) and thus, discuss **H** 3 and **H** 4. Last, we discuss further findings.

General Remarks. We use the tool R, version 4.4.1, for data analysis and visualisation. The survey took about 40 min. 133 participants submitted the completed questionnaire. 44 were randomized to the *Running-Text* and 47 to the *Graph-Tree* group, 42 to the *Text-Tree*. From the total number of participants, 37% had no tutorial, 41% had a brief tutorial, and 22% had an extended version of the tutorial. In Table 2, we present the distribution of participants per group.

Table 2. Baseline data of the study.

Model	Had tutorial	n	Score logic test	Had logic class
Text	No	16 (12%)	2.4 ± 0.6	5 (31%)
Text	Yes	28 (21%)	2.5 ± 0.8	11 (39%)
TextTree	No	15 (11%)	2.6 ± 0.5	1 (7%)
TextTree	Yes	12 (9%)	2.3 ± 0.8	3 (25%)
TextTree	Extended	15 (11%)	2.5 ± 0.7	7 (47%)
ADT	No	19 (14%)	2.2 ± 0.9	4 (21%)
ADT	Yes	14 (11%)	2.1 ± 0.9	6 (43%)
ADT	Extended	14 (11%)	2.4 ± 0.6	7 (50%)

4.1 Pre-task

We give a descriptive overview of the performance in the pre-task. The logical questions were answered correctly with an average score of 2.39 (± 0.77) out of three possible points with no significant differences between the subgroups. 32 % of the participants attended a logic lecture at least once, with 34 %, 26 % and 35 % for Running-Text, Text-Tree and Graph-Tree respectively. However, there were significant differences in the subgroups by tutorial (see Table 2). For instance, only one participant attended a logic lecture in the group Text-Tree representation with no tutorial. Hence, without adjustment, this sampling would confound the overall study result. Therefore, we adjust all the following statistical models w.r.t. participation in a logic class as the independent variable.

4.2 Main-task

Figure 4 shows the results of the main-task. Our measure is the number of correctly scored questions per attack scenario. We first give a short overview of the key insights and then examine hypotheses **H** 1 and **H** 2.

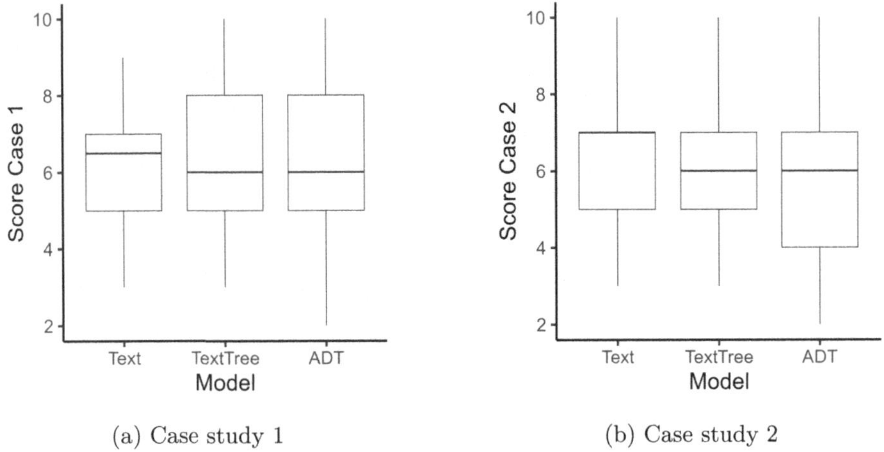

(a) Case study 1

(b) Case study 2

Fig. 4. Box-plot of the number of correctly scored questions (maximum 11 points) over the different groups for each case study. Outcomes were similar in all groups with no statistically significant difference.

The number of correctly scored questions achieved by the participants in the *main*-task were similar in all groups (see Figure Fig. 4) with an overall mean of 6.29 ± 1.82 and 6.17 ± 1.89 for case study one and two, respectively, out of a maximum of eleven points in each of the cases.

However, as mentioned earlier, we want to ensure sampling does not confound the overall study result. Hence, we apply a linear model to adjust for taking a logic class and to adjust the significance threshold (α-value) for the multiple tests executed correctly.

Interpretation. The results show no significant difference in the participants' overall performance depending on the chosen attack scenario representation or if they had a tutorial in advance (see Table 3). However, attending a logic class improved the overall score by 1.3 points (around 5%) on average with statistical significance. Thus, neither a graphical representation nor tutorial length enhances understanding of an attack scenario. So, we refute both **H** 1 and **H** 2.

4.3 Post-task

Lastly, we mention and evaluate how participants perceive the different representations. To this end, we use linear regression to determine subjective feelings of

Table 3. Summary of regression coefficients on the overall score for the tutorial and the model types. Results were insignificant except for the attendance of a logic class previous to the study, which was highly significant (p=0.012 on α=0.05). Empty rows denote the reference value.

Characteristic	Beta (Estimated effect)	SE (Standard error)	p-value (Statistical significance)[1]
Tutorial			
No	—	—	
Yes	0.61	0.556	0.3
Extended	0.49	0.688	0.5
Model			
Text	—	—	
TextTree	-0.12	0.648	0.8
ADT	-0.36	0.617	0.6
Attended logic class			
No	—	—	
Yes	1.3	0.526	**0.012***

[1] *p<0.05; **p<0.01; ***p<0.001

Abbreviations: CI = Confidence Interval, SE = Standard Error

familiarity, frustration, understanding, and correctness dependent on the model, the tutorial type and the logical class participation. It is interesting to note that the Text-Tree representation performance is worse in three categories. The following section discusses the participants' perceptions of familiarity, understandability, frustration, and correction. The full results are summarised in Table 4.

Perceived Ease of Use:

Familiarity. None of the independent variables (Representation, Tutorial, Logic class, Points in main task) used for the model had a statistically significant influence on the participants' familiarity with the representations.

Frustration. The analysis of frustration showed that the participants felt significantly more frustrated with the Text-Tree representation. The other independent variables showed no significant impact.

Perceived Usefulness:

Understandability. Participants with the Text-Tree representation felt they understood the task less than in other groups. However, they showed the same level of comprehension in the main task. Additionally, subjective understandability significantly improved by tutorial length.

Correctness. Participants using a Text-Tree representation were statistically significantly less confident in their skills. An extended tutorial slightly failed with a positive estimate of the test of significance ($p = 0.051$). Overall, the participants reliably estimated the number of questions answered correctly.

Table 4. Summary of regressions coefficients on the tutorial and model types' subjective perception categories. The Text-Tree representation is significantly worse in three categories, while an extended tutorial had a benefit in one of four categories. Explanations on the column names can be found in Table 3. Points questionnaire denotes the number of correctly answered questions in both case studies.

	Familiarity			Frustration			Understandability			Correctness		
Characteristic	**Beta**	**SE**	**p-value**[1]	**Beta**	**SE**	**p-value**[1]	**Beta**	**SE**	**p-value**[1]	**Beta**	**SE**	**p-value**[1]
Model												
Text	—	—		—	—		—	—		—	—	
TextTree	-0.92	0.641	0.2	-1.7	0.703	**0.015***	-2.6	0.595	**<0.001*****	-2.0	0.515	**<0.001*****
ADT	0.50	0.611	0.4	0.00	0.670	>0.9	-0.90	0.567	0.12	-0.87	0.491	0.079
Tutorial												
No	—	—		—	—		—	—		—	—	
Yes	-0.10	0.553	0.9	-0.60	0.606	0.3	-0.17	0.513	0.7	-0.47	0.444	0.3
Extended	0.57	0.645	0.4	1.1	0.708	0.11	1.3	0.599	**0.034***	1.0	0.519	0.051
Attended logic class												
No	—	—		—	—		—	—		—	—	
Yes	-0.61	0.535	0.3	-1.0	0.587	0.077	-0.02	0.497	>0.9	-0.41	0.430	0.3
Points questionnaire	0.16	0.084	0.062	0.16	0.092	0.088	0.01	0.078	>0.9	0.32	0.068	**<0.001*****

[1] *p<0.05; **p<0.01; ***p<0.001

Abbreviations: CI = Confidence Interval, SE = Standard Error

Interpretation. The groups with an extended tutorial had a significantly better subjective impression of the task regarding understandability than those without a short tutorial. There was no significant difference between the other two subgroups. Additionally, in the categories of Understandability and Correctness, participants rated the Text-Tree model statistically significantly worse. Therefore, we can neither refute nor support **H** 4, as it might depend on the type of graphical model. While the Text-Tree performed worse then the others, the Graph-Tree performed equally to the Running-Text.

The overall number of correctly scored questions in the case study had a highly significant impact on the felt correctness of the task but no significant effect on the other dependent variables. Thus, we accept **H** 3 for correctness on all three representations.

4.4 Discussion

In the adjusted analysis, we found a significant beneficial effect of participation in a logic class.[2] This is to be expected, as logic classes are designed to train a formal form of reasoning, which can be applied to many contexts. However, it implies that the way computer scientists describe security systems may be less accessible to people who have no or little experience with such topics.

In subjective analysis, a reduced tree-structured text, the Text-Tree representation, resulted in more frustration, less understanding and less confidence in their abilities than the other groups. While the Text-Tree representation may, on the first look, offer a helpful reduction of the contents, the unfamiliarity outweighed the benefits of the format. On the other hand, attack-defense trees offer more explicit visual hierarchy and information via icons that result in a similar level of subjective perception than the sole display of text.

Increasing the length of the tutorial has been an independent positive influence on subjective understandability. Hence, laypeople can only solve security tasks with preparation, but a thorough introduction may facilitate their use of the models more regularly. There was no extended tutorial for the Running-Text group, so the quantitative interpretation might be limited.

5 Potential Implications

The observed result that logic classes have a beneficial effect on the performance in the study task needs to be further examined. On the one hand, it may only be a proxy variable for another beneficial influence, such as generally close contact with the relevant education. On the other hand, there has been discussion over the last decades whether it was even possible to teach logic at all e.g. [24,32]. University students seem to significantly improve their reasoning abilities over the process of their studies [2,24]. The effect in [24] was bigger in social sciences like medicine and psychology, than in chemistry. This may be due to the more probabilistic scenarios encountered in the study of life sciences. However, it is not feasible to let laypeople undergo a full or even multiple university courses in advance to use security models. Also, it does not support the claimed ease of use of such models.

The efforts to improve cognitive abilities with "brain training"-activities have shown effects with much smaller efforts, but mostly on tasks of high similarity to the trained ones [32]. The transferability of effects of such broad training on ADT is therefore unlikely. Yet, it may be possible to improve laypeople's performance with specific training in a reasonable amount of time. [28] suggests that it may be possible to do so within a couple of hours training by an expert.

Nevertheless, training potential users of the models may be a possible solution to improve performance, increasing the accessibility of the models for laypeople is a more realistic way to enhance their use and acceptance in potential industrial

[2] This may not be the case for the logical questions in the beginning, as the type of question is likely known to the general public.

applications. Therefore, we have to find potential competences that result from logic classes, and *improve the ADT in a way that lowers the level of competences needed.*

Logical competences taught in university classes are to enable students to use the tools and strategies for the problems they encounter in their curricula [13]. Therefore, the focus is more on enabling, rather than formal backgrounds. [17] goes in-depth on potential goal descriptions for informal logic curricula which we were using in our statements. The main focus is here on the creation and validation of logical arguments. On higher levels, students should also be able to divide an argument into sections and discuss their relations.

Suggestions for ADT Extensions

As we can expect laypeople to only have lower-level logical skills, we assume, that the current representation of security models is too much at once for the untrained person to process and interpret. Thus, we suggest the usage of tailored "hybrid" models, i.e. combinations of the representations Graph-Tree and Running-Text, that also allow for the reduction of content on display. In a non-formal way, one can allow users to collapse or unfold the subtrees they are interested in. Additionally, tooltips automatically generated in natural language as descriptions for collapsed subtrees can be introduced to avoid peripheral subtrees with little significance to unnecessarily increase the tree size for the user (see Fig. 5).

Domain-Knowledge. More formally, we can use domain-knowledge (see Definition 2) to define abstraction and pruning operations on attack-defense trees (see Sect. 2).

Definition 2. *A competence profile for the users of* ADT *can be defined as follows:*

- C *be a set of competences*
- $\mathsf{comp}\colon \mathsf{BE} \rightarrow 2^{\mathsf{C}}$ *be the competency assignment function mapping basic events to the set of competences required to understand them*
- *Let* $\mathsf{comp}(g)$ *for* $g \in \mathsf{G}$ *be the set of competences required to understand all children of an inner node. It is recursively defined on the ADT as* $\mathsf{comp}(g) = \bigcup_{v \in \{v \in \mathsf{V} \mid (v,g) \in \mathsf{E}\}} \mathsf{comp}(v)$
- $P \subseteq \mathsf{C}$ *be a* competency profile *(of the person using the attack-defense tree)*

In this work we interpret competences as knowledge or skills, that are required to understand or execute a task, as it is done for instance in the NICE guidelines for cyber security [1].

Abstraction allows us to hide detailed attack steps and focus on major attack goals instead. The more abstract model keeps the benefit of a visual hierarchy that the Graph-Tree offers but also keeps the familiarity of Running-Text, both of which have been shown feasible in our study to understand the used ADT. Formally, this extension is based on *abstractions* of subgraphs, merging them into single nodes. The concept of abstraction is present in many works on verification [3].

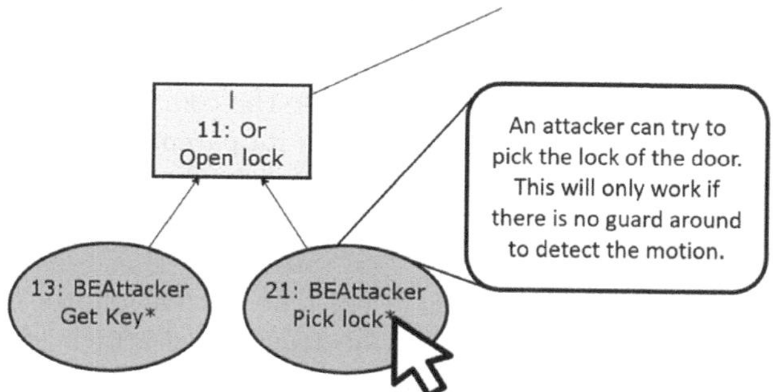

Fig. 5. Cutout with collapsed nodes from the first task (see Fig. 1). Details are hidden behind a mouse over, as the general concept of the parent nodes should be clear to laypeople. Existence of details is marked by a star.

To abstract a specific node, the node and its siblings under the same parent node are merged/collapsed into the parent node. This is formally done by removing the edges and nodes in the child-subtrees of the parent node. In the next step the parent node is transformed into a basic event representing the collapsed sub-tree (see Fig. 5). This process does not hinder the analytical process of bottom-up analysis as for instance described in [10] as we can see the concrete nodes that are merged as an ADT rooted in the parent node and therefore transfer the analytic results in the newly generated basic event.

As an intuition for the overall abstraction we want to find the nodes closest to the root where the user has none of the necessary competences to reduce the size as much as possible. So, starting from the top we recursively check the nodes for eligibility. Then, we create the intersection of the user competence profile and the necessary competences for the node $I_v = P \cap \mathsf{comp}(v)$ and use it as follows:

- If $I_v = \emptyset$ the user has no competences for the subtree $\rightarrow$ Merge the subtree with its siblings.
- If $I_v = \mathsf{comp}(v)$[3] the user has all competences in the subtree $\rightarrow$ Stop evaluation for the subtree and keep it as is.

[3] This corresponds to $\mathsf{comp}(v) \subseteq P$.

- If $I_v \neq \mathsf{comp}(v)$ and $v \in \mathsf{BE}$ the user does not have all necessary competences $\rightarrow$ Merge the node with its siblings[4]
- If $I_v \neq \mathsf{comp}(v)$, $I_v \neq \emptyset$ and $v \in \mathsf{G} \rightarrow$ Continue evaluating the children of the node

Pruning focuses on cutting out parts of the tree, without collapsing parts the users may understand. For instance, a normal employee at a sales corporation will likely not have the power to change the company-wide server hardware to increase security. On the other hand, the CEO is likely not interested in parts of the model that offer only small benefits in security and/or have very high costs to implement (see Fig. 6). We can therefore use the competence definition from above. But rather than merging the node into its parent node, we just remove the subtree and the outgoing edges from the model. Therefore, this extension is based on defining *pruning* (not displaying all the subtrees), a concept dual to abstraction[5].

To the best of our knowledge, there exist no current efforts in the formal methods community to add pruning or abstraction to attack trees and their extensions. However, there exists a tool for ADT that allows for new domains to be added as plug-ins [10].

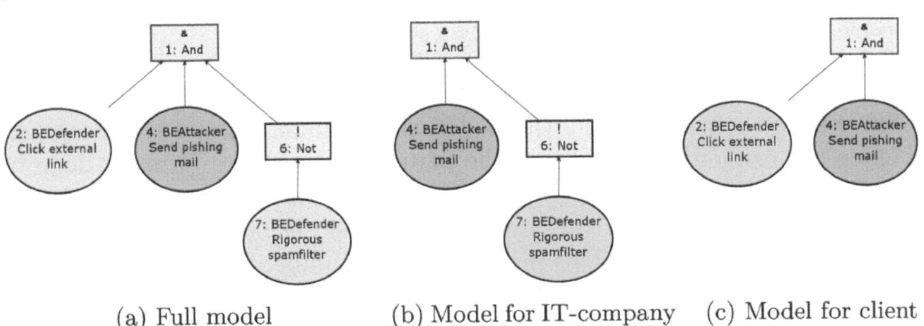

(a) Full model (b) Model for IT-company (c) Model for client

Fig. 6. Model for a phishing attack on a company, that has an external IT-department. (a) shows the complete model, while (b) shows the pruned version with all elements that can be observed/intervened with by the external IT-company. Accordingly, (c) shows all elements that a normal employee at the company can observe/interact with.

Summary. Pruning retains the details of topics the user might have a special interest in, while in abstraction the siblings of the selected node are also merged in the parent node. However, this will likely result in a more substantial size

[4] This behaviour implies, as mentioned above, that competences are mandatory to understand a node.

[5] In the sense of category theory, prunings are subobjects, corresponding to monomorphisms, and abstractions are quotient objects, corresponding to epimorphisms.

reduction of the model and therefore a simpler output. In both cases we can annotate the affected nodes with footnotes including a natural language description of the removed/collapsed part of the model.

Additionally, the analysis of the simplified models is not standardised yet. While for abstraction some domains like probabilities, delays and costs can still be calculated by using the properties of the collapsed subtree, the capabilities will be limited when the order of element execution matters, or more complex domains are used. Therefore, we currently suggest using the concrete model for the underlying analysis and display the properties at the corresponding nodes in the simplified model.

6 Conclusion and Future Work

This paper sets out to evaluate the impact of different representations on the objective understanding of attack scenarios. In a surprising deviation from similar studies involving domain experts, our research reveals that the specific representation of the attack scenario is inconsequential for laypeople. In other words, participants could grasp security-related insights from all the provided representations. However, we observed a significant positive influence from taking a logic class before the survey.

Our survey raises numerous intriguing avenues for future research. Two, in particular, stand out. Firstly, the manner in which computer scientists articulate attack scenarios could be less effective for laypeople with limited or no exposure to formal reasoning. This could necessitate a fundamental shift in the design of models when targeting laypeople. Secondly, whether logic classes designed to train a formal form of reasoning are more beneficial to training laypeople in security than teaching them different graphical representations of attack scenarios.

Other study questions may include the participants' effort to grasp the attack scenarios. In particular, how much time is required to reach the same understanding in each representation. Another line of work is the analysis of adequate training resources to empower laypeople in interpreting and using this formalism. Lastly, future research should develop model representations that do not lose their analytic properties but improve usability for laypeople (see Sect. 5). Let us emphasize that while significant effort has been spent on extending ADT to improve their usability w.r.t. to the modelling power, e.g. [7,11,12] , the modelling ease and explainability has received much less attention.

It is important to note that available analysis and verification methods for graphical security models and their potential to effectively communicate security risks to *domain experts* are of their own interest. Independent surveys will be needed for that group, as their skills and aims differ hugely. This survey explicitly aims to help answer the question of whether graphical security models can be a valuable part of risk communications to *laypeople* only. Further research, as outlined above, can make the formalism more appealing to this target group.

Acknowledgement. We thank the recent anonymous reviewers for their comments, that significantly improved the message of this paper.

This research has received funding from the European Union under Grant Agreement No. 101171844, project Intelligence-Oriented Verification&Controller Synthesis (InOVationCS), and from the European Union'Fs Horizon Europe program under Grant Agreement No. 101212818. Views and opinions expressed are, however, those of the authors only and do not necessarily reflect those of the European Union or European Research Executive Agency. Neither the European Union nor the granting authority can be held responsible for them.

This research has also received funding from the MUNI Award in Science and Humanities MUNI/I/1757/2021 of the Grant Agency of Masaryk University, the German Academic Scholarship Foundation and project Proven Security for systems with human interaction (ProSec) funded by the German Federal Ministry of Education and Research (Bundesministerium für Bildung und Forschung) and supported by Software Campus performed in collaboration of TUM and DATEV eG.

A Remaining Representations

A.1 Running-Text Representation [Case 1]

The following text describes how an attacker might enter a company building by attacking its front door. Of course, the attacker can always open the door using brute force.

There are additional ways to attack the door: lock picking, for instance, is another way to access the building. Additionally, suppose the attacker managed to steal the keys, make a copy, and return the keys without getting noticed. In that case, the attacker could also access the building by unlocking the door with the key. The attacker needs to return the keys. Otherwise, the owners of the company notice that they are missing, and the attack would fail.

The company creates a defense strategy. First, to avoid brute force attacks, they have reinforced the door. Hence, the attacker will not be able anymore to perform brute force attacks. Moreover, the company wants to be protected against attacks that are performed by lock picking. Hence, they establish a security team passing by the door. If the team sees motion on the lock, they will prevent the attacker from picking the lock.

A.2 Graph-Tree Representation [Case 2]

(see Fig. 7).

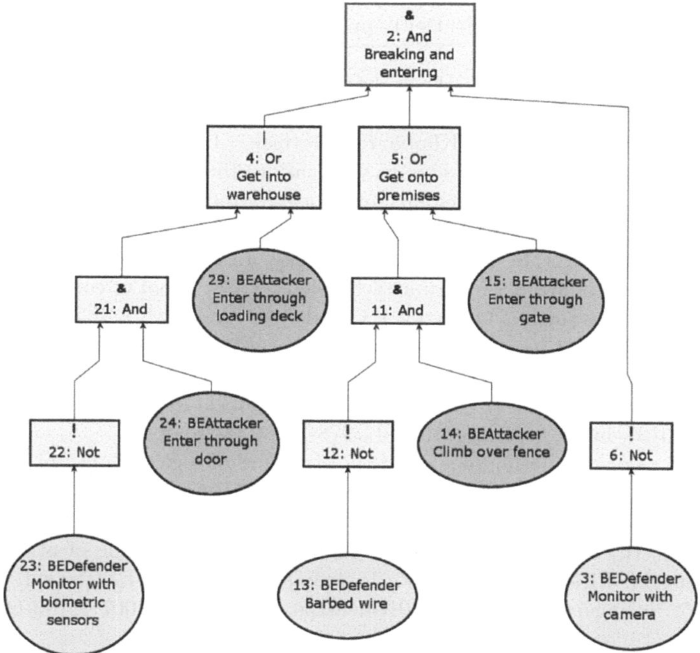

Fig. 7. Attack scenario 2 represented as Graph-Tree.

References

1. Alsmadi, I., Easttom, C.: The NICE Cyber Security Framework. Springer, Cham (2020)
2. Attridge, N., Aberdein, A., Inglis, M.: Does studying logic improve logical reasoning? (2016)
3. Baier, C., Katoen, J.P.: Principles of Model Checking. MIT Press, Cambridge (2008)
4. Berkowitz, M., Stern, E.: Which cognitive abilities make the difference? Predicting academic achievements in advanced stem studies. J. Intell. **6** (2018)
5. Broccia, G., ter Beek, M.H., Lluch Lafuente, A., Spoletini, P., Ferrari, A.: Assessing the understandability and acceptance of attack-defense trees for modelling security requirements. In: International Working Conference on Requirements Engineering: Foundation for Software Quality, pp. 39–56. Springer, Cham (2024)
6. Bronkhorst, H., Roorda, G., Suhre, C., Goedhart, M.: Logical reasoning in formal and everyday reasoning tasks. Int. J. Sci. Math. Educ. **18** (2019). https://doi.org/10.1007/s10763-019-10039-8

7. Buldas, A., Gadyatskaya, O., Lenin, A., Mauw, S., Trujillo-Rasua, R.: Attribute evaluation on attack trees with incomplete information. Comput. Secur. **88** (2020). https://doi.org/10.1016/J.COSE.2019.101630
8. Chowdhury, P.D., Hallett, J., Patnaik, N., Tahaei, M., Rashid, A.: Developers are neither enemies nor users: they are collaborators. In: 2021 IEEE Secure Development Conference (SecDev), pp. 47–55 (2021). https://doi.org/10.1109/SecDev51306.2021.00023
9. Chuttur, M.Y.: Overview of the technology acceptance model: origins, developments and future directions (2009)
10. Dorfhuber, F., Eisentraut, J., Klioba, K., Křetínský, J.: QuADTool: attack-defense-tree synthesis, analysis and bridge to verification. In: International Conference on Quantitative Evaluation of Systems and Formal Modeling and Analysis of Timed Systems, pp. 52–71. Springer, Cham (2024)
11. Eisentraut, J., Holzer, S., Klioba, K., Křetínský, J., Pin, L., Wagner, A.: Assessing security of cryptocurrencies with attack-defense trees: proof of concept and future directions. In: Cerone, A., Ölveczky, P.C. (eds.) ICTAC 2021. LNCS, vol. 12819, pp. 214–234. Springer, Cham (2021). https://doi.org/10.1007/978-3-030-85315-0_13
12. Eisentraut, J., Křetínský, J.: Expected cost analysis of attack-defense trees. In: Parker, D., Wolf, V. (eds.) QEST 2019. LNCS, vol. 11785, pp. 203–221. Springer, Cham (2019). https://doi.org/10.1007/978-3-030-30281-8_12
13. Fillion, N.: Logical methodology and the structure of logic syllabi. In: Research in History and Philosophy of Mathematics: The CSHPM 2022, pp. 1–14. Springer, Cham (2023)
14. Hermanns, H., Krämer, J., Krčál, J., Stoelinga, M.: The value of attack-defence diagrams. In: Piessens, F., Viganò, L. (eds.) POST 2016. LNCS, vol. 9635, pp. 163–185. Springer, Heidelberg (2016). https://doi.org/10.1007/978-3-662-49635-0_9
15. Hong, J.B., Kim, D.S., Chung, C.J., Huang, D.: A survey on the usability and practical applications of graphical security models. Comput. Sci. Rev. **26**, 1–16 (2017). https://doi.org/10.1016/j.cosrev.2017.09.001. https://www.sciencedirect.com/science/article/pii/S1574013716301083
16. IBM: Cost of a data breach IBM report (2024). https://www.ibm.com/reports/data-breach. Accessed 07 Oct 2024
17. Ikuenobe, P.: Teaching and assessing critical thinking abilities as outcomes in an informal logic course. Teach. High. Educ. **6**(1), 19–32 (2001)
18. Kordy, B., Mauw, S., Radomirović, S., Schweitzer, P.: Foundations of attack-defense trees. In: Proceedings of the 7th International Conference on Formal Aspects of Security and Trust, FAST 2010, pp. 80–95. Springer, Heidelberg (2011). http://dl.acm.org/citation.cfm?id=1964555.1964561
19. Kordy, B., Piètre-Cambacédès, L., Schweitzer, P.: Dag-based attack and defense modeling: don't miss the forest for the attack trees. Comput. Sci. Rev. **13** (2013). https://doi.org/10.1016/j.cosrev.2014.07.001
20. Lallie, H., Debattista, K., Bal, J.: Evaluating practitioner cyber-security attack graph configuration preferences. Comput. Secur. **79** (2018). https://doi.org/10.1016/j.cose.2018.08.005
21. Lallie, H.S., Debattista, K., Bal, J.: An empirical evaluation of the effectiveness of attack graphs and fault trees in cyber-attack perception. IEEE Trans. Inf. Forensics Secur. **13**(5), 1110–1122 (2018). https://doi.org/10.1109/TIFS.2017.2771238

22. Lallie, H.S., Debattista, K., Bal, J.: A review of attack graph and attack tree visual syntax in cyber security. Comput. Sci. Rev. **35**, 100219 (2020). https://doi.org/10.1016/j.cosrev.2019.100219. https://www.sciencedirect.com/science/article/pii/S1574013719300772
23. Marangunić, N., Granić, A.: Technology acceptance model: a literature review from 1986 to 2013. Univ. Access Inf. Soc. **14**, 81–95 (2015)
24. Nisbett, R.E., Fong, G.T., Lehman, D.R., Cheng, P.W.: Teaching reasoning. Science **238**(4827), 625–631 (1987)
25. Norman, D.A.: The Design of Everyday Things. Basic Books Inc., USA (2002)
26. Oliveira, D., Rosenthal, M., Morin, N., Yeh, M., Cappos, J., Zhuang, Y.: It's the psychology stupid: how heuristics explain software vulnerabilities and how priming can illuminate developer's blind spots (2014). https://doi.org/10.1145/2664243.2664254
27. Opdahl, A.L., Sindre, G.: Experimental comparison of attack trees and misuse cases for security threat identification. Inf. Softw. Technol. **51**(5), 916–932 (2009)
28. Schiele, N.D., Gadyatskaya, O.: A limited technical background is sufficient for attack-defense tree acceptability. arXiv preprint arXiv:2502.11920 (2025)
29. Schneier, B.: Attack trees, modeling security threats. Dr. Dobb's Journal (1999). https://www.schneier.com/academic/archives/1999/12/attack_trees.html
30. Segers, E., Verhoeven, L.: How logical reasoning mediates the relation between lexical quality and reading comprehension. Reading Writing **29** (2016). https://doi.org/10.1007/s11145-015-9613-9
31. Shostack, A.: Threat Modeling: Designing for Security. Wiley, Hoboken (2014)
32. Simons, D.J., et al.: Do "brain-training" programs work? Psychol. Sci. Public Interest **17**(3), 103–186 (2016)
33. Steve, M.: Special report: Cyberwarfare in the c-suite. https://cybersecurityventures.com/hackerpocalypse-cybercrime-report-2016/. Accessed 26 Mar 2022
34. Tatam, M., Shanmugam, B., Azam, S., Kannoorpatti, K.: A review of threat modelling approaches for apt-style attacks. Heliyon **7**(1), e05969 (2021). https://doi.org/10.1016/j.heliyon.2021.e05969. https://www.sciencedirect.com/science/article/pii/S2405844021000748
35. Widel, W., Audinot, M., Fila, B., Pinchinat, S.: Beyond 2014: formal methods for attack tree-based security modeling. ACM Comput. Surv. (CSUR) **52**(4), 1–36 (2019)

MPL—A Flexible Multiprecision Library

Jonathan Tanner and Christoph Haase(✉)

Department of Computer Science, University of Oxford, Oxford, UK
{jonathan.tanner,christoph.haase}@cs.ox.ac.uk

Abstract. Multiprecision arithmetic is required in many applications, notably safety critical areas. It carries, however, a substantial performance impact compared to fixed precision arithmetic. Since a significant part of this is due to allocation and memory fragmentation, a substantial speed up can be obtained by optimising for small numbers by storing them inline on the stack rather than on the heap. Libraries implementing such an optimisation typically fix the range of numbers considered small. However, optimal performance requires customising this range depending on the problem. The contribution of this tool paper is to introduce MPL, a library for arbitrary fixed precision and multiprecision arithmetic, which allows developers to customise the range of small numbers based on the knowledge of their problem at compile time. We experimentally demonstrate that MPL can deliver significant speed-ups when benchmarked against GMP and CLN, both running microbenchmarks on our library. MPL is released under a permissive BSD license, and we also provide a full integration of MPL with cvc5, enabling using MPL as a back end in cvc5.

1 Introduction

The goal of this tool paper is to describe an approach to multiprecision arithmetic that is complementary to existing ones, the motivation behind it, implementation and technical details, and its experimental evaluation. Traditional arithmetic on computers uses a fixed precision that is, to a large extent, dictated by the hardware platform on which code runs, requiring the programmer to align with the machine-level precision when they write a program. This means that if the runtime data exceed these limits it will overflow and cause errors. This can be somewhat overcome with floating point arithmetic, which does not suffer from overflows. However, floating point arithmetic has limited precision and still also has a fixed upper bound beyond which it is unable to represent finite numbers.

Fixed-precision arithmetic is a result of technical limitations and rather foreign to how humans perform arithmetic, which is one reason why several high-level programming languages transparently support arbitrary precision arithmetic. An example is Python, in which integers support arbitrary precision by default. However, this significantly increases the overhead of all arithmetic operations. Furthermore, in many application domains, fixed precision arithmetic is not just a nuisance, but may lead to incorrect results, which is particularly problematic in safety critical areas. For instance, when deciding a system of linear

A. Goharshady and C. Haase (Eds.): SETTA 2025, LNCS 16458, pp. 78–90, 2026.
https://doi.org/10.1007/978-981-95-7826-9_5

equations, fixed precision arithmetic may lead to rounding errors that can result in incorrectly asserting that a given system of linear equations is infeasible. For this reason, SMT-solvers such as Z3 [4], MathSAT [3], or cvc5 [1] incorporate multiprecision arithmetic libraries such as GMP [5] or CLN [7].

GMP and CLN differ in that the former always dynamically allocates memory depending on the size required to represent a number whereas CLN only dynamically allocates memory for integers larger than 30 bits; smaller numbers are stored inline. This means that CLN can be dramatically faster when performing operations on numbers smaller than the 31 bits threshold, which is hard-coded in CLN. This *small number optimisation* in CLN makes sense, since a majority of integers occurring at runtime will often not exceed this threshold. Nevertheless, since, in general, the denominator of a rational increases with the product of the denominators of the inputs, simply adding 30 rationals may already cause the denominator to exceed the 30 bit threshold. Moreover, there are many application scenarios where multiprecision arithmetic is required, yet numbers encountered in practice are "small" yet larger than 30 bits, cf. [10, Fig. 6d] for an example in compiler optimisation. In cryptographic applications, numbers of fixed bit length are common, e.g., private keys in many elliptic curve cryptographic algorithms have bit length 256 or less. For another example, when computing the exact determinant of an $n \times n$ matrix whose largest entry has bit length L, Bareiss' algorithm [2], for instance, only produces numbers of bit length $O(n \cdot (\log n + L))$. While linear in n and L and not fitting into machine words, those numbers can still be comparably small for reasonably sized matrices. There are also applications such as neural networks, where it has been demonstrated that networks have a minimum bitsize below which their performance suffers majorly [8]. This means that, as the boundaries of neural networks are being pushed, it may be required to have bitwidth greater than machine native yet not of arbitrarily large bitwidth. These and other examples motivate optimising for small numbers, however, which numbers are considered "small" depends on the application.

Another approach to reducing the overhead of multiprecision arithmetic is *transprecision*. This is a technique where a calculation is performed at a given fixed precision, checking for overflows, aborting and rerunning the entire calculation at a higher precision if an overflow occurs. If well engineered, transprecision can be demonstrated to give a significant speedup in many settings over multiprecision libraries such as GMP and CLN, in particular since transprecision enables using vectorisation techniques. As a drawback, transprecision is challenging from an engineering perspective as a program must be architected around transprecision due to the requirement to perform the same calculation at different precisions. Recently, Pitchanathan et al. [10] developed a transprecision approach for high-performance arbitrary precision arithmetic in a library for manipulating sets definable in Presburger arithmetic. This followed on from previous work showing the benefits of transprecision when solving systems of linear inequalities [6]. Pitchanathan et al. [10] state as an open problem to develop an approach that matches the empirical performance of transprecision approaches yet does not come at the significant engineering overhead.

Library	Small optimisation size	Development cost	Compile-time cost	Flexibility of representation	Language
GMP	None	Low	Low	No	C
CLN	30	Low	Low	No	C++
FPL transprecision	16 & 64	High	High	No	C++
MPL	**Flexible**	**Low**	**High**	**Yes**	**C++**

Fig. 1. Different multiprecision libraries

Unsurprisingly, there is no one-size-fits-all solution to multiprecision arithmetic. Depending on the application domain, there are, roughly speaking, three types of cost to consider when judging the suitability of an approach to multiprecision arithmetic: runtime cost, compile time cost, and development time cost. Traditional C based multiprecision libraries like GMP are fast at compile time and relatively easy to use at development time; they are, however, suboptimal at runtime. At the other end of the scale, techniques like transprecision can get extremely good runtime performance, however the significant use of templates means that compile time suffers and the requirement that the entire program be templated on the precision adds a major burden at development time. It is no coincidence that the only uses of transprecision are in greenfield projects; it would be almost impossible to add transprecision to, say, an existing SMT solver; such an endeavour would be essentially a complete rewrite. CLN sits somewhere in between, providing a fixed width of 30 bits up until which it stores numbers inline before switching to GMP (or GMP-like algorithms). Figure 1 summarises the different strengths and weaknesses of the existing approaches discussed so far, together with *MPL*, the library presented in this paper.

MPL is a possible approach to the open problem identified by Pitchanathan et al. [10]. The aim of this paper is to describe the design and an implementation of MPL, a portable and flexible multiprecision library, with the following features:

- support for arbitrary fixed precision and multiprecision arithmetic
- support for user-defined data structures for storing numbers (called *containers* henceforth)
- comes equipped with containers optimised for "small" numbers in a way that is configurable at compile time
- minimal development time overhead compared to machine integers or GMP
- outperforms GMP for numbers of small and medium bit width; and outperforms CLN for numbers not fitting within CLN's fixed 30 bit optimisation
- competitive with GMP and CLN at large bit widths
- extensively tested and can directly be used as a back end for cvc5, passing the full cvc5 test suite; cf. Appendix A for some further details
- open-source[1] under a permissive 3 clause BSD license

[1] MPL: https://github.com/aDifferentJT/MPL
cvc5 integration:https://github.com/aDifferentJT/cvc5.

Our library is based on the approach that Alexander Stepanov pioneered in the Standard Template Library for C++ [11], much of which was later made a part of the C++ standard library. That library built on the ideas of generic programming to decouple algorithms from data structures. This gives the major advantage that adding a new representation does not require reimplementing the algorithms. This means that users with particular requirements can select the best data structure to fit those requirements. With existing libraries, not only does the user get no choice of representation, but the developers of the library had to make that choice at the beginning of the project, limiting their ability to make an informed choice. We elaborate further on technical design choices underlying MPL in Sects. 2 and 3.

In Sect. 4, we benchmark MPL against GMP and CLN, including MPL using a number of different containers. We compare their performance using microbenchmarks consisting of arithmetic operations on both integers and rationals, and finding primes of fixed bit width using the Miller-Rabin test.

2 Small Numbers Belong on the Stack

In a modern computer, one of the slowest operations is accessing memory. This can be multiple orders of magnitude slower than other primitive operations, and newer generations of hardware are only widening that gap. This means that memory layout can be extremely important for performance. Memory is laid out in two main pools, the stack and the heap. The stack is used for local variables of which the size is statically known, whereas the heap, or free store, is a less structured pool of memory from which memory can be dynamically requested. Since multiprecision integers can be of arbitrary size, it is unavoidable that the heap will be needed for sufficiently large integers. However, this is problematic for performance for two reasons. Firstly, memory allocation is not free, and secondly, the memory obtained from an allocator is not going to be in the cache. This performance impact can be mitigated by storing integers on the stack, as space on the stack can be allocated at much lower cost and is much more cache friendly. However, with very limited exceptions, the size of the data placed on the stack must be known statically at compile time. This means that only small integers can be stored thus, but since most integers are small, storing them on the stack can still provide a major benefit in performance.

It has been observed that the strategy of storing data on the stack, whenever possible, can lead to dramatic performance improvements. For instance, the observation that most strings at runtime are short is what motivated engineers at Facebook to replace the representation of strings with a representation that can store strings of up to 23 characters on the stack [9]. This change in representation resulted in a performance gain of 1% across *all of* Facebook. The discussions from [9] around strings and the empirical success of such small string optimisations inspired the development of this library.

Another advantage of storing numbers on the stack is seen when temporaries occur, e.g., when computing a value as a sequence of different operations.

Since allocating and deallocating space on the heap is comparatively expensive, code using traditional multiprecision libraries must be careful not to generate temporaries. This can be seen when comparing the performance of the two functions in Fig. 2b under GMP. When run on our benchmarking infrastructure,

```
mpz_class test1() {
  mpz_class x = 42;
  mpz_class y = 42;
  for (int i=0; i<100; i+=1) {
    x += y;
    x += y;
  }
  return x;
}
```

(a) Code avoiding temporaries

```
mpz_class test2() {
  mpz_class x = 42;
  mpz_class y = 42;
  for (int i=0; i<100; i+=1) {
    mpz_class z = y + y;
    x += z;
  }
  return x;
}
```

(b) Code with temporaries

Fig. 2. The impact of temporaries

cf. Sect. 4, `test1()` takes an average of 1.1 µs whereas `test2()` takes 3.5 µs. This is because `test2()` has to allocate storage for the $y + y$ temporary. The above example demonstrates a remarkable difference between what one may conventionally consider to be equivalent code. In particular, to be optimal, code must be written carefully considering such issues, which makes development more difficult.

However, the algorithmic work is extremely similar between these two tests, and so with an implementation that can eliminate allocation for small numbers, this difference can be almost entirely eliminated, making development easier. This will be further discussed in Sect. 4.

3 Design and Implementation

When designing a data structure for efficiently representing integers there are two conflicting interests that must be balanced. Firstly, and as previously discussed, heap allocations are expensive, so storing small numbers inline is desirable. Secondly, accessing the data without a significant overhead is important. These two interests conflict, the first requires multiple different representations, which implies that every operation would start with a condition, this then leads to a large potential overhead, e.g., due to branch mispredictions.

These are similar concerns to those faced in the storage of strings, however there are two key differences. Firstly, and to our benefit, integers can be sign extended while maintaining the same value, this means that not every size needs to be representable. It is, e.g., acceptable to have a small representation that does not track the size. Secondly, and to our detriment, efficiently processing multiprecision integers requires storing them in chunks of machine integer width, henceforth assumed to be 64 bits. This eliminates the ability to use some of the tricks used for strings without major waste of space. For example, given a 24

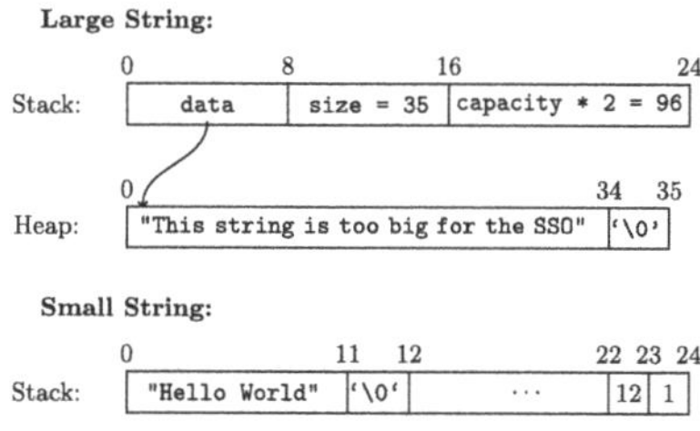

(a) A representation similar to that used by libc++

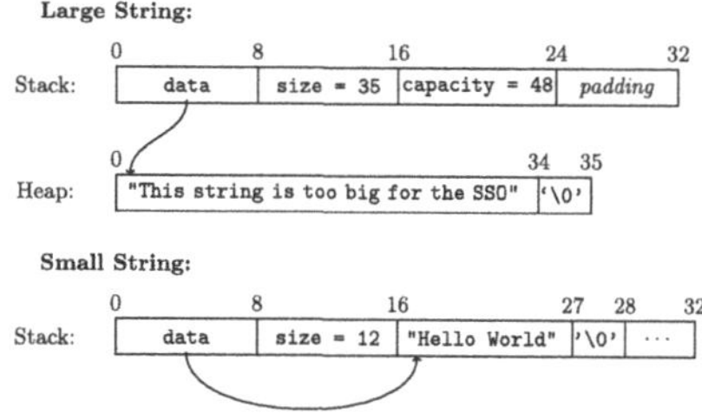

(b) A representation similar to that used by libstdc++

Fig. 3. Small string optimisations

byte structure, a string implementation can use 1 byte for flags and metadata and leave 23 bytes for string data. However, an integer implementation that uses 1 byte for a flag sacrifices 7 bytes to padding in order to satisfy alignment rules.

There are multiple different approaches used in practice for strings. Figure 3a shows a simplification of the libc++ approach, distinguishing small and large strings using a flag in the final bit. Facebook's `FBString` [9] uses a similar representation, with which they demonstrated a 1% speedup across their entire codebase compared to the older, naïve implementation.

In contrast, Fig. 3b shows libstdc++'s implementation, which appears at first glance to be significantly less efficient, using a larger structure (32 bytes, not 24) and only supporting 15 characters of small string, as opposed to 21. However, this is done with good reason, storing the data and size at the same locations in both representations allows the `data`, `size`, `begin`, and `end` functions to be branch free, only a couple of instructions each. There is a cost to this, namely that moving such a data structure now requires checking whether this is a small representation and if so, adjusting the data pointer. Thus, which representation is better depends on the relative frequencies of these operations. Microsoft's STL also uses a similar technique.

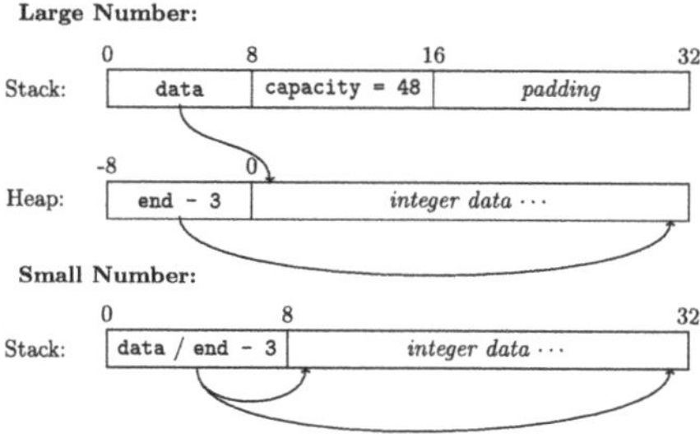

Fig. 4. An efficient representation for integers used in MPL

Both implementations are more efficient than naïve string implementations for two main reasons, firstly the allocation of memory on the heap is not free, and secondly these implementations decrease cache misses by reducing memory fragmentation.

For integers, we evaluated containers based on both of these ideas, all available in MPL. However, the representation that appeared to work best in most of our test cases is based upon the libstdc++ approach, though taking advantage of the different properties of integers by eliminating storing the size from the small representation. In more detail, for numbers that are not small, this representation stores the end pointer on the heap prior to the integer data, cf. Fig. 4. Thus it can be accessed by `*(data - 1)`.[2] In a small number, `*(data - 1)` will be equal to `data`. If instead of storing the end pointer in the large number we store `end - 3`, then for a large number we calculate `end = *(data - 1) + 3`. Doing this for a small number gets us `end = *(data - 1) + 3 = data + 3`, which is exactly the end of that small number. This technique allows us to support 24 bytes of small integer buffer in a 32 byte structure while maintaining the property that `data`, `size`, `begin`, and `end` are all branch free. In the actual implementation of MPL, the size of the small integer buffer is actually a template parameter and so can be customised, though in our evaluation, 24 bytes appeared a reasonable choice. Making the critical operations of `data`, `size`, `begin`, and `end` branch free not only increases performance for small numbers, but also minimises overhead of operations on large numbers relative to a naïve implementation. This is important because the cost of branch mis-prediction can be very high on a modern processor.

Decoupling Algorithms from Data Structures. Alexander Stepanov's Standard Template Library (STL) [11] for C++, developed in the early 1990s, was a very influential example of generic programming in API design, and it very heavily inspired the C++ standard library. A fundamental principle of the design of this library is that algorithms are defined independently of the containers, this has several main benefits. Firstly, this can decrease the amount of code to write, as if there are n algorithms and m containers the amount of code

```
struct container {
  virtual auto length() const -> std::size_t = 0;
  virtual auto operator[](std::size_t i) const -> int = 0;
};
auto sum(container const & xs) {
  auto acc = 0;
  for (std::size_t i = 0; i < xs.length(); i += 1) {
    acc += xs[i];
  }
  return acc;
}
```

Fig. 5. An example showing dynamic dispatch

[2] All pointer arithmetic is in multiples of 8 bytes.

is $n + m$ not $n \times m$. Furthermore, this can make the code much easier to test, because there is both less code and the algorithms can be tested with simpler containers before more complicated ones. Secondly, this allows users to define a new container and, as long as it complies with the defined requirements, standard algorithms can be used. This then makes it much easier to select the best container for a task, as the container selection can be done independently of the choice of algorithm. In many languages such decoupling carries an inherent runtime cost, as it requires some form of dynamic dispatch at runtime within the algorithm depending on the type of the container. This is because many languages only have dynamic polymorphism, which works as in the example in Fig. 5.

There is one sum function, and what is passed into sum is a pointer to a container, within that container is a pointer to a vtable, and within that vtable are the pointers to the functions `length` and `operator[]` that are applicable to this container. This means that `xs[i]` will require two extra pointer indirections, plus the overhead of the function call. This being an indirect call, it will cause a stall in the CPU's pipeline. Furthermore, it means that the call cannot be inlined, and that can have a major performance impact. Inlining is not only a valuable optimisation in and of itself but also enables many other optimisations. One option that some compilers can use is speculative devirtualisation. In the example above, GCC 13.2 does this but Clang 17.0.1 does not.[3] This is a technique where the compiler looks up the address that would be called through virtual dispatch, and then compares that address to the address of a particular concrete implementation. If these addresses match then an inlined version of this function can be used, which enables many other optimisations to occur.

However C++, through its template system, also provides static polymorphism implemented through monomorphisation. This is a technique where the compiler does not actually compile a polymorphic function into a polymorphic implementation, but rather each time the function is used, a monomorphic implementation is generated. The disadvantages of this are several, firstly, the same polymorphic function can potentially be generated many times for different parameter types leading to a significant increase in executable size. Secondly, the implementation must be available when the function is used, which makes it impossible to use incremental compilation to compile the implementation separately and improve compile times during development. On top of this where multiple translation units are used, multiple copies of the same template instantiation may be generated and then discarded by the linker, this further increases compilation times. However, monomorphisation carries the major benefit of eliminating the runtime overhead of any form of dynamic dispatch, as well as giving the compiler knowledge of the concrete types allowing significant optimisations.

These benefits have proven extremely valuable in allowing the STL, and the C++ standard library in succession, to effectively perform such a decoupling while still retaining optimal performance. MPL benefits similarly from this approach in its API design.

[3] Both the latest version of GCC and Clang at the time of writing.

4 Empirical Evaluation

We empirically evaluated MPL on three classes of benchmarks. All results were obtained on a MacBook Pro (13-in, 2020, Four Thunderbolt 3 ports) with an Intel(R) Core(TM) i5-1038NG7 CPU, connected to power and with fans manually set to maximum speed.

Basic Arithmetic Operations on Integers and Rationals. These benchmarks compute $\sum_{i=0}^{n} f(x_i, y_i)$ for random $x_i, y_i \in \mathbb{N}$ (for Fig. 6a, b, and c), and for random $x_i, y_i \in \mathbb{Q}$ (for Fig. 6d and e), n being the size of the test vectors, in our testing 100, and f being the operation being benchmarked. To generate random integers up to a given magnitude (k), random integers were generated uniformly in the range $[0, 10^k)$. To generate random rationals up to a given magnitude, random integers up to that magnitude were generated as above, and used as the numerators and denominators.

To robustly measure the performance of such short operations, we used Google Benchmark, a library for accurately timing C++ functions. The results are displayed in Figs. 6a and d. GMP performance is shown in black, CLN in orange, and MPL in blue, brown and purple: blue is MPL using `std::vector` from the standard library as the container, in purple MPL using a custom container applying a small number optimisation similar to Fig. 3a. In brown is MPL using the container depicted in Fig. 4.

We see that CLN does very well for very small numbers, but performance quickly degrades, in fact for integer division, the CLN results had to be excluded as they quickly left the chart. MPL using vectors is slightly worse than GMP, likely due to the large engineering efforts gone into GMP. The two different MPL containers show different trade-offs between the size of the small cutoff and the performance overhead. The branch-free version shown in Fig. 4 seems to give a very good trade-off, particularly since it displays no measurable detriment to performance on large numbers compared to using vectors.

On rationals, the situation is different, since storing rationals in canonical form requires frequent GCD calculations, there is more room for algorithmic optimisations. This can be seen in Fig. 6d by the extent to which MPL using vectors is outperformed by GMP, despite using similar containers. However, MPLs optimised containers are able to yield performance competitive to GMP, demonstrating the benefits of the containers supplied by MPL. In particular, at medium bit lengths, MPL outperforms CLN.

Primality Tests at Fixed Bit Width. The benchmarks were obtained by performing a Miller-Rabin primality test on 100000 randomly generated integers of a given magnitude. The results are shown in Fig. 6f, normalised to the performance in GMP depicted in black with CLN depicted in orange and MPL in blue. Since bitwidths are known at compile time, MPL is able to use a static array and so is able to optimise very well and to outperform both GMP and CLN by a significant margin over a wide range of bitwidths.

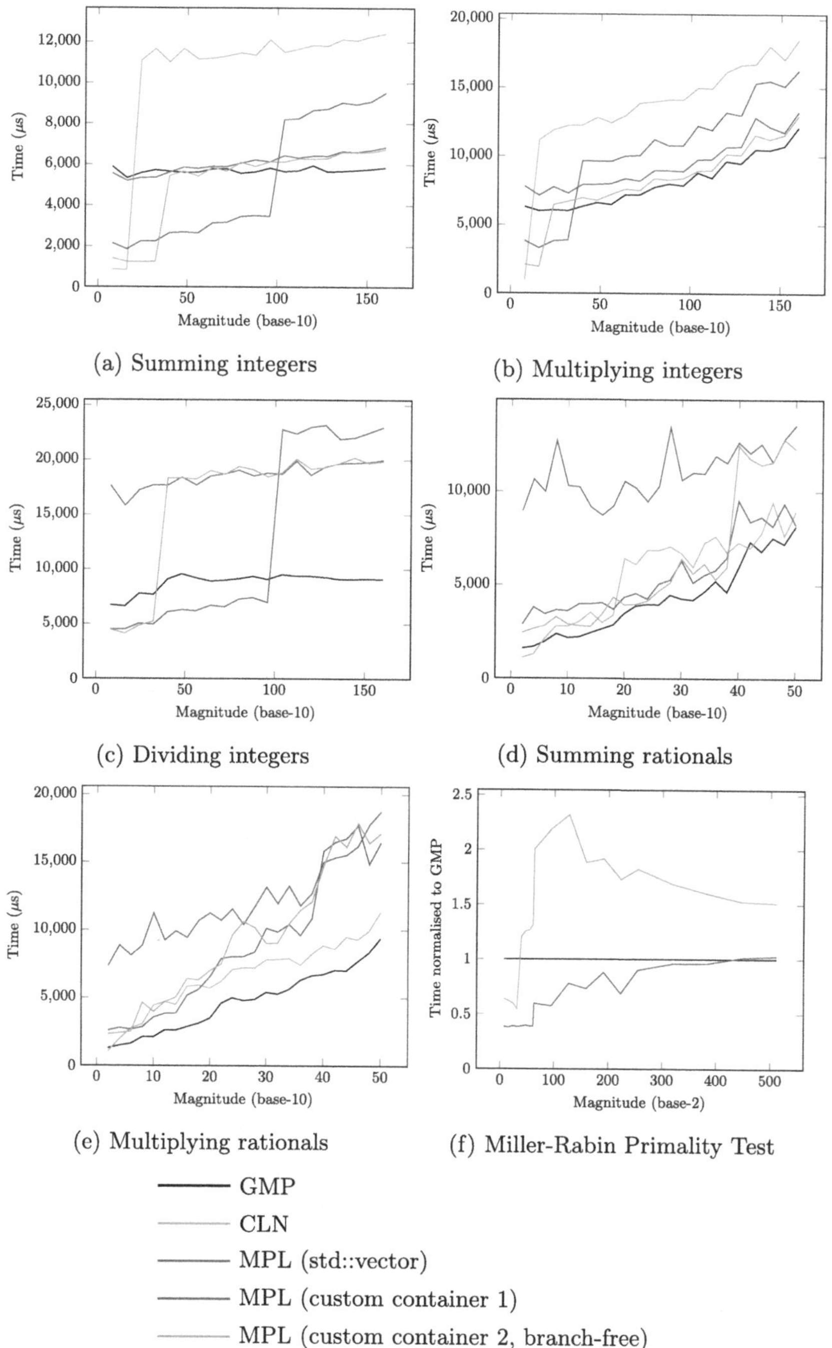

Fig. 6. Microbenchmarks for a range of magnitudes

Performance When Redundant Copies Are Included. When programming in C++ it can be easy to inadvertently force extraneous copies. As discussed in Sect. 2, this majorly impacts performance when copies must allocate. To highlight the benefits of the design choices underlying MPL, in Appendix B we perform an equivalent to the previous benchmarks where the functions take arguments by value, not reference. This shows MPL in a much more favourable light compared to GMP.

Acknowledgements. We would like to thank the SETTA'25 reviewers for their comments and suggestions. This work is part of a project that has received funding from the European Research Council (ERC) under the European Union's Horizon 2020 research and innovation programme (Grant agreement No. 852769, ARiAT).

A MPL as a cvc5 Back End

We fully integrated MPL as a back end multiprecision library for cvc5, and pass all of cvc5's regression tests.

Tests in this regression test suite are intentionally small and fast. CLN is very optimised for these cases and always outperforms MPL. We also explored if and where, without any further changes to cvc5 or its default configuration, MPL can outperform GMP. This is shown in the following table (Fig. 7).

Test	GMP	MPL	P value
regress1/sygus/temp_input_to_synth_ic-error-121418.sy	0.279	0.206	4.0e-22
regress0/fp/fp-set-comprehension-basic.smt2	0.166	0.162	5.8e-03
regress2/bv/opStructure_MBA_6.scrambled.min.smt2	1.504	1.152	6.9e-19
regress0/fp/bvcomp-rewrite.smt2	0.193	0.189	5.6e-02
regress2/sygus/pbe_bvurem.sy	0.703	0.588	8.2e-12
regress1/rr-verify/bool-crci.sy	0.301	0.296	3.9e-03
regress1/fp/rti_3_5_bug_report.smt2	0.869	0.793	1.0e-06
regress1/rr-verify/fp-arith.sy	0.854	0.655	3.1e-15
regress0/smtlib/reset-force-logic.smt2	0.123	0.122	5.9e-02
regress1/sygus/pLTL_5_trace.sy	0.749	0.634	1.5e-12
regress1/fp/fp_to_real.smt2	0.269	0.259	6.0e-06
regress1/rr-verify/bv-term.sy	1.404	1.242	1.4e-12

Fig. 7. Regression tests where MPL outperforms GMP. All times are in seconds.

We performed Welch's t-test on the results and from this we can conclude that MPL, even on such small test cases, is able to statistically significantly outperform a highly-optimised library like GMP that cvc5 uses by default.

Further optimising the implementation of MPL allowing it to outperform CLN or GMP as a cvc5 backend on substantially more test cases and benchmarks is beyond the scope of this paper and left for future work.

B Benchmarks with Temporaries

In Fig. 8 we present benchmarks similar to those in Fig. 6, but with extraneous copies introduced by passing by value instead of by reference, and we see that

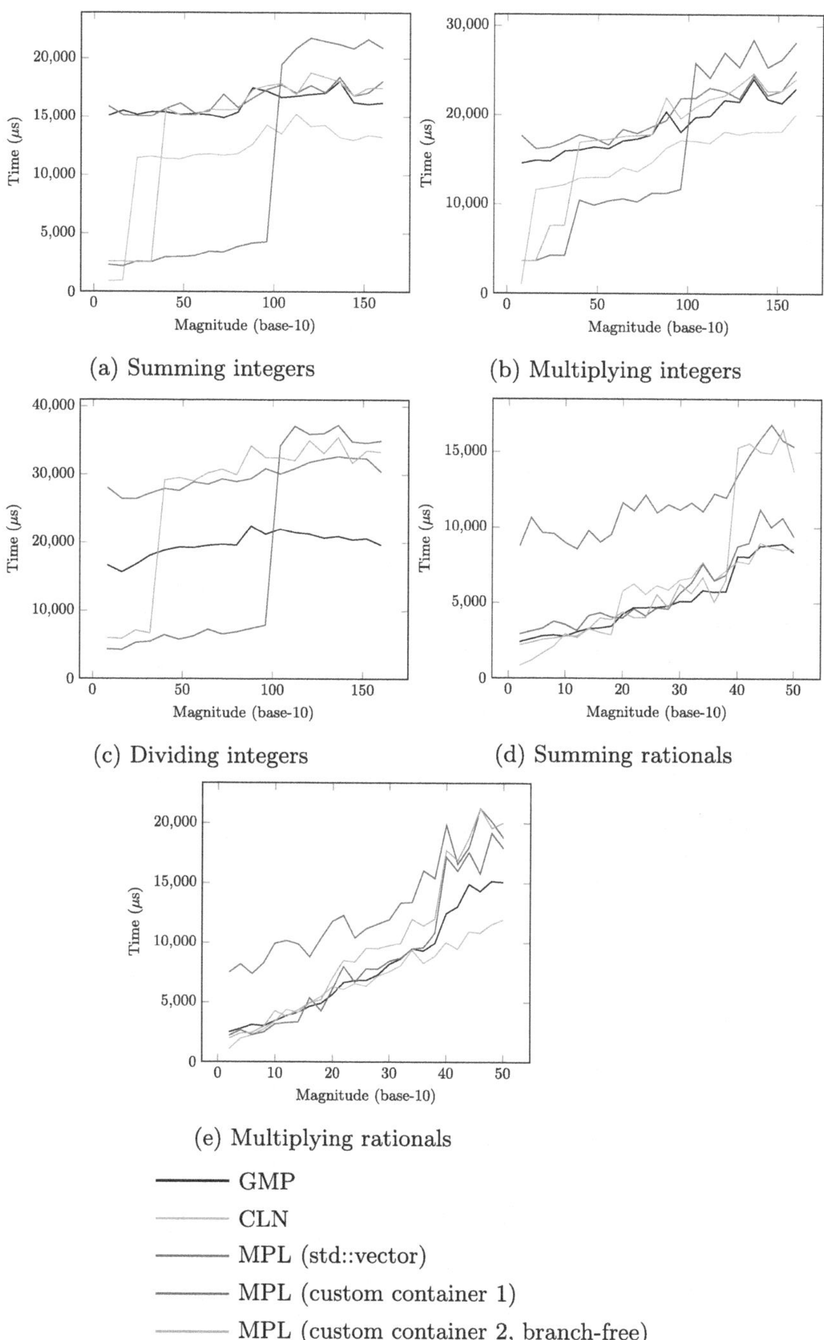

Fig. 8. Microbenchmarks for a range of magnitudes, with extraneous copies

GMP performs substantially worse. The other implementations see a similar performance drop once they transition to their large representations, which happens first for CLN, and later for MPL, according to the different containers used by MPL.

References

1. Barbosa, H., et al.: cvc5: a versatile and industrial-strength SMT solver. In: Fisman, D., Rosu, G., (eds.) Tools and Algorithms for the Construction and Analysis of Systems, pp. 415–442. Springer, Cham (2022)
2. Bareiss, E.H.: Sylvester's identity and multistep integer-preserving gaussian elimination. Math. Comput. **22**(103), 565–578 (1968). http://www.jstor.org/stable/2004533
3. Cimatti, A., Griggio, A., Schaafsma, B.J., Sebastiani, R.: The MathSAT5 SMT solver. In: Piterman, N., Smolka, S.A. (eds.) Tools and Algorithms for the Construction and Analysis of Systems, pp. 93–107. Springer, Heidelberg (2013)
4. de Moura, L., Bjørner, N.: Z3: an efficient SMT solver. In: Ramakrishnan, C.R., Rehof, J. (eds.)Tools and Algorithms for the Construction and Analysis of Systems, pp. 337–340. Springer, Heidelberg (2008)
5. Granlund, T., The GMP Development Team: GNU MP: The GNU Multiple Precision Arithmetic Library, 6.2.1 edition (2023). http://gmplib.org/
6. Grosser, T., et al.: Fast linear programming through transprecision computing on small and sparse data. Proc. ACM Program. Lang. **4**(OOPSLA), 195 (2020)
7. Haible, B., Kreckel, R.B.: CLN, a Class Library for Numbers, 1.3.6 edition (2022). https://www.ginac.de/CLN/
8. Li, Z., Ma, Y., Vajiac, C., Zhang, Y.: Exploration of numerical precision in deep neural networks (2018). http://arxiv.org/abs/1805.01078
9. Ormrod, N.: The strange details of std::string at Facebook. https://www.youtube.com/watch?v=kPR8h4-qZdk
10. Pitchanathan, A., Ulmann, C., Weber, M., Hoefler, T., Grosser, T.: FPL: fast presburger arithmetic through transprecision. Proc. ACM Program. Lang. **5**(OOPSLA) (2021). https://doi.org/10.1145/3485539
11. Plauger, P.J., Lee, M., Musser, D., Stepanov, A.A.: C++ Standard Template Library, 1st edn. Prentice Hall PTR, USA (2000)

Logic and Theorem Proving

A Generic Dynamic Logic for Program Reasoning Based on Operational Semantics

Yuanrui Zhang(✉) and Zhibin Yang

Collage of Software, Nanjing University of Aeronautics and Astronautics, Nanjing, China
yuanruizhang@nuaa.edu.cn

Abstract. Dynamic logic is a valuable formalism that has many applications in ensuring the correctness of safety-critical systems. We present a novel theory of parameterized dynamic logic, namely DL_p, for specifying and reasoning about program models based on their operational semantics. Different from most dynamic logics that deal with regular expressions or a particular type of models, DL_p allows arbitrary forms of programs and formulas according to specific domains. It provides a language-independent proof calculus under dynamic-logic settings, supporting symbolic-execution-based reasoning with a general notion of labels for capturing program configurations. To admit certain infinite proof deductions caused by loop programs, we adapt the cyclic proof approach to the theory of DL_p by building a cyclic proof structure specific to DL_p. The soundness of DL_p is analyzed and formally proved. A case study displays an instantiation of DL_p in particular domains, demonstrating the potential usage of DL_p in program verification.

Keywords: Dynamic Logic · Program Deduction · Verification Framework · Cyclic Proof · Operational Semantics · Symbolic Execution

1 Introduction

Dynamic logic [20] has proven to be a valuable formalism for specifying and reasoning about different types of programs. It has been successfully applied to domains such as process algebras [6], programming languages [5], synchronous systems [49,50], hybrid systems [35,36] and probabilistic systems [26,34]. These theories have inspired the development of related verification tools for safety-critical systems, such as KIV [39], KeY [43], KeYmaera [37], and the tools developed in [14,50]. Recent developments in dynamic logic include a range of extensions aimed at addressing contemporary challenges, such as ensuring the correctness of blockchain systems [23], describing hyperproperties [19], and verifying quantum computations [14,47]. It also has attracted attention as a promising framework for "incorrectness reasoning", as explored recently in [33,51].

A. Goharshady and C. Haase (Eds.): SETTA 2025, LNCS 16458, pp. 93–112, 2026.
https://doi.org/10.1007/978-981-95-7826-9_6

As an extension of modal logic, dynamic logic embeds a program α into the modality $\Box$ of a modal formula $\Box\phi$ as a form: $[\alpha]\phi$, meaning that after all executions of α, formula ϕ holds. This so-called "dynamic formula" allows multiple and nested modalities in forms like $[\alpha]\phi \to \langle\beta\rangle\psi$ and $[\alpha]\langle\beta\rangle\phi$ (where $\langle\cdot\rangle$ is the dual modality of $[\cdot]$), being able to directly express and reason about more complex program properties than Hoare triple $\{\phi\}\alpha\{\psi\}$ in Hoare logics (e.g. [22,40]). Particularly, when restricting a program α to be deterministic, formulas $\phi \to [\alpha]\psi$ and $\phi \to \langle\alpha\rangle\psi$ exactly capture the meanings of partial and total correctness of program α respectively in Hoare logics.

Program logics, like standard dynamic logics [20] and Hoare logics [22], are usually in explicit forms. When applying them to a certain system model or computer program, new theories are required to adapt to the target languages. For instance, to apply first-order dynamic logic (FODL) to the verification of Java programs, many primitives in Java and inference rules specific to the structures of Java need to be added into the FODL theory (cf. [5]). Otherwise, additional language transformations are inevitable, causing loss of critical program structural information during deductions. However, many languages in reality, such as AADL, UML/MARTE, Esterel [7], Java, C, etc., often have complex structures. Building a specific logic theory for them requires a lot of work. Moreover, the proof system of a logic theory is often error prone, thus requiring validation of its soundness (and even completeness), which also can be costly. One example is that Verifiable C [3] spends nearly 40,000 lines of Coq code to define and validate its logic theory for C programming language based on separation logic [40].

Another main issue is that the proof systems of these program logics are often based on programs' denotational semantics (cf. [20]) (, in which the semantics of a program is usually interpreted as a set of behavioral traces). For many interesting computer systems and programs, on the other hand, operational semantics—which describes that how a program α under a configuration σ (denoted by (α, σ)) is transitioned to another program α' under a configuration σ' (denoted by (α', σ'))—is in their nature. In these cases, the consistency from denotational semantics to operational semantics has to be validated (cf. [31,41]). This thus increases the burden of using the logic theories. Moreover, the denotational semantics of some languages are not compositional w.r.t. some of their language operators. Typical examples are synchronous programming languages like Esterel [8] and Quartz [17]. For these models, reasoning based on operational semantics is more direct, in the sense that we do not need to perform extra program transformations. [17] shows an example of non-compositional derivations of Quartz programs that rely on heavy program transformations.

This paper focuses on a theoretical solution of the above two problems in existing dynamic-logic theories. We present a novel dynamic logic called "parameterized dynamic logic" (abbreviated as DL_p) for reasoning about programs based on their operational semantics. Generally speaking, DL_p is a unified dynamic-logic theory modulo programs' operational semantics. It provides a language-independent verification framework in which program deductions rely solely on program transitions of a universal form: $(\alpha, \sigma) \longrightarrow (\alpha', \sigma')$ (for arbitrary $\alpha, \alpha', \sigma, \sigma'$). Instead of carefully designing rules according to programs' denotational semantics, the inference rules for program transitions can be built directly from the operational semantics of programs. Their validations are straightforward without the need of additional proofs.

The methodology of reasoning based on operational semantics has been proposed and studied for years within different mathematical theories, among them the work based on rewriting logics [12,41,42,45], set theory and coinduction [27,31], and program updates [4,5,35] are closest to our work (see Sect. 6 for a detailed comparison). Except a few work such as [21,32], to the best of our knowledge, most of the previous work has not yet addressed a similar approach under dynamic-logic settings, i.e., to provide an efficient logical calculus for deriving dynamic formulas. In our opinion, it is valuable to fill in this gap.

Illustration of Main Idea. Informally, DL_p treats program α and formula ϕ of $[\alpha]\phi$ as 'parameters', while introducing 'labels' σ as program configurations to capture current program states for symbolic executions. The structures of α, ϕ and σ are irrelevant to the main skeleton of the verification framework. In DL_p, we derive a labelled DL_p dynamic formula $\sigma : [\alpha]\phi$ instead of $[\alpha]\phi$. When σ represents an arbitrary configuration, $\sigma : [\alpha]\phi$ exactly captures the same meaning as $[\alpha]\phi$.

To see how we can benefit from deriving a labelled DL_p formula, consider a simple example. We want to prove a formula $\phi_1 =_{df} (x \geq 0 \rightarrow [x := x+1]x > 0)$ in FODL [38], where x is a variable ranging over integers $\mathbb{Z}$. Intuitively, formula ϕ_1 means that if $x \geq 0$ holds, then $x > 0$ holds after assigning the expression $x + 1$ to x. In FODL, to derive ϕ_1, we apply rule:

$$\frac{\phi[x/e]}{[x := e]\phi}\ {\scriptstyle (x:=e)}$$

for assignment on formula $[x := x + 1]x > 0$ by substituting x of $x > 0$ with $x+1$, and obtain $x+1 > 0$. Formula ϕ_1 thus becomes $\phi_1' =_{df} (x \geq 0 \rightarrow x+1 > 0)$, which is true for any $x \in \mathbb{Z}$.

In DL_p, however, formula ϕ_1 can be expressed as a form: $\psi_1 =_{df} (t \geq 0 \rightarrow \{x \mapsto t\} : [x := x + 1]x > 0)$. In ψ_1, formula $[x := x + 1]x > 0$ is labelled by configuration $\{x \mapsto t\}$, which means that variable x stores value t (with t a free variable). With a label explicitly showing up, to derive formula ψ_1, we instead directly perform a program transition of $x := x + 1$ as:

$$(x := x + 1, \{x \mapsto t\}) \longrightarrow (\downarrow, \{x \mapsto t + 1\}), \qquad (ex\ x := e)$$

which assigns the value $t + 1$ to x afterwards. Here $\downarrow$ indicates a program termination. Formula ψ_1 thus becomes $\psi_1' =_{df} (t \geq 0 \rightarrow \{x \mapsto t + 1\} : x > 0)$, by replacing the part '$\{x \mapsto t\} : [x := x+1]$' with its execution result '$\{x \mapsto t+1\}$'. Formula $\{x \mapsto t + 1\} : x > 0$ exactly means $t + 1 > 0$, by replacing x with its current value $t + 1$. So from ψ_1' we obtain formula $t \geq 0 \rightarrow t + 1 > 0$, which is exactly formula ϕ_1' (modulo free-variable renaming).

In the above example, the form of the transition ($ex\ x := e$) directly comes from the operational semantics of the assignment $x := e$. It is universal for all types of program transitions. By choosing different labels one can specify the rules for different languages. On the other hand, rule ($x := e$) here is actually a special assignment rule in FODL. It cannot be directly applied to other languages, for example, a Java statement $x := new\ C(...)$ that creates a new object of class C (cf. [5]).

Main Contributions and Challenges. In this paper, we firstly define the syntax and semantics of DL_p based on the standard theory of propositional dynamic logic (PDL) [16]. The challenge of this part is to find a suitable way to define the semantics of DL_p (Definition 4), since its ingredients are all unknown parameters. Following the conventions of defining a dynamic logic [20], we propose a so-called "program-labelled" (PL) Kripke structure (Definition 2) to support describing the operational semantics of programs in arbitrary forms. And we follow an approach similar in [15] to propose a labelled sequent calculus (Sect. 3.1) for symbolic-execution-based reasoning. But here the forms of labels in DL_p can be an explicit program structure rather than just an abstract state in [15] (see Sect. 6).

After defining the logic theory, we build a cyclic verification framework for DL_p. Cyclic proof approach (cf. [11]) is a powerful technique to admit a certain type of infinite deductions (i.e. "cyclic proofs") caused by symbolic executions of programs with loop structures (Sect. 3.3). It has been attracting more and more attention and recently has been applied to many logic theories such as [2,24,48]. We investigate this approach and adapt it to the theory of DL_p. The main challenges of this part are (1) identifying a sound cyclic proof system, where the most critical work is to design rule (Sub) and the "substitutions of labels" (Definition 7); and (2) constructing a cyclic proof structure, where the key step is to define "progressive derivation traces" (Definition 9). At last, as an important contribution, we prove the soundness of our cyclic proof system (Sect. 5).

To sum up, the main contributions of this paper are threefold:

- We define the syntax and semantics of DL_p formulas.
- We build a labelled proof system for DL_p.
- We construct a sound cyclic proof system for DL_p and prove its soundness.

The rest of the paper is organized as follows. Section 2 defines the syntax and semantics of DL_p formulas. In Sect. 3, we propose a cyclic proof system for DL_p. In Sect. 4, we give an example of cyclic deductions of DL_p formulas. Section 5 analyzes and proves the soundness of DL_p. Section 6 introduces related work, while Sect. 7 makes a conclusion and discusses about future work. Due to the space limit, some more details of this work is given in an extended version of this paper online [1].

2 Dynamic Logic DL_p

The theory of DL_p extends PDL [16] by permitting the program α and formula ϕ in modalities $[\alpha]\phi$ to take arbitrary forms, subject to a restriction condition

(Definition 10). A brief introduction to PDL and FODL is given in the online report [1].

We assume two pre-defined sets $\mathbf{P}$ and $\mathbf{F}$, namely *parameters* of DL_p. $\mathbf{P}$ is a set of programs, in which we distinguish a special program $\downarrow \in \mathbf{P}$ called *termination*. $\mathbf{F}$ is a set of formulas.

Definition 1 (DL_p Formulas). *A dynamic logical formula ϕ w.r.t. parameters $\mathbf{P}$ and $\mathbf{F}$, called a "parameterized dynamic logic" (DL_p) formula, is defined as follows in BNF form:*

$$\phi =_{df} F \mid \neg\phi \mid \phi \wedge \phi \mid [\alpha]\phi,$$

where $F \in \mathbf{F}$, $\alpha \in \mathbf{P}$. We denote the set of DL_p formulas as $\mathfrak{F}_{dlp}$.

Intuitively, formula $[\alpha]\phi$ means that after all executions of program α, formula ϕ holds. $\langle\cdot\rangle$ is the dual operator of $[\cdot]$. Formula $\langle\alpha\rangle\phi$ is expressed as $\neg[\alpha]\neg\phi$. Other formulas with logical connectives such as $\vee$ and $\rightarrow$ can be expressed by formulas with $\neg$ and $\wedge$ accordingly. Note that in a DL_p formula, there can be multiple and nested modalities, e.g., both $[\alpha]\phi \rightarrow \langle\beta\rangle\psi$ and $[\alpha]((\langle\beta\rangle\phi)$ are legal DL_p formulas.

Following the convention of defining a dynamic logic (cf. [20]), we introduce a novel Kripke structure to tackle parameterized program behaviours in $\mathbf{P}$.

Definition 2 (Program-Labelled Kripke Structure). *A "program-labelled" (PL) Kripke structure w.r.t. parameters $\mathbf{P}$ and $\mathbf{F}$ is a triple*

$$K(\mathbf{P}, \mathbf{F}) =_{df} (\mathcal{S}, \longrightarrow, \mathcal{I}),$$

where S is a set of worlds; $\longrightarrow \subseteq \mathcal{S} \times (\mathbf{P} \times \mathbf{P}) \times \mathcal{S}$ is a set of relations labelled by program pairs, in the form of $w_1 \xrightarrow{\alpha/\alpha'} w_2$ for some $w_1, w_2 \in \mathcal{S}$, $\alpha, \alpha' \in \mathbf{P}$; $\mathcal{I} : \mathbf{F} \rightarrow \mathcal{P}(\mathcal{S})$ is an interpretation of formulas in $\mathbf{F}$ on the power set of worlds, satisfying that $w \not\xrightarrow{\downarrow/\alpha} \cdot$ for any $w \in \mathcal{S}$ and $\alpha \in \mathbf{P}$ (capturing the meaning of program $\downarrow$).

PL Kripke structures differ from the Kripke structures of PDL by introducing program-labelled relations $w_1 \xrightarrow{\alpha/\alpha'} w_2$, which describe programs' transitional behaviours. Intuitively, it means that from world w_1, program α is transitioned to program α', ending with world w_2.

Below in this paper, **our discussion is always based on an assumed PL Kripke structure namely** $K(\mathbf{P}, \mathbf{F}) = (\mathcal{S}, \longrightarrow, \mathcal{I})$, where transitional behaviours $\longrightarrow$ is usually captured by a set of inference rules on program transitions (see Sect. 3.2), as the operational semantics of $\mathbf{P}$.

Example 1 (An Instantiation of Programs and Formulas). Consider a while program *WP* in an instantiation namely $\mathbf{P}_W$ of parameter $\mathbf{P}$:

$$WP =_{df} \{while\ (n > 0)\ do\ s := s + n\ ;\ n := n - 1\ end\}.$$

Given an initial value of variables n and s, program *WP* computes the sum from n to 1 stored in the variable s. The underlying theory of programs $\mathbf{P}_W$ is the arithmetic number theory in integer domain $\mathbb{Z}$. Let Var_W be the set of integer variables. $x := e$ is an assignment, which assigns the value of expression e to variable x. In the PL Kripke structure $K_W = (\mathcal{S}_W, \longrightarrow, \mathcal{I}_K)$ for $\mathbf{P}_W$, a world $w \in \mathcal{S}_W$ is a mapping $w : Var_W \to \mathbb{Z}$ from variables to integers. Programs' transitional behaviours of $\mathbf{P}_W$ is captured by the relations on K_W. For example, we have a relation $w \xrightarrow{x:=x+1/\downarrow} w[x \mapsto w(x)+1]$, where $w[x \mapsto v]$ is a mapping that only differs from w on mapping x to value v. The formulas in while programs namely $\mathbf{F}_W$ are the usual arithmetic first-order logical formulas in integer domain $\mathbb{Z}$.

Definition 3 (Execution Path). *An "execution path" on K is a finite sequence of relations on $\longrightarrow$: $w_1 \xrightarrow{\alpha_1/\beta_1} ... \xrightarrow{\alpha_n/\beta_n} w_{n+1}$ $(n \geq 0)$ satisfying that $\beta_n \in \{\downarrow\}$, and $\beta_i = \alpha_{i+1} \notin \{\downarrow\}$ for all $1 \leq i < n$.*

In Definition 3, the execution path is sometimes simply written as a sequence of worlds: $w_1...w_{n+1}$. When $n = 0$, the execution path is a single world w_1 (without any relations on $\longrightarrow$).

Definition 4 (Semantics of DL_p Formulas). *Given a DL_p formula ϕ, the satisfaction of ϕ by a world $w \in S$ under K, denoted by $K, w \models \phi$, is inductively defined as follows:*

1. *$K, w \models F$ where $F \in \mathbf{F}$, if $w \in \mathcal{I}(F)$;*
2. *$K, w \models \neg\phi$, if $K, w \not\models \phi$;*
3. *$K, w \models \phi \wedge \psi$, if $K, w \models \phi$ and $K, w \models \psi$;*
4. *$K, w \models [\alpha]\phi$, if for all execution paths of the form: $w \xrightarrow{\alpha/\cdot} ... \xrightarrow{\cdot/\downarrow} w'$ for some $w' \in \mathcal{S}$, $K, w' \models \phi$.*

According to the definition of operator $\langle\cdot\rangle$, its semantics is defined such that $K, w \models \langle\alpha\rangle\phi$, if there exists an execution path of the form $w \xrightarrow{\alpha/\cdot} ... \xrightarrow{\cdot/\downarrow} w'$ for some $w' \in \mathcal{S}$ such that $K, w' \models \phi$.

A DL_p formula ϕ is called *valid* w.r.t. K, denoted by $K \models \phi$ (or simply $\models \phi$), if $K, w \models \phi$ for all $w \in \mathcal{S}$.

Example 2 (DL_p Specifications). A property of program *WP* (Example 1) is described as the following formula

$$(n \geq 0 \wedge n = N \wedge s = 0) \to [WP](s = ((N+1)N)/2),$$

which means that given an initial condition of n and s, after executing *WP*, s equals to $((N+1)N)/2$, which is the sum of $1 + 2 + ... + N$, with N a free variable in $\mathbb{Z}$. We will prove an equivalent labelled version of this formula in DL_p in Sect. 4.

3 A Cyclic Proof System for DL_p

We propose a cyclic proof system for DL_p. We firstly propose a labelled proof system P_{dlp} to support reasoning based on symbolic executions (Sect. 3.2). Then we construct a cyclic proof structure for system P_{dlp}, which support deriving infinite proof trees under certain conditions (Sect. 3.3). Section 3.1 introduces the notions of labelled sequent calculus and cyclic proof.

3.1 Prerequisites

Labelled Sequent Calculus. We assume a set $\mathbf{L}$ of labels as a *parameter* of DL_p. A label mapping $\mathfrak{m} : \mathbf{L} \to \mathcal{S}$ maps each label of $\mathbf{L}$ to a world of set $\mathcal{S}$. Denote the set of all label mappings as $\mathbf{M}$. A *labelled DL_p formula* is of the form $\sigma : \phi$, where $\sigma \in \mathbf{L}$ and $\phi \in \mathfrak{F}_{dlp}$. Denote the set of all labelled DL_p formulas as $\mathfrak{F}_{ldlp}$.

From program-labelled relations defined in Definition 2 we introduce symbolic executions of programs as a type of abstract transitions on labels and program terminations. A *program transition* is a relation of the form $\sigma \xrightarrow{\alpha/\alpha'} \sigma'$ (also written as $(\alpha, \sigma) \longrightarrow (\alpha', \sigma')$ below) between labels and labelled by a program pair, with $\sigma, \sigma' \in \mathbf{L}$ and $\alpha, \alpha' \in \mathbf{P}$. Call pair (α, σ) a *program state.* We use $\mathfrak{F}_{pt}$ to represent the set of all program transitions. A *program termination* is a relation of the form $\sigma \Downarrow \alpha$ between a label and a program, where $\sigma \in \mathbf{L}$ and $\alpha \in \mathbf{P}$. The set of all program terminations is denoted by $\mathfrak{F}_{ter}$.

A *sequent* is a logical argumentation of the form: $\Gamma \Rightarrow \Delta$, where Γ and Δ are finite multi-sets of formulas, called the *left side* and the *right side* of the sequent respectively. We use dot $\cdot$ to express Γ or Δ when they are empty sets. Intuitively, a sequent $\Gamma \Rightarrow \Delta$ means that if all formulas in Γ hold, then one of formulas in Δ holds. We use ν to represent a sequent.

A *labelled sequent* is a sequent in which each formula is a formula in $\mathfrak{F}_{ldlp} \cup \mathfrak{F}_{pt} \cup \mathfrak{F}_{ter}$. We use τ to represent a formula of a labelled sequent.

Definition 5 (Semantics of Formulas in Labelled Sequents). *Given a labelled sequent ν and a label mapping $\mathfrak{m} \in \mathbf{M}$, the satisfaction relation $K, \mathfrak{m} \models \tau$ of a formula τ in ν under K is defined as follows according to the different cases of τ:*

1. *$K, \mathfrak{m} \models \sigma : \phi$, if $K, \mathfrak{m}(\sigma) \models \phi$;*
2. *$K, \mathfrak{m} \models \sigma \xrightarrow{\alpha/\alpha'} \sigma'$, if $\mathfrak{m}(\sigma) \xrightarrow{\alpha/\alpha'} \mathfrak{m}(\sigma')$ is a relation on K;*
3. *$K, \mathfrak{m} \models \sigma \Downarrow \alpha$, if there exists an execution path $\mathfrak{m}(\sigma) \xrightarrow{\alpha/\cdot} ... \xrightarrow{\cdot/\downarrow} w$ on K for some world $w \in \mathcal{S}$.*

A formula τ in a labelled sequent is *valid*, denoted by $K \models \tau$ (or simply $\models \tau$), if $K, \mathfrak{m} \models \tau$ for all $\mathfrak{m} \in \mathbf{M}$. According to the meaning of a sequent above, a labelled sequent $\Gamma \Rightarrow \Delta$ is *valid*, if for every $\mathfrak{m} \in \mathbf{M}$, $K, \mathfrak{m} \models \tau$ for all $\tau \in \Gamma$ implies $K, \mathfrak{m} \models \tau'$ for some $\tau' \in \Delta$.

For a multi-set Γ of formulas, we write $K, \mathfrak{m} \models \Gamma$ to mean that $K, \mathfrak{m} \models \tau$ for all $\tau \in \Gamma$.

Example 3 (Instantiation of Labels). In while programs, we consider a type of labels namely $\mathbf{L}_W$ of the form: $\{x_1 \mapsto e_1, ..., x_n \mapsto e_n\}$ $(n \geq 0)$ as program configurations, where each variable $x_i \in Var_W$ stores a unique value of arithmetic expression e_i $(1 \leq i \leq n)$. To make it simple, we restrict that variables $x_1, ...x_n$ must appear in the discussed programs and any free variable in $e_1, ..., e_n$ cannot be any of $x_1, ..., x_n$. For example, in program *WP* (Example 1), $\{n \mapsto N, s \mapsto 0\}$ is a configuration that maps n to value N (as a free variable) and s to 0.

Example 4 (Instantiation of Label Mappings). In while programs, we consider a set $\mathbf{M}_W$ of label mappings where each label mapping is associated to a world, denoted by $\mathfrak{m}_w$ for some $w \in \mathcal{S}_W$. Given a configuration $\sigma =_{df} \{x_1 \mapsto e_1, ..., x_n \mapsto e_n\}$ $(n \geq 1)$, $\mathfrak{m}_w(\sigma)$ is defined as a world such that (1) $\mathfrak{m}_w(\sigma)(x_i) = w(e_i)$ for each x_i $(1 \leq i \leq n)$; (2) $\mathfrak{m}_w(\sigma)(y) = w(y)$ for other variable $y \in Var_W$. Where $w(e_i)$ returns a value by substituting each free variable x of e_i with value $w(x)$. For example, let $w(N) = 5$, then we have $\mathfrak{m}_w(\{n \mapsto N, s \mapsto 0\})(n) = w(N) = 5$, $\mathfrak{m}_w(\{n \mapsto N, s \mapsto 0\})(s) = 0$. In fact, in this case, $\mathfrak{m}_w(\{n \mapsto N, s \mapsto 0\}) = w$.

An *inference rule* is of the form $\frac{\nu_1 \quad ... \quad \nu_n}{\nu}$, where each of ν, ν_i $(1 \leq i \leq n)$ is also called a *node*. Each of $\nu_1, ..., \nu_n$ is called a *premise*, and ν is called the *conclusion*, of the rule. The semantics of the rule is that the validity of sequents $\nu_1, ..., \nu_n$ implies the validity of sequent ν. A formula τ of node ν is called the *target formula* if except τ other formulas are kept unchanged in the derivation from ν to some node ν_i $(1 \leq i \leq n)$. And in this case other formulas except τ in node ν are called the *context* of ν. A formula pair (τ_1, τ_2) with τ_1 in ν and τ_2 in some ν_i is called a *conclusion-premise* (CP) pair of the derivation from ν to ν_i.

Proof and Preproof and Cyclic Proof. A *proof tree* (or *proof*) is a finite tree structure formed by making derivations backward from a root node. In a proof tree, a node is called *terminal* if it is the conclusion of an axiom.

In the cyclic proof approach (cf. [11]), a *preproof* is an infinite proof tree (i.e. some of its derivations contain infinitely many nodes) in which there exist non-terminal leaf nodes, called *buds*. Each bud is identical to one of its ancestors in the tree. The ancestor identical to a bud ν is called a *companion of* ν. A *derivation path* in a preproof is an infinite sequence of nodes $\nu_1\nu_2...\nu_m...$ $(m \geq 1)$ starting from the root node ν_1, where each node pair (ν_i, ν_{i+1}) $(i \geq 1)$ is a CP pair of a rule. A proof tree is *cyclic*, if it is a preproof in which there exists a "progressive derivation trace", whose definition depends on specific logic theories (see Definition 9 later for DL_p), over every derivation path.

A *proof system* P consists of a finite set of inference rules. We say that a node ν can be derived from P, denoted by $P \vdash \nu$, if a proof tree can be constructed (with ν the root node) by applying the rules in P, which satisfies either (1) all of its leaf nodes terminate or (2) it is a cyclic proof tree.

3.2 A Proof System for DL_p

The labelled proof system P_{dlp} of DL_p is defined as: $P_{dlp} =_{df} P_{ldlp} \cup P_{pt} \cup P_{ter}$, where P_{ldlp} is a set of *core rules* listed in Table 2, P_{pt} and P_{ter} are two finite pre-defined sets of rules according to parameter $\mathbf{P}$.

Sets P_{pt} and P_{ter} are for deriving program transitions $\mathfrak{F}_{pt}$ and terminations $\mathfrak{F}_{ter}$ respectively. Each rule in P_{pt} (resp. P_{ter}) has a restricted form: $\dfrac{\Gamma_1 \Rightarrow \Delta_1 \quad ... \quad \Gamma_n \Rightarrow \Delta_n}{\Gamma \Rightarrow \tau, \Delta}$, where $n \geq 0$, $\tau \in \mathfrak{F}_{pt}$ (resp. $\tau \in \mathfrak{F}_{ter}$), τ is the target formula of the rule.

P_{pt} and P_{ter} are assumed to be *sound and complete* for the operational semantics of $\mathbf{P}$ in the sense of the following definition.

Table 1. Partial Inference Rules for Program Transitions of While Programs

$$\frac{}{\Gamma \Rightarrow (x := e, \sigma) \longrightarrow (\downarrow, \sigma^x_e), \Delta}\ {\scriptstyle (x:=e)} \qquad \frac{\Gamma \Rightarrow (\alpha_1, \sigma) \longrightarrow (\alpha'_1, \sigma'), \Delta}{\Gamma \Rightarrow (\alpha_1; \alpha_2, \sigma) \longrightarrow (\alpha'_1; \alpha_2, \sigma'), \Delta}\ {\scriptstyle (;)}$$

$$\frac{\Gamma \Rightarrow (\alpha_1, \sigma) \longrightarrow (\downarrow, \sigma'), \Delta}{\Gamma \Rightarrow (\alpha_1; \alpha_2, \sigma) \longrightarrow (\alpha_2, \sigma'), \Delta}\ {\scriptstyle (;\downarrow)} \qquad \frac{\Gamma, \sigma : \phi \Rightarrow (\alpha, \sigma) \longrightarrow (\alpha', \sigma'), \Delta \quad \Gamma \Rightarrow \phi : \sigma, \Delta}{\Gamma \Rightarrow (\mathit{while}\ \phi\ \mathit{do}\ \alpha\ \mathit{end}, \sigma) \longrightarrow (\alpha';\ \mathit{while}\ \phi\ \mathit{do}\ \alpha\ \mathit{end}, \sigma'), \Delta}\ {\scriptstyle (wh1)}$$

$$\frac{\Gamma, \sigma : \phi \Rightarrow (\alpha, \sigma) \longrightarrow (\downarrow, \sigma'), \Delta \quad \Gamma \Rightarrow \sigma : \phi, \Delta}{\Gamma \Rightarrow (\mathit{while}\ \phi\ \mathit{do}\ \alpha\ \mathit{end}, \sigma) \longrightarrow (\mathit{while}\ \phi\ \mathit{do}\ \alpha\ \mathit{end}, \sigma'), \Delta}\ {\scriptstyle (wh1\downarrow)} \qquad \frac{\Gamma \Rightarrow \sigma : \neg\phi, \Delta}{\Gamma \Rightarrow (\mathit{while}\ \phi\ \mathit{do}\ \alpha\ \mathit{end}, \sigma) \longrightarrow (\downarrow, \sigma), \Delta}\ {\scriptstyle (wh2)}$$

Table 2. Rules P_{ldlp} for the Proof System of DL_p

$$\frac{\{\Gamma \Rightarrow \sigma' : [\alpha']\phi, \Delta\}_{(\alpha', \sigma') \in \Phi}}{\Gamma \Rightarrow \sigma : [\alpha]\phi, \Delta}\ {\scriptstyle 1\ ([\alpha]R)}, \quad \text{where } \Phi =_{df} \{(\alpha', \sigma') \mid P_{dlp} \vdash (\Gamma \Rightarrow \sigma \xrightarrow{\alpha/\alpha'} \sigma', \Delta)\}$$

$$\frac{\Gamma, \sigma' : [\alpha']\phi \Rightarrow \Delta}{\Gamma, \sigma : [\alpha]\phi \Rightarrow \Delta}\ {\scriptstyle 1\ ([\alpha]L)}, \quad \text{if } P_{dlp} \vdash (\Gamma \Rightarrow \sigma \xrightarrow{\alpha/\alpha'} \sigma', \Delta)$$

$$\frac{\sigma : \phi}{\sigma : [\downarrow]\phi}\ {\scriptstyle ([\downarrow])} \quad \Bigg| \quad \frac{}{\Gamma \Rightarrow \Delta}\ {\scriptstyle 2\ (Ter)} \quad \Bigg| \quad \frac{\Gamma \Rightarrow \Delta}{\mathit{Sub}(\Gamma) \Rightarrow \mathit{Sub}(\Delta)}\ {\scriptstyle 3\ (Sub)} \quad \Bigg| \quad \frac{}{\Gamma, \sigma : \phi \Rightarrow \sigma : \phi, \Delta}\ {\scriptstyle (ax)}$$

$$\frac{\Gamma \Rightarrow \sigma : \phi, \Delta \quad \Gamma, \sigma : \phi \Rightarrow \Delta}{\Gamma \Rightarrow \Delta}\ {\scriptstyle (Cut)} \quad \Bigg| \quad \frac{\Gamma \Rightarrow \Delta}{\Gamma \Rightarrow \sigma : \phi, \Delta}\ {\scriptstyle (WkR)} \quad \Bigg| \quad \frac{\Gamma \Rightarrow \Delta}{\Gamma, \sigma : \phi \Rightarrow \Delta}\ {\scriptstyle (WkL)} \quad \Bigg| \quad \frac{\sigma : \phi, \sigma : \phi}{\sigma : \phi}\ {\scriptstyle (Con)}$$

$$\frac{\Gamma, \sigma : \phi \Rightarrow \Delta}{\Gamma \Rightarrow \sigma : \neg\phi, \Delta}\ {\scriptstyle (\neg R)} \quad \Bigg| \quad \frac{\Gamma \Rightarrow \sigma : \phi, \Delta}{\Gamma, \sigma : \neg\phi \Rightarrow \Delta}\ {\scriptstyle (\neg L)} \quad \Bigg| \quad \frac{\Gamma \Rightarrow \sigma : \phi, \Delta \quad \Gamma \Rightarrow \sigma : \psi, \Delta}{\Gamma \Rightarrow \sigma : \phi \wedge \psi, \Delta}\ {\scriptstyle (\wedge R)} \quad \Bigg| \quad \frac{\Gamma, \sigma : \phi, \sigma : \psi \Rightarrow \Delta}{\Gamma, \sigma : \phi \wedge \psi \Rightarrow \Delta}\ {\scriptstyle (\wedge L)}$$

[1] $\alpha \notin \{\downarrow\}$. [2] for each $\sigma : \phi \in \Gamma \cup \Delta$, $\phi \in \mathbf{F}$; Sequent $\Gamma \Rightarrow \Delta$ is valid. [3] *Sub* is given by Definition 7.

Definition 6 (Assumptions on P_{dlp}). *System P_{dlp} is assumed to satisfy the following properties:*

1. *Soundness of P_{pt} and P_{ter}. All rules of P_{pt} and P_{ter} are sound.*
2. *Completeness w.r.t. K. For any $\sigma \in \mathbf{L}$, Γ and $\mathfrak{m} \in \mathbf{M}$ with $\mathfrak{m} \models \Gamma$, if $\mathfrak{m}(\sigma) \xrightarrow{\alpha/\alpha'} w$ is a relation on K for some $\alpha, \alpha' \in \mathbf{P}$ and $w \in \mathcal{S}$, then there exists a label $\sigma' \in \mathbf{L}$ such that $\mathfrak{m}(\sigma') = w$ and $P_{dlp} \vdash (\Gamma \Rightarrow \sigma \xrightarrow{\alpha/\alpha'} \sigma')$.*

Example 5 (Instantiation of $\mathfrak{F}_{pt}$). Table 1 displays a set $(\mathfrak{F}_{pt})_W$ of partial inference rules for the transitions of while programs. Here σ^x_e represents a configuration that stores variable x as value e, while storing other variables as the same value as σ.

Through the rules in P_{ldlp}, a labelled DL_p formula can be transformed into proof obligations as non-dynamic formulas, which can then be encoded and verified accordingly through, for example, an SAT/SMT checking procedure. The rules for other operators like $\vee$, $\rightarrow$ can be derived accordingly using the rules in Table 2.

The illustration of each rule in Table 2 is as follows. We use a double-lined inference form: $\dfrac{\phi_1 \quad \dots \quad \phi_n}{\phi}$ to represent both rules $\dfrac{\Gamma \Rightarrow \phi_1, \Delta \quad \dots \quad \Gamma \Rightarrow \phi_n, \Delta}{\Gamma \Rightarrow \phi, \Delta}$ and $\dfrac{\Gamma, \phi_1 \Rightarrow \Delta \quad \dots \quad \Gamma, \phi_n \Rightarrow \Delta}{\Gamma, \phi \Rightarrow \Delta}$, provided any context Γ and Δ.

Rules ($[\alpha]R$) and ($[\alpha]L$) reason about dynamic parts of labelled DL_p formulas. Both rules rely on side deductions: '$P_{dlp} \vdash (\Gamma \Rightarrow \sigma \xrightarrow{\alpha/\alpha'} \sigma', \Delta)$' as sub-proof procedures of program transitions. In rule ($[\alpha]R$), $\{...\}_{(\alpha',\sigma')\in\Phi}$ represents the collection of premises for all program states $(\alpha', \sigma') \in \Phi$. By the finiteness of system P_{dlp}, set Φ must be finite (because only a finite number of forms (α', σ') can be derived). So rule ($[\alpha]R$) only has a finite number of premises. When Φ is empty, the conclusion terminates. Compared to rule ($[\alpha]R$), rule ($[\alpha]L$) has only one premise for some program state (α', σ').

Rule ($[\downarrow]$) deals with the situation when the program is a termination $\downarrow$. Its soundness is straightforward by the semantics of $\downarrow$ in Definition 2.

Rule (*Ter*) indicates that one proof branch terminates when all labelled formulas do not contain any dynamic parts.

Rule (*Sub*) describes a specialization process for labelled DL_p formulas. For a set A of labelled formulas, $Sub(A) =_{df} \{Sub(\sigma) : \phi \mid (\sigma : \phi) \in A\}$, with *Sub* an abstract notion of substitution defined as follows in Definition 7. Intuitively, if sequent $\Gamma \Rightarrow \Delta$ is valid, then its one of special cases $Sub(\Gamma) \Rightarrow Sub(\Delta)$ is also valid. Rule (*Sub*) plays an important role in constructing a bud in a cyclic proof structure (Sect. 3.3). See Sect. 4 for more details.

Definition 7 (Substitution of Labels). *A 'substitution' $\eta : \mathbf{L} \rightarrow \mathbf{L}$ is a function on $\mathbf{L}$ satisfying that for any label mapping $\mathfrak{m} \in \mathbf{M}$, there exists a label mapping $\mathfrak{m}'(\mathfrak{m}, \eta)$ (determined only by $\mathfrak{m}$ and η) such that $\mathfrak{m}'(\sigma) = \mathfrak{m}(\eta(\sigma))$ for all labels $\sigma \in \mathbf{L}$.*

Definition 7 will be used in the proof of soundness of rules P_{ldlp} and the cyclic proof system of DL_p.

Rules from (ax) to ($\wedge L$) are the "labelled versions" of the corresponding rules inherited from traditional first-order logic. Their meanings are classical and we omit their discussions here.

Theorem 1. *Each rule from P_{ldlp} in Table 2 is sound.*

Following the above explanations, Theorem 1 can be proved according to the semantics of labelled DL_p formulas under the assumption of Definition 6. See Appendix A of [1] for more details.

3.3 Construction of a Cyclic Proof Structure for DL_p

In an ordinary proof system we usually expect a finite proof tree. However, in system P_{dlp}, a branch of a proof tree does not always terminate, because the process of symbolically executing a program via rule $([\alpha]R)$ or/and rule $([\alpha]L)$ might not stop. This is well-known when a program has an explicit/implicit loop structure that may run infinitely. For example, a while program $W =_{df}$ *while true do* $x := x + 1$ *end* will proceed infinitely as the following program transitions: $(W, \{x \mapsto 0\}) \longrightarrow (W, \{x \mapsto 1\}) \longrightarrow ....$

In this paper, we build a cyclic labelled proof system for DL_p, in order to recognize and admit potential infinite derivations as above when deriving labelled DL_p formulas $\mathfrak{F}_{ldlp}$ using the rules in P_{ldlp}. Based on the notion of preproof (Sect. 3.1), we build a cyclic proof structure for system P_{dlp}, where the key part is to introduce the notion of progressive derivation traces in DL_p (Definition 9). Section 5 will further show that a cyclic proof of DL_p ensures a valid conclusion.

Next we first introduce the notion of progressive derivation traces for DL_p, then we define the cyclic proof structure for DL_p, as a special case of the notion already given in Sect. 3.1.

Definition 8 (Derivation Traces). *A "derivation trace" over a derivation path $\mu_1\mu_2...\mu_k\nu_1\nu_2...\nu_m...$ $(k \geq 0, m \geq 1)$ is an infinite sequence $\tau_1\tau_2...\tau_m...$ of formulas with each formula τ_i $(1 \leq i \leq m)$ in node ν_i. Each CP pair (τ_i, τ_{i+1}) $(i \geq 1)$ of derivation (ν_i, ν_{i+1}) satisfies special conditions as follows according to (ν_i, ν_{i+1}) being the different instances of rules from P_{ldlp}:*

1. *If (ν_i, ν_{i+1}) is an instance of rule $([\alpha]R)$, $([\alpha]L)$, $([\downarrow])$, $(\neg R)$, $(\neg L)$, $(\wedge R)$ or $(\wedge L)$, then either τ_i is the target formula and τ_{i+1} is its replacement by application of the rule, or $\tau_i = \tau_{i+1}$;*
2. *If (ν_i, ν_{i+1}) is an instance of rule (Sub), then $\tau_i = Sub(\sigma) : \phi$ and $\tau_{i+1} = \sigma : \phi$ for some $\sigma \in \mathbf{L}$ and $\phi \in \mathfrak{F}_{dlp}$;*
3. *If (ν_i, ν_{i+1}) is an instance of other rules, then $\tau_i = \tau_{i+1}$.*

Definition 9 (Progressive Derivation Traces). *In a preproof of system P_{dlp}, given a derivation trace $\tau_1\tau_2...\tau_m...$ over a derivation path $...\nu_1\nu_2...\nu_m...$ $(m \geq 1)$ starting from τ_1 in node ν_1, a CP pair (τ_i, τ_{i+1}) $(1 \leq i \leq m)$ of derivation (ν_i, ν_{i+1}) is called a "progressive step", if (τ_i, τ_{i+1}) is the following CP pair of an instance of rule $([\alpha]R)$:*

$$\frac{... \quad \nu_{i+1} :: (\Gamma \Rightarrow \tau_{i+1} :: (\sigma' : [\alpha']\phi), \Delta) \quad ...}{\nu_i :: (\Gamma \Rightarrow \tau_i :: (\sigma : [\alpha]\phi), \Delta),} \scriptstyle ([\alpha]R);$$

or the following CP pair of an instance of rule ($[\alpha]L$)*:*

$$\frac{\nu_{i+1} :: (\Gamma, \tau_{i+1} :: (\sigma' : [\alpha']\phi) \Rightarrow \Delta)}{\nu_i :: (\Gamma, \tau_i :: (\sigma : [\alpha]\phi) \Rightarrow \Delta)} \; ([\alpha]L),$$

provided with an additional side deduction $P_{dlp} \vdash (\Gamma \Rightarrow \sigma' \Downarrow \alpha', \Delta)$.

If a derivation trace has an infinite number of progressive steps, we say that the trace is 'progressive'.

The additional side condition of the instance of rule ($[\alpha]L$) is the key to prove the corresponding case in Lemma 1 (see Appendix A of [1]).

Table 3. Derivations of Property ν_1

$$\dfrac{\dfrac{\dfrac{}{17}\,(Ter)}{3}\,(WkR) \quad \dfrac{\dfrac{\dfrac{\dfrac{\dfrac{\dfrac{\dfrac{16}{15}\,(WkL)}{14}\,(Sub)}{11}\,(WkL) \quad \dfrac{\dfrac{}{13}\,(Ter)}{12}\,(WkR)}{10}\,(Cut)}{9}\,([\alpha]R)}{5}\,([\alpha]R) \quad \dfrac{\dfrac{\dfrac{}{8}\,(Ter)}{7}\,([\downarrow])}{6}\,([\alpha]R)}{4}\,(\vee L)}{2}\,(Cut)}{\nu_1 : 1}\,(Sub)$$

(dotted back-link from 16 to 2)

Definitions of other symbols:
$WP =_{df} \{while\ (n > 0)\ do\ s := s + n\ ;\ n := n - 1\ end\}$
$\alpha_1 =_{df} s := s + n\ ;\ n := n - 1$
$\phi_1 =_{df} (s = ((N + 1)N)/2)$
$\sigma_1 =_{df} \{n \mapsto N, s \mapsto 0\}$
$\sigma_2 =_{df} \{n \mapsto N - m, s \mapsto (2N - m + 1)m/2\}$
$\sigma_3 =_{df} \{n \mapsto N - m, s \mapsto (2N - (m + 1) + 1)(m + 1)/2\}$
$\sigma_4 =_{df} \{n \mapsto N - (m + 1), s \mapsto (2N - (m + 1) + 1)(m + 1)/2\}$

1:	$\sigma_1 : n \geq 0$	$\Rightarrow$	$\sigma_1 : [while\ (n > 0)\ do\ \alpha_1\ end]\phi_1$
2:	$\sigma_2 : n \geq 0$	$\Rightarrow$	$\underline{\sigma_2 : [while\ (n > 0)\ do\ \alpha_1\ end]\phi_1}$
3:	$\sigma_2 : n \geq 0$	$\Rightarrow$	$\sigma_2 : [while\ (n > 0)\ do\ \alpha_1\ end]\phi_1, \sigma_2 : (n > 0 \vee n \leq 0)$
17:	$\sigma_2 : n \geq 0$	$\Rightarrow$	$\sigma_2 : (n > 0 \vee n \leq 0)$
4:	$\sigma_2 : n \geq 0, \sigma_2 : (n > 0 \vee n \leq 0)$	$\Rightarrow$	$\underline{\sigma_2 : [while\ (n > 0)\ do\ \alpha_1\ end]\phi_1}$
5:	$\sigma_2 : n \geq 0, \sigma_2 : n > 0$	$\Rightarrow$	$\underline{\sigma_2 : [while\ (n > 0)\ do\ \alpha_1\ end]\phi_1}$
9:	$\sigma_2 : n \geq 0, \sigma_2 : n > 0$	$\Rightarrow$	$\underline{\sigma_3 : [n := n - 1;\ while\ (n > 0)\ do\ \alpha_1\ end]\phi_1}$
10:	$\sigma_2 : n \geq 0, \sigma_2 : n > 0$	$\Rightarrow$	$\underline{\sigma_4 : [while\ (n > 0)\ do\ \alpha_1\ end]\phi_1}$
11:	$\sigma_2 : n \geq 0, \sigma_2 : n > 0, \sigma_4 : n \geq -1, \sigma_4 : n \geq 0$	$\Rightarrow$	$\underline{\sigma_4 : [while\ (n > 0)\ do\ \alpha_1\ end]\phi_1}$
14:	$\sigma_4 : n \geq -1, \sigma_4 : n \geq 0$	$\Rightarrow$	$\underline{\sigma_4 : [while\ (n > 0)\ do\ \alpha_1\ end]\phi_1}$
15:	$\sigma_2 : n \geq -1, \sigma_2 : n \geq 0$	$\Rightarrow$	$\underline{\sigma_2 : [while\ (n > 0)\ do\ \alpha_1\ end]\phi_1}$
16:	$\sigma_2 : n \geq 0$	$\Rightarrow$	$\underline{\sigma_2 : [while\ (n > 0)\ do\ \alpha_1\ end]\phi_1}$
12:	$\sigma_2 : n \geq 0, \sigma_2 : n > 0$	$\Rightarrow$	$\sigma_4 : [while\ (n > 0)\ do\ \alpha_1\ end]\phi_1, \sigma_4 : n \geq -1, \sigma_4 : n \geq 0$
13:	$\sigma_2 : n \geq 0, \sigma_2 : n > 0$	$\Rightarrow$	$\sigma_4 : n \geq -1, \sigma_4 : n \geq 0$
6:	$\sigma_2 : n \geq 0, \sigma_2 : n \leq 0$	$\Rightarrow$	$\sigma_2 : [while\ (n > 0)\ do\ \alpha_1\ end]\phi_1$
7:	$\sigma_2 : n \geq 0, \sigma_2 : n \leq 0$	$\Rightarrow$	$\sigma_2 : [\downarrow]\phi_1$
8:	$\sigma_2 : n \geq 0, \sigma_2 : n \leq 0$	$\Rightarrow$	$\sigma_2 : (s = ((N + 1)N)/2)$

Theorem 2. *Every cyclic proof of system* P_{dlp} *has a sound conclusion.*

In Sect. 5, we will analyze and prove Theorem 2 under a restriction on **P**.

Since DL_p is not a specific logic, it is impossible to discuss about its decidability, completeness or whether it is cut-free without any restrictions on parameters **P**, **F** and **L**. One of our future work will focus on analyzing under what restrictions, these properties can be obtained in a general sense.

4 Case Study– A Cyclic Deduction for While Programs

We give an example to show how a DL_p formula can be derived according to rules in Table 2. We prove the property in Example 2, which can be captured by the following equivalent labelled sequent

$$\nu_1 =_{df} \sigma_1 : n \geq 0 \Rightarrow \sigma_1 : [WP](s = ((N+1)N)/2),$$

where $\sigma_1 =_{df} \{n \mapsto N, s \mapsto 0\}$, describing the initial configuration of *WP*.

Table 3 shows its derivations. We omit all side deductions as sub-proof procedures in instances of rule $([\alpha]R)$ derived using the inference rules in Table 1. Non-primitive rule $(\vee L)$ can be derived by the rules for $\neg$ and $\wedge$ accordingly.

The derivation from sequent 1 to 2 is according to rule (Sub), where the substitution *Sub* of labels defined in Definition 7 is instantiated as function $(\cdot)[e/x]$. Informally, for any label σ, $\sigma[e/x]$ returns the label by substituting each free variable x of σ with term e. We observe that $\sigma_1 = \sigma_2[0/m]$, so sequent 1 is a special case of sequent 2 by substitution $(\cdot)[0/m]$. Intuitively, label σ_2 captures the program configuration after the mth loop $(m \geq 0)$ of program *WP*. This step is crucial as starting from sequent 2, we can find a bud node—16—that is identical to node 2.

The derivation from sequent 2 to $\{3, 4\}$ provides a lemma: $\sigma_2 : (n > 0 \vee n \leq 0)$, which is trivially valid. Sequent 16 indicates the end of the $(m+1)$th loop of program *WP*. From node 10 to 16, we transform the formulas on the left side into a trivial logical equivalent form in order to apply rule (Sub) from sequent 14 to 15. Sequent 14 is a special case of sequent 15 since $\sigma_4 = \sigma_2[m+1/m]$.

The whole proof tree is cyclic because the only derivation path: $2, 4, 5, 9, 10, 11, 14, 15, 16, 2, ...$ has a progressive derivation trace whose elements are underlined in Table 3.

Compared to the deduction processes in traditional dynamic logics and Hoare logics, a notable feature of the above deduction process is that the search for a loop invariant is reflected in looking for a suitable configuration (i.e. σ_2). One advantage brought by this cyclic derivation approach is that it does not rely on the inference rule for decomposing an explicit loop structure (here *while...do...end*), which also makes it easily amendable for reasoning about programs with implicit loop structures, such as CCS-like process algebras [29,30] and some synchronous languages [8,44].

As a demonstration of its powerfulness, in Appendix B of [1], we briefly introduce another instantiation of DL_p for the synchronous language Esterel [8] and show a cyclic derivation of an Esterel program. That example can better highlight the advantages of DL_p since the loop structures of some Esterel programs are implicit. In [1], we also briefly show that FODL [38] can be instantiated in DL_p.

5 Soundness of Cyclic Proof System P_{dlp}

In this section, we prove Theorem 2 under a restriction on **P** given as in Definition 10.

An execution path (Definition 3) $w_1...w_n$ ($n \geq 1$) is called *minimum*, if there are no two relations $w_i \xrightarrow{\alpha_i/\cdot} \cdot$ and $w_j \xrightarrow{\alpha_j/\cdot} \cdot$ for some $1 \leq i < j < n$ such that $w_i = w_j$ and $\alpha_i = \alpha_j$. Intuitively, in a minimum execution path, there are no two relations starting from the same world and program.

Definition 10. (Termination Finiteness). *In PL Kripke structure K, a program $\alpha \in \mathbf{P}$ satisfies the "termination finiteness" property, if for a world $w \in \mathcal{S}$, there is only a finite number of minimum execution paths starting from a relation of the form $w \xrightarrow{\alpha/\cdot} \cdot$.*

The programs satisfying termination finiteness are in fact a rich set, including, for example, all the programs whose behaviour is deterministic, such as while programs discussed in this paper, programming languages like Esterel, C, Java, etc. There exist non-deterministic programs that fall into this category. For example, automata that have non-deterministic transitions and a finite number of states. More on this restriction will be discussed in our future work.

Main Idea. We follow the main idea behind [10] to prove Theorem 2 by contradiction. The key point is that, if the conclusion of a cyclic proof is invalid, then there must exist an *invalid derivation path* in which each node is invalid, and one of its progressive traces would lead to an infinite descent sequence of some well-founded set (introduced below), which violates the definition of the well-foundedness (cf. [13]) itself.

Below we firstly introduce the well-founded relation $\prec_m$ we will rely on, then we focus on the main skeleton of proving Theorem 2. Other proof details are given in Appendix A of the online report [1].

Well-Foundedness and Relation $\preceq_m$. Given a set S and a partial-order relation $\preceq$ on S, $\preceq$ is called a *well-founded relation* over S, if for any element a in S, there is no infinite descent sequence: $a \succ a_1 \succ a_2 \succ ...$ in S. Set S is called a *well-founded* set w.r.t. $\preceq$.

Definition 11. (Relation $\preceq_m$). *Given two finite sets C_1 and C_2 of finite execution paths, $C_1 \preceq_m C_2$ is defined if either (1) $C_1 = C_2$; or (2) set C_1 can be obtained from C_2 by replacing (or removing) one or more elements of C_2 each with a finite number of elements, such that for each replaced element tr, its replacements $tr_1, ..., tr_n$ ($n \geq 1$) in C_1 are proper suffixes of tr.*

$\preceq_m$ is a partial-order relation. The proof is given in Appendix A of [1].

Example 6. Let $C_1 = \{tr_1, tr_2, tr_3\}$, where $tr_1 =_{df} ww_1w_2w_3w_4, tr_2 =_{df} ww_1w_5w_6w_7$ and $tr_3 =_{df} ww_8$; $C_2 = \{tr'_1, tr'_2\}$, where $tr'_1 =_{df} w_1w_2w_3w_4, tr'_2 =_{df} w_1w_5w_6w_7$. We see that tr'_1 is a proper suffix of tr_1 and tr'_2 is a proper suffix of tr_2. C_2 can be obtained from C_1 by replacing tr_1 and tr_2 with tr'_1 and tr'_2 respectively, and removing tr_3. Hence $C_2 \preceq_m C_1$. Since $C_1 \neq C_2$, $C_2 \prec_m C_1$.

Proposition 1. *Relation $\preceq_m$ is a well-founded relation.*

We omit the proof of Proposition 1. Relation $\preceq_m$ is just a special case of the "multi-set ordering" introduced in [13], where it has been proved to be well-founded.

Proof Skeleton of Theorem 2. Below we give the main skeleton of the proof by skipping the details of the proof of Lemma 1, which can be found in Appendix A of [1].

Following the main idea above, we first introduce the concept of "execution paths of a dynamic DL_p formula". They are the elements of a well-founded relation $\preceq_m$. Next, we propose Lemma 1, which plays a key role in the proof of Theorem 2 that follows.

Given two execution paths $w_1...w_n$ and $w'_1w'_2...w'_m$ $(n, m \geq 1)$, *path concatenation* $\cdot$ is a partial function defined such that $(w_1...w_n) \cdot (w'_1w'_2...w'_m) =_{df} w_1...w_nw'_2...w'_m$, if $w_n = w'_1$.

Definition 12 (Execution Paths of Dynamic Formulas). *Given a world $w \in \mathcal{S}$ and a dynamic formula ϕ, the execution paths $EX(w, \phi)$ of ϕ w.r.t. w is inductively defined according to the structure of ϕ as follows:*

1. $EX(w, [\alpha]F) =_{df} mex(w, \alpha)$, *where* $F \in \mathbf{F}$;
2. $EX(w, [\alpha]\phi_1) =_{df} mex(w, \alpha) \cup \{tr_1 \cdot tr_2 \mid tr_1 \in mex(w, \alpha), tr_2 \in EX((tr_1)_e, \phi_1)\}$;
3. $EX(w, \neg\phi_1) =_{df} EX(w, \phi_1)$;
4. $EX(w, \phi_1 \wedge \phi_2) =_{df} EX(w, \phi_1) \cup EX(w, \phi_2)$.

Where
$mex(w, \alpha) =_{df} \{w...w' \mid w \xrightarrow{\alpha/\cdot} ... \xrightarrow{\cdot/\downarrow} w'$ *is a min. exec. path for some* $w' \in \mathcal{S}\}$ *is the set of all minimum paths of* α *starting from world* w.

We call $\mathfrak{m} \in \mathbf{M}$ a *counter-example mapping* of a node ν, if it makes ν invalid.

Lemma 1. *In a cyclic proof (where there is at least one derivation path), let $(\sigma : \phi, \sigma' : \phi')$ be a step of a derivation trace over a derivation (ν, ν') of an invalid derivation path, where $\phi, \phi' \in \mathfrak{F}_{dlp}$. For any set $EX(\mathfrak{m}(\sigma), \phi)$ of $\sigma : \phi$ w.r.t. a counter-example mapping $\mathfrak{m}$ of ν, there exists a counter-example mapping $\mathfrak{m}'$ of ν' and a set $EX(\mathfrak{m}'(\sigma'), \phi')$ of $\sigma' : \phi'$ such that $EX(\mathfrak{m}'(\sigma'), \phi') \preceq_m EX(\mathfrak{m}(\sigma), \phi)$. Moreover, if $(\sigma : \phi, \sigma' : \phi')$ is a progressive step, then $EX(\mathfrak{m}'(\sigma'), \phi') \prec_m EX(\mathfrak{m}(\sigma), \phi)$.*

Intuitively, Lemma 1 helps us discover suitable execution-path sets imposed by a well-founded relation $\preceq_m$ between them in an invalid derivation path.

Based on Proposition 1 and Lemma 1, we give the proof of Theorem 2 as follows.

Proof (Proof of Theorem 2). By contradiction. Let the progressive trace be $\tau_1\tau_2...\tau_k...$ over a derivation path $...\nu_1\nu_2...\nu_k...$ $(k \geq 1)$ starting from τ_1 in ν_1, where $\tau_i =_{df} \sigma_i : \phi_i$ $(i \geq 1)$, each ν_i $(i \geq 1)$ is invalid.

Since ν_1 is invalid, let $\mathfrak{m}_1$ be one of its counter-example mappings. By Lemma 1, from $EX(\mathfrak{m}_1(\sigma_1), \phi_1)$, there exists an infinite sequence of sets $EX_1, ..., EX_k, ...$ $(k \geq 1)$, where each $EX_i =_{df} EX(\mathfrak{m}_i(\sigma_i), \phi_i)$ $(i \geq 1)$ with $\mathfrak{m}_i$ a counter-example mapping of node ν_i, and which satisfies that $EX_1 \succeq_m ... \succeq_m EX_k \succeq_m ....$ Moreover, since trace $\tau_1\tau_2...\tau_k...$ is progressive (Definition 9), there must be an infinite number of $j \geq 1$ such that $EX_j \succ_m EX_{j+1}$. This thus forms an infinite descent sequence w.r.t. $\prec_m$, violating the well-foundedness of relation $\preceq_m$ (Proposition 1).

6 Related Work

The idea of reasoning about programs based on their operational semantics is not new. Previous work such as [12,41,42,45] in the last decade has addressed this issue using theories based on rewriting logic [28]. Matching logic [41] is based on patterns and pattern matching. Its basic form, a reachability rule $\varphi \Rightarrow \varphi'$ (where $\Rightarrow$ has another meaning from its use in this paper), captures whether pattern φ' is reachable from pattern φ in a given pattern reachability system. Based on matching logic, one-path and all-paths reachability logics [42,45] were developed by enhancing the expressive power of the reachability rule. A more powerful matching μ-logic [12] was proposed by adding a least fixpoint μ-binder to matching logic.

In these theories, 'patterns' are more general structures. So to encode the dynamic forms $[\alpha]\phi$ in DL_p requires additional work and program transformations. On the other hand, dynamic logics like DL_p provide more direct ways to express and reason about complex before-after and temporal program properties with their modalities $[\cdot]$ and $\langle\cdot\rangle$. In terms of expressiveness, matching logic and one-path reachability logic cannot capture the semantics of modality $[\cdot]$ when the programs are non-deterministic (which means that there are more than one execution path). We conjecture that matching μ-logic can encode DL_p, as it has been claimed that it can encode traditional dynamic logics (cf. [12]).

[31] proposed a general program verification framework based on coinduction. Using the terminology in this paper, a program specification $\sigma : [\alpha]\phi$ can be expressed as a pair $((\alpha, \sigma), P(\phi))$ in [31], with $P(\phi)$ a set of program states capturing the semantics of formula ϕ. A method was designed to derive a program specification in a coinductive way according to the operational semantics of (α, σ). Following [31], [27] also proposed a general framework for program reasoning, but via big-step operational semantics. Unlike the frameworks in [31] and [27] which are directly built up on mathematical set theory, DL_p is in logical forms, and is based on a cyclic deduction approach rather than coinduction. In terms of expressiveness, the meaning of modality $\langle\cdot\rangle$ in DL_p cannot be expressed in the framework of [31].

The structure 'updates' adopted in work [4,5,35] are "delay substitutions" of variables and terms. They in fact can be defined as a special case of the more general labels in DL_p by choosing suitable label mappings accordingly.

The proof system of DL_p relies on the cyclic proof theory which firstly arose in [46] and was later developed in different logics such as [10,11]. [25] proposed a complete cyclic proof system for μ-calculus, which subsumes PDL [16] in its expressiveness. In [15], the authors proposed a complete labelled cyclic proof system for PDL. Both logics in [15,25] are propositional and cannot be used to prove many valid formulas in particular domains, for example, the arithmetic first-order formulas in number theory as shown in our example. The labelled form of DL_p formula $\sigma : [\alpha]\phi$ is inspired from [15], where a label is just a variable of worlds in a traditional Kripke structure. On the other hand, the labels in DL_p allow arbitrary terms from actual program configurations.

There has been some other work for generalizing the theories of dynamic logics, such as [21,32]. However, generally speaking, they neither consider structures as general as allowed by programs and configurations in DL_p, nor adopt a similar approach for reasoning about programs. [32] proposed a complete generic dynamic logic for monads of programming languages. In the dynamic logic proposed in [21], more general programs can be reasoned about than regular expressions of PDL, based on so-called "interaction-based" behaviours. But there program transitions are captured by abstract actions in a form e.g. $\alpha \xrightarrow{a} \beta$, where no explicit structures of program configurations are allowed. And yet no proof systems have been built for that logic.

7 Conclusion and Future Work

In this paper, we propose a novel dynamic logic DL_p that supports reasoning about general forms of programs and formulas based on programs' operational semantics. We mainly build the theory of DL_p and propose a sound cyclic proof system of DL_p that is proved to be useful and applicable. As the main theoretical result we prove the soundness of DL_p.

On theoretical aspects, we are interested in obtaining a complete proof system by fixing the parameters of DL_p in some algebraic domains, e.g., a multi-sorted signature for imperative programs as in [18]. We also want to analyze whether our framework can be adapted to a wider range of program behaviours, i.e., to relax the property Definition 10. From an applied perspective, we are carrying out a full mechanization of DL_p in Coq [9]. To see the full potential of DL_p, we will try to instantiate more types of programs or system models in DL_p, and to specify and verify their properties using DL_p formulas.

References

1. https://github.com/yrz5a/setta2025-onlineReport.git
2. Afshari, B., Enqvist, S., Leigh, G.E.: Cyclic proofs for the first-order μ-calculus. Logic J. IGPL **32**(1), 1–34 (2022)
3. Appel, A.W., Dockins, R., et al.: Program Logics for Certified Compilers. Cambridge University Press, Cambridge (2014)
4. Beckert, B., Bruns, D.: Dynamic logic with trace semantics. In: Bonacina, M.P. (ed.) CADE 2013. LNCS (LNAI), vol. 7898, pp. 315–329. Springer, Heidelberg (2013). https://doi.org/10.1007/978-3-642-38574-2_22

5. Beckert, B., Klebanov, V., Weiß, B.: Dynamic logic for Java. In: Deductive Software Verification – The KeY Book. LNCS, vol. 10001, pp. 49–106. Springer, Cham (2016). https://doi.org/10.1007/978-3-319-49812-6_3
6. Benevides, M.R., Schechter, L.M.: A propositional dynamic logic for concurrent programs based on the π-calculus. In: M4M 2009, pp. 49–64. Elsevier (2010)
7. Berry, G., Cosserat, L.: The ESTEREL synchronous programming language and its mathematical semantics. In: Brookes, S.D., Roscoe, A.W., Winskel, G. (eds.) CONCURRENCY 1984. LNCS, vol. 197, pp. 389–448. Springer, Heidelberg (1985). https://doi.org/10.1007/3-540-15670-4_19
8. Berry, G., Gonthier, G.: The ESTEREL synchronous programming language: design, semantics, implementation. Sci. Comput. Program. **19**(2), 87–152 (1992)
9. Bertot, Y., Castéran, P.: Interactive Theorem Proving and Program Development - Coq'Art: The Calculus of Inductive Constructions. Texts in Theoretical Computer Science. An EATCS Series, Springer, Heidelberg (2004). https://doi.org/10.1007/978-3-662-07964-5
10. Brotherston, J., Bornat, R., Calcagno, C.: Cyclic proofs of program termination in separation logic. SIGPLAN Not. **43**(1), 101–112 (2008)
11. Brotherston, J., Simpson, A.: Complete sequent calculi for induction and infinite descent. In: LICS 2007, pp. 51–62 (2007)
12. Chen, X., Rosu, G.: Matching *mu*-logic. In: LICS 2019, pp. 1–13. IEEE Computer Society (2019)
13. Dershowitz, N., Manna, Z.: Proving termination with multiset orderings. In: Maurer, H.A. (ed.) ICALP 1979. LNCS, vol. 71, pp. 188–202. Springer, Heidelberg (1979). https://doi.org/10.1007/3-540-09510-1_15
14. Do, C.M., Takagi, T., Ogata, K.: Automated quantum protocol verification based on concurrent dynamic quantum logic. ACM Trans. Softw. Eng. Methodol. (2024). Accepted
15. Docherty, S., Rowe, R.N.S.: A non-wellfounded, labelled proof system for propositional dynamic logic. In: Cerrito, S., Popescu, A. (eds.) TABLEAUX 2019. LNCS (LNAI), vol. 11714, pp. 335–352. Springer, Cham (2019). https://doi.org/10.1007/978-3-030-29026-9_19
16. Fischer, M.J., Ladner, R.E.: Propositional dynamic logic of regular programs. J. Comput. Syst. Sci. **18**(2), 194–211 (1979)
17. Gesell, M., Schneider, K.: A Hoare calculus for the verification of synchronous languages. In: PLPV 2012, pp. 37–48. Association for Computing Machinery (2012)
18. Goguen, J.A., Malcolm, G.: Algebraic Semantics of Imperative Programs. The MIT Press, Cambridge (1996)
19. Gutsfeld, J.O., Müller-Olm, M., Ohrem, C.: Propositional dynamic logic for hyperproperties. In: 31st International Conference on Concurrency Theory (CONCUR), pp. 50:1–50:22 (2020)
20. Harel, D., Kozen, D., Tiuryn, J.: Dynamic Logic. MIT Press, Cambridge (2000)
21. Hennicker, R., Wirsing, M.: A generic dynamic logic with applications to interaction-based systems. In: ter Beek, M.H., Fantechi, A., Semini, L. (eds.) From Software Engineering to Formal Methods and Tools, and Back. LNCS, vol. 11865, pp. 172–187. Springer, Cham (2019). https://doi.org/10.1007/978-3-030-30985-5_11
22. Hoare, C.A.R.: An axiomatic basis for computer programming. Commun. ACM **12**(10), 576–580 (1969)
23. Icard, B.: A dynamic logic for information evaluation in intelligence (2024). https://arxiv.org/abs/2405.19968

24. Jones, E., Ong, C.H.L., Ramsay, S.: CycleQ: an efficient basis for cyclic equational reasoning. In: Proceedings of the 43rd ACM SIGPLAN International Conference on Programming Language Design and Implementation. PLDI 2022, pp. 395–409. Association for Computing Machinery, New York, NY, USA (2022)
25. Jungteerapanich, N.: A tableau system for the modal μ-calculus. In: Giese, M., Waaler, A. (eds.) TABLEAUX 2009. LNCS (LNAI), vol. 5607, pp. 220–234. Springer, Heidelberg (2009). https://doi.org/10.1007/978-3-642-02716-1_17
26. Kozen, D.: A probabilistic pdl. J. Comput. Syst. Sci. **30**(2), 162–178 (1985)
27. Li, X., Zhang, Q., Wang, G., Shi, Z., Guan, Y.: Reasoning about iteration and recursion uniformly based on big-step semantics. In: Qin, S., Woodcock, J., Zhang, W. (eds.) SETTA 2021. LNCS, vol. 13071, pp. 61–80. Springer, Cham (2021). https://doi.org/10.1007/978-3-030-91265-9_4
28. Meseguer, J.: Twenty years of rewriting logic. J. Logic Algebr. Program. **81**(7), 721–781 (2012)
29. Milner, R.: A Calculus of Communicating Systems. Springer, Heidelberg (1982). https://doi.org/10.1007/3-540-10235-3
30. Milner, R., Parrow, J., Walker, D.: A calculus of mobile processes, i. Inf. Comput. **100**(1), 1–40 (1992)
31. Moore, B., Peña, L., Rosu, G.: Program verification by coinduction. In: Ahmed, A. (ed.) ESOP 2018. LNCS, vol. 10801, pp. 589–618. Springer, Cham (2018). https://doi.org/10.1007/978-3-319-89884-1_21
32. Mossakowski, T., Schröder, L., Goncharov, S.: A generic complete dynamic logic for reasoning about purity and effects. Form. Asp. Comput. **22**(3–4), 363–384 (2010)
33. O'Hearn, P.W.: Incorrectness logic. Proc. ACM Program. Lang. **4**(POPL) (2019)
34. Pardo, R., Johnsen, E.B., et al.: A specification logic for programs in the probabilistic guarded command language. In: Seidl, H., Liu, Z., Pasareanu, C.S. (eds.) ICTAC 2022. LNCS, vol. 13572, pp. 369–387. Springer, Cham (2022). https://doi.org/10.1007/978-3-031-17715-6_24
35. Platzer, A.: Differential dynamic logic for verifying parametric hybrid systems. In: Olivetti, N. (ed.) TABLEAUX 2007. LNCS (LNAI), vol. 4548, pp. 216–232. Springer, Heidelberg (2007). https://doi.org/10.1007/978-3-540-73099-6_17
36. Platzer, A.: Logical Foundations of Cyber-Physical Systems. Springer, Cham (2018). https://doi.org/10.1007/978-3-319-63588-0
37. Platzer, A., Quesel, J.-D.: KeYmaera: a hybrid theorem prover for hybrid systems (system description). In: Armando, A., Baumgartner, P., Dowek, G. (eds.) IJCAR 2008. LNCS (LNAI), vol. 5195, pp. 171–178. Springer, Heidelberg (2008). https://doi.org/10.1007/978-3-540-71070-7_15
38. Pratt, V.R.: Semantical considerations on Floyd-Hoare logic. In: Annual IEEE Symposium on Foundations of Computer Science (FOCS), pp. 109–121. IEEE Computer Society (1976)
39. Reif, W.: The Kiv-approach to software verification. In: Broy, M., Jähnichen, S. (eds.) KORSO: Methods, Languages, and Tools for the Construction of Correct Software. LNCS, vol. 1009, pp. 339–368. Springer, Heidelberg (1995). https://doi.org/10.1007/BFb0015471
40. Reynolds, J.: Separation logic: a logic for shared mutable data structures. In: Proceedings 17th Annual IEEE Symposium on Logic in Computer Science, pp. 55–74 (2002)
41. Roşu, G., Ştefănescu, A.: Towards a unified theory of operational and axiomatic semantics. In: Czumaj, A., Mehlhorn, K., Pitts, A., Wattenhofer, R. (eds.) ICALP 2012. LNCS, vol. 7392, pp. 351–363. Springer, Heidelberg (2012). https://doi.org/10.1007/978-3-642-31585-5_33

42. Rosu, G., Stefanescu, A., Ciobâcá, S., Moore, B.M.: One-path reachability logic. In: LICS 2013, pp. 358–367 (2013)
43. Rustan, K., Leino, M.: Verification of Object-Oriented Software. The KeY Approach, Lecture Notes in Computer Science (LNCS), vol. 4334. Springer, Cham (2007). https://doi.org/10.1007/978-3-642-31762-0
44. Schneider, K., Brandt, J.: Quartz: a synchronous language for model-based design of reactive embedded systems. In: Ha, S., Teich, J. (eds.) Handbook of Hardware/Software Codesign, pp. 1–30. Springer, Dordrecht (2017). https://doi.org/10.1007/978-94-017-7267-9_3
45. Ştefănescu, A., Ciobâcă, Ş, Mereuta, R., Moore, B.M., Şerbănută, T.F., Roşu, G.: All-path reachability logic. In: Dowek, G. (ed.) RTA 2014. LNCS, vol. 8560, pp. 425–440. Springer, Cham (2014). https://doi.org/10.1007/978-3-319-08918-8_29
46. Stirling, C., Walker, D.: Local model checking in the modal mu-calculus. Theor. Comput. Sci. **89**(1), 161–177 (1991)
47. Takagi, T., Do, C.M., Ogata, K.: Automated quantum program verification in dynamic quantum logic. In: Gierasimczuk, N., Velázquez-Quesada, F.R. (eds.) DaLí 2023. LNCS, vol. 14401, pp. 68–84. Springer, Cham (2024). https://doi.org/10.1007/978-3-031-51777-8_5
48. Tellez, G., Brotherston, J.: Automatically verifying temporal properties of pointer programs with cyclic proof. J. Autom. Reason. **64**(3), 555–578 (2020)
49. Zhang, Y., Mallet, F., Liu, Z.: A dynamic logic for verification of synchronous models based on theorem proving. Front. Comput. Sci. **16**(4) (2022)
50. Zhang, Y., Wu, H., Chen, Y., Mallet, F.: A clock-based dynamic logic for the verification of CCSL specifications in synchronous systems. Sci. Comput. Program. **203**, 102591 (2021)
51. Zilberstein, N., Dreyer, D., Silva, A.: Outcome logic: a unifying foundation for correctness and incorrectness reasoning. Proc. ACM Program. Lang. **7**(OOPSLA1) (2023)

HHLPar: Automated Theorem Prover for Parallel Hybrid Communicating Sequential Processes

Xiangyu Jin[1,2], Bohua Zhan[3], Shuling Wang[2,4](✉), and Naijun Zhan[5]

[1] Key Laboratory of System Software and State Key Laboratory of Computer Science, Institute of Software Chinese Academy of Sciences, Beijing, China
[2] University of Chinese Academy of Sciences, Beijing, China
{jinxy,wangsl}@ios.ac.cn
[3] Huawei Technologies Co., Ltd., Beijing, China
zhanbohua@huawei.com
[4] National Key Laboratory of Space Integrated Information System, Institute of Software Chinese Academy of Sciences, Beijing, China
[5] School of Computer Science, Peking University, Beijing, China
njzhan@pku.edu.cn

Abstract. We introduce HHLPar, a tool for verifying hybrid systems modeled in Hybrid Communicating Sequential Processes (HCSP). HHLPar is based on a Hybrid Hoare Logic for HCSP, which enables reasoning about both the continuous-time properties of differential equations and the communication and parallel composition of HCSP processes. This is achieved through the use of specialized trace assertions and their synchronization. The logic has been formalized and proven sound in Isabelle/HOL, providing a reliable foundation for the verification. HHLPar implements the logic in Python and supports automated verification: On one hand, it provides functions for symbolically decomposing HCSP processes, generating assertions for individual sequential processes, and then composing them via synchronization to obtain the final specification for the entire parallel HCSP process; On the other hand, it is integrated with external solvers for handling differential equations and real arithmetic properties. The resulting assertions are sufficiently expressive to deduce both the state properties at termination and the continuous-time invariants maintained throughout the execution of processes, which are critical for ensuring system safety. Finally, we present the main issues related to the implementation of HHLPar and demonstrate its applicability through a case study involving a simplified cruise control system.

Keywords: Hybrid System · Hybrid Hoare Logic · Interactive and Automated Theorem Proving

1 Introduction

Hybrid systems involve complex interactions between continuous-time evolving physical processes and discrete control systems. In networked applications such as cyber-physical systems, communication and parallel composition play a critical role in

A. Goharshady and C. Haase (Eds.): SETTA 2025, LNCS 16458, pp. 113–133, 2026.
https://doi.org/10.1007/978-981-95-7826-9_7

enabling interactions among distributed components, to facilitate the coordination of concurrent behaviors and the exchange of data across subsystems. However, ensuring the safety of such systems is highly challenging due to their inherent complexity, which stems from the interplay of continuous dynamics, discrete transitions, and the need for synchronization between parallel components. Formal verification has been widely recognized in both academic community and industry as an important approach to ensure correctness of hybrid systems. Especially, a verification tool that is sound and capable of producing trustworthy results and meanwhile supporting automation in verification process is essential for the practical design of safety-critical systems.

There are two mainstream verification techniques of hybrid systems: model checking and deductive verification. Model checking verifies a system model, typically represented as hybrid automata [1], by exhaustively computing and checking all reachable system states. However, this approach faces intrinsic challenges due to the infinite state domains and the increasing complexity of hybrid systems. On the other hand, deductive verification conducts proof via logical reasoning by induction on system models and reasons about continuous evolution represented as ordinary differential equations (ODEs) with the help of differential invariants [10,11,16]. A prerequisite for deductive verification of hybrid systems is to have a compositional modelling language for hybrid systems and meanwhile a specification logic for reasoning about the formal models such that the verification of a complex system can be reduced to the verification of decomposed components of the system. Differential dynamic logic ($d\mathcal{L}$) [2,12,13,15] is a first-order dynamic logic proposed for specifying and verifying hybrid systems modelled as hybrid programs. Its soundness has been proved in Isabelle/HOL and Coq in [3]. Its prover KeYmaera [17] supports automatic proof search of rules of $d\mathcal{L}$ and integrates with computer algebra tools for solving differential equations and real arithmetic formulas. Its successor KeYmaera X [7] enhances automation and provides stronger soundness guarantees through a small, trusted prover kernel. However, $d\mathcal{L}$ lacks direct support for communication and parallel composition, which are ubiquitous in practical cyber-physical systems. The verification of hybrid systems with communication and parallel composition poses additional challenges due to the need to account for concurrent interactions, synchronization and the resulting complex, non-deterministic behaviors arising from distributed components.

Hybrid CSP (HCSP) [8,27] extends Hoare's CSP [9] by including ODEs to model continuous dynamics. It leverages the communication and parallel composition features of CSP to enable the flexible interactions between continuous physical processes and discrete control systems. The specification logic and verification of HCSP have been studied by extending the classical Hoare logic to handle both continuous evolution and communication based parallel composition. One line of the work [10,21] utilizes Duration Calculus (DC), which is an interval-based temporal logic with binary modality chop and was extended to specify continuous-time properties, but the DC-based reasoning system is quite complicated and in consequence the tool support for verifying HCSP under this approach is limited to interactive theorem proving in Isabelle/HOL [22], which imposes a significant proof burden on users. To overcome these limitations, an alternative Hybrid Hoare Logic (HHL) was developed by introducing trace-based assertions into first-order logic [26]. This logic proposes traces composed of both communication and continuous-time events, and handles parallel composition of processes through trace synchronization. Building on this logic, the HHL prover was implemented, as illustrated in Fig. 1, providing a more automated and user-friendly verification tool for HCSP.

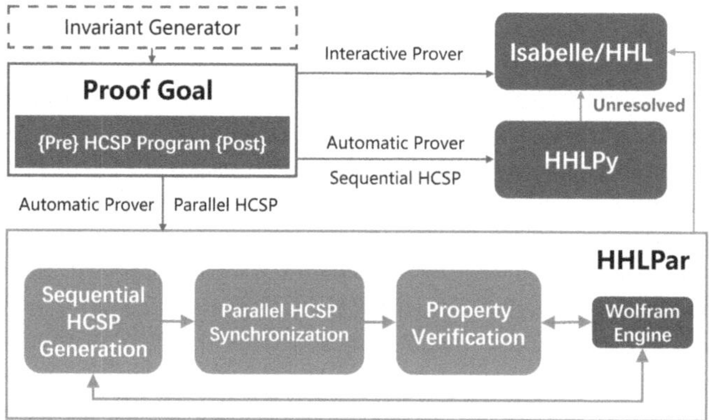

Fig. 1. Architecture of HHLProver.

As shown by Fig. 1, the HHL prover comprises four parts: an Invariant Generator for synthesizing differential invariants of ODEs and supplying them to other modules; HHLPy [20], an automatic verifier for verifying sequential HCSP, particularly ODEs, based on differential invariants; HHLPar, an automatic verifier for HCSP with communication and concurrency; and Isabelle/HHL, an interactive theorem prover for HHL. Both HHLPy and HHLPar are designed to automate verification, while unproven conditions are passed to the interactive mode of HHL prover, i.e. Isabelle/HHL. HCSP captures flexible interactions among multiple processes via communication, which is typical in cyber-physical systems, while HHLPy is restricted to single, sequential processes—this limitation motivates our work.

In this paper, we present HHLPar, the automated theorem prover for HCSP in concurrent setting, including its assertions, inference rules and implementation. HHLPar builds upon the HHL in [26] but differs in several key aspects. The HHL in [26] defines a generalized trace-based logic and a weakest precondition-style proof system, which is proved to be relative complete and very expressive, but faces difficulty in automating the verification of parallel composition. Instead, HHLPar proposes an explicit assertion language for specifying traces, and provides a set of inference rules for constructing assertions of sequential processes and a set of synchronization rules for constructing assertions of parallel processes constituting their specification. This constructive style logic sacrifices the relative completeness of the original logic but enables the automation of HCSP reasoning. The soundness of these inference rules underlying HHLPar has been formally verified in Isabelle/HOL. Meanwhile, we implemented the algorithms for operating assertions in Python, which supports the automated theorem proving of HCSP processes by performing symbolic decomposition and reasoning based on the logic's inference rules. It also inherits HHLPy's integration with the external Wolfram Engine for automatically solving ODEs and reasoning about logical formulas.

The assertions in specification generated by HHLPar are sufficiently expressive to describe the behavior of processes. Also, it is strong enough to enable the derivation of logical formula properties over process variables. In this paper we have developed a set of inference rules specifically for deriving two different forms of properties from the generated assertions automatically. The first class is properties of final states at termination which is also a concern of classical Hoare logic and HHLPy. The second class is continuous-time invariants held throughout the execution which ensure that the system meets the requirements over all continuous time intervals. These properties are crucial for assessing system safety. To demonstrate the usability of HHLPar, we applied it to verify a simplified cruise control system, successfully automating the verification of its safety requirement.

After reviewing the related work, the remainder of the paper is structured as follows. Section 2 provides a brief overview of HCSP. Section 3 introduce the assertions we proposed and its corresponding specification modified from HHL. Section 4 and Sect. 5 introduce inference rules of how to construct assertions in specification for both sequential and parallel HCSP, respectively. Section 6 gives the rules for proving properties of specific forms from assertions. Section 7 discusses the key implementation aspects in both Isabelle/HOL and HHLPar, and demonstrates the application of HHLPar through a case study. The accompanying code, including the formalization and soundness proof of the logic in Isabelle/HOL, the Python implementation and the case study, is available at https://github.com/AgHHL/gHHL2024.git.

1.1 Related Work

Model checking tools of hybrid systems endeavor to compute reachable states of continuous dynamics efficiently in an algorithmic approach, by achieving high scalability while maintaining high accuracy, e.g. the representative PHAVer [5] for linear hybrid automata, HSolver [19] and SpaceEx [6] for both linear and non-linear dynamics. Deduction verification tools are developed upon program logics and conduct proofs via theorem proving. KeYmaera [17] and its successor KeYmaera X [7] are automated and interactive theorem provers built upon differential dynamic logic ($d\mathcal{L}$) [12,13,15], which proposes a complete set of rules [14,18] for reasoning about continuous dynamics such as differential invariants, differential weakening, differential cut, and differential ghosts. Both the tools combine deductive reasoning of $d\mathcal{L}$, real algebraic and computer algebraic provers for automated verification. Foster et al. [4] proposed a semantic verification framework for hybrid systems using the Isabelle/HOL proof assistant and then extended it to IsaVODEs [25]. The related work on specification and verification of HCSP have been discussed in the introduction. In contrast, HHLPar extends HHLPy [20] to support the parallel fragment of HCSP, encompassing communication, parallel composition and continuous evolution. HHLPar inherits HHLPy's integration with external solvers for real arithmetic and ODEs, and further enables automated deductive verification of communication and parallel composition through specialized assertions and synchronization. Both HHLPy and HHLPar are integrated to HHL prover in order to improve its automation, as indicated in Fig. 1.

2 An Overview of HCSP

As an extension of Communicating Sequential Processes (CSP [9]), Hybrid CSP (HCSP) is a formal modeling language for hybrid systems. It introduces Ordinary Differential Equations (ODEs) to model continuous evolution and interrupts. In HCSP, communication is the sole mechanism for data exchange between processes, and shared variables among parallel processes are explicitly prohibited. This section is extracted from [26], which plays the foundation of the logic in this paper. For self-containedness, we provide a brief overview.

Syntax. Below, we present the syntax for HCSP. Here c and c_i denote sequential processes, while pc and pc_i denote parallel processes. $\dot{x}$ represents the first-order derivative of x w.r.t. time, $\overrightarrow{x}$ (resp. $\overrightarrow{e}$) denotes a vector of variables (expressions). ch refers to a channel name, and ch_i* denotes either an input event $ch_i?x$ or output event $ch_i!e$. L is a non-empty set of indices, cs is a set of channel names. B and e represent Boolean and arithmetic expressions, respectively.

$$\begin{aligned} c \ ::= {} & \text{skip} \mid x := e \mid ch?x \mid ch!e \mid c_1 \sqcup c_2 \mid c_1; c_2 \mid c^* \mid \text{if } B \text{ then } c_1 \text{ else } c_2 \mid \\ & \langle \dot{\overrightarrow{x}} = \overrightarrow{e} \& B \rangle \mid \text{wait } e \mid \langle \dot{\overrightarrow{x}} = \overrightarrow{e} \& B \propto c \rangle \trianglerighteq \|_{i \in L}(ch_i* \rightarrow c_i) \\ pc ::= {} & c \mid pc_1 \|_{cs} pc_2 \end{aligned}$$

The input $ch?x$ receives a value through channel ch and assigns it to variable x, while the output $ch!e$ sends the value of e through ch. Both statements may block, waiting for the corresponding dual party to be ready. The continuous evolution $\langle \dot{\overrightarrow{x}} = \overrightarrow{e} \& B \rangle$ evolves continuously according to the given ODE $\dot{\overrightarrow{x}} = \overrightarrow{e}$ as long as the open *domain* B holds, and terminates whenever B becomes false. The wait statement wait e keeps variables unchanged except that a period of time determined by e progresses. Communication interruption $\langle \dot{\overrightarrow{x}} = \overrightarrow{e} \& B \propto c \rangle \trianglerighteq \|_{i \in L}(ch_i* \rightarrow c_i)$ evolves according to the ODE $\dot{\overrightarrow{x}} = \overrightarrow{e}$ until it is preempted by one of the communication events ch_i*, followed by the corresponding c_i; or until it violated the domain condition B, followed by the execution of c. The parallel composition $pc_1 \|_{cs} pc_2$ executes pc_1 and pc_2 independently, except that all communication events over the common channels in cs are synchronized between pc_1 and pc_2. No same channel direction (e.g. $ch!$) occurs in both pc_1 and pc_2. The meaning of other statements such as assignment, internal choice, sequential composition, and so on, follow their standard definitions.

The following example models a moving vehicle operating in parallel with its discrete controller. The vehicle's motion is governed by an ODE, where s represents the trajectory, v the velocity and a the acceleration. Every d time units, the continuous evolution is interrupted by the controller. During each interruption, the controller senses the trajectory and the velocity of the vehicle through input $p2c?x$, computes the new acceleration and sends it to the vehicle via $c2p!contl(x)$. The vehicle then follows this updated acceleration in the next time period.

$$(\dot{s} = v, \dot{v} = a \trianglerighteq \|(p2c!(s, v) \rightarrow c2p?a))^* \|(\text{wait } d; p2c?x; c2p!contl(x))^*$$

Semantics. Figure 2 presents part of the big-step semantics of HCSP, defined as a set of transition rules. Each transition takes the form $(c, s) \Rightarrow (s', tr)$, indicating that c carries initial state s to final state s', producing a trace tr. Here states $s, s' \in \mathit{Vars} \rightarrow \mathit{Values}$ are mappings from variables to values. A trace tr is an ordered sequence of events generated during the execution of an HCSP process. It can be an empty trace ϵ, a single event, or the concatenation $tr_1^\frown tr_2$ of two traces tr_1 and tr_2, defined recursively. An event describes an observable step in the behavior of a process. There are two types of events: A *communication event* $\langle ch\triangleright, v\rangle$, where $\triangleright$ is ? or !, indicating input and output, and v is a value transmitted during the communication; a *continuous event* $\langle d, \overrightarrow{p}, rdy\rangle$, where d is a positive value specifying the duration of this event, $\overrightarrow{p}$ a continuous function from $[0, d]$ to states, describing the evolution of states over time, and rdy is the set of channels that are waiting for communication during this duration.

$$\frac{}{(ch!e, s) \Rightarrow (s, \langle ch!, s(e)\rangle)}\ \text{Out-1} \qquad \frac{}{(ch!e, s) \Rightarrow (s, \langle d, I_s, \{ch!\}\rangle^\frown\langle ch!, s(e)\rangle)}\ \text{Out-2}$$

$$\frac{\forall t \in [0, d).\, s[\overrightarrow{x} \mapsto \overrightarrow{p}(t)](B) \quad \neg s[\overrightarrow{x} \mapsto \overrightarrow{p}(d)](B)}{(\langle \dot{\overrightarrow{x}} = \overrightarrow{e}\&B\rangle, s) \Rightarrow (s[\overrightarrow{x} \mapsto \overrightarrow{p}(d)], \langle d, \overrightarrow{p}, \{\}\rangle)}\ \text{Cont}$$

$$\frac{\forall t \in [0, d).\, s[\overrightarrow{x} \mapsto \overrightarrow{p}(t)](B) \quad i \in L \quad ch_i* = ch!e \quad (c_i, s[\overrightarrow{x} \mapsto \overrightarrow{p}(d)]) \Rightarrow (s', tr)}{\begin{array}{c}(\langle \dot{\overrightarrow{x}} = \overrightarrow{e}\&B \propto c\rangle \trianglerighteq \talloblong_{i\in L}(ch_i* \rightarrow c_i), s) \Rightarrow \\ (s', \langle d, \overrightarrow{p}, rdy(\cup_{i\in L} ch_i*)\rangle^\frown\langle ch!, s[\overrightarrow{x} \mapsto \overrightarrow{p}(d)](e)\rangle^\frown tr)\end{array}}\ \text{Int-1}$$

$$\frac{\forall t \in [0, d).\, s[\overrightarrow{x} \mapsto \overrightarrow{p}(t)](B) \quad \neg s[\overrightarrow{x} \mapsto \overrightarrow{p}(d)](B) \quad (c, s[\overrightarrow{x} \mapsto \overrightarrow{p}(d)]) \Rightarrow (s', tr)}{\begin{array}{c}(\langle \dot{\overrightarrow{x}} = \overrightarrow{e}\&B \propto c\rangle \trianglerighteq \talloblong_{i\in L}(ch_i* \rightarrow c_i), s) \Rightarrow \\ (s', \langle d, \overrightarrow{p}, rdy(\cup_{i\in L} ch_i*)\rangle^\frown tr)\end{array}}\ \text{Int-2}$$

$$\frac{(c_1, s_1) \Rightarrow (s_1', tr_1) \quad (c_2, s_2) \Rightarrow (s_2', tr_2) \quad tr_1 \|_{cs} tr_2 \Downarrow tr}{(c_1 \|_{cs} c_2, s_1 \uplus s_2) \Rightarrow (s_1' \uplus s_2', tr)}\ \text{Par}$$

Fig. 2. Part of big-step semantics of HCSP

Rules (Out-1) and (Out-2) define two cases for communication: one where the communication occurs immediately, and another where it occurs after a delay of d time units. During the waiting period, I_s represents an identity function that maps time to the initial state. Rule (Cont) defines the behavior of the continuous evolution, which terminates after time d due to the violation of domain B. This results in a continuous event with duration d and function $\overrightarrow{p}$, where $\overrightarrow{p}$ is a solution of the ODE $\dot{\overrightarrow{x}} = \overrightarrow{e}$ satisfying the initial condition $\overrightarrow{p}(0) = s(\overrightarrow{x})$. Rule (int-1) defines that the ODE is interrupted after $d > 0$ time duration, by the occurrence of a communication over channel ch, and then the subsequent process c_i is executed; Rule (int-2) defines that the ODE terminates due to the violation of B, without any communication among $\{ch_i\}$ being able to occur, and then the subsequent process c is executed. Other similar cases, e.g. interruption by an input event, are not listed here. Rule (Par) defines the semantics of the parallel composition, which results in the disjoint union of the states (denoted by $s_1 \uplus s_2$) and the synchronization of the traces (denoted by $tr_1 \|_{cs} tr_2 \Downarrow tr$), of the two respective processes.

Especially, the trace synchronization relation $tr_1\|_{cs}tr_2 \Downarrow tr$ can be derived according to the structures of traces tr_1 and tr_2. Part of the derivation rules is given below. An output event synchronizes with the corresponding input event (SyncIO). When an external communication event occurs on one side, it does not need to synchronize with the other side (NoSyncIO); When both sides are continuous events, then the continuous events of the same length will synchronize if they have compatible ready sets (SWait), denoted by compat, meaning that no input and output along a same channel occur simultaneously in the two ready sets (otherwise the corresponding communication must occur immediately).

$$\frac{ch \in cs \quad tr_1\|_{cs}tr_2 \Downarrow tr}{\langle ch!, v\rangle^\frown tr_1\|_{cs}\langle ch?, v\rangle^\frown tr_2 \Downarrow tr}\text{SyncIO} \qquad \frac{ch \notin cs \quad tr_1\|_{cs}tr_2 \Downarrow tr}{\langle ch\triangleright, v\rangle^\frown tr_1\|_{cs}tr_2 \Downarrow \langle ch\triangleright, v\rangle^\frown tr}\text{NoSyncIO}$$

$$\frac{tr_1\|_{cs}tr_2 \Downarrow tr \quad \mathrm{compat}(rdy_1, rdy_2) \quad d > 0}{\langle d, \overrightarrow{p}_1, rdy_1\rangle^\frown tr_1\|_{cs}\langle d, \overrightarrow{p}_2, rdy_2\rangle^\frown tr_2 \Downarrow \langle d, \overrightarrow{p}_1 \uplus \overrightarrow{p}_2, (rdy_1 \cup rdy_2) - cs\rangle^\frown tr}\text{SWait}$$

The full definition of the trace synchronization function and big-step semantics used in this paper are shown in the complement document[1].

3 Assertions and Specifications

We will introduce an assertion language for explicitly specifying traces, which serves as the foundation for the inference rules of constructing specifications of HCSP in the following sections. The assertion language, with its explicit syntactic forms, enables automated processing of inference rules for verifying HCSP processes. Building on these assertions, we further propose a novel specification form tailored for HCSP.

3.1 Syntax and Semantics

The syntax of the assertion language is defined below: P, Q represent assertions, cm is a list of tuples recording the assertion information for channels, I is a path condition.

$$\begin{aligned}
P, Q \ &::= \mathsf{true} \mid \mathsf{false} \mid P \bar{\wedge} Q \mid P \bar{\vee} Q \mid \uparrow b \mid P[\overrightarrow{x} := \overrightarrow{e}] \mid \mathsf{init} \\
&\quad \mid \mathsf{wait_in}(I, ch, \{\mathsf{d}, \mathsf{v} \Rightarrow P\}) \mid \mathsf{wait_outv}(I, ch, e, \{\mathsf{d} \Rightarrow P\}) \mid \mathsf{wait}(I, e, \{\mathsf{d} \Rightarrow P\}) \\
&\quad \mid \mathsf{interrupt}(I, e, \{\mathsf{d} \Rightarrow P\}, cm) \mid \mathsf{interrupt}_\infty(I, cm) \mid \mathsf{Rec}\ R.\ P \bar{\vee} F(R) \\
cm \ &::= \epsilon \mid (ch?, \{\mathsf{d}, \mathsf{v} \Rightarrow P\}) \cdot cm \mid (ch!, h, \{\mathsf{d} \Rightarrow P\}) \cdot cm \\
I \ &::= \mathsf{id} \mid \overrightarrow{x} \rightarrowtail f(\overrightarrow{x}, t) \mid \mathsf{inv} \mid I[\overrightarrow{x} := \overrightarrow{e}] \mid I_1 \uplus I_2
\end{aligned}$$

where b and inv are boolean expressions, e is a real expression, $\{\mathsf{d}, \mathsf{v} \Rightarrow P\}$ represents a function mapping from real valued variables d and v to assertions($\{\mathsf{d} \Rightarrow P\}$ is similar), for example, $\{\mathsf{d}, \mathsf{v} \Rightarrow \mathsf{init}[x := x + \mathsf{d}][y := \mathsf{v}]\}$. Here, d and v are two special bounded variables introduced to synchronize communication between parallel processes: d denotes the transmitted value and v denotes the time of occurrence, which will be resolved when the dual events in parallel processes synchronize. cm is a list of tuples or triples recording the communication branches used in interrupt. Rec

[1] https://github.com/AgHHL/gHHL2024/blob/main/complement.pdf.

defines a recursive assertion where P acts as the guard ensuring the recursion terminates. Here F is a generator function defined inductively according to the syntax of the assertion language which can be atomic or non-atomic assertion containing a hole indicating the position where a recursion happens. For example, $F(R)$ can be $R[x := 0]$ or $\mathsf{wait}(I, e, \{\mathsf{d} \Rightarrow R[x := x+1]\})$.

We first define the semantics of path conditions. A path condition I is a predicate interpreted over the starting state, the time and the state, denoted by $(s_0, t, s) \models I$. It describes the relationship between the starting state s_0 and the state s at time t during the evolution. As defined by the semantics, id states that s keeps the same as the initial state s_0; $\overrightarrow{x} \rightarrowtail f(\overrightarrow{x}, t)$ substitutes $\overrightarrow{x}$ to the value defined by f at time t; inv means that state s at t satisfies the invariant inv; the substitution $I[\overrightarrow{x} := \overrightarrow{e}]$ updates the value of $\overrightarrow{x}$ at initial state to be the one of $\overrightarrow{e}$. Intuitively, we use id to describe the constant duration and use f and inv to handle the ODE with explicit solutions or with differential invariants.

$$
\begin{aligned}
(s_0, t, s) \models \mathsf{id} &\triangleq s = s_0 \\
(s_0, t, s) \models \overrightarrow{x} \rightarrowtail f(\overrightarrow{x}, t) &\triangleq s = s_0[\overrightarrow{x} \mapsto f(s_0(\overrightarrow{x}), t)] \\
(s_0, t, s) \models \mathsf{inv} &\triangleq \mathsf{inv}(s) \\
(s_0, t, s) \models I[\overrightarrow{x} := \overrightarrow{e}] &\triangleq (s_0[\overrightarrow{x} \mapsto s_0(\overrightarrow{e})], t, s) \models I \\
(s_0, t, s) \models I_1 \uplus I_2 &\triangleq \exists\, s_{01}\, s_{02}\, s_1\, s_2 .\, s_0 = s_{01} \uplus s_{02} \wedge s = s_1 \uplus s_2 \wedge \\
&\qquad (s_{01}, t, s_1) \models I_1 \wedge (s_{02}, t, s_2) \models I_2
\end{aligned}
$$

Next, we introduce the semantics of the assertions. An assertion P is interpreted over an initial state, current state and a trace, denoted by $(s_0, s, tr) \models P$. The assertions true, false, $P \bar{\wedge} Q$, $P \bar{\vee} Q$ are defined similar to the propositional logic. $\uparrow b$ lifts a boolean expression on starting state as a boolean assertion, i.e. b holds at the starting state. $P[\overrightarrow{x} := \overrightarrow{e}]$ means that P holds under the starting state updated by assigning $\overrightarrow{x}$ to $\overrightarrow{e}$. init means that the state equals starting state and the trace is empty.

$$
\begin{aligned}
(s_0, s, tr) \models\, \uparrow b &\triangleq b(s0) \\
(s_0, s, tr) \models P \bar{\wedge} Q &\triangleq (s_0, s, tr) \models P \wedge (s_0, s, tr) \models Q \\
(s_0, s, tr) \models P \bar{\vee} Q &\triangleq (s_0, s, tr) \models P \vee (s_0, s, tr) \models Q \\
(s_0, s, tr) \models P[\overrightarrow{x} := \overrightarrow{e}] &\triangleq (s_0[\overrightarrow{x} \mapsto s_0(\overrightarrow{e})], s, tr) \models P \\
(s_0, s, tr) \models \mathsf{init} &\triangleq s_0 = s \wedge tr = \epsilon
\end{aligned}
$$

We then introduce the semantics of assertions specifying the behavior of input, output, continuous evolution and interrupt respectively:

- $(s_0, s, tr) \models \mathsf{wait\_in}(I, ch, \{\mathsf{d}, \mathsf{v} \Rightarrow P\})$ iff one of the following is satisfied:

  1. $(s_0, s, tr') \models P|_{\mathsf{d}=0, \mathsf{v}=v} \wedge tr = \langle ch?, v\rangle ^\frown tr'$
  2. $(s_0, s, tr') \models P|_{\mathsf{d}=d, \mathsf{v}=v} \wedge d > 0 \wedge \overrightarrow{p}(0) = s_0 \wedge \forall t \in [0, d].\, (s_0, t, \overrightarrow{p}(t)) \models I$ $\wedge tr = \langle d, \overrightarrow{p}, \{ch?\}\rangle ^\frown \langle ch?, v\rangle ^\frown tr'$

- $(s_0, s, tr) \models \mathsf{wait\_outv}(I, ch, e, \{\mathsf{d} \Rightarrow P\})$ iff one of the following is satisfied:

  1. $(s_0, s, tr') \models P|_{\mathsf{d}=0} \wedge tr = \langle ch!, s_0(e)\rangle ^\frown tr'$
  2. $(s_0, s, tr') \models P|_{\mathsf{d}=d} \wedge d > 0 \wedge \overrightarrow{p}(0) = s_0 \wedge \forall t \in [0, d].\, (s_0, t, \overrightarrow{p}(t)) \models I$ $\wedge tr = \langle d, \overrightarrow{p}, \{ch!\}\rangle ^\frown \langle ch!, s_0(e)\rangle ^\frown tr'$

- $(s_0, s, tr) \models \mathsf{wait}(I, e, \{\mathsf{d} \Rightarrow P\})$ iff one of the following is satisfied:

  1. $(s_0, s, tr) \models P|_{\mathsf{d}=0} \wedge s_0(e) \leq 0$
  2. $(s_0, s, tr') \models P|_{\mathsf{d}=s_0(e)} \wedge s_0(e) > 0 \wedge \overrightarrow{p}(0) = s_0 \wedge \forall t \in [0, s_0(e)].\, (s_0, t, \overrightarrow{p}(t)) \models I$ $\wedge tr = \langle s_0(e), \overrightarrow{p}, \{\}\rangle^\frown tr'$

- $(s_0, s, tr) \models \mathsf{interrupt}(I, e, \{\mathsf{d} \Rightarrow P\}, cm)$ iff one of the following is satisfied:

  1. $(s_0, s, tr) \models P|_{\mathsf{d}=0} \wedge s_0(e) \leq 0$
  2. $(s_0, s, tr') \models P|_{\mathsf{d}=s_0(e)} \wedge s_0(e) > 0 \wedge \overrightarrow{p}(0) = s_0 \wedge \forall t \in [0, s_0(e)].\, (s_0, t, \overrightarrow{p}(t)) \models I$ $\wedge tr = \langle s_0(e), \overrightarrow{p}, rdy(cm)\rangle^\frown tr'$
  3. $(s_0, s, tr') \models P_i|_{\mathsf{d}=0, \mathsf{v}=v} \wedge cm[i] = (ch_i?, \{\mathsf{d}, \mathsf{v} \Rightarrow P_i\}) \wedge tr = \langle ch_i?, v\rangle^\frown tr'$
  4. $(s_0, s, tr') \models P_i|_{\mathsf{d}=d, \mathsf{v}=v} \wedge cm[i] = (ch_i?, \{\mathsf{d}, \mathsf{v} \Rightarrow P_i\}) \wedge 0 < d \leq s_0(e)$ $\wedge \overrightarrow{p}(0) = s_0 \wedge \forall t \in [0, d].\, (s_0, t, \overrightarrow{p}(t)) \models I \wedge tr = \langle d, \overrightarrow{p}, rdy(cm)\rangle^\frown \langle ch_i?, v\rangle^\frown tr'$
  5. $(s_0, s, tr') \models P_i|_{\mathsf{d}=0} \wedge cm[i] = (ch_i!, h, \{\mathsf{d} \Rightarrow P_i\}) \wedge tr = \langle ch_i!, h(0)\rangle^\frown tr'$
  6. $(s_0, s, tr') \models P_i|_{\mathsf{d}=d} \wedge cm[i] = (ch_i!, h, \{\mathsf{d} \Rightarrow P_i\}) \wedge 0 < d \leq s_0(e)$ $\wedge \overrightarrow{p}(0) = s_0 \wedge \forall t \in [0, d].\, (s_0, t, \overrightarrow{p}(t)) \models I \wedge tr = \langle d, \overrightarrow{p}, rdy(cm)\rangle^\frown \langle ch_i!, h(d)\rangle^\frown tr'$

- $(s_0, s, tr) \models \mathsf{interrupt}_\infty(I, cm)$ iff one of the following is satisfied:

  1. $(s_0, s, tr') \models P_i|_{\mathsf{d}=0, \mathsf{v}=v} \wedge cm[i] = (ch_i?, \{\mathsf{d}, \mathsf{v} \Rightarrow P_i\}) \wedge tr = \langle ch_i?, v\rangle^\frown tr'$
  2. $(s_0, s, tr') \models P_i|_{\mathsf{d}=d, \mathsf{v}=v} \wedge cm[i] = (ch_i?, \{\mathsf{d}, \mathsf{v} \Rightarrow P_i\}) \wedge 0 < d$ $\wedge \overrightarrow{p}(0) = s_0 \wedge \forall t \in [0, d].\, (s_0, t, \overrightarrow{p}(t)) \models I \wedge tr = \langle d, \overrightarrow{p}, rdy(cm)\rangle^\frown \langle ch_i?, v\rangle^\frown tr'$
  3. $(s_0, s, tr') \models P_i|_{\mathsf{d}=0} \wedge cm[i] = (ch_i!, h, \{\mathsf{d} \Rightarrow P_i\}) \wedge tr = \langle ch_i!, h(0)\rangle^\frown tr'$
  4. $(s_0, s, tr') \models P_i|_{\mathsf{d}=d} \wedge cm[i] = (ch_i!, h, \{\mathsf{d} \Rightarrow P_i\}) \wedge 0 < d$ $\wedge \overrightarrow{p}(0) = s_0 \wedge \forall t \in [0, d].\, (s_0, t, \overrightarrow{p}(t)) \models I \wedge tr = \langle d, \overrightarrow{p}, rdy(cm)\rangle^\frown \langle ch_i!, h(d)\rangle^\frown tr'$

As defined by wait_in, the first case corresponds to communicating immediately, so the delay d is 0, the input value v can be any real number v which can't be determined by itself. We use the notation $P|_{\mathsf{d}=0,\mathsf{v}=v}$ to represent the assertion obtained by replacing the appearance of d and v in P with value 0 and v. The second case corresponds to communicating after waiting for time $d > 0$. The path taken by the state during waiting is given by $\overrightarrow{p}$, which satisfies the path condition I. wait_out is defined similarly, but unlike the input case, the output value is determined by e and the map $\{\mathsf{d} \Rightarrow P\}$ is only over the delay d. For the wait assertion, e is a real expression specifying the wait time and the map in this assertion only has one argument over delay d.

The interrupt assertion covers two main categories of termination for the ODE. One occurs when the ODE evolves for zero or more time units and then terminates due to violating the domain. The other happens when the ODE, after evolving for zero or more time units, is interrupted by an input or output event. In the definition of interrupt assertion, e specifies the *maximum* waiting time of the interrupt, P specifies the remaining behavior if the waiting stops upon reaching the time bound e, cm specifies the list of communications that can happen at any time not exceeding $s_0(e)$. cm is given by a list of elements like $\langle ch_i?, \{\mathsf{d}, \mathsf{v} \Rightarrow P_i\}\rangle$ or $\langle ch_i!, g, \{\mathsf{d} \Rightarrow P_i\}\rangle$, which specifies what happens after the corresponding interrupt is triggered, where g is a function mapping from delay to the output value and $rdy(cm)$ denotes the ready set of communications in cm.

There is an important special case: often we know the maximum waiting time may be infinite, for example when the domain of the ODE is true, the system can only execute the next command when a communication occurs. We denote this case by assertion $\mathsf{interrupt}_\infty(I, cm)$.

Finally, we introduce the recursion assertion:

$$(s_0, s, tr) \models \mathsf{Rec}\ R.\ P \bar{\vee} F(R) \text{ iff } (s_0, s, tr) \models P \text{ or } (s_0, s, tr) \models F(\mathsf{Rec}\ R.\ P \bar{\vee} F(R))$$

We can deduce that $(s_0, s, tr) \models \mathsf{Rec}\ R.\ P \bar{\vee} F(R)$ iff $\exists n.\, (s_0, s, tr) \models F^n(P)$ where $F^n \triangleq F(F^{n-1}(P))$ and n is a natural number.

3.2 Specification

In previous HHL [26], the specification of a HCSP process pc takes the form of Hoare triple $\{Pre\}\, pc\, \{Post\}$, where Pre and $Post$ are predicates on state and trace. We use $(s, tr) \models Pre$ to denote that the state s and the trace tr satisfy the predicate Pre ($Post$ is similar). Note that, an assertion Q is a predicate over three elements: initial state s_0, current state s and a trace tr, thus $Q(s_0)$ can be seen as a predicate on state and trace, e.g. $(s, tr) \models Q(s_0) \equiv (s_0, s, tr) \models Q$. The validity of a Hoare triple is defined in terms of big-step semantics as follows:

$$\{Pre\}\, pc\, \{Post\} \triangleq$$
$$\forall s_1\ s_2\ tr\ tr'.\, (s_1, tr) \models Pre \longrightarrow (pc, s_1) \Rightarrow (s_2, tr') \longrightarrow (s_2, tr^\frown tr') \models Post$$

In this paper, we utilize a new method of specification definition named spec_of based on Hoare triples:

$$\mathsf{spec\_of}(pc, Q) \quad \triangleq \quad \forall s_0.\, \{s = s_0 \wedge tr = \epsilon\}\, pc\, \{(s, tr) \models Q(s_0)\}$$

where the assertion Q describes the relationship between the initial state s_0, the final state s and the produced trace tr. This specification means that if this process starts with a state s_0, then when the process terminates, the end state and the trace produced should meet the predicate $Q(s_0)$.

Next, we give some useful characteristics and lemmas on predicates and assertions. Given two predicates G_1 and G_2 , we define the entailment between G_1 and G_2 as:

$$G_1 \Longrightarrow_a G_2 \quad \triangleq \quad \forall\, s\ tr.\, (s, tr) \models G_1 \longrightarrow (s, tr) \models G_2$$

Obviously, this entailment relationship satisfies the transitivity and reflexivity. There are some common entailment rules, for example introduction and elimination rules for conjunction or disjunction. Some special notes of entailment related to monotonicity and substitution of assertions are stated in the following.

The assertions wait_in, wait_outv, wait, etc. all satisfy monotonicity rules on the initial state s_0, that reduce entailment relations among assertions to entailments on its components. For example, monotonicity of wait_in take the following form:

$$\frac{\forall d\ v.\, P_1|_{\mathsf{d}=d, \mathsf{v}=v}(s_0) \Longrightarrow_a P_2|_{\mathsf{d}=d, \mathsf{v}=v}(s_0)}{\mathsf{wait\_in}(I, ch, \{\mathsf{d}, \mathsf{v} \Rightarrow P_1\})(s_0) \Longrightarrow_a \mathsf{wait\_in}(I, ch, \{\mathsf{d}, \mathsf{v} \Rightarrow P_2\})(s_0)}$$

This rule permits deducing entailment between two wait_in assertions that differ only in the ensuing parameters. There are similar rules for wait_outv, wait, interrupt and interrupt$_\infty$. By these rules, we can assert that all the functions from assertions to assertions constructed by the forms introduced satisfies monotonicity.

The commutativity with existential quantifier for assertions is like the following:

$$\mathsf{wait\_in}(I, ch, \{\mathsf{d}, \mathsf{v} \Rightarrow \exists x.\, P\})(s_0) \Longrightarrow_a \exists x.\, \mathsf{wait\_in}(I, ch, \{\mathsf{d}, \mathsf{v} \Rightarrow P\})(s_0)$$

Other forms of assertions in our logic have similar results. So far, both the monotonicity and commutativity conditions are proved to hold for the assertions defined at the beginning of this section. We proved in Isabelle that the Rec assertion is the least fixed point under the assumption that F is monotonic with respect to logical implication and commutative with existential quantifier.

Besides, performing substitution $[x := e]$ on assertions such as wait_in can be reduced to performing the same operations on its components. For example, the entailment rule for wait_in is:

$$\mathsf{wait\_in}(I, ch, \{\mathsf{d}, \mathsf{v} \Rightarrow P\})[x := e](s_0) \Longrightarrow_a \mathsf{wait\_in}(I[x := e], ch, \{\mathsf{d}, \mathsf{v} \Rightarrow P[x := e]\})(s_0)$$

4 Inference Rules for Sequential HCSP

In this section, we introduce the inference rules for generating assertions of sequential HCSP processes. For each sequential HCSP construct, we define the rule for it where it is followed by a subsequent process c. This is because different processes can have varying effects on the traces of the sequentially composed c. Notably, the rules for the constructs alone can be derived by substituting c with skip and applying the skip rule.

For skip, assignment, input, output, wait and if commands, we have following rules:

$$\frac{}{\mathsf{spec\_of}(\mathsf{skip}, \mathsf{init})} \qquad \frac{\mathsf{spec\_of}(c, Q)}{\mathsf{spec\_of}(\mathsf{skip}; c, Q)} \qquad \frac{\mathsf{spec\_of}(c, Q)}{\mathsf{spec\_of}(x := e; c, Q[x := e])}$$

$$\frac{\mathsf{spec\_of}(c_1; c, P) \quad \mathsf{spec\_of}(c_2; c, Q)}{\mathsf{spec\_of}(\text{if } B \text{ then } c_1 \text{ else } c_2; c, (\uparrow (B) \bar{\wedge} P) \bar{\vee} (\uparrow (\neg B) \bar{\wedge} Q))}$$

$$\frac{\mathsf{spec\_of}(c, Q)}{\mathsf{spec\_of}(ch?x; c, \mathsf{wait\_in}(\mathsf{id}, ch, \{\mathsf{d}, \mathsf{v} \Rightarrow Q[x := \mathsf{v}]\}))}$$

$$\frac{\mathsf{spec\_of}(c, Q)}{\mathsf{spec\_of}(ch!e; c, \mathsf{wait\_outv}(\mathsf{id}, ch, e, \{\mathsf{d} \Rightarrow Q\}))}$$

$$\frac{\mathsf{spec\_of}(c, Q)}{\mathsf{spec\_of}(\text{wait } e; c, \mathsf{wait}(\mathsf{id}, e, \{\mathsf{d} \Rightarrow Q\}))}$$

For the nondeterministic repetition command, we have the following rule:

$$\frac{\mathsf{spec\_of}(c', P) \quad \forall\, cc\, Q.\, \mathsf{spec\_of}(cc, Q) \longrightarrow \mathsf{spec\_of}(c; cc, F(Q))}{\mathsf{spec\_of}(c^*; c', \mathsf{Rec}\ R.\ P \bar{\vee} F(R))}$$

In this rule, P represents the assertion of proceeding directly to subsequent processes without executing the loop and F represents the change in assertion resulting from executing once loop. This recursion assertion can be seen as the loop invariant of repetition.

We now state the rules for continuous evolution. If the (unique) solution to the ODE is known, the predicate $\mathsf{paramODEsol}(\dot{\overrightarrow{x}} = \overrightarrow{e}, B, f, e)$ is introduced: $\dot{\overrightarrow{x}} = \overrightarrow{e}$ is an equation between variables and their derivative expressions; B is a predicate on the state, specifying the open boundary condition; $f(\overrightarrow{x}, t)$ is the solution of $\dot{\overrightarrow{x}} = \overrightarrow{e}$ at time t; e maps the starting state to the length of time for the unique solution of the ODE reaching the boundary. We can then state the inference rule for the continuous evolution as follows:

$$\frac{\mathsf{paramODEsol}(\dot{\overrightarrow{x}} = \overrightarrow{e}, B, f, e) \quad \mathsf{lipschitz}(\dot{\overrightarrow{x}} = \overrightarrow{e}) \quad \mathsf{spec\_of}(c, Q)}{\mathsf{spec\_of}(\langle \dot{\overrightarrow{x}} = \overrightarrow{e} \& B\rangle; c, \mathsf{wait}(\overrightarrow{x} \rightarrowtail f(\overrightarrow{x}, t), e, \{\mathsf{d} \Rightarrow Q[\overrightarrow{x} := f(s_0(\overrightarrow{x}), \mathsf{d})]\}))}$$

The meaning of this rule is as follows. Suppose $\dot{\overrightarrow{x}} = \overrightarrow{e}$ with boundary condition B has solution f with time given by e (both functions of s_0) and the lipschitz predicate ensures that there is a unique solution to this ODE, then the specification of $\langle \dot{\overrightarrow{x}} = \overrightarrow{e} \& B\rangle; c$ first evolves along the path $\overrightarrow{p}(t) = s0[\overrightarrow{x} \mapsto f(s_0(\overrightarrow{x}), t)]$ for time $s_0(e)$, then followed by the behavior of c as specified by Q starting from the updated state $s_0[\overrightarrow{x} := f(s_0(\overrightarrow{x}), \mathsf{d})]$.

Next, we show how to use differential invariants to reason about continuous evolution. We define predicate $\mathsf{paramODEInv}(\dot{\overrightarrow{x}} = \overrightarrow{e}, inv, pp)$, meaning that if the starting state of ODE satisfies the condition pp, then all the states along the ODE $\dot{\overrightarrow{x}} = \overrightarrow{e}$ satisfy the invariant inv. Before applying this rule, we should have inv and corresponding differential methods provided. The predicate is verified using the technology introduced in [15,20].

$$\frac{\mathsf{paramODEInv}(\dot{\overrightarrow{x}} = \overrightarrow{e}, B, inv, pp) \quad \mathsf{lipschitz}(\dot{\overrightarrow{x}} = \overrightarrow{e}) \quad \mathsf{spec\_of}(c, Q)}{\begin{array}{c}\mathsf{spec\_of}(\langle \dot{\overrightarrow{x}} = \overrightarrow{e} \& B\rangle; c, (\uparrow (\neg B) \bar{\wedge} Q) \bar{\vee} \uparrow (\neg pp \wedge B) \bar{\vee} \\ \exists T\, \overrightarrow{nx}. (\uparrow (pp \wedge B) \bar{\wedge} \mathsf{wait}(inv, T, \{d \Rightarrow (\uparrow (inv \wedge bound(B)) \bar{\wedge} Q)[\overrightarrow{x} := \overrightarrow{nx}]\})))\end{array}}$$

This rule includes three cases via disjunction: (1) If the boundary is violated at the beginning, then the ODE terminates at once and satisfies the specification of c. (2) The second case is when the condition pp does not hold. Although we do not desire this situation to arise, it must be included to ensure the correctness of the specification. We expect $\neg pp$ to conflict with other conditions in the subsequent verification and counteract this case, indicating that this case will not happen. (3) The last case states that it will stop at some state satisfying both the invariant and the boundary of B. (During implementation, we will introduce new variables T and $\overrightarrow{nx}$ to avoid Existential quantifier.)

The inference rules for interrupt command can be seen as the combination of rules for ODE, input and output. The detailed rules can be found in the complement document.

Below we give an example to illustrate how to generate the specifications of sequential HCSP processes by applying these rules.

Example 1. This example illustrates handling of delay and communication events.

$$c \triangleq ch_2?x; \text{wait } 1; ch_1!x$$

The specification of c is generated by the following steps:

$$\begin{aligned}
&1: \mathsf{spec_of}(ch_1!x, \mathsf{wait_outv}(\mathsf{id}, ch_1, x, \{\mathsf{d1} \Rightarrow \mathsf{init}\}))\\
&2: \mathsf{spec_of}(\mathsf{wait}(1); ch_1!x, \mathsf{wait}(\mathsf{id}, 1, \{\mathsf{d2} \Rightarrow \mathsf{wait_outv}(\mathsf{id}, ch_1, x, \{\mathsf{d1} \Rightarrow \mathsf{init}\})\}))\\
&3: \mathsf{spec_of}(ch_2?x; \mathsf{wait}(1); ch_1!x, \mathsf{wait_in}(\mathsf{id}, ch_2, \{\mathsf{d3}, \mathsf{v3} \Rightarrow\\
&\quad \mathsf{wait}(\mathsf{id}, 1, \{\mathsf{d2} \Rightarrow \mathsf{wait_outv}(\mathsf{id}, ch_1, x, \{\mathsf{d1} \Rightarrow \mathsf{init}\})\})[x := \mathsf{v3}]\}))\\
&4: \mathsf{spec_of}(ch_2?x; \mathsf{wait}(1); ch_1!x, \mathsf{wait_in}(\mathsf{id}, ch_2, \{\mathsf{d3}, \mathsf{v3} \Rightarrow\\
&\quad \mathsf{wait}(\mathsf{id}[x := \mathsf{v3}], 1, \{\mathsf{d2} \Rightarrow \mathsf{wait_outv}(\mathsf{id}[x := \mathsf{v3}], ch_1, \mathsf{v3}, \{\mathsf{d1} \Rightarrow \mathsf{init}\})\})\}))
\end{aligned}$$

At Step 4, we obtain the final specification of c, which can be understood as follows: Starting from state s_0, first waits for input along channel ch_2, after receiving input value $\mathsf{v3}$ at time $\mathsf{d3}$, then waits for time 1 with state $s_0[x := \mathsf{v3}]$, then waits for output along channel ch_1 with state $s_0[x := \mathsf{v3}]$, that occurs at time $\mathsf{d1}$. The output value is $\mathsf{v3}$, and the final state after output is $s_0[x := \mathsf{v3}]$.

5 Inference Rules for Parallel HCSP

In this section, we introduce the inference rules for constructing assertions of parallel processes by synchronization. In order to handle parallel processes, we define operator $\mathsf{sync}(chs, P_1, P_2)$ denoting the synchronization if given two assertions P_1 and P_2 for two processes and the set of common channels chs through which communications occur between them:

$$\begin{aligned}
(s_0, s, tr) \models \mathsf{sync}(chs, P_1, P_2) \text{ iff } \exists\, s_{01}\ s_{02}\ s_1\ s_2\ tr_1\ tr_2. s_0 = s_{01} \uplus s_{02} \wedge s = s_1 \uplus s_2 \wedge\\
(s_{01}, s_1, tr_1) \models P_1 \wedge (s_{02}, s_2, tr_2) \models P_2 \wedge tr_1 \|_{chs} tr_2 \Downarrow tr
\end{aligned}$$

By the above definition of sync, we can easily obtain the following conclusion:

$$\frac{\mathsf{spec\_of}(c_1, P_1) \quad \mathsf{spec\_of}(c_2, P_2)}{\mathsf{spec\_of}(c_1 \|_{chs} c_2, \mathsf{sync}(chs, P_1, P_2))}$$

However, we can't intuitively derive valid information from the definition of this operator. Our objective is to find an assertion Q within our assertion language that can replace $\mathsf{sync}(chs, P_1, P_2)$, ensuring that Q is logically implied by $\mathsf{sync}(chs, P_1, P_2)$ and thus satisfies the above specification. We conclude this motivation to reach the following inference rule for parallel composition:

$$\frac{\mathsf{spec\_of}(c_1, P_1) \quad \mathsf{spec\_of}(c_2, P_2) \quad \forall\, s_0.\, \mathsf{sync}(chs, P_1, P_2)(s_0) \Longrightarrow_a Q(s_0)}{\mathsf{spec\_of}(c_1 \|_{chs} c_2, Q)}$$

We hope that Q reserves the whole behaviour of parallel process to facilitate verification of the system in subsequent steps. For example, the trivial true is always satisfactory, but we can't get any valid information from it. Thus, our proof system contains a set of inference rules for reasoning about the parallel synchronization of assertions in the form of $\mathsf{sync}(chs, P, Q)(s_0) \Longrightarrow_a Q(s_0)$.

By repeatedly using synchronization rules (as well as monotonicity rules and other entailments among assertions), we can gradually reduce an assertion headed by sync into one without sync operators. For the sake of brevity, we select a representative case to illustrate the synchronization rules. The following rule states that, when the channels of two sides match, the communication occurs immediately, determining the time variable d with 0 and the value variable v with $e(s_0)$, and then the procedure of synchronization continues to the tail assertions P_1 and P_2.

$$\frac{ch_1 \in chs \quad ch_2 \in chs \quad ch_1 = ch_2}{\begin{array}{c}\mathsf{sync}(chs, \mathsf{wait\_in}(I_1, ch_1, \{\mathsf{d}, \mathsf{v} \Rightarrow P_1\}), \mathsf{wait\_outv}(I_2, ch_2, e, \{\mathsf{d} \Rightarrow P_2\}))(s_0) \Longrightarrow_a \\ \mathsf{sync}(chs, P_1|_{\mathsf{d}=0,\mathsf{v}=s_0(e)}, P_2|_{\mathsf{d}=0})(s_0)\end{array}} \text{InOut1}$$

We present other rules in the complement document and explain their intuitive meanings. The soundness of these rules have been formally proven by combining the definition of operator sync and the trace synchronization relation as introduced in Sect. 2.

Example 2. This example demonstrates the handling of communication synchronization and loop. It repeatedly sends the same value x from the left to the right, with z received on the right, and then sends $z + 1$ back from the right to the left.

$$c_1 \triangleq (ch_1!x; ch_2?y)^* \qquad c_2 \triangleq (ch_1?z; ch_2!(z+1))^*$$

By applying the rules for input, output, sequential composition and repetition, we can derive $\mathsf{spec\_of}(c_1, P_1)$ and $\mathsf{spec\_of}(c_2, P_2)$ with

$$\begin{aligned} P_1 \triangleq\ & \mathsf{Rec}\ R_1.\ \mathsf{init} \bar{\vee} \mathsf{wait\_outv}(\mathsf{id}, ch_1, x, \{\mathsf{d}_1 \Rightarrow \\ & \quad \mathsf{wait\_in}(\mathsf{id}, ch_2, \{\mathsf{d}_2, \mathsf{v}_2 \Rightarrow R_1[x := \mathsf{v}_2]\})\}) \\ P_2 \triangleq\ & \mathsf{Rec}\ R_2.\ \mathsf{init} \bar{\vee} \mathsf{wait\_in}(\mathsf{id}, ch_1, \{\mathsf{d}_1, \mathsf{v}_1 \Rightarrow \\ & \quad \mathsf{wait\_outv}(\mathsf{id}[z := \mathsf{v}_1], ch_2, \mathsf{v}_1 + 1, \{\mathsf{d}_2 \Rightarrow R_2[z := \mathsf{v}_1]\})\}) \end{aligned}$$

According to the rule for synchronization of two recursion assertions, we can derive

$$\mathsf{sync}(\{ch_1, ch_2\}, P_1, P_2)(s_0) \Longrightarrow_a \mathsf{Rec}\ R.\ \mathsf{init} \bar{\vee} R[z := s_0(x)][y := s_0(x) + 1](s_0)$$

As indicated by the final specification, the internal communications over the common channel set $\{ch_1, ch_2\}$ are hidden and unobservable. The effect of the parallel composition of c_1 and c_2 is to repeatedly assign z the value of x and assign y the value of $x + 1$ to their joint state s_0, iterated any number of times.

6 Property Verification

Till now, we have introduced the inference rules to generate the assertion Q satisfying $\mathsf{spec\_of}(pc, Q)$, for either sequential or parallel processes pc. As defined by the semantics of assertions in Sect. 3, Q captures the trace execution history of pc

over time up to the termination of pc. However, deriving the properties of process pc (related to variables) during execution directly from assertion Q is far from intuitive. In this section, we present how to verify properties of a process in a fixed form of $(s, tr) \models Post \triangleq q_1(s) \wedge \mathsf{trl}(tr, q_2)$ where s and tr represent the final state and trace at termination, q_1 and q_2 are boolean expressions on state, and

$$\mathsf{trl}(tr, q) \triangleq \forall i.\, tr[i] = \langle d, \overrightarrow{p}, rdy\rangle \longrightarrow (\forall t \in [0, d].\, q(\overrightarrow{p}(t)))$$

Intuitively speaking, $Post$ holds for final state s and trace tr, iff q_1 holds for the final state s, and q_2 holds for each continuous state in tr, i.e. it holds almost everywhere during the whole execution of pc (except for some discrete events). In the following, we will call q_1 and q_2 postcondition and trace invariant respectively. Together with the definition of specification, we conclude the following inference rule:

$$\frac{\forall\, s_0\, s\, tr.\, p(s_0) \longrightarrow (s_0, s, tr) \models Q \longrightarrow (s, tr) \models Post \quad \mathsf{spec\_of}(pc, Q)}{\{Pre\}\, pc\, \{Post\}}$$

where $(s, tr) \models Pre \triangleq p(s) \wedge tr = \epsilon$ which represents that the process pc starts from an initial state satisfying precondition p and an empty trace. Next, we present how to derive the first antecedent of the above rule for different forms of assertions. We only consider closed processes pc for which all communications are internal, thus no communications are contained in Q any more as all internal communications are reduced during synchronization, as shown in rule InOut1.

For the init assertion, we have:

$$\frac{\forall s.\, p(s) \longrightarrow q_1(s)}{p(s_0) \longrightarrow (s_0, s, tr) \models \mathsf{init} \longrightarrow q_1(s) \wedge \mathsf{trl}(tr, q_2)}$$

since $\mathsf{init}(s_0, s, tr)$ implies $s = s_0$ and $tr = \epsilon$.

For the wait assertion, we have

$$\frac{\begin{array}{c} p(s_0) \wedge s_0(e) > 0 \wedge t \geq 0 \wedge t \leq s_0(e) \longrightarrow (s_0, t, s) \models I \longrightarrow q_2(s) \\ p(s_0) \wedge s_0(e) > 0 \longrightarrow (s_0, s, tr) \models P|_{\mathsf{d}=s_0(e)} \longrightarrow q_1(s) \wedge \mathsf{trl}(tr, q_2) \\ p(s_0) \wedge s_0(e) \leq 0 \longrightarrow (s_0, s, tr) \models P|_{\mathsf{d}=0} \longrightarrow q_1(s) \wedge \mathsf{trl}(tr, q_2) \end{array}}{p(s_0) \longrightarrow (s_0, s, tr) \models \mathsf{wait}(I, e, \{\mathsf{d} \Rightarrow P\}) \longrightarrow q_1(s) \wedge \mathsf{trl}(tr, q_2)}$$

where the wait time is evaluated (either positive or not) to determine the remaining part and check the trace invariant from the path condition.

For pure assertion, we have:

$$\frac{p(s_0) \wedge b(s_0) \longrightarrow (s_0, s, tr) \models Q \longrightarrow (s, tr) \models Post}{p(s_0) \longrightarrow (s_0, s, tr) \models (\uparrow b \bar{\wedge} Q) \longrightarrow (s, tr) \models Post}$$

For substitution, we have:

$$\frac{\forall s_0\, s\, tr.\, (\exists v.\, p[v/x] \wedge x = e[v/x])(s_0) \longrightarrow (s_0, s, tr) \models Q \longrightarrow (s, tr) \models Post}{p(s_0) \longrightarrow (s_0, s, tr) \models Q[x := e] \longrightarrow (s, tr) \models Post}$$

As shown in this rule, we change the initial state from s_0 to $s_0[x \mapsto e]$, thus the precondition p needs to be rewritten on the new state while maintaining the equivalence.

For disjunction, we have:

$$\frac{\begin{array}{c} p(s_0) \longrightarrow (s_0, s, tr) \models Q_1 \longrightarrow (s, tr) \models Post \\ p(s_0) \longrightarrow (s_0, s, tr) \models Q_2 \longrightarrow (s, tr) \models Post \end{array}}{p(s_0) \longrightarrow (s_0, s, tr) \models Q_1 \bar{\vee} Q_2 \longrightarrow (s, tr) \models Post}$$

For recursion assertion, we have:

$$\frac{\begin{array}{c} \forall s.\, p(s) \longrightarrow loop(s) \\ \forall s_0\, s\, tr.\, loop(s_0) \longrightarrow (s_0, s, tr) \models P \longrightarrow (s, tr) \models Post \\ \forall Q\, s_0\, s\, tr.\, (\forall s_0\, s\, tr.\, loop(s_0) \longrightarrow (s_0, s, tr) \models Q \longrightarrow (s, tr) \models Post) \\ \longrightarrow loop(s_0) \longrightarrow (s_0, s, tr) \models F(Q) \longrightarrow (s, tr) \models Post \end{array}}{p(s_0) \longrightarrow (s_0, s, tr) \models (\mathsf{Rec}\ R.\ P \bar{\vee} F(R)) \longrightarrow (s, tr) \models Post}$$

In this rule we need to provide a loop invariant $loop$ and prove three conditions for $loop$ to be an invariant. The first two conditions states the precondition implies the loop invariant and the base assertion P implies postcondition under the invariant. The intuitive meaning of the last one is that, for any assertion Q, $F(Q)$ satisfying property $Post$ under loop invariant $loop$ can be deduced from that Q satisfying property $Post$ under $loop$. From this condition, we can extend the property to the general recursion $\mathsf{Rec}\ R.\ P \bar{\vee} F(R)$. Since once loop means once F applied to the assertion P, if we can prove $F(Q)$ satisfying the property $Post$ from any Q have already meets it, then we can extend to $F^n(P)$ for any nature number n of the loop times.

We demonstrate the usage of these rules by the following example involving delay and loop.

Example 3.

$$c \triangleq (\mathsf{wait}\ 1; x := x + 1)^*$$

For process c, it's easy to find that if the initial state s_0 satisfies $x = 1$, then $x > 0$ will hold for the final state at termination and also for each continuous state during the execution. This property can be described in Hoare triples as:

$$\{p(s) \wedge tr = \epsilon\}\, c\, \{q_1(s) \wedge \mathsf{trl}(tr, q_2)\}$$

where we define $p \triangleq x = 1$, $q_1 \triangleq x > 0$ and $q_2 \triangleq x > 0$. To prove this triple, we apply the main inference rule resulting in two premises.

$$\mathsf{spec\_of}(c, \mathsf{Rec}\ R.\ \mathsf{init} \bar{\vee} \mathsf{wait}(\mathsf{id}, 1, \{\mathsf{d} \Rightarrow R[x := x + 1]\}))$$

which can be derived by the sequential inference rules in Sect. 4, and

$$p(s_0) \longrightarrow (s_0, s, tr) \models (\mathsf{Rec}\ R.\ \mathsf{init} \bar{\vee} \mathsf{wait}(\mathsf{id}, 1, \{\mathsf{d} \Rightarrow R[x := x{+}1]\})) \longrightarrow q_1(s) \wedge \mathsf{trl}(tr, q_2)$$

which can be derived by rules in this section according to the structures of assertions by providing the loop invariant $loop \triangleq x > 0$. The detailed proof can be seen in the complement document.

7 Implementation and Case Study

In this section, we present the implementation of HHLPar and demonstrate its application through a case study. We formalize the underlying logic and establish its soundness using Isabelle/HOL, thereby ensuring the correctness of the proof system. In addition to providing a correctness guarantee for the HHL logic, the Isabelle implementation also enables the interactive verification of HCSP by applying the appropriate inference rules. HHLPar is built on this logic and aims to enhance the automation of proof procedures.

Algorithm 1. Main algorithm of HHLPar

Input: precondition p, HCSP process pc, postcondition q_1, trace invariant q_2, additional: ode invariants ode_inv, loop invariants $loop\_inv$
Output: Success/Fail

1: **function** ASSERTION(pc, ode_inv)
2:     **if** $pc = pc_1 \|_{chs} pc_2$ **then**
3:         $P_1 \leftarrow$ ASSERTION(pc_1, ode_inv)
4:         $P_2 \leftarrow$ ASSERTION(pc_2, ode_inv)
5:         **return** PARSYN(chs, P_1, P_2)
6:     **else**
7:         **return** SEQGEN(pc, ode_inv)
8:     **end if**
9: **end function**
10: $P \leftarrow$ ASSERTION(pc, ode_inv)
11: **if** PROVER($P, p, q_1, q_2, loop\_inv$) **then**
12:     **return** Success
13: **else**
14:     **return** Fail
15: **end if**

7.1 HHLPar in Python

We introduce HHLPar from two aspects: the overall structure, and the main implementation issues in Python.

HHLPar in a Nutshell The main algorithm of the HHLPar tool is illustrated in Algorithm 1. The tool accepts as input: a precondition, a HCSP process to be verified, a postcondition and a trace invariant, as well as additional invariants for ODEs and loops, if they are present. The verification process is carried out through three main steps: Sequential Generation, Parallel Synchronization, and Property Verification. The first step processes the sequential components of pc and generates their assertions, and then the second step generates the assertion of pc through synchronization of sequential ones. After these two steps, an assertion Q satisfying spec_of(pc, Q) will be obtained. The last step verifies whether postcondition and trace invariant hold for given precondition, with a result returned.

Implementation in Python. HHLPar implement the following three functionalities in the algorithm.

Sequential Generation. We implemented the function for generating assertions of sequential HCSP satisfying the specification. When dealing with ODEs, if the differential invariants are not provided, this function will invoke the Wolfram Engine to compute solutions in symbolic form and compute the maximum waiting time based on constraint. For the sake of expressiveness and convenience, we choose to create a fresh time variable representing the length of this duration and record the constraints of this time variable in a boolean expression. For example, $\langle \dot{x} = 1 \& x < 5 \rangle$ corresponds to $\uparrow (t_1 = 5 - x) \bar{\wedge} \mathsf{wait}(x \rightarrowtail x + t, t_1, \{\mathsf{d} \Rightarrow \mathsf{init}[x := x + \mathsf{d}]\})$. If differential invariants are provided, this function will check whether the invariants are correct.

Parallel Synchronization. We implemented the synchronization function which accepting two assertions and the communication channel set and then producing the parallel assertion. Note that variables in different processes are independent and cannot be shared in HCSP. Consequently, when same variable names occur in parallel processes and subsequently in their specifications, we consider them different. Therefore, before synchronization of assertions, we assign process names to different parallel processes and their corresponding assertions in the implementation.

Property Verification. We implemented the verifying function which takes an assertion (the result of the previous steps), three boolean expressions representing the precondition on the initial state s_0, the postcondition on the final state s and the trace invariant on the trace tr separately and additional loop invariants as inputs. When applying the rules, the expression on initial state s_0 will be constantly updated. When the assertion is a recursion, we need to prove that the loop invariant is maintained over each loop iteration. This function will invoke the Wolfram Engine to check all the logical formulas in premises. If all of them are valid, the algorithm will stop successfully, indicating that this property is indeed satisfied with respect to the assertion and precondition, and in consequence it holds for the process being verified with the given Hoare triples.

7.2 Case Study

We experimented with a series of examples to test HHLPar across various situations. In this section, we illustrate its ability to handle simple branches in bulk through one case study, demonstrating how HHLPar can effectively verify processes involving ODEs, interrupts, communications, repetition and parallel composition involved.

The simplified case study of a cruise control system (CCS) is taken from [23], for which the verification was performed via interactive theorem proving. Compared to [24], we have implemented the algorithm for assertions to prove final properties of the process, and the whole procedure of verification is automated. The model of the CCS comprises two parts: a controller (Control) and a physical plant (Plant). The Plant process models the vehicle's movement, continuously evolving along a given ODE. The evolution is periodically interrupted by the transmission of velocity v and position p to the Control, followed by the reception of updated acceleration a.

$$Plant \triangleq ch1!v; ch2!p; (ch3?a; \langle \dot{p} = v, \dot{v} = a \& \mathsf{true} \propto \mathsf{skip}\rangle \trianglerighteq [][ch1!v \rightarrow ch2!p])^*$$

The Control process computes and sends the appropriate vehicle acceleration, determined by the received velocity and position, with respect to a period T.

$$\begin{aligned}
Control \triangleq\ & ch1?v; ch2?p; (pp := p + v \cdot T + \tfrac{1}{2} \cdot da \cdot T^2; vv := v + da \cdot T;\\
& (\text{if } 2 \cdot am \cdot (op - pp) \geq vm^2 \text{ then } vlm := vm^2 \text{ else}\\
& \quad \text{if } op - pp > 0 \text{ then } vlm := 2 \cdot am \cdot (op - pp) \text{ else } vlm := 0);\\
& (\text{if } vv \leq 0 \| vv^2 \leq vlm \text{ then } a := da \text{ else } (pp := p + v \cdot T;\\
& \quad (\text{if } 2 \cdot am \cdot (op - pp) \geq vm^2 \text{ then } vlm := vm^2 \text{ else}\\
& \quad\quad \text{if } op - pp > 0 \text{ then } vlm := 2 \cdot am \cdot (op - pp) \text{ else } vlm := 0);\\
& \quad \text{if } v \leq 0 \| v^2 \leq vlm \text{ then } a := 0 \text{ else } a := -am));\\
& ch3!a; \text{wait } T; ch1?v; ch2?p)^*
\end{aligned}$$

where constants T, op, ad, am represent the time period, the position of obstacle, the fixed acceleration during speeding up and deceleration separately, and the variable vlm is the upper limit of velocity based on the concept of Maximum Protection Curve.

In this case, the parallel process $Plant\|_{ch1,ch2,ch3}Control$ is provided to the tool HHLPar. The tool automatically gives *Plant* (and *Control*) and all the variables appearing in them a prefix name A (and B) and the loop invariant inv are provided below:

$$\begin{gathered}
BT > 0 \wedge Bam > 0 \wedge Bda > 0 \wedge Bvm > 0 \wedge Ap \leq Bop \wedge Av = Bv \wedge Ap = Bp\\
\wedge ((2 \cdot Bam \cdot (Bop - Ap) \geq Bvm^2 \wedge Av \leq Bvm) \vee\\
(2 \cdot Bam \cdot (Bop - Ap) < Bvm^2 \wedge (Av \leq 0 \vee Av^2 \leq 2 \cdot Bam \cdot (Bop - Ap))))
\end{gathered}$$

under the following provided precondition, denoted by *Init*:

$$\begin{gathered}
BT > 0 \wedge Bam > 0 \wedge Bda > 0 \wedge Bvm > 0 \wedge Ap \leq Bop\\
\wedge ((2 \cdot Bam \cdot (Bop - Ap) \geq Bvm^2 \wedge Av \leq Bvm) \vee\\
(2 \cdot Bam \cdot (Bop - Ap) < Bvm^2 \wedge (Av \leq 0 \vee Av^2 \leq 2 \cdot Bam \cdot (Bop - Ap))))
\end{gathered}$$

indicating the requirements on constants and that the initial position does not exceed the obstacle and the initial velocity is within the MPC, and $Ap \leq Bop$ provided as both the postcondition and trace invariant, denoted by *Safe*, HHLPar finally returns "pass". This indicates that the following specification is proved:

$$\{Init(s) \wedge tr = \epsilon\}\ Plant\|_{ch1,ch2,ch3}Control\ \{Safe(s) \wedge \mathsf{trl}(tr, Safe)\}$$

8 Conclusion

We presented HHLPar, an automated theorem prover for verifying parallel HCSP processes, which cover basic ingredients of hybrid and cyber-physical systems including discrete control, continuous dynamics, communication, interrupts and parallel composition. HHLPar implements a Hybrid Hoare Logic, that is composed of a set of inference rules for reasoning about sequential HCSP processes and a set of inference rules for reasoning about parallel HCSP processes, with the help of specialized assertions and their synchronization. HHLPar provides both guarantee to soundness from the formalization of the logic in Isabelle/HOL and automation via symbolically decomposing and executing HCSP processes according to the logic and the integration with external solvers to handle differential equations and real arithmetic properties. In the future, we will consider to develop more efficient rules for reasoning about ODEs and loops in HHLPar and also apply HHLPar to a wider range of practical case studies.

Acknowledgements. This work was supported by the National Key R&D Program of China under grant No. 2022YFA1005101 and No. 2022YFA1005103, the Natural Science Foundation of China (NSFC) under grants No. 62432005, No. 62032024, and No. 62192732.

References

1. Alur, R., Courcoubetis, C., Henzinger, T.A., Ho, P.-H.: Hybrid automata: an algorithmic approach to the specification and verification of hybrid systems. In: Grossman, R.L., Nerode, A., Ravn, A.P., Rischel, H. (eds.) HS 1991-1992. LNCS, vol. 736, pp. 209–229. Springer, Heidelberg (1993). https://doi.org/10.1007/3-540-57318-6_30
2. Bohrer, R., Rahli, V., Vukotic, I., Völp, M., Platzer, A.: Formally verified differential dynamic logic. In: Proceedings of the 6th ACM SIGPLAN Conference on Certified Programs and Proofs, pp. 208–221 (2017)
3. Bohrer, R., Rahli, V., Vukotic, I., Völp, M., Platzer, A.: Formally verified differential dynamic logic. In: Proceedings of the 6th ACM SIGPLAN Conference on Certified Programs and Proofs, CPP 2017, Paris, France, 16–17 January 2017, pp. 208–221. ACM (2017)
4. Foster, S., Huerta y Munive, J.J., Gleirscher, M., Struth, G.: Hybrid systems verification with Isabelle/HOL: simpler syntax, better models, faster proofs. In: Huisman, M., Păsăreanu, C., Zhan, N. (eds.) FM 2021. LNCS, vol. 13047, pp. 367–386. Springer, Cham (2021). https://doi.org/10.1007/978-3-030-90870-6_20
5. Frehse, G.: PHAVer: algorithmic verification of hybrid systems past HyTech. Int. J. Softw. Tools Technol. Transf. **10**(3), 263–279 (2008)
6. Frehse, G.: SpaceEx: scalable verification of hybrid systems. In: Gopalakrishnan, G., Qadeer, S. (eds.) CAV 2011. LNCS, vol. 6806, pp. 379–395. Springer, Heidelberg (2011). https://doi.org/10.1007/978-3-642-22110-1_30
7. Fulton, N., Mitsch, S., Quesel, J.-D., Völp, M., Platzer, A.: KeYmaera X: an axiomatic tactical theorem prover for hybrid systems. In: Felty, A.P., Middeldorp, A. (eds.) CADE 2015. LNCS (LNAI), vol. 9195, pp. 527–538. Springer, Cham (2015). https://doi.org/10.1007/978-3-319-21401-6_36
8. He, J.: From CSP to hybrid systems. In: A Classical Mind, pp. 171–189. Prentice Hall International (UK) Ltd. (1994)
9. Hoare, C.A.R.: Communicating Sequential Processes. Prentice-Hall (1985)
10. Liu, J., Lv, J., Quan, Z., Zhan, N., Zhao, H., Zhou, C., Zou, L.: A calculus for hybrid CSP. In: Ueda, K. (ed.) APLAS 2010. LNCS, vol. 6461, pp. 1–15. Springer, Heidelberg (2010). https://doi.org/10.1007/978-3-642-17164-2_1
11. Liu, J., Zhan, N., Zhao, H.: Computing semi-algebraic invariants for polynomial dynamical systems. In: EMSOFT'11, pp. 97–106. ACM (2011)

12. Platzer, A.: Differential dynamic logic for hybrid systems. J. Autom. Reason. **41**(2), 143–189 (2008)
13. Platzer, A.: Logical Analysis of Hybrid Systems. Springer, Heidelberg (2010). https://doi.org/10.1007/978-3-642-14509-4
14. Platzer, A.: A complete uniform substitution calculus for differential dynamic logic. J. Autom. Reason. **59**(2), 219–265 (2017)
15. Platzer, A.: Logical Foundations of Cyber-Physical Systems. Springer, Cham (2018). https://doi.org/10.1007/978-3-319-63588-0
16. Platzer, A., Clarke, E.M.: Computing differential invariants of hybrid systems as fixedpoints. In: CAV'08, LNCS, vol. 5123, pp. 176–189 (2008)
17. Platzer, A., Quesel, J.-D.: KeYmaera: a hybrid theorem prover for hybrid systems (system description). In: Armando, A., Baumgartner, P., Dowek, G. (eds.) IJCAR 2008. LNCS (LNAI), vol. 5195, pp. 171–178. Springer, Heidelberg (2008). https://doi.org/10.1007/978-3-540-71070-7_15
18. Platzer, A., Tan, Y.K.: Differential equation invariance axiomatization. J. ACM **67**(1), 6:1–6:66 (2020)
19. Ratschan, S., She, Z.: Safety verification of hybrid systems by constraint propagation-based abstraction refinement. ACM Trans. Embed. Comput. Syst. **6**(1), 8 (2007)
20. Sheng, H., Bentkamp, A., Zhan, B.: HHLPy: practical verification of hybrid systems using Hoare Logic. In: FM 2023. LNCS, vol. 14000, pp. 160–178. Springer, Cham (2023). https://doi.org/10.1007/978-3-031-27481-7_11
21. Wang, S., Zhan, N., Guelev, D.: an assume/guarantee based compositional calculus for hybrid CSP. In: Agrawal, M., Cooper, S.B., Li, A. (eds.) TAMC 2012. LNCS, vol. 7287, pp. 72–83. Springer, Heidelberg (2012). https://doi.org/10.1007/978-3-642-29952-0_13
22. Wang, S., Zhan, N., Zou, L.: An improved HHL prover: an interactive theorem prover for hybrid systems. In: Butler, M., Conchon, S., Zaïdi, F. (eds.) ICFEM 2015. LNCS, vol. 9407, pp. 382–399. Springer, Cham (2015). https://doi.org/10.1007/978-3-319-25423-4_25
23. Xu, X., Wang, S., Zhan, B., Jin, X., Talpin, J.-P., Zhan, N.: Unified graphical co-modeling, analysis and verification of cyber-physical systems by combining AADL and Simulink/Stateflow. Theor. Comput. Sci. **903**, 1–25 (2022)
24. Xu, X., et al.: Case Study: Modeling, Simulation, Verification, and Code Generation of an Automatic Cruise Control System, pp. 226–246. Springer, Cham (2024). https://doi.org/10.1007/978-3-031-66673-5_12
25. Huerta y Munive, J.J., Foster, S., Gleirscher, M., et al.: IsaVODEs: interactive verification of cyber-physical systems at scale. J. Autom. Reason. **68**(4), 21 (2024)
26. Zhan, N., Jin, X., Zhan, B., Wang, S., Guelev, D.P.: A generalized hybrid Hoare logic. CoRR, abs/2303.15020 (2023)
27. Chaochen, Z., Ji, W., Ravn, A.P.: A formal description of hybrid systems. In: Alur, R., Henzinger, T.A., Sontag, E.D. (eds.) HS 1995. LNCS, vol. 1066, pp. 511–530. Springer, Heidelberg (1996). https://doi.org/10.1007/BFb0020972

Separation Logic with Heap Variables: A Decision Procedure and Its Application

Xie Li[1,2(✉)], Yutian Zhu[1,2], Taolue Chen[3], Fu Song[1,2], and Zhilin Wu[1,2]

[1] State Key Laboratory of Computer Science, Institute of Software, Chinese Academy of Sciences, Beijing, China
{lixie19,zhuyt,songfu,wuzl}@ios.ac.cn
[2] University of Chinese Academy of Sciences, Beijing, China
[3] Birkbeck, University of London, London, UK
t.chen@bbk.ac.uk

Abstract. We propose Separation Logic with Heap Variables (SLHV), an extension of separation logic which introduces explicit heap variables in conjunction with separating conjunction and classical Boolean operations. We provide a decision procedure for the satisfiability of SLHV by reducing to the satisfiability of quantifier-free linear integer arithmetic. We implement a prototype solver for SLHV based on Z3, which, together with the encoding of heap-manipulating C programs as SLHV formulas, gives rise to a new bounded model checker for heap-manipulating C programs. The experimental results show the efficacy of our approach.

1 Introduction

Heap-manipulating programs are prevailing in computer software, but are notoriously difficult to guarantee their correctness. Separation Logic (SL [1,2]) has been the *de facto* logic for reasoning about heaps in the past two decades. One of the motivations of the current work is to apply software (bounded and unbounded) model checking to heap-manipulating program verification. Consider a heap-manipulating C program (Listing 1.1), which is slightly adapted from a program in the `memsafety` folder of SV-COMP 2024 [3]. It first allocates a block of memory pointed to by the pointer `x` of type `R` (Line 4), updates its field a (Line 5), then deallocates the memory (Line 6). Next, it allocates a new block of memory pointed to by the pointer `y` of type `R` (Line 7), and finally deallocates this memory again (Lines 8–9). Note that `y` is freed twice if `x` and `y` are equal.

```
1  typedef struct R {int a; int b;} R;
2  void main() {
3    R* x = NULL; R* y = NULL;
4    x = malloc(sizeof(R));
5    x->a = 10;
6    free(x);
7    y = malloc(sizeof(R));
8    if (x == y) {free(y)};
9    free(y);
10 }
```

Listing 1.1. A heap-manipulating C program P

A. Goharshady and C. Haase (Eds.): SETTA 2025, LNCS 16458, pp. 134–153, 2026.
https://doi.org/10.1007/978-981-95-7826-9_8

To apply model checking, we need to specify the evolution of memory states before and after each statement. Take `x = malloc(sizeof(R))` as an example. We introduce a heap variable $\mathfrak{h}$ to specify the (already allocated) memory cells, an auxiliary heap variable $\mathfrak{s}$ to store the memory size owned by each pointer, and a program variable x, where both $\mathfrak{h}$ and $\mathfrak{s}$ are partial functions. Their respective "primed" versions $\mathfrak{h}'$, $\mathfrak{s}'$ and x' are also introduced to specify their values after the execution of the statement. In particular, when the memory is allocated, we set $\mathfrak{s}(x) = 2$ (as R declared at Line 1 contains two integer fields); when the memory is deallocated, x becomes undefined in $\mathfrak{s}'$, indicating that the memory pointed to by x is freed. The readers may expect a formula

$$\exists \mathfrak{h}_1.\exists z.\exists d_1.\exists d_2.\ \mathfrak{h}' = \mathfrak{h} \uplus \mathfrak{h}_1 \wedge \mathfrak{h}_1 = z \mapsto d_1 \uplus z+1 \mapsto d_2 \wedge \mathfrak{s}' = \mathfrak{s} \uplus z \mapsto 2 \wedge x' = z$$

where the heap constraint $\mathfrak{h}_1 = z \mapsto d_1 \uplus z+1 \mapsto d_2$ stands for a memory block of length 2 starting from the location z and ending at $z+1$, and the points-to heap term $z \mapsto 2$ means that the size of the block allocated for z is 2; moreover, $\uplus$ is the disjoint union connector (a.k.a., separating conjunction in SL).

In general, model checking heap-manipulating programs requires encoding the transition relation of the program states as a logic formula, and then deciding the satisfiability of the resulting formula. An observation is that the current SL does not fit this purpose, mostly because it has no explicit reference to heap variables/states, which would be necessary to express how the heap evolves when moving from one state to another.

To remedy this, we propose *Separation Logic with Heap Variables* (SLHV) where explicit heap variables (e.g., $\mathfrak{h}, \mathfrak{h}', \mathfrak{s}, \mathfrak{s}'$ in the above example) are introduced, enabling a convenient means to describe the relationship between heaps before and after executing a statement. Furthermore, inherited from separation logic, SLHV retains the separating conjunction which can specify the shape of heaps. We show that SLHV is expressive enough to capture both the SL [1,2] and the theory of arrays [4] that has been widely-used for verification [5–8].

However, logic solely is insufficient to support software model checking. With the introduction of SLHV, a decision procedure for its satisfiability problem is indispensable. This is challenging as SLHV admits classical Boolean operators, second-order heap variables, in addition to separating conjunction. In this paper, we propose a decision procedure based on a characterization of an SLHV formula being satisfiable. In particular, we formulate constraints over the heap terms of a given SLHV formula. We then show that these constraints can be encoded in (quantifier-free) linear integer arithmetic (LIA), the satisfiability of which is well-known in NP. These together yield an NP decision procedure for checking satisfiability of SLHV, and more importantly, pave a way for an efficient tool, as LIA has been integrated into SMT solvers. This result confirms that SLHV achieves a dedicate balance between expressiveness and practical tractability, which is crucial for model checking of heap-manipulating programs.

To demonstrate the potential of SLHV, we consider bounded model checking (BMC for short) of C programs but focus on heap manipulating operations such as `malloc` and `free` (which means that mostly we only consider the `int` type).

SLHV integrates heap variables, separating conjunction, and classical Boolean operators into a unified logical framework, thus enables to encode the transition relation of a heap-manipulating C program naturally as a logic formula. This leads to a more principled, connaturally neater and potentially more efficient approach for BMC of heap-manipulating C programs than the previous ones.

As a proof of concept, we implement a solver Z3-SLHV for the satisfiability of SLHV based on Z3 [9]. To demonstrate the potential of SLHV for program verification, we also develop a prototype bounded model checker SELO for heap-manipulating C programs, by adapting the bounded model checker ESBMC [10], where Z3-SLHV is harnessed for solving verification conditions.

We evaluate Z3-SLHV and SELO using a collection of 20 BMC problem instances (each of which comprises one C program and one memory safety property), derived from the `memsafety` folder of SV-COMP 2024. The experimental results show the effectiveness of our approach and shed insight on the performance of the decision procedure. In particular, Z3-SLHV solves all the 229 SLHV formulas generated from the 20 BMC instances (note that ESBMC may generate multiple formulas from one BMC instance), where the solving time ranges over 0.01–24.46 s (average 0.87 s). Moreover, SELO can verify all the 20 BMC instances with largely comparable time as ESBMC.

Structure. Section 3 gives the decision procedure for satisfiability of SLHV without block predicates. Section 3 gives the decision procedure for satisfiability of SLHV. Section 4 shows the encoding of heap-manipulating programs. Section 5 reports the results for bounded model checking, including the implementation and evaluation. Section 6 discusses the related work and Sect. 7 concludes the paper. The source code of Z3-SLHV and SELO and all the benchmarks can be found at https://anonymous.4open.science/r/SLHV.

2 Separation Logic with Heap Variables (SLHV)

Let $\mathbb{N}$ (resp. $\mathbb{Z}$) be the set of natural numbers (resp. integers). For $m, n \in \mathbb{N}$ with $m < n$, $[m, n)$ denotes the set $\{m, \ldots, n-1\}$ and $[n]$ denotes $\{1, \ldots, n\}$.

Intuitively, a *heap* gives a mapping table, each entry of which maps a location to a location/value. For simplicity, we assume that the locations are encoded by natural numbers with 0 reserved for the special location null, and the values are from $\mathbb{Z}$. Formally, a *heap* is a partial function $h : \mathbb{N} \rightharpoonup \mathbb{Z}$ such that the domain of h, denoted by $\mathrm{dom}(h)$, is finite. Let $\mathbb{H}$ denote the set of heaps, which is typically ranged over by $h, h', h_1, \ldots$. Moreover, $h_\varnothing \in \mathbb{H}$ denotes the heap with $\mathrm{dom}(h_\varnothing) = \varnothing$. To define SLHV, we introduce a set $\mathcal{I}$ of *integer variables* ranged over by $x, x_1, \ldots$ and a set $\mathcal{H}$ of *heap variables* ranged over by $\mathfrak{h}, \mathfrak{h}_1, \ldots$.

Syntax. The syntax of SLHV is defined as follows:

$$
\begin{array}{llr}
it & ::= x \mid n \mid it + it \mid it - it \mid n \cdot it & \text{(integer terms)}\\
ht & ::= \mathtt{emp} \mid \mathfrak{h} \mid it \mapsto it \mid ht \uplus ht & \text{(heap terms)}\\
\varphi_a & ::= it \lhd it \mid ht \bowtie ht & \text{(atomic formulas)}\\
\varphi & ::= \varphi_a \mid \exists x.\varphi \mid \exists \mathfrak{h}.\varphi \mid \varphi \wedge \varphi \mid \varphi \vee \varphi & \text{(formulas)}
\end{array}
$$

where $n \in \mathbb{Z}$, $\lhd \in \{=, \neq, \leqslant, <\}$, and $\bowtie \in \{=, \neq\}$.

In particular, $it_1 \mapsto it_2$ is referred to as a *points-to heap term* (which intuitively is an entry of the heap as a mapping table). Moreover, atomic formulas of the form $ht_1 = ht_2$ and $ht_1 \neq ht_2$ are referred to as *heap equalities* and *heap inequalities*; those of the form $it_1 \lhd it_2$ are referred to as *pure constraints*. Points-to heap terms and heap variables are called *atomic heap terms*.

Note that SLHV only allows *existential* quantifiers and formulas in the positive normal form (i.e., negation is excluded), in light of a trade-off between expressiveness (in particular, our application) and decidability/complexity.

For convenience, we introduce the following syntactic sugar:

$$x \in ht \stackrel{\text{def}}{=} \exists \mathfrak{h}.\exists y.\ ht = \mathfrak{h} \uplus x \mapsto y \text{ and } x \notin ht \stackrel{\text{def}}{=} x \leqslant 0 \vee \exists \mathfrak{h}.\exists y.\ \mathfrak{h} = ht \uplus x \mapsto y.$$

For an SLHV formula φ, let $\mathsf{IVars}(\varphi)$ and $\mathsf{HVars}(\varphi)$ denote the set of all the integer variables and heap variables occurring in φ, respectively.

Semantics. A *store* $\rho : \mathsf{IVars}(\varphi) \to \mathbb{Z} \uplus \mathsf{HVars}(\varphi) \to \mathbb{H}$ is a function that assigns integers (resp. heaps) to integer (resp. heap) variables. An SLHV formula φ is interpreted over a store ρ. First of all, the interpretation $[\![\cdot]\!]_\rho$ of terms w.r.t. a store ρ is defined as follows, where $\perp$ denotes the undefined function.

- $[\![x]\!]_\rho = \rho(x)$, $[\![n]\!]_\rho = n$, $[\![it_1 \pm it_2]\!]_\rho = [\![it_1]\!]_\rho \pm [\![it_2]\!]_\rho$, $[\![n \cdot it]\!]_\rho = n \cdot [\![it]\!]_\rho$.
- $[\![\mathfrak{h}]\!]_\rho = \rho(\mathfrak{h})$, $[\![\mathtt{emp}]\!]_\rho = h_\varnothing$.
- $[\![it_1 \mapsto it_2]\!]_\rho = \begin{cases} h, \text{ if } [\![it_1]\!]_\rho > 0 \text{ where } \mathrm{dom}(h) = \{[\![it_1]\!]_\rho\}, h([\![it_1]\!]_\rho) = [\![it_2]\!]_\rho \\ \perp, \text{ otherwise.} \end{cases}$
- $[\![ht_1 \uplus ht_2]\!]_\rho = \begin{cases} [\![ht_1]\!]_\rho \cup [\![ht_2]\!]_\rho, & \text{if } \mathrm{dom}([\![ht_1]\!]_\rho) \cap \mathrm{dom}([\![ht_2]\!]_\rho) = \varnothing, \\ \perp, & \text{otherwise.} \end{cases}$

The semantics of SLHV is then defined as the satisfaction relation $\rho \models \varphi$.

- $\rho \models it_1 \lhd it_2$ if $[\![it_1]\!]_\rho \lhd [\![it_2]\!]_\rho$; $\rho \models ht_1 = ht_2$ if $[\![ht_1]\!]_\rho = [\![ht_2]\!]_\rho \neq \perp$;
- $\rho \models ht_1 \neq ht_2$ if $\perp \neq [\![ht_1]\!]_\rho \neq [\![ht_2]\!]_\rho \neq \perp$;
- $\rho \models \exists x.\varphi$ if there exists an integer $n \in \mathbb{Z}$ such that $\rho[n/x] \models \varphi$;
- $\rho \models \exists \mathfrak{h}.\varphi$ if there exists a heap $h \in \mathbb{H}$ such that $\rho[h/\mathfrak{h}] \models \varphi$;
- $\rho \models \varphi_1 \wedge \varphi_2$ if $\rho \models \varphi_1$ and $\rho \models \varphi_2$; $\rho \models \varphi_1 \vee \varphi_2$ if $\rho \models \varphi_1$ or $\rho \models \varphi_2$.

Since the disjoint union $\uplus$ is associative and commutative, all heap terms ht can be flattened into the form of $\mathfrak{h}_1 \uplus \ldots \uplus \mathfrak{h}_k \uplus it_1 \mapsto it'_2 \uplus \ldots \uplus it_l \mapsto it'_l$. For two heap terms ht and ht', ht is a sub-term of ht', written as $ht \preceq_{\mathsf{st}} ht'$, if ht' can be rewritten as $ht \uplus ht''$. For instance, $\mathfrak{h}_1 \preceq_{\mathsf{st}} \mathfrak{h}_1 \uplus \mathfrak{h}_2 \uplus \mathfrak{h}_3$ and $\mathfrak{h}_1 \uplus \mathfrak{h}_3 \preceq_{\mathsf{st}} \mathfrak{h}_1 \uplus \mathfrak{h}_2 \uplus \mathfrak{h}_3$.

An SLHV formula is in *normal form*, if it is in the prenex normal form $\exists \sigma_1. \ldots .\exists \sigma_m.\varphi$ and all the heap terms of the form $\mathfrak{h} \uplus \mathtt{emp}$ are reduced to $\mathfrak{h}$.

We also observe that heap inequality $ht_1 \neq ht_2$ can be rewritten as

$$\begin{aligned}\exists x, y_1, y_2, \mathfrak{h}, \mathfrak{h}', \mathfrak{h}_1, \mathfrak{h}_2 . ht_1 = \mathfrak{h}_1 \bigwedge ht_2 = \mathfrak{h}_2 \bigwedge \\ \begin{pmatrix} (x \in ht_1 \wedge x \notin ht_2) \bigvee (x \notin ht_1 \wedge x \in ht_2) \bigvee \\ (ht_1 = \mathfrak{h} \uplus x \mapsto y_1 \wedge ht_2 = \mathfrak{h}' \uplus x \mapsto y_2 \wedge y_1 \neq y_2) \end{pmatrix}\end{aligned}$$

Note that $ht_1 = \mathfrak{h}_1$ is used to enforce the condition $\bot \neq [\![ht_1]\!]_\rho$ in semantics, similarly for $ht_2 = \mathfrak{h}_2$. As a result, in the rest of the paper, we only consider flattened SLHV formulas which are in normal forms and heap-inequality free.

Expressiveness. We show that SLHV is sufficiently expressive to subsume separation logic and capture the satisfiability of theory of arrays.

Separation Logic (SL) [2]. The syntax of SL is defined as follows.

$$\begin{array}{rcll} t & ::= & x \mid n \mid t+t \mid t-t \mid n \cdot t & \text{(location terms)} \\ \Pi & ::= & t \lhd t \mid \Pi \wedge \Pi & \text{(pure formulas)} \\ F & ::= & \texttt{emp} \mid t \mapsto t \mid F * F & \text{(spatial formulas)} \\ \varphi & ::= & \exists \boldsymbol{x}.\ \Pi : F \mid \varphi \vee \varphi & \text{(SL formulas)} \end{array}$$

where $n \in \mathbb{Z}$, and $\lhd \in \{=, \neq, \leqslant, <\}$.

Similar to SLHV, the heap in SL is a finite partial function from locations to values/locations. An SL formula $\exists \boldsymbol{x}.\ \Pi : F$ defines a symbolic heap, where $\boldsymbol{x}$ is the set of involved location variables. The operator $*$ is the separating conjunction. The other terms and formulas are interpreted as usual.

Fix an SL formula $\exists \boldsymbol{x}.\ \Pi : F$. We can translate it into an equisatisfiable SLHV formula $\exists \boldsymbol{x}.\ \exists \boldsymbol{\mathfrak{h}}.\ \Pi \wedge [\![F]\!]$, where $\boldsymbol{\mathfrak{h}}$ is the set of heap variables involved in $[\![F]\!]$ which is inductively defined as follows:

- $[\![\texttt{emp}]\!] \stackrel{\text{def}}{=} \mathfrak{h}_{\texttt{emp}} = \texttt{emp}$, $\quad [\![t_1 \mapsto t_2]\!] \stackrel{\text{def}}{=} \mathfrak{h}_{t_1 \mapsto t_2} = t_1 \mapsto t_2$,
- $[\![F_1 * F_2]\!] \stackrel{\text{def}}{=} \mathfrak{h}_{F_1 * F_2} = \mathfrak{h}_{F_1} \uplus \mathfrak{h}_{F_2} \wedge [\![F_1]\!] \wedge [\![F_2]\!]$.

It is easy to see that the resulting SLHV formula $\exists \boldsymbol{x}.\ \exists \boldsymbol{\mathfrak{h}}.\ \Pi \wedge [\![F]\!]$ is equisatisfiable with the SL formula $\exists \boldsymbol{x}.\ \Pi : F$.

Theory of Arrays [4]. Note that SLHV cannot express that a heap represents continuous memory region. However, we shall show that an equisatisfiable SLHV formula can be constructed in linear time from a formula in theory of arrays. Similar to SLHV, we assume that both the index domain and element domain of arrays are $\mathbb{Z}$ and consider LIA over them. The theory of arrays is defined as:

$$\begin{array}{rll} it & ::= i \mid n \mid it + it \mid it - it \mid n \cdot it & \text{(index terms)} \\ et & ::= x \mid n \mid et + et \mid et - et \mid n \cdot et \mid \texttt{read}(at, it) & \text{(element terms)} \\ at & ::= A \mid \texttt{write}(at, it, et) & \text{(array terms)} \\ \varphi_a & ::= it \lhd it \mid et \lhd et \mid at \bowtie at & \text{(atomic formulas)} \\ \varphi & ::= \varphi_a \mid \exists i.\varphi \mid \exists x.\varphi \mid \exists A.\varphi \mid \varphi \wedge \varphi \mid \varphi \vee \varphi & \text{(formulas)} \end{array}$$

where $n \in \mathbb{Z}$, $\lhd \in \{=, \neq, \leqslant, <\}$, and $\bowtie \in \{=, \neq\}$. Intuitively, $\texttt{read}(at, it)$ returns the it-th element of the array ar; $\texttt{write}(at, it, et)$ returns the array at in which the it-th element is replaced by et. The semantics of the other terms and formulas are defined as usual.

Fix a formula φ in the array theory. Clearly, we can assume that $et_1 \lhd et_2$ is of the form $x \lhd \texttt{read}(A, it)$ or $x \lhd et$ such that et is $\texttt{read}$-free, and $at_1 \bowtie at_2$ is of the form $A_1 \bowtie A_2$ or $A_1 \bowtie \texttt{write}(A_2, it, x)$.

Since this theory does not constrain the domain of array variables, defining an array variable as a partial function does not affect the satisfiability of φ. We use a heap variable $\mathfrak{h}_A$ to represent an array variable A in φ. Moreover, we utilize a bijection $\eta : \mathbb{Z} \to \mathbb{N}$ between indices and locations defined as $\eta(m) = 2m$ if $m \geq 0$ and $-2m - 1$ if $m < 0$. Intuitively, η is used to map a non-negative (resp. negative) index of the array to a positive even (resp. odd) location of the heap. We define $[\![\varphi]\!]$ inductively as follows.

- $[\![it_1 \lhd it_2]\!] \stackrel{\text{def}}{=} it_1 \lhd it_2$; (Note that we cannot use $\eta(it_1) \lhd \eta(it_2)$ here.)
- $[\![x \lhd \texttt{read}(A, it)]\!] \stackrel{\text{def}}{=} \exists \mathfrak{h}', x'.(\mathfrak{h}_A = \mathfrak{h}' \uplus 2 \cdot it \mapsto x' \wedge x \lhd x' \wedge it \geq 0) \vee (\mathfrak{h}_A = \mathfrak{h}' \uplus -2 \cdot it - 1 \mapsto x' \wedge x \lhd x' \wedge it < 0)$, where $\mathfrak{h}'$ is a fresh heap variable and x' is a fresh integer variable;
- $[\![x \lhd et]\!] \stackrel{\text{def}}{=} x \lhd et$, where et is read-free;
- $[\![A_1 \bowtie A_2]\!] \stackrel{\text{def}}{=} \mathfrak{h}_{A_1} \bowtie \mathfrak{h}_{A_2}$;
- $[\![A_1 \bowtie \texttt{write}(A_2, it, x)]\!] \stackrel{\text{def}}{=} \exists \mathfrak{h}', x'.(\mathfrak{h}_{A_2} = \mathfrak{h}' \uplus 2 \cdot it \mapsto x' \wedge \mathfrak{h}_{A_1} \bowtie \mathfrak{h}' \uplus 2 \cdot it \mapsto x \wedge it \geq 0) \vee (\mathfrak{h}_{A_2} = \mathfrak{h}' \uplus -2 \cdot it - 1 \mapsto x' \wedge \mathfrak{h}_{A_1} \bowtie \mathfrak{h}' \uplus -2 \cdot it - 1 \mapsto x \wedge it < 0)$, where $\mathfrak{h}'$ is a fresh heap variable and x' is a fresh integer variable;
- $[\![\exists i.\varphi']\!] \stackrel{\text{def}}{=} \exists i.[\![\varphi']\!]$, $[\![\exists x.\varphi']\!] \stackrel{\text{def}}{=} \exists x.[\![\varphi']\!]$, $[\![\exists A.\varphi']\!] \stackrel{\text{def}}{=} \exists \mathfrak{h}_A.[\![\varphi']\!]$;
- $[\![\varphi_1 \wedge \varphi_2]\!] \stackrel{\text{def}}{=} [\![\varphi_1]\!] \wedge [\![\varphi_2]\!]$, $[\![\varphi_1 \vee \varphi_2]\!] \stackrel{\text{def}}{=} [\![\varphi_1]\!] \vee [\![\varphi_2]\!]$.

It is straightforward to show that the resulting SLHV formula $[\![\varphi]\!]$ is equisatisfiable with the original formula φ in the theory of arrays.

3 Decision Procedure for Satisfiability

Given an SLHV formula φ, the satisfiability problem is to decide whether there is a store ρ such that $\rho \models \varphi$. Our main result is as follows.

Theorem 1. *The satisfiability of* SLHV *is* NP*-complete.*

It is sufficient to show the upper bound, as the NP-hardness follows from the satisfiability of propositional logic. One way to reduce propositional satisfiability is to introduce, for each Boolean variable q, two integer variables x_q and y_q. Then the satisfiability of propositional formula can be encoded into an LIA formula (which is clearly subsumed by SLHV) by replacing each atomic literal q with $x_q > y_q$ and its negation $\neg q$ with $x_q \leqslant y_q$. We assume that φ is a conjunction of atomic formulas of the form $it_1 \lhd it_2$ and $ht_1 = ht_2$. For SLHV formulas containing disjunctions, we can one can guess a disjunct of the disjunctive normal forms and solve the satisfiability problem for each disjunct accordingly.

Notations. We write φ_p for the conjunction of the formulas of the form $it_1 \lhd it_2$ in φ. We denote by $\mathsf{HEQ}(\varphi)$ the set of heap equalities $ht_1 = ht_2$ in φ, by $\mathsf{HT}(\varphi)$ the set of heap terms ht_1, ht_2 such that $ht_1 = ht_2 \in \mathsf{HEQ}(\varphi)$, by $\mathsf{PT}(\varphi)$ the set of points-to heap terms in φ. For a heap term ht, let $\mathsf{AHT}(ht)$ denote the set of atomic heap terms occurring in ht. (In particular, $\mathsf{AHT}(\texttt{emp}) = \varnothing$.) Finally, $\mathsf{AHT}(\varphi) := \bigcup_{ht \in \mathsf{HT}(\varphi)} \mathsf{AHT}(ht)$. For instance, for $\varphi \equiv \mathfrak{h}_1 = \mathfrak{h}_2 \uplus x \mapsto y \wedge \mathfrak{h}_3 =$

P1. ψ is satisfiable and $\psi \models \varphi_p$. (**ψ strengthens φ_p.**)
P2. $\{(ht_1, ht_2) \in \mathsf{AHT}(\varphi) \times \mathsf{AHT}(\varphi) \mid \exists ht' \in \mathscr{H}.\ ht_1 \uplus ht_2 \preceq_{\mathsf{st}} ht'\} \subseteq \boxtimes$. (**$\boxtimes$ inherits the domain-disjointness brought upon by $\uplus$.**)
P3. $\{(ht_1, ht_2) \in (\mathsf{AHT}(\varphi) \cup \{\mathtt{emp}\}) \times \mathscr{H} \mid ht_1 \neq \mathtt{emp} \implies ht_1 \preceq_{\mathsf{st}} ht_2\} \cup \{(ht_1, ht_2), (ht_2, ht_1) \mid ht_1 = ht_2 \in \mathsf{HEQ}(\varphi)\} \subseteq \sqsubseteq$. (**$\sqsubseteq$ inherits $\preceq_{\mathsf{st}}$.**)
P4. If $(it_1 \mapsto it_2, it'_1 \mapsto it'_2) \in \boxtimes$, then $\psi \models it_1 \neq it'_1$. (**$\boxtimes$ between two points-to terms implies inequality of locations.**)
P5. If $it_1 \mapsto it_2 \sqsubseteq it'_1 \mapsto it'_2$, then $\psi \models it_1 = it'_1 \wedge it_2 = it'_2$. (**$\sqsubseteq$ between two points-to terms implies equality of locations.**)
P6. If $ht \neq \mathtt{emp}$ and $it_1 \mapsto it_2 \sqsubseteq ht$, then $it_1 \mapsto it_2 \sqsubseteq a$ for some $a \in \mathsf{AHT}(ht)$. (**$\sqsubseteq$ between a points-to term and a heap term implies $\sqsubseteq$ between a points-to term and an atomic heap term.**)
P7. If $it_1 \mapsto it_2 \sqsubseteq ht$, $it'_1 \mapsto it'_2 \sqsubseteq ht$, then either $(it_1 \mapsto it_2, it'_1 \mapsto it'_2) \in \boxtimes$, or $it_1 \mapsto it_2 \sqsubseteq it'_1 \mapsto it'_2$ and $it'_1 \mapsto it'_2 \sqsubseteq it_1 \mapsto it_2$. (**If two points-to terms are sub-heaps of the same heap term, then they are either domain-disjoint or equal.**)
P8. If $ht_1 \sqsubseteq ht_2$, $ht_2 \sqsubseteq ht_3$, then $ht_1 \sqsubseteq ht_3$. (**$\sqsubseteq$ is transitive.**)
P9. If $\{ht_1, ht_2, ht_3, ht_4\} \subseteq \mathsf{HT}(\varphi) \cup \mathsf{AHT}(\varphi)$, $ht_1 \sqsubseteq ht_3$, $ht_2 \sqsubseteq ht_4$, $(ht_3, ht_4) \in \boxtimes$, then $(ht_1, ht_2) \in \boxtimes$. (**$\boxtimes$ between two heap terms implies $\boxtimes$ between their sub-heap terms.**)
P10. There does not exist $it_1 \mapsto it_2 \in \mathscr{H}$ such that $it_1 \mapsto it_2 \sqsubseteq \mathtt{emp}$. (**No points-to terms are sub-heaps of emp.**)

Fig. 1. Properties encoding the satisfiability of φ

$\mathfrak{h}_2 \uplus x \mapsto z$, $\mathsf{HT}(\varphi) = \{\mathfrak{h}_1, \mathfrak{h}_2 \uplus x \mapsto y, \mathfrak{h}_3, \mathfrak{h}_2 \uplus x \mapsto z\}$, $\mathsf{PT}(\varphi) = \{x \mapsto y, x \mapsto z\}$, and $\mathsf{AHT}(\varphi) = \{\mathfrak{h}_1, \mathfrak{h}_2, x \mapsto y, \mathfrak{h}_3, x \mapsto z\}$.

Let $\mathscr{H} = \mathsf{HT}(\varphi) \cup \mathsf{AHT}(\varphi) \cup \{\mathtt{emp}\}$. We shall reduce checking the satisfiability of φ to checking the existence of a structure $(\psi, \boxtimes, \sqsubseteq)$ satisfying the properties **P1-P10** (see Fig. 1), where ψ is a Linear Integer Arithmetic (LIA) formula, $\boxtimes \subseteq \mathscr{H} \times \mathscr{H}$ specifies the domain-disjointness relation, and $\sqsubseteq \subseteq \mathscr{H} \times \mathscr{H}$ specifies the subheap relation. Recall that the theory of LIA consist of arithmetic atomic formulas of the form $\sum_i a_i x_i \bowtie c$ where a_i's and c are integer constants and x_i's are integer variables, and $\lhd \in \{=, \neq, \leqslant, <\}$.

Let φ be an SLHV formula that is a conjunction of atomic formulas. We have the following proposition.

Proposition 1. *There exists a structure $(\psi, \boxtimes, \sqsubseteq)$ satisfying **P1–P10** if and only if there exists a store ρ such that $\rho \models \varphi$.*

We proceed to show that the existence of a structure $(\psi, \boxtimes, \sqsubseteq)$ can be encoded by an LIA formula ψ'. To this end, we introduce Boolean variables to represent the relations $\boxtimes$ and $\sqsubseteq$ so that the constraints **P1-P10** can be encoded. For each pair $(ht_1, ht_2) \in \mathscr{H} \times \mathscr{H}$, we introduce a Boolean variable idj_{ht_1, ht_2} for $ht_1 \boxtimes ht_2$ and a Boolean variable ish_{ht_1, ht_2} for $ht_1 \sqsubseteq ht_2$.

We then construct $\psi' \stackrel{\text{def}}{=} \psi'_{init} \wedge \psi'_{pto} \wedge \psi'_{ish} \wedge \psi'_{idj} \wedge \psi'_{cons}$, where

- ψ'_{init} encodes **P1-P3** and is defined by

$$
\begin{aligned}
&\varphi_p \wedge \bigwedge_{\substack{ht_1, ht_2 \in \mathsf{AHT}(\varphi), \\ \exists ht' \in \mathscr{H}. ht_1 \uplus ht_2 \leq_{\mathsf{st}} ht'}} idj_{ht_1, ht_2} \wedge \bigwedge_{ht \in \mathscr{H}} ish_{\mathtt{emp}, ht} \\
&\wedge \bigwedge_{\substack{ht_1 \in \mathsf{AHT}(\varphi), \\ ht_2 \in \mathscr{H} \setminus \{\mathtt{emp}\}, ht_1 \leq_{\mathsf{st}} ht_2}} ish_{ht_1, ht_2} \wedge \bigwedge_{ht_1 = ht_2 \in \mathsf{HEQ}(\varphi)} (ish_{ht_1, ht_2} \wedge ish_{ht_2, ht_1}),
\end{aligned}
$$

- ψ'_{pto} encodes **P4-P7** and is defined by

$$
\begin{aligned}
&\bigwedge_{\{it_1 \mapsto it_2, it'_1 \mapsto it'_2\} \subseteq \mathscr{H}} (idj_{it_1 \mapsto it_2, it'_1 \mapsto it'_2} \rightarrow it_1 \neq it'_1) \wedge \\
&\bigwedge_{\{it_1 \mapsto it_2, it'_1 \mapsto it'_2\} \subseteq \mathscr{H}} (ish_{it_1 \mapsto it_2, it'_1 \mapsto it'_2} \rightarrow (it_1 = it'_1 \wedge it_2 = it'_2)) \wedge \\
&\bigwedge_{\{it_1 \mapsto it_2, ht\} \subseteq \mathscr{H}, ht \neq \mathtt{emp}} \left(ish_{it_1 \mapsto it_2, ht} \rightarrow \bigvee_{a \in \mathsf{AHT}(ht)} ish_{it_1 \mapsto it_2, a} \right) \wedge \\
&\bigwedge_{\{it_1 \mapsto it_2, it'_1 \mapsto it'_2, ht\} \subseteq \mathscr{H}} \left(\begin{array}{l} (ish_{it_1 \mapsto it_2, ht} \wedge ish_{it'_1 \mapsto it'_2, ht}) \rightarrow \\ \left(\begin{array}{l} idj_{it_1 \mapsto it_2, it'_1 \mapsto it'_2} \vee \\ (ish_{it_1 \mapsto it_2, it'_1 \mapsto it'_2} \wedge ish_{it'_1 \mapsto it'_2, it_1 \mapsto it_2}) \end{array} \right) \end{array} \right),
\end{aligned}
$$

- ψ'_{ish} encodes **P8** and is defined by

$$
\bigwedge_{\{ht_1, ht_2, ht_3\} \subseteq \mathscr{H}} ((ish_{ht_1, ht_2} \wedge ish_{ht_2, ht_3}) \rightarrow ish_{ht_1, ht_3}),
$$

- ψ'_{idj} encodes **P9** and is defined by

$$
\bigwedge_{\{ht_1, ht_2, ht_3, ht_4\} \subseteq \mathsf{HT}(\varphi) \cup \mathsf{AHT}(\varphi)} ((ish_{ht_1, ht_3} \wedge ish_{ht_2, ht_4} \wedge idj_{ht_3, ht_4}) \rightarrow idj_{ht_1, ht_2}),
$$

- ψ'_{cons} encodes **P10** and is defined as $\bigwedge_{it_1 \mapsto it_2 \in \mathscr{H}} \neg ish_{it_1 \mapsto it_2, \mathtt{emp}}$.

Example 1. We use the following SLHV formula φ to illustrate the encoding of its satisfiability as an LIA formula ψ',

$$
\begin{aligned}
\varphi ::= \; & (\mathfrak{h}_1 = \mathfrak{h}_2 \uplus x_1 \mapsto y_1) \wedge (\mathfrak{h}_1 = \mathfrak{h}_3 \uplus x_2 \mapsto y_2) \wedge (\mathfrak{h}_2 = \mathfrak{h}_4 \uplus x_2 \mapsto y_3) \wedge \\
& x_1 \neq x_2 \wedge y_2 \neq y_3.
\end{aligned}
$$

φ is unsatisfiable, because

- From that $x_2 \mapsto y_2$ is a subheap of $\mathfrak{h}_3 \uplus x_2 \mapsto y_2$ and $\mathfrak{h}_1 = \mathfrak{h}_3 \uplus x_2 \mapsto y_2$, $x_2 \mapsto y_2$ is a subheap of $\mathfrak{h}_1$.
- From that $x_2 \mapsto y_2$ is a subheap of $\mathfrak{h}_1$ and $\mathfrak{h}_1 = \mathfrak{h}_2 \uplus x_1 \mapsto y_1$, $x_2 \mapsto y_2$ is a subheap of $\mathfrak{h}_2 \uplus x_1 \mapsto y_1$. Thus $x_2 \mapsto y_2$ is a subheap of $\mathfrak{h}_2$ or a subheap of $x_1 \mapsto y_1$. Moreover, from $x_1 \neq x_2$, $x_2 \mapsto y_2$ is not a subheap of $x_1 \mapsto y_1$. Hence $x_2 \mapsto y_2$ is a subheap of $\mathfrak{h}_2$.

- From $\mathfrak{h}_2 = \mathfrak{h}_4 \uplus x_2 \mapsto y_3$, $x_2 \mapsto y_2$ is a subheap of $\mathfrak{h}_4$ or a subheap of $x_2 \mapsto y_3$. From $y_2 \neq y_3$, $x_2 \mapsto y_2$ cannot be a subheap of $x_2 \mapsto y_3$. As a result, $x_2 \mapsto y_2$ is a subheap of $\mathfrak{h}_4$.
- From the domain disjointness of $\mathfrak{h}_4$ and $x_2 \mapsto y_3$, we deduce the domain disjointness of $x_2 \mapsto y_2$ and $x_2 \mapsto y_3$, a contradiction.

We deduce the unsatisfiability of ψ' by a parallel argument. According to the construction, $\psi' = \psi'_{init} \wedge \psi'_{pto} \wedge \psi'_{ish} \wedge \psi'_{idj} \wedge \psi'_{cons}$.

- From $\psi'_{init} \models ish_{x_2 \mapsto y_2, \mathfrak{h}_3 \uplus x_2 \mapsto y_2} \wedge ish_{\mathfrak{h}_3 \uplus x_2 \mapsto y_2, \mathfrak{h}_1}$ and

$$\psi'_{ish} \models (ish_{x_2 \mapsto y_2, \mathfrak{h}_3 \uplus x_2 \mapsto y_2} \wedge ish_{\mathfrak{h}_3 \uplus x_2 \mapsto y_2, \mathfrak{h}_1}) \rightarrow ish_{x_2 \mapsto y_2, \mathfrak{h}_1},$$

  we deduce $\psi' \models ish_{x_2 \mapsto y_2, \mathfrak{h}_1}$.
- Then from $\psi'_{init} \models ish_{\mathfrak{h}_1, \mathfrak{h}_2 \uplus x_1 \mapsto y_1}$ and

$$\psi'_{ish} \models (ish_{x_2 \mapsto y_2, \mathfrak{h}_1} \wedge ish_{\mathfrak{h}_1, \mathfrak{h}_2 \uplus x_1 \mapsto y_1}) \rightarrow ish_{x_2 \mapsto y_2, \mathfrak{h}_2 \uplus x_1 \mapsto y_1},$$

  we deduce $\psi' \models ish_{x_2 \mapsto y_2, \mathfrak{h}_2 \uplus x_1 \mapsto y_1}$. From $\psi'_{pto} \models ish_{x_2 \mapsto y_2, x_1 \mapsto y_1} \rightarrow (x_2 = x_1 \wedge y_2 = y_1)$ and $\psi' \models x_1 \neq x_2$, we know $\psi' \models \neg ish_{x_2 \mapsto y_2, x_1 \mapsto y_1}$. Moreover, from $\psi'_{pto} \models ish_{x_2 \mapsto y_2, \mathfrak{h}_2 \uplus x_1 \mapsto y_1} \rightarrow (ish_{x_2 \mapsto y_2, \mathfrak{h}_2} \vee ish_{x_2 \mapsto y_2, x_1 \mapsto y_1})$ and $\psi' \models ish_{x_2 \mapsto y_2, \mathfrak{h}_2 \uplus x_1 \mapsto y_1}$, we deduce $\psi' \models ish_{x_2 \mapsto y_2, \mathfrak{h}_2}$.
- From $\psi'_{pto} \models ish_{\mathfrak{h}_2, \mathfrak{h}_4 \uplus x_2 \mapsto y_3}$, $\psi' \models ish_{x_2 \mapsto y_2, \mathfrak{h}_2}$ and $\psi'_{ish} \models (ish_{x_2 \mapsto y_2, \mathfrak{h}_2} \wedge ish_{\mathfrak{h}_2, \mathfrak{h}_4 \uplus x_2 \mapsto y_3}) \rightarrow ish_{x_2 \mapsto y_2, \mathfrak{h}_4 \uplus x_2 \mapsto y_3}$, we deduce $\psi' \models ish_{x_2 \mapsto y_2, \mathfrak{h}_4 \uplus x_2 \mapsto y_3}$. Then from $\psi'_{pto} \models ish_{x_2 \mapsto y_2, \mathfrak{h}_4 \uplus x_2 \mapsto y_3} \rightarrow (ish_{x_2 \mapsto y_2, \mathfrak{h}_4} \vee ish_{x_2 \mapsto y_2, x_2 \mapsto y_3})$, we have $\psi' \models ish_{x_2 \mapsto y_2, \mathfrak{h}_4} \vee ish_{x_2 \mapsto y_2, x_2 \mapsto y_3}$. From $\psi'_{pto} \models ish_{x_2 \mapsto y_2, x_2 \mapsto y_3} \models (x_2 = x_2 \wedge y_2 = y_3)$ and $\psi'_{init} \models y_2 \neq y_3$, we deduce $\psi' \models \neg ish_{x_2 \mapsto y_2, x_2 \mapsto y_3}$. Then from $\psi' \models ish_{x_2 \mapsto y_2, \mathfrak{h}_4} \vee ish_{x_2 \mapsto y_2, x_2 \mapsto y_3}$, we have $\psi' \models ish_{x_2 \mapsto y_2, \mathfrak{h}_4}$.
- From $\psi'_{init} \models idj_{\mathfrak{h}_4, x_2 \mapsto y_3}$,

$$\psi'_{idj} \models (ish_{x_2 \mapsto y_2, \mathfrak{h}_4} \wedge ish_{x_2 \mapsto y_3, x_2 \mapsto y_3} \wedge idj_{\mathfrak{h}_4, x_2 \mapsto y_3}) \rightarrow idj_{x_2 \mapsto y_2, x_2 \mapsto y_3},$$

  and $\psi' \models ish_{x_2 \mapsto y_2, \mathfrak{h}_4} \wedge ish_{x_2 \mapsto y_3, x_2 \mapsto y_3}$, we deduce $\psi' \models idj_{x_2 \mapsto y_2, x_2 \mapsto y_3}$. Finally, from $\psi'_{pto} \models idj_{x_2 \mapsto y_2, x_2 \mapsto y_3} \rightarrow x_2 \neq x_2$, we conclude that $\psi' \models x_2 \neq x_2$. Therefore, ψ' is unsatisfiable.

□

Complexity. For a given SLHV disjunction-free formula φ, the size of the set of heap terms $\mathscr{H}$ is linear in the sum of the number of atomic heap terms and the number of atomic propositions in φ. The size of the LIA formula ψ' to which the satisfiability reduced to is polynomial in the size of $\mathscr{H}$. It is well-known that the satisfiability of quantifier-free LIA formulas is in NP [11], hence the satisfiability of SLHV is in NP.

4 Bounded Model Checking

In this section, we show how to encode the transition relation of heap-manipulating C statements as an SLHV formula. We restrict to memory allocations of constant sizes. Moreover, we assume the *recyclable* memory model, that is, once a memory region is freed, it can be reallocated later. For convenience, we shall use control flow graphs as a representation of C programs.

Definition 1 (Control Flow Graphs). *A* control flow graph *(CFG) G is a tuple $(\mathcal{L}, \mathcal{B}, E, l_0, l_f)$, where $\mathcal{L}$ is a finite set of program counters (pc for short), $\mathcal{B}$ is a finite set of basic blocks, $E \subseteq \mathcal{L} \times \mathcal{B} \times \mathcal{L}$ is the edge relation, $l_0 \in \mathcal{L}$ is the initial pc, and $l_f \in \mathcal{L}$ is the final pc. We require that E is complete, i.e., for each $l \in \mathcal{L}$ with $l \neq l_f$, there are $B \in \mathcal{B}$ and $l' \in \mathcal{L}$ such that $(l, B, l') \in E$.*

Each *basic block* in a CFG is a sequence of statements which are defined by the following syntactic rules,

$$stmt \stackrel{\text{def}}{=} \texttt{skip} \mid v := e \mid \texttt{assume}(be) \mid p := \texttt{malloc}(n) \mid \\ \texttt{free}(pe) \mid \texttt{store}(pe, e) \mid v := \texttt{load}(pe)$$

where $n \in \mathbb{N}$, v is a variable, e is an expression and pe, be are used to denote pointer and Boolean expressions respectively. We also require that the statements in a basic block are in single-static-assignment (SSA) form.

Remark 1. It is not hard to see that the aforementioned syntactic rules are sufficiently expressive to capture the typical statements in heap-manipulating C programs. For example, consider the C statement x = p->f that reads the value of the field f of the pointer p of a struct type (say str) and assigns it to x. Provided with the typing information of str, one can obtain the offset $o_f \in \mathbb{N}$ of the field f with respect to p. Then x = p->f can be rewritten as $x := \texttt{load}(p + o_f)$. Moreover, the statement p->f = 10 that writes 10 to the field f of the pointer p can be rewritten as $\texttt{store}(p + o_f, 10)$.

Below, we first show how the transition relation of a CFG can be encoded as an SLHV formula (Sect. 4.1). Once the transition relation is available, one can specify various memory safety properties, e.g., memory leak, invalid free, or invalid dereference (technically, we adapt the transition relation by adding some Boolean variables to facilitate the specification; cf. Sect. 4.2).

4.1 Encoding the Transition Relation of a Control Flow Graph

Let $G = (\mathcal{L}, \mathcal{B}, E, l_0, l_f)$ be a CFG. We first introduce some notations. Then we encode the semantics of the statements as SLHV formulas. Afterwards, we encode G as a transition relation.

Let X_G denote the set of (integer, location and Boolean) variables appearing in G. For convenience, we often write X_G as a vector $\overrightarrow{x}$. We use M_G to denote the set of constants m that appear in the statements $\texttt{malloc}(m)$ of G. In the encoding below, we shall use $\mathfrak{h}, \mathfrak{h}_i, \mathfrak{h}'$ to represent heaps and $\mathfrak{s}, \mathfrak{s}_i, \mathfrak{s}'$ to represent the sizes of the allocated memory blocks.

We start with some syntactic sugar.

- $\psi_{uc} \stackrel{\text{def}}{=} \bigwedge_{x \in X_G} x' = x$, ("uc" is an abbreviation of "unchanged")
- $\psi_{ucmo}(x) \stackrel{\text{def}}{=} \bigwedge_{z \in X_G \setminus \{x\}} z' = z$, ($\psi_{ucmo}(x)$ intuitively means that the values of variables are unchanged except for x.)
- $x = read(\mathfrak{h}, pe) \stackrel{\text{def}}{=} \exists \mathfrak{h}_1.\ \mathfrak{h} = \mathfrak{h}_1 \uplus pe \mapsto x$,
- $\mathfrak{h}' = write(\mathfrak{h}, pe, e) \stackrel{\text{def}}{=} \exists \mathfrak{h}_1, z.\ \mathfrak{h} = \mathfrak{h}_1 \uplus pe \mapsto z \wedge \mathfrak{h}' = \mathfrak{h}_1 \uplus pe \mapsto e$.

The encoding of `malloc`, `free`, `store` and `load` in SLHV is as follows.

$$\begin{aligned}
\varphi_{p:=\texttt{malloc}(n)}(\mathfrak{h}, \mathfrak{h}', \mathfrak{s}, \mathfrak{s}', \overrightarrow{x}, \overrightarrow{x'}) \stackrel{\text{def}}{=} \exists y, z_0, \cdots, z_{n-1}.\ & \\
\mathfrak{h}' = \mathfrak{h} \uplus \biguplus_{i \in [0, n-1]} y + i \mapsto z_i \wedge p' = y \wedge & \\
\mathfrak{s}' = \mathfrak{s} \uplus y \mapsto n \wedge \psi_{ucmo}(p). &
\end{aligned}$$

$$\begin{aligned}
\varphi_{\texttt{free}(pe)}(\mathfrak{h}, \mathfrak{h}', \mathfrak{s}, \mathfrak{s}', \overrightarrow{x}, \overrightarrow{x'}) \stackrel{\text{def}}{=} \exists z_0, \cdots, z_{\max(M_G)-1}, x_s.\ & \\
\psi_{uc} \wedge \mathfrak{s} = \mathfrak{s}' \uplus pe \mapsto x_s \wedge & \\
\bigvee_{n \in M_G} (x_s = n \wedge \mathfrak{h} = \mathfrak{h}' \uplus \biguplus_{j \in [0, n-1]} pe + j \mapsto z_j). &
\end{aligned}$$

$$\varphi_{\texttt{store}(pe,e)}(\mathfrak{h}, \mathfrak{h}', \mathfrak{s}, \mathfrak{s}', \overrightarrow{x}, \overrightarrow{x'}) \stackrel{\text{def}}{=} \mathfrak{h}' = write(\mathfrak{h}, pe, e) \wedge \psi_{uc} \wedge \mathfrak{s}' = \mathfrak{s}.$$

$$\varphi_{v:=\texttt{load}(pe)}(\mathfrak{h}, \mathfrak{h}', \mathfrak{s}, \mathfrak{s}', \overrightarrow{x}, \overrightarrow{x'}) \stackrel{\text{def}}{=} v' = read(\mathfrak{h}, pe) \wedge \psi_{ucmo}(v) \wedge \mathfrak{h}' = \mathfrak{h} \wedge \mathfrak{s}' = \mathfrak{s}.$$

Note that when a memory block denoted by pe is freed, pe is also removed from the domain of $\mathfrak{s}$, which is guaranteed by the formula $\mathfrak{s} = \mathfrak{s}' \uplus pe \mapsto x_s$.

A basic block B is a sequence $s_1; s_2; \cdots; s_n$ of statements, hence is encoded as

$$\begin{aligned}
\mathcal{T}_B(\mathfrak{h}_0, \mathfrak{h}_n, \mathfrak{s}_0, \mathfrak{s}_n, \overrightarrow{x_0}, \overrightarrow{x_n}) \stackrel{\text{def}}{=} \exists \mathfrak{h}_1, \ldots \mathfrak{h}_{n-1}, \mathfrak{s}_1, \ldots, \mathfrak{s}_{n-1}, \overrightarrow{x_1}, \ldots, \overrightarrow{x_{n-1}}.\ & \\
\bigwedge_{i=1}^{n} \varphi_{s_i}(\mathfrak{h}_{i-1}, \mathfrak{s}_{i-1}, \overrightarrow{x_{i-1}}; \mathfrak{h}_i, \mathfrak{s}_i, \overrightarrow{x_i}), &
\end{aligned}$$

where $\mathfrak{h}_i, \mathfrak{s}_i, \overrightarrow{x_i}$ (for $i \in [0, n]$) record the state of the heap, heap-size information and values of variables after executing the first i statements in B.

Finally, we define the transition relation of G as

$$\mathcal{T}_G(pc, \mathfrak{h}, \mathfrak{s}, \overrightarrow{x}; pc', \mathfrak{h}', \mathfrak{s}', \overrightarrow{x'}) \stackrel{\text{def}}{=} \bigvee_{(l,B,l') \in E} \mathcal{T}_{(l,B,l')},$$

where

- pc, pc' are the program counters before and after a basic block of G,
- $\mathfrak{h}, \mathfrak{h}'$ denote the states of heaps,
- $\mathfrak{s}, \mathfrak{s}'$ denote the mappings from the starting addresses of allocated memory regions to their sizes,

- $\overrightarrow{x}$, $\overrightarrow{x}'$ represent the values of pointer/integer variables,
- $\mathcal{T}_{(l,B,l')}$ is the formula corresponding to the edge (l, B, l') and can be expressed as

$$\begin{aligned}\mathcal{T}_{(l,B,l')} \stackrel{\text{def}}{=} \; & \exists \mathfrak{h}_0, \mathfrak{h}_n. \exists \mathfrak{s}_0, \mathfrak{s}_n. \exists \overrightarrow{x_0}, \overrightarrow{x_n}. \\ & pc = l \wedge pc' = l' \wedge \overrightarrow{x} = \overrightarrow{x_0} \wedge \overrightarrow{x}' = \overrightarrow{x_n} \wedge \\ & \mathfrak{h} = \mathfrak{h}_0 \wedge \mathfrak{h}' = \mathfrak{h}_n \wedge \mathfrak{s} = \mathfrak{s}_0 \wedge \mathfrak{s}' = \mathfrak{s}_n \wedge \\ & \mathcal{T}_B(\mathfrak{h}_0, \mathfrak{h}_n, \mathfrak{s}_0, \mathfrak{s}_n, \overrightarrow{x_0}, \overrightarrow{x_n}),\end{aligned}$$

where n is the number of statements in B.

Example 2. We use the following example to demonstrate the encoding of the transition relation of the CFG G corresponding to the program P in Listing 1.1 (see Fig. 2). In G, the assignment `x1->a = 10` can be rewritten as `store`(`x1`, 10), since `a` is the first field of the structure `R`. Moreover, `sizeof(R)` is 2.

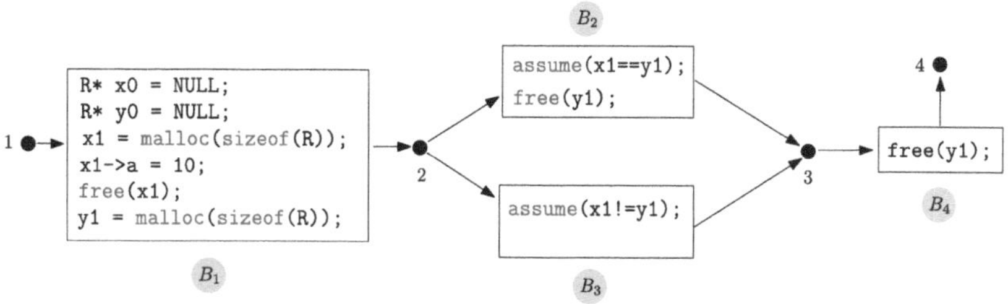

Fig. 2. The control flow graph of P in Listing 1.1

The transition relation of G can be expressed as

$$\begin{aligned}& \mathcal{T}_G(pc, \mathfrak{h}, \mathfrak{s}, x0, y0, x1, y1; pc', \mathfrak{h}', \mathfrak{s}', x0', y0', x1', y1') \stackrel{\text{def}}{=} \\ & \mathcal{T}_{(1,B_1,2)} \vee \mathcal{T}_{(2,B_2,3)} \vee \mathcal{T}_{(2,B_3,3)} \vee \mathcal{T}_{(3,B_4,4)},\end{aligned}$$

where pc, pc' are the variables to denote the program counters before and after applying a block respectively.

Recall that M_G denotes the finite set of constant sizes in the `malloc` statements of G. It is easy to see that $M_G = \{2\}$ since `sizeof(R)` is 2. Then

$$
\begin{aligned}
\mathcal{T}_{(1,B_1,2)} \stackrel{\text{def}}{=} & \exists z_1, z_2, d_1, d_2, d_3, d_5, d_6, d_7, \mathfrak{h}_1, \mathfrak{h}_2, \mathfrak{h}_3, \mathfrak{h}_4, \mathfrak{h}_5, \mathfrak{h}_6, \mathfrak{s}_1, \mathfrak{s}_2, \mathfrak{s}_3. \\
& pc = 1 \wedge x0' = \mathsf{null} \wedge \mathsf{y0}' = \mathsf{null} \wedge \\
& \underbrace{\mathfrak{h}_1 = \mathfrak{h} \uplus z_1 \mapsto d_1 \uplus z_1 + 1 \mapsto d_2 \wedge \mathfrak{s}_1 = \mathfrak{s} \uplus z_1 \mapsto 2 \wedge x1' = z_1}_{\text{allocation for } x1} \wedge \\
& \underbrace{\mathfrak{h}_1 = \mathfrak{h}_2 \uplus x1' \mapsto d_3 \wedge \mathfrak{h}_3 = \mathfrak{h}_2 \uplus x1' \mapsto 10}_{\text{store 10 to } x1} \wedge \\
& \underbrace{\left(\mathfrak{s}_1 = \mathfrak{s}_2 \uplus x1' \mapsto 2 \wedge \mathfrak{h}_3 = \mathfrak{h}_4 \uplus \mathfrak{h}_5 \wedge \mathfrak{h}_5 = x1' \mapsto d_4 \uplus x1' + 1 \mapsto d_5\right)}_{\text{deallocation for } x1} \wedge \\
& \underbrace{\mathfrak{h}_6 = \mathfrak{h}_4 \uplus z_2 \mapsto d_6 \uplus z_2 + 1 \mapsto d_7 \wedge \mathfrak{s}_3 = \mathfrak{s}_2 \uplus z_2 \mapsto 2 \wedge y1' = z_2}_{\text{allocation for } y1} \wedge \\
& \mathfrak{h}' = \mathfrak{h}_6 \wedge \mathfrak{s}' = \mathfrak{s}_3 \wedge pc' = 2.
\end{aligned}
$$

Finally, $\mathcal{T}_{(2,B_2,3)}$, $\mathcal{T}_{(2,B_3,3)}$, and $\mathcal{T}_{(3,B_4,4)}$ can be defined in a similar way. □

4.2 Encoding of Memory-Safety Issues

We show how to specify various memory issues, namely, memory leak, invalid free, or invalid dereference, in the BMC of C programs. In some cases, we adapt the transition relation by adding some Boolean variables in order to ease the specification.

Memory Leak. For memory leak, the k-step BMC of G is encoded by

$$
\varphi^{(k)}_{G,ml} \stackrel{\text{def}}{=} \bigvee_{i \in [k]} \Big(pc_0 = l_0 \wedge \mathfrak{h}_0 = \mathtt{emp} \wedge \mathfrak{s}_0 = \mathtt{emp} \wedge (\bigwedge_{j \in [i]} \mathcal{T}^j_G) \wedge pc_i = l_f \wedge \mathfrak{h}_i \neq \mathtt{emp} \Big),
$$

where $\mathcal{T}^j_G$ is obtained from $\mathcal{T}_G$ by replacing pc and pc' with pc_{j-1} and pc_j respectively, $\mathfrak{h}$ and $\mathfrak{h}'$ with $\mathfrak{h}_{j-1}$ and $\mathfrak{h}_j$ respectively, and so on.

To ease the encoding of invalid free (resp. invalid dereferences), we introduce the Boolean variable b_{if} (resp. b_{id}), which encodes whether invalid free (resp. invalid dereference) has occurred before or not. We update the values of b_{if} (resp. b_{id}) during the execution of the statements.

Invalid Free. For each statement s, except for the statement of the form $\mathtt{free}(pe)$, the atomic formula $b_{if} \leftrightarrow b'_{if}$ is added as a conjunct of φ_s that has been constructed before. For the statement $\mathtt{free}(pe)$, $\varphi_{\mathtt{free}(pe)}$ is adapted into $\varphi_{\mathtt{free}(pe),if}$ defined as follows.

$$
\begin{aligned}
\varphi_{\mathtt{free}(pe),if} \stackrel{\text{def}}{=} & (b_{if} \wedge b'_{if}) \vee (pe \neq 0 \wedge pe \notin \mathfrak{h} \wedge b'_{if}) \vee \\
& \exists z_0, \cdots, z_{\max(MS_G)-1}, x_s.\ \neg b_{if} \wedge \neg b'_{if} \wedge \psi_{uc} \wedge \\
& \mathfrak{s} = \mathfrak{s}' \uplus pe \mapsto x_s \wedge \bigvee_{n \in MS_G} (x_s = n \wedge \mathfrak{h} = \mathfrak{h}' \uplus \biguplus_{j \in [0,n-1]} pe + j \mapsto z_j).
\end{aligned}
$$

Let $\mathcal{T}_{G,if}$ denote the transition relation that is adapted from $\mathcal{T}_G$ for encoding invalid free. Then for invalid free, the k-step BMC of G is encoded by

$$\varphi_{G,if}^{(k)} \stackrel{\text{def}}{=} \bigvee_{i \in [k]} (pc_0 = l_0 \wedge \mathfrak{h}_0 = \texttt{emp} \wedge \mathfrak{s}_0 = \texttt{emp} \wedge \neg b_{if,0} \wedge (\bigwedge_{j \in [i]} \mathcal{T}_{G,if}^j) \wedge b_{if,i}).$$

Invalid Dereference. For each statement s that contains no dereferences, the atomic formula $b_{id} \leftrightarrow b'_{id}$ is added as a conjunct of φ_s. Let $\varphi_{s,id}$ denote the resulting formula. For the statement `load` or `store`, we illustrate the adaptation of φ_s to $\varphi_{s,id}$ by considering $s \equiv x := \texttt{load}(pe)$,

$$\begin{aligned}\varphi_{x:=\texttt{load}(pe),id} \stackrel{\text{def}}{=} & (b_{id} \wedge b'_{id}) \vee (pe \not\in \mathfrak{h} \wedge b'_{id}) \vee (\neg b_{id} \wedge \neg b'_{id} \wedge \\ & x' = read(\mathfrak{h}, pe) \wedge \psi_{ucmo}(x) \wedge \mathfrak{h}' = \mathfrak{h} \wedge \mathfrak{s}' = \mathfrak{s}).\end{aligned}$$

Let $\mathcal{T}_{G,id}$ denote the transition relation that is adapted from $\mathcal{T}_G$ for encoding invalid dereference. For invalid dereference, the k-step BMC of G is encoded by

$$\varphi_{G,id}^{(k)} \stackrel{\text{def}}{=} \bigvee_{i \in [k]} (pc_0 = l_0 \wedge \mathfrak{h}_0 = \texttt{emp} \wedge \mathfrak{s}_0 = \texttt{emp} \wedge \neg b_{id,0} \wedge (\bigwedge_{j \in [i]} \mathcal{T}_{G,id}^j) \wedge b_{id,i}).$$

5 Implementation and Evaluation

We implement our decision procedure for SLHV based on Z3 [9] as a solver Z3-SLHV. As a prototype, we directly encode SLHV formulas as LIA formulas. (We anticipate that it would, when integrated in the DPLL or CDCL framework, exhibit better performance.) To demonstrate the potential of SLHV for program verification, we implement a prototype bounded model checker SELO for verifying heap-manipulating C programs, by adapting the ESBMC [10], where the verification conditions are solved by Z3-SLHV.

SELO currently targets three types of memory safety properties, i.e., invalid free (IF), invalid dereference (ID) and memory leak (ML). Note that the current encoding does not support `union`, `memset`, `memcpy`, `malloc` with variable memory-size or unbounded loops.

Benchmarks. To evaluate the performance of Z3-SLHV and SELO, we consider the 44 BMC problem instances from the `memsafety` folder of SV-COMP 2024 [3], each of which comprises a pair of C program and memory safety property. After excluding the unsupported programs and manually processing programs (e.g., inlining functions), we obtain 20 BMC problem instances yielding 229 SLHV formulas, whose statistics are given in Table 1.

Table 1. Statistics of the benchmarks.

#instances	avg #LOC	min #LOC	max #LOC
20	25	17	64
#formulas	avg #AHT	min #AHT	max #AHT
229	16	2	67

Table 2. Experiment results of Z3-SLHV.

	SAT	UNSAT	Solved
#formulas	26	203	229
avg time (seconds)	1.01	0.93	0.94
min time (seconds)	0.01	0.01	0.01
max time (seconds)	20.02	24.46	24.46

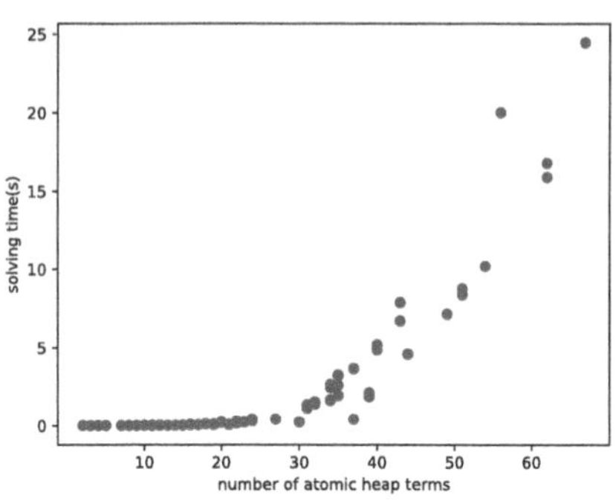

Fig. 3. Distribution of solving time.

All experiments are conducted on a 13th-Gen Intel Core i7-13700 CPU with 128 GB memory. The execution time budget per instance is set as 900 s.

Results of Z3-SLHV. Table 2 reports the results of Z3-SLHV, which can solve all the 229 formulas, 0.94 s. For the 26 satisfiable (resp. 203 unsatisfiable) formulas, the average is 1.01 s (resp. 0.93 s) and the maximum is 20.02 s (resp. 24.46 s). Figure 3 depicts the distribution of solving time w.r.t. the number of atomic heap terms. Clearly, the time increases moderately when the number of atomic heap terms is less than 30, but sharply afterwards. However, we also observe that the solving time is also dependent on the structure of formula.

Results of SELO. Table 3 reports the results of SELO, where manually preprocessed benchmarks have postfix `-mutate` in their names. To cross-check the verification results and demonstrate the efficiency of SELO, we also report the results of ESBMC with Z3 as the backend solver. SELO can verify all the 20 BMC instances, with almost the same verification results as ESBMC. The only exception is `cmp-freed-ptr-mutate` where SELO reports invalid free (IF) error while ESBMC reports SAFE (highlighted in red in Table 3).

This discrepancy attributes to the adopted memory model. SELO uses a recyclable memory model while ESBMC uses a non-recyclable memory model where the addresses of the allocated (even freed) memory should be monotonically increasing. Remarkably, the recyclable memory model showcases the advantage of SLHV, which is arguably more faithful to the actual behavior of C programs.

Note that the ID&IF results on `960521-1-2-mutate` and `global-atexit-5` mean that two memory safety properties are violated, though the invalid free (IF) error is caused by the invalid dereference (ID) error. Finally, we remark that SELO is mainly for demonstrating the potential of SLHV for program verification (hence is not optimized), on some instances (e.g., `test-0232-2-mutate`, `test-0513-mutate`, and `test-0232-3-mutate`) it is not as competitive as mature tools such as ESBMC.

Table 3. Experiment results of SELO and ESBMC.

Name	#LOC	SELO		ESBMC	
		Result	Time	Result	Time
960521-1-1-mutate	17	IF	**0.05 s**	IF	0.09 s
960521-1-2-mutate	26	ID&IF	**0.04 s**	ID&IF	0.06 s
960521-1-2	26	SAFE	0.45s	SAFE	**0.06 s**
960521-1-3-mutate	17	ID	**0.03 s**	ID	0.06 s
cmp-freed-ptr-mutate	21	IF	**0.01 s**	**SAFE**	0.06 s
global-atexit	28	SAFE	0.10 s	SAFE	0.10 s
global-atexit-1-mutate	23	ML	**0.03 s**	ML	0.06 s
global-atexit-1	21	ML	0.06 s	ML	0.06 s
global-atexit-2-mutate	22	ML	**0.05 s**	ML	0.06 s
global-atexit-2	21	ML	**0.05 s**	ML	0.06 s
global-atexit-3	20	ML	0.07 s	ML	**0.06 s**
global-atexit-5	30	ID&IF	0.15 s	ID&IF	**0.06 s**
test-0019-1	18	SAFE	0.89 s	SAFE	**0.06 s**
test-0019-2	19	ML	1.07 s	ML	**0.06 s**
test-0019-1-mutate	18	ML	0.70 s	ML	**0.06 s**
test-0019-2-mutate	20	ML	1.33 s	ML	**0.06 s**
test-0232-1	26	ML	0.28 s	ML	**0.07 s**
test-0232-2-mutate	34	SAFE	33.62s	SAFE	**0.10s**
test-0513-mutate	64	SAFE	91.37s	SAFE	**1.00s**
test-0232-3-mutate	34	IF	82.82s	IF	**0.13s**

6 Related Work

In this section, we discuss the related work which we classify into three categories.

Logics for Heaps. Various logics have been proposed to specify heap structures, apart from separation logic. Recently, explicit theory of heaps are studied [12,13], where heaps are modeled as algebraic data types (with operations such as `alloc`, `read`, `write`), and heap variables (second-order variables of heap sort) can be used to represent heaps explicitly. Although these logics can express heaps freely, they are inconvenient for specifying the disjointness of subheaps.

To the best of our knowledge, [14] is the first to introduce explicit heap variables in separation logic, where SLHV can be considered as a fragment tailored for software model checking purposes. However, the motivation of [14] is different from ours, hence the logic therein is much more expressive than what it needed for our purpose (i.e., automated program verification); for instance, it is largely in the context of Coq. Importantly, our logic enjoys an efficient decision procedure.

The concept of spatial interpolants has been proposed to refine counterexamples in shape analysis of heap-manipulating programs [15,16]. However, symbolic transition relations of heap-manipulating programs required by standard software model checking algorithms are still missing therein.

Decision Procedures for SL. Decision procedures for SL have been investigated extensively. Polynomial-time decision procedures are proposed in [17] for checking satisfiability and entailment of SL with singly linked lists. [18] provides a decision procedure, setting the satisfiability problem (almost) completely. [19,20] focus on the symbolic heap fragments for list segments and binary trees, and provide complete proof systems. For SL with general inductive definitions (SLID), [21] establishes fundamental decidability and complexity results for the entailment problem. [22] proposes a compositional fragment equipped with an incomplete decision procedure. [23,24] provide complete decision procedures for the entailment problem by reducing to the language inclusion problem of tree automata. [25] studies separation logic with a simply-nonlinear compositional inductive predicate, and gives polynomial-time decision procedures for satisfiability and entailment. Furthermore, [26,27] investigate array separation logic (a variant of separation logic in which the data structures are continuous blocks of allocated memory) and its variants, and obtain some complexity results on satisfiability, entailment, model checking and bi-abduction.

For SL with data constraints, [28,29] consider quantifier-free and Bernays-Schönfinkel-Ramsey fragments where the constraints for data values are from SMT theories. Decision procedures for these fragments are obtained by translating to second-order formulas with quantifiers over a domain of sets and uninterpreted functions. As the satisfiability of second-order formulas is undecidable in general, it is unclear how the approach in [28,29] can be extended to deal with heap variables. Compared with the encoding of SL into existential second order logic in [30], our contribution is not merely theoretical because SLHV exposes a single first order heap variable and admits a compact SMT encoding that we implement in a prototype. Translating SLHV into the setting in [30] is nontrivial, it may requires several uninterpreted function symbols to simulate heap variables and heap terms, together with explicit disjointness constraints for separating conjunction, which complicates the translation pipeline and model extraction rather than only enlarging the search space. Finally, we mention work considering decision procedures for SLID extended with data and size constraints, e.g., [31–37].

Bounded Model Checking. As mentioned before, various bounded model checkers for heap-manipulating programs have been developed, including SeaBMC [38] LLBMC [39], CBMC [40,41] and ESBMC [10], where arrays or uninterpreted functions are used to model heaps indirectly. Therefore, the heap manipulating programs are encoded in variants of extensions of theory of arrays or uninterpreted functions where memory-related functions and predicates are needed.

7 Conclusion

We have proposed SLHV, an extension of separation logic with explicit heap variables. We provided a decision procedure for its satisfiability which has been implemented as a solver based on Z3 and applied in bounded model checking heap-manipulating programs. We believe that SLHV provides a more elegant way of modeling heap-manipulating programs, compared to the existing way of modeling heaps by arrays. The decision procedure and the solver pave the way for automated verification of this class of programs.

Future work includes introducing a predicate **blk** to describe the (continuous) memory blocks of unbounded sizes as well as improving the Z3-SLHV solver, in particular, integrating the decision procedure within the DPLL/CDCL framework. Moreover, we plan to study unbounded model checking of heap-manipulating programs.

References

1. O'Hearn, P., Reynolds, J., Yang, H.: Local reasoning about programs that alter data structures. In: Fribourg, L. (ed.) CSL 2001. LNCS, vol. 2142, pp. 1–19. Springer, Heidelberg (2001). https://doi.org/10.1007/3-540-44802-0_1
2. Reynolds, J.C.: Separation logic: a logic for shared mutable data structures. In: Proceedings of the 17th IEEE Symposium on Logic in Computer Science, pp. 55–74 (2002)
3. Beyer, D.: Memory-safety track of SV-COMP 2024 benchmarks. https://gitlab.com/sosy-lab/benchmarking/sv-benchmarks/-/tree/main/c/mem-safety
4. McCarthy, J.: Towards a mathematical science of computation. In: Proceedings of the 2nd IFIP Congress on Information Processing, pp. 21–28 (1962)
5. Suzuki, N., Jefferson, D.: Verification decidability of Presburger array programs. J. ACM **27**(1), 191–205 (1980)
6. Burch, J.R., Dill, D.L.: Automatic verification of pipelined microprocessor control. In: Dill, D.L. (ed.) CAV 1994. LNCS, vol. 818, pp. 68–80. Springer, Heidelberg (1994). https://doi.org/10.1007/3-540-58179-0_44
7. Falke, S., Merz, F., Sinz, C.: Extending the theory of arrays: memset, memcpy, and beyond. In: Cohen, E., Rybalchenko, A. (eds.) VSTTE 2013. LNCS, vol. 8164, pp. 108–128. Springer, Heidelberg (2014). https://doi.org/10.1007/978-3-642-54108-7_6
8. Bradley, A.R., Manna, Z., Sipma, H.B.: What's decidable about arrays? In: Emerson, E.A., Namjoshi, K.S. (eds.) VMCAI 2006. LNCS, vol. 3855, pp. 427–442. Springer, Heidelberg (2005). https://doi.org/10.1007/11609773_28
9. de Moura, L., Bjørner, N.: Z3: an efficient SMT solver. In: Ramakrishnan, C.R., Rehof, J. (eds.) TACAS 2008. LNCS, vol. 4963, pp. 337–340. Springer, Heidelberg (2008). https://doi.org/10.1007/978-3-540-78800-3_24
10. Gadelha, M.Y.R., Monteiro, F.R., Morse, J., Cordeiro, L.C., Fischer, B., Nicole, D.A.: ESBMC 5.0: an industrial-strength C model checker. In: Proceedings of the 33rd ACM/IEEE International Conference on Automated Software Engineering, ASE 2018, pp. 888–891 (2018)
11. Haase, C.: A survival guide to Presburger arithmetic. ACM SIGLOG News **5**(3), 67–82 (2018)

12. Esen, Z., Rümmer, P.: Reasoning in the theory of heap: satisfiability and interpolation. In: LOPSTR 2020. LNCS, vol. 12561, pp. 173–191. Springer, Cham (2021). https://doi.org/10.1007/978-3-030-68446-4_9
13. Esen, Z., Rümmer, P.: An SMT-LIB theory of heaps. In: Proceedings of the 20th Internal Workshop on Satisfiability Modulo Theories. Volume 3185 of CEUR Workshop Proceedings, pp. 38–53 (2022)
14. Nanevski, A., Vafeiadis, V., Berdine, J.: Structuring the verification of heap-manipulating programs. In: Proceedings of the 37th ACM SIGPLAN-SIGACT Symposium on Principles of Programming Languages, POPL, pp. 261–274. ACM (2010)
15. Albargouthi, A., Berdine, J., Cook, B., Kincaid, Z.: Spatial interpolants. In: Vitek, J. (ed.) ESOP 2015. LNCS, vol. 9032, pp. 634–660. Springer, Heidelberg (2015). https://doi.org/10.1007/978-3-662-46669-8_26
16. Holík, L., Hruška, M., Lengál, O., Rogalewicz, A., Vojnar, T.: Counterexample validation and interpolation-based refinement for forest automata. In: Bouajjani, A., Monniaux, D. (eds.) VMCAI 2017. LNCS, vol. 10145, pp. 288–309. Springer, Cham (2017). https://doi.org/10.1007/978-3-319-52234-0_16
17. Cook, B., Haase, C., Ouaknine, J., Parkinson, M., Worrell, J.: Tractable reasoning in a fragment of separation logic. In: CONCUR 2011, pp. 235–249 (2011)
18. Brotherston, J., Fuhs, C., Perez, J.A.N., Gorogiannis, N.: A decision procedure for satisfiability in separation logic with inductive predicates. In: LICS 2014, pp. 25:1–25:10 (2014)
19. Berdine, J., Calcagno, C., O'Hearn, P.W.: Symbolic execution with separation logic. In: Yi, K. (ed.) APLAS 2005. LNCS, vol. 3780, pp. 52–68. Springer, Heidelberg (2005). https://doi.org/10.1007/11575467_5
20. Hou, Z., Goré, R., Tiu, A.: Automated theorem proving for assertions in separation logic with all connectives. In: CADE 2015, pp. 501–516 (2015)
21. Antonopoulos, T., Gorogiannis, N., Haase, C., Kanovich, M.I., Ouaknine, J.: Foundations for decision problems in separation logic with general inductive predicates. In: FoSSaCS 2014, pp. 411–425 (2014)
22. Enea, C., Lengal, O., Sighireanu, M., Vojnar, T.: Compositional entailment checking for a fragment of separation logic. Technical report FIT-TR-2014-01, FIT, Brno University of Technology. APLAS 2014 (2014)
23. Iosif, R., Rogalewicz, A., Simacek, J.: The tree width of separation logic with recursive definitions. In: CADE 2013, pp. 21–38 (2013)
24. Iosif, R., Rogalewicz, A., Vojnar, T.: Deciding entailments in inductive separation logic with tree automata. In: ATVA 2014, pp. 201–218 (2014)
25. Chen, T., Song, F., Wu, Z.: Tractability of separation logic with inductive definitions: beyond lists. In: Proceedings of the 28th International Conference on Concurrency Theory. Volume 85 of LIPIcs, pp. 37:1–37:17 (2017)
26. Brotherston, J., Gorogiannis, N., Kanovich, M.I., Rowe, R.: Model checking for symbolic-heap separation logic with inductive predicates. In: POPL 2016, pp. 84–96 (2016)
27. Brotherston, J., Gorogiannis, N., Kanovich, M.: Biabduction (and related problems) in array separation logic. In: de Moura, L. (ed.) CADE 2017. LNCS (LNAI), vol. 10395, pp. 472–490. Springer, Cham (2017). https://doi.org/10.1007/978-3-319-63046-5_29
28. Reynolds, A., Iosif, R., Serban, C., King, T.: A decision procedure for separation logic in SMT. In: Proceedings of the 14th International Symposium on Automated Technology for Verification and Analysis, pp. 244–261 (2016)

29. Reynolds, A., Iosif, R., Serban, C.: Reasoning in the Bernays-Schönfinkel-Ramsey fragment of separation logic. In: Bouajjani, A., Monniaux, D. (eds.) VMCAI 2017. LNCS, vol. 10145, pp. 462–482. Springer, Cham (2017). https://doi.org/10.1007/978-3-319-52234-0_25
30. Brochenin, R., Demri, S., Lozes, É.: On the almighty wand. Inf. Comput. **211**, 106–137 (2012)
31. Chin, W., David, C., Nguyen, H.H., Qin, S.: Automated verification of shape, size and bag properties via user-defined predicates in separation logic. Sci. Comput. Program. **77**(9), 1006–1036 (2012)
32. Gu, X., Chen, T., Wu, Z.: A complete decision procedure for linearly compositional separation logic with data constraints. IJCAR **2016**, 532–549 (2016)
33. Tatsuta, M., Le, Q.L., Chin, W.: Decision procedure for separation logic with inductive definitions and Presburger arithmetic. In: APLAS 2016, pp. 423–443 (2016)
34. Le, Q.L., Sun, J., Chin, W.: Satisfiability modulo heap-based programs. In: CAV 2016, pp. 382–404 (2016)
35. Reynolds, A., Iosif, R., Serban, C., King, T.: A decision procedure for separation logic in SMT. In: ATVA 2016, pp. 244–261 (2016)
36. Xu, Z., Chen, T., Wu, Z.: Satisfiability of compositional separation logic with tree predicates and data constraints. Technical report, State Key Laboratory of Computer Science, Institute of Software, Chinese Academy of Sciences (2017)
37. Gao, C., Chen, T., Wu, Z.: Separation logic with linearly compositional inductive predicates and set data constraints. In: Catania, B., Královič, R., Nawrocki, J., Pighizzini, G. (eds.) SOFSEM 2019. LNCS, vol. 11376, pp. 206–220. Springer, Cham (2019). https://doi.org/10.1007/978-3-030-10801-4_17
38. Priya, S., Su, Y., Bao, Y., Zhou, X., Vizel, Y., Gurfinkel, A.: Bounded model checking for LLVM. In: Proceedings of the 22nd Formal Methods in Computer-Aided Design, pp. 214–224 (2022)
39. Merz, F., Falke, S., Sinz, C.: LLBMC: bounded model checking of C and C++ programs using a compiler IR. In: Joshi, R., Müller, P., Podelski, A. (eds.) VSTTE 2012. LNCS, vol. 7152, pp. 146–161. Springer, Heidelberg (2012). https://doi.org/10.1007/978-3-642-27705-4_12
40. Clarke, E., Kroening, D., Lerda, F.: A tool for checking ANSI-C programs. In: Jensen, K., Podelski, A. (eds.) TACAS 2004. LNCS, vol. 2988, pp. 168–176. Springer, Heidelberg (2004). https://doi.org/10.1007/978-3-540-24730-2_15
41. Kroening, D., Tautschnig, M.: CBMC – C bounded model checker. In: Ábrahám, E., Havelund, K. (eds.) TACAS 2014. LNCS, vol. 8413, pp. 389–391. Springer, Heidelberg (2014). https://doi.org/10.1007/978-3-642-54862-8_26

VQCS: Verified Quantity Calculus System

Zhengpu Shi(✉)

Suzhou City University, Suzhou 215104, China
zhengpushi@szcu.edu.cn

Abstract. The complexity of unit systems for physical quantities and their informal treatment pose potential risk of errors in engineering and mathematical reasoning. Moreover, existing formal verification tools lack support for reasoning involving physical quantities with units. To address this, we propose VQCS (Verified Quantity Calculus System), a formal system implemented in the Rocq theorem prover. Its main contributions are as follows. First, we construct a unit system based on dimensional analysis, defining the syntax and semantics of units while supporting both manual and automatic conversion between units of the same kind. Second, we establish a quantity calculus system over abstract data types. Third, we define concrete quantity calculus systems over the real numbers and real vectors, enabling unit-aware computations for common mathematical derivations in engineering applications. Finally, we instantiate the system with the International System of Units (SI) and provide several case studies demonstrating its practical utility. The VQCS framework is released as an open-source Rocq library, providing a verifiable infrastructure for quantity calculus in engineering modeling.

Keywords: Formal Verification · Dimensional Analysis · Unit Conversion · Theorem Proving · Rocq

1 Introduction

1.1 Background

The mathematical expressions of physical quantities, which represent phenomena quantitatively, consist of numerical values and units. The definition and manipulation of units constitute unit calculus. The manipulation of quantities themselves constitutes quantity calculus. As such, quantity calculus fundamentally depends on unit calculus. For instance, velocity is defined as the ratio of length to time quantities. Using length units meter (m), kilometer (km) and time units second (s), hour (h), we derive velocity units $\mathsf{m/s}$ and $\mathsf{km/h}$. Given $\mathsf{km} = 1000\,\mathsf{m}$ and $\mathsf{h} = 3600\,\mathsf{s}$, we obtain $\mathsf{km/h} = \frac{1}{3.6}\,\mathsf{m/s}$, enabling conversion of $v = 90\,\mathsf{km/h}$ to $v = 25\,\mathsf{m/s}$.

Quantities and their units historically varied across regions and eras but now adhere to unified standards. The International System of Quantities (ISQ) governs physical quantities, while the International System of Units (SI) standardizes units. Although alternative systems exist (e.g., imperial, Gaussian/CGS), their precise definitions are ultimately based on SI [7].

A. Goharshady and C. Haase (Eds.): SETTA 2025, LNCS 16458, pp. 154–173, 2026.
https://doi.org/10.1007/978-981-95-7826-9_9

Mathematical expressions of physical quantities must satisfy both *numerical correctness* and *dimensional homogeneity*. However, unit system diversity (e.g., coexistence of SI and imperial units) coupled with informal handling methods can introduce critical errors during system design. Unit-related miscalculations have caused catastrophic failures, such as Air Canada Flight 143's fuel exhaustion due to unit confusion (requiring a glide landing) [10] and the Mars Climate Orbiter's destruction from imperial/metric unit inconsistency [9].

1.2 Critical Challenges in Unit-Aware Verification

Formal verification of unit-aware computations faces several challenges:

- Traditional engineering mathematics lacks formal unit specifications, leading to ambiguous interpretations (e.g., inconsistent unit usage in manual derivations, natural language annotations may be ambiguous).
- Dimensionally invalid operations (e.g., adding velocity to mass) cannot be detected at compile-time in informal systems.
- Manual unit conversions between systems (e.g., km/h $\leftrightarrow$ m/s) disrupts automated verification workflows.

1.3 VQCS System Design

To address these challenges, we present VQCS (Verified Quantity Calculus System), whose architecture is depicted in Fig. 1.

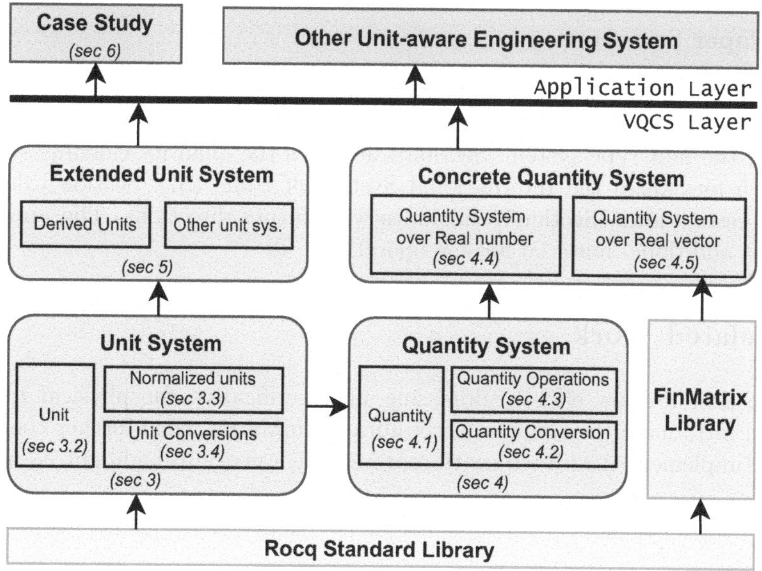

Fig. 1. Architecture of VQCS

Here, the VQCS Layer represents our developed quantity calculus system, while the Application Layer encompasses case studies and future unit-aware engineering systems. VQCS is further divided into two tiers: a core unit system with quantity system, and concrete implementations. Additionally, an existing formally verified matrix library *FinMatrix* [13,14] is utilized in the quantity system over real vector spaces. Detailed descriptions follow in subsequent sections.

1.4 Key Contributions

- **Formalized Unit Modeling**: Constructs hierarchical unit algebras based on type theory with SI base units $(\mathsf{T}, \mathsf{L}, \mathsf{M}, \mathsf{I}, \Theta, \mathsf{N}, \mathsf{J})$ as atomic types and derived units through power products (e.g., $\mathsf{N} \triangleq \mathsf{kg}\cdot\mathsf{m}\cdot\mathsf{s}^{-2}$). Thus removing ambiguities of informal descriptions.
- **Dimensional Homogeneity Enforcement**: Enforces dimensional homogeneity constraints through dynamic checking for validating physical operations (e.g., velocity $\times$ time $\rightarrow$ displacement; velocity $+$ mass $\rightarrow$ invalid quantity (`Qinvalid`)).
- **Extensible Architecture**: Supports polymorphic quantity types for matrices/tensors, enabling multiphysics coupling analysis.
- **System Completeness**: Implements full SI standards with non-SI units (e.g., minutes, electronvolts) and covers arithmetic, trigonometric, exponential functions, and matrix operations for engineering derivations.
- **Automated Verification Infrastructure**: Develops metaprogramming tactics for unit equivalence proofs and seamless unit conversions.

1.5 Paper Structure

The remainder of this paper is organized as follows. Section 2 reviews related work. Section 3 presents the core design of VQCS, including dimensional algebra and the unit type system. Section 4 develops the quantity calculus system. Section 5 formalizes the International System of Units (SI). Section 6 demonstrates case studies. Section 7 concludes with future directions. The appendix provides additional material for key operations.

2 Related Work

This section reviews efforts addressing unit verification for physical quantities and introduces the formal matrix library FinMatrix, then further contrasts VQCS (implemented in Rocq) with representative works to highlight its unique value.

Theorem Prover Extensions. Hayes and Mahony pioneered unit type systems in the Z specification language [5]. However, their static typing approach requires manual function-based definitions for each unit (e.g., $\mathsf{m.kg.s}^{-2}$ as $\mathsf{R} \odot \mathsf{U.L.M.T}^{-2}$), resulting in complexity. Their implementation offers limited operations and lacks full SI formalization, restricting practical utility. Foster and Wolff formalized physical quantities and units in Isabelle/HOL [1,2], supporting SI and imperial units. Nevertheless, their design exhibits limitations: incoherent units lack rigorous definitions (e.g., 2 minute merely represents (2×60) second without native minute support), and it omits advanced operations like trigonometric functions and vector support.

VQCS vs. Isabelle/HOL (Foster et al.): Enhancing Theorem-Prover-Based Unit Reasoning. To address the gaps in Foster et al.'s Isabelle/HOL framework, VQCS introduces targeted improvements in **operation coverage** and **automation**—two critical requirements for engineering-oriented unit-aware computations. First, in terms of operation support: Foster et al.'s work is limited to scalar quantities, failing to handle vector/matrix operations or trigonometric functions that are essential for scenarios like structural mechanics (e.g., force vector analysis) or signal processing. VQCS integrates the formally verified FinMatrix library [13,14] to natively support vector-valued and matrix-valued quantities, enabling unit-propagating operations such as dot products ($\langle q_1, q_2 \rangle$) and cross products ($q_1 \times q_2$) (Sect. 4.5). It also implements unit-aware trigonometric functions (e.g., qsin, qasin) that enforce radian-only arguments, preventing dimensionally invalid computations (e.g., sin(5m)) that the Isabelle/HOL framework cannot detect [2]. Second, regarding automation of unit conversion: While Foster et al.'s framework requires manual lemma definitions for unit conversions (e.g., explicitly stating "1minute = 60second"), VQCS eliminates this overhead via its normalized unit form ($N \triangleq \mathbb{R} \times D$) and automated tactics. The u2n function automatically computes a unit's coefficient and dimensional exponents, and the ueq tactic (See Sect. 3.3) fully automates equivalence proofs for both base and derived units (e.g., verifying $\mathsf{Pa} \equiv \mathsf{N/m}^2$, see Example 4). For dynamic conversion, VQCS's q2qu function handles unit conversions (e.g., 6000mV $\rightarrow$ 6V) whether or not a specific target unit is provided—a capability absent in Foster et al.'s Isabelle/HOL work.

Domain-Specific Languages. Wang et al. designed the ATPRDL language for train control systems [12], implementing dimensional checking via string matching. However, it lacks formal unit semantic models, making unit conversions and complex operations intractable. Physical modeling languages like Modelica support unit declarations [15], but their validation relies on runtime numerical computations rather than formal verification of unit consistency.

Type System Enhancements. F#'s Units of Measure [8] enables compile-time unit checking via type annotations but lacks dimensional algebra support, preventing dynamic relationships between derived units. Physics engines (e.g., OpenMM [11]) embed unit systems for simulation but prioritize numerical computation over formal verification.

VQCS vs. Haskell (Gundry): Beyond Compile-Time Unit Checking. Among programming-language-based unit validation approaches, Gundry's Haskell typechecker plugin is a representative effort, enabling compile-time unit checking via type annotations (e.g., declaring velocity as $\mathsf{DoubleMeasure}[\mathsf{Length}, \mathsf{Time}^{-1}]$) [4]. While this efficiently rejects dimensionally invalid operations (e.g., adding velocity to mass) during compilation, VQCS differs fundamentally in **verification depth** and **flexibility**: 1. Formal proof of correctness: Gundry's plugin focuses on "error detection" but cannot formally prove the correctness of unit-aware computations. VQCS leverages Rocq's theorem-proving capabilities to verify end-to-end engineering derivations—for example, in the free fall case study (Example 11), it proves that computed velocity ($v = g \cdot t$) and distance ($s = \frac{1}{2}g \cdot t^2$) have valid units ($\mathsf{m/s}$ and m, respectively) using the qeqR tactic. 2. Dynamic error handling: Gundry's strict compile-time checks prevent programs with potential dynamic unit invalidity (e.g., sensor data with variable units) from compiling. VQCS adopts a flexible dynamic approach via the Qinvalid constructor (Sect. 4.1), allowing programs to run and handle invalid cases at runtime (e.g., logging errors instead of crashing)—a critical feature for real-world engineering systems.

FinMatrix Library. We utilize the FinMatrix library, a dependently-typed formal matrix library supporting infinitely nested tensor types [13,14]. Its integration with our quantity calculus system enables unit-aware mathematical derivations with vector and matrix structures—a key advantage over scalar-only frameworks like Foster et al.'s Isabelle/HOL work and Gundry's Haskell plugin.

3 Unit System

All units are constructed from a set of base units and a coefficient according to specific rules. To semantically unify the concept of units, we compute the coefficient and dimensional exponents of each unit based on the principles of dimensional analysis. Furthermore, if the coefficient and all dimensional exponents of a unit are known, a unique normal form for the unit can be generated through a deterministic method. These operations of decomposing and generating units bridge their syntax and semantics, forming the foundation for unit conversion.

3.1 Base Units

The SI system defines seven base units, whose names, symbols, corresponding physical quantities, and dimensional symbols are listed in Table 1 (Appendix).

According to dimensional analysis theory [3,6], the dimension of each unit u takes the form of a product of basic dimensional exponents:

$$[u] \sim \mathsf{T}^{\alpha}\mathsf{L}^{\beta}\mathsf{M}^{\gamma}\mathsf{I}^{\delta}\Theta^{\epsilon}\mathsf{N}^{\zeta}\mathsf{J}^{\eta} \quad (1)$$

where $\alpha, \beta, \ldots$ are the dimensional exponents of u with respect to base dimensions $\mathsf{T}, \mathsf{L}, \ldots$. Henceforth, we use dimensional symbols to represent base units and denote the base unit type as $\mathbf{BU}$.

The formal definition of base units in Rocq is:

```
1  Inductive BaseUnit : Set := | BUTime | BULength | BUMass | BUCurrent
2    | BUTemperature | BUAmount | BULuminous
3  Notation "&T" := (BUTime). Notation "&L" := (BULength).
```

3.2 Unit Syntax

Physically, $\mathsf{N} \cdot \mathsf{m}$ and $\mathsf{m} \cdot \mathsf{N}$ represent identical units, indicating that distinct syntactic forms may represent the same physical unit. Our formal system syntactically distinguishes between such representations.

Unit Type. Based on dimensional theory, we propose a constructive approach to unit formation. Syntactically, units are formed through these rules: A real number is a dimensionless unit, a base unit is a unit, a unit may be inverted, and units may be multiplied. The formation rules for the *unit type* (denoted as $\mathbf{U}$) are given in BNF notation:

$$(u : \mathbf{U}) ::= (r : \mathbb{R}) \mid (b : \mathbf{BU}) \mid /u \mid u * u \tag{2}$$

For example, rpm (revolutions per minute) is defined as $1/(60 * \text{'s})$, where 's is the base unit second (see Sect. 5). The formal Rocq definition is:

```
1  Inductive Unit : Set :=
2    | Unone (coef:R) :> Unit | Ubu (bu : BaseUnit) :> Unit
3    | Uinv (u : Unit) | Umul (u1 u2 : Unit).
4  Notation "u1 * u2" := (Umul u1 u2) : Unit_scope.
5  Notation " / u" := (Uinv u) : Unit_scope.
6  Notation "u1 / u2" := (u1 * (/ u2)) : Unit_scope.
```

Here, `Unone` represents a dimensionless unit with a coefficient. `Ubu` constructs a unit from a base unit. The notation ":>" enables automatic type coercion. We establish `Unit_scope` as a dedicated notation scope.

Using this type, we can represent physical units:

Example 1 (Unit Examples).

```
1  Let m := &L. Let kg := &M. Let s := &T. (* meter,kilogram,second *)
2  Let hour := 3600 * s. (* hour *)
3  Let m3 := m ^ 3. (* cubic meter *)
4  Let N := 1 * (kg * m) / (s * s). (* newton *)
5  Let N' := (1 * kg / s) * (m / s). (* newton *)
```

Last two examples shows different syntactic representations of Newton unit.

Last two examples show different syntactic representations of the Newton unit. Such syntactic distinction is common—for instance, $\mathsf{N} \cdot \mathsf{m}$ (torque) and $\mathsf{m} \cdot \mathsf{N}$ are also $\mathsf{Umul}(u_1, u_2)$-ordered differently in syntax, but they are physically equivalent. In VQCS, this equivalence is verified via the u2n normalization function (see Sect. 3.3 for details on u2n and unit semantics, where the normalization function and its role in defining unit semantics are formally introduced)—since real multiplication (for coefficients) and additive summation (for dimensional exponents) are commutative, u2n maps both $\mathsf{Umul}(u_1, u_2)$ and $\mathsf{Umul}(u_2, u_1)$ to the same normalized form $(\mathbb{R} \times D)$. A concise proof example is as follows:

```
1  Let m := &L. Let N := 1 * (&M * &L) / (&T * &T). (* Define N *)
2  Let N_m := N * m. (* N.m *)
3  Let m_N := m * N. (* m.N *)
4  Lemma Nm_eq_mN : N_m == m_N. Proof. ueq. Qed. (* Full automated *)
```

Unit Coefficient. The *unit coefficient* $\tau(u)$ denotes the numerical factor when expressing u in base units, with type $\mathbf{U} \to \mathbb{R}$:

$$\tau(r : \mathbb{R}) \mapsto r \quad \tau(b : \mathbf{BU}) \mapsto 1 \quad \tau(/u) \mapsto /(\tau(u)) \quad \tau(u_1 * u_2) \mapsto \tau(u_1) * \tau(u_2) \tag{3}$$

Unit Dimensional Exponent. The *dimensional exponent* $\delta(u, b)$ specifies the power of base unit b in u, with type $\mathbf{U} \times \mathbf{BU} \to \mathbb{Z}$:

$$\begin{array}{ll} \delta(r : \mathbb{R}, b) \mapsto 0 & \delta(b' : \mathbf{BU}, b) \mapsto b' = b \ ?\ 1 : 0 \\ \delta(/u', b) \mapsto -\delta(u', b) & \delta(u_1 * u_2, b) \mapsto \delta(u_1, b) + \delta(u_2, b) \end{array} \tag{4}$$

For example, square meter (m^2) has $\delta = 2$ for L and $\delta = 0$ for others.

Constructing Units from Base Exponents. Given base unit $b : \mathbf{BU}$ and exponent $z : \mathbb{Z}$, we can construct a unique unit b^z. For natural $n : \mathbb{N}$, multiply n instances of b (via `ugenByBUNat`). For negative z, apply inversion to the positive exponent result. Formalized as:

```
1  Fixpoint ugenByBUNat (b : BaseUnit) (n : nat) : Unit :=
2    match n with | O => 1 | S O => b | S n' => (ugenByBUNat b n') * b
       end.
3  Definition ugenByBU (b : BaseUnit) (z : Z) : Unit :=
4    match z with | Z0 => 1
5    | Zpos p => ugenByBUNat b (Pos.to_nat p)
6    | Zneg p => / (ugenByBUNat b (Pos.to_nat p)) end.
```

Unit Construction from Components. Given unit $u : \mathbf{U}$, base unit $bu : \mathbf{BU}$, and exponent $z : \mathbb{Z}$, we can construct a unit $b^z \cdot u$ by:

$$\texttt{ucons}(u, b, z) = \begin{cases} u & \text{if } z = 0 \\ \texttt{ugenByBU}(b, z) \cdot u & \text{otherwise} \end{cases}$$

Equational properties of `ucons` are listed in Table 2 (Appendix).

3.3 Unit Semantics

The semantics of a unit is determined by its scaling coefficient and complete set of dimensional exponents.

Dimensional Exponent Type. The type of *(complete) dimensional exponents* of a unit form a 7-tuple type: $\mathbf{D} \triangleq \mathbb{Z}^7$. Formally:

```
1  Definition Dims := (Z * Z * Z * Z * Z * Z * Z)
```

We define essential operations on $\mathbf{D}$:

1. Zero exponents (dimensionless). $\texttt{dzero} \triangleq (0, 0, 0, 0, 0, 0, 0)$.
2. Boolean equality. $\texttt{deqb} : \mathbf{D} \to \mathbf{D} \to \mathbb{B}$ (component-wise AND of equalities).
3. Addition. $\texttt{dplus} : \mathbf{D} \to \mathbf{D} \to \mathbf{D}$ (component-wise sum).
4. Negation. $\texttt{dopp} : \mathbf{D} \to \mathbf{D}$ (component-wise negation).
5. Scalar multiplication. $\mathsf{dscal} : \mathbb{Z} \to \mathbf{D} \to \mathbf{D}$ (component-wise scaling).

Computing Dimensional Exponents. For any unit $u : \mathbf{U}$, its dimensional exponent tuple is computed by $\Delta : \mathbf{U} \to \mathbf{D}$:

$$\Delta(u) \mapsto (\delta(u, \mathsf{T}), \delta(u, \mathsf{L}), \delta(u, \mathsf{M}), \delta(u, \mathsf{I}), \delta(u, \Theta), \delta(u, \mathsf{N}), \delta(u, \mathsf{J})) \quad (5)$$

Normalized Form Type. The *normalized form* of a unit is a pair comprising its coefficient and dimensional exponent tuple, with type $\mathbf{N} \triangleq \mathbb{R} \times \mathbf{D}$. Essential operations on $\mathbf{N}$ are following:

1. Identity. $\texttt{nOne} \triangleq (1, \texttt{dzero})$
2. Boolean equality. $\texttt{neqb} : \mathbf{N} \to \mathbf{N} \to \mathbb{B}$
3. Multiplication. $\texttt{nmul}(n_1, n_2) \triangleq (n_1.1 \cdot n_2.1,\ \texttt{dplus}(n_1.2, n_2.2))$
4. Inversion. $\texttt{ninv}(n) \triangleq (1/n.1,\ \texttt{dopp}(n.2))$
5. Division. $\texttt{ndiv}(n_1, n_2) \triangleq \texttt{nmul}(n_1, \texttt{ninv}(n_2))$

Computing Normalized Form. The normalization function $\mathtt{u2n} : \mathbf{U} \to \mathbf{N}$ is defined as: $\mathtt{u2n}(u) \triangleq (\tau(u), \Delta(u))$. Two units u_1 and u_2 are semantically equivalent if and only if $\mathtt{u2n}(u_1) = \mathtt{u2n}(u_2)$.

Semantic equivalence is formally defined in Rocq:

```
1  Definition ueq (u1 u2 : Unit) : Prop := u2n u1 = u2n u2.
2  Infix "==" := (ueq) (at level 70) : Unit_scope.
```

Automated Equivalence Proofs. Semantic equivalence proofs are automated using the following tactic:

```
1  Ltac ueq := compute; f_equal; try lra; try field.
```

This tactic handles goals of form $u_1 == u_2$ by following steps:

- `compute`: Fully reduces the goal to $(c_1, d_1) = (c_2, d_2)$.
- `f_equal`: Splits into subgoals $c_1 = c_2$ and $d_1 = d_2$.
- Solves $d_1 = d_2$ automatically.
- Uses real arithmetic tactics for $c_1 = c_2$, such as `lra` and `field`.

3.4 Conversions Between Normalized Forms

Convertibility of Normalized Forms. Two normalized forms are mutually convertible when they share identical dimensional exponents but differ only in their coefficients. For example, seconds and minutes exhibit such convertibility. Conversely, forms with different dimensions (e.g., seconds vs. meters) are inconvertible. We formalize this as a boolean predicate $\mathtt{ncvtbleb} : \mathbf{N} \to \mathbf{N} \to \mathbb{B}$:

```
1  Definition ncvtbleb (m n : Nunit) : bool := deqb m.2 n.2.
```

Conversion Between Normalized Forms. For convertible forms, we compute a real-valued conversion factor. Given source $src : \mathbf{N}$ and reference $ref : \mathbf{N}$ forms, the conversion factor of src relative to ref is $\frac{src.1}{ref.1}$. Formally:

```
1  Definition nconvRate (src ref : Nunit) : option R :=
2    if ncvtbleb src ref then Some (src.1 / ref.1) else None.
```

To avoid ambiguity, conversions attach the reference form to the result:

```
1  Definition nconv (src ref : Nunit) : option (R * Nunit) :=
2    if ncvtbleb src ref then Some (src.1 / ref.1, ref) else None.
```

Since units ($\mathbf{U}$) convert to normalized forms via u2n, this indirectly enables unit conversions. Example 2 demonstrates this.

Example 2 (Unit Conversion Example). The conversion factor from hours to minutes is 60:

```
1    Goal nconvRate (u2n 'hrs) (u2n 'min) = Some 60.
2    Proof. compute; f_equal; lra. Qed.
```

Converting hours to seconds yields (3600, 's):

```
1    Goal nconv (u2n 'hrs) (u2n 's) = Some (3600, (u2n 's)).
2    Proof. compute; repeat f_equal; lra. Qed.
```

Note: `'s`, `'min`, and `'hrs` are defined in Sect. 5.

4 Physical Quantity Calculus System

The calculus of physical quantities needs to follow specific rules. For instance, only physical quantities with the same or convertible units can be compared or undergo addition or subtraction. Also, in trigonometric calculations, the units of physical quantities must be radians; if degrees are used, a prior conversion is necessary to avoid incorrect results. Based on the unit system introduced in Sect. 3, this section constructs a physical quantity calculus system. It supports multiple data types, including real numbers, vectors, and matrices, to meet the diverse numerical representation needs of physical quantities.

4.1 Quantity Type

A physical quantity combines numerical value information with unit information.

Definition of Quantity Type. The quantity type must represent both valid and invalid quantities. For example: Time and length are distinct physical quantities, but their addition is meaningless and should yield an invalid quantity. To support this, we define the quantity type $\mathbf{Q}$ for a numerical type $\mathbf{A}$ as:

$$\mathbf{Q} \triangleq (\mathbf{A} \times \mathbf{N}) + \mathrm{INVALID} \tag{6}$$

Formally, we implement this using an option-like structure:

```
1  Inductive Quantity {A : Type} :=
2    | Qmake (v : A) (n : Nunit)     (* valid quantity   *)
3    | Qinvalid.                     (* invalid quantity *)
4  Notation "!!" := Qinvalid (at level 3) : Quantity_scope.
```

We use the `Quantity_scope` notation scope and define "`!!`" for invalid case. Convenience constructors for quantity are defined:

```
1  Definition u2q {A} (v : A) (u : Unit) := Qmake v (u2n u).
2  Definition a2q {A} (v : A) := Qmake v nOne.
```

Here, u2q(v, u) constructs from value v and syntactic unit u, a2q(v) creates dimensionless quantity with value v.

Basic Operations on Quantity Type. For a valid quantity $q : \mathbf{Q}$ ($q \neq$ `!!`), it contains three components: $q = (v, c, d)$ where:

- $v : \mathbf{A}$ is the numerical value.
- $c : \mathbb{R}$ is the unit coefficient.
- $d : \mathbf{D}$ is the dimensional exponents.

We define projection functions:

- `qval` : $\mathbf{Q} \rightarrow$ option $\mathbf{A}$ extracts the numerical value.
- `qcoef` : $\mathbf{Q} \rightarrow$ option $\mathbb{R}$ extracts the unit coefficient.
- `qdim` : $\mathbf{Q} \rightarrow$ option $\mathbf{D}$ extracts the dimensional exponents.

4.2 Quantity Conversion

Quantities sharing identical dimensional exponents but differing only in coefficients are mutually convertible and can be transformed to new units. For example, quantities in seconds and minutes are convertible. Under the quantity type definition (Sect. 4.1), valid quantities $q_1, q_2 : \mathbf{Q}$ decompose into:

$$q_1 = (v_1, c_1, d_1), \qquad q_2 = (v_2, c_2, d_2) \tag{7}$$

Dimensional analysis requires that for physically equivalent quantities:

$$c_1 \cdot v_1 = c_2 \cdot v_2 \tag{8}$$

where:

- $v_1, v_2 : \mathbf{A}$ are numerical values.
- $c_1, c_2 : \mathbb{R}$ are unit coefficients.
- $d_1, d_2 : \mathbf{D}$ are dimensional exponents, and $d_1 = d_2$.

Equation (8) provides the computational basis for quantity conversion. Note that the $\cdot$ operation has type $\mathbb{R} \rightarrow \mathbf{A} \rightarrow \mathbf{A}$ since v_i are polymorphic in $\mathbf{A}$. We formalize this context:

```
1   Context {A} (ARmul : R -> A -> A). (* scalar multiplication *)
```

Conversion to Normalized Form. Given source quantity $q_{src} = (v_{src}, c_{src}, d_{src})$ and reference normalized form $n_{ref} = (c_{ref}, d_{ref})$, conversion is possible when $d_{src} = d_{ref}$. The converted quantity is:

$$q' = \left(\frac{c_{src}}{c_{ref}} \cdot v_{src},\ c_{ref},\ d_{ref} \right) \tag{9}$$

Formalized as q2qn:

```
1  Definition q2qn (q : Quantity) (ref : Nunit) : Quantity :=
2    match q with
3    | Qmake v n => if ncvtbleb n ref
4        then Qmake (ARmul (n.1 / ref.1) v) ref else !!
5    | !! => !!
6    end.
```

This satisfies Equation (8) by construction.

Conversion to Syntactic Unit. Using q2qn and u2n, we define conversion with a syntactic unit $uref : \mathbf{U}$:

```
1  Definition q2qu (q : Quantity) (uref : Unit) : Quantity :=
2    q2qn q (u2n uref).
```

4.3 Quantity Operations

Dimensional analysis requires that quantities must share identical units for addition and comparison, while unary operations may impose specific unit requirements. As established in Sect. 4.2, dimensionally compatible quantities can be converted to common units. We design operations considering dimensional consistency and convertibility. Since many operations follow similar patterns, we first define generic operation templates before implementing specific ones (addition, multiplication, etc.).

Generic Unary Operation. For any quantity q and unary operation $f : \mathbf{A} \to \mathbf{A}$ on the numerical type, define the *unary quantity operation* qop1:

$$\mathtt{qop1}(f, q) \triangleq \begin{cases} (f(v), n) & \text{if } q = (v, n) \\ !! & \text{otherwise} \end{cases} \tag{10}$$

Generic Binary Operation with Identical Units. For quantities q_1, q_2 and binary operation $f : \mathbf{A} \to \mathbf{A} \to \mathbf{A}$, define the *binary quantity operation with identical units* qop2:

$$\mathtt{qop2}(f, q_1, q_2) \triangleq \begin{cases} (f(v_1, v_2), n_1) & \text{if } q_1 = (v_1, n_1) \wedge q_2 = (v_2, n_2) \wedge n_1 = n_2 \\ !! & \text{otherwise} \end{cases} \tag{11}$$

Addition, Negation, and Subtraction. For quantities q_1, q_2:

- *Addition* ($\mathtt{qadd} : q_1 + q_2$), applies numerical addition when units are identical (wrapper with qop2).

- *Negation* ($\texttt{qopp} : -q$), negates numerical value while preserving units (wrapper with $\texttt{qop1}$).
- *Subtraction* ($\texttt{qsub} : q_1 - q_2$), defined as $q_1 + (-q_2)$.

If the numerical type $\mathbf{A}$ with addition is associative/commutative, so is qadd.

Multiplication, Reciprocal, and Division.

- *Multiplication* ($\texttt{qmul} : q_1 * q_2$), multiplies numerical values and normalized unit forms.
- *Reciprocal* ($\texttt{qinv} : /q$), takes numerical reciprocal and unit inverse.
- *Division* ($\texttt{qdiv} : q_1/q_2$), defined as $q_1 * (/q_2)$.

Example: $(2, \mathsf{s}) * (5, \mathsf{m}) = (10, \mathsf{m} \cdot \mathsf{s})$ where $\mathsf{m} \cdot \mathsf{s}$ is the normalized product form.

4.4 Real-Valued Quantities

When the numerical type supports extended operations, additional functionality can be derived for quantities. For real numbers $\mathbb{R}$ and n-dimensional vectors $\mathbb{R}^n$, we instantiate and extend operations accordingly. To accommodate potential interactions between scalar and vector quantities, distinct notations are employed.

Derived Operations for Real Scalars. Operations for real-valued quantities (**QuR**) are largely derived from the polymorphic calculus, as shown below. For more details, see Table 3 (Appendix).

- Scalar multiplication: $r \cdot q$ $(r \in \mathbb{R})$
- Exponentiation: q^z $(z \in \mathbb{Z})$
- Trigonometric functions (radian arguments)

Integer Roots of Real Quantities. Engineering applications often require roots of quantities. Such as: $\sqrt{100\ \mathsf{m}^2} = 10\ \mathsf{m}$, $\sqrt[3]{27\ \mathsf{m}^3} = 3\ \mathsf{m}$. We define the integer root operation $\texttt{qrootR} : \mathbf{QuR} \to \mathbb{Z} \to \mathbf{QuR}$:

$$\texttt{qrootR}(q, z) \triangleq \begin{cases} \left(v^{1/z}, \texttt{nroot}(n, z)\right) & q = (v, n) \wedge v \geq 0 \text{ (for even } z) \wedge \\ & \text{each element of } \texttt{dims}(n) \text{ divides } z. \\ !! & \text{otherwise} \end{cases} \tag{12}$$

where, $v^{1/z}$ is the real root operation, $\mathsf{nroot}(n, z)$ computes the z-th root of normalized unit n. This operation imposes strict dimensional constraints:

1. For even roots: $v \geq 0$ and positive unit coefficients.
2. Dimensional exponents must be divisible by z (e.g., $\sqrt{\mathsf{m}^3}$ is invalid).

Detailed preconditions and error cases exceed our current scope.

4.5 Vector-Valued Quantities

For quantities with real vector numerical values (termed vector quantities), most operations derive from the polymorphic calculus (Sect. 4.3).

Component Extraction. A fundamental operation is component extraction: `qnthRV` : **QuRV** $\rightarrow$ `fin` n $\rightarrow$ **QuR**. This constructs a real-valued quantity from the i-th vector component and the original unit. For an n-dimensional vector quantity q, its i-th component is denoted $q.[i]$. Constant-dimension vectors support shorthand notations ($q.1, q.2$):

```
1  Definition qnthRV {n} (q : QuRV n) (i : fin n) : QuR :=
2    match q with
3    | Qmake v n => Qmake (v i) n (* get component, preserve unit *)
4    | !! => !!                  (* propagate invalid *)
5    end.
6  Notation "q .[ i ]" := (qnthRV q i) : QuRV_scope. (* i-th element *)
7  Notation "q .1" := (q.[#0]) : QuRV_scope.   (* q.2 similarly *)
```

Vector-Specific Operations. Since the numerical component is a vector, we define additional operations:

- *Dot Product* (`qdotRV`): $\langle \mathbf{q}_1, \mathbf{q}_2 \rangle$: **QuRV** $\rightarrow$ **QuRV** $\rightarrow$ **QuR**, computes scalar product of vectors and multiplies normalized units.
- *Cross Product* (`qcrossRV3`): $\mathbf{q}_1 \times \mathbf{q}_2$: **QuRV** $\rightarrow$ **QuRV** $\rightarrow$ **QuRV**, computes vector product and multiplies normalized units.

Formal definitions:

```
1  Definition qdotRV {n} (q1 q2 : QuRV n) : QuR :=
2    match q1, q2 with
3    | Qmake v1 n1, Qmake v2 n2 => Qmake (vdot v1 v2) (nmul n1 n2)
4    | _, _ => !!
5    end.
6  Definition qcrossRV3 (q1 q2 : QuRV 3) : QuRV 3 :=
7    match q1, q2 with
8    | Qmake v1 n1, Qmake v2 n2 => Qmake (v3cross v1 v2) (nmul n1 n2)
9    | _, _ => !!
10   end.
11 Notation "'< q1 , q2 >" := (qdotRV q1 q2) : QuRV_scope.
12 Notation "q1 \x q2" := (qcrossRV3 q1 q2) : QuRV_scope.
```

Here, `vdot` and `v3cross` are defined vector operations in FinMatrix. Further development and verification of vector operations remain future work.

5 The International System of Units (SI)

Using the unit system formalized in Sect. 3, we implement all units defined in the SI. We define SI units using the syntactic unit type **U** and verify their semantics and equivalence through normalized forms **N**. Custom notations represent SI unit symbols, consistently prefixed with a single quote (except in Sect. 5.1). For example, 's denotes the second unit of time.

5.1 SI Prefixes

The International Bureau of Weights and Measures (BIPM) defines 24 SI prefixes, with the complete list referred in Table 7 in SI Brochure [7]. We implement these using underscore-prefixed notations. For example, the milli (10^{-3}) prefix is formalized as:

```
1  Definition milli (u : Unit) : Unit := 1e-3 * u.
2  Notation "'_m' x" := (milli x) (at level 5, right associativity).
```

where Rocq recognizes 1e-3 as scientific notation for 10^{-3}. Thus, given 's (seconds), _m 's represents milliseconds.

5.2 Base Units

Base unit definitions establish named constants with dedicated notations. All seven SI base units follow this pattern:

Example 3 (Second Definition). The second (time) is defined as:

```
1  Definition second := BUTime. (* base unit for time *)
2  Notation "'s" := second (at level 5) : SI_scope.
```

This uses the **BU** type for semantic clarity while enabling automatic promotion to **U** via the Ubu constructor.

5.3 Derived Units

The SI defines 22 derived units with specific names and symbols. The complete list is shown in Table 4 in SI Brochure [7].

Example 4 (Definition of Pascal Pressure Unit) The pressure unit pascal has the English name "pascal" and symbol Pa. Expressed in SI base units, it is $\mathsf{kg} \cdot \mathsf{m}^{-1} \cdot \mathsf{s}^{-2}$. It can also be defined using other SI units: N/m^2 or J/m^3. It is formally defined as:

```
1  Definition pascal := 'kg * (/'m) * (/'s²).
2  Notation "'Pa" := (pascal) (at level 5) : SI_scope.
```

Verify $\mathsf{Pa} = \mathsf{N}/\mathsf{m}^2$ and $\mathsf{Pa} = \mathsf{J}/\mathsf{m}^3$:

```
1  Lemma pascal_spec : 'Pa == 'N / 'm^2. Proof. ueq. Qed.
2  Lemma pascal_spec2 : 'Pa == 'J / 'm^3. Proof. ueq. Qed.
```

These verifications are automated, benefiting from the computational design.

We have verified the mutual definition rules for all derived units. Cross-verification ensures definitional consistency throughout the SI hierarchy.

5.4 Accepted Non-SI Units

Although the SI is widely adopted globally, many non-SI units remain in use across scientific, technical, and commercial literature. Due to historical and cultural influences, these units have not been fully replaced by SI units. The International Committee for Weights and Measures (CIPM) provides a list of acceptable non-SI units, including hour, minute, degreer, and so on. Their formal names and symbols are listed in Table 8 in SI Brochure [7].

Example 5 (Definitions of Minute, Hour, and Day). The formal definitions and verifications for minute, hour, and day units are presented below:

```
1  Definition minute := 60 * 's. Notation "'min" := minute.
2  Definition hour := 60 * 'min. Notation "'hrs" := hour.
3  Definition day := 24 * 'hrs. Notation "'d" := day.
```

Verification of equivalence relationships shows definitional consistency:

```
1  Lemma hour2second : 'hrs == 3600 * 's. Proof. ueq. Qed.
2  Lemma day2second : 'd == 86400 * 's. Proof. ueq. Qed.
3  Lemma day2minute : 'd == 1440 * 'min. Proof. ueq. Qed.
```

6 Experiments

We present examples demonstrating the basic usage of the quantity calculus system (Sect. 4) and the International System of Units (Sect. 5).

6.1 Simple Applications of Real-Valued Quantities

This section demonstrates basic usage of real-valued quantities (Sect. 4.4) through simple applications.

Example 6 (Unit Conversion). Convert 6000 mV to V, yielding 6 V:

```
1  Goal q2quR (u2qR 6000 _m 'V) 'V = (u2qR 6 'V). Proof. qeqR. Qed.
```

Here: `_m` is the milli prefix, `_m 'V` constructs mV unit, `u2qR 6000 _m 'V` creates quantity (6000 mV), `q2quR q 'V` converts quantity q to volts, `qeqR` automates real-valued quantity proofs.

Example 7 (Addition with Identical Units). Add 3 s and 2 s, yielding 5 s:

```
1    Goal (u2qR 3 's) + (u2qR 2 's) = (u2qR 5 's). Proof. qeqR. Qed.
```

Example 8 (Manual Conversion and Addition). Add 1 min and 60 s by converting minutes to seconds:

```
1    Goal q2quR (u2qR 1 'min) 's + (u2qR 60 's) = u2qR 120 's.
2    Proof. qeqR. Qed.
```

Convert seconds to minutes instead:

```
1    Goal u2qR 1 'min + q2quR (u2qR 60 's) 'min = u2qR 2 'min.
2    Proof. qeqR. Qed.
```

Example 9 (Division). Divide 10 m by 5 m/s, yielding 2 s:

```
1    Goal (u2qR 10 'm) / (u2qR 5 ('m/'s)
2    Proof. qeqR. Qed.
```

Example 10 (Root Extraction). Cube root of 1000 cm^3 yields 10 cm:

```
1    Goal qrootR (u2qR 1000 (_c 'm ^ 3)
2    Proof. qeqR. ra. Qed.
```

6.2 Comprehensive Applications of Real-Valued Quantities

We present relatively complete yet concise applications for clarity.

Example 11 (Free Fall Motion). Consider free fall motion starting at time $t = 0$. Compute velocity and distance at: (1) $t_1 = 30$ seconds. (2) $t_2 = 1$ minute. Given gravitational acceleration $g = 9.8$ m/s^2.

Solution: First define known quantities:

```
1    Let g := u2qR 9.8 ('m/('s^2))
2    Let t1 := u2qR 30 's.    Let t2 := u2qR 1 'min.
```

Then compute velocities ($v_i = g \cdot t_i$) and distances ($s_i = \frac{1}{2}gt_i^2$):

```
1    Let v1 := t1 * g.    Let v2 := t2 * g.
2    Let s1 := (1/2)
3    Let s2 := (1/2)
```

Verify $v_1 = 294$ m/s and $s_1 = 4410$ m with automatic unit inference:

```
1    Goal v1 = u2qR 294 ('m/'s)
2    Goal s1 = u2qR 4410 'm. Proof. qeqR. Qed.
```

Directly verify the numerical value of v_1 (unit: m/s):

```
1    Goal qval v1 = Some 294. Proof. qeqR. Qed.
```

6.3 Simple Applications of Vector-Valued Quantities

This section demonstrates basic usage of vector-valued quantities (Sect. 4.5) through simple applications.

Example 12 **(Scalar Multiplication, Component Extraction, and Dot Product).** Given: velocity vector $\mathbf{v} = [1, 2, 3]^\mathrm{T}$ m/s in 3D space, time $t = 5$ s. The displacement is computed as $\mathbf{s} = t \cdot \mathbf{v} = [5, 10, 15]^\mathrm{T}$ m:

```
1  Let v := @u2qRV 3 (l2v [1;2;3]) ('m/'s)
2  Let t := u2qR 5 's. Let s := t * v.
3  Goal s = u2qRV (l2v [5;10;15]) 'm. Proof. qeqRV. Qed.
```

where, l2v converts a list to a vector, u2qRV constructs a vector-valued quantity.

Verify the i-th component of $\mathbf{s}$ is 5 m:

```
1  Goal s.1 = u2qR 5 'm. Proof. qeqRV. Qed.
```

Verify the dot product $\langle \mathbf{v}, \mathbf{v} \rangle = 14\ \mathrm{m}^2/\mathrm{s}^2$:

```
1  Goal <v, v> = u2qR 14 (('m/'s)^2)
```

7 Conclusion

This paper presents the Verified Quantity Calculus System (VQCS), an integrated framework providing precise tooling for describing, manipulating, and verifying mathematical expressions involving physical units. VQCS encompasses a formal calculus of units, real-valued and vector-valued quantity calculi built upon foundational abstract types, and a formalized implementation of the International System of Units (SI). By embedding physical intuition into rigorous mathematical foundations, VQCS enables highly automated verification of unit consistency and dimensional accuracy within complex derivations. This establishes a robust foundation for ensuring the correctness of physical computations, particularly vital for safety-critical and high-reliability engineering applications. VQCS thus contributes essential infrastructure for formal metrology, empowering engineers to identify and resolve unit-related errors early in the design process, thereby streamlining development and enhancing system reliability. The framework is open-source: https://zhengpushi.github.io/projects/VQCS.

Future research will focus on enhancing VQCS's practical utility and integration. Key directions include: formalizing measurement systems; extending VQCS for comprehensive unit-aware modeling of large-scale engineering systems, with rigorous evaluation of runtime and memory performance for operations involving large matrices/tensors; developing quantity calculi for diverse data types, including strategies for handling numerical issues like floating-point errors; and creating domain-specific languages to enable standalone verification tools accessible to engineers without theorem proving expertise. Complementary efforts will explore integration with platforms like Simulink and conduct further validation in realistic scenarios.

Acknowledgments. I would like to thank Gang Chen and Hao Deng for their advice about unit system design, and my colleagues for their discussions and suggestions.

A Appendix: Selected Definitions and Properties

Herein are the verified properties and key definitions in VQCS. For the complete catalog, refer to https://zhengpushi.github.io/projects/VQCS/v1.0/toc.html.

Table 1. SI Base Units

Unit Name	Unit Symbol	Physical Quantity	Dimensional Symbol	Typical Symbol
Second	s	Time	T	t
Meter	m	Length	L	l, x, r
Kilogram	kg	Mass	M	m
Ampere	A	Electric Current	I	I, i
Kelvin	K	Thermodynamic Temperature	Θ	T
Mole	mol	Amount of Substance	N	n
Candela	cd	Luminous Intensity	J	I_v

Table 2. Properties related to the ucons operation

Lemma Name	Property	Explanation
ucoef_inj_exp	$u :: (b, z_1) = u :: (b, z_2) \rightarrow z_1 = z_2$	Injective in exponents.
ucoef_inj_Unit	$u_1 :: (b, z) = u_2 :: (b, z) \rightarrow u_1 = u_2$	Injective in initial units.
ucoef_ucons	$\tau(u :: (b, z)) = \tau(u)$	Coefficient unchanged after connection.
udim_ucons_same	$\delta(u :: (b, z), b) = \delta(u, b) + z$	Dimension for b after b^z connection.

Table 3. Operations of quantity calculus over real numbers

Type or Function	Meaning	Definition	Notation
QuR	Real quantity type	@Quantity $\mathbb{R}$	
u2qR($x : \mathbb{R}, u$: QuR) : QuR	Construct quantity from x and unit u	u2q(x, u)	
qaddR(q_1 q_2 : QuR) : QuR	Addition of quantities	qadd(Rplus, q_1, q_2)	$q_1 + q_2$
qoppR(q : QuR) : QuR	Negation	qopp(Ropp, q)	$-q$
qmulR(q_1 q_2 : QuR) : QuR	Multiplication	qmul(Rmult, q_1, q_2)	$q_1 \cdot q_2$
qpowR(q : QuR, $z : \mathbb{Z}$) : QuR	Integer power	qpow(Rmult, q, z)	q^z
qinvR(q : QuR) : QuR	Inverse	qinv(Rinv, q)	$1/q$
qabs(q : QuR) : QuR	Absolute value	qop1(Rabs, q)	
qsin(q : QuR) : QuR	Sine	qdim0op1(sin, q)	'sin q
qasin(q : QuR) : QuR	Arcsine	qdim0op1(asin, q)	'asin q

References

1. Foster, S., Wolff, B.: A sound type system for physical quantities, units, and measurements. Archive of Formal Proofs (2020). https://isa-afp.org/entries/Physical_Quantities.html, Formal proof development
2. Foster, S., Wolff, B.: Automated reasoning for physical quantities, units, and measurements in Isabelle/HOL (2023). https://arxiv.org/abs/2302.07629
3. Gao, G.: Fundamentals of Dimensional Analysis. Science Press, China (2020). (in Chinese)
4. Gundry, A.: A typechecker plugin for units of measure: Domain-specific constraint solving in GHC Haskell. ACM SIGPLAN Not. **50**(12), 11–22 (2015). https://doi.org/10.1145/2887747.2804305
5. Hayes, I.J., Mahony, B.P.: Using units of measurement in formal specifications. Formal Asp. Comput. **7**(3), 329–347 (1995). https://doi.org/10.1007/BF01211077
6. Liang, C., Cao, Z.: Dimensional Analysis: Theory and Application. Science Press, China (2020). (in Chinese)
7. des Poids et Mesures (BIPM), B.I.: Le Système International d'Unités (SI) [The International System of Units]. BIPM, France, 9 edn. (2019). https://www.bipm.org/utils/common/pdf/si-brochure/SI-Brochure-9.pdf, available online at BIPM website
8. Microsoft: Units of measure (f#) (2024). https://learn.microsoft.com/en-us/dotnet/fsharp/language-reference/units-of-measure
9. NASA: Mars Climate Orbiter Mishap Investigation Board - Phase I Report. NASA Lessons Learned Information System (1999). https://llis.nasa.gov/lesson/641. Accessed 29 July 2024
10. Nelson, W.H.: The gimli glider. Soaring Mag. (1997). http://www.wadenelson.com/gimli.html, 2800 Words including sidebars
11. OpenMM Team: OpenMM: High performance, customizable molecular simulation (2017–2025). https://openmm.org. Accessed 31 May 2024
12. Shang, W., et al.: A dimensional analysis method for the requirements model of railway control software. Chin. J. Comput. **43**(11), 2152–2165 (2020). https://doi.org/10.11897/SP.J.1016.2020.02152. (in Chinese)
13. Shi, Z., Chen, G.: CoQ formalization of orientation representation: matrix, Euler angles, axis-angle and quaternion. In: Marmsoler, D., Sun, M. (eds.) Formal Aspects of Component Software. FACS '24, pp. 79–96. Springer, Cham (2024). https://doi.org/10.1007/978-3-031-71261-6_5
14. Shi, Z., Chen, G.: Formal verification of executable matrix inversion via adjoint matrix and Gaussian elimination. In: Proceedings of the 26th International Symposium on Principles and Practice of Declarative Programming. PPDP '24. Association for Computing Machinery, New York, NY, USA (2024). https://doi.org/10.1145/3678232.3678242
15. Tiller, M.: Introduction to Physical Modeling with Modelica. Springer, Cham (2001). https://doi.org/10.1007/978-1-4615-1561-6

Automata

Efficient Decomposition Identification of Deterministic Finite Automata from Examples

Junjie Meng[1], Jie An[2](✉), Yong Li[3](✉), Andrea Turrini[3,4](✉), Fanjiang Xu[2], Naijun Zhan[5], and Miaomiao Zhang[1](✉)

[1] School of Computer Science and Technology, Tongji University, Shanghai, China
{2311452,miaomiao}@tongji.edu.cn
[2] National Key Laboratory of Space Integrated Information System, Institute of Software, Chinese Academy of Sciences, Beijing, China
{anjie,fanjiang}@iscas.ac.cn
[3] Key Laboratory of System Software (Chinese Academy of Sciences), Institute of Software, Chinese Academy of Sciences, Beijing, China
{liyong,turrini}@ios.ac.cn
[4] Institute of Intelligent Software Guangzhou, Guangzhou, China
[5] School of Computer Science and MOE Key Laboratory of High Confidence Software Technologies, Peking University, Beijing, China
njzhan@pku.edu.cn

Abstract. The identification of deterministic finite automata (DFAs) from labeled examples is a cornerstone of automata learning, yet traditional methods focus on learning monolithic DFAs, which often yield a large DFA lacking simplicity and interoperability. Recent work addresses these limitations by exploring DFA decomposition identification problems (DFA-DIPs), which model system behavior as intersections of multiple DFAs, offering modularity for complex tasks. However, existing DFA-DIP approaches depend on SAT encodings derived from Augmented Prefix Tree Acceptors (APTAs), incurring scalability limitations due to their inherent redundancy.

In this work, we advance DFA-DIP research through studying two variants: the traditional Pareto-optimal DIP and the novel states-optimal DIP, which prioritizes a minimal number of states. We propose a novel framework that bridges DFA decomposition with recent advancements in automata representation. One of our key innovations replaces APTA with 3-valued DFA (3DFA) derived directly from labeled examples. This compact representation eliminates redundancies of APTA, thus drastically reducing variables in the improved SAT encoding. Experimental results demonstrate that our 3DFA-based approach achieves significant efficiency gains for the Pareto-optimal DIP while enabling a scalable solution for the states-optimal DIP.

Keywords: DFA decomposition · DFA identification · Model learning · Passive learning · SAT solving · Grammatical inference

A. Goharshady and C. Haase (Eds.): SETTA 2025, LNCS 16458, pp. 177–195, 2026.
https://doi.org/10.1007/978-981-95-7826-9_10

1 Introduction

The identification of Deterministic Finite Automata (DFAs) from labeled examples is a fundamental problem in computer science, with applications in inference of network invariants [7], grammatical inference [10], model checking [15], reinforcement learning [13], etc. Known as passive model learning [19], classical methods focus on inferring a single DFA from examples. The generated DFA may have a large size and thus suffers from a lack of simplicity and interpretability, as a single DFA representing complex system behaviors can have a very intricate structure.

To address this issue, recent research [13] has moved toward the *DFA decomposition identification problem* (DFA-DIP), i.e., inferring a group of DFAs from examples, where their conjunction language includes all positive examples and excludes all negative examples. This approach allows for capturing sub-tasks performed by the system, with system behavior being described as the intersection of the languages from several DFAs, thereby improving interpretability.

Existing DFA identifying approaches [9,20,21] typically first employ a data structure called the Augmented Prefix Tree Acceptor (APTA) [3] to represent the labeled examples and then encode the identification of the minimal DFA from the APTA as a satisfiability (SAT) problem for Boolean formulas. The number of Boolean variables required in the SAT problem grows polynomially with the size of the constructed APTA. However, the size of the APTA increases dramatically with both the number and the length of the examples, since every prefix of the examples corresponds to a unique state in the APTA. This results in a corresponding increase in the number of Boolean variables and, consequently, the size of the SAT problem, posing a significant challenge to SAT solvers.

To alleviate this challenge, a recent work [5] extends the technique presented in [4] to construct the minimal 3-valued DFA (3DFA) consistent with the given examples, i.e., the 3DFA accepts all positive examples and rejects all negative examples. According to its definition, APTA can be viewed as a specific kind of 3DFA. The constructed minimal 3DFA is dramatically smaller than the original APTA. Hence, the proposed method via minimal 3DFAs in [5] significantly improves the DFA identification.

Since the state-of-the-art algorithm for identifying DFA decompositions [13] still relies on the basic APTA construction, a natural improvement would be to apply this minimal 3DFA construction to further reduce the number of Boolean variables required. However, our findings suggest that the minimal 3DFA construction from [5] *cannot* be directly applied to the current DFA decomposition learning framework [13]. This is because with a minimal 3DFA, its structural characteristics are different from those of the prefix tree, which makes the original encoding no longer applicable (cf. Sect. 4).

Contributions. To advance the DFA decomposition identification research, we make several contributions in this paper, as summarized below:

- We review the Pareto-optimal DIP studied in [13] and introduce a novel DFA-DIP, named the states-optimal DIP, that prioritizes decompositions with smaller state spaces (Sect. 3).
- We propose a new method for constructing a succinct 3DFA consistent with the given examples and an improved SAT encoding via 3DFA, both tailored for DFA-DIPs (Sect. 4).
- We propose a method for solving the novel states-optimal DIP (Sect. 5).
- We have implemented the improved method for solving the Pareto-optimal DIP by replacing the original encoding via APTA in [13] with our improved encoding via 3DFA, and have also implemented our method for solving the states-optimal DIP. The experimental results show that our new 3DFA construction significantly reduces the number of states compared to using APTA and dramatically improves the efficiency in solving the Pareto-optimal DIP. Additionally, we present preliminary experiments on the novel states-optimal DIP, highlighting the scalability of our method (Sect. 6).

The omitted proofs and additional experimental results are available in the companion technical report [14].

Related Work. We review the most related work on DFA identification from examples. The most common approach is the evidence driven state-merging (EDSM) algorithm [12]. It first constructs an APTA consistent with the given examples, and then iteratively applies a state-merging procedure until no valid merges are left. However, the issue of this algorithm is that it terminates at a local optimum. Current SAT-based methods typically construct an APTA first, and then reduce the problem to a SAT solving problem [9], with its help. These approaches return a minimal DFA. Several works [17,18,20,21] have improved the second step by proposing symmetry-breaking techniques and compact SAT encoding. More recently, the first step, which is an APTA construction, has been improved in [5] by extending the technique in [4] to construct a minimal 3DFA consistent with the given examples, instead of an APTA. The minimal 3DFA requires fewer states than APTA. Here, minimality is in terms of the number of states in the constructed 3DFA. However, all these works only consider learning a *single* DFA from the examples. In contrast to them, [13] introduces DFA-DIP and extends the SAT encoding via APTA to infer DFA decompositions under their so-called Pareto-optimal partial order. As the minimal 3DFA cannot directly be used for DFA-DIP, our work proposes a method to construct a non-minimal 3DFA with fewer states than APTA and an improved SAT encoding for DFA-DIP. All the works above, including ours, focus on learning *unknown* DFA decompositions from examples. When the finite-state automata to decompose are known, specific approaches [1,6,11] can be used.

2 Preliminaries

In this paper, given $n \in \mathbb{N}$, we denote by $[n]$ the set $\{1, 2, \ldots, n\}$. We fix a finite alphabet Σ of letters. A *word* u is a finite sequence of letters in Σ. We denote by

ε the empty word and with Σ^* the set of all finite words, and let $\Sigma^+ = \Sigma^* \setminus \{\varepsilon\}$. Given a word u, we denote by $|u|$ the *length* of u ($|\varepsilon| = 0$) and by $u[i]$ the i-th letter of u for $0 \leq i < |u|$. Given two words u and v, we denote by $u \cdot v$ (for short uv) their concatenation. We say that a word u is a *prefix* of a word w if $w = u \cdot v$ for some word $v \in \Sigma^*$. We denote by $\mathsf{prefixes}(u)$ the set of all prefixes of u and we extend it to a set of words S in the usual way, i.e., $\mathsf{prefixes}(S) = \bigcup_{u \in S} \mathsf{prefixes}(u)$.

Transition Systems. A *deterministic* transition system (TS) is a tuple $\mathcal{T} = (Q, \iota, \delta)$, where Q is a finite set of states, $\iota \in Q$ is the initial state, and $\delta\colon Q \times \Sigma \to Q$ is a transition function. We also extend δ from letters to words in the usual way, by letting $\delta(q, \varepsilon) = q$ and $\delta(q, a \cdot u) = \delta(\delta(q, a), u)$, where $u \in \Sigma^*$ and $a \in \Sigma$. The *run* of a TS $\mathcal{T}$ on a finite word u of length n is the sequence of states $\rho = q_0 q_1 \cdots q_n \in Q^+$ such that, for every $0 \leq i < n$, $q_{i+1} = \delta(q_i, u[i])$.

Definition 1 (Deterministic finite automata). *A deterministic finite automaton (DFA) is a tuple $\mathcal{A} = (\mathcal{T}, A)$, where $\mathcal{T}$ is a deterministic TS and $A \subseteq Q$ is a set of* accepting *states.*

A run is *accepting* (respectively, *rejecting*) if it ends in an accepting (resp. rejecting) state. A finite word $u \in \Sigma^*$ is *accepted* (resp. *rejected*) by $\mathcal{A}$ if it has an accepting (resp. rejecting) run on u. It is easy to extend DFAs to process languages with “don't-care” words.

Definition 2 (3-valued DFAs [5]). *A 3-valued DFA (3DFA) is a triple $\mathcal{A} = (\mathcal{T}, A, R)$, where $\mathcal{T}$ is a deterministic TS and A, R, and $D = Q \backslash (A \cup R)$ partition the set of states Q, where $A \subseteq Q$ is the set of* accepting *states, $R \subseteq Q$ is the set of* rejecting *states, and the remaining states D are called* don't-care *states.*

3DFAs map all words in Σ^* to *three* values: accepting (+), rejecting (−), and don't-care (?), where they are accepting if they have an accepting run, rejecting if they have a rejecting run, and don't-care otherwise. Note that DFAs are a special type of 3DFAs with only accepting and rejecting states. We denote the language of $\mathcal{A}$ by $\mathcal{L}(\mathcal{A})$, i.e., the set of words accepted by $\mathcal{A}$.

3 Problem Formalization

In this work, we consider two specific DFA decomposition identification problems (DIPs). One is the Pareto-optimal DIP established in [13], and the other is the states-optimal DIP we introduce in this paper. Before formally presenting the two DIPs, we recall the definition of DFA decompositions.

Definition 3 (DFA decomposition [13]). *Let $\mathcal{H}$ be the set of all DFAs over Σ. A $(m_1, \ldots, m_n)$-DFA decomposition is a tuple of n DFAs $(\mathcal{A}_1, \ldots, \mathcal{A}_n) \in \mathcal{H}^n$ such that each DFA $\mathcal{A}_i$ has m_i states and $m_1 \leq m_2 \leq \cdots \leq m_n$.*

A decomposition $(\mathcal{A}_1, \ldots, \mathcal{A}_n)$ accepts a word u if and only if all DFAs accept u, i.e., $u \in \mathcal{L}(\mathcal{A}_i)$ for all $1 \leq i \leq n$; a word that is not accepted is rejected. Therefore its language $\mathcal{L}(\mathcal{A}_1, \ldots, \mathcal{A}_n)$ is the intersection of the languages of the individual DFAs, i.e., $\mathcal{L}(\mathcal{A}_1, \ldots, \mathcal{A}_n) = \bigcap_{1 \leq i \leq n} \mathcal{L}(\mathcal{A}_i)$. We say $(m_1, \ldots, m_n)$ is the *states allocation* of the DFA decomposition $(\mathcal{A}_1, \ldots, \mathcal{A}_n)$.

DFA Decomposition Identification Problem (DFA-DIP). Given a set of labeled examples $S = (S^+, S^-)$ where S^+ contains positive examples and S^- contains negative examples, respectively, a general DFA-DIP asks to identify a DFA decomposition consistent with the example set S; formally, it asks to find a DFA decomposition $(\mathcal{A}_1, \ldots, \mathcal{A}_n)$ for a given integer $n \in \mathbb{N}$ that satisfies:

C1 Consistency: $S^+ \subseteq \mathcal{L}(\mathcal{A}_1, \ldots, \mathcal{A}_n)$ and $S^- \subseteq \Sigma^* \setminus \mathcal{L}(\mathcal{A}_1, \ldots, \mathcal{A}_n)$.

Obviously, the identification problem of monolithic DFAs is a special case of DFA-DIP with $n = 1$, i.e., learning a single DFA from examples. We say a DFA decomposition $(\mathcal{A}_1, \cdots, \mathcal{A}_n)$ is *consistent* with S if it satisfies **C1**.

To compare decompositions, a *Pareto-optimal partial order* $\prec$ has been introduced in [13]. Formally, given a $(m_1, \ldots, m_n)$-DFA decomposition $(\mathcal{A}_1, \ldots, \mathcal{A}_n)$ and a $(m'_1, \ldots, m'_n)$-DFA decomposition $(\mathcal{A}'_1, \ldots, \mathcal{A}'_n)$, we say $(\mathcal{A}_1, \ldots, \mathcal{A}_n) \prec (\mathcal{A}'_1, \ldots, \mathcal{A}'_n)$ if $m_i \leq m'_i$ for all $1 \leq i \leq n$ and there exists $1 \leq j \leq n$ such that $m_j < m'_j$. If so, we say that $(\mathcal{A}_1, \ldots, \mathcal{A}_n)$ *dominates* $(\mathcal{A}'_1, \ldots, \mathcal{A}'_n)$.

As incomparable decompositions exist, they can form a Pareto frontier of solutions to the Pareto-optimal DIP defined as follows:

Pareto-Optimal DIP [13]. Given a set of labeled examples $S = (S^+, S^-)$ and an integer $n \in \mathbb{N}$, find a $(m_1, \ldots, m_n)$-DFA decomposition $(\mathcal{A}_1, \ldots, \mathcal{A}_n)$ such that (i) it satisfies **C1**, and (ii) there does not exist a decomposition satisfying **C1** dominating it under the Pareto-optimal partial order $\prec$.

In this paper, we also introduce a novel DFA-DIP—states-optimal DIP—which depends on the number of states and the *entropy* of a decomposition defined as follows.

Definition 4 (Entropy of DFA decomposition). *Given a $(m_1, \ldots, m_n)$-DFA decomposition $(\mathcal{A}_1, \ldots, \mathcal{A}_n)$, its entropy is defined as*

$$\mathcal{E}(\mathcal{A}_1, \ldots, \mathcal{A}_n) = -\sum_{i=1}^{n} P(i) \log_2 P(i)$$

where $P(i) = m_i / \sum_{j=1}^{n} m_j$ for $1 \leq i \leq n$.

Based on Definition 4, we present a *states-optimal preorder* as follows. Given a $(m_1, \ldots, m_n)$-DFA decomposition $(\mathcal{A}_1, \ldots, \mathcal{A}_n)$ and a $(m'_1, \ldots, m'_l)$-DFA decomposition $(\mathcal{A}'_1, \ldots, \mathcal{A}'_l)$, we say $(\mathcal{A}_1, \ldots, \mathcal{A}_n) \lessdot (\mathcal{A}'_1, \ldots, \mathcal{A}'_l)$ if $\sum_{i=1}^{n} m_i < \sum_{j=1}^{l} m'_j$, or $\mathcal{E}(\mathcal{A}_1, \ldots, \mathcal{A}_n) \geq \mathcal{E}(\mathcal{A}'_1, \ldots, \mathcal{A}'_l)$ if $\sum_{i=1}^{n} m_i = \sum_{j=1}^{l} m'_j$. The preorder reflects that we prefer a DFA decomposition that has the minimal number of states or, for the same number of states, it contains more individual DFAs with similar (smaller) size.

A decomposition with a higher entropy value indicates a more evenly distributed state allocation among DFAs, leading to a more flexible and potentially more generalizable representation of the input data. In contrast, lower entropy values suggest that the state allocation is concentrated in fewer DFAs, which may reduce the system's ability to capture diverse structural variations in the

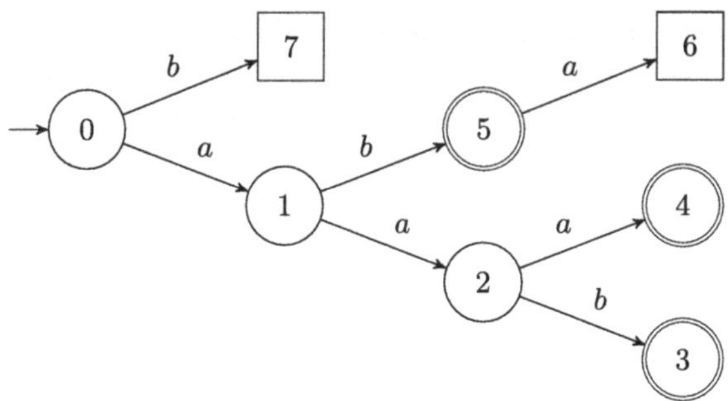

Fig. 1. The APTA consistent with the examples $S^+ = \{aab, aaa, ab\}$ and $S^- = \{b, aba\}$, where an accepting node is represented by a double circle and a rejecting node by a square.

data. Note that the states-optimal preorder does not require two DFA decompositions having the same number of DFAs, as does the Pareto-optimal partial order. Therefore, the states-optimal preorder is a total preorder.

States-Optimal DIP. Given a set of labeled examples $S = (S^+, S^-)$, find a $(m_1, \ldots, m_n)$-DFA decomposition $(\mathcal{A}_1, \ldots, \mathcal{A}_n)$ for some $n \in \mathbb{N}$ such that it is a minimal decomposition w.r.t. the states-optimal preorder $\lessdot$ satisfying **C1**.

Note that the states-optimal DIP does not require a given input n to restrict the number of DFAs in the resulted DFA decomposition. Of course, a specific variant is to find a states-optimal decomposition with a given input n.

4 An Improved SAT Encoding of DFA-DIP via 3DFAs

In this section, we first briefly review the existing encoding via APTA proposed in [13], then present our improved SAT encoding of DFA-DIP via 3DFA. We describe a challenge in utilizing minimal 3DFAs [5] within our encoding at last.

4.1 Existing Encoding via APTAs

In [13], Lauffer *et al.* proposed a SAT encoding method for DFA-DIP by extending the SAT encoding for identifying a single DFA from examples [9,17,18,20]. Their encoding reduces DFA-DIP into a graph coloring problem where the graph is in fact an APTA, a tree-based 3DFA. In the graph coloring problem, the state of each node of the tree structure, each edge of the tree, and for each state, each transition of the DFA, can be represented by a different color variable [9].

In an APTA, each state corresponds to a unique prefix of a word in the set of examples $S = (S^+, S^-)$ that we also write as $S = S^+ \cup S^-$. First, one can define a function $f\colon \mathsf{prefixes}(S) \to \mathbb{N}_S$ where $\mathbb{N}_S = \{0, \ldots, |\mathsf{prefixes}(S)| - 1\}$. Intuitively, f maps each prefix $u \in \mathsf{prefixes}(S)$ to a state in the APTA represented by a unique number in $\mathbb{N}_S$. Formally, an APTA $\mathcal{P}$ of S is a 3DFA $(\mathcal{T}, A, R)$ where the TS $\mathcal{T}$

Fig. 2. The two DFAs of the $(2,2)$-DFA decomposition $(\mathcal{A}_1, \mathcal{A}_2)$ consistent with the examples $S = (S^+, S^-)$ from Fig. 1.

consists of the set of states $\mathbb{N}_S$, the initial state $f(\varepsilon)$, and the transition function δ defined as $\delta(i,a) = j$ if $f(u) = i$ and $f(ua) = j$ where $u, ua \in \mathsf{prefixes}(S)$ and $a \in \Sigma$; we define the sets A and R as $A = \{ i \in \mathbb{N}_S \mid f(u) = i \text{ for some } u \in S^+ \}$ and $R = \{ i \in \mathbb{N}_S \mid f(u) = i \text{ for some } u \in S^- \}$. For example, Fig. 1 shows the APTA generated from the set of examples $S = (S^+, S^-)$ where $S^+ = \{aab, aaa, ab\}$, $S^- = \{b, aba\}$, and $f = \{\varepsilon \mapsto 0, a \mapsto 1, aa \mapsto 2, aab \mapsto 3, aaa \mapsto 4, ab \mapsto 5, aba \mapsto 6, b \mapsto 7\}$. The set of accepting states is $A = \{3,4,5\}$ and the set of rejecting states is $R = \{6,7\}$.

Given a positive integer $n \in \mathbb{N}$, the state-of-the-art encoding method associates the APTA states with the states of each DFA $\mathcal{A}_i$ in the $(m_1, \ldots, m_n)$-DFA decomposition $(\mathcal{A}_1, \ldots, \mathcal{A}_n)$. More precisely, given an APTA consistent with the examples S and an allocation of states $(m_1, \ldots, m_n)$, each unknown DFA $\mathcal{A}_i$ gets assigned m_i states and the encoding associates each APTA state with one of the $\mathcal{A}_i$'s m_i states, subject to a set of constraints, such as each accepting (rejecting, resp.) APTA state should be associated with an accepting (a rejecting, resp.) DFA state. APTA states with the same (DFA-indexed) state variable will be identified as the same state in the corresponding DFA. For instance, for each APTA state $v \in \mathbb{N}_S$, a state variable $x^k_{v,i}$ represents it is associated with the i-th state in the k-th DFA. Considering the APTA in Fig. 1, if we would like to generate a $(2,2)$-DFA decomposition $(\mathcal{A}_1, \mathcal{A}_2)$, we need 32 state variables $x^k_{v,i}$. Besides these variables, the encoding method requires other variables to represent the transition relations and the accepting conditions. Based on the coloring, several constraints imposed by **C1** – such as a positive example must be accepted by all DFAs and a negative example must be rejected by at least one DFA – will be encoded into a SAT problem. The complete list of Lauffer's encoding [13] can be found in the companion technical report [14]. Figure 2 presents the identified $(2,2)$-DFA decomposition $(\mathcal{A}_1, \mathcal{A}_2)$ consistent with the APTA in Fig. 1.

4.2 Our Improved Encoding via 3DFAs

The existing approaches [9,13,17,18,20] face a critical challenge: the size of the APTA grows dramatically with both the number and the length of examples S as APTA associates each prefix in $\mathsf{prefixes}(S)$ with a unique node. As mentioned earlier, the increase in the number of nodes in the APTA leads to more encoding variables, which in turn increases the size of the resulting SAT problem [16,20]. Consequently, the smaller the APTA size is, the easier the SAT problem will be.

In light of this, to obtain smaller APTAs, [5] proposed to construct the *minimal* 3DFA for S by merging equivalent nodes. Moreover, inspired by [4], the minimal 3DFA can even be constructed incrementally from the set S if the examples in S are sorted by the standard lexicographical order. Following [4,5], we also propose an incremental construction of 3DFAs by merging equivalent nodes. Differently from [5], our construction, rather than looking for the minimal 3DFA, requires that every rejecting word in S^- must reach a unique state in the constructed 3DFA. That is, we only merge equivalent accepting or "don't-care" states. In what follows, we first introduce our construction of 3DFAs starting from APTAs and then the improved encoding via 3DFAs. Afterwards, we reveal the reason why it is important to associate every rejecting word with a unique state in the 3DFA.

3DFA Construction. For simplicity, we assume that the full APTA $\mathcal{P}$ of S is given. Note that our 3DFA can also be constructed on-the-fly from S using the same techniques as [4,5]. Since our goal is to associate each rejecting word with a unique state and merge as many other states as possible, our reduction process works in a backward manner as follows.

Initially, we collapse all accepting nodes without outgoing transitions into one representative state and store it in a hash map called `Register`. Since all rejecting nodes are inequivalent to other states, each rejecting node will be stored as its own representative in the `Register`.

Our reduction process then iteratively traverses the APTA nodes in a backward manner from leaves towards the root and process the 3DFA as follows. In each iteration, we first collect the states whose all successors are representative states in `Register`, and then identify equivalent states with the following two conditions:

- both states must be either accepting or don't-care states, and
- for every input letter $a \in \Sigma$, either they both have no successors or both have the same successor in `Register`.

We thus create a state representative for each equivalent class, i.e., a set of equivalent states, and store the representative in `Register`. Further, all states that have a representative in `Register` will be replaced by their representative in the updated 3DFA.

Our construction repeats the reduction process until all states, including the initial one, are processed, resulting in a 3DFA consistent with S.

Theorem 1. *Given a set of examples $S = (S^+, S^-)$, the 3DFA construction produces a 3DFA consistent with S.*

Note that our 3DFA can also be constructed *on the fly* from S in the same manner as in [5] if the example words are taken out from S in the standard lexicographical order.

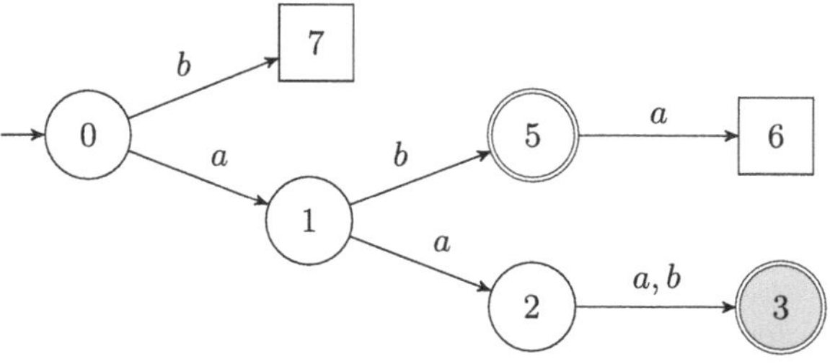

Fig. 3. The 3DFA $\mathcal{A} = (\mathcal{T}, A, R)$ constructed from the APTA in Fig. 1, where $A = \{3, 5\}$ and $R = \{6, 7\}$.

Table 1. Size comparison between 3DFAs and APTAs. "Length" indicates the length of each word.

$\|\Sigma\|$	Length	Automata Size	
		3DFA	APTA
5	5	1,255	3,214
5	6	4,449	13,634
5	7	13,787	53,277
5	8	43,064	209,721
5	9	136,019	835,954
5	10	443,763	3,369,694

Observe that every rejecting word in S^- leads the constructed 3DFA to a unique rejecting state by construction. In fact, we can get the following stronger result, that we will use later in our SAT encoding phase.

Lemma 1. *Let $\mathcal{A} = (\mathcal{T}, A, R)$ be the outcome of the 3DFA construction, where $\mathcal{T} = (Q, \iota, \delta)$. For two different prefixes $u, u' \in \mathsf{prefixes}(S)$, we have $\delta(\iota, u) \neq \delta(\iota, u')$ if either $u \in \mathsf{prefixes}(S^-)$ or $u' \in \mathsf{prefixes}(S^-)$.*

For instance, as shown in Fig. 3, this construction process can merge the states $\{3, 4\}$ of the APTA in Fig. 1 reached by positive examples into a representative state 3. Although this simple example does not clearly show the advantage of the construction, Table 1 presents the size comparison between APTAs and our constructed 3DFAs in terms of the number of states on a number of cases from parity game solving [5]. We can see that the resulting 3DFAs exhibit significantly smaller sizes than the original APTAs. Therefore, using 3DFAs instead of APTAs requires dramatically fewer variables and fewer constraints in our improved encoding given below, yielding easier SAT problems and thus faster solving speed in general than those via APTAs, as confirmed by the experiments in Sect. 6.

SAT Encoding via 3DFAs. We now present the standard SAT encoding for solving the DFA-DIP problem [13] adapted to our 3DFAs. Note that we also use the symmetry breaking techniques proposed in [17,18] to further improve our SAT encoding, just like in [13]. In what follows, we focus on our major encoding. Given the 3DFA $\mathcal{A} = (\mathcal{T}, A, R)$ with $\mathcal{T} = (Q, \iota, \delta)$ consistent with S, we are looking for a consistent DFA decomposition $(\mathcal{A}_1, \ldots, \mathcal{A}_n)$ of S where the state allocation is $(m_1, \ldots, m_n)$ for a given $n \in \mathbb{N}$. To encode the DFA-DIP, we use the following three types of variables:

1. **State variables** $x^k_{v,i}$, where $k \in [n]$, $v \in Q$, and $i \in [m_k]$. $x^k_{v,i} \equiv 1$ iff the state v of the 3DFA and the state i in the DFA $\mathcal{A}_k$ can both be reached on some word $u \in \Sigma^*$ from their initial states.
2. **Transition relation variables** $e^k_{l,i,j}$, where $k \in [n]$, $l \in \Sigma$, and $i, j \in [m_k]$. $e^k_{l,i,j} \equiv 1$ iff DFA $\mathcal{A}_k$ has a transition from state i to state j over the letter l.
3. **Acceptance variables** z^k_i, where $k \in [n]$ and $i \in [m_k]$. $z^k_i \equiv 1$ iff the state i of DFA $\mathcal{A}_k$ is an accepting state.

Recall that A (resp., R) is the set of accepting (resp., rejecting) states in the 3DFA $\mathcal{A}$. We now give the list of constraints for the SAT encoding. First of all, we require that each individual automaton $\mathcal{A}_i$ should be a DFA. That is, $\mathcal{A}_i$ must be deterministic and also complete.

D1 Determinism. For a state i and a letter l in $\mathcal{A}_k$, there is at most one successor:

$$\bigwedge_{l \in \Sigma} \bigwedge_{k \in [n]} \bigwedge_{\substack{i,j,t \in [m_k] \\ j<t}} e^k_{l,i,j} \implies \neg e^k_{l,i,t}.$$

D2 Completeness. For a state i and a letter l in $\mathcal{A}_k$, there must be a successor:

$$\bigwedge_{l \in \Sigma} \bigwedge_{k \in [n]} \bigwedge_{i \in [m_k]} \bigvee_{j \in [m_k]} e^k_{l,i,j}.$$

Second, we require that the DFA decomposition $(\mathcal{A}_1, \cdots, \mathcal{A}_n)$ should be consistent with S, so to satisfy **C1**.

R1 Positive Consistency. Every positive example in S^+ must be accepted by all individual DFAs, i.e., by each DFA $\mathcal{A}_k$ where $k \in [n]$. It follows that, if $x^k_{v,i} \equiv 1$, then all positive examples leading the 3DFA $\mathcal{A}$ to an accepting state v must also make $\mathcal{A}_k$ reach an accepting state, i.e., state i must also be an accepting state.

$$\bigwedge_{v \in A} \bigwedge_{k \in [n]} \bigwedge_{i \in [m_k]} x^k_{v,i} \implies z^k_i.$$

R2 Negative Consistency. Each negative example in S^- should be rejected by at least one individual DFA $\mathcal{A}_k$. That is, if $x^k_{v,i} \equiv 1$, then the example leading the 3DFA $\mathcal{A}$ to a rejecting state v must also make $\mathcal{A}_k$ reach a rejecting state as well, i.e., state i of $\mathcal{A}_k$ should also be rejecting.

$$\bigwedge_{v \in R} \bigvee_{k \in [n]} \bigwedge_{i \in [m_k]} x^k_{v,i} \implies \neg z^k_i.$$

To further enforce the DFA decomposition to be consistent with S, we also need to perform the product of the 3DFA $\mathcal{A}$ and each individual DFA $\mathcal{A}_k$ in order to build the transition system of each $\mathcal{A}_k$, where $k \in [n]$. That is, $x^k_{v,i} \equiv 1$ also means that in the product automaton of $\mathcal{A}$ and $\mathcal{A}_k$, the pair of states (v, i) is seen as a product state and it is reached from the initial product state $(r, 1)$ over some word $u \in \Sigma^*$. The constraints are listed below:

T1 Initialization. The initial state r of 3DFA $\mathcal{A}$ should always be associated with the initial state 1 for each DFA $\mathcal{A}_k$:

$$\bigwedge_{k\in[n]} x^k_{r,1}$$

T2 State Correspondence. Each state v of 3DFA $\mathcal{A}$ must be associated with one state in each DFA $\mathcal{A}_k$, i.e., $x^k_{v,i} \equiv 1$ for some state i in $\mathcal{A}_k$:

$$\bigwedge_{v\in Q} \bigwedge_{k\in[n]} \bigvee_{i\in[m_k]} x^k_{v,i}.$$

T3 Transition Relation. For each $k \in [n]$, in the product automaton of $\mathcal{A}$ and $\mathcal{A}_k$, if the product state (v, i) is reachable from the initial product state $(r, 1)$, and there is a transition from state i to j over letter a in $\mathcal{A}_k$, then the product state $(\delta(v, a), j)$ is also reachable.

$$\bigwedge_{v\in Q} \bigwedge_{k\in[n]} \bigwedge_{i,j\in[m_k]} \bigwedge_{a\in l(v)} (x^k_{v,i} \land e^k_{a,i,j}) \implies x^k_{\delta(v,a),j}$$

where $l(v)$ is the set of letters on the outgoing transitions from state v.

In addition to the above constraints, Lauffer *et al.* [13] also proposed an optimization as follows.

O1 Each state v in the 3DFA can only be associated with at most one state i in each individual DFA $\mathcal{A}_k$.

$$\bigwedge_{v\in Q} \bigwedge_{k\in[n]} \bigwedge_{i,j\in[m_k],i<j} \neg x^k_{v,i} \lor \neg x^k_{v,j}.$$

This constraint holds in the APTA because each state v corresponds to a unique prefix $u \in \mathsf{prefixes}(S)$. Since both $\mathcal{A}$ and $\mathcal{A}_k$ are deterministic, the product state (v, i) reached from the initial product state $(r, 1)$ over u must be unique. That is, there will be a unique i in $\mathcal{A}_k$ to make $x^k_{v,i}$ be true.

However, this constraint might not be true when we use a 3DFA for our encoding. For instance, consider the 3DFA $\mathcal{A}$ in Fig. 3: we can see that there are two words that can make $\mathcal{A}$ reach state 3, namely aaa and aab. In our target DFA $\mathcal{A}_k$, these two words might lead to two different states, say i and j. It then follows that we have both $x^k_{3,i} \equiv 1$ and $x^k_{3,j} \equiv 1$, which obviously violates the constraint **O1**. This will prevent us from finding a consistent DFA decomposition $(\mathcal{A}_1, \ldots, \mathcal{A}_n)$ with the state allocation $(m_1, \ldots, m_n)$.

Nonetheless, we observe that during the construction of the 3DFA, it is easy to identify those states that correspond to multiple different prefix words in $\mathsf{prefixes}(S)$. Indeed, we can just record the representative states which correspond to multiple equivalent states, denoted by M. That is, for each state $v \in M$, there must be two different prefixes $u, u' \in \mathsf{prefixes}(S)$ such that $v = \delta(r, u) = \delta(r, u')$. In fact, M must not contain the states corresponding to a prefix in $\mathsf{prefixes}(S^-)$ as guaranteed by Lemma 1. The set of states in $\mathcal{A}$ that is associated with a unique prefix word in $\mathsf{prefixes}(S)$ is $Q \setminus M$. Therefore, we can replace the constraint **O1** with the following constraint:

O1' Each state v in the 3DFA that does not correspond to multiple equivalent states can only be associated with at most one state i in each individual DFA $\mathcal{A}_k$.

$$\bigwedge_{v \in Q \setminus M} \bigwedge_{k \in [n]} \bigwedge_{i,j \in [m_k], i<j} \neg x^k_{v,i} \vee \neg x^k_{v,j}.$$

Clearly, by Lemma 1, all states having a path to a rejecting state in $\mathcal{A}$ belong to $Q \setminus M$.

Let $\varphi^{\mathcal{A},n}_{(m_1,\ldots,m_n)}$ be the conjunction of the constraints **D1-2**, **R1-2**, **T1-3**, and **O1'**. Then, we get the following result.

Theorem 2. *Let $\mathcal{A}$ be the 3DFA consistent with the examples S and $n \in \mathbb{N}$. $\varphi^{\mathcal{A},n}_{(m_1,\ldots,m_n)}$ is satisfiable if, and only if, there exists a $(m_1,\ldots,m_n)$-DFA decomposition $(\mathcal{A}_1,\ldots,\mathcal{A}_n)$ consistent with S.*

Encoding Size. The size of the formula $\varphi^{\mathcal{A},n}_{(m_1,\ldots,m_n)}$ is determined by the conjunction of each constraint above. Let m be the maximal number that occurs in $(m_1,\ldots,m_n)$. The contribution of each constraint to the formula size is:

- (**D1-2**): $O(|\Sigma| \cdot n \cdot m^3) + O(|\Sigma| \cdot n \cdot m^2)$;
- (**R1-2**): $O(|Q^+| \cdot n \cdot m) + O(|Q^-| \cdot n \cdot m)$;
- (**T1-3**): $O(n) + O(|Q| \cdot n \cdot m) + O(|Q| \cdot n \cdot m^2)$; and
- (**O1'**): $O(|Q \setminus M| \cdot n \cdot m^2)$.

The overall size is thus $O(|\Sigma| \cdot n \cdot m^3) + O(|Q| \cdot n \cdot m^2)$.

4.3 Why Not Use Minimal 3DFAs

Our 3DFA construction is inspired by the one of `DFAMiner` [5], with the main difference being that we do not generate the minimal 3DFA recognizing S. In the minimal 3DFA generated by `DFAMiner`, all rejecting states that cannot reach a rejecting state are merged together. For instance, in Fig. 3, both rejecting states 6 and 7 do not reach another rejecting state, so in the minimal 3DFA, these two states will be merged. This also means that the two rejecting words b and aba will correspond to the same state, say v, in the minimal 3DFA $\mathcal{A}$. However, this would make the meaning of constraint **R2** imprecise: by constraint **R2**, we want every word to be rejected by at least one individual DFA, but the

Algorithm 1: State-optimal DIP Solving

```
   Input: The labeled examples S = (S+, S-)
   Output: A DFA decomposition D for the states-optimal DIP
 1 A ← 3DFAConstruction(S);        ▷ Construct a 3DFA from the examples
 2 N ← 2;    ▷ Initial total number of states in possible decompositions
 3 while true do
 4 |   M ← ComputeStatesAllocation(N, 2);     ▷ Get all possible states
   |   allocations under N
 5 |   foreach (m_1, ..., m_n) ∈ M do
 6 |   |   SAT, D ← Solve((m_1, ..., m_n), A);
 7 |   |   if SAT then
 8 |   |   |   return D;
 9 |   |   end
10 |   end
11 |   N ← N + 1;
12 end
```

constraint actually says that we have at least one individual DFA that rejects a word associated with the rejecting state v. This means that it is *not* guaranteed that every word in S^- reaching v will be rejected. This means, for instance, that for b and aba in Fig. 3, it may happen that only b is rejected by some individual DFA but aba is totally ignored and thus not rejected by any DFA. This kind of issues can lead to inconsistent DFA decompositions from the SAT solver and we indeed observed them in the experiments when we directly used the minimal 3DFA in our encoding.

In light of this, it is clear why we require in our construction that every rejecting word must be associated with a unique state in the constructed 3DFA or, equivalently, that every rejecting state in the APTA must not be equivalent to any other states. We are now ready to introduce in the next section the overall algorithm for finding consistent DFA decompositions.

5 Identification Algorithms for DFA Decomposition

In this section, we present identification algorithms for two DFA decomposition problems: the Pareto-optimal DIP and the states-optimal DIP.

For the Pareto-optimal DIP, our algorithm builds on top of the approach of [13], where we replace their SAT encoding via APTA with our enhanced 3DFA-based encoding. The detailed algorithm can be found in the full version [14]. As the experimental results in Sect. 6 show, this modification yields significant improvement. Therefore, in what follows, we focus on our method for solving the new states-optimal DIP, which is summarized as Algorithm 1.

Given a set of labeled examples $S = (S^+, S^-)$, Algorithm 1 first builds a 3DFA consistent with S (Line 1) according to Sect. 4.2 and then looks for the decomposition with the minimal total number of states, starting with $N =$

Algorithm 2: ComputeStatesAllocation

Input: N: the total number of states in unknown decompositions
k: the minimum number of states in each DFA
Output: $\mathcal{M}$: all possible states allocations of unknown decompositions

```
1 M ← {N};
2 for m ← k to N do                          ▷ Current DFA has m states
3   if m ≤ N − m then          ▷ Still enough states left for the next DFA
4     M' ← ComputeStatesAllocation(N − m, m);
5     M ← M ∪ ({m} × M');    ▷ Add the new states allocations to M
6   end
7 end
8 Sort M in descending order by entropy (see Definition 4);
9 return M;
```

2 (Line 2) and incrementing it until a suitable decomposition is found. This is achieved by computing all possible states allocations $\mathcal{M}$ (Line 4) having N total states by calling Algorithm 2, which ensures that every states allocation $(m_1, \ldots, m_n) \in \mathcal{M}$ satisfies: (1) the total number of states is N (i.e., $\sum_{i=1}^{n} m_i = N$), (2) every corresponding DFA has at least 2 states[1] (i.e., $m_i \geq 2$ for all $1 \leq i \leq n$), and (3) allocated states are in ascending order (i.e., $m_i \leq m_{i+1}$ for all $1 \leq i < n$). As a result, Algorithm 2 enumerates all possible combinations where the number of DFAs n will range from 1 to $\lfloor \frac{N}{2} \rfloor$. For instance, for $N = 10$, Algorithm 2 returns the following states allocations:

$$\{(2,2,2,2,2),(2,2,3,3),(2,2,2,4),(3,3,4),(2,4,4),(2,3,5),\\(2,2,6),(5,5),(4,6),(3,7),(2,8),(10)\}.$$

After calling Algorithm 2, for every possible states allocation $(m_1, \ldots, m_n) \in \mathcal{M}$, Algorithm 1 applies our encoding method and calls a SAT solver to determine whether there is a $(m_1, \ldots, m_n)$-DFA decomposition $\mathcal{D}$ for the state-optimal DIP (Line 6). If so, it returns it (Line 8). Otherwise, it means that there is no solution under the current total number of states N, so we increase it (Line 11).

Note that, in Algorithm 1, we increase the total number of states N by 1 in each round. For every fixed N, Algorithm 2 sorts the states allocations in descending order based on their entropy values (Line 8). Therefore, they work together to keep the states-optimal preorder defined in Sect. 3. Theorem 3 shows the termination and the correctness of Algorithm 1.

Theorem 3 (Termination and Correctness). *Let $S = (S^+, S^-)$ be a given set of labeled examples. Algorithm 1 terminates and returns a correct DFA decomposition $\mathcal{D} = (\mathcal{A}_1, \ldots, \mathcal{A}_n)$ for the states-optimal DIP.*

[1] As the constraint **D2** in Sect. 4.2 requires that every state in the generated DFAs should have a transition for every action in Σ, the generated DFAs are complete DFAs. Since a complete DFA with a single state will either accept or reject all words, we skip such naïve DFAs and thus every DFA should have at least 2 states.

Complexity Analysis. It can be observed that there is always a correct decomposition $\mathcal{D} = (\mathcal{A}_1, \ldots, \mathcal{A}_n)$ when $N = 2 + \sum_{u \in S^-} (|u| + 2)$, where a 2-states DFA $\mathcal{A}_1$ accepts all words and every other DFA rejects one negative example $u \in S^-$. Therefore, the loop iterations in Algorithm 1 are bounded by $1 + \sum_{u \in S^-} (|u| + 2)$, as N starts with 2 and it is increased by 1 every round. In every loop, the recursive generation of all possible states allocations under a given N in Algorithm 2 is dominated by the integer partition problem. According to the Hardy-Ramanujan formula [8], the asymptotic estimation of the number of states allocations is $|\mathcal{M}| \sim \frac{e^{\pi\sqrt{2N/3}}}{4N\sqrt{3}}$, which shows that the growth of $|\mathcal{M}|$ is subexponential in N.

It is not hard to have a simple variant of Algorithm 1 with a given integer n restricting the number of DFAs in the decomposition. It can be done by checking if a combination has at most n DFAs before adding it to $\mathcal{M}$ in Algorithm 2.

6 Experimental Evaluation

We have implemented our approach[2] on top of the tool developed in [13] and we used as benchmarks pairs of sets of examples representing partially-ordered tasks (cf. [13, Section III.C]), where we vary the numbers of tasks, the maximum length of each sequence of tasks, and the number of samples in each positive and negative sets; for each combination, we randomly generate 10 instances, provided they can be generated, by following the generation strategy[3] in [13]. Let ParetoAPTA, Pareto3DFA, and StatesOptimalDIP denote the original tool from [13], its version using our 3DFA encoding (cf. Sect. 4), and by our method for solving states-optimal DIP (cf. Sect. 5), respectively. We ran the tools on a desktop machine with an i7-4790 CPU and 16 GB of memory running Ubuntu Server 24.04.2 and we used BenchExec [2] to trace and constrain the tools' executions: we allowed each benchmark to use 15 GB of memory and imposed a time limit of 10 minutes of wall-clock time.

6.1 Comparison Between ParetoAPTA and Pareto3DFA on Solving Pareto-Optimal DIP

In Table 2 we report on how ParetoAPTA and Pareto3DFA performed on 460 benchmarks with 2 tasks ($|\Sigma| = 2$) and 1090 benchmarks with 4 tasks ($|\Sigma| = 4$) when changing the number of DFAs in the decomposition. As we can see from the table, ParetoAPTA can scale to 5 DFAs for the $|\Sigma| = 2$ benchmarks, but it already struggles at 3 DFAs when $|\Sigma| = 4$. By just replacing the original APTA encoding with our 3DFA-based one, Pareto3DFA has been able to solve all benchmarks except for one case up to 6 DFAs. We have also run Pareto3DFA up to 10 DFAs, obtaining success everywhere except for 2 and 3 timeouts on $|\Sigma| = 4$ for 9 and 10 DFAs, respectively.

[2] Available at: https://github.com/MJJ-Shuai/dfa_decomposed_3DFA.

[3] See https://github.com/mvcisback/dfa-identify.

Table 2. Overview of the outcomes of the encoding experiments

Tool	Result	No. of DFAs, $\|\Sigma\| = 2$					No. of DFAs, $\|\Sigma\| = 4$				
		2	3	4	5	6	2	3	4	5	6
PARETOAPTA [13]	Success	460	460	460	456	92	1058	129	85	72	72
	Memoryout	0	0	0	4	397	21	467	981	989	978
	Timeout	0	0	0	0	1	11	3	24	29	40
PARETO3DFA (ours)	Success	460	460	460	460	460	1090	1090	1090	1090	1089
	Timeout	0	0	0	0	0	0	0	0	0	1

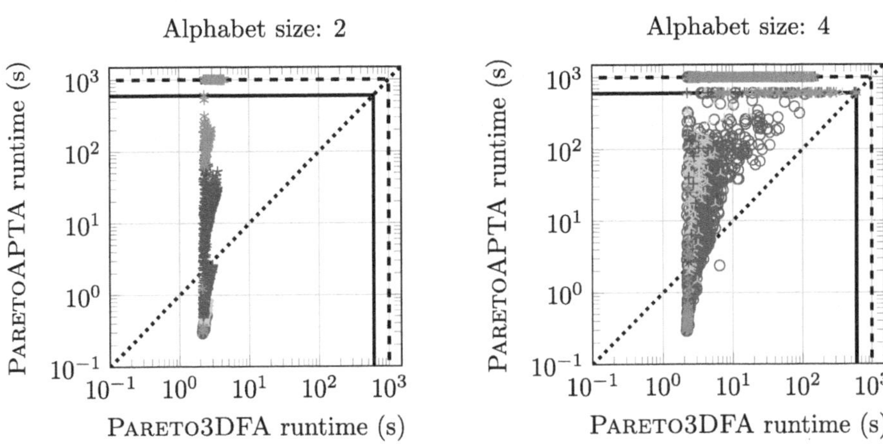

Fig. 4. Running time comparison between PARETOAPTA and PARETO3DFA

In Fig. 4 we show the runtime comparison between two methods PARETOAPTA and PARETO3DFA on all 1550 experiments considered in Table 2. The scatter plots in the figure have logarithmic axes and marks above the dotted diagonal line mean that PARETOAPTA took more time than PARETO3DFA to solve the same benchmark; the solid line at 600 s represents the timeout we imposed to the experiments while marks on the dashed line at 1000 s stand for experiments where the corresponding tool went memoryout.

As we can see from the plots, except for the cases taking very limited time, our PARETO3DFA always significantly outperforms PARETOAPTA in the running time, while producing DFAs with the same number of states as PARETOAPTA on the commonly solved cases. For benchmarks requiring at least 5 s to be computed by both tools, PARETO3DFA is 1.4–80.3 times faster than PARETOAPTA; for at least 10 s, the speedup lies in 2.8–40.5.

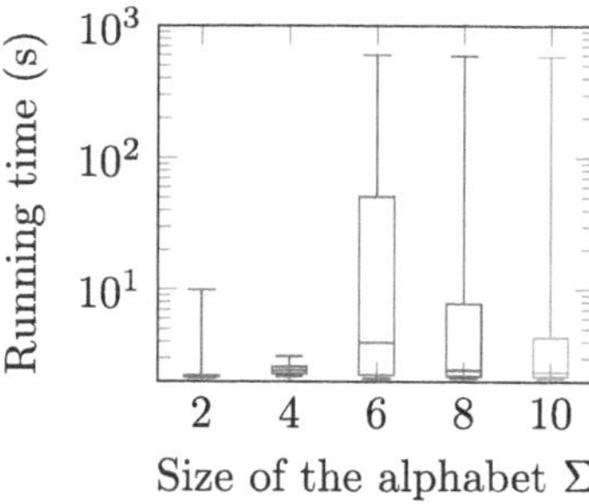

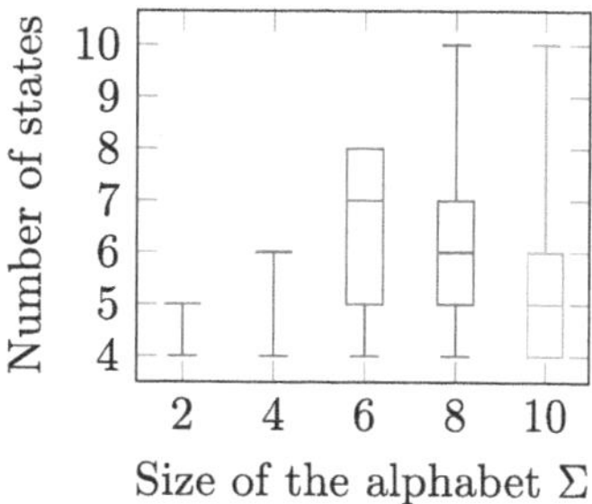

Fig. 5. Box plots for the StatesOptimalDIP experiments

6.2 The Scalability for Our Method on Solving States-Optimal DIP

To evaluate how StatesOptimalDIP is able to scale with more challenging benchmarks, we ran it on the same benchmarks used for Table 2 as well as on 1150, 1190, and 1210 benchmarks with $|\Sigma| = 6$, $|\Sigma| = 8$, and $|\Sigma| = 10$, respectively. StatesOptimalDIP has completed successfully all experiments for $|\Sigma| \in \{2, 4\}$; for $|\Sigma| = 6$ it solved 919 cases and went timeout on 231, while for $|\Sigma| = 8$ it solved 689 cases and went timeout on 501, and for $|\Sigma| = 10$ it solved 783 cases and went timeout on 427; no failure by memoryout happened.

The box plots in Fig. 5 show the distribution of the running time and of the number of states relative to the successfully solved benchmarks. As we can see from the plots, StatesOptimalDIP is really fast for the simpler benchmarks with $|\Sigma| \in \{2, 4\}$, taking less than 1 s and needing between 4 and 6 states to solve each of them. For the more demanding benchmarks ($|\Sigma| \in \{6, 8, 10\}$), more states are necessary (at most 10), so by Algorithm 1 more cycles in the loop, more decompositions, and larger encoding formulas are generated and evaluated, as reflected by the higher running times shown in the plot on the left of Fig. 5.

7 Conclusion

In this paper we considered two DFA decomposition identification problems: the Pareto-optimal DIP, studied by Lauffer *et al.* in [13], and the states-optimal DIP that we introduced in this paper. To solve the former problem, we proposed an improved SAT encoding via 3DFA; compared to the encoding via APTA [13], our method reduces the number of required encoding variables, thus significantly improving the efficiency, as confirmed by the experimental results, showing that our method is dramatically faster than the state-of-the-art method from [13]. We also proposed a solution method for the novel states-optimal DIP, and the experimental results on a large set of benchmarks demonstrate its scalability.

For future work, we consider further improving the practical efficiency in running time. One possibility is to find a novel encoding method where the input is a fixed total number of states N of the decomposition, but not a states allocation. In this way, if the answer is UNSAT, we can just increase the total number of states N without computing all possible states allocations suitable for the current N.

Acknowledgments. We thank the anonymous reviewers for their useful remarks that helped us improve the quality of the paper.

Work supported in part by the National Key R&D Program of China (Grant No. 2022YFA1005101), by the Natural Science Foundation of China (NSFC) (Grants Nos. W2511064, 62472316, 62192732, 62032024, and 62032019), by the ISCAS Basic Research (Grant Nos. ISCAS-JCZD-202406 and ISCAS-JCZD-202302), by the CAS Project for Young Scientists in Basic Research (Grant No. YSBR-040), and by the ISCAS New Cultivation Project ISCAS-PYFX-202201. This project is part of the European Union's Horizon 2020 research and innovation programme under the Marie Skłodowska-Curie grant no. 101008233.

References

1. Ashar, P., Devadas, S., Newton, A.R.: Finite State Machine Decomposition, pp. 117–168. Springer, Boston (1992)
2. Beyer, D., Löwe, S., Wendler, P.: Reliable benchmarking: requirements and solutions. Int. J. Softw. Tools Technol. Transf. **21**(1), 1–29 (2019)
3. Coste, F., Nicolas, J.: How considering incompatible state mergings may reduce the DFA induction search tree. In: Honavar, V., Slutzki, G. (eds.) ICGI 1998. LNCS, vol. 1433, pp. 199–210. Springer, Heidelberg (1998). https://doi.org/10.1007/BFb0054076
4. Daciuk, J., Mihov, S., Watson, B.W., Watson, R.E.: Incremental construction of minimal acyclic finite state automata. Comput. Linguist. **26**(1), 3–16 (2000)
5. Dell'Erba, D., Li, Y., Schewe, S.: DFAMiner: mining minimal separating DFAs from labelled samples. In: FM 2024. LNCS, vol. 14934, pp. 48–66. Springer, Cham (2024)
6. Egri-Nagy, A.: Applications of automata theory and algebra via the mathematical theory of complexity to biology, physics, psychology, philosophy, and games. Artif. Life **17**(2), 141–143 (2011)
7. Grinchtein, O., Leucker, M., Piterman, N.: Inferring network invariants automatically. In: Furbach, U., Shankar, N. (eds.) IJCAR 2006. LNCS (LNAI), vol. 4130, pp. 483–497. Springer, Heidelberg (2006). https://doi.org/10.1007/11814771_40
8. Hardy, G.H., Ramanujan, S.: Asymptotic formulae in combinatory analysis. Proc. Lond. Math. Soc. **s2-17**(1), 75–115 (1918)
9. Heule, M.J.H., Verwer, S.: Exact DFA identification using SAT solvers. In: Sempere, J.M., García, P. (eds.) ICGI 2010. LNCS (LNAI), vol. 6339, pp. 66–79. Springer, Heidelberg (2010). https://doi.org/10.1007/978-3-642-15488-1_7
10. de la Higuera, C.: A bibliographical study of grammatical inference. Pattern Recogn. **38**(9), 1332–1348 (2005)
11. Kupferman, O., Mosheiff, J.: Prime languages. Inf. Comput. **240**, 90–107 (2015)
12. Lang, K.J., Pearlmutter, B.A., Price, R.A.: Results of the Abbadingo one DFA learning competition and a new evidence-driven state merging algorithm. In: Honavar, V., Slutzki, G. (eds.) ICGI 1998. LNCS, vol. 1433, pp. 1–12. Springer, Heidelberg (1998). https://doi.org/10.1007/BFb0054059

13. Lauffer, N., Yalcinkaya, B., Vazquez-Chanlatte, M., Shah, A., Seshia, S.A.: Learning deterministic finite automata decompositions from examples and demonstrations. In: FMCAD 2022, pp. 1–6. IEEE (2022)
14. Meng, J., et al.: Efficient decomposition identification of deterministic finite automata from examples. arXiv abs/2509.24347 (2025). https://arxiv.org/abs/2509.24347
15. Neider, D.: Computing minimal separating DFAs and regular invariants using SAT and SMT solvers. In: Chakraborty, S., Mukund, M. (eds.) ATVA 2012. LNCS, pp. 354–369. Springer, Heidelberg (2012). https://doi.org/10.1007/978-3-642-33386-6_28
16. Neider, D.: Applications of automata learning in verification and synthesis. Ph.D. thesis, RWTH Aachen University (2014)
17. Ulyantsev, V., Zakirzyanov, I., Shalyto, A.: BFS-based symmetry breaking predicates for DFA identification. In: Dediu, A.-H., Formenti, E., Martín-Vide, C., Truthe, B. (eds.) LATA 2015. LNCS, vol. 8977, pp. 611–622. Springer, Cham (2015). https://doi.org/10.1007/978-3-319-15579-1_48
18. Ulyantsev, V., Zakirzyanov, I., Shalyto, A.: Symmetry breaking predicates for SAT-based DFA identification. arXiv abs/1602.05028 (2016)
19. Vaandrager, F.W.: Model learning. Commun. ACM **60**(2), 86–95 (2017)
20. Zakirzyanov, I., Morgado, A., Ignatiev, A., Ulyantsev, V., Marques-Silva, J.: Efficient symmetry breaking for SAT-based minimum DFA inference. In: Martín-Vide, C., Okhotin, A., Shapira, D. (eds.) LATA 2019. LNCS, vol. 11417, pp. 159–173. Springer, Cham (2019). https://doi.org/10.1007/978-3-030-13435-8_12
21. Zakirzyanov, I., Shalyto, A., Ulyantsev, V.: Finding all minimum-size DFA consistent with given examples: SAT-based approach. In: Cerone, A., Roveri, M. (eds.) SEFM 2017. LNCS, vol. 10729, pp. 117–131. Springer, Cham (2018). https://doi.org/10.1007/978-3-319-74781-1_9

Monitoring

FLARE — Monitoring for the Regulatory Requirements of a Drone Case Study

Sean Fenech(✉), Christian Colombo, Gordon Pace, and Axel Curmi

University of Malta, Msida MSD2080, Malta
{sean.fenech.23,christian.colombo,gordon.pace,axel.curmi}@um.edu.mt

Abstract. As regulatory requirements for software systems in the European Union continue to evolve, there is growing pressure to embed mechanisms into deployed systems that ensure both operational trustworthiness and legal accountability. Frameworks such as the AI Act and the Cyber Resilience Act introduce obligations related to cybersecurity, incident response, transparency, and auditability, particularly for high-risk and autonomous systems. These demands go beyond traditional verification and increasingly call for runtime components capable of monitoring behaviour, detecting non-compliance, and preserving forensic evidence. In this work, we present FLARE, a runtime verification tool that combines automated monitoring with tamper-evident logging to support regulatory compliance. Building on existing runtime verification techniques, FLARE enables the construction of both a system harness that monitors live interactions with the environment and flags policy violations; and a forensic node, capable of recording verifiable logs. We demonstrate the application of FLARE on a waste-identification and localisation drone, a cyber-physical system subject to multiple legal and safety constraints. Our case study shows how FLARE can support legal and operational requirements while introducing minimal overhead, providing a practical path towards compliance-aware software instrumentation.

Keywords: runtime verification · regulatory compliance · forensic node

1 Introduction

The regulatory demands for the transparency, security and auditability of digital systems—particularly those deployed in safety- or mission-critical domains—are becoming increasingly more stringent. Within the European Union, the *AI Act* and the *Cyber Resilience Act (CRA)* (amongst other technology regulation) highlight the growing expectation that deployed systems should not only behave correctly but should also be built to support investigation and accountability in the event of a failure or breach.

As part of this shift, we are seeing regulatory bodies starting to provide requirements for the technical architecture of trustworthy digital systems. One of

A. Goharshady and C. Haase (Eds.): SETTA 2025, LNCS 16458, pp. 199–219, 2026.
https://doi.org/10.1007/978-981-95-7826-9_11

the early adopters of such an approach is the *Malta Digital Innovation Authority (MDIA)* and the *Technology Assurance and Recognition Framework (TARF)* [23] with associated proposed guidelines for assessing AI systems [24]. For AI systems registered under the TARF, the proposed guidelines require two core architectural components that systems are required to include: (i) a *system harness*; and (ii) a *forensic node*. The system harness wraps around the main application logic to enable real-time monitoring of system-environment interactions, helping detect policy violations or anomalies during operation. The forensic node, on the other hand, serves as a tamper-evident event logger, storing runtime data securely to support audits or legal compliance checks after the fact. Together, these components form the backbone of systems that are not only functionally sound, but verifiably accountable.

In this paper we explore how runtime verification (RV)—a formal method typically used for checking temporal properties during system execution—can be adapted to support compliance with these regulatory requirements. RV has traditionally focused on monitoring and potentially intervening with the system-under-scrutiny in a manner that aligns closely with the system harness component requirements. By incorporating tamper-evident storage in its execution, RV can also provide a strategically-placed forensic node component.

In this paper, we introduce FLARE, a runtime verification tool that couples Larva (a Java-based RV tool) with SealFS, a file system offering tamper-evident logging. The result is a tool that not only checks compliance with runtime properties but also produces tamper-evident audit trails, allowing it to fulfil the roles of both a system harness and a forensic node.

To validate this approach, we apply FLARE to a *waste-identification and localisation drone*—a cyber-physical system that operates under a mix of safety, environmental, and data protection constraints. We demonstrate how FLARE can monitor and record key behaviours relevant to regulatory compliance, including geofencing, speed and altitude constraints, signal strength, and privacy concerns, using a risk-based approach to selective event logging.

The remainder of this paper is structured as follows: Sect. 2 gives an overview of the regulatory landscape, and Sect. 3 discusses the combination of the underlying technologies—Larva for runtime monitoring and SealFS for tamper-evident logging. Section 4 describes a waste detection and localisation project, detailing how the system harness and forensic node requirements were realised for this case study. Next, we present our empirical evaluation, including performance and overhead measurements in Sect. 5. Finally, we discuss related work and limitations in Sect. 6 and conclude in Sect. 7.

2 The Regulatory Landscape

The need for the regulation of digital technologies has been increasingly recognised in the past years. Before then, high-risk domains had their own domain-specific legislation to address risk of failure. For instance, in the case of medical devices, regulation going back to the 1990s was applicable to software components of such devices, which was then made more explicit and stringent in the

2010s e.g. the European Union's Medical Devices Regulation[1]. Regulation of software used in aviation can be traced back to the 1980s,[2] and was strengthened over time. In contrast, we are now starting to see legislation addressing digital solutions in general or for more specific technologies. At an EU level, one finds, for instance, the EU Cybersecurity Act [16], the NIS2 Directive [17], the EU AI Act [18], and more recently, the EU Cyber Resilience Act [19]. One can also find such regulation appearing at a national level, such as the *Innovative Technology Arrangement Act* set up in Malta [14,21], covering blockchain and distributed ledger technologies but later widened to cover the whole class of critical systems.

The definition of AI in the EU AI Act is rather wide: *"machine-based system designed to operate with varying levels of autonomy and that may exhibit adaptiveness after deployment and that, for explicit or implicit objectives, infers, from the input it receives, how to generate outputs such as predictions, content, recommendations, or decisions that can influence physical or virtual environments"* [18][3] The aim of the regulation is that AI systems are safe and respect fundamental rights whilst promoting trustworthy innovation, and takes a risk-based approach to regulatory requirements: (i) *prohibited artificial intelligence practices* as identified in the Act include: systems using subliminal techniques, ones which distort the behaviour of persons on the basis of their age, disability or a specific social or economic situation, use of biometric data to categorise individuals, inferring personal information such as race, political opinions, etc., some uses of real-time remote biometric identification systems in publicly accessible spaces, and AI systems to infer emotions of a natural person in workplace areas; (ii) *high-risk AI systems* and their operators regulated under specific stringent requirements and obligations include: AI in critical infrastructure, education, essential private and public services, law enforcement; and (iii) *certain AI systems* such as chatbots and content-generation systems being subject to rules covering transparency, market placement, monitoring, surveillance and enforcement.

Various data-centric obligations arise from this new suite of regulations, including ones which address functional correctness and ones which address legal compliance. Given the importance of technical auditing and to enable replayability and availability of evidence in case of failures, the AI Act specifically requires logging capabilities for high-risk systems which are *"designed to ensure a level of traceability of the AI system's operation that is appropriate to the intended purpose of the system, the level of risk and the obligations laid down in this Regulation"* (see Article 19: Automatically Generated Logs[4] and Arti-

[1] Regulation (EU) 2017/745.

[2] For instance, ED-12 (EUROCAE) was a de facto standard for certifying airborne software required at a national level by a number of countries in Europe in the 1980s.

[3] In 2025, the European Commission has published more extensive guidelines on the definition of AI systems spanning over 13 pages [20].

[4] https://artificialintelligenceact.eu/article/19/.

cle 12: Record-Keeping[5]). Similar constraints arise in the Cyber Resilience Act (CRA): Annex I, Sect. 1(3d)[6], requires that, *"where applicable, products with digital elements shall protect the integrity of stored, transmitted or otherwise processed data, personal or other, commands, programs and configuration against any manipulation or modification not authorised by the user, as well as report on corruptions"*.

The control objectives to be used in conformity assessments for the EU AI Act are still under development. Thus, we will be referring to the AI regulatory guidelines set up in Malta in 2019 [24], where specific control objectives were proposed [26], allowing us to concretely explore the use of runtime verification and other formal methods in a regulatory context.

It is worth adding that the AI Act also entails the setting up of AI regulatory sandboxes to allow for *"the development of tools and infrastructure for testing, benchmarking, assessing and explaining dimensions of AI systems relevant for regulatory learning, such as accuracy, robustness and cybersecurity as well as measures to mitigate risks to fundamental rights, environment and the society at large"* [18]. Such a technical assurance sandbox was set up in Malta in 2020 [28], which also allows us to consider the impact of the use of our approach within that context.

The approach adopted in the regulatory guidelines developed in Malta is closely aligned with that of the EU AI Act, focusing on the trustworthiness of AI solutions through regulatory processes and obligations, as well as technical audits or assessments against control objectives. These cover a variety of aspects of the system under review, ranging from the processes in place (e.g. auditing of design and development processes) and technical assessment (e.g. functional correctness and measures mitigating data and bias risks including ones potentially arising post deployment), to appropriate support measures (e.g. appropriate measures in place to address risks such as cybersecurity and the handling of personal data, and compliance engines).

Of particular interest to this paper are control objectives covering components intended to support monitoring of the live system, including the *system harness* and the *forensic node*[7]:

System harness: The guidelines make it a requirement that an AI system should include an *ITA Harness*[8] [25]. The harness must surround the underlying system (see Fig. 1), providing a safety net (i) enabling the monitoring environmental interaction to ensure compliance with the documented expected behaviour; (ii) enabling identification of anomalies it detects e.g. out-of-bounds inputs and outputs. Note that the harness encompasses not only the core system (the dotted box and the bottom box), but also the data collection and processing engines

[5] https://artificialintelligenceact.eu/article/12/.

[6] https://european-cyber-resilience-act.com/Cyber_Resilience_Act_Annex_1.html.

[7] A more thorough overview of the approach adopted by Malta can be found in [15].

[8] *Innovative Technology Arrangement* (ITA) term broadly refers to digital systems encompassed by the legislation, including AI systems deployed in critical areas.

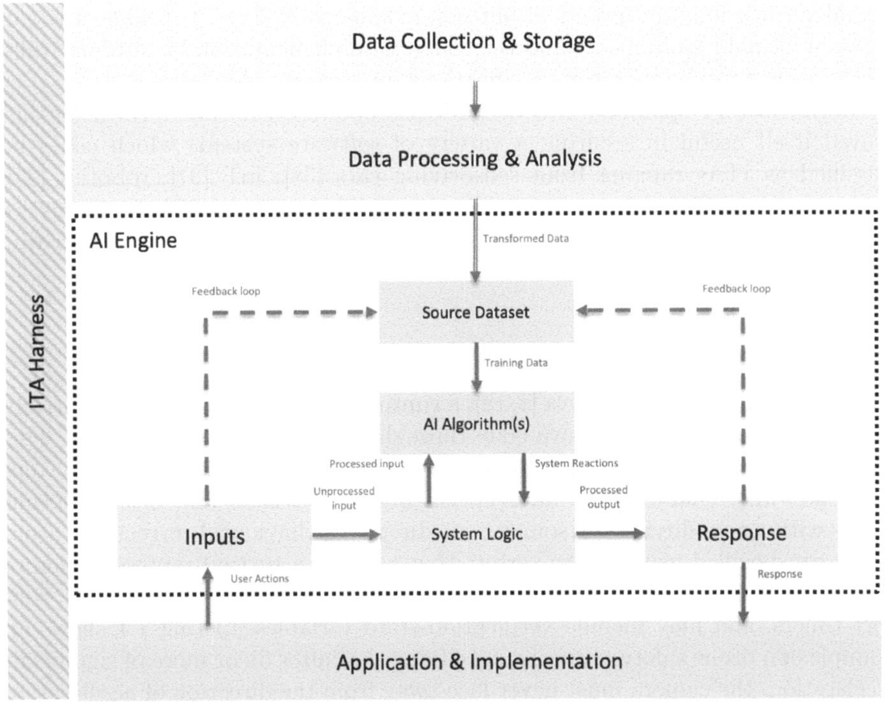

Fig. 1. ITA Harness around an AI system (taken from [25]).

(the top two boxes), as well as the training process (if applicable). This enables its use, not only to enable assessment of the system, but also to collect information and detect anomalies elsewhere e.g. detecting potential bias during the data collection phase. It is worth adding that the control objectives require the technical auditors to review that the implementation of the harness is as specified in the regulatory guidelines i.e. collects all relevant information and events faithfully.

Forensic node: The Forensic Node is intended to be a data repository to store all relevant events and information during the runtime of the AI-ITA in real-time, and in a secure tamper-proof manner. In conjunction with the system harness, this allows for offline assessment of the system's control effectiveness during audits and would support legal compliance investigations. Although the official guidelines architectural diagram (Fig. 1) does not show the forensic node, it is mentioned that it would typically feed off the system harness or be an integral part of it.

3 Runtime Verification and Trustable Logs

In the context of safety- and mission-critical software, runtime verification (RV) [10] has emerged as a compromise between full-state but non-scalable formal verification, and practical but non-exhaustive testing. It bridges the gap between formal requirements and the concrete implementation by automatically synthesising runtime monitor specifications into executable code.

As its history spanning two decades has shown[9], runtime verification has proved itself useful in securing a variety of software systems which could be classified as ITAs ranging from self-driving cars [38], IoT [37], robotics [35], smart contracts [2], and not least AI systems [6]. Inspired by these works, we turn to RV in the context of new regulatory challenges and adapt an existing tool for the job.

3.1 Larva

In this paper, we build on Larva [8,12], a runtime verification tool which natively supports the monitoring of Java code through AspectJ[10] instrumentation. This is achieved by weaving additional monitoring code into the application at compile/load time, enabling the interception of method calls and other relevant events without modifying the source code directly. Behavioural correctness properties are specified using Larva scripts that capture a textual representation of DATE automata [11]. These symbolic automata communicate via channels, support timers, and may include verification-state variables. Listing 1.1 shows an example of a drone safety property, specifying that after 5 s or more of significant acceleration, the camera must never face away from the direction of acceleration (depicted in Fig. 2).

Line 2 declares any necessary variables, in this case consisting of a single timer object. Lines 3–9 identify the traced method calls that trigger state transitions and initialise timer objects. Lines 11–16 define the states of the automaton, identifying the starting, normal and bad ones. Lines 17–29 specify the state transitions, with each transition also qualified by an event, a guard condition, and the action performed (within `[]` and separated by `\\`). Intuitively, the automaton starts in state `LowAcc` and moves to `Acc` upon a high acceleration event. The clock is reset so that it stores the length of time in which the drone has been accelerating. If 5 s elapse, the clock triggers the transition to the `Acc5s` state if its field of vision is aligned with the moving direction, or bad state `Acc5sLW` if otherwise.

```
1 GLOBAL {
2   VARIABLES { Clock c; }
3   EVENTS {
4     HA() = {...} %% High Acceleration
5     LA() = {...} %% Low Acceleration
6     L() = {...} %% Looking
7     LAw() = {...} %% Looking Away
8     Clock() = {c@5}
9   }
```

[9] https://runtime-verification.github.io/events — international event series held annually since 2001.
[10] https://www.eclipse.org/aspectj/.

```
10  PROPERTY cameraProperty {
11  STATES {
12    BAD { Acc5sLW } %% Low Acc and Looking Away
13    NORMAL { Acc %% Accelerating
14             Acc5s } %% Accelerating for >5s
15    STARTING { LowAcc } %% Low Acceleration
16  }
17  TRANSITIONS {
18    LowAcc -> Acc [HA\\c1.reset();]
19    LowAcc -> LowAcc [L\!look\look=true;]
20    LowAcc -> LowAcc [LAw\look\look=false;]
21    Acc -> LowAcc [LA\\c1.off();]
22    Acc -> Acc5s [Clock\look\]
23    Acc -> Acc5sLW [Clock\!look\]
24    Acc -> Acc [L\!look\look=true;]
25    Acc -> Acc [LAw\look\look=false;]
26    Acc5s -> LowAcc [LA\\]
27    Acc5s -> Acc5sLW [LAw\\look=false;]
28    Acc5sLW -> Acc5s [L\\look=true;]
29    Acc5sLW -> LowAcc [LA\\] } } }
```

Listing 1.1. Larva script for: *After 5 seconds or more of significant acceleration, the camera must never face away from the direction of acceleration.*

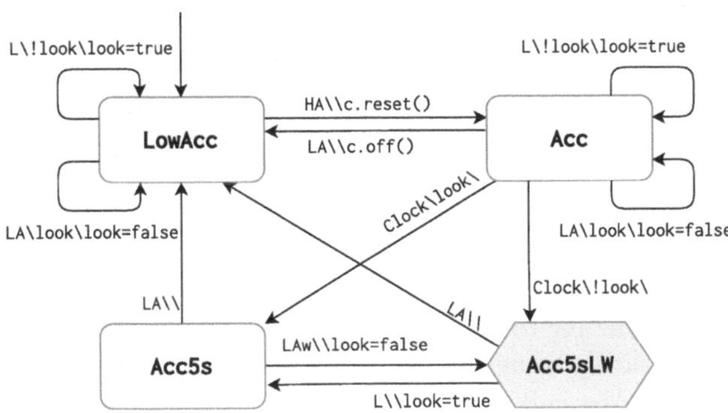

Fig. 2. Visual representation of the property and corresponding Larva listing.

Since DATEs allow unrestricted Java code as transition guards and actions, their expressivity is equivalent to that of Java. If used appropriately, DATE specifications should support modular design complementing the main system implementation, potentially sharing underlying modules. As such, DATEs can also express complex properties requiring statistical reasoning or learning-based anomaly detection.

Importantly, the choice of the events, which trigger automata transitions, should reflect points in the system execution where monitoring checks should be carried out. Selecting the right points of entry for the monitor is crucial to access the relevant data context for the property at hand, as well as to detect any violations as early as possible. Through AspectJ, compiled monitoring code is automatically injected into the system code, avoiding manual modification of the underlying system.

3.2 Tamper-Evident Logging

Runtime verification is tightly coupled with logging because it frequently operates directly on system logs [3] and the output it generates could also constitute important log material [22]. In this sense, RV can serve as a gatekeeper of the forensic node, acting as an event collector, filter, processor, and enhancer. This natural fit is the motivation for considering the integration of RV with tamper-evident logging.

At the core of tamper-evident logging lies the principle of forward integrity [4], which ensures that once a log entry is committed, it cannot be modified or deleted without detection —even if future keys or the system itself are compromised at any privilege level. This is typically achieved through a variety of cryptographic primitives such as hash chains [33]. Importantly, such systems must strike a balance between computational cost, hardware dependencies, and compatibility with existing infrastructure—particularly in resource-constrained and/or online environments.

SealFS [29,36] is a stackable Linux file system, authenticating data as it is written to log files using a one-time-use keystream. By supporting append-only operations, SealFS ensures that once data is written, it cannot be altered without detection. A copy of the keystream is stored securely on an external system that is disconnected after setup. This is then used to verify the integrity of the logs when required, e.g. for forensic analysis purposes.

3.3 Runtime Verification with Tamper-Evident Logging

Building on the existing RV tool Larva, we have modified its open source compiler to have it automatically generate monitors whose output is committed to a tamper-evident file. We call this FLARE since it provides Forensic Logs for Auditing Runtime Events.

The tool's architecture, depicted in Fig. 3, closely follows that of Larva with the additional machinery to provide out-of-the-box tamper-evident logging. The process of using the tool is split into two stages: compilation and runtime execution, corresponding to the upper and lower parts of Fig. 3 respectively.[11] Note that in the diagram, black arrows represent the creation or passing of a file or process. Yellow arrows represent data being consumed and generated at runtime, and purple arrows represent procedures relevant to SealFS.

Stage 1 (Compilation): Starting off with the application to be monitored and the monitoring script (properties), the user uses the FLARE compiler to generate:

[11] The tool and the script with the properties can be accessed from https://github.com/SeanFenech/FLARE.

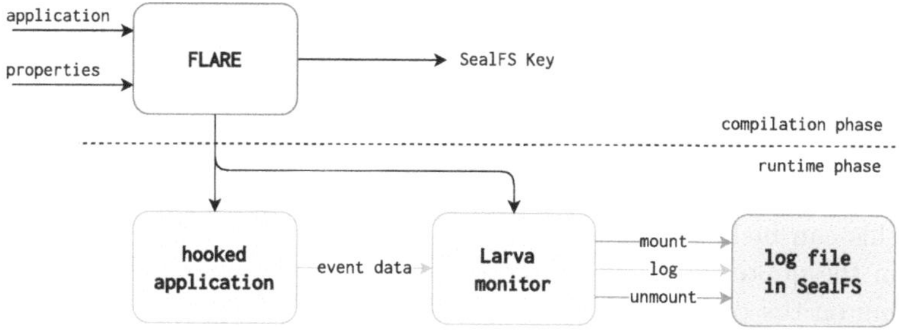

Fig. 3. FLARE combines Larva with SealFS.

(i) the hooked application, i.e., the application plus AspectJ files, which extracts events from the application, (ii) the monitor itself with abilities to setup tamper-evident logging via SealFS, and (iii) the cryptographic key used by SealFS to ensure tamper resistance. This is later also used to verify the logs.

Stage 2 (Runtime Execution): Executing the FLARE-generated code, two things happen: (i) Upon initialisation, the monitor starts by mounting SealFS[12]. (ii) The hooked application automatically starts sending events to the monitor as they occur. As the monitor starts receiving events, it starts processing them as happens with normal monitoring. In the background, a separate thread is launched which is responsible for writing the logs produced by FLARE to a file under the SealFS mount-point. This approach enables the log writing to be asynchronous to its processing, as the latter must keep up with incoming events from the target application or otherwise slow the application's progress. The log-writing thread can then take priority when events are less frequent or require less computational effort to process. Upon application exit, the monitor unmounts SealFS and the logs remain available for the user to access and/or verify them whenever necessary.

3.4 Tamper-Evident Runtime Verification for Compliance

System Harness. To satisfy the requirements set out in the regulatory guidelines, a system harness must *"safeguard the operation of the AI-ITA by actively checking that the user actions (inputs), system reactions (outputs), and any other behaviour is within the expected boundaries of the operation of the AI-ITA and any exceptions trigger the appropriate failure modes"*.

Larva, and by extension FLARE, can act as this harness since it provides: *Active checking:* As a runtime verification tool, FLARE runtime-monitors the system's state and events, including inputs, outputs, and its behaviour more generally. Specification of expected operational boundaries can be defined through

[12] Note that root privileges are required for this operation. However, this still does not allow for the application to tamper with logs written to SealFS without invalidating them.

formal properties. Sitting at a higher level of abstraction, such formal specifications are automatically compiled into code to minimise the possibility of bugs being introduced if implementing the checks by hand.

Appropriate automated triggering: Specific reactions can be programmed alongside the specification to trigger system steering code in response to policy violations. This can include, but is not limited to, triggering failure modes as mentioned in the quoted document. Importantly, such reactions need to be timely, depending on the context.

Forensic Node. To qualify as a forensic node under the regulatory framework, a component has to satisfy three conditions[13]:

Completeness: "All relevant events and data are recorded faithfully in real-time." A strict interpretation of completeness—recording all events—is rarely feasible, especially in constrained or resource-sensitive environments such as drones. In such cases, a risk-based approach could be necessary to select which event streams need to be logged and at which frequency.

Soundness: Data is *"stored in a tamper-proof and accurate manner"*. Tamper-evident storage is achieved through the use of SealFS, which provides strong cryptographic guarantees that logged data has not been altered. SealFS allows for verification of the integrity of log files—a core requirement in any forensic investigation.

Availability: "Processes are in place to ensure timely access to this information." Logs must be accessible and verifiable in a timely fashion, for example when needed for a forensic investigation. This aspect will be evaluated empirically later in the paper.
Having established FLARE as a valid candidate to meet regulatory requirements, the next section introduces the case study, explaining the risk elements that need to be handled by the assurance components.

4 Waste Detection and Localisation Case Study

Manual litter collection can be a costly process involving a number of steps: litter needs to be visually located (possibly from some distance) by having personnel searching for it within an area under consideration; after which, the litter needs to be precisely located (possibly requiring a vehicle), picked up, and sorted according to type (paper, plastic, glass, etc.).

From such a traditional perspective that assumes no use of technology, efforts in litter collection are typically focused and optimised for urban contexts for a number of practical reasons emanating from the fact that rural areas are typically unstructured, variable, and spread over a relatively large area: (i) visual detection is easier when litter lies on a uniform surface, such as roads or pavements; (ii)

[13] See page 6 of the Guidelines [27].

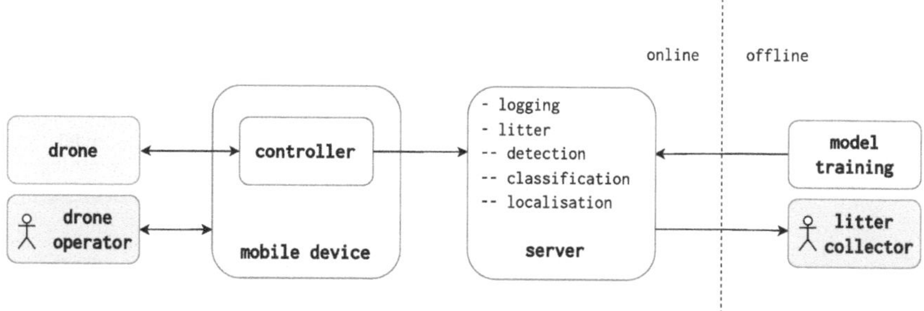

Fig. 4. The setup of the AWIGS project without monitoring.

infrastructure typically found in an urban context limits the areas where litter might be, thus providing a smaller search space; (iii) litter collection is harder when access to particular areas is limited, particularly for vehicles.

Novel and recent developments in AI provide an opportunity to address the challenges described above to carry out sustainable, efficient, and large-scale litter collection in rural areas. An ongoing project, Aerial Waste Identification and Geolocation System (AWIGS), aims to use aerial images captured from different altitudes to automate the search and geolocation process for litter in a vast area. Referring to Fig. 4, the drone sends telemetry data and footage to the controller which in turn displays the video feed to the human operator. The data is further forwarded to a cloud server from where it is processed (using image processing techniques from [31,32]). Litter geolocation information is subsequently forwarded to human litter collectors. Even though the process currently relies on humans to collect litter, this setup still brings along various technical, safety, and regulatory risks and challenges.

In [13], the authors have identified a number of risks organised under the headings data, functionality, regulatory, and safety. Based on these risks, we have derived a number of properties to be monitored, constituting the system harness.

Regulatory Risk: UAV Regulations: Following Maltese drone regulations, it must be ensured that the drone remains below the maximum height (60 m) and that it remains within its predefined flight area (and outside the restricted zones). Furthermore, the drone's speed should not exceed a particular threshold, depending on the altitude—lower threshold at lower altitudes. Similarly, the threshold is lowered when the remote control (RC) signal is weak since this poses a greater risk as the operator may not have sufficient control over the drone.

Safety Risk: To mitigate safety risks, it must be ensured that the drone remains in range from the takeoff location, and that the signal strength remains above an acceptable threshold. The battery cell consistency and temperature should also be monitored to detect early warning signs of wear. Wind speed is a major factor in safe drone navigation. For this reason, this needs to be monitored, giving particular attention to high wind speeds or sudden large changes.

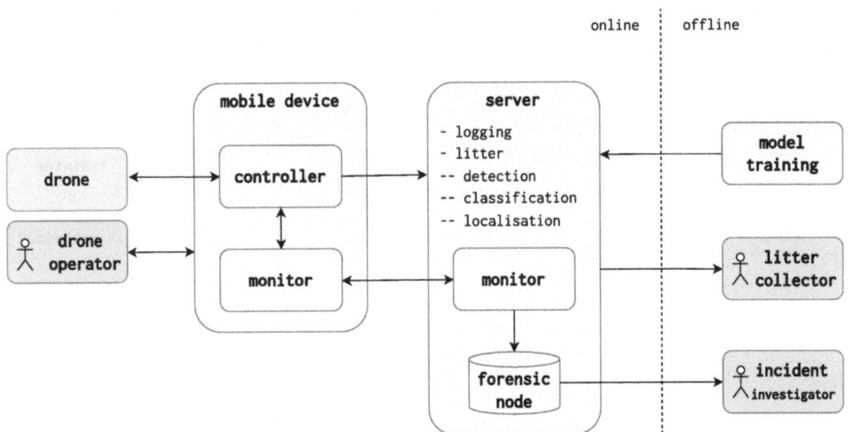

Fig. 5. The setup of the AWIGS project with monitoring components and the forensic node.

Data Risk: To ensure correct detection and classification of litter, even before training begins, it must be ensured that the training and evaluation datasets have sufficient variety and size. This would involve checking the overall dataset sizes and their distribution across different categories. Required data includes the dataset itself, the counts of objects per category, as well as the various environments (e.g., beach, forest, etc.) where the litter is found. This applies both to initial training and eventual re-training of the models.

Regulatory Risk: Privacy Concerns When the drone scans areas for litter, there is a significant probability of capturing identifiable data of individuals or vehicles within the drone's field of view. To avoid non-compliance to privacy regulations, such elements need to be detected and anonymised, for example through blurring/masking people and vehicles with solid colour boxes.

4.1 Monitoring Setup

Taking the above into consideration, we proceed to propose a modified AWIGS setup which incorporates the system harness and the forensic node. Given the time-sensitive nature of monitor feedback, the monitor should receive the data stream with minimal delay. For this reason, as shown in Fig. 5, we split the monitor into two parts: the monitor which handles the drone receives the feed directly from the controller, by-passing the server, and being able to give immediate feedback to the human drone operator. On the other hand, the monitor which handles AI components can operate on the server, dealing with more expensive, yet less time-sensitive checks. The two monitoring components would interact with each other: in one direction, from the mobile device to the server to log the monitor output in the forensic node. In the other direction, actionable insights from the server-side monitor can be sent back to the controller. For example, one could suggest that the operator takes the drone lower or revisits a particular area at a slower speed if the footage was not clear enough for a reliable classification.

As expected, safety and regulatory risks related to UAV regulations tend to be more time sensitive. What follows is a list of such properties that are ideally checked directly on the mobile device linked to the controller: high wind speed check; battery monitoring in relation to charge and health status; GPS and remote control signal strength monitoring; speed check in relation to altitude and signal strength; position monitoring for inbound altitude, coordinates, and distance from the controller; ensuring that during consistent acceleration the drone's camera axis matches that of the drone acceleration direction.

FLARE code needed to monitor such properties is identical to that required by Larva as provided in the example in Sect. 3.1 (corresponding to the latter property in the list above).

While we could use FLARE to actively intervene (e.g. overriding the human operator in certain exceptional scenarios), in the current phase of the project, the system does not yet support direct automated feedback. Instead, the tool acts as a watchdog: upon detecting non-compliance, FLARE issues alerts to the human operator, who remains the only agent authorised to modify system behaviour. As noted in [25], ultimately the *"harness is not intended to be a replacement for human-level checks"*. Rather, it provides a safety net that detects and communicates anomalies, ensuring operational awareness and supporting legal defensibility.

Concerning data risk and privacy concerns, such properties are typically less clearcut to monitor. For example, the data risk can be kept under watch through proxy measures, e.g. dataset distribution throughout ongoing training updates. Tackling privacy concerns adds another layer of uncertainty; while the harness would be able to ensure that the algorithm used has a high accuracy score, it wouldn't be able to check with certainty that there are no privacy issues without using alternative models (which would themselves not be 100% theoretically accurate). These properties are not yet implemented but are planned to be added once the project reaches the corresponding development phase.

4.2 Forensic Node Data Collection

To avoid storing excessive amounts of data on the forensic node, a risk-based approach has been adopted, taking into consideration the properties being monitored and assessing both the likelihood and impact of potential system failures or legal breaches. Through this exercise, we have identified the set of events necessary to support a meaningful forensic investigation, should the need for one arise. For instance, in the context of operator control risk, critical data includes RC connection strength, speed, and altitude. Events related to these parameters are logged at higher frequencies, while lower-risk parameters (e.g. GPS signal strength above thresholds) are recorded less frequently (see Table 1). The balance between extra overhead and the quantity of data collected can vary greatly, even within different contexts of our use case. For our proof of concept we have chosen the frequencies of 1 Hz and 0.1 Hz based on the feedback we received from the domain experts. This balancing act ensures that the system remains responsive and efficient while still capturing essential evidence for post-incident analysis.

Table 1. Events and the frequency at which they are logged

Event	Condition	Freq. (Hz)
Position update	alt > 60 m, in restricted area, >115 m from takeoff	1
	otherwise	0.1
Battery update	Low battery health, or charge < 20%	1
	otherwise	0.1
	Takeoff/landing	F^{14}
RC Signal update	Low RC signal strength	1
	otherwise	0.1
GPS Signal update	Low GPS signal strength	1
	otherwise	0.1

[14] The frequency at which the controller receives signals—in our case $F = 10/s$.

The FLARE code snippet in Listing 1.2 shows events being received from the controller and their parameters being stored within the monitor (see lines 3–8). At second and ten-second intervals a number of data fields are logged (see lines 10–11). Similarly, at critical events such as takeoff and landing, data is logged as frequently as the system allows (see lines 13–14).

FLARE offers the possibility of encrypting the data stored in the logfile. However, this is optional as this is not a requirement of the forensic node. In our case study we have not used this feature.

```
1 ...
2 TRANSITIONS {
3   normal -> normal [dataAltitude\\l_altitude = altitude; lt_altitude = time
        ;]
4   normal -> normal [dataGPS\\l_satellites = satellites;
5                       lt_satellites = time; l_gpsLevel = gpsLevel;
                            lt_gpsLevel = time;]
6   normal -> normal [goodCellConsistency\\d_goodCellConsistency = true;]
7   normal -> normal [badCellConsistency\\d_goodCellConsistency = false;]
8   normal -> normal [veryBadCellConsistency\\d_goodCellConsistency = false;]
9   ...
10  normal -> normal [dataClock1\\logData(d_location,d_rc,d_gps,d_battery);dc1
        .reset();]
11  normal -> normal [dataClock10\\logData(true, true, true, true); dc10.reset
        ();]
12  ...
13  normal -> normal [takeOff\\logData(true, false, false, false);]
14  normal -> normal [landing\\logData(true, false, false, false);]
15  ... } ...
```

Listing 1.2. Larva script: *Logging relevant data at the right frequencies.*

4.3 Lessons Learnt from Implementation

The main implementation process involved the encoding of the identified properties into DATEs. Once DATEs were formatted into a complete Larva script, these were ready for compilation by FLARE. From that stage, the compilation process automatically generates the necessary code. While there is a learning curve when using the tool for the first time, our experience has shown that this moderate. Perhaps what remains a significant challenge is that the testing process of the RV process itself is not typically automated as industrial Java systems. Indeed, the way the monitor integrates with the system through AspectJ and its output in the dedicated text file, makes automated testing cumbersome to set up. For this reason, testing was carried out manually. Beyond the actual implementation of the requirements, a significant step in this project was the capturing of the requirements themselves. As our previous experiences with runtime verification applications in industry have shown [9], bridging this gap comes with its own set of challenges. To facilitate communication, we organised several meetings with the domain experts to ensure that the requirements truly reflected the intended semantics. Such meetings were also crucial in understanding the risks involved and, subsequently, in establishing the right frequency of events to be processed and logged for each type (as expressed in Table 1). Crucially, we aimed to ensure that the risk appetite of the domain experts is correctly translated into the corresponding numbers.

We estimate the number of hours used by the runtime verification engineer (the main author of this paper) as listed in Table 2.

Table 2. Number of hours used by the runtime verification engineer.

Task	Hours
Designing properties and communicating with domain experts	40
Expressing properties as DATEs and writing Larva script	25
Testing and debugging	20
Validation with domain experts and the resulting fine-tuning	15

5 Empirical Evaluation

Increased security always comes with a tradeoff. Given the additional cryptographic operations carried out by FLARE, one would expect an overhead penalty over the original tool Larva. Furthermore, since a major concern for a system harness is its ability to react in an appropriately timely manner, one would also need to assess whether this is adequate for drone monitoring. Secondly, since the monitoring output is being used as a forensic node, in line with the requirements, we need to ensure that data is accessible without undue delay.

5.1 Measuring Monitoring Latency

The aim of our experiment is to have a clear indication of the additional latency introduced by the new monitoring tool. Using Larva as a baseline, we analyse the performance of FLARE on actual drone flight data. For this reason we use a simulated telemetry generation process, triggering events with 100ms delay between each data record. The experiment consisted of processing 153,226 records which translates to a little over 4 h (number of records multiplied by 100ms) worth of data from the drone. The experiment was run on a virtual machine running Ubuntu 22.04.5 LTS, with the 5.15.0-119-generic kernel, through VirtualBox 7.0.20 and Vagrant 2.4.1, given 4GB RAM and 4/8 CPUs. The virtual machine ran on an Intel i7-8565U CPU 1.80GHz, 4 Cores, 8 Logical Processors, with 8GB DDR4 RAM.

Given the 100ms delay between each data record received from the drone, the small additional processing time required by FLARE was not discernable, both tools took 4.26 h (reflecting the time taken to simulate all the events) with FLARE taking 11ms longer. The reason for this small difference is that the 100ms delays allows enough time for FLARE to catch up after each event. Therefore, to obtain a measurable difference between the monitoring tools, we also simulated the monitoring process without any delays. The results are shown in Table 3. As expected due to the cryptographic operations involved, FLARE took more time to process the data: a 38% increase. The data generated by the monitor increased by 15% namely due to the metadata added to the logfile.

Since our main concern is the latency introduced through monitoring, we also divided the monitoring time by the number of samples processed. The result is in the order of hundreds of microseconds—leading to an insignificant increase in latency. Of course one would expect these numbers to be bigger if monitoring is carried out on a mobile device, but even with an order of magnitude higher, latency would still be a modest one.

To explore how the monitoring overhead increases as the data increases, we ran both versions on the data available twice. While this could vary depending on the properties monitored, in this case, the monitoring time and the data generated grew linearly (i.e., doubled). More precisely, the monitoring time for Larva increased by 57% while the monitoring time for FLARE increased by 93%. As expected, the data generated by the monitors doubled exactly.

Table 3. Monitoring data and SealFS verification for different setups.

Setup	Larva	FLARE	Larva ×2	FLARE ×2
Total Monitoring Time (s)	43.41	59.89	68.24	115.30
Monitoring Time per Sample (μs)	283	391	223	376
Data generated (MB)	218.47	250.86	437.02	501.78
SealFS verification (s)	N/A	31.56	N/A	62.82

Finally, due to the forensic node requirement of timely access to the stored data, we consider this element for our implementation. Reading from our forensic node is not different from reading a file on a standard operating system. However, verifying the integrity of the data requires processing time as shown in Table 3. For example 500MB of data took a little over one minute to verify. To ensure that the verification time remains manageable (depending on the context), one could have separate log files, for example one log file for each hour of operation. In our case, using simple proportion, one hour of operation would require around 8 s to verify.

5.2 Discussion

The results presented above suggest that FLARE introduces manageable overheads in terms of performance and storage, even when integrated with cryptographic logging via SealFS. In our experiments, the system handled over four hours' worth of drone telemetry with negligible latency, demonstrating that compliance-aware monitoring and forensic capabilities can be introduced without undermining the responsiveness or reliability of real-time systems.

The linear relationship observed between data size and verification time also supports the practical viability of forensic node deployment, particularly when logs are segmented appropriately. In our case, 500MB of data could be verified in just over one minute, suggesting that the forensic verification process scales well and can meet the availability requirements defined by the regulatory guidelines.

That said, the current implementation is not without its limitations:

Key Depletion: SealFS consumes a finite keystream for tamper-evident logging. Although sufficient for our case study, this could become a bottleneck in long-running or high-frequency logging scenarios. Future versions could integrate ratcheting-based key regeneration [29] to address this.

Crash Resilience: If the system crashes between event occurrence and log writing, that event may be lost, and the monitor's state reset. Future iterations could explore persistent monitor state snapshots to support recovery.

Meta-event Visibility: Events involving the monitoring infrastructure itself—e.g., system reboots, monitor initialisation, or failures—currently fall outside the visibility scope of FLARE. These may need to be captured via a complementary "meta-level" forensic mechanism to ensure completeness of the forensic narrative.

6 Related Work

Runtime verification allows the monitoring of system behaviour against formalised specifications. While the combination of RV with tamper-evident storage has been previously discussed [1,7], to the best of our knowledge, FLARE is the first open-source tool that provides an integrated pipeline supporting both runtime monitoring and verifiable logging out-of-the-box.

That said, several other RV tools could, in principle, be extended to fulfil the system harness role described in regulatory frameworks. One notable example is JavaMOP [5], which supports the specification of monitoring properties using multiple logic formalisms. Crucially, JavaMOP also supports a corrective process, enabling not just passive observation but also the execution of predefined actions in response to violations—a capability also offered by Larva and required to instantiate an active system harness. With additional support for secure logging (e.g. via integration with SealFS or another cryptographically-verifiable backend), JavaMOP could similarly provide a sound basis for building compliance-aware systems.

Beyond SealFS, tamper-evident logging has been implemented in various contexts through a number of tools such as EmLog [34], Custos [30], and QED[14]. These tools are generally focused on ensuring the integrity of recorded data, but do not provide mechanisms for high-level behavioural monitoring or compliance reasoning. As such, they serve well as forensic storage layers but do not meet the broader objectives of a system harness as described in regulatory frameworks.

The combination of Larva and SealFS represents one possibility out of many others (e.g., those mentioned above). For the purposes of the proof of concept implementation presented in this work, the chosen tools ticked all the boxes.

7 Conclusions and Future Work

In this paper, we presented FLARE, a runtime verification tool designed to meet emerging regulatory requirements through tamper-evident logging. By integrating runtime verification with SealFS-based storage, FLARE offers a pragmatic solution for achieving compliance with frameworks such as the EU AI Act and the Cyber Resilience Act, particularly in the context of cyber-physical systems like drones. Our case study demonstrates that runtime verification, when combined with secure logging, can provide a lightweight yet robust layer of assurance, improving auditability, forensic capabilities, and regulatory alignment without imposing prohibitive overheads.

The experimental results show that the additional monitoring overhead introduced by FLARE remains manageable, and the approach scales linearly with the data generated. We also highlight important considerations for deploying forensic nodes in practice, including the need for risk-based data prioritisation and timely access to verified logs.

As the project evolves, we plan to implement the data-focused properties, particularly for the subsystems involving image processing, where balanced training data and privacy pose additional challenges. Looking ahead, we can also consider extending FLARE with code attestation capabilities to further strengthen trust guarantees. Furthermore, expanding the tool's validation across multiple case studies will help assess its generalisability to a broader range of AI-driven and safety-critical systems.

[14] https://github.com/BBVA/qed.

Ultimately, FLARE represents a step towards bridging the gap between formal methods research and real-world demands of regulated digital technologies.

Acknowledgments. We gratefully acknowledge support from the Aerial Waste Identification and Geolocation System (AWIGS) project, funded by Xjenza Malta and led by Dylan Seychell, with key feedback from Matthias Bartolo and Gabriel Hili.

References

1. Abela, R., et al.: Runtime verification for trustworthy computing. In: Proceedings of the Third Workshop on Agents and Robots for reliable Engineered Autonomy, AREA@ECAI 2023, Krakow, Poland, 1st October 2023. EPTCS, vol. 391, pp. 49–62 (2023). https://doi.org/10.4204/EPTCS.391.7
2. Azzopardi, S., Ellul, J., Pace, G.J.: Monitoring smart contracts: contractlarva and open challenges beyond. In: Runtime Verification (RV 2018). Lecture Notes in Computer Science, vol. 11237, pp. 113–137 (2018). https://doi.org/10.1007/978-3-030-03769-7_8
3. Barringer, H., Groce, A., Havelund, K., Smith, M.H.: An entry point for formal methods: Specification and analysis of event logs. In: Proceedings of the Workshop on Formal Methods for Aerospace (FMA). Electronic Proceedings in Theoretical Computer Science, vol. 20, pp. 16–21 (2009). https://doi.org/10.4204/EPTCS.20.2
4. Bellare, M., Yee, B.S.: Forward integrity for secure audit logs. Technical report CS98-580, Department of Computer Science and Engineering, University of California at San Diego (November 1997)
5. Chen, F., Rosu, G.: Java-mop: A monitoring oriented programming environment for java. In: Halbwachs, N., Zuck, L.D. (eds.) Tools and Algorithms for the Construction and Analysis of Systems, 11th International Conference, TACAS 2005, Held as Part of the Joint European Conferences on Theory and Practice of Software, ETAPS 2005, Edinburgh, UK, April 4–8, 2005, Proceedings. Lecture Notes in Computer Science, vol. 3440, pp. 546–550. Springer (2005). https://doi.org/10.1007/978-3-540-31980-1_36
6. Cheng, C., Nührenberg, G., Yasuoka, H.: Runtime monitoring neuron activation patterns. In: Design, Automation and Test in Europe (DATE), pp. 300–303 (2019). https://doi.org/10.23919/DATE.2019.8714971
7. Colombo, C., Curmi, A., Abela, R.: RVsec: towards a comprehensive technology stack for secure deployment of software monitors. In: Proceedings of the 7th ACM International Workshop on Verification and Monitoring at Runtime Execution, VORTEX 2024, Vienna, Austria, 19 September 2024, pp. 13–18. ACM (2024). https://doi.org/10.1145/3679008.3685542
8. Colombo, C., Pace, G.J.: Runtime verification using LARVA. In: RV-CuBES 2017. An International Workshop on Competitions, Usability, Benchmarks, Evaluation, and Standardisation for Runtime Verification Tools, September 15, 2017, Seattle, WA, USA. Kalpa Publications in Computing, vol. 3, pp. 55–63. EasyChair (2017). https://doi.org/10.29007/N7TD
9. Colombo, C., Pace, G.J.: Industrial experiences with runtime verification of financial transaction systems: Lessons learnt and standing challenges. In: Bartocci, E., Falcone, Y. (eds.) Lectures on Runtime Verification - Introductory and Advanced

Topics, Lecture Notes in Computer Science, vol. 10457, pp. 211–232. Springer (2018). https://doi.org/10.1007/978-3-319-75632-5_7
10. Colombo, C., Pace, G.J.: What is Runtime Verification, pp. 9–15. Springer International Publishing (2022). https://doi.org/10.1007/978-3-031-09268-8_2
11. Colombo, C., Pace, G.J., Schneider, G.: Dynamic event-based runtime monitoring of real-time and contextual properties. In: Cofer, D.D., Fantechi, A. (eds.) Formal Methods for Industrial Critical Systems, 13th International Workshop, FMICS 2008, L'Aquila, Italy, September 15–16, 2008, Revised Selected Papers. Lecture Notes in Computer Science, vol. 5596, pp. 135–149. Springer (2008). https://doi.org/10.1007/978-3-642-03240-0_13
12. Colombo, C., Pace, G.J., Schneider, G.: LARVA – safer monitoring of real-time java programs (tool paper). In: Seventh IEEE International Conference on Software Engineering and Formal Methods, SEFM 2009, Hanoi, Vietnam, 23–27 November 2009, pp. 33–37. IEEE Computer Society (2009). https://doi.org/10.1109/SEFM.2009.13
13. Colombo, C., Pace, G.J., Seychell, D.: Runtime verification and AI: addressing pragmatic regulatory challenges. In: Bridging the Gap Between AI and Reality - Second International Conference, AISoLA 2024, Crete, Greece, October 30 - November 3, 2024, Proceedings. Lecture Notes in Computer Science, vol. 15217, pp. 225–241. Springer (2024). https://doi.org/10.1007/978-3-031-75434-0_16
14. Ellul, J., Galea, J., Ganado, M., Mccarthy, S., Pace, G.J.: Regulating Blockchain, DLT and Smart Contracts: a technology regulator's perspective. ERA Forum **21**(2), 209–220 (2020). https://doi.org/10.1007/s12027-020-00617-7
15. Ellul, J., et al.: Regulating artificial intelligence: a technology regulator's perspective. In: ICAIL '21: Eighteenth International Conference for Artificial Intelligence and Law, São Paulo Brazil, June 21–25, 2021, pp. 190–194. ACM (2021). https://doi.org/10.1145/3462757.3466093
16. European Union: Regulation (EU) 2019/881 of the European Parliament and of the Council of 17 April 2019 on ENISA (the European Union Agency for Cybersecurity) and on information and communications technology cybersecurity certification and repealing Regulation (EU) (2019)
17. European Union: Directive (EU) 2022/2555 of the European Parliament and of the Council of 14 December 2022 on measures for a high common level of cybersecurity across the Union, amending Regulation (EU) (2022)
18. European Union: Proposal for a Regulation of the European Parliament and of the Council laying down harmonised rules on artificial intelligence (Artificial Intelligence Act) and amending certain Union legislative acts (2024)
19. European Union: Regulation (EU) 2024/2847 of the European Parliament and of the Council of 23 October 2024 on horizontal cybersecurity requirements for products with digital elements and amending Regulations (EU) (2024)
20. European Union: Approval of the content of the draft Communication from the Commission – Commission Guidelines on the definition of an artificial intelligence system established by Regulation (EU) 2024/1689 (AI Act) (2025)
21. Government of Malta: Innovative Technology Arrangements and Services Act (2018)
22. Havelund, K., Joshi, R.: Experience with rule-based analysis of spacecraft logs. In: Artho, C., Ölveczky, P.C. (eds.) Formal Techniques for Safety-Critical Systems - Third International Workshop, FTSCS 2014, Luxembourg, November 6–7, 2014. Revised Selected Papers. Communications in Computer and Information Science, vol. 476, pp. 1–16. Springer (2014). https://doi.org/10.1007/978-3-319-17581-2_1

23. Malta Digital Innovation Authority: Technology assessment recognition framework: Guidelines for applicants, assessors and other stakeholders, G-SPG-012 Rev. 1, 2023
24. Malta Digital Innovation Authority: AI ITA Guidelines (October 2019). https://mdia.gov.mt/app/uploads/2024/07/AI-ITA-Guidelines-03OCT19.pdf
25. Malta Digital Innovation Authority: AI ITA Nomenclature (October 2019). https://mdia.gov.mt/app/uploads/2024/07/AI-ITA-Nomenclature-03OCT19.pdf
26. Malta Digital Innovation Authority: AI System Auditor Control Objectives (October 2019). https://www.mdia.gov.mt/wp-content/uploads/2022/11/AI-ITA-SA-Control-Objectives-03OCT19.pdf
27. Malta Digital Innovation Authority: Forensic Node Guidelines (September 2019). https://mdia.gov.mt/app/uploads/2022/11/Forensic-Node-Guidelines.pdf
28. Malta Digital Innovation Authority: Technology Assurance Sandbox v2.0 Programme Guidelines (June 2020). https://www.mdia.gov.mt/wp-content/uploads/2022/11/MDIA-Technology-Assurance-Sandbox-TAS-Programme-Guidelines.pdf
29. Muzquiz, G.G., Soriano-Salvador, E.: Sealfsv2: combining storage-based and ratcheting for tamper-evident logging. Int. J. Inf. Sec. **22**(2), 447–466 (2023). https://doi.org/10.1007/S10207-022-00643-1
30. Paccagnella, R., et al.: Custos: Practical tamper-evident auditing of operating systems using trusted execution. In: 27th Annual Network and Distributed System Security Symposium, NDSS 2020, San Diego, California, USA, February 23–26, 2020. The Internet Society (2020). https://doi.org/10.14722/ndss.2020.24065
31. Pisani, D., Seychell, D., Schembri, M.: Detecting litter from aerial imagery using the SODA dataset. In: 2024 IEEE 22nd Mediterranean Electrotechnical Conference (MELECON) (2024). https://doi.org/10.1109/MELECON56669.2024.10608507
32. Schembri, M., Seychell, D.: Small object detection in highly variable backgrounds. In: 2019 IEEE 11th International Symposium on Image and Signal Processing and Analysis (ISPA), pp. 32–37 (2019). https://doi.org/10.1109/ISPA.2019.8868719
33. Schneier, B., Kelsey, J.: Secure audit logs to support computer forensics. ACM Trans. Inf. Syst. Secur. **2**(2), 159–176 (1999). https://doi.org/10.1145/317087.317089
34. Shepherd, C., Akram, R.N., Markantonakis, K.: EmLog: Tamper-resistant system logging for constrained devices with TEEs. CoRR abs/1712.03943 (2017). 10.48550/arXiv. 1712.03943
35. Shivakumar, S., Torfah, H., Desai, A., Seshia, S.A.: SOTER on ROS: a run-time assurance framework on the robot operating system. In: Runtime Verification (RV 2020). Lecture Notes in Computer Science, vol. 12399, pp. 184–194 (2020). https://doi.org/10.1007/978-3-030-60508-7_10
36. Soriano-Salvador, E., Muzquiz, G.G.: SealFS: storage-based tamper-evident logging. Comput. Secur. **108**, 102325 (2021). https://doi.org/10.1016/J.COSE.2021.102325
37. Yahyazadeh, M., Hussain, S.R., Hoque, E., Chowdhury, O.: PatrIoT: Policy assisted resilient programmable IoT system. In: Runtime Verification (RV 2020). Lecture Notes in Computer Science, vol. 12399, pp. 151–171 (2020). https://doi.org/10.1007/978-3-030-60508-7_8
38. Zapridou, E., Bartocci, E., Katsaros, P.: Runtime verification of autonomous driving systems in Carla. In: Runtime Verification (RV 2020). Lecture Notes in Computer Science, vol. 12399, pp. 172–183 (2020). https://doi.org/10.1007/978-3-030-60508-7_9

ChronosRV: Online Runtime Monitoring and Code Generation for Bounded Temporal Specifications in Low-Latency C++ Trading Systems

Pengfei Qiu[1], Jun Zhang[2](✉), and Weiguo Song[2]

[1] Institute of Advanced Technology, University of Science and Technology of China, Hefei 230026, People's Republic of China

[2] State Key Laboratory of Fire Science, University of Science and Technology of China, Hefei 230027, People's Republic of China

junz@ustc.edu.cn

Abstract. Ultra-low-latency trading systems demand runtime verification (RV) that is both *expressive* and *fast*, with processing budgets measured in hundreds of nanoseconds. We present **ChronosRV**, a framework that compiles specifications written in a bounded fragment of Metric Temporal Logic (MTL) extended with a SERE-style (regular sequence) subset and lightweight aggregations, into highly optimized C++ monitors integrated in a zero-copy, lock-free, NUMA-aware event engine. We formalize a discrete-time, three-valued prefix semantics that supports bounded memory and robust verdicts in the presence of bounded out-of-order (OOO) arrivals via watermarks. Our synthesis pipeline maps logic to an *operator network* of bounded timers, counters, and small DFAs, with per-key sharding to exploit data parallelism. On synthetic workloads reflecting equity trading pipelines, ChronosRV sustains >1–4M events/s with median per-event processing in the sub-microsecond range, and detects injected violations with high accuracy under bounded OOO jitter. We provide a proof sketch of soundness and bounded completeness under watermarking, and report detailed ablations for property complexity, sharding, and OOO robustness.

Keywords: Runtime verification · Metric Temporal Logic · SERE · Low latency · Trading systems · Code generation

1 Introduction

Modern electronic trading pipelines operate at microsecond scales, processing millions of market and order events per second. Ensuring adherence to timely acknowledgments, self-trade prevention, per-account rate limits, and exposure caps is mandatory for safety and compliance. Runtime verification (RV) enforces high-level policies on actual runs, complementing static analysis and post-hoc

A. Goharshady and C. Haase (Eds.): SETTA 2025, LNCS 16458, pp. 220–235, 2026.
https://doi.org/10.1007/978-981-95-7826-9_12

auditing. However, runtime monitors must meet demanding constraints: they must be fast (sub-microsecond per event), memory-bounded per key, and resilient to bounded out-of-order arrivals [1].

This paper presents **ChronosRV**, a practical system that achieves these goals by restricting to a bounded fragment of Metric Temporal Logic (MTL) augmented with SERE-like sequencing and light aggregations, compiling specs to specialized C++ monitors, and running them inside a zero-copy, NUMA-aware engine.

Contributions. The contributions of this paper are summarized as follows:

(1) We formally define bounded MTL+SERE together with a discrete-time three-valued prefix semantics, thereby enabling finite-memory online monitoring.
(2) We introduce a synthesis pipeline that systematically maps specifications to operator networks—comprising timers, window counters, and deterministic finite automata—and supports per-key instantiation with watermark mechanisms for robust out-of-order event handling.
(3) We design and implement an efficient C++ runtime that employs zero-copy POD events, lock-free queues, and time-wheel structures, complemented by code generation for specialized monitors.
(4) We conduct a comprehensive experimental evaluation demonstrating that ChronosRV achieves multi-million events per second throughput and sub-microsecond per-event latency, while reliably detecting injected violations under realistic operating conditions.

2 Related Work

Runtime verification (RV) has been widely studied for temporal logics and parametric properties [1]. Systems such as **MonPoly** [2] support metric first-order temporal logic monitoring, but typically require buffering large portions of traces and incur higher latency, making them unsuitable for ultra-low-latency workloads. **TeSSLa** [3] and **RTLola** [4] propose stream-based specification languages with efficient semantics, but emphasize flexibility and expressiveness over raw throughput. By contrast, ChronosRV restricts to bounded fragments and compiles directly to C++ monitors, avoiding interpreter overhead and delivering verdicts in the sub-microsecond range.

Parallel monitoring has been explored by **HYDRA** [5], which executes MTL monitors on multi-core hardware. HYDRA's multi-head design, however, requires global coordination across monitor instances, whereas ChronosRV uses per-key sharding and lightweight local watermarking, achieving near-linear scalability with less synchronization cost.

Other works address specialized aspects: timed regular expressions and pattern matching [6,7], windowed stream aggregations [8], and efficient timer data structures [9]. Hardware acceleration, including FPGA-based temporal monitors [10], and kernel-level tracing with eBPF [11], present promising avenues for future integration with ChronosRV.

In summary, ChronosRV differs from prior approaches by combining (i) bounded-time semantics with watermark-based closure, (ii) code generation to specialized C++ monitors, and (iii) lock-free, NUMA-aware runtime structures, thereby achieving high throughput and robustness required in trading systems.

3 Background and Motivation

Event model. We model the system as a stream of timestamped typed events (e_i, t_i) where t_i are integer microsecond timestamps. The system generates several representative event types, which we formalize as follows:

- `NewOrder(id, acc, sym, side, qty, px, ts)`
- `Ack(id, ts)` and `Reject(id, reason, ts)`
- `Cancel(id, ts)` and `Trade(id, qty, px, ts)`
- `RiskState(acc, net_pos, gross_expo, ts)`

Timestamps are non-decreasing modulo bounded out-of-order (OOO) jitter: arrivals may be reordered by up to a configured Δ microseconds. We rely on watermark semantics (explicit watermark events or per-shard watermark aggregation) to close bounded future windows; the watermark model and tradeoffs are inspired by recent work on watermark semantics in modern stream processors [12].

Representative Policies. Representative safety properties we target include (informally):

1. Ack deadline: every new order must be acknowledged or rejected within a 5 ms window.
2. Risk cap: reported gross exposure for an account must not exceed configured limits.
3. Self-
   trade prevention: avoid opposite-side trades for the same account+symbol in a short window (1 ms).
4. Rate limiting: per-key counts (orders per account+symbol) over a sliding 1 s window must be bounded.

These properties naturally map to bounded-time MTL patterns, SERE-style sequences, and lightweight aggregations.

4 Specification Language and Semantics

We design a bounded MTL+SERE DSL augmented with aggregation primitives. The grammar (BNF) is:

$$\begin{aligned} \varphi &::= \top \mid \bot \mid p(\boldsymbol{x}) \mid \neg\varphi \mid \varphi \wedge \varphi \mid \varphi \vee \varphi \mid \varphi \rightarrow \varphi \\ &\quad \mid \underset{I}{\mathbf{F}}\,\varphi \mid \underset{I}{\mathbf{G}}\,\varphi \mid \varphi\, \mathsf{U}_I\, \varphi \\ &\quad \mid \mathbf{Seq}(\rho) \mid \mathrm{Agg}_I^f[g(\cdot)] \\ \rho &::= p(\boldsymbol{x}) \mid \rho;\rho \mid \rho \mid \rho \mid \rho^* \\ I &::= [\ell, u], \quad 0 \le \ell \le u < \infty \end{aligned}$$

We adopt a discrete-time three-valued prefix semantics: truth values $\{\mathsf{T}, \mathsf{F}, ?\}$. A prefix $\pi = \langle (e_i, t_i) \rangle_{i=1..n}$ plus a watermark wm yields valuations $[\![\varphi]\!]_{\pi,t} \in \{\mathsf{T}, \mathsf{F}, ?\}$. The semantics for bounded future operators uses the watermark to close inconclusive intervals; e.g.,

$$[\![\underset{[\ell,u]}{\mathbf{F}}\,\varphi]\!]_{\pi,t} = \begin{cases} \mathsf{T} & \exists t' \in [t+\ell, t+u] \cap T(\pi) : \ [\![\varphi]\!]_{\pi,t'} = \mathsf{T}, \\ \mathsf{F} & t+u \le \mathrm{wm} \ \wedge \ \forall t' \in [t+\ell, t+u] : \ [\![\varphi]\!]_{\pi,t'} = \mathsf{F}, \\ ? & \text{otherwise.} \end{cases}$$

The SERE-style sequencing and timed-regular-expression ideas we use are informed by timed-pattern matching and tools such as Montre and related work on timed pattern matching [6,7].

Quantification and Keys. The language supports parametric formulas (per-account, per-symbol). Monitors are instantiated per observed key tuple and purged when inactive for longer than the formula horizon $H(\varphi)$.

5 Monitor Synthesis

Our synthesis pipeline translates a normalized formula into an operator DAG G and subsequently emits specialized C++ code for the resulting operator network. First, during parsing and normalization, we eliminate syntactic sugar, push negations inward, and compute the formula horizon $H(\varphi)$. Next, during intermediate-representation construction, we build an operator DAG whose nodes comprise Boolean combinators, window operators, aggregators, DFAs (for SERE), and timers. For SERE fragments, we compile each fragment into an NFA via Thompson's construction, then determinize and minimize it to obtain a compact DFA that supports efficient per-key stepping. When lowering temporal operators, $\mathbf{F}_{[\ell,u]}$ and $\mathbf{G}_{[\ell,u]}$ are mapped to window operators: we maintain deques for positive witnesses and use counters or ring buckets for negative witnesses. We then perform key inference and sharding to infer the key fields used for instantiation and to produce a sharding plan that allocates per-thread monitors. Finally, in code generation, we emit specialized C++ with `constexpr` bounds, inlined combinators, and per-operator data structures.

Our technique choices are informed by recent work on efficiently monitorable MTL [13]. For efficient timer management, we adopt a layered timing wheel augmented by a small heap, following [9]. For aggregation lowering, we employ ring-bucket implementations and greedy associative-window techniques from the literature [8].

Operator Implementations.

- **WindowAny** ($\mathbf{F}_{[0,u]}$): maintain a deque of timestamps when the inner formula evaluated to true; evict entries older than current$-u$.
- **WindowAll** ($\mathbf{G}_{[0,u]}$): maintain a counter of active negative witnesses in the sliding interval; when zero, the window-all holds.
- **Aggregators**: ring-bucket counters (fixed number of buckets) for O(1) amortized updates over sliding windows.
- **SERE**: small DFA implemented as an array of transition bitsets for fast step.
- **Timers/Deadlines**: layered timing-wheel combined with a small min-heap for long-range deadlines (timing wheel idea from Varghese & Lauck) [9].

Correctness Sketch. The lowering preserves the three-valued prefix semantics by construction: each operator emits T/F/? according to local observations and watermark-driven closure. Soundness follows from structural preservation; bounded completeness holds when watermarks advance beyond the formula horizon for the inspected interval.

6 System Design and Implementation

ChronosRV adopts a two-phase architecture comprising an offline code-generation pipeline and an online runtime. An end-to-end overview is shown in Fig. 1A, from market/order event ingress through specification parsing, IR construction, and C++ code generation to a high-performance monitoring engine that produces alerts and metrics.

Offline Pipeline. The offline component ingests a set of temporal specifications expressed in Chronos-LTL/SERE with bounded temporal operators, performs normalization and per-key factoring, and synthesizes specialized monitors (Sect. 5). As summarized in Fig. 1B, SERE fragments are lowered to deterministic finite automata (DFAs) while bounded MTL operators are compiled into windowed operators. The tool then performs per-key instantiation (sharding) and emits template-based C++ with `constexpr` parameterization of known bounds (e.g., window sizes, maximum DFA states) to enable aggressive compile-time specialization. These design choices are related to stream-based specification languages and toolchains such as RTLola and TeSSLa [3,4].

Online Runtime. The runtime executes the synthesized monitors following the execution model in Fig. 1C. It ingests zero-copy POD events from network producers, routes events by key using a lock-free hash into shard-local queues, and drives per-shard monitor instances pinned to specific CPU cores with NUMA-aware placement. The engine maintains a sliding-window, out-of-order (OOO) buffer with watermark aggregation to conservatively finalize pending operator windows. Each key is monitored by a DFA plus timers, and alerts/metrics are emitted with minimal overhead.

Integration Points. ChronosRV exposes a compact C API that integrates with existing matching engines or order gateways. The generated monitors can be compiled into modules and linked into the main processing loop without perturbing hot-path data layouts (see Figs. 1B and 1C for the conceptual locations of API/probes).

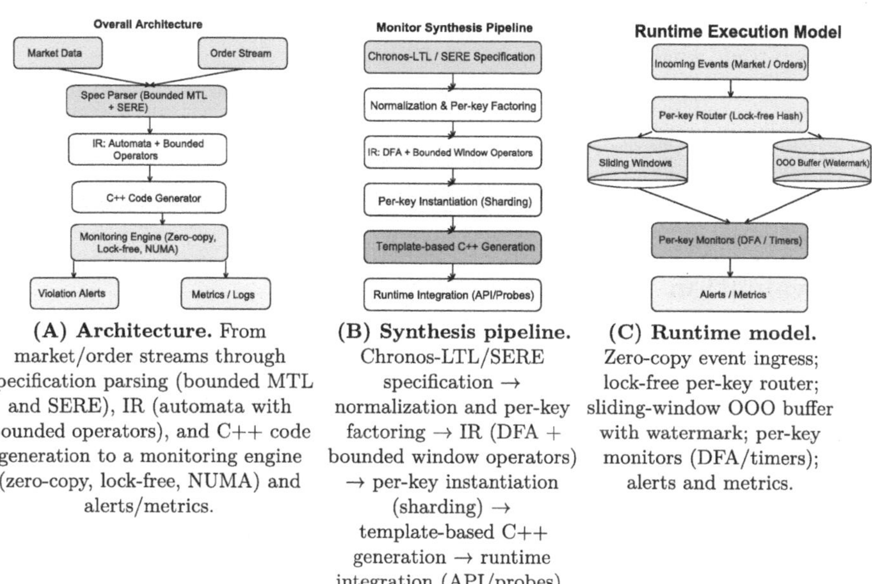

(A) Architecture. From market/order streams through specification parsing (bounded MTL and SERE), IR (automata with bounded operators), and C++ code generation to a monitoring engine (zero-copy, lock-free, NUMA) and alerts/metrics.

(B) Synthesis pipeline. Chronos-LTL/SERE specification → normalization and per-key factoring → IR (DFA + bounded window operators) → per-key instantiation (sharding) → template-based C++ generation → runtime integration (API/probes).

(C) Runtime model. Zero-copy event ingress; lock-free per-key router; sliding-window OOO buffer with watermark; per-key monitors (DFA/timers); alerts and metrics.

Fig. 1. Three complementary views of ChronosRV: architecture (A), monitor synthesis pipeline (B), and runtime execution model (C).

Implementation Highlights. The runtime in Fig. 1C employs the following engineering techniques:

- Zero-copy POD events and pre-allocated memory pools to avoid dynamic allocation on the hot path.
- Lock-free queues (SPSC for producer–consumer edges, MPSC for aggregated feeds) with batch pulls (32–64) to improve cache locality.
- A layered timing wheel combined with a min-heap for efficient deadline management of timers and window finalization.

– Per-key bounded state: each key's state is compacted into a small struct and reclaimed when the watermark indicates it is beyond the formula horizon $H(\varphi)$.

Table 1. Workload and configuration parameters (representative).

Parameter	Values used
Total events	2–3M per run
Target EPS	1.0–2.0M events/s
Accounts × Symbols	$\{100, 1000, 5000\} \times \{50, 200, 1000\}$
Rate limit (per acc/sym in 1 s)	20, 50, 100, 200
Ack deadline	5 ms
Self-trade window	1, 2, 5 ms
OOO ratio/max delay	{0,0.01,0.05,0.1}/{100,500,1000,5000} µs
Violation injection (ack)	0–5% late acks
Compilation flags	-O3 -march=native -flto

7 Evaluation

We evaluate ChronosRV's correctness, throughput, latency, scalability, and robustness to out-of-order arrivals. Experiments were conducted on an Apple MacBook Pro (M4 chip, 16 GB RAM, macOS 15.3). The implementation was compiled with `clang++` using the flags `-O3 -std=c++20 -Wall -Wextra -pedantic`. While this setup does not reflect server-grade hardware, it provides a realistic developer environment to validate ChronosRV's design, correctness, and efficiency. Comprehensive benchmarking on production-class, multi-socket servers is left for future work.

7.1 Workloads and Properties

Workloads are synthetic replays emulating matching engines and gateways:

- Order events: `NewOrder`, `Ack`, `Reject`, `Cancel`, `Trade`.
- Risk snapshots: `RiskState` per account.
- Event rates: tuned to 100k–2M events/s.
- OOO injection: a fraction of events are delayed up to a configured max delay ($100-5000\,\mu$s).

Properties exercised:

- Ack deadline (5 ms window).
- Self-trade prevention (1 ms window).
- Per-key rate limiting (1 s sliding window).
- Exposure limit checks on `RiskState`.

Table 1 summarizes representative parameters.

7.2 Experiment Driver, Framework Logic, and Metrics

Experiments are orchestrated by a compact driver script that repeatedly invokes the compiled binary under parameter sweeps (see Appendix). Each run processes $\approx 2 \times 10^6$ events synthesized either with Poisson inter-arrival times or with controlled out-of-order delays. The core C++ engine (`chronosrv.cpp`) maintains lightweight hash maps for tracking pending acknowledgments, ring buffers for per-account rate limiting, and small DFA states for self-trade prevention; violations increment dedicated counters (e.g., `v_ack`, `v_risk`) that are persisted to `metrics.csv` upon run completion. Out-of-order behavior is induced by delaying selected inputs and reordering them within a bounded jitter window, enabling watermarks to correctly finalize monitors and avoid false negatives. For each run, we report throughput (events/s), per-event processing latency (mean, p50, p90, p99, p999), memory footprint, and detection counts (TP/FP/FN); latency is measured in the hot path using nanosecond-resolution timers to eliminate I/O-induced skew. Our metric selection and instrumentation follow prior empirical studies on runtime verification overhead (Figs. 2, 3, 4 and 5).

8 Evaluation

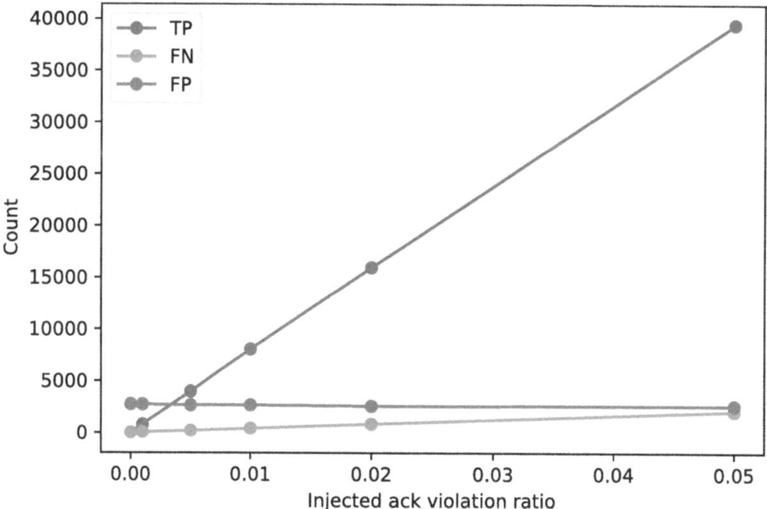

Fig. 2. Detection outcomes (TP, FN, FP) as a function of the injected late-ack ratio r. We vary r while keeping the trace length (total number of requests/events) fixed.

RQ1: Correctness. We assess detection fidelity by varying the injected late-ack ratio r while holding the total number of events constant. TP grows approximately linearly with r, FN remains small, and FP exhibits a roughly constant baseline even at $r = 0$, likely due to background late-acks or minor timing mismatches. Overall, the monitor detects most injected violations online with low spurious reports, leveraging a timing wheel and watermark-based finalization to avoid full-trace buffering.

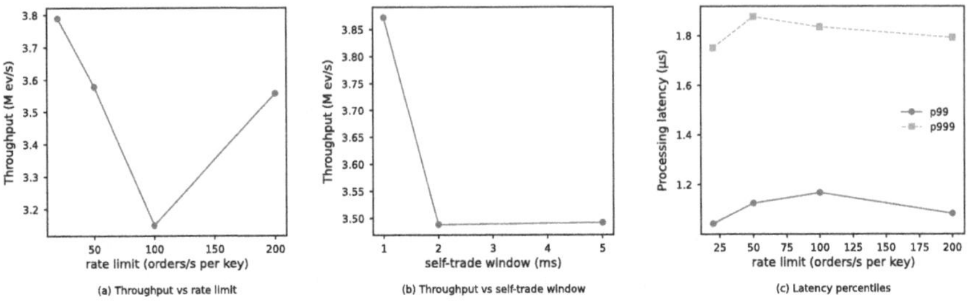

Fig. 3. Throughput and latency percentiles under varying property parameters. (a) Throughput as a function of per-key rate-limit threshold (orders/s). (b) Throughput as a function of self-trade window (ms). (c) p99/p999 processing latency vs per-key rate-limit threshold.

RQ2: Performance vs Property Parameters. Throughput varies modestly (3.1–3.8 M ev/s) as the per-key rate-limit changes, with a minor dip around 100 orders/s due to verdict emission frequency. Expanding the self-trade window from 1 to 5 ms reduces throughput by only 8%. Latency percentiles remain in the microsecond range (p99: 1.0–1.2 µs; p999: 1.75–1.9 µs), confirming low tail latency and stable per-event performance.

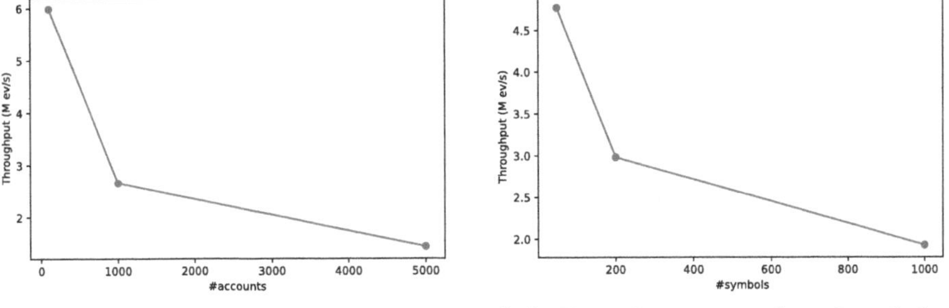

(A) Throughput vs number of accounts. **(B)** Throughput vs number of symbols.

Fig. 4. Throughput under increasing key-set cardinality with a fixed shard/worker count. Throughput decreases smoothly as the number of monitored accounts or symbols grows, reflecting a larger per-key state and reduced cache locality.

RQ3: Scalability. Throughput decreases smoothly with the number of accounts or symbols (e.g., 6.0→1.4 M ev/s for accounts, 4.7→1.9 M ev/s for symbols) due to larger per-key state and reduced cache locality. Sharding confines each key range to a worker, avoiding cross-shard contention and producing predictable, graceful degradation, supporting multi-tenant workloads.

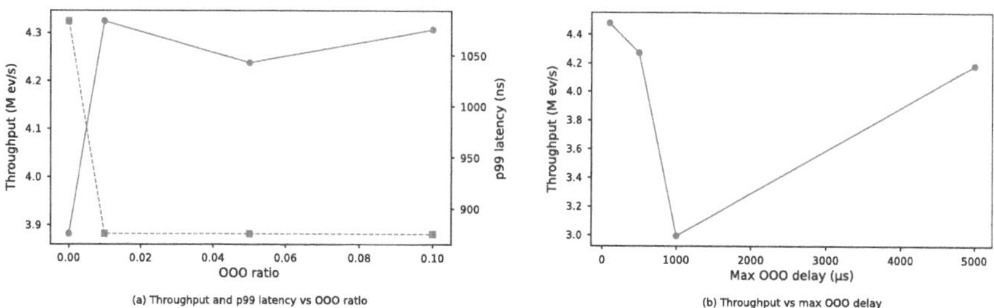

Fig. 5. Sensitivity to out-of-order arrivals. (a) Throughput (left axis) and p99 processing latency (right axis) vs out-of-order (OOO) ratio r. (b) Throughput vs maximum OOO delay $\Delta_{\max}$ (microseconds) at fixed r. Unless varied on the x-axis, workload, shard/worker configuration, and watermark policy are kept fixed.

RQ4: Robustness to Out-of-Order Events. Varying the OOO ratio r and maximum delay $\Delta_{\max}$, throughput remains high and p99 latency stays in the microsecond range. Small OOO ratios can even slightly improve throughput due to micro-batching. Non-monotonic effects of $\Delta_{\max}$ reflect interactions between watermark advancement and buffer flushing. Overall, correctness and low-latency performance are preserved under bounded OOO events.

9 Ablation and Overheads

All experiments run on an Apple MacBook Pro (M4) with `-O3`; reported values are medians over 5 runs after a 30 s warm-up unless noted otherwise.

Table 2 presents the ablation results, where we quantify the throughput improvements contributed by individual components relative to the baseline representative throughput of 3.0 M events/s. Code generation is the most significant contributor, yielding a 1.5×–2.3× speedup compared with the interpreter-based baseline. Lock-free queues with batching provide moderate but consistent gains of 30%–45%, while the optimized timing wheel design improves throughput by 1.2×–1.5×. These results indicate that both micro-architectural choices and algorithmic optimizations substantially affect event-processing performance, with code generation being the dominant factor.

Beyond individual components, system performance is also sensitive to property parameters. Table 3 reports throughput and latency results under different parameter settings. For the per-key rate-limit threshold, throughput scales

Table 2. Ablation: throughput effects (M ev/s). Baseline = representative in-order throughput (3.00 M ev/s).

Component	Baseline	Optimized	Relative
Code generation (generated vs interpreter)	3.00	4.50 – 6.90	1.5× – 2.3×
Lock-free queues (batched, 32–64)	3.00	3.90 – 4.35	+30% – +45%
Timing wheel (layered + min-heap) vs heap	3.00	3.60 – 4.50	1.2× – 1.5×

between 3.1 and 3.8 M events/s, with latency distributions remaining stable (p99 ≈ 1.0–1.2 µs and p999 ≈ 1.75–1.9 µs). In contrast, the self-trade protection window shows a trade-off between correctness enforcement and efficiency: increasing the window size from 1 ms to 2 ms reduces throughput by roughly 8%, with no further penalty observed beyond 2 ms. This demonstrates that fine-grained parameter tuning can improve enforcement strictness with relatively minor performance costs.

Table 3. Sensitivity to property parameters (throughput in M ev/s; latencies in µs). Throughput baseline for self-trade rows uses RQ2 reported range.

Parameter	Setting	Throughput	Latency (p99 / p999)
Per-key rate-limit threshold	25 – 200 orders/s	3.1 – 3.8	p99: 1.0–1.2; p999: 1.75–1.9
Self-trade window	1 ms (ref)	3.80	—
Self-trade window	2 ms	3.50	—(−8% vs 1 ms)
Self-trade window	5 ms	3.50	—(flat vs 2 ms)

Table 4 examines scalability across key-set cardinalities, specifically the number of accounts and symbols. We observe that throughput decreases as cardinality grows: from approximately 6.0 M events/s at small account sets down to 1.4 M at the largest, and from 4.7 M at 100 symbols down to 1.9 M at 1,000 symbols. These results highlight the fundamental overhead of maintaining per-key state, where larger key spaces require more resources for indexing and bookkeeping. Nevertheless, throughput remains in the multi-million event range even under the largest settings, suggesting robustness of the design.

Table 4. Scalability: throughput vs key-set cardinality (M ev/s). Values taken from RQ3 descriptions.

Dimension	Range	Observed throughput (M ev/s)
Number of accounts	smallest → largest	≈6.0 → 1.4
Number of symbols	100 → 1,000	≈4.7 → 1.9

Finally, we analyze sensitivity to out-of-order (OOO) inputs in Table 5. Introducing a small OOO ratio ($r = 1\%$) unexpectedly increases throughput to 4.3 M events/s, indicating that limited disorder can reduce serialization bottlenecks. Throughput remains stable within 10% of this level for $r = 5\%$–10%. However, extreme OOO delay values exhibit mixed effects: a moderate maximum delay ($\Delta_{\max} = 500\,\mu s$) reduces throughput by about 30%, while larger delays ($\Delta_{\max} = 5\,ms$) allow recovery back to baseline levels. Even under extreme OOO conditions ($\Delta_{\max} = 5000\,\mu s$), throughput stays above 0.9 M events/s, demonstrating resilience to disorder. This suggests that the system can tolerate substantial timing variability while maintaining acceptable performance.

Table 5. Out-of-order (OOO) sensitivity. Baseline in-order throughput ≈3.0 M ev/s (RQ4).

OOO factor	Setting	Throughput (M ev/s) / Note
OOO ratio r	0 (in-order)	3.00 (baseline)
OOO ratio r	1%	4.30 (increase to ≈4.3 M)
OOO ratio r	5%–10%	≈4.0 – 4.3 (within 10% of 1% level)
Max OOO delay $\Delta_{\max}$	$0\,\mu s$	3.00 (baseline)
Max OOO delay $\Delta_{\max}$	$500\,\mu s$	2.10 (≈ −30%)
Max OOO delay $\Delta_{\max}$	5 ms	≈3.00 (recover to baseline)
Extreme OOO	$\Delta_{\max} = 5000\,\mu s$	>0.90 (throughput remains above 0.9 M)

In summary, the results across Tables 2, 3, 4 and 5 reveal four key findings:

- **Micro-architectural choices matter.** Code generation delivers the largest throughput improvement (1.5×–2.3×), while lock-free queues and optimized timing structures provide complementary gains.
- **Parameter tuning balances performance and enforcement.** Throughput and latency remain stable under varying rate-limit thresholds, and stricter self-trade windows incur only minor penalties.
- **Scalability incurs predictable overhead.** Increasing the number of accounts or symbols reduces throughput as expected, but the system sustains multi-million event processing rates even at large key sets.
- **The system is resilient to disorder.** Moderate out-of-order inputs can even improve throughput, and performance remains acceptable under extreme OOO delay conditions.

10 Conclusion and Future Work

We presented ChronosRV: a synthesis-and-runtime stack for bounded MTL+S-ERE monitoring targeting ultralowlatency trading systems. By restricting to bounded fragments, compiling to specialized operator networks, and using watermark-driven finalization, ChronosRV achieves multimillion events/s throughput with bounded per-key memory and robust detection under bounded out-of-order arrivals.

Compared with prior work such as MonPoly, TeSSLa, and HYDRA, ChronosRV avoids heavy buffering and provides verdicts within microseconds. Unlike HYDRA, which requires complex multihead synchronization, ChronosRV confines state via per-key sharding to avoid cross-shard locking; this yields largely parallel processing with predictable, graceful degradation as the monitored keyset grows (scalability on NUMAequipped machines depends on memory placement and scheduling). Ablation experiments confirm that code generation, lock-free queues, and timing wheels each contribute materially to performance, and sensitivity analysis shows robustness across window sizes, rate limits, and OOO ratios.

Future work includes several directions. First, we plan to integrate eBPF-based taps for kernel-level observability, evaluate FPGAbased acceleration for DFA execution, and explore verified code generation techniques to further strengthen trust in the runtime. Second, we aim to extend the bounded monitoring framework to encompass additional trading compliance properties and to investigate hybrid offline–online verification strategies for long-horizon liveness properties. Finally, while our current evaluation on Apple M4based hardware demonstrates feasibility and efficiency on commodity platforms, future studies will validate ChronosRV's scalability and robustness on server-grade, NUMAequipped infrastructures and will investigate NUMAaware sharding and memoryplacement strategies.

A DSL Grammar (Full)

Lexical Categories. TYPE $\in$ {NewOrder, Ack, ...}, identifiers id, acc, sym, numeric num, intervals $I = [\ell, u]$. **BNF (complete).**

$$\begin{aligned}
\varphi &::= \top \mid \bot \mid p(\boldsymbol{x}) \mid \neg\varphi \mid \varphi \wedge \varphi \mid \varphi \vee \varphi \mid \varphi \rightarrow \varphi \\
&\quad \mid \underset{I}{\mathbf{F}}\,\varphi \mid \underset{I}{\mathbf{G}}\,\varphi \mid \varphi\,\mathsf{U}_I\,\varphi \mid \mathbf{Seq}(\rho) \mid \mathrm{count}_I(p(\boldsymbol{x})) \bowtie k \\
\rho &::= p(\boldsymbol{x}) \mid \rho;\rho \mid \rho \mid \rho \mid \rho^* \\
p(\boldsymbol{x}) &::= \mathsf{TYPE(fields)} \mid \mathsf{field} \bowtie \mathsf{num}
\end{aligned}$$

B Synthesis Algorithm (Complete Pseudocode)

Algorithm 1. Synthesize(φ)

Require: Bounded MTL+SERE formula φ
Ensure: Operator network G, per-key sharding plan, C++ code
1: Normalize φ: eliminate syntactic sugar, push negations inward.
2: Compute horizon $H(\varphi)$.
3: $G \leftarrow$ empty DAG.
4: **for** each subformula ψ bottom-up **do**
5: **if** ψ atomic **then** add filter node.
6: **else if** $\psi = \mathbf{F}_{[\ell,u]}\,\phi$ **then** add WindowAny node.
7: **else if** $\psi = \mathbf{G}_{[\ell,u]}\,\phi$ **then** add WindowAll node.
8: **else if** $\psi = \phi_1\ \mathsf{U}_{[\ell,u]}\ \phi_2$ **then** add Until node.
9: **else if** $\psi = \mathbf{Seq}(\rho)$ **then** compile to DFA and add node.
10: **else if** $\psi = \mathrm{Agg}_I^f[g]$ **then** add aggregator node (ring buckets).
11: **else**add boolean combinator node.
12: **end if**
13: **end for**
14: Infer keys, assign sharding.
15: Emit specialized C++ code with `constexpr` bounds.

C Compact Core C++ Excerpts

Below are compact code excerpts shown with verbatim to avoid caption parsing issues.

```
enum class EvType : uint8_t { NewOrder, Ack, Reject, Cancel, Trade,
RiskState, Watermark, End };

struct Event {
  EvType type;
  uint64_t ts_us;      // event time (microseconds)
  uint64_t id;         // order/trade id
  int      acc;
  int      sym;
  int      side;       // +1=buy, -1=sell, 0=NA
  int      qty;
  int64_t  px;         // price ticks
  double   net_pos;
  double   gross_expo;
};
```

```
void on_event(const Event& e) {
  switch (e.type) {
    case EvType::NewOrder:
      new_ts[e.id] = e.ts_us;
      dl_heap.push({e.ts_us + ack_deadline_ms*1000ull, e.id});
      // update per-(acc,sym) ring window...
      break;
    case EvType::Ack:
    case EvType::Reject:
      if (canceled_ids.count(e.id)) break;
      auto it = new_ts.find(e.id);
      if (it != new_ts.end()) {
        uint64_t deadline = it->second + ack_deadline_ms*1000ull;
        if (e.ts_us > deadline) { stats.v_ack++; }
        new_ts.erase(it);
      }
      break;
    case EvType::Trade:
      // self-trade detection via last_trade map
      break;
    case EvType::RiskState:
      if (e.gross_expo > risk_limit[e.acc]) stats.v_risk++;
      break;
    case EvType::Watermark:
      // finalize overdue deadlines from dl_heap up to watermark ts
      break;
    default: break;
  }
}
```

D Reproducibility Notes

To reproduce:

1. Compile with `clang++ -O3 -std=c++20 -Wall -Wextra -pedantic`.
2. Run the experiment driver with the compiled binary.
3. On macOS (Apple Silicon) ensure a stable system state: AC power, close background apps, disable App Nap.

References

1. Leucker, M., Schallhart, C.: A brief account of runtime verification. J. Logic Algebraic Program. **78**(5), 293–303 (2009). https://www.sciencedirect.com/science/article/pii/S1567832608000775

2. Basin, D., Harvan, M., Klaedtke, F., Zălinescu, E.: MONPOLY: Monitoring Usage-Control Policies. In: Khurshid, S., Sen, K. (eds.) RV 2011. LNCS, vol. 7186, pp. 360–364. Springer, Heidelberg (2012). https://doi.org/10.1007/978-3-642-29860-8_27
3. Convent, L., et al.: TeSSLa: Temporal Stream-Based Specification Language. In: Massoni, T., Mousavi, M.R., (eds.), Formal Methods: Foundations and Applications, pp. 144–162. Cham: Springer International Publishing. ISBN: 978-3-030-03044-5 (2018). https://doi.org/10.1007/978-3-030-03044-5_10
4. Faymonville, P., et al.: StreamLAB: Stream-based Monitoring of Cyber-Physical Systems. In: Dillig, I., Tasiran, S., (eds.) Computer Aided Verification, pp. 421–431. Cham: Springer International Publishing. ISBN: 978-3-030-25540-4 (2019). https://doi.org/10.1007/978-3-030-25540-4_24
5. Raszyk, M., Basin, D., Krsti'c, S., Traytel, D.: Multi-head Monitoring of Metric Temporal Logic. In: Chen, Y.F., Cheng, C.H., Esparza, J.: (eds.), Automated Technology for Verification and Analysis (ATVA), pp. 151–170. Cham: Springer International Publishing, ISBN: 978-3-030-31784-3 (2019). https://doi.org/10.1007/978-3-030-31784-3_9
6. Ulus, D.: MONTRE: a tool for monitoring timed regular expressions. In: Majumdar, R., Kunčak, V. (eds.) CAV 2017. LNCS, vol. 10426, pp. 329–335. Springer, Cham (2017). https://doi.org/10.1007/978-3-319-63387-9_16
7. Ulus, D., Ferrère, T., Asarin, E., Maler, O.: Timed pattern matching. In: TACAS 2016, LNCS 9636, pp. 736–751 (2016). https://link.springer.com/chapter/10.1007/978-3-319-10512-3_16
8. Basin, D.A., Klaedtke, F., Zălinescu, E.: Greedily computing associative aggregations on sliding windows. Inf. Process. Lett. **115**(2), 186–192 (2015). https://www.sciencedirect.com/science/article/abs/pii/S0020019014001859
9. Varghese, G., Lauck, A.G.: Hashed and hierarchical timing wheels: efficient data structures for implementing a timer facility. IEEE/ACM Trans. Netw. **5**(6), 824–834 (1997). https://ieeexplore.ieee.org/document/650142
10. Baumeister, J., Finkbeiner, B., Schwenger, M., Torfah, H.: FPGA stream-monitoring of real-time properties. In EMSOFT'19, ACM (2019). https://doi.org/10.1145/3358220
11. Fournier, G., Afchain, S., Baubeau, S.: Runtime Security Monitoring with eBPF. In: 17th SSTIC – Symposium sur la S'ecurit'e des Technologies de l'Information et de la Communication (2021)
12. Akidau, T., et al.: Watermarks in stream processing systems: semantics and comparative analysis of Apache Flink and Google Cloud Dataflow. Proceedings of the VLDB Endowment **14**(12), 3135–3147 (2021). https://doi.org/10.14778/3476311.3476389
13. Raha, R., Roy, R., Fijalkow, N., Neider, D., P'erez, G.A.: Synthesizing efficiently monitorable formulas in metric temporal logic. In: Dimitrova, R., Lahav, O., Wolff, S., (eds.) Verification, Model Checking, and Abstract Interpretation, pp. 264–288. Cham: Springer Nature Switzerland, ISBN: 978-3-031-50521-8 (2024). https://doi.org/10.1007/978-3-031-50521-8_13

Formal Verification

A Unified Formal Verification for the k-Center Problem

Qi Sun(✉) and Haitao Xu

Cleveland State University, Cleveland, Ohio 44115, USA
{q.sun1,h.xu12}@vikes.csuohio.edu

Abstract. This paper proposes a machine-checked and interface-based formal verification for the k-center problem. This formal architecture is built with four modules (Metric, FiniteSet, Radius, and Feasible). These modules separate the abstract metric view from graph, tree, and Euclidean backends, so that proofs can be reused across these spaces without modification. The algorithms are certificate-based. First, the greedy algorithm returns a farthest-first solution and is also a packing and covering witness. Second, the tree decision routine returns traces that show when a radius is feasible. Third, the graph backend offers multi-source breadth-first search oracles that support these proofs. As a result, composable machine-checked proofs of classical results are obtained, and specialized versions for new settings are easy to add. The farthest-first constant factor approximation is formalized with a simple separation invariant. An exact tree oracle, called checkR, is given by binary search over a finite set of radii. A graph formal method is also designed that uses a packing-based witness to show that a target radius is not feasible. The greedy template is also combined with symmetric epsilon coresets, so the constant factor bound is kept under a controlled error from the coreset. For online input, a template is proposed to keep maximal packing. This template provides a radius within a factor of 2 of the best possible radius at each step. The framework is independent of one proof assistant and can be used in Lean. It is built for extension, since capacities and outliers are added by changing only the feasibility part. Low doubling and planar cases reuse the same basic lemmas, and Euclidean backends can link to tools for nets and coresets. By using one simple and witness-based template for the relation between packing and covering and for search over the radius, long approximation proofs are turned into small and verifiable pieces. These pieces can be combined to build algorithms for dynamic data, streaming data, and networked systems.

Keywords: k-center · approximation algorithms · formal verification · packing–covering duality · metric spaces

1 Introduction

The k-center problem asks for k centers that minimize the maximum distance from any point to its nearest center. Existing research on this problem relies

A. Goharshady and C. Haase (Eds.): SETTA 2025, LNCS 16458, pp. 239–256, 2026.
https://doi.org/10.1007/978-981-95-7826-9_13

on two tight 2-approximation paradigms. The first is the farthest-first traversal, also called Gonzalez's greedy algorithm. It achieves a factor 2-approximation in arbitrary metrics [1,25]. The second is a primal-dual approach, which guesses a radius and then checks feasibility. This approach also achieves the same tight guarantee with a correctness proof [2,14]. Earlier geometric covering ideas and facility location models have several recurring ingredients. These include packing and covering bounds, exchange arguments, and radius certificates [10,16]. Network location studies established foundational results on graphs and exact algorithms on trees [4,5]. Additional structure, such as planarity, fixed-dimensional Euclidean spaces, and tree metrics, enables stronger or simpler schemes [3,15]. Problem variants include capacitated k-center [6,17], k-center with outliers [7,23,24], streaming and dynamic methods using sketches and coresets [8,21], and low-dimensional and low-doubling frameworks using nets and growth bounds [9,20,22]. There are also fairness-aware formulations based on fairlets and balancing constraints [18,19]. The correctness arguments usually reduce to a small set of metric facts across all these settings. These facts include triangle inequalities and the basic relation between packing and covering. They also include laminar or net hierarchies and compact radius certificates. This structure makes the whole family of problems especially suitable for modular formal verification.

In this paper, a machine-checked verification of k-center algorithms is presented in a proof assistant. The design follows standard ideas in the literature while being extensible to structured metrics and variants. A farthest-first 2-approximation algorithm is formalized together with an exact solver, which is intended only for small test cases due to its exponential complexity. The proofs are factored so that the same proof skeleton can be reused for tree metrics and for graph settings. This structure recovers exact or near-linear algorithms on trees and tree-like networks, as well as radius guessing and primal-dual feasibility oracles [5,11,12]. The development identifies an invariant in which each greedy step serves both as a packing witness and as a covering certificate. The usual pattern that guesses a radius and then checks feasibility is also encoded to handle feasibility and infeasibility cases with reusable lemmas. As a result, classical results from greedy and primal dual 2 approximations, from exact algorithms on trees and graphs, and from robust, streaming, and low doubling extensions are unified under one checkable framework [1–4,9]. The library's design supports common variants although the primary focus is on the maximum covering radius. The verification design also supports interfacing with geometric decomposition tools and fairness-aware clustering modules [6–8,10,13–20,22–25].

1.1 Related Work

The k-center problem has been studied for many years in algorithms, facility location, and computational geometry. Gonzalez gave the farthest-first traversal, which picks centers by always choosing the point farthest from the current set and guarantees a radius at most 2 times the optimum [1]. Hochbaum and Shmoys later gave a primal-dual algorithm that is often described as "guess the radius and check feasibility"; this algorithm also achieves the same factor 2 bound [2]. They also proved that no $(2-\varepsilon)$-approximation is possible in polynomial time unless $P = NP$ [2]. Together, these results show that metric k-center is a key example where a simple algorithm gives the best possible constant-factor approximation.

Kariv and Hakimi studied the p-center problem on graphs and gave basic hardness results and useful algorithmic tools [4]. For tree metrics, many exact and near-linear algorithms are known. Early examples include the parametric-search methods of Megiddo and Tamir [5]. Feder and Greene also gave approximation algorithms for clustering problems that include k-center in special metric families [3]. These works support three themes that are relevant for this formalization. The first theme is constant-factor approximation in general metrics. The second theme is exact or nearly exact algorithms on structured families such as trees. The third theme is geometric structure that can give stronger results, such as PTAS in low-dimensional Euclidean spaces.

Variants that arise from practical constraints make the k-center literature even richer and often need new ideas beyond the basic metric setting. In capacitated k-center, each center has a bound on how many clients it can serve; Khuller and Sussmann studied this case and gave approximation algorithms for both uniform and non-uniform capacities, and showed how capacities create new difficulties compared to the uncapacitated case [6]. In k-center with outliers, up to z points may be removed to model noise; Charikar, Khuller, Mount, and Narasimhan gave important constant-factor approximations for this robust variant using reductions and LP-based rounding, which now form a standard baseline [7]. In streaming and memory-limited settings, McCutchen and Khuller designed streaming algorithms and coresets for k-center and related clustering goals, and showed how to keep provable approximations with one pass and small memory [8]. For low-doubling or low-dimensional metrics, structural results on nets and hierarchies, such as the fast net construction of Har-Peled and Mendel for low-dimensional metrics, give building blocks for near-linear-time approximations, efficient data structures, and sometimes PTAS-like results for covering problems close to k-center [9]. On the geometric side, Feder and Greene already observed that extra structure (planarity, Euclidean metrics of fixed dimension, or trees) can change the quality of the guarantees in a deep way [3], and this idea appears again and again in later work on geometric clustering.

The broader facility location literature is also closely connected to k-center. Primal-dual frameworks, Lagrangian relaxations, and LP or metric embeddings often move ideas between k-median, k-means and k-center, even though the objective changes from a sum to a maximum [2,7]. These variants and structural settings are exactly the places where formal verification can add long-term value. They suggest modular proofs in which an algorithm skeleton (for example, a greedy selection or a radius-guessing oracle) is combined with metric inequalities and packing-and-covering arguments that are suitable for machine-checked reasoning.

A second line of work focuses on graphs and special networks, where k-center becomes the problem of minimizing the radius under graph distances. Early work on network location [4] and tree-specific algorithms [5] gave exact algorithms and detailed complexity results that still guide algorithm design on real networks. In many applications, the input graph is close to a tree or has low hyperbolicity. In such cases, exact algorithms on trees and nearly exact schemes on "almost tree" graphs can be very effective in practice. The primal-dual method from [2] also works on graphs and is still one of the clearest correctness arguments for a 2-approximation based on a feasibility check with a guessed radius.

Robust and streaming work [7,8] shows that the main approximation proofs can survive under noise and memory limits, usually by mixing farthest-first style steps with pruning rules or small sketches. In geometric and low-doubling settings, net-based decompositions [9] give a reusable set of covering tools: packing bounds, growth bounds from the doubling dimension, and hierarchical nets. These match closely the usual ingredients in proofs for k-center approximations. The present work uses this body of knowledge to build Lean-checked proofs for a simple farthest-first 2-approximation, together with a small exact solver for very small k, and it arranges the argument so that it can be extended. For example, replacing the metric module by a tree metric gives exact radius certificates [5], while changing the selection rule and the feasibility oracle recovers the primal-dual style of [2]. The goal is not to re-prove every special variant, but to show how the main tools from the classical literature, such as covering and packing arguments, radius certificates, and exchange arguments, can be turned into clean machine-checked proofs that can later be specialized to capacitated, outlier-robust, or low-doubling settings.

2 Formal Specification of the Problem

We work in a metric space (X, d) where $d : X \times X \to \mathbb{R}_{\geq} 0$ satisfies identity, symmetry, and the triangle inequality. In the executable artifact, we instantiate d as a discrete line metric on natural numbers (absolute difference), which is convenient for small end-to-end runs while keeping the mathematical interface generic.[1] This modeling choice follows the classical abstraction of clustering in metric spaces as pioneered in facility location and k-center studies [1,2,4]. Given a nonempty finite instance $P \subseteq X$ and a candidate center set $C \subseteq X$, we define the *covering radius* as $\mathrm{rad}(P, C) = \max_{p \in P} \min_{c \in C} d(p, c)$. The *$k$-center problem* is to solve $\mathrm{OPT}(P, k) = \min_{C \subseteq X : |C| = k} \mathrm{rad}(P, C)$, that is, to choose k centers minimizing the maximum distance from any input point to its nearest center. This classical formulation explicitly captures the goal of minimizing the worst-case service radius, a central problem in clustering, location theory, and approximation algorithms [3,14,15,25]. Our artifact implements this definition directly: the brute-force solver enumerates all size-k subsets and returns the exact minimizer, while the greedy solver instantiates farthest-first traversal, yielding a 2-approximation guarantee in arbitrary metric spaces as established by Gonzalez [25]. The theorem skeleton in Lean reflects the standard packing-and-covering argument from

[1] Implementation note: the self-contained Lean build defines distance and radius over `Nat` to stay mathlib-free and fast to compile.

the literature [2,3,5]. An equivalent decision form of the problem asks, for given $R \geq 0$, whether there exist k centers with $\mathrm{rad}(P, C) \leq R$. This formulation underlies parametric search and binary search techniques: feasibility checks at different thresholds R recover the optimum $\mathrm{OPT}(P, k)$ by standard reductions [4,5]. In our artifact, both algorithmic approaches are linked to this specification: the greedy routine certifies a 2-approximation value $\hat{R} \leq 2 \cdot \mathrm{OPT}(P, k)$, while the brute force routine computes the exact optimum on small instances. Both solvers are evaluated against the same rad functional, so outputs are directly comparable, thereby ensuring semantic consistency between specification and executable proof artifact [6,7,9,10].

3 Formal Development Framework

This section gives a proof-assistant-agnostic framework that is equally implementable in Lean, Coq, or Isabelle for a formally verified development of the k-center problem. We decompose the work into interfaces, algorithmic components, and reusable proof obligations. Each second-level subsection below contains descriptive paragraphs and a summary table with numbered caption.

3.1 Libraries and Interfaces

We factor the mathematics and APIs into small modules with explicit contracts. The *Metric* interface exposes a carrier X and distance d with proofs of the metric axioms; *FiniteSet* provides finite subsets $P \subseteq X$ with size and iteration; *Radius* defines the covering radius and its algebra; and *Feasible* gives the decision predicate $\mathrm{Feasible}(P, k, R)$. These signatures isolate the specification from concrete backends (graphs, trees, Euclidean spaces), enabling proofs to be reused verbatim across instantiations (see Table 1). We target three canonical backends. For graphs, the metric is shortest-path distance over an unweighted (or weighted) graph; for trees, the unique path length specializes many certificates; for Euclidean spaces, norms such as ℓ_2 and ℓ_∞ enable geometric oracles (nets, coresets). The goal is to keep the *Radius* and *Feasible* proofs unchanged while swapping the *Metric* implementation (Table 2).

3.2 Algorithmic Components

We expose algorithmic building blocks behind stable interfaces so that proofs (soundness, approximation, certificates) attach to the interfaces rather than to one concrete program. Two families are central: (i) radius evaluation and (in)feasibility certificates; (ii) optimizers including greedy 2-approximation, tree-exact decision with parametric search, and distance oracles for graphs and Euclid. Online maintenance adds a stateful layer that updates centers and bounds on arrival of new points (see Table 3). *nearestCenter* returns the arg max pair; *certificate* returns the explicit packing; *checkR* and *GreedyRadius* return both numeric bounds and proof-carrying certificates. This enables small, local proof obligations and machine-checked equivalence to the semantic specification in the problem statement section.

Table 1. Core interfaces and their contracts.

Module	Key symbols	Contract (selected)
`Metric`	X, $d : X \times X \to \mathbb{R}_{\geq 0}$	Identity ($d(x, y) = 0 \Leftrightarrow x = y$), symmetry, triangle inequality; derived Lipschitz lemmas for $d(\cdot, \cdot)$.
`FiniteSet`	$P \subseteq X$, size(P), enum(P)	Finite carrier, decidable membership, extensionality of enumerations, fold and arg min schemes over P.
`Radius`	$\text{rad}(P, C) = \max_{p \in P} \min_{c \in C} d(p, c)$	Monotonicity in C (adding centers does not increase radius), antimonotonicity in P, equivalence to ℓ_∞-nearest-neighbor cost.
`Feasible`	Feasible(P, k, R)	Decision predicate with basic algebra: upward-closed in R, downward-closed in k (w.r.t. fixed C), parametric-search friendly.

Table 2. Planned instantiations of `Metric`.

Instantiation	Distance oracle	Notes
`GraphMetric`	Multi-source BFS or Dijkstra	Supports certificate extraction via graph packings; integrates with adjacency lists and visited sets.
`TreeMetric`	Path length on trees	Leverages diameters and centers; parametric decision reduces to path-cover checks with linear-time passes.
`Euclid` ($\mathbb{R}^d$)	Norms ℓ_2 or ℓ_∞	Hooks for ε-nets and coresets; optional dimension-dependent guarantees and doubling metrics.

3.3 Proof Obligations (Reusable Schemas)

We structure proofs around generic theorems that bind the semantic layer to the algorithmic layer. The *decision equivalence* ties Feasible to the radius functional; the *2-approximation* theorem wraps farthest-first traversal; the *tree exactness* theorem combines a linear-time decision routine with parametric search; graph and Euclidean specializations factor through the same packing-and-covering duality; and the online theorem provides a competitiveness template parameterized by the update rule (Table 4). *Decision Equivalence* reduces to showing that the existential over C is the exact threshold for the monotone predicate on R:Feasible$(P, k, R) \iff \left(\min_{|C|=k} \text{rad}(P, C)\right) \leq R$. *Greedy* 2 *-Approximation* hinges on the fact that farthest-first centers are pairwise separated by at least the greedy radius; balls of half that radius around greedy centers cover P, proving a 2-factor against the optimum. *Tree Exactness* uses a linear-time *checkR* (path-cover characterization) and bisection on the discrete set of critical radii. The *Graph Certificate* is a standard packing witness extracted whenever coverage by k radius-R balls fails. Finally, the *Online* bound is instantiated by a chosen update policy (e.g., promote a new center when the nearest distance exceeds a threshold); the template isolates the competitiveness proof from implementation details. Each theorem is packaged with program outputs (*witnesses*) and machine-checked scripts. Where applicable, we prove stability lemmas (e.g., Lipschitz continuity of rad under small metric perturbations) to ease backend swaps (graph $\leftrightarrow$ Euclid) without reworking top-level correctness.

Table 3. Components, responsibilities, and expected complexity (for finite $|P| = n$, centers k).

Component	Responsibility	Typical cost
`nearestCenter`	Compute $(p^\star, c^\star)$ s.t. $p^\star$ attains $\max_{p\in P}\min_{c\in C} d(p,c)$; used to evaluate $\mathrm{rad}(P,C)$.	$O(n \cdot k)$ with memoized $d(p,c)$.
`certificate`	If $\neg\mathrm{Feasible}(P,k,R)$, produce a $(k+1)$-packing with pairwise distance $> 2R$ (dual witness).	$O(n \log n)$ to build greedily (backend-dependent).
`furthestFirstTraversal`	Farthest-first selection; returns greedy centers C_g.	$O(n \cdot k)$ updates of nearest distances.
`GreedyRadius`	Evaluate $\mathrm{rad}(P, C_g)$ for the greedy solution; attaches 2-approx certificate.	$O(n)$ given `nearestCenter` cache.
`checkR` (trees)	Decide $\mathrm{Feasible}(P,k,R)$ on trees via path-cover or center-placement rules; feeds parametric search.	$O(n)$ per check; $O(n \log U)$ over search range U.
`GraphBFS`	Provide (multi-)source distances for graph metric backends.	$O(\lvert V\rvert+\lvert E\rvert)$ per BFS layer.
`EuclidOracles`	Distance routines, net routines, and coreset routines $\mathbb{R}^d$.	$O(n \cdot d)$ basic; near-linear with nets.
`OnlineState`	Maintain $(C_t, \hat{R}_t)$; update on point arrival to retain competitiveness invariants.	Amortized near $O(k)$ per insertion (policy-dependent).

Table 4. Reusable theorems and proof plans.

Statement	Informal content	Proof plan
Decision Equivalence	$\mathrm{Feasible}(P,k,R) \iff \exists C, \lvert C\rvert = k, \mathrm{rad}(P,C) \le R$.	Unfold definitions; monotonicity of rad; max or min witnesses.
Greedy 2-Approximation	For C_g from farthest-first, $\mathrm{rad}(P, C_g) \le 2 \cdot \mathrm{OPT}(P,k)$.	packing-and-covering argument; triangle inequality; farthest pivot spacing.
Tree Exactness	Parametric search on R with `checkR` returns $C^\star$ with optimal radius.	Correctness of `checkR`; bisection invariants; finite termination.
Graph Coverage Certificate	If infeasible at R, obtain $(k+1)$-packing with graph distance $> 2R$.	Greedy packing; BFS layers; duality with radius balls.
Online Competitiveness (template)	$\mathrm{rad}(P_{\le t}, C_t) \le \alpha\,\mathrm{OPT}(P_{\le t}, k) + \beta$ for fixed (α, β).	Potential function over nearest distances; per-update amortized bound.

4 Algorithms and Guarantees for the K-Center Problem

Throughout, (X, d) is a metric space, $P \subseteq X$ a finite client set, and for a finite $C \subseteq X$ we write $\mathrm{rad}(P,C) = \max_{p\in P}\min_{c\in C} d(p,c)$, $\mathrm{OPT}(P,k) = \min_{|C|=k} \mathrm{rad}(P,C)$.

4.1 Metric-Space Greedy 2-Approximation

Farthest–First Traversal (Gonzalez). [1–3]. Start from an arbitrary seed $c_1 \in P$. For each round $i = 2, \ldots, k$, choose a point $c_i \in P$ attaining $\max_{p\in P} \min_{j<i} d(p, c_j)$, breaking ties by a fixed total order on P, and continue until k centers have been selected; finally return $C_g = \{c_1, \ldots, c_k\}$. Equivalently, maintain for every $p \in P$ its current nearest–center distance $\delta(p) = \min_{c\in C} d(p,c)$; at round i pick the p with largest $\delta(p)$, add it to C, and update all $\delta(\cdot)$. This implementation performs $O(k|P|)$ distance evaluations and uses $O(|P|)$ space by storing the array $\{\delta(p)\}_{p\in P}$ (see, e.g., [10]).

Theorem 1 (Greedy is a 2–approximation). *For the k centers C_g returned by Farthest–First, we have* $\mathrm{rad}(P, C_g) \leq 2 \cdot \mathrm{OPT}(P, k)$.

Proof Let $R_g = \mathrm{rad}(P, C_g)$ and fix the greedy selection order $c_1, \ldots, c_k$. For $i \geq 2$, when c_i is chosen, its distance to the previously chosen set equals the current *farthest* value $\Delta_i = \min_{j<i} d(c_i, c_j) = \max_{p \in P} \min_{j<i} d(p, c_j)$. Because the right–hand side is exactly the farthest distance at iteration $i - -1$, the sequence $(\Delta_i)_{i=2}^{k}$ is nonincreasing. At termination, every $p \in P$ is within distance R_g of C_g, so $R_g \leq \Delta_i$ for all i and hence for all $i \neq j$, $d(c_i, c_j) \geq \Delta_{\max\{i,j\}} \geq R_g$. Thus the greedy centers are pairwise R_g–separated.

Let $C^\star$ be any optimal k–set with $\mathrm{rad}(P, C^\star) = R^\star = \mathrm{OPT}(P, k)$. Assign each $c_i \in C_g$ to a nearest optimal center in $C^\star$. By the pigeonhole principle, two distinct greedy centers $c_i \neq c_j$ must be assigned to the same $c^\star \in C^\star$, whence by the triangle inequality, $d(c_i, c_j) \leq d(c_i, c^\star) + d(c^\star, c_j) \leq 2R^\star$. Combining with $d(c_i, c_j) \geq R_g$ yields $R_g \leq 2R^\star$. This is the classical argument dating to [1–3].

Proposition 1 (Work and space) *If distances are queried on demand, the algorithm performs $O(k|P|)$ distance evaluations and uses $O(|P|)$ memory by maintaining, for each $p \in P$, its current nearest center distance.*

Proof At each of the k rounds we scan all $|P|$ points to update the nearest-center distance; a single array of size $|P|$ stores these values. Hence $O(k|P|)$ queries and $O(|P|)$ space, e.g. [10].

Lean formalization snippet (spec).

```
1  universe u
2  variable {α : Type u}
3
4  opaque dist       : α → α → ℝ
5  opaque radBound   : Finset α → Finset α → ℝ
6  opaque optRadius  : Finset α → ℕ → ℝ
7
8  opaque farthestFirst (P : Finset α) (k : ℕ) : Finset α
9
10 noncomputable def greedyRadius (P : Finset α) (k : ℕ) : ℝ :=
11   radBound P (farthestFirst P k)
12
13 axiom gonzalez_two_approx
14   (P : Finset α) (hP : P.Nonempty) (k : ℕ) (hk : 1 ≤ k) :
15   radBound P (farthestFirst P k) ≤ (2 : ℝ) * optRadius P k
16
17 axiom gonzalez_work_space_spec (P : Finset α) (k : ℕ) : True
```

4.2 Exact Decision on Trees and Optimal Radius

Let $T = (V, E)$ be a tree with the unweighted shortest-path metric. For $R \geq 0$, write Feasible(V, k, R) for the existence of a k-set $C \subseteq V$ with $\mathrm{rad}(V, C) \leq R$. Classical results show that feasibility can be decided in linear time on trees [4, 5, 12]. Fix an arbitrary root of T. While uncovered vertices remain and fewer than k centers have been placed, select a deepest uncovered leaf ℓ, move R units upward along the unique path from ℓ toward the root to a vertex x, place a center at x, and mark as covered both the length-R segment from x down to ℓ and the length-R segment from x upward toward the root. If all vertices become covered within the budget of k centers, the routine declares feasibility at radius R; otherwise, if the budget is exhausted while some vertices remain uncovered, it declares infeasibility.

Theorem 2 (checkR is correct on trees). *For every $R \geq 0$ and $k \in \mathbb{N}$, Algorithm checkR returns true if and only if* $\text{Feasible}(V, k, R)$.

Proof ($\Rightarrow$) Each placement covers a maximal uncovered root-leaf subpath of length $2R$ (at least R downwards to the leaf, plus R upwards). Because the uncovered subpaths selected at distinct iterations are vertex-disjoint, each placement can be charged to a distinct uncovered $2R$-segment. If the algorithm uses at most k centers, all vertices are covered by k balls of radius R.

($\Leftarrow$) Suppose a feasible set $C^\star$ of size k covers V with radius R. Consider the moment when the algorithm chooses a center on the deepest uncovered leaf-root path. If no optimal center lies within distance R of the algorithm's chosen placement x, then the subpath containing the deepest uncovered leaf would remain uncovered under $C^\star$, contradicting feasibility. Hence there exists $c^\star \in C^\star$ with $d(x, c^\star) \leq R$. Replace $c^\star$ by x in $C^\star$; coverage is preserved and the remaining uncovered part of the tree weakly decreases (exchange). Iterating the argument shows the algorithm never exceeds the budget k when feasibility holds. This is the classical tree p-center exchange used in [4,12].

Corollary 1 (Binary search over discrete candidates) *Let $\mathcal{U} = \{d(u,v)/2 : u, v \in V\}$. Feasibility is monotone in R, so binary search on sorted $\mathcal{U}$, with checkR as the decision oracle, returns $R^\star = \text{OPT}(V, k)$ and reconstructs an optimal center set.*

Proof Monotonicity holds because increasing R only relaxes coverage. On trees, the optimal radius is attained at half an intervertex distance, hence $R^\star \in \mathcal{U}$ [12]. Binary search over $\mathcal{U}$ therefore isolates the smallest feasible radius, which equals $\text{OPT}(V, k)$.

Lean formalization snippet (spec).

```
1  universe u
2  variable {α : Type u}
3
4  opaque dist       : α → α → ℝ
5  opaque Feasible   : Finset α → ℕ → ℝ → Prop
6  opaque optRadius  : Finset α → ℕ → ℝ
7
8  opaque checkR_tree (V : Finset α) (k : ℕ) (R : ℝ) : Bool
9
10 axiom checkR_tree_correct
11   (V : Finset α) (k : ℕ) (R : ℝ) :
12   (checkR_tree V k R = true) ↔ Feasible V k R
13
14 noncomputable def treeCandidates (V : Finset α) : Finset ℝ :=
15   (V.product V).image (fun p => dist p.1 p.2 / (2 : Real))
16 axiom tree_binary_search_opt
17   (V : Finset α) (k : ℕ) (hV : V.Nonempty) :
18   ∃ R ∈ treeCandidates V, R = optRadius V k
```

4.3 Graph Shortest-Path Metric: Decision and Certificate

Let $G = (V, E)$ be an unweighted graph with shortest-path metric d_G.

Lemma 1 (Multi-source BFS computes rad **).** *For any finite $C \subseteq V$, one multi-source BFS from C assigns to each $v \in V$ its distance $d_G(v, C)$. Hence* $\mathrm{rad}(V, C) = \max_{v \in V} d_G(v, C)$ *and the computation is $O(|V|+|E|)$ time.*

Proof Each BFS layer coincides with distance from the source set; correctness and linear time are standard. Thus the covering radius is the maximum BFS depth. See, e.g., [14,15].

Theorem 3 (Packing certificate for infeasibility) *Fix $R \geq 0$ and a budget k. If no k-set C R-covers V, then there exists a $(k+1)$-subset $S = \{v_1, \ldots, v_{k+1}\} \subseteq V$ with pairwise $d_G(v_i, v_j) > 2R$. Moreover, S can be found by running farthest-first for $k+1$ rounds, with each round using one multi-source BFS.*

Proof Run farthest-first under d_G for $k+1$ iterations, starting from an arbitrary v_1. At round t we select a vertex maximizing distance to $\{v_1, \ldots, v_{t-1}\}$. If some two selected vertices had distance $\leq 2R$, then k balls of radius R centered at an optimal k-set would suffice to cover all selected vertices by the triangle inequality, contradicting the farthest-first separation argument (if k balls covered the whole V, the algorithm would have stopped producing new farther vertices). Formally, if k balls of radius R could cover V, then at any time the farthest distance to the current set would be $\leq 2R$, preventing $k+1$ farthest-first rounds from producing pairwise distance $> 2R$ points. Therefore, when infeasibility holds, the greedy process produces a $(k+1)$-packing with all pairwise distances $> 2R$. Each round's farthest distance is obtained by a BFS from the current set, so the total time is $O(k(|V|+|E|))$. See [14,15].

Lean formalization snippet (spec).

```
1  /- Context: dist, radBound, and isPacking are defined elsewhere. -/
2
3  opaque bfsRad (V : Finset α) (C : Finset α) : ℕ
4
5  opaque packingCertificate (V : Finset α) (k : ℕ) (R : ℝ) :
6    Option (Finset α)
7
8  /-- Soundness: if packingCertificate returns S, then |S| = k+1
9      and it is a packing at scale 2*R (i.e., pairwise distance > 2R). -/
10 axiom packingCertificate_sound
11   (V : Finset α) (k : ℕ) (R : ℝ) :
12   ∀ S, packingCertificate V k R = some S →
13     S.card = k + 1 ∧ isPacking (2*R) S
```

4.4 Euclidean K-Center via Coresets

Let $P \subset \mathbb{R}^d$. An *ε-coreset* $Q \subseteq P$ for k-center means that for every k-set C,

$$\mathrm{rad}(P, C) \leq (1+\varepsilon)\,\mathrm{rad}(Q, C) \quad \text{and} \quad \mathrm{rad}(Q, C) \leq (1+\varepsilon)\,\mathrm{rad}(P, C).$$

Theorem 4 (Coreset stability and composition with greedy) *If Q is an ε-coreset for P, then* $\mathrm{OPT}(Q,k) \leq (1+\varepsilon)\,\mathrm{OPT}(P,k)$ *and, if $C_g(Q)$ is the greedy 2-approximation computed on Q, then* $\mathrm{rad}\big(P, C_g(Q)\big) \;\leq\; 2(1+\varepsilon)\,\mathrm{OPT}(P,k)$.

Proof Let $C_Q^\star$ be optimal for Q. By the first inequality, $\mathrm{OPT}(P,k) \leq (1+\varepsilon)\mathrm{rad}(Q, C_Q^\star) = (1+\varepsilon)\mathrm{OPT}(Q,k)$, so $\mathrm{OPT}(Q,k) \leq (1+\varepsilon)\mathrm{OPT}(P,k)$. For the composition with greedy,

$$\mathrm{rad}\big(P, C_g(Q)\big) \;\leq\; (1+\varepsilon)\,\mathrm{rad}\big(Q, C_g(Q)\big) \;\leq\; (1+\varepsilon)\cdot 2\,\mathrm{OPT}(Q,k) \;\leq\; 2(1+\varepsilon)\,\mathrm{OPT}(P,k),$$

by Theorem 1. Coreset constructions satisfying the symmetric distortion above are well known in low-dimensional metrics; see [9,20–22].

Lean formalization snippet (spec).

```
1  universe u
2  variable {α : Type u}
3
4  opaque radBound   : Finset α → Finset α → ℝ
5  opaque optRadius  : Finset α → ℕ → ℝ
6
7  def isKCoreset (P Q : Finset α) (k : ℕ) (ε : ℝ) : Prop :=
8    ∀ C : Finset α, C.card = k →
9      (radBound P C ≤ (1 + ε) * radBound Q C) ∧
10     (radBound Q C ≤ (1 + ε) * radBound P C)
11
12 opaque farthestFirst (S : Finset α) (k : ℕ) : Finset α
13
14 noncomputable def greedyOn (Q : Finset α) (k : ℕ) : Finset α :=
15   farthestFirst Q k
16
17 axiom gonzalez_two_approx_on
18   (Q : Finset α) (k : ℕ) :
19   radBound Q (greedyOn Q k) ≤ 2 * optRadius Q k
20
21 axiom coreset_stability_spec
22   (P Q : Finset α) (k : ℕ) (ε : ℝ)
23   (h : isKCoreset P Q k ε) :
24   optRadius Q k ≤ (1 + ε) * optRadius P k ∧
25   radBound P (greedyOn Q k) ≤ 2 * (1 + ε) * optRadius P k
```

4.5 Online (Incremental) Template via Packing

Let $(P_t)_{t\geq 1}$ be a stream with $P_{\leq t} = \{p_1, \ldots, p_t\}$ and suppose we maintain at time t a set $S_t \subseteq P_{\leq t}$ that is a maximal R_t-packing (pairwise distances $> 2R_t$ and no $p \in P_{\leq t}$ is at distance $> 2R_t$ from all of S_t).

Proposition 2 (Maximal packing $\Rightarrow$ $2R_t$-cover) *If S_t is a maximal R_t-packing of $P_{\leq t}$, then* $\mathrm{rad}(P_{\leq t}, S_t) \leq 2R_t$.

Proof If some $p \in P_{\leq t}$ had $d(p,s) > 2R_t$ for all $s \in S_t$, then $S_t \cup \{p\}$ would still be an R_t-packing, contradicting maximality. Hence every p is within $2R_t$ of S_t, i.e. covered. This is the bottleneck packing-covering duality used repeatedly for k-center; see, e.g., [14,15].

Corollary 2 (A generic 2-competitive template) *If a policy maintains $|S_t| \leq k$ for all t and updates (R_t) only when $|S_t|$ would exceed k, then* $\mathrm{rad}(P_{\leq t}, S_t) \leq 2\,\mathrm{OPT}(P_{\leq t}, k)$ *for all t (taking $R_t \leq \mathrm{OPT}(P_{\leq t}, k)$ whenever $|S_t| \leq k$), hence a factor-2 competitive ratio in radius.*

Proof By Proposition 2, $\mathrm{rad}(P_{\leq t}, S_t) \leq 2R_t$. While $|S_t| \leq k$, the packing size is a feasible certificate that $R_t \leq \mathrm{OPT}(P_{\leq t}, k)$ by the duality: if $|S_t| > k$, then R_t is too small; conversely $|S_t| \leq k$ implies R_t is not smaller than the optimal radius. Combining gives the bound.

Lean formalization snippet (spec).

```
1  universe u
2  variable {α : Type u}
3
4  opaque coverWithin        (R : ℝ) (P S : Finset α) : Prop
5  opaque radBound           (P C : Finset α) : ℝ
6  opaque optRadius          (P : Finset α) (k : ℕ) : ℝ
7  opaque isMaximalPacking (R : ℝ) (P S : Finset α) : Prop
8
9  axiom maximalPacking_twoR_cover
10   {P S : Finset α} {R : ℝ} :
11   isMaximalPacking R P S → coverWithin (2 * R) P S
12
13 axiom coverWithin_radBound
14   {P S : Finset α} {R : ℝ} :
15   coverWithin R P S → radBound P S ≤ R
16
17 axiom maxpack_opt_duality
18   {P S : Finset α} {R : ℝ} {k : ℕ} :
19   isMaximalPacking R P S → S.card ≤ k → R ≤ optRadius P k
20
21 axiom online_two_competitive
22   (P≤ : ℕ → Finset α) (S : ℕ → Finset α) (R : ℕ → ℝ) (k : ℕ)
23   (hmax    : ∀ t, isMaximalPacking (R t) (P≤ t) (S t))
24   (hbudget : ∀ t, (S t).card ≤ k)
25   (hupdate : ∀ t, (S t).card > k → R (t + 1) > R t) :
26   ∀ t, radBound (P≤ t) (S t) ≤ 2 * optRadius (P≤ t) k
```

In Subsect. 4.4, the symmetric coreset assumption is standard for low-dimensional metrics; see, e.g., [9,20–22]. In doubling metrics, nets and coresets with such two-sided distortion are available from [9]. The tree decision routine and the binary-search scheme (Subsect. 4.2) follow classical p-center techniques [4,5,12]. The greedy factor-2 guarantee (Subsect. 4.1) is the standard packing-covering argument [1–3].

5 Formalization and Reusable Lemmas

We formalize reusable predicates and lemmas that support the algorithms and guarantees in Sect. 4.1-4.5. Throughout (X, d) is a metric space, $P \subseteq X$ is finite and nonempty, and for a finite $C \subseteq X$, $\mathrm{rad}(P, C) = \max_{p \in P} \min_{c \in C} d(p, c)$, $\mathrm{OPT}(P, k) = \min_{|C|=k} \mathrm{rad}(P, C)$. For $R \geq 0$, we write $\mathrm{cover}(R; P, C)$ for the predicate that every $p \in P$ is within distance $\leq R$ of some $c \in C$, and $\mathrm{Feasible}(P, k, R)$ for the existence of a k-set C with $\mathrm{cover}(R; P, C)$.

5.1 Core Predicates and Monotonicity

Lemma 2 (Monotonicity in centers) *If* $C \subseteq C'$, *then* $\mathrm{rad}(P, C') \leq \mathrm{rad}(P, C)$.

Proof For each $p \in P$, $\min_{c' \in C'} d(p, c') \leq \min_{c \in C} d(p, c)$ since the minimum is taken over a superset. Maximizing over p preserves the inequality.

Lemma 3 (Monotonicity in radius) *If* $\mathrm{Feasible}(P, k, R)$ *holds and* $R' \geq R$, *then* $\mathrm{Feasible}(P, k, R')$ *holds.*

Proof A cover at radius R remains a cover at any larger radius R' by monotonicity of the balls.

Lemma 4 (Nearest-center is *1* -Lipschitz). *For any fixed finite* C *and any* $p, p' \in X$,

$$\left|\min_{c \in C} d(p, c) - \min_{c \in C} d(p', c)\right| \leq d(p, p'). \tag{1}$$

Proof For every $c \in C$, $|d(p, c) - d(p', c)| \leq d(p, p')$ by the triangle inequality; taking minima preserves a 1-Lipschitz bound.

Lean formalization snippet (spec).

```
1  opaque dist       : α → α → ℝ
2  opaque radBound  : Finset α → Finset α → ℝ
3
4  /-- Feasible(P,k,R) := ∃ C, C.card ≤ k ∧ ∀ p ∈ P, ∃ c ∈ C, dist p c ≤ R -/
5  def Feasible (P : Finset α) (k : ℕ) (R : ℝ) : Prop :=
6    ∃ C : Finset α, C.card ≤ k ∧ ∀ {p}, p ∈ P → ∃ c ∈ C, dist p c ≤ R
7
8
9  axiom rad_monotone_centers {P C C' : Finset alpha} (hsub : C \subseteq C') :
10   radBound P C' <= radBound P C
11
12 lemma feasible_mono_R {P : Finset alpha} {k : Nat} {R R' : Real}
13   (hRR' : R <= R') (h : Feasible P k R) : Feasible P k R' := by
14   h = (C, hCk, hcov)
15   intro p hp
16   rcases h with (C, hCk, hcov)
17   use hcov hp = (c, hcC, hpc)
18   rcases hcov hp with (c, hcC, hpc)
19   exact (c, hcC, le_trans hpc hRR')
```

5.2 Packing–Covering Duality

Definition 1 (Packing at scale R **).** *A finite* $S \subseteq P$ *is an* R*-packing if* $d(x, y) > 2R$ *for all distinct* $x, y \in S$. *It is maximal if no* $p \in P$ *can be added while preserving the property.*

Lemma 5 (Packing ⇒ infeasibility). *If* $S \subseteq P$ *is an* R*-packing with* $|S| = k{+}1$, *then* $\mathrm{Feasible}(P, k, R)$ *is false.*

Proof Assume a k-set C satisfies cover$(R; P, C)$. Each $s \in S$ lies in some ball $B_R(c)$ with $c \in C$. Two packing points cannot share the same $B_R(c)$ because then they would be at distance $\leq 2R$, contradicting the packing. Hence k balls cover at most k points of S, impossible for $|S| = k+1$. This bottleneck duality underlies the k-center lower-bound certificates; cf. [14].

Proposition 3 (Maximal packing $\Rightarrow$ $2R$ -cover). *If S is a maximal R-packing in P, then* $\text{rad}(P, S) \leq 2R$.

Proof If some $p \in P$ had $d(p, s) > 2R$ for all $s \in S$, then $S \cup \{p\}$ would still be an R-packing, contradicting maximality. Therefore $P \subseteq \bigcup_{s \in S} B_{2R}(s)$.

Lean formalization snippet (spec).

```
universe u
variable {α : Type u}

opaque coverWithin        : ℝ → Finset α → Finset α → Prop
opaque radBound           : Finset α → Finset α → ℝ
opaque isMaximalPacking : ℝ → Finset α → Finset α → Prop

axiom maximalPacking_twoR_cover
  {P S : Finset α} {R : ℝ} :
  isMaximalPacking R P S → coverWithin (2 * R) P S

axiom radBound_le_of_cover
  {P S : Finset α} {R : ℝ} :
  coverWithin R P S → radBound P S ≤ R

lemma rad_le_from_maxpack
  {P S : Finset α} {R : ℝ}
  (h : isMaximalPacking R P S) :
  radBound P S ≤ 2 * R :=
by
  exact radBound_le_of_cover (maximalPacking_twoR_cover h)
```

5.3 Greedy Separation Invariant (Reusable)

Let $C_g = \{c_1, \ldots, c_k\}$ be the farthest-first centers (Sect. 4.1) and $R_g = \text{rad}(P, C_g)$.

Lemma 6 (Separation and maximality of C_g). *We have $d(c_i, c_j) \geq R_g$ for all $i \neq j$, and C_g is a maximal R_g-packing in P.*

Proof At round i the chosen c_i maximizes the nearest-distance to $\{c_1, \ldots, c_{i-1}\}$; the farthest value is nonincreasing across rounds and at termination bounded below by R_g. Hence $d(c_i, c_j) \geq R_g$. If some p had $d(p, C_g) > R_g$, then R_g would not be the maximum nearest-distance, contradicting the definition of rad. See [1,2].

Lemma 7 (Separation and maximality of C_g.) *We have $d(c_i, c_j) \geq R_g$ for all $i \neq j$, and C_g is a maximal R_g-packing in P.*

Proof At round i the chosen c_i maximizes the nearest-distance to $\{c_1, \ldots, c_{i-1}\}$. The farthest value is nonincreasing across rounds and, at termination, equals $\max_{p \in P} \min_{c \in C_g} d(p, c) = R_g$. Hence for all $i \neq j$, $d(c_i, c_j) \geq R_g$. If some $p \in P$ had $d(p, C_g) > R_g$, then R_g would not be the maximum nearest-distance, contradicting the definition of rad. See [1,2].

Lean formalization snippet (spec).

```
universe u
variable {α : Type u} [PseudoMetricSpace α]

constant radBound : Finset α → Finset α → ℝ

opaque farthestFirst (P : Finset α) (k : ℕ) : Finset α

noncomputable def greedyRadius (P : Finset α) (k : ℕ) : ℝ :=
  radBound P (farthestFirst P k)

def isPacking (R : ℝ) (S : Finset α) : Prop :=
  ∀ {x y}, x ∈ S → y ∈ S → x ≠ y → dist x y ≥ R

def isMaximalPacking (R : ℝ) (P S : Finset α) : Prop :=
  isPacking R S ∧ ∀ {p}, p ∈ P → ∃ s ∈ S, dist p s ≤ R

axiom farthestFirst_pairwise_separation
  (P : Finset α) (k : ℕ) :
  let Cg := farthestFirst P k; let Rg := greedyRadius P k
  in ∀ {x y}, x ∈ Cg → y ∈ Cg → x ≠ y → dist x y ≥ Rg

axiom farthestFirst_maximal_packing
  (P : Finset α) (k : ℕ) :
  let Cg := farthestFirst P k; let Rg := greedyRadius P k
  in isMaximalPacking Rg P Cg

lemma farthestFirst_separation_and_maximal
  (P : Finset α) (k : ℕ) :
  let Cg := farthestFirst P k; let Rg := greedyRadius P k in
  (∀ {x y}, x ∈ Cg → y ∈ Cg → x ≠ y → dist x y ≥ Rg) ∧
  isMaximalPacking Rg P Cg := by
  intro;exact (farthestFirst_pairwise_separation P k,
       farthestFirst_maximal_packing P k)
```

5.4 Parametric Search and Discrete Candidates

Lemma 8 (Feasibility monotone ⇒ binary search correctness). *Let* $\mathcal{U} \subseteq \mathbb{R}_{\geq 0}$ *be finite and contain* $R^\star = \text{OPT}(P, k)$. *If* $R \mapsto \text{Feasible}(P, k, R)$ *is monotone (Lemma 3), then binary search on sorted* $\mathcal{U}$ *returns* $R^\star$.

Proof Feasible radii form an initial segment of $\mathcal{U}$ whose smallest feasible element is $R^\star$. Binary search maintains the invariant that the boundary between false or true lies in the current interval; termination yields $R^\star$. For classical bottleneck parametric schemes see [5,14].

Lean formalization snippet (spec).

```
universe u
variable {α : Type u}

opaque Feasible : Finset α → ℕ → ℝ → Prop

def isMinFeasible (U : Finset ℝ) (P : Finset α) (k : ℕ) (R : ℝ) : Prop :=
  Feasible P k R ∧ ∀ R' ∈ U, R' < R → ¬ Feasible P k R'

axiom bsearch_finite_monotone
  (P : Finset α) (k : ℕ)
  (U : Finset ℝ) (Rstar : ℝ)
  (hmem  : Rstar ∈ U)
  (hmono : ∀ {R R'}, R ≤ R' → Feasible P k R → Feasible P k R')
  (hstar : Feasible P k Rstar)
  (hinit : ∀ R ∈ U, R < Rstar → ¬ Feasible P k R) :
  ∃ R ∈ U, isMinFeasible U P k R
```

5.5 Complexity and Resource Specifications

Theorem 5 (Asymptotic specifications (verifiable claims).) *(i) Farthest-first uses $O(k|P|)$ distance evaluations and $O(|P|)$ memory (array of nearest-center distances). (ii) On graphs, multi-source BFS is $O(|V|+|E|)$ per call; k rounds for packing and certificates cost $O(k(|V|+|E|))$. (iii) On trees, binary search over a finite candidate set with a linear-time decision routine costs $O(|V|\log|\mathcal{U}|)$.*

Proof (i) Maintain and update the nearest-distance for each p at each of k rounds; see [10, Ch. 3]. (ii) BFS is linear-time; repetition across k rounds scales the cost [14,15]. (iii) Combine Lemma 8 with a linear-time decision on trees as in Sect. 4.2 and [4,5,12].

Lean formalization snippet (spec).

```
universe u
variable {α : Type u}

axiom farthestFirst_cost_spec
  (P : Finset α) (k : ℕ) : True

axiom bfs_cost_spec
  (V : Finset α) (E : Finset (α * α)) (S : Finset α) : True

axiom tree_bsearch_cost_spec
  (V : Finset α) (k : ℕ) : True
```

6 Conclusion

This paper presents a framework to build and verify algorithms for the k-center problem. A small set of modules (Metric, FiniteSet, Radius, and Feasible) separates the problem meaning from the data structure used in the backend. This design lets one proof work for many metrics, such as graphs, trees, and Euclidean spaces. The algorithms return certificates that explain why the answer is correct. For example, the greedy method returns both a packing and a covering.

The tree method returns a record that shows why a radius is feasible or infeasible. On graphs, tools based on multi-source breadth-first search give short and clear machine-checked proofs of known results. Backend components can change without changing the main proofs.

The framework covers several key results. It gives the constant-factor bound for the greedy farthest-first method. It gives an exact algorithm on trees that searches over a set of radii. It also gives a graph-based method that uses a packing to prove that a target radius is not feasible. The greedy template also works with coresets and keeps the same constant-factor bound. For online inputs, a template that keeps a maximal packing gives a radius within a factor of two of the optimum at each step. The design does not depend on one proof assistant and can be adapted to Lean, Coq, or Isabelle. New features are easy to add. Capacity limits or outliers only require changes to the feasibility test. Core lemmas can be reused for special cases, such as low-doubling metrics or planar graphs. Euclidean code can connect to existing tools for nets and coresets.

Clear templates for packing, covering, and radius search turn long textbook proofs into small, reusable, and machine-checkable code units. These units can be combined to build new algorithms for dynamic data, streaming data, and networked systems.

References

1. Gonzalez, T.F.: Clustering to minimize the maximum intercluster distance. Theor. Comput. Sci. **38**, pp. 293–306 (1985)
2. Hochbaum, D.S., Shmoys, D.B.: A best possible heuristic for the k-center problem. Math. Oper. Res. **10**(2), 180–184 (1985)
3. Tamas, F., Greene, D. H.: Optimal algorithms for approximate clustering. In: Proceedings of the Twentieth Annual ACM Symposium on Theory of Computing (STOC), pp. 434–444 (1988)
4. Kariv, O., Hakimi, S.L.: An algorithmic approach to network location problems. part 1: the p-centers. SIAM J. Appl. Math. **37**(3), 513–538 (1979)
5. Megiddo, N., Tamir, A.: On the complexity of locating linear facilities in the plane. SIAM J. Comput. **12**(1), 182–196 (1983)
6. Khuller, S., Sussmann, Y.J.: The capacitated k-center problem. SIAM J. Discret. Math. **13**(3), 403–418 (2000)
7. Moses, C., Khuller, S., Mount, D. M., Narasimhan, G.: Algorithms for facility location problems with outliers. In: Proceedings of the Twelfth Annual ACM–SIAM Symposium on Discrete Algorithms (SODA), pp. 642–651 (2001)
8. McCutchen, R. M., Khuller, S.: Streaming algorithms for clustering with outliers. In: Proceedings of the 16th Annual European Symposium on Algorithms (ESA), pp. 165–176 (2008)
9. Har-Peled, S., Mendel, M.: Fast construction of nets in low dimensional metrics and their applications. SIAM J. Comput. **35**(5), 1148–1184 (2006)
10. Dorit, S. H.: Approximation algorithms for NP-hard problems. PWS Publishing, (1997)
11. Tamir, A.: Obnoxious facility location on graphs and trees. Oper. Res. Lett. **19**(1), 1–7 (1996)

12. Hakimi, S.L., Schmeichel, A.: p-Centers on a Tree. Networks **13**(3), 293–307 (1983)
13. Plesník, J.: A heuristic for the p-center problem in graphs. Discret. Appl. Math. **17**(3), 263–268 (1987)
14. Hochbaum, D.S., Shmoys, D.B.: A unified approach to approximation algorithms for bottleneck problems. J. ACM **33**(3), 533–550 (1986)
15. Feder, T., Greene, D.H.: Approximate clustering and its application to network design. J. Comput. Syst. Sci. **45**(2), 233–284 (1992)
16. Teofilo, G. F.: Covering a set of points in multidimensional space. Theor. Comput. Sci. **21**, pp. 113–135 (1982)
17. Sharma, A., Keswani, M.P.: A note on capacitated k-center. Inf. Process. Lett. **106**(4), 152–155 (2008)
18. Deeparnab, C., Negahbani, M.: Generalized k-center: fairness, outliers, and robustness. In: Proceedings of the 44th International Colloquium on Automata, Languages, and Programming (ICALP), pp. 67:1–67:14 (2017)
19. Flavio, C., Kumar, R., Lattanzi, S., Vassilvitskii, S.: Fair clustering through fairlets. In: Proceedings of the 31st Conference on Neural Information Processing Systems (NeurIPS), pp. 5029–5037 (2017)
20. Pankaj, A. K., Ben-Avraham, R., Har-Peled, S., Yu, H.: Near-linear time approximation schemes for clustering in low-dimensional metrics. In: Proceedings of the 31st International Colloquium on Automata, Languages and Programming (ICALP), pp. 49–60 (2004)
21. Gerhard, F., Sohler, C.: Coresets in dynamic geometric data streams. In: Proceedings of the 37th Annual ACM Symposium on Theory of Computing (STOC), pp. 209–217 (2005)
22. Sariel, H.:Geometric approximation algorithms. American Mathematical Society(2011)
23. Sanjeev, D., Marathe, M.V., Ravi, S. S., Taylor, D.S., Widmayer, P.: Approximation algorithms for clustering to minimize the maximum intercluster distance. In: Proceedings of the 11th Annual ACM–SIAM Symposium on Discrete Algorithms (SODA), pp. 436–445 (2000)
24. Omid, A., et al.: Approximation schemes for clustering with outliers in doubling metrics. In: Proceedings of the 29th Annual ACM–SIAM Symposium on Discrete Algorithms (SODA), pp. 1529–1543 (2018)
25. Teofilo, G. F.: Clustering to minimize the maximum intercluster distance. In: Proceedings of the Sixteenth Annual ACM Symposium on Theory of Computing (STOC), pp. 516–524 (1985)

WEX: Formal Specifications for Windows in Stream Processing

S. Hitarth[1(✉)] and M. Praveen[2,3]

[1] Hong Kong University of Science and Technology, Hong Kong, China
hsinghab@connect.ust.hk
[2] Chennai Mathematical Institute, Chennai, India
praveenm@cmi.ac.in
[3] CNRS IRL ReLaX, Chennai, India

Abstract. A key operation in processing an unbounded data stream is windowing, which extracts finite portions of streams for further handling. The existing frameworks and query languages either require windows to be defined using ad hoc imperative languages or are limited to rudimentary constructs such as time- or count-based windows. We propose **W**indow **EX**pression, a formal specification for precisely expressing windowing constructs based on monadic second-order logic. WEX can naturally express traditional windowing constructs such as sliding windows and tumbling windows, as well as more complex windows whose start and end indices are triggered based on the satisfaction of given logical conditions. After introducing a model of *symbolic automata with lookbacks* over an alphabet theory, we present another equivalent representation of WEX based on symbolic regular expressions. The precise semantics of windowing enable static analysis over WEX. In particular, we show that, in general,it is undecidable to check whether a WEX allows an unbounded number of overlapping windows. However, when the data stream is over a finite alphabet, or the alphabet theory has the so-called *completion property*, the problem becomes decidable.

Keywords: Stream processing · Formal Specification · Symbolic Regular Expressions · Monadic Second-Order Logic

1 Introduction

Stream Processors. Traditional ways of storing and querying data do not work well in scenarios where data is being generated continuously and quick decisions need to be taken. For example, in hospital intensive care units, signals from multiple devices need to be monitored and the occurrence of any anomaly should raise alarms immediately. Stream Processors are programs that consume and produce such unbounded streams of data. They are applied in many areas, ranging from

M. Praveen—was partially support by the Infosys foundation.

A. Goharshady and C. Haase (Eds.): SETTA 2025, LNCS 16458, pp. 257–276, 2026.
https://doi.org/10.1007/978-981-95-7826-9_14

detecting who is controlling the ball in soccer matches [21] to detecting irregularities in heartbeat rhythms in implantable cardioverter-defibrillators (ICDs) [1] and continuous analysis of RFID readings to track valid paths of shipments in inventory management systems [25]. One common aspect is that they produce output within a bounded amount of time, during which they can only read a bounded portion of the input.

Windows. Windows define a span of positions along a stream that the program can use as a unit to perform computations on and are fundamental to stream processors. Stream processors allow the end-users to specify windows using their specification language, however, not all of them allow end-users to define customized windows.

Example 1. Suppose we want to generate the so-called *sliding windows* of size 5 and offset 2, i.e., each window will span 5 data elements and the next window will be generated by sliding the current window by 2 data elements. This is illustrated in Fig. 1.

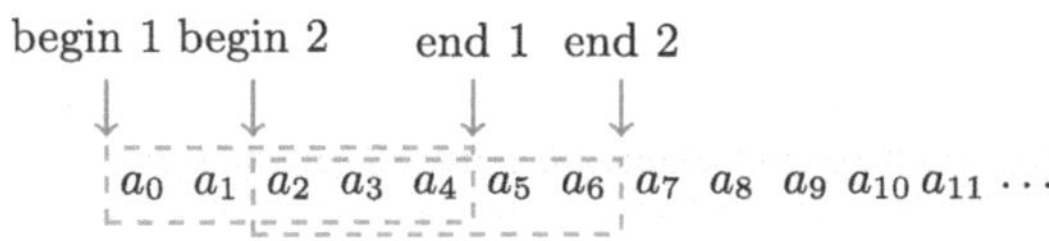

Fig. 1. Illustration of Windows: Two windows $a_0a_1a_2a_3a_4$ and $a_2a_3a_4a_5a_6$ are generated.

The survey [6, Table IV] mentions thirty-four processors, of which six allow user-defined windows. Four of them allow only time-based or count-based windows. The other two (Esper [12] and IBM System S [17]) allow customizable windows based on other criteria, but they must be written in imperative programming languages.

The syntax of many languages used in stream processors extend database query languages. Relational database query processing arguably derives a significant portion of its robustness from the fact that it is based on relational algebra that is expressively equivalent to first-order logic [5]. But for streaming processing, the fundamental linear order of arrival is not part of the syntax, which may be important for certain applications.

Window EXpressions. We introduce a novel method of defining windows called **WEX** based on the Monadic Second Order (MSO) logic of one successor. MSO includes the linear order of arrival as a basic building block. Apart from easily expressing practical queries, we get other advantages from concepts and constructs in formal language theory. The equivalence of MSO with regular expressions allows us to design another equivalent representation for defining windows that is arguably easier to understand for end users compared to logic-based syntax [23]. In particular, we give two equivalent definitions of WEX, one based on MSO and another based on regular expressions. The equivalence with automata allows us to design a procedure that automatically produces windows from a data stream according to specifications.

Example 2. Informally, WEX specifies windows with a logical formula $\phi(x_s, x_e)$ over two special free variables x_s (start) and x_e (end), such that the span (a, b) of a word w is a window if $w \models \phi(a, b)$.

For instance, the sliding windows from Example 1 can be *captured* by the following formula in the theory of linear arithmetic:

$$\phi(x_s, x_e) :- \exists n \in \mathbb{N}, x_s = 2 \cdot n \wedge x_e = x_s + 5.$$

Motivating Example. Sequence of stock prices as they are traded in the market is a natural data stream. Detecting trends in such streams is widely used in both stock markets and algorithmic trading [21]. Assume that the average price of a stock is emitted every minute as a stream.

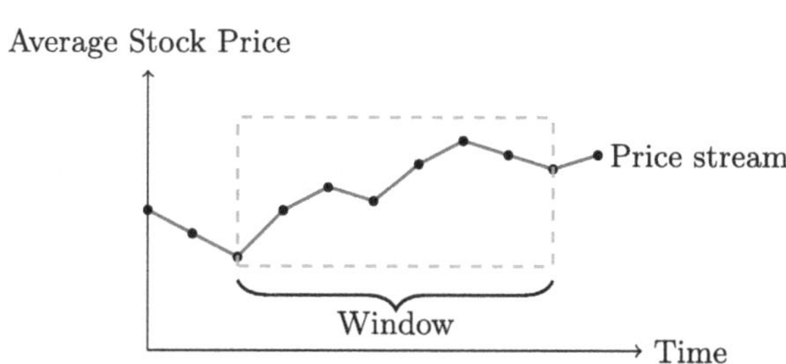

Fig. 2. Stock price stream with average values emitted every minute. A window (highlighted) is used to detect a potentially downward trend.

We are interested in detecting *a trend* with the following behaviour, illustrated in Fig. 2. The window opens right after the price starts to increase after having gone down at least twice consecutively. Inside the window, the price may fluctuate, but is not allowed to go down twice in a row. The window closes right when the price goes down twice consecutively. Such a window captures a phase that is mostly increasing with occasional dips, ending with a potential downward trend.

This kind of pattern cannot be specified by simple operators such as sliding or tumbling windows as they are purely time or count-based. Nor do existing algebraic or stream-monitoring frameworks support such event-based windows defined rigorously as first-class objects: they typically require imperative definitions of windows in some ad hoc language. In contrast, our formalism (WEX) can precisely define such intricate patterns. A key motivation for WEX is to formalize such informal requirements, which are otherwise prone to misunderstanding. We will formalize this with WEX in Sect. 3.1.

Overlapping Windows. It is possible that a window specification results in a large number of windows overlapping at the same position of a data stream, overwhelming the stream processor. This is usually handled by engines using load shedding—dropping off information items from the stream at runtime when load becomes too high. This may be acceptable if it is caused by high input rate, but not if there is a design fault in the window definition. We study the crucial problem of checking whether the number of windows overlapping at a single position is potentially unbounded for a given window definition. This problem is undecidable in general for infinite alphabets. We show that this is decidable when the alphabet is finite and also when the alphabet theory has the so-called *completion property*.

Data Streams and Symbolic MSO. Data elements in a stream are usually numerical or similar values from an infinite domain. Symbolic MSO [8] is meant to deal with infinite alphabets. The atomic formulas of this logic can check the properties of input symbols using predicates over the infinite alphabet. This also has automata counterparts, called symbolic automata [9] and symbolic regular expressions [24]. We will define these terms in the next section. Our window expressions can be expressed using a guarded variant Symbolic MSO. The advantage of high expressiveness of Symbolic MSO outweigh the disadvantage of undecidability of many static analysis problems over Symbolic MSO. Moreover, we identify a fragment for which it is decidable, even for symbolic automata.

Contributions and structure. The main contributions of this paper are:

- In Sect. 2, we introduce a variant of symbolic automata with lookbacks (k-SLA). We estabilish certain closure properties of k-SLA to define symbolic regular expressions equivalent to it. We then prove that our automata model is equivalent to the Symbolic Monadic Second Order logic based on [8].
- In Sect. 3, we define the two formalism of WEX based on a guarded fragment of S-MSO and symbolic regular expressions. In Sect. 3.1, we provide a few applications of WEX to specify complicated windowing.
- We prove the decidability of the unboundedness of overlapping windows for restricted classes of window expressions in Sect. 4.
- Finally, we present an algorithm for a stream processor based on WEX in Sect. 5 that uses *panes* to avoid duplicate computations.

Related works. Mamouras et al. extended regular expressions in [19] with operators to handle quantitative data for processing data streams. In their work, windows have to be defined as derived operators or written in external code, in contrast to our formalisms where windows are treated as first-class objects and defining them is a basic construct. A model called data transducers is used in [2] for implementing data stream processors, but again windows are not part of the core specification language.

In runtime monitoring frameworks Lola/RTLola [4,7,14], one can define simple windows such as tumbling windows and sliding windows. In [15], a formal framework based on models of computation is developed for complex event processing. They also work on data streams, but windows as we consider here are not of particular interest there. Algebraic systems for generating windows from streams are considered in [20,22], and they study properties of window definitions that are useful for query optimization and related static analysis tasks. The windows are defined via algebraic constraints over the timestamps of the streaming data, and not the actual values of the data. Moreover, their goal is not to integrate window definitions in the syntax of query languages, which we do here.

In database theory, *spanners* are used for information extraction from a document. Spans, like windows, are contiguous substrings of the document identified by the starting and ending indices. Formal spanners introduced in [13] are conceptually closest to WEX, as both use regular expressions to select intervals over a sequence. The key distinction is that spanners work in an offline setting; they assume access to the whole document. In contrast, our setting is online, and the window boundaries must be determined in a 0-*delay manner*, i.e., windows are selected based on data up to the current position and cannot depend on unseen future data. Another key difference in formalism is that WEX supports alphabet theories, allowing window selection based on predicates over an infinite domain.

2 Symbolic Automata, Expressions and MSO

We assume that data streams are infinite sequences of letters from an infinite alphabet Σ. Given a word $w \in \Sigma^*$ and $i, j \in \mathbb{N}$, $w[i:j]$ represents the contiguous substring of w starting from i^{th} index to j^{th} index, both inclusive. We start indexing from 0. Let $w[i] = w[i:i]$ and $w[:k]$ be the suffix of w of length $k+1$.

We introduce the model of k-symbolic automata, which is a variant of symbolic automata with lookback. We refer to [8,9,24] for details. In standard automata and MSO, transitions, and atomic formulas can check that the symbol at a position is equal to some particular letter in a finite alphabet. In Symbolic automata and MSO, we can instead check that the symbol at a position satisfies some property specified in the first-order logic. For example, an atomic formula of symbolic MSO can check that an input symbol is an even number, which can be specified in first-order logic over $\mathbb{N}$ with addition.

Definition 1. *An* ***alphabet theory*** *is a tuple* $\mathcal{A} = (\Sigma, V, \Psi_V)$ *such that* Σ *is a (finite or infinite) alphabet and* Ψ_V *is a set of first-order formulas with free variables* V *closed under boolean connectives* $\{\vee, \wedge, \neg\}$ *with* $\bot, \top \in \Psi_V$. *Given* $\psi \in \Psi_V$ *and a valuation* $\nu : V \to \Sigma$, *it should be decidable to check whether* $\nu \models_{\mathcal{A}} \psi$.

We use $\models_{\mathcal{A}}$ to denote the models relation in the alphabet theory, to distinguish it from models relation in other logics. We use a variation of symbolic automata that can read symbols in the previous k positions, for a fixed k, in addition to the current symbol. We call them k-symbolic lookback automata (k-*SLA*), similar to k-symbolic lookback transducers introduced in [11].

Definition 2. *A* **k-*symbolic lookback automata*** *(k-SLA) is a tuple* $S = (\mathcal{A}, Q, q_0, F, \delta)$ *where* $\mathcal{A} = (\Sigma, V, \Psi_V)$ *is an alphabet theory with* $V = (x_{-k}, \ldots, x_0)$ *as a set of* $k+1$ lookback variables, *Q is a finite set of states, $q_0 \in Q$ is the initial state, $F \subseteq Q$ is the set of final states, and $\delta : Q \times Q \to \Psi_V$ is the transition function.*

Given a word w of length $|w| = k+1$, $v_V(w) : V \mapsto \Sigma$ denotes a valuation such that $v_V(w)(x_{-j}) = w[k-j]$ for all $j \in [0, k]$. We define the **run** *of S on a word $w \in \Sigma^*$ of length $n \geq k+1$ to be a sequence $(q_0, q_1, \ldots, q_{n-k-1})$ of states such that it starts from the initial state q_0, and for all $i \in [k, n-1]$ we have $v_V(w[i-k : i]) \models_{\mathcal{A}} \delta(q_{i-k}, q_{i-k+1})$.*

If $q_{n-k-1} \in F$, then the run is accepting, and the word is **accepted** *by S. If there is no accepting run, the word is* **rejected***. The run is not defined for words of length less than $k+1$, which are all rejected by a k-SLA.*

The **language** *accepted by S is $L(S) = \{w \in \Sigma^* \mid w \text{ is accepted by } S\}$.*

Definition 3. *If $\delta(q_i, q_j) = \varphi$, then φ is called the guard of the transition $q_i \xrightarrow{\varphi} q_j$. A k-SLA is* **deterministic** *if for every $q, q', q'' \in Q$ with $q' \neq q''$, $\delta(q, q') \wedge \delta(q, q'')$ is unsatisfiable.*

We say a k-SLA is **clean** *if every $\delta(q, q')$ is either $\bot$ or is satisfiable. We can easily construct an equivalent clean k-SLA for any k-SLA by replacing all the unsatisfiable guards by $\bot$.*

k-concatenation We define a variant of concatenation, called k-concatenation, denoted by $\cdot_k$.

Definition 4. *Given two strings $w_1 = wv$ and $w_2 = vw'$ and $|v| = k$, we define the* **k-*concatenation*** *$w_1 \cdot_k w_2 = wvw'$. If the last k letters of w_1 do not exactly match with first k letters of w_2, or length of either word is less than k, then the concatenation is undefined. The k-concatenation of two languages L_1 and L_2 is defined as $L_1 \cdot_k L_2 = \{wvw' \in \Sigma^* \mid wv \in L_1, vw' \in L_2 \text{ and } |v| = k\}$.*

Example 3. For 2-concatenation, $abaa \cdot_2 aaba = abaaba$, while $abab \cdot_2 aaba$ is undefined.

The usual closure properties are satisfied by k-*SLA*, which we establish next. The results given in this section are easy adaptations of similar results for finite alphabets.

Lemma 1 (Determinization). *Given a k-SLA $S = (\mathcal{A}, Q, q_0, F, \delta)$, we can construct a deterministic k-SLA $S' = (\mathcal{A}, Q', q_0', F', \delta')$ such that $L(S) = L(S')$.*

Proof. We can assume, WLOG, that S is clean. Let $q \in Q$ and $\mathbf{q} \subseteq Q$. We will first define the following useful notation.

$$\begin{aligned} \delta_S(q) &= \{(q, \delta(q, q'), q') \neq \bot \mid q' \in Q\} \\ \delta_S(\mathbf{q}) &= \cup_{q \in \mathbf{q}} \delta_S(q) \\ Target(\mathbf{t}) &= \{q' \mid (q, \varphi, q') \in \mathbf{t}\} \\ Cond((q, \varphi, q')) &= \varphi \end{aligned}$$

Let $Q' = 2^Q$. To define the transition function δ', we will define the outgoing transition from each $\mathbf{q} \subseteq Q$. For each subset $\mathbf{t} \subseteq \delta_S(\mathbf{q})$ let

$$\varphi_{\mathbf{t}} = (\bigwedge_{t \in \mathbf{t}} Cond(t)) \wedge (\bigwedge_{t \in \delta_S(\mathbf{q}) \setminus \mathbf{t}} \neg Cond(t))$$

.

If $\varphi_{\mathbf{t}}$ is satisfiable, then define $\delta'(\mathbf{q}, Target(\mathbf{t})) = \varphi_T$, otherwise $\delta'(\mathbf{q}, Target(\mathbf{t})) = \bot$. For all sets $\mathbf{q'} \subseteq Q$ which are not equal to $Target(\mathbf{t})$ for any $\mathbf{t} \subseteq \delta_S(\mathbf{q})$, we define $\delta'(\mathbf{q}, \mathbf{q'})) = \bot$.

Define $q_0' = \{q_0\}$ and $F' = \{\mathbf{q} \subseteq Q \mid \exists q \in \mathbf{q}. q \in F\}$.

To see that S' is deterministic, note that for every two outgoing transition from a state $\mathbf{q} \in Q'$ with guard $\varphi_{\mathbf{t}}$ and $\varphi_{\mathbf{t'}}$ with $\mathbf{t} \neq t'$, $\varphi_{\mathbf{t}} \wedge \varphi_{\mathbf{t'}}$ is unsatisfiable. It follows because, WLOG, if $t \in \mathbf{t}$ and $t \notin \mathbf{t'}$, then $\varphi_{\mathbf{t}}$ will have the conjunct $Cond(t)$ while $\varphi_{\mathbf{t'}}$ will have $\neg Cond(t)$.

It's trivial to verify that S' accepts the same language as S. □

Definition 5. *We complement languages of k-SLAs with respect to strings of length at least $k+1$. The* ***complement*** *of a language of k-SLA is defined as $\overline{L(S)} = (\Sigma^{k+1} \cdot \Sigma^*) \setminus L(S)$. The following result follows from the previous one.*

Lemma 2 (Complementation). *Given a k-SLA S, we can construct a k-SLA S' such that $L(S') = \overline{L(S)}$.*

Proof (Sketch). Proof is similar to the standard NFA complementation procedure. We first determinize S and then swap the final states with non-final states. □

Product construction works on *k-SLA* as usual. Given two *k-SLA* $S_1 = (\mathcal{A}, Q_1, q_0^1, F_1, \delta_1)$ and $S_2 = (\mathcal{A}, Q_2, q_0^2, F_2, \delta_2)$, the product of S_1 and S_2 is $S = (\mathcal{A}, Q_1 \times Q_2, (q_0^1, q_0^2), F, \delta)$ where $F = \{(q_1, q_2) \mid q_1 \in F_1 \textit{ and } q_2 \in F_2\}$ and $\delta((q_1, q_2), (q_1', q_2')) = \delta_1(q_1, q_1') \wedge \delta(q_2, q_2')$ for all $q_1, q_1' \in Q$ and $q_2, q_2' \in Q_2$.

Lemma 3 (Intersection). *Given two k-SLA $S_1 = (\mathcal{A}, Q_1, q_0^1, F_1, \delta_1)$ and $S_2 = (\mathcal{A}, Q_2, q_0^2, F_2, \delta_2)$, let the product of S_1 and S_2 be S. Then, $L(S) = L(S_1) \cap L(S_2)$.*

The languages of *k-SLA* are also closed under union, which can be proved as usual by taking disjoint union of two automata.

Lemma 4. *The languages of k-SLA are closed under k-concatenation.*

Proof. Let *k-SLA* $S_1 = (\mathcal{A}, Q_1, q_0^1, F_1, \delta_1)$ and $S_2 = (\mathcal{A}, Q_2, q_0^2, F_2, \delta_2)$. The construction is similar to that in case of finite automata. Formally, construct a *k-SLA* $S = (\mathcal{A}, Q_1 \cup Q_2, q_0^1, F_2, \delta)$ with

$$\delta(q, q') = \begin{cases} \delta_1(q, q'), & \text{if } q, q' \in Q_1 \\ \delta_2(q, q'), & \text{if } q, q' \in Q_2 \\ \delta_2(q_0^2, q'), & \text{if } q \in F_1, q' \in Q_2 \\ \bot, & \text{otherwise} \end{cases}$$

In the third case above, S non-deterministically switches from S_1 to S_2. The proof of correctness is routine. □

2.1 Symbolic Regular Expressions

Symbolic Regular Expressions (SRE). SREs are regular expressions over an alphabet theory.

Definition 6. *Given an alphabet theory $\mathcal{A} = (\Sigma \cup \{\varepsilon\}, V, \Psi_V)$, the set of* ***Symbolic Regular Expressions*** *is defined by the grammar:*

$$R :- [\varphi] \mid R + R \mid R \cdot_k R \mid R^*,$$

where $\varphi \in \Psi_V$.

The semantics of SRE are defined as follows: $L([\varphi]) :- \{w \in \Sigma^{k+1} \mid v_V(w) \models_{\mathcal{A}} \varphi\}$, $L(R_1 + R_2) :- L(R_1) \cup L(R_2)$, $L(R_1 \cdot_k R_2) :- L(R_1) \cdot_k L(R_2)$ and $L(R^*) :- \bigcup_{1 \leq n \in \mathbb{N}} L(R^n)$.

Lemma 5. *For every SRE R there is a k-SLA S (and vice versa) such that $L(S) = L(R)$.*

Proof (omitted). Trivial proof via same constructions as for finite alphabet.

2.2 S-MSO: Symbolic Monadic Second Order

We define Symbolic Monadic Second Order (S-MSO) logic from [8] with support for lookback variables.

Definition 7. *Given an alphabet theory $\mathcal{A} = (\Sigma, V, \Psi_V)$, The syntax of S-MSO over $\mathcal{A}$ is defined by the following grammar: $\phi ::= [\varphi](x) \mid x < y \mid X(x) \mid \neg\phi \mid \phi \wedge \phi \mid \exists x\ \phi \mid \exists X\ \phi$, where $\varphi \in \Psi_V$, lower case letters x, y, z are first-order variables and upper case letters X, Y, Z are second order variables. Note that the lookback variables in V can occur only in formula from Ψ_V.*

Semantics of S-MSO. Let ϕ be an S-MSO formula with free variables $FV(\phi)$. Consider a word $w \in \Sigma^*$ with $|w| \geq k+1$ and a map $\theta : FV(\phi) \to [k, |w|-1] \cup 2^{[k,|w|-1]}$, where the first order variables are mapped to $[k, |w|-1]$ and second order variables are mapped to $2^{[k,|w|-1]}$. Given a substring $w' = a_0 \ldots a_k$ of w of size $k+1$, we define $\nu[w'] : V \to \Sigma$ to be a map with $\nu[w'](x_{i-k}) = a_i$ for all $i \in [0, k]$. The semantics of S-MSO with k-lookback is as follows.

$$\begin{aligned}
w, \theta &\models [\varphi](x) &&\Leftrightarrow v_V(w[\theta(x) - k : \theta(x)]) \models_{\mathcal{A}} \varphi \\
w, \theta &\models x < y &&\Leftrightarrow \theta(x) < \theta(y) \\
w, \theta &\models X(x) &&\Leftrightarrow \theta(x) \in \theta(X) \\
w, \theta &\models \neg\phi &&\Leftrightarrow w, \theta \not\models \phi \\
w, \theta &\models \phi_1 \wedge \phi_2 &&\Leftrightarrow w, \theta \models \phi_1 \text{ and } w, \theta \models \phi_2 \\
w, \theta &\models \exists x\ \phi(x) &&\Leftrightarrow \exists i \in [k, |w|-1] \text{ such that } w, \theta[x \mapsto i] \models \phi(x) \\
w, \theta &\models \exists X\ \phi(X) &&\Leftrightarrow \exists I \in 2^{[k,|w|-1]} \text{ such that } w, \theta[X \mapsto I] \models \phi(X)
\end{aligned}$$

Equivalence of S-MSO and *k-SLA*. To prove that *k-SLA* and S-MSO are equally expressive, the following extension of alphabet theories is helpful.

Definition 8. *The extension of an alphabet theory* $\mathcal{A} = (\Sigma, V, \Psi_V)$ *with a boolean variable* x *is a new alphabet theory* $\mathcal{A}_x = (\Sigma \times \{0,1\}, V, \Psi_V \times \{x = 0, x = 1\})$ *such that for any* $a \in \Sigma$ *and* $b, b' \in \{0,1\}$, $(a,b) \models (\varphi, x = b')$ *if and only if* $a \models_{\mathcal{A}} \varphi$ *and* $b = b'$. *We denote the extension by* n *boolean variables* $x_1, x_2, \ldots, x_n$ *by* $\mathcal{A}_{(x_1, x_2, \ldots, x_n)}$.

Let $x_1, \ldots, x_n$ denote first order variables and $X_1, \ldots, X_m$ denote the second order variables for an S-MSO formula ϕ. Given a word $w \in \Sigma^*$ and a map θ, let us define a word over extended alphabet theory $w_\theta \in (\Sigma \times \{0,1\}^{n+m})^*$ as

$$w_\theta[i] = (w[i], e_1(\theta(x_1), i), \ldots, e_1(\theta(x_n), i), e_2(\theta(X_1), i), \ldots e_2(\theta(X_m), i)),$$

where $e_1(n, i) = 1$ if $n = i$ else 0, and $e_2(I, i) = 1$ if $i \in I$ else 0. Recall that this is similar to the usual construction one does while showing equivalence of MSO and finite automata.

Lemma 6. *Let* $\mathcal{A} = (\Sigma, V, \Psi_V)$ *be an alphabet theory, and* $w \in \Sigma^*$ *be any word.*

- *For every S-MSO formula* ϕ *over the free variables* $\{x_1, \ldots, x_n, X_1, \ldots, X_m\}$, *there exists an k-SLA* S *over the extended alphabet theory* $\mathcal{A}_{(x_1, \ldots, x_n, X_1, \ldots, X_m)}$ *such that* $w \models \phi \iff w \in L(S)$.
- *For every k-SLA* S *there exists an equivalent S-MSO sentence* ϕ *such that* $w \in L(S) \iff w \models \phi$.

Proof (sketch). Let $\phi(x_1, \ldots, x_n, X_1, \ldots, X_m)$ be a S-MSO formula with first order free variables $\{x_1, \ldots, x_n\}$ and second order free variables $\{X_1, \ldots, X_n\}$. A construction similar to that of MSO over finite alphabets will give a *k-SLA* S over the extended alphabet theory $\mathcal{A}_{(x_1, \ldots, x_n, X_1, \ldots, X_m)}$, such that $w, \theta \models \phi$ if and only if the word $w_\theta \in (\Sigma \times \{0,1\}^{n+m})^*$ is accepted by S.

Conversely, given a *k-SLA* over the alphabet theory $\mathcal{A} = (\Sigma, V, \Psi_V)$, we can construct a S-MSO formula ϕ over $\mathcal{A}$ with no free variables such that $w \in \Sigma^*$ is accepted by S if and only if $w \models \phi$ using the standard automata to MSO construction and replacing the letters with predicates $\varphi \in \Phi_V$. □

The expressive power of symbolic lookback automata and symbolic MSO are useful for designing parsing algorithms and specification languages as we will see subsequently. But, unfortunately, the expressive power is enough to simulate Turing machines and static analysis problems are undecidable.

Theorem 1. *The problems of checking non-emptiness of languages of k-SLAs and satisfiability of S-MSO formulas are undecidable.*

Proof (sketch). The k-*SLA* automata work over infinite domains and transitions can relate values at a position with previous values. This can be used to simulate counter machines. The domain is the set $\mathbb{N}$ of natural numbers and the counters are simulated by numerical fields in the input stream. An incrementing transition of the counter machine can be simulated by a transition of a k-*SLA*, by requiring that the next value of the corresponding field is one more than the previous one. Decrementing and zero testing transitions can be similarly simulated. This is a standard trick used for models dealing with infinite domains, e.g., [10,11].

3 WEX: Defining Windows with S-MSO

A window in a data stream is a pair (i_b, i_e) of indices that indicate where the window begins and ends. In this section, we explain how windows can be defined with S-MSO over an alphabet theory $\mathcal{A}$, and also show an expressively equivalent representation using symbolic regular expressions. Some proofs omitted due to space constraints are available in the full version [16].

We designate first-order variables x_b, x_e for denoting the beginning and ending indices of windows. We use S-MSO formulas to specify which indices can begin and end windows. The end of a window should be detected as soon as it arrives in the stream, so the decision about whether a position is the end of a window should be made based only on the stream data that has been read so far. We enforce this in S-MSO formulas by guarding the quantifiers.

$$\phi := [\varphi](x) \mid x < x' \mid X(x) \mid \neg\phi \mid \phi \vee \phi \mid \exists x \leq x_e\ \phi \mid \exists X \subseteq [0, x_e]\ \phi \tag{1}$$

The above syntax is a guarded fragment of S-MSO—$\exists x \leq x_e\ \phi$ is syntactic sugar for $\exists x(x \leq x_e\ \wedge\ \phi)$ and $\exists X \subseteq [0, x_e]\ \phi$ is syntactic sugar for $\exists X(\forall y(X(y) \Rightarrow y \leq x_e)\ \wedge\ \phi)$.

Definition 9. *Let $x_b \leq x_e\ \wedge\ \phi(x_b, x_e)$ be a S-MSO formula in the guarded fragment given in* (1)*, with x_b and x_e being free variables. A pair (i_b, i_e) of indices of a word w is said to be a window recognized by $x_b \leq x_e\ \wedge\ \phi(x_b, x_e)$ if $i_b \leq i_e$ and $w \models \phi(i_b, i_e)$*

To reduce clutter, we don't explicitly write the condition $x_b \leq x_e$ but assume that it is present in all window specifications. Whether a pair (i_b, i_e) is recognized as a window by $\phi(x, y)$ in a word w depends only on the word $w[0 : i_e]$.

End users of streaming data processors may not be familiar with logic based languages. It's a general observation that specifications based on regular expressions are easier to understand compared to those based on logic. Next we give a way of defining windows based on symbolic regular expressions, that is expressively equivalent to the one above based on S-MSO.

Definition 10. *A Window EXpression (**WEX**) is a set $\mathcal{R} = \{(r_1, r_1'), \ldots (r_l, r_l')\}$. For every i, r_i, r_i' are symbolic regular expressions over an alphabet theory $\mathcal{A}$.*

Given a word $w \in \Sigma^*$, a pair $(i_b, i_e) \in [k, |w|-1]^2$ is said to be ***recognized as a window*** *by $\mathcal{R}$ if there exists $(r, r') \in \mathcal{R}$ such that $w[0 : i_b - 1] \in L(r)$ and $w[i_b - k : i_e] \in L(r')$.*

Intuitively, one can think of r as a *prefix automaton* that decides where the window can begin, and r' as a *window automaton* that decides where the window can end. We need to include the k proceeding symbols before i_b as r' is a k-*SLA* that needs access to k symbols to start reading from index i_b.

Lemma 7. *Given a S-MSO formula $\phi(x_b, x_e)$ in the guarded fragment given in* (1)*, we can effectively construct a window expression $\mathcal{R} = \{(r_1, r'_1), \ldots, (r_l, r'_l)\}$ such that for every word w, the set of windows recognized by $\phi(x_b, x_e)$ is the same as that recognized by $\mathcal{R}$.*

Proof (Sketch). We take the automaton corresponding to the S-MSO formula ϕ and split it at a transition that reads the symbol at position x_b. Each such split results in a pair of expressions.

Lemma 8. *Given a WEX $\mathcal{R} = \{(r_1, r'_1), \ldots, (r_l, r'_l)\}$ over $\mathcal{A}$, we can effectively construct a S-MSO formula $\phi(x_b, x_e)$ in the guarded fragment given in* (1) *such that, for every word w, the set of windows recognized by $\mathcal{R}$ is same as that recognized by $\phi(x_b, x_e)$.*

3.1 Examples from Practical Applications

In this section, we give a few examples from practical applications of stream processing, to illustrate how WEX can express queries with clearly specified semantics. Let us denote the atomic formula in alphabet theory that is always true by $\top$ with $L(\top) = \Sigma^{k+1}$.

1. Trends in stock markets Continuing the motivating example from the introduction, we formalize the windowing construct with WEX by fixing the theory of reals with lookback variable set $V = \{x_{-2}, x_{-1}, x_0\}$ as the alphabet theory. We first define the following atomic formulas: $D_2 := x_{-2} > x_{-1} \wedge x_{-1} > x_0$ and $U_1 := x_0 > x_{-1}$. The formula D_2 is true at a position if it follows two consecutive decrements in the average stock price, and U_1 is true at a position if the stock price has just increased. The WEX $R = (PA, WA)$ where $PA = \top^* \cdot_3 [D_2]$ and $WA = U_1 \cdot_3 [\neg D_2]^* \cdot_3 [D_2]$ precisely specifies the windowing construct illustrated in Fig. 2 that we wished to capture.

2. Arrhythmia Detection An ICD delivers shocks to restore normal heartbeat when it detects arrhythmia [1]. For our purposes, the input stream is a sequence $\{h_i\}_i$, where h_i is the ith measurement from a heartbeat spectrogram. A sequence value h_i is *peaking* if $h_i \geq \max(h_{i-1}, h_{i+1})$ and $h_i \geq p$, for some predefined threshold p.

We fix the theory of reals with $k = 2$ and three lookback variables $V = \{x_{-2}, x_{-1}, x_0\}$ as the alphabet theory. Let $R = (PA, WA)$ be a WEX, where $PA = \top^*$ and $WA = [x_{-1} > x_{-2} \wedge x_{-1} > x_0 \wedge x_{-1} > p]$. On processing an input stream with R, the output will be a stream of windows $w_i = hh'$, such that the first value h is peaking.

4 Window Overlap Problem

Consider the WEX $((a+b)^*, a^*b)$ over the finite alphabet $\Sigma = \{a, b\}$. A window can start at any position but must end at the letter b. Applied to the input stream $a^n b$, this WEX accepts $n+1$ windows, each of the form $a^i b$ for $i \in [0, n]$, all mutually overlapping. However, if we restrict the input streams to those that do not have a^c as an infix, for some constant c, the same WEX will always have a bound on the number overlapping windows. In particular, there are at most c overlapping windows at any time.

A natural problem arises to determine whether a given WEX allows unbounded number of overlapping windows. The answer to this depends on whether the input data stream follows any pattern in relation to the window expressions. This motivates formally defining the class of streams under consideration. As we will see later, other than the theoretical nicety, this problem has a practical importance in determining whether a stream processor can require unbounded amount of memory when processing a stream for a given WEX.

Input Specifier for Streams. To formalize which streams are to be considered, we use **input specifiers**, which are prefix-closed k-*SLA*s, i.e., if w is accepted then every prefix of w of length greater than k is also accepted. We can think of a specifying automaton S as being in an "accepting zone" or in a "rejecting zone", it starts in an accepting zone and switches to the rejecting zone at most once. A stream is said to *conform* to an input specifier if it never enters the rejecting zone while reading the stream.

Definition 11 (Window Overlap Problem). *Two windows* ***overlap*** *if the intervals defining them intersect. Given a WEX R and an input specifier S over alphabet theory $\mathcal{A}$, determine whether for each $n \in \mathbb{N}$, there exists a stream s_n conforming to S such that there exists at least n mutually overlapping windows accepted by R over the stream s_n.*

In general, the window overlap problem is undecidable, just like the problem of checking non-emptiness of languages of k-*SLA*s. We identify a fragment for which it is decidable.

Definition 12. *An alphabet theory $\mathcal{A} = (\Sigma, V, \Psi_V)$ is called* ***simple*** *if Ψ_V is restricted to boolean combination of atomic formulas of the form $R(x_1, \ldots, x_l)$, where R is a relation symbol. In particular, we don't allow quantifiers in formulae.*

Checking non-emptiness of the languages of a k-*SLA* over a simple alphabet theory is also undecidable, if the equality relation and one more relation symbol are present (see [10, Theorem 10.1]). Hence, the window overlap problem also remains undecidable over them.

We further restrict simple alphabet theories by adapting the concept of the *completion property* [10, Sect. 4].

Definition 13. *Suppose Φ is a set of atomic formulas over the set of variables V, $V' \subseteq V$ and $\Phi \upharpoonright V' \subseteq \Phi$ is the set of those formulas in Φ that only use variables in V'.*

A simple alphabet theory is said to have the ***completion property*** *if for every satisfiable set of formulas Φ, for every subset $V' \subseteq V$ and every partial valuation $v' : V' \rightarrow \Sigma$ that satisfies all the constraints in $\Phi \upharpoonright V'$, there exists an extension $v : V \rightarrow \Sigma$ of v' that satisfies all the constraints in Φ.*

The theory of integers with the binary relation $<$ does not satisfy the completion property. Consider the set of formulas $\{x < y, x < z, z < y\}$ and a partial valuation $v' : \{x \mapsto 1, y \mapsto 2\}$. It satisfies $x < y$, but it cannot be extended to include a mapping for z such that $x < z$ and $z < y$ (i.e., z is strictly between x and y), since there is no integer strictly between 1 and 2. The theory of rational or real numbers with $<$ satisfy the completion property. For theories with linear orders, the completion property is closely related to the denseness of the domain [10, Lemma 5.3]. Note that the completion property depends upon both the domain and the relations. For example, theory of rational or real numbers with the binary relations $<$ and $+$ (addition) does **not** have completion property.

Theorem 2. *The Window Overlap Problem is decidable for WEX over simple alphabet theory with completion property.*[1]

Lemma 9. *Given a WEX as a pair (PA, WA) of deterministic k-SLAs over an alphabet theory with the completion property, and an input specifier S, the number of overlapping windows will be unbounded over streams in S iff there exist words w_1, w_2, w_3 and a state q of WA such that*

1. *There is a path from q to a final state in which no transition has the guard $\bot$ (we say that q is not a dead state in this case),*
2. *in the input specifier S, $init_S \xrightarrow{w_1} s \xrightarrow{w_2} s \xrightarrow{w_3} s$, such that s is an accepting state,*
3. *$init_{PA} \xrightarrow{w_1} p \xrightarrow{w_2} p \xrightarrow{w_3} p$, where p is a final state of PA,*
4. *$init_{WA} \xrightarrow{w_1[:k]w_2} q$, $q \xrightarrow{w_1[:k]w_2} q \xrightarrow{w_3} q$ and*
5. *the runs $s \xrightarrow{w_1[:k]w_2} s \xrightarrow{w_3} s$, $p \xrightarrow{w_1[:k]w_2} p \xrightarrow{w_3} p$, $q \xrightarrow{w_1[:k]w_2} q \xrightarrow{w_3} q$ satisfy the following: the sequence of transitions used while reading the first k letters of w_2 is the same sequence used for reading the first k letters of w_3.*

Proof. ($\Rightarrow$) Let w be a stream conforming with S for which there are at least n overlapping windows. There must exist an increasing sequence of positions (or time instants) $(t_i)_i$ corresponding to the start index of the overlapping windows, such that $w_n[0 : t_i] \in L(PA)$. Let $w_n = w[0 : t_n]$.

Let Q_{PA}, Q_{WA}, Q_S be the set of states in PA, WA, S respectively. Let T_{PA}, T_{WA} and T_S be the set of k-tuples of transitions inPA, WA and S respectively. Let $\mathbb{T}$ be the set of all functions of the form $Q_{WA} \rightarrow T_{WA}$. We will use

[1] Recall that for finite alphabets, the set of formula Φ is an empty set. Therefore, they trivially are simple and have completion property.

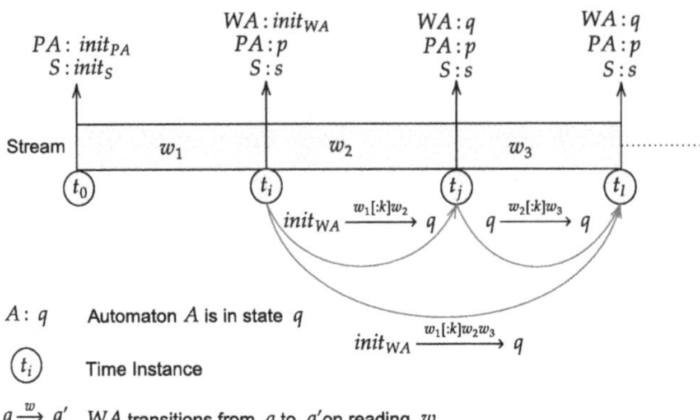

Fig. 3. Illustration of the stream used in Proof of Lemma 9.

the set of colors $C = \mathbb{T} \times 2^{Q_{WA} \times Q_{WA}}$ to color the edges of a graph we define later. Let r be the Ramsey number $R(n_1, n_2, \ldots, n_{|C|})$, where $n_1 = n_2 = \ldots = n_{|C|} = 2|Q_{PA}||Q_S||T_{PA}||T_S| + 1$. We set $n = r$ and construct a complete graph G with the set $\{t_i\}$ as vertices. For every two instants t_i, t_j with $i < j$, we add an edge with color $(T_i, \{(q_1, q_2) \mid q_1, q_2 \in Q_{WA}, q_1 \xrightarrow{w_n[t_i+1-k:t_j]} q_2\})$, where $T_i \in \mathbb{T}$ is the function such that $T_i(q)$ is the sequence of k transitions executed in *WA* if it starts at the instant t_i in state q. We infer from Ramsey's theorem that the graph G will have a monochromatic clique of size $2|Q_{PA}||Q_S||T_{PA}||T_S| + 1$.

We infer from the pigeonhole principle that this monochromatic clique contains at least three time instants, say $t_i < t_j < t_l$, at which *PA* and S are in the same pair of states, say p in *PA* and s in S, both of which are accepting states in their respective automata. Also, the sequence of k transitions executed in *PA* (resp. S) from t_i, t_j, t_l are same. Now, consider the instances of window automaton *WA* initiated at the instants t_i, t_j and t_l.

Fig. 3 may help parse the following argument. Let $init_{WA} \xrightarrow{w_n[t_i+1-k:t_j]} q$ for some state q. Since the edges between t_i, t_j, t_l all have the same color, $init_{WA} \xrightarrow{w_n[t_i+1-k:t_l]} q$. Since *WA* is deterministic and $t_i < t_j < t_l$, we can split $init_{WA} \xrightarrow{w_n[t_i+1-k:t_l]} q$ into $init_{WA} \xrightarrow{w_n[t_i+1-k:t_j]} q$ and $q \xrightarrow{w_n[t_j+1-k:t_l]} q$. Since (t_i, t_j) and (t_j, t_l) have the same colour, we infer that $q \xrightarrow{w_n[t_i+1-k:t_j]} q$. Let $w_1 = w_n[0 : t_i]$, $w_2 = w_n[t_i + 1 : t_j]$ and $w_3 = w_n[t_j + 1 : t_l]$. We have $init_{PA} \xrightarrow{w_1} p \xrightarrow{w_2} p \xrightarrow{w_3} p$, $init_S \xrightarrow{w_1} s \xrightarrow{w_2} s \xrightarrow{w_3} s$, p (resp. s) is accepting in *PA* (resp. S), $init_{WA} \xrightarrow{w_1[:k]w_2} q$, $q \xrightarrow{w_1[:k]w_2} q \xrightarrow{w_3} q$ and the runs $s \xrightarrow{w_1[:k]w_2} s \xrightarrow{w_3} s, p \xrightarrow{w_1[:k]w_2} p \xrightarrow{w_3} p, q \xrightarrow{w_1[:k]w_2} q \xrightarrow{w_3} q$ satisfy the following: the sequence of transitions used while reading the first k letters of w_2 is the same sequence used for reading the first k letters of w_3.

($\Leftarrow$) We will construct a word $w^i = w_1 \cdot w_2^0 \cdots w_2^i$ for each $i \geq 0$ such that $init_S \xrightarrow{w^i} s$, $init_{PA} \xrightarrow{w^i} p$ and $init_{WA} \xrightarrow{w_2^0} q \xrightarrow{w_2^1} \cdots q \xrightarrow{w_2^i} q$. We let $w^{-1} = w_1$ for convenience. For every i, there will be a new window starting at $|w_1|+|w_2^0 \cdots w_2^i|$. The state $init_{WA}$ will be updated to q after reading w_2^{i+1} and keeps coming back to q after reading w_2^j for $j > i+1$. Therefore, none of these windows will close during the processing of w_i. Since q is not a dead state, the stream can be extended with a suffix to realize arbitrarily many overlapping windows. All w_2^i will be built from w_2 using the completion property, ensuring that w_2^{i+1} makes the automaton behave exactly like w_2^i did. We will do this with an inductive construction, for which we need to introduce some terminology.

Suppose w is a stream. Consider the substring of w between positions $i-k$ to i. We would like to capture the constraints put on this substring by some transition τ executed by an automaton at the $(i+j)^{\text{th}}$ position, where $j \in [0,k]$. For that transition, the values for lookback variables $x_{-k}, \ldots, x_{-j}$ are given by $w[i-k+j], \ldots, w[i]$ respectively. For a transition τ and $j \in [0,k]$, let $\Phi(\tau) \upharpoonright j$ be the set of all atomic formulas ϕ occurring in the guard of τ such that only the lookback variables $x_{-k}, \ldots, x_{-j}$ are used in ϕ. For such an atomic formula ϕ, let $\phi[\rightarrow j]$ be the formula obtained from ϕ by replacing every lookback variable x_{-l} by x_{-l+j} (this results in the values for lookback variables $x_{-k+j}, \ldots, x_0$ of $\phi[\rightarrow j]$ being given by $w[i-k+j], \ldots, w[i]$ respectively). In the run $init_S \xrightarrow{w_1} s \xrightarrow{w_2} s \xrightarrow{w_3} s$, let τ_i be the transition executed while reading the ith letter of w_2w_3. For $i \in [0, |w_2|-1]$, the constraints satisfied by the substring $w_1w_2[|w_1|+i-k : |w_1|+i]$ for this run is $\cup_{j\in[0,k]}\{\phi[\rightarrow j] \mid \phi \in \Phi(\tau_{i+j}) \upharpoonright j, v_V(w_1w_2[|w_1|+i-k : |w_1|+i]) \models \phi[\rightarrow j]\} \cup \cup_{j\in[0,k]}\{\neg\phi[\rightarrow j] \mid \phi \in \Phi(\tau_{i+j}) \upharpoonright j, v_V(w_1w_2[|w_1|+i-k : |w_1|+i]) \not\models \phi[\rightarrow j]\}$. Let us call this set Γ_i^S. We similarly define the set Γ_i^P for the run $init_{PA} \xrightarrow{w_1} p \xrightarrow{w_2} p \xrightarrow{w_3} p$. In the run $q \xrightarrow{w_1[:k]w_2} q \xrightarrow{w_3} q'$, let τ_i be the transition executed while reading the ith letter of w_2w_3. For $i \in [0, |w_2|-1]$, the constraints satisfied by the substring $(w_1[:k]w_2)[i:i+k]$ for this run is $\cup_{j\in[0,k]}\{\phi[\rightarrow j] \mid \phi \in \Phi(\tau_{i+j}) \upharpoonright j, v_V((w_1[:k]w_2)[i:i:k]) \models \phi[\rightarrow j]\} \cup \cup_{j\in[0,k]}\{\neg\phi[\rightarrow j] \mid \phi \in \Phi(\tau_{i+j}) \upharpoonright j, v_V((w_1[:k]w_2)[i:i+k]) \not\models \phi[\rightarrow j]\}$. Let us call this set Γ_i^W.

We claim that for every $i \geq 0$, there exists string w_2^i such that $|w_2^i| = |w_2|$ and for every $j \in [0, |w_2|-1]$, $v_V(w^i[|w^{i-1}|+j-k : |w^{i-1}|+j])$ satisfies all the constraints in $\Gamma_j^S \cup \Gamma_j^P \cup \Gamma_j^W$. This is sufficient to establish the result, since all the automata S, PA, WA can repeat the same sequence of transitions for w_2^{i+1} as the sequence for w_2^i. We prove the claim by induction on i. For the base case $i = 0$, we set $w_2^0 = w_2$ and the claim is satisfied by definition. For the induction step, suppose we have defined up to w_2^i as claimed. We define $w_2^{i+1}[j]$ for every $j \in [0, |w_2|-1]$ by secondary induction on j.

For the base case, $j = 0$, by the primary induction hypothesis, $v_V(w^i[:k+1])$ satisfies all the constraints in $\Gamma_{|w_2|-1}^S \cup \Gamma_{|w_2|-1}^P \cup \Gamma_{|w_2|-1}^W$. Let $V' = V \setminus \{x_0\}$. Since the first k transitions for w_3 are same as the first k transitions for w_2, we infer that $v_{V'}(w^i[:k])$ satisfies those formulas in $\Gamma_0^S \cup \Gamma_0^P \cup \Gamma_0^W$ that don't use x_0. By the completion property, $v_{V'}(w^i[:k])$ can be extended to include a valuation for x_0 so that the resulting valuation satisfies all the formulas in $\Gamma_0^S \cup \Gamma_0^P \cup \Gamma_0^W$. This new valuation for x_0 is the value we set for $w_2^{i+1}[0]$. The induction step for $j+1$ is similar. This completes the induction step and hence establishes the result. □

Deciding the Window Overlap Problem. The characterization of Lemma 9 can now be used to obtain a decision procedure for the window overlap problem, provided the alphabet theory itself is decidable. This involves checking that there exist words w_1, w_2, w_3 as claimed above, which can be done using symbolic models, which decompose the problem into an automata-theoretic problem over finite alphabets and satisfiability of formulas in the alphabet theory.

Decidability for window overlap problem for decidable alphabet theories with the completion property can be proven by using techniques similar to those of [10, Theorem 4.4] (attributed originally to [3]). This, when converted to terminology used in this paper, states that *checking non-emptiness of the language of a k-SLA can be reduced to checking satisfiability of a finite set of formulas in the alphabet theory, provided it is simple and has the completion property.*

5 Stream Processor for WEX with Panes

In this section, we present the pseudocode of a stream processor that takes a WEX and incoming streaming data and produces windows as specified in the expressions. For modeling purposes, we treat a stream as an infinite string in Σ^ω. The data present in a window is usually processed to produce an aggregate value, such as the average of some field, sum of all entries in a window, etc. If some positions of the stream belong to multiple windows, performing the same computation multiple times could be inefficient. One way to avoid this is to subdivide windows into *panes* [18] and then aggregate the values of those panes that make up a window. For example, suppose the average of a numerical field is to be computed for every window. If within the span of a window, other windows start, then the window is subdivided into panes as shown in Fig. 4.

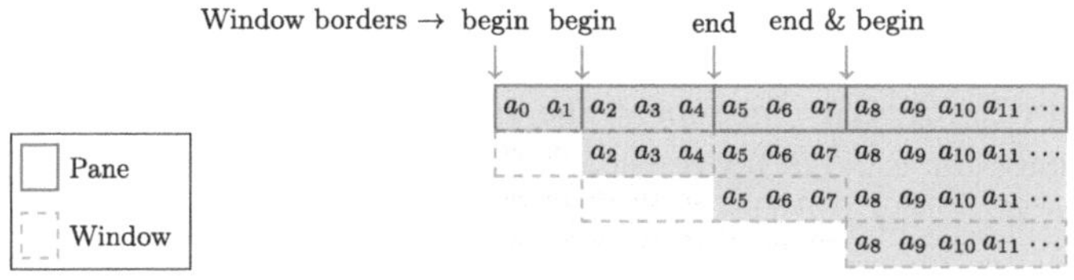

Fig. 4. Paning: Start a new pane at each instant when a window begins or ends.

For each pane, the average and number of entries in the tuple is computed and stored. When the window ends, these can be used to compute the average of the whole window. The exact computation to be performed in panes is application dependent. We assume that a class is provided to do that computation. In our processor, we ensure that the class methods are called at the correct positions in the stream.

The pseudocode of the processor is shown in Algorithm 1. For simplicity of presentation, we show the processor for one pair of expressions (r, r'). We further assume that the pair has been converted to a pair (PA, WA) of prefix and window k-*SLA*, both deterministic. It is routine to extend the processor to handle multiple pairs. The main idea is that we run the prefix automaton, and whenever it reaches a final state, we spawn a new copy of window automaton. A new window is produced when one of the spawned window automaton reaches its final state. We also perform *garbage collection* by removing window automaton which are in dead state.

The variable *PrefixState* stores the current state of the prefix automaton *PA*. The variable *WindowStartIndices* stores a mapping $\mathit{WindowStartIndices} : Q \to 2^{\mathbb{N}}$, which tracks multiple copies of the window automaton *WA*, as explained next. A copy of *WA* is started at any position of the input stream that is potentially a start position of a window. If such a copy started at position x is currently in state q, then $x \in \mathit{WindowStartIndices}(q)$. In other words, all the copies of *WA* that are currently in state q are tracked by storing their starting positions in $\mathit{WindowStartIndices}(q)$.

Simultaneously, we generate panes with the following strategy:

- Start a new pane at every possible beginning of a new window, i.e., whenever the prefix automaton reaches an accepting state.
- End the current pane whenever a new pane must be created because a window begins or ends

The correctness of the algorithm, formalized in the following results, follows directly from algorithm's execution.

Lemma 10 (Main loop invariant). *The following hold at the start of every iteration of the main loop of the processor (line 9), where n is the position of the last symbol read from the input channel I :*

1. *PrefixState stores the state of PA after reading $w[0:n]$.*
2. *For every position $i < n$ such that PA reaches a final state on reading $w[0:i]$, if $init_{WA} \xrightarrow{w[i+1:n]} q$ and q is not a dead-state, then $i+1 \in \mathit{WindowStartIndices}(q)$.*

Corollary 1. *The processor produced by the Algorithm 1, given the input pair (PA, WA) and the stream w, will add $(x+1, y)$ to the output stream iff $w[0:x] \in L(PA)$ and $w[x+1:y] \in L(WA)$.*

Memory Requirement of Stream Processor. In the processor produced by the Algorithm 1, *WindowStartIndices* and P are variables that store starting positions of windows and panes respectively. If the number of starting positions or the number of panes is too large, the memory required to store them will also be large. It is decidable to check whether the memory requirement is unbounded for a given WEX and input specifier, when the alphabet theory has the completion property, as this problem is equivalent to the window overlap problem.

Input : A pair of k-*SLA*s $\mathcal{R} = (PA, WA)$, channels I, O for input, output
Result: Stream from I decomposed into windows according to $\mathcal{R}$ and output into O
Nomenclature: Q, Q': set of states of *PA*, *WA*
Function *main* **is**

```
    PrefixState := q0 ;                          /* q0 is the initial state of PA */
    WindowStartIndices(q') := ∅ for all q' ∈ Q';
    w_block := read first k elements of I;
    x := k − 1;
    p := new Pane(StartIndex = 0, EndIndex = k − 1);
    Update value of p to the aggregate of w_block;
    P := {p} ;                                   /* P is the set of Panes */
9   while input stream I is live do
        σ := next item in I;
        w_block := w_block[−k + 1 : 0] · σ;
        startNewPane := False;
        if PrefixState is a final state of PA then
14          Add the index (x + 1) to WindowStartIndices(init_WA) (init_WA is the
             initial sate of WA);
            startNewPane := True;
        end
        foreach q_f ∈ Q' such that q_f is a final state of WA and
             WindowStartIndices(q_f) ≠ ∅ do
19          Add (x', x) to the output stream O for each index
             x' ∈ WindowStartIndices(q_f), along with the aggregate of those
             panes in P that are between x' and x;
            startNewPane := True;
        end
        foreach q_d ∈ Q' such that q_d is a dead state of WA do
            WindowStartIndices(q_d) := ∅;
        end
        if startNewPane == True then
            p.EndIndex = x; p = newPane(); P.add(p);
        end
        p.add_element(σ) ;      /* update the current pane with the newly
         read symbol */
        Let x_min be the minimum of the indices in the range of
         WindowStartIndices;
        From P, delete those panes that end before x_min;
        Update PrefixState to new state of PA by reading w_block;
        foreach {q ∈ Q'} do
            Q_pred = {q' ∈ Q' | q is the w_block successor of q' in WA};
34          WindowStartIndices'(q) = ∪_{q'∈Q_pred} WindowStartIndices(q');
        end
36      WindowStartIndices := WindowStartIndices' ;          /* simultaneous
         update */
        x += 1;
    end
end
```

Algorithm 1: Stream processor to extract windows from a stream

6 Conclusion

A common feature is to process data from multiple streams simultaneously, to perform computations. An open problem is to integrate this feature into the formal framework of WEX. Another important direction is to characterize the fragments with decidable window overlap problem beyond the completion property. It would also be valuable to study the complexity of this problem, the heuristics and algorithms that can perform well in practice. Finally, an orthogonal direction is to investigate query optimization over WEX, i.e., finding an equivalent WEX with lower memory or computational requirements.

Acknowledgment. We thank the anonymous reviewers for their critical reading of our paper and valuable feedback, which greatly improved its quality.

References

1. Abbas, H., et al.: Quantitative regular expressions for arrhythmia detection. IEEE/ACM Trans. Comput. Biol. Bioinf. **16**(5), 1586–1597 (2019). https://doi.org/10.1109/TCBB.2018.2885274
2. Alur, R., Mamouras, K., Stanford, C.: Modular quantitative monitoring. Proc. ACM Program. Lang. **3**(POPL) (2019). https://doi.org/10.1145/3290363
3. Balbiani, P., Condotta, J.F.: Computational complexity of propositional linear temporal logics based on qualitative spatial or temporal reasoning. In: FroCoS, pp. 162–176. Springer-Verlag, Berlin, Heidelberg (2002)
4. Baumeister, J., Finkbeiner, B., Schirmer, S., Schwenger, M., Torens, C.: Rtlola cleared for take-off: monitoring autonomous aircraft (2020). https://arxiv.org/abs/2004.06488
5. Codd, E.F.: Relational completeness of data base sublanguages. In: Database Systems, pp. 65–98. Prentice-Hall (1972)
6. Cugola, G., Margara, A.: Processing flows of information: from data stream to complex event processing. ACM Comput. Surv. **44**(3) (2012). https://doi.org/10.1145/2187671.2187677
7. D'Angelo, B., et al.: Lola: runtime monitoring of synchronous systems. In: 12th International Symposium on Temporal Representation and Reasoning (TIME'05), pp. 166–174 (2005). https://api.semanticscholar.org/CorpusID:15173372
8. D'Antoni, L., Veanes, M.: Monadic second-order logic on finite sequences. SIGPLAN Not. **52**(1), 232–245 (2017). https://doi.org/10.1145/3093333.3009844
9. D'Antoni, L., Veanes, M.: The power of symbolic automata and transducers. In: Computer Aided Verification, pp. 47–67. Springer (2017)
10. Demri, S., D'Souza, D.: An automata-theoretic approach to constraint LTL. Inf. Comput. **205**(3), 380–415 (2007). https://doi.org/10.1016/j.ic.2006.09.006
11. D'Antoni, L., Veanes, M.: Extended symbolic finite automata and transducers. Formal Meth. Syst. Des. **47**(1), 93–119 (2015). https://doi.org/10.1007/s10703-015-0233-4
12. EsperTech: Esper. https://www.espertech.com/esper/
13. Fagin, R., Kimelfeld, B., Reiss, F., Vansummeren, S.: Document spanners: a formal approach to information extraction. J. ACM **62**(2), 1–51 (2015). https://doi.org/10.1145/2699442

14. Faymonville, P., Finkbeiner, B., Schirmer, S., Torfah, H.: A stream-based specification language for network monitoring. In: Runtime Verification: 16th International Conference, RV 2016, Madrid, Spain, September 23–30, 2016, Proceedings, pp. 152–168. Springer (2016)
15. Grez, A., Riveros, C., Ugarte, M.: A formal framework for complex event processing. In: ICDT. LIPIcs, vol. 127, pp. 5:1–5:18. Schloss Dagstuhl, Dagstuhl, Germany (2019). https://doi.org/10.4230/LIPIcs.ICDT.2019.5
16. Hitarth, S., Praveen, M.: Wex: formal specifications for windows in stream processing (2025). https://arxiv.org/abs/2209.04244
17. IBM Research: IBM system S. https://researcher.watson.ibm.com/researcher/view_group_subpage.php?id=2534
18. Li, J., Maier, D., Tufte, K., Papadimos, V., Tucker, P.A.: No pane, no gain: efficient evaluation of sliding-window aggregates over data streams. SIGMOD Rec. **34**(1), 39–44 (2005). https://doi.org/10.1145/1058150.1058158
19. Mamouras, K., Raghothaman, M., Alur, R., Ives, Z.G., Khanna, S.: StreamQRE: modular specification and efficient evaluation of quantitative queries over streaming data. In: PLDI, pp. 693–708. ACM, New York, NY, USA (2017). https://doi.org/10.1145/3062341.3062369
20. Patroumpas, K., Sellis, T.: Window specification over data streams. In: EDBT, pp. 445–464. Springer (2006)
21. Perera, S., Suhothayan, S.: Solution patterns for realtime streaming analytics. In: Proceedings of the 9th ACM International Conference on Distributed Event-Based Systems, pp. 247–255. DEBS '15, ACM (2015). https://doi.org/10.1145/2675743.2774214
22. Petit, L., Labbé, C., Roncancio, C.L.: An algebric window model for data stream management. In: Proceedings of the Ninth ACM International Workshop on Data Engineering for Wireless and Mobile Access, pp. 17–24. ACM (2010). https://doi.org/10.1145/1850822.1850826
23. Vardi, M.Y.: The rise and fall of LTL. In: GandALF (2011)
24. Veanes, M., de Halleux, P., Tillmann, N.: Rex: Symbolic regular expression explorer. In: 2010 Third International Conference on Software Testing, Verification and Validation, pp. 498–507 (2010). https://doi.org/10.1109/ICST.2010.15
25. Wang, F., Liu, P.: Temporal management of RFID data. In: Proceedings of the 31st International Conference on Very Large Data Bases, pp. 1128–1139. VLDB '05, VLDB Endowment (2005)

Efficient Algorithms for Partial Constraint Satisfaction Problems over Control-Flow Graphs

Xuran Cai(✉) and Amir Kafshdar Goharshady

Department of Computer Science, University of Oxford, Oxford, UK
{xuran.cai,amir.goharshady}@cs.ox.ac.uk

Abstract. In this work, we focus on the Partial Constraint Satisfaction Problem (PCSP) over control-flow graphs (CFGs) of programs. PCSP serves as a generalization of the well-known Constraint Satisfaction Problem (CSP). In the CSP framework, we define a set of variables, a set of constraints, and a finite domain D that encompasses all possible values for each variable. The objective is to assign a value to each variable in such a way that all constraints are satisfied. In the graph variant of CSP, an underlying graph is considered, and we have one variable corresponding to each vertex of the graph and one or several constraints corresponding to each edge. In PCSPs, we allow for certain constraints to be violated at a specified cost, aiming to find a solution that minimizes the total cost. Numerous classical compiler optimization tasks can be framed as PCSPs over control-flow graphs. Examples include Register Allocation, Lifetime-optimal Speculative Partial Redundancy Elimination (LOSPRE), and Optimal Placement of Bank Selection Instructions. On the other hand, it is well-known that control-flow graphs of structured programs are sparse and decomposable in a variety of ways. In this work, we rely on the Series-Parallel-Loop (SPL) decompositions as introduced by [7]. Our main contribution is a general algorithm for PCSPs over SPL graphs with a time complexity of $O(|G| \cdot |D|^6)$, where $|G|$ represents the size of the control-flow graph. Note that for any fixed domain D, this yields a linear-time solution. Our algorithm can be seen as a generalization and unification of previous SPL-based approaches for register allocation and LOSPRE. In addition, we provide experimental results over another classical PCSP task, i.e., Optimal Bank Selection, achieving runtimes four times better than the previous state of the art.

Keywords: Structured Programs · Compiler Optimization · Control-flow Graphs · Graph Decompositions · Partial Constraint Satisfaction Problems

1 Introduction

CSP and PCSP. Constraint Satisfaction Problems (CSPs) provide an expressive framework for a wide variety of tasks in different fields, especially in compiler optimization. CSPs involve determining values for variables while adhering

A. Goharshady and C. Haase (Eds.): SETTA 2025, LNCS 16458, pp. 277–295, 2026.
https://doi.org/10.1007/978-981-95-7826-9_15

to constraints that define permissible combinations of these values [25]. Many common graph-related problems, such as the graph coloring problem, can be formulated as CSPs. However, there are instances where it may be infeasible or impractical to find complete solutions that satisfy every constraint. In such cases, we may aim for partial solutions, specifically by satisfying the maximum number of constraints or assigning a cost to each unsatisfied constraint and minimizing the total cost, which comes to the area of Partial Constraint Satisfaction Problems(PSCPs) [30].

PCSPs have a wide array of applications. A notable example that translates elegantly into the PCSP framework is the MAX-SAT problem [31]. Additionally, various compiler optimization tasks, particularly those related to graph theory, can be represented as PCSPs. Examples include register allocation [7], lifetime-optimal speculative partial redundancy elimination [6], and optimal placement of bank selection instructions [32].

The NP-hardness of PCSPs, even with a domain size of 3, is established through an easy reduction from the 3-coloring problem in graphs. In [31], it was shown via a reduction from MAX-SAT that PCSPs are NP-hard even when all domains are restricted to size two. Computational experiments support these findings in practical scenarios [31].

Efficient PCSP Algorithms. Although both CSP and PCSP are NP-hard, efficient polynomial-time algorithms exist when the underlying primal graph is a tree or has a tree-like structure [18,24,35]. Even in the absence of such structures, recognizing that a problem can be viewed as containing a tree or being part of a tree-like structure remains beneficial and leads to effective heuristics [18,19]. A significant advancement in PCSP algorithms was obtained by [30], utilizing tree decompositions. This approach provides an efficient parameterized algorithm based on the treewidth of the graph. Treewidth is a measure of tree-likeness. Intuitively speaking, graphs of treewidth t can be decomposed into small sets of vertices, each of size at most $t+1$ that are connected to each other in a tree-like formation.

Control-flow Graphs and their Sparsity. The control-flow graph (CFG) of a program is defined as a graph where each vertex represents a statement in the program, and a directed edge exists between two vertices if their corresponding statements can be executed in succession. Some applications adopt a slightly coarser definition of CFGs, where each vertex corresponds to a basic block of program statements. In both instances, it is well established that the control-flow graphs of real-world programs are sparse, often resembling trees, and can be decomposed into sets of vertices, each containing at most 8 vertices that are interconnected in a tree-like fashion. More formally, CFGs of structured goto-free programs have a treewidth of at most 7 [40]. This notable result has been leveraged in various areas, including program analysis, compiler optimization, and model checking, where the small treewidth property enables faster algorithms for μ-calculus model checking [36], data-flow analysis [11,27], Markov Decision Processes (MDPs) [1,3,15], reachability analysis [9,37], algebraic program analysis [10,14,16], register allocation [4,33], cache management [2,12], and equality saturation [26].

The original treewidth bound established in [40] applied to Pascal and C programs, but subsequent research has extended this result to other programming languages, including Ada [5], Java [13,29], and Solidity [8], as well as to path decompositions [17]. However, there are also negative findings indicating that bounded treewidth does not always facilitate verification [22].

In the context of register allocation, the recent work [7] introduced a new decomposition concept known as Series-Parallel-Loop (SPL), which precisely captures the set of control-flow graphs for structured goto-free programs and formalizes their sparsity. We build upon the same decomposition concept but show that it has a much higher potential than the authors of [7] imagined and can be exploited to solve a significantly wider family of problems than the register allocation task investigated in [7].

Our Contribution. In this work, we focus on the general family of Partial Constraint Satisfaction Problems (PCSPs) over the CFGs of structured goto-free programs. Our approach is a generalization of [7] and [6], and thus contains register allocation and LOSPRE as special cases. We develop a *linear-time* algorithm for PCSPs. Specifically, we leverage the sparsity of CFGs and their SPL decompositions to design an algorithm with a runtime of $O(n \cdot |D|^6)$, where n is the number of lines in the program and D is the domain of variables. Unlike the method in [30], we do not rely on tree decompositions. Thus, there is no extra parameter such as treewidth. Instead, we use SPL decompositions [7]. This choice results in a significantly simpler algorithm since SPL decompositions accurately represent the set of CFGs, allowing us to avoid solving the problem on a broader set of graphs than necessary. Moreover, SPL decompositions take into account the direction of edges in the CFG.

On the experimental side, we apply our general solution to the problem of Optimal Placement of Bank Selection Instructions, comparing it with the state-of-the-art approach of [32]. The simplicity of our algorithm yields practical benefits. We present extensive experimental results conducted on the Small Device C Compiler (SDCC), a highly optimized compiler based on [20,21]. Our algorithm achieves substantial performance improvements over [32].

Organization. Section 2 presents a formal definition of SPL decompositions, following [7]. Section 3 covers our main contribution: a linear-time algorithm for general PCSPs over control-flow graphs that exploits SPL decompositions. This is followed by the example use-case in Bank Selection in Sect. 4. Finally, Sect. 5 reports our experimental results.

2 SPL Decompositions

We will build our algorithm on top of a decomposition method introduced in [7]. This decomposition method is called SPL (Series-Parallel-Loop) and is an extension of series-parallel graphs with an extra loop operation. It is shown in [7] that a graph is a CFG of a structured program if and only if it has an SPL decomposition.

Structured Programs. [40] We say a program is structured if it can be generated using the following grammar:

$$\begin{aligned} P := \epsilon \mid \texttt{break} \mid \texttt{continue} \mid P; P \\ \mid \texttt{if } \varphi \texttt{ then } P \texttt{ else } P \texttt{ fi} \mid \texttt{while } \varphi \texttt{ do } P \texttt{ od}. \end{aligned} \tag{1}$$

Here, ϵ is any atomic operation that has no effect on control flow, such as an assignment to a variable. It is easy to define other structures such as `for` and `switch` as syntactic sugar. See [40] for details. We say a program generated by the grammar above is *closed* if every `break` and `continue` statement appears inside a `while` loop's body.

SPL Graphs. [7] An SPL graph $G = (V, E, S, T, B, C)$ is a directed graph (V, E) with four distinct special nodes $S, T, B, C \in V$, which are respectively called the *start*, *terminate*, *break* and *continue* nodes, generated by the grammar below:

$$G := A_\epsilon \mid A_{\texttt{break}} \mid A_{\texttt{continue}} \mid G \otimes G \mid G \oplus G \mid G^{\circledast} \tag{2}$$

We now explain the atomic graphs and operations in this grammar.

Atomic SPL Graphs. There are three different atomic SPL graphs: A_ϵ, $A_{\texttt{break}}$, and $A_{\texttt{continue}}$, corresponding to the programs ϵ, `break` and `continue`, respectively. All of them contain only the four special nodes and only one edge as shown in Fig. 1.

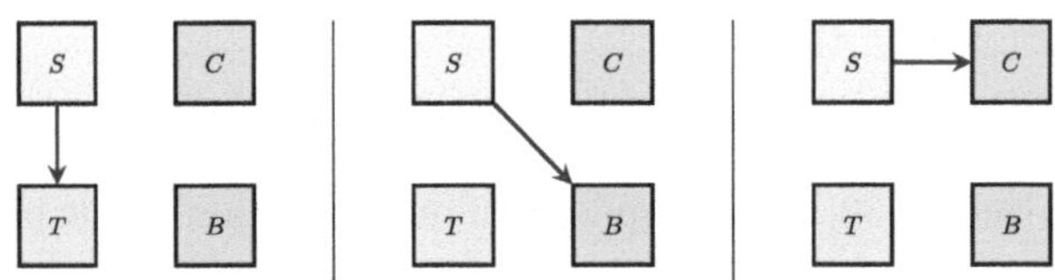

Fig. 1. Atomic SPL graphs: A_ϵ (left), $A_{\texttt{break}}$ (middle), and $A_{\texttt{continue}}$ (right) [7].

SPL Operations. SPL defines three operations. Let $G_1 = (V_1, E_1, S_1, T_1, B_1, C_1)$ and $G_2 = (V_2, E_2, S_2, T_2, B_2, C_2)$ be two disjoint SPL graphs. Then, the graphs obtained by the following operations are also SPL graphs.

1. *Series Operation.* $G_1 \otimes G_2$ is generated by taking the union of G_1 and G_2 and merging the pairs of vertices $M = (T_1, S_2)$, $B = (B_1, B_2)$, and $C = (C_1, C_2)$. The distinguished vertices of $G_1 \otimes G_2$ are (S_1, T_2, B, C). It is easy to verify that the series operation is associative. Figure 2 shows two examples of the series operation. Intuitively, if G_1 is the CFG of a program P_1 and G_2 is the CFG of P_2 then $G_1 \otimes G_2$ is the CFG of the program $P_1; P_2$.

2. *Parallel Operation.* $G_1 \oplus G_2$ is generated by taking union of G_1 and G_2 and merging the pairs of vertices $S = (S_1, S_2)$, $T = (T_1, T_2)$, $B = (B_1, B_2)$, and $C = (C_1, C_2)$. The special vertex tuple of $G_1 \otimes G_2$ is (S, T, B, C). Fig. 3 shows an example of this operation. Informally, if G_1 and G_2 are the CFGs of the programs P_1 and P_2, respectively, then $G_1 \oplus G_2$ is the CFG of the program `if` φ `then` P_1 `else` P_2 `fi`.
3. *Loop Operation.* $G_1^{\circledast}$ is generated by adding four new vertices S, T, B, C to G_1 and then adding the following edges: $(S, S_1), (S, T), (T_1, S), (C_1, S)$, and (B_1, T). The special vertex tuple of $G_1^{\circledast}$ is (S, T, B, C). Fig. 4 shows an example of the loop operation. Intuitively, if G_1 is the CFG of the program P_1, then $G_1^{\circledast}$ is the CFG of the loop with P_1 as its body, i.e. `while` φ `do` P_1 `od`.

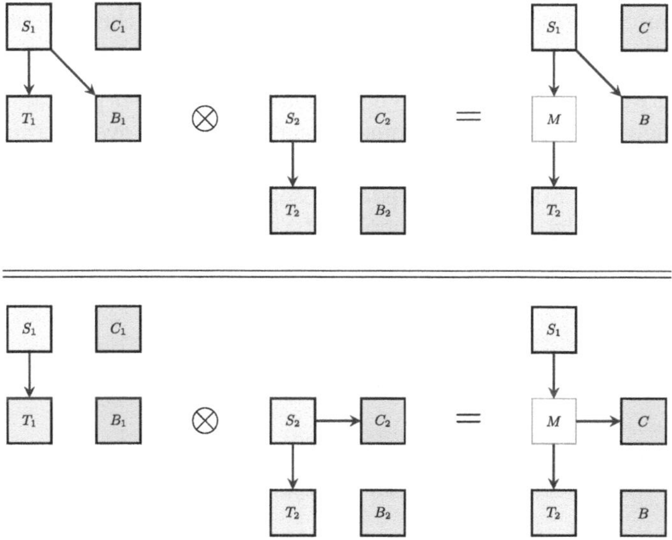

Fig. 2. Two examples of the series operation $\otimes$, taken from [7].

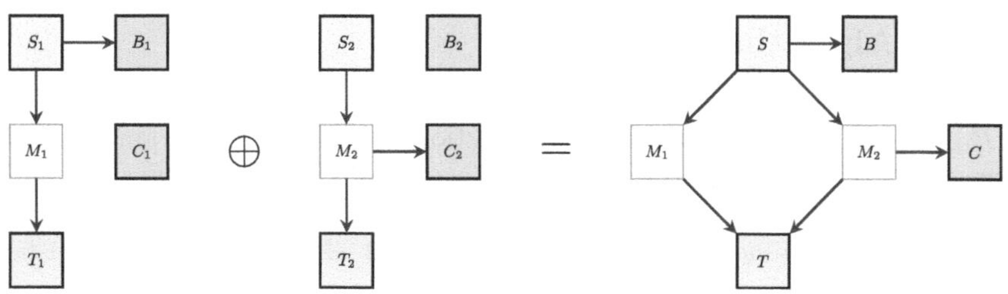

Fig. 3. An example of the parallel operation $\oplus$ [7].

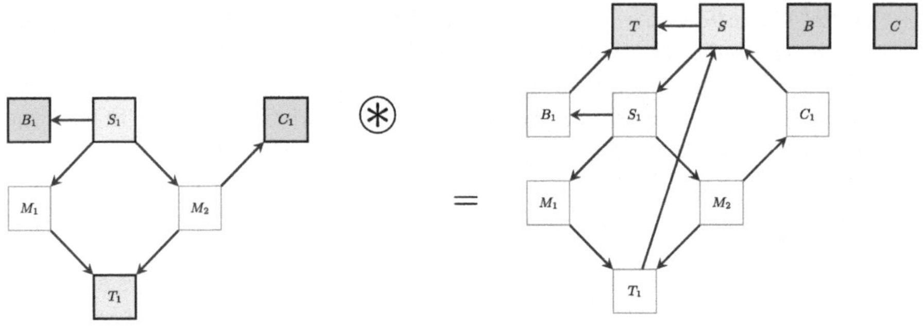

Fig. 4. An example of the loop operation $^{\circledast}$ [7].

We say an SPL graph $G = (V, E, S, T, B, C)$ is *closed* if there are no incoming edges to the vertices B and C.

SPLs as CFGs. Given the above definitions of structured programs and SPL graphs, we have the following homomorphism which maps every structured program to its control-flow graph. Moreover, this homomorphism preserves closedness, i.e. closed programs are mapped to closed graphs. A graph is an SPL graph if and only if it is the control-flow graph of a program [7].

$$\mathsf{cfg}(\epsilon) = A_\epsilon \;\; \mathsf{cfg}(\texttt{break}) = A_{\texttt{break}} \;\; \mathsf{cfg}(\texttt{continue}) = A_{\texttt{continue}}$$

$$\mathsf{cfg}(P_1; P_2) = \mathsf{cfg}(P_1) \otimes \mathsf{cfg}(P_2)$$

$$\mathsf{cfg}(\texttt{if}\ \varphi\ \texttt{then}\ P_1\ \texttt{else}\ P_2\ \texttt{fi}) = \mathsf{cfg}(P_1) \oplus \mathsf{cfg}(P_2)$$

$$\mathsf{cfg}(\texttt{while}\ \varphi\ \texttt{do}\ P_1\ \texttt{od}) = \mathsf{cfg}(P_1)^{\circledast}$$

SPL Decompositions. Given a closed program P, we can first parse it based on the grammar (1) to generate a parse tree. Subsequently, by applying the homomorphism above to this parse tree, we can derive a parse tree according to (2) for its control-flow graph. We use the term *SPL decomposition* to refer to the parse tree of the CFG according to (2). It is easy to verify that this process takes linear time. See Fig. 5 as an example.

3 Our Algorithm

CSP. The well-known Constraint Satisfaction Problem (CSP) framework [25] defines a tuple $\langle V, D, C\rangle$, where V is a finite set of variables, D is the domain set for all $v \in V$, and C is a set of constraints[1]. A CSP is solved by finding an assignment of values to the variables such that all constraints are satisfied. When applied to graphs, we treat each node as a variable and each edge as

[1] Our algorithm can be trivially extended to support different domains for variables.

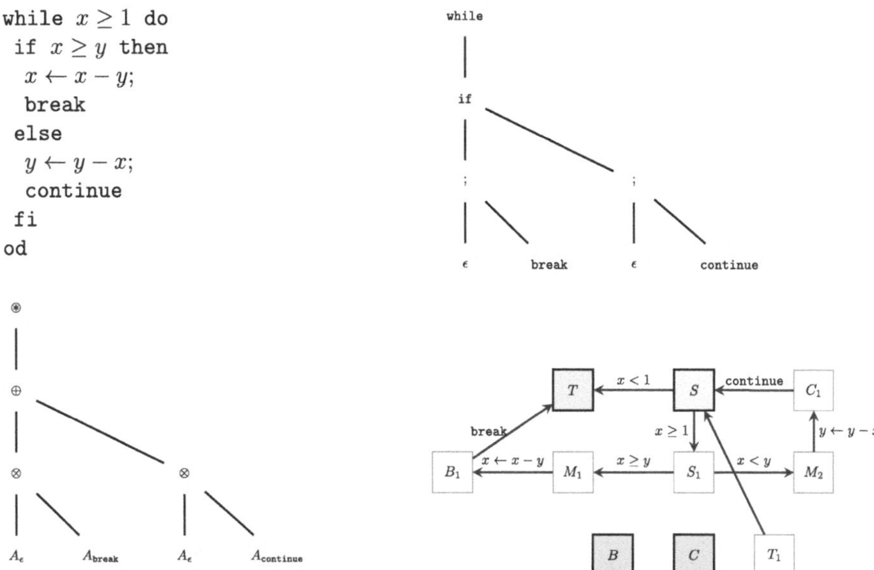

Fig. 5. A program P (top left), its parse tree (top right), the corresponding parse tree of $G = \mathsf{cfg}(P)$ (bottom left) and the graph $G = \mathsf{cfg}(P)$ (bottom right) [7]. The edges of the graph are labeled according to the statements in the program.

a constraint, with the stipulation that constraints exist only between adjacent nodes. For example, the graph coloring problem can be formulated as a CSP. Considering the graph 6, given three colors, we want to color the graph so that no two adjacent nodes share the same color. We can consider each node to be a variable, and each edge imposes a constraint that the colors of adjacent nodes must differ, then this graph coloring problem is a typical CSP. It is well-known that the graph coloring problem is NP-hard even when limiting the domain set to only three colors, which implies that the CSP problem is also NP-hard.

PCSP. In the context of graph-based PCSPs (Partial Constraint Satisfaction Problems) [25], we allow certain constraints to be violated at a specified cost, with the goal of finding a solution that minimizes this cost. To define the cost, we introduce a cost function $c(e, b_0, b_1)$, where e is the edge, and b_0 and b_1 are the values assigned to the two nodes connected by the edge. If b_0 and b_1 do not violate the constraints, the cost is 0; otherwise, a positive cost is assigned. Our objective is to find:

$$\min_{A} \sum_{e \in E} c(e, A(v_0), A(v_1))$$

where $A : V \to D$ is a valuation that maps each node to a domain element.

Figure 6 with two colors is an example. Similar to CSP, we consider each node as a variable and each color as a value. We define the cost function as follows:

$$c(e, b_0, b_1) = \begin{cases} 0 & \text{if } b_0 \neq b_1 \\ 1 & \text{if } b_0 = b_1 \end{cases}$$

In this scenario, the minimum cost is 1, as the edge connecting nodes B and C incurs a cost of 1, while all other edges do not contribute to the cost. It is straightforward to verify that this configuration constitutes a valid solution to the PCSP problem, as it is impossible to color the figure using only two colors in a manner that satisfies the constraints. If we assign an infinite cost to the constraints, the problem reduces to the CSP. Thus, PCSP is NP-hard, too.

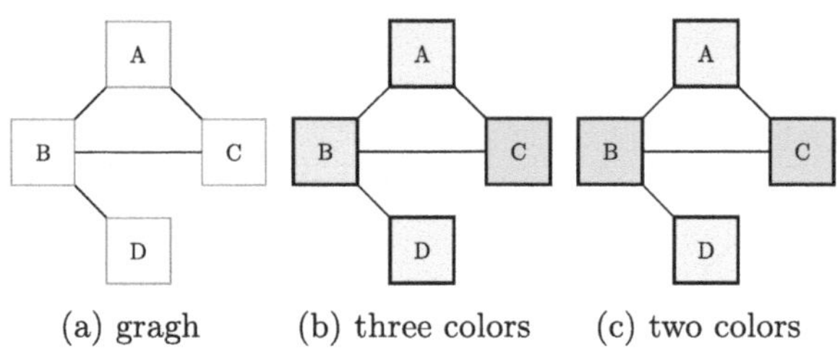

Fig. 6. Graph Coloring.

Our Setting. We consider a PCSP instance in which the underlying graph is the control-flow graph of a structured goto-free program. Our goal is to use the SPL decomposition of the control-flow graph to obtain an efficient algorithm. As we will see further below, this is motivated by the fact that many classical problems in program analysis and compiler optimization are defined over the control-flow graphs and are special cases of PCSP.

Our SPL-Based Algorithm. Our algorithm proceeds with a bottom-up dynamic programming on the SPL decomposition. Note that each node u of the SPL decomposition corresponds to an SPL subgraph $G_u = (V_u, E_u, S_u, T_u, B_u, C_u)$ of G which is either an atomic SPL graph (when u is a leaf) or obtained by applying one of the SPL operations to the graphs corresponding to the children of u. Let $\Gamma_u = \{S_u, T_u, B_u, C_u\}$ be the set of special vertices of G_u. Let $X : \Gamma_u \to D$ be the assignment for the vertices in Γ_u. We define a dynamic programming variable $\mathsf{dp}[u, X]$. Our goal is to compute this dynamic programming value such that

$$\mathsf{dp}[u, X] = \min_{A} \sum_{e \in E_u} c(e, A(v_0), A(v_1))$$

where the minimum is taken over all assignments A to the vertices of G_u that agree with X on the special vertices. In other words, $A(v) = X(v)$ for all $v \in \Gamma_u$. We now show how our algorithm computes these $\mathsf{dp}[\cdot, \cdot]$ values at every kind of node in the SPL decomposition:

1. *Atomic Nodes*: If G_u is an atomic SPL graph, then the only vertices in G_u are the four special vertices. Therefore, we must have $A = X$. Our algorithm sets
$$\mathtt{dp}[u, X] = \sum_{e \in E_u} c(e, X(v_0), X(v_1))$$
2. *Series Nodes*: Suppose $G_u = G_v \otimes G_w$ where v and w are the children of u in the SPL decomposition. Let X_i be the assignment for the special vertices/variables in Γ_i for $i \in \{u, v, w\}$. We say that X_u and X_w are compatible and write $X_u \leftrightharpoons X_w$ if the following conditions satisfied:
   - $X_u(S_u) = X_v(S_v)$;
   - $X_u(B_u) = X_v(B_v)$;
   - $X_u(C_u) = X_v(C_v)$.

   Intuitively, compatibility means that the assignments X_u and X_v return the same value when given the same vertex/variable.
   Now consider X_u and X_w. We say that X_u and X_w are compatible and write $X_u \leftrightharpoons X_w$ if the following conditions are satisfied:
   - $X_u(T_u) = X_w(T_w)$;
   - $X_u(B_u) = X_w(B_w)$;
   - $X_u(C_u) = X_w(C_w)$.

   The intuition is the same as the previous case, except that we now have $T_u = T_w$. Finally, we say that X_v and X_w are compatible and write $X_v \leftrightharpoons X_w$ if
   - $X_v(T_v) = X_w(S_w)$.

   This is because T_v and S_w are the same vertex of the CFG.
   Given the definition above, our algorithm simply sets
$$\mathtt{dp}[u, X_u] = \min_{\substack{X_u \leftrightharpoons X_v \\ X_u \leftrightharpoons X_w \\ X_v \leftrightharpoons X_w}} \mathtt{dp}[v, X_v] + \mathtt{dp}[w, X_w].$$
   This is because every edge in G_u appears in either G_v or G_w but not both. Thus, the cost of the edges would simply be the sum of their costs in the two subgraphs.
3. *Parallel Nodes:* We can handle parallel nodes in the same manner as series nodes, i.e., finding compatible assignments at both children. To be more precise, let $G_u = G_v \oplus G_w$. The compatibility conditions are now changed to simple equality. This is because the parallel operation merges the respective start, terminate, break and continue vertices in G_v and G_w. In some cases, repeated edges may be introduced, e.g., both graphs v and w have edges connecting the S vertex and the B vertex. These two edges represent the same edge in graph u, so we only need to calculate the cost once. Let's create a set E' that contains all such edges.
   With the same argument as in the previous case, our algorithm sets
$$\mathtt{dp}[u, X_u] = \min_{\substack{X_u \leftrightharpoons X_v \\ X_u \leftrightharpoons X_w \\ X_v \leftrightharpoons X_w}} \mathtt{dp}[v, X_u] + \mathtt{dp}[w, X_u] - \sum_{e \in E'} c(e).$$

4. *Loop Nodes:* Finally, we should handle the case where $G_u = G_v^{\circledast}$. By construction, in comparison to G_v, the graph G_u has four new vertices

$$\Gamma_u = \{S_u, T_u, B_u, C_u\}$$

and three new edges

$$E_{\text{new}} = \{(S_u, S_v), (S_u, T_u), (T_v, S_u))\}.$$

Knowing X_u and X_v is sufficient to calculate the costs of our new edges. Let us denote the cost of a new edge e based on X_u and X_v by $c(e)$. Our algorithm sets

$$\mathtt{dp}[u, X_u] = \min \mathtt{dp}[v, X_v] + \sum_{e \in E_{\text{new}}} c(e).$$

After computing all the $\mathtt{dp}[\cdot, \cdot]$ values, our solution, i.e., the minimum possible cost, is given by $\min_X \mathtt{dp}[r, X]$ where r is the root node of the SPL decomposition and $X : \Gamma_r \to D$ is an assignment for the special vertices of the root SPL graph. The exact assignment for every node can be easily tracked and updated during the dynamic programming.

Let us now analyze the time complexity of each step of our algorithm:

- *Atomic nodes:* As we only have four vertices in an atomic graph and each of them have $|D|$ possible values, the time complexity is $O(|D|^4)$. To slightly optimize the runtime, we can only consider the connected vertices and ignore disconnected vertices, which, by definition, have no constraints on them. As there are at most two connected vertices in atomic nodes, the time complexity is $O(|D|^2)$.
- *Series nodes:* When doing computations for a series node, there are a total of eight special vertices that need to be considered, but as we also need to consider the compatibility, there are three pairs among them that are guaranteed to have the same values. Thus, the time complexity is $O(|D|^5)$, as we only need to consider value for five independent variables.
- *Parallel nodes:* The analysis is similar to a series node, except that there are four pairs of vertices that need to have the same value. Thus, the time complexity is $O(|D|^4)$.
- *Loop nodes:* This is also similar to the previous cases, but no vertices are merged and should have the same value. Thus, the time complexity is $O(|D|^8)$. However, we know that the C_u and B_u are not connected to any other vertex after the loop operation. So, we can temporarily ignore them, reducing the time complexity to $O(|D|^6)$.

Thus, the dynamic programming computations at each node of the SPL decomposition can be done in $O(|D|^6)$. Moreover, the SPL decomposition has the same asymptotic size as the control-flow graph. Therefore, the overall runtime of our algorithm is in $O(|G| \cdot |D|^6)$.

Before discussing the placement of the bank selection problem, let's first present how two other applications [6,7] that have utilized SPL-decomposition can be considered as instances of the PCSP.

Register Allocation. Here we show how Register Allocation [7] is a special case of PCSP. Suppose we are given a program P with control-flow graph $G = \mathsf{cfg}(P) = (V, E, S, T, B, C)$. Let $[r] = \{0, 1, \ldots, r-1\}$ be the set of available registers and $\mathbb{V}$ the set of our program variables. Every variable $v \in \mathbb{V}$ has a lifetime $< v$ which is a connected subgraph of G. Since lifetimes can be computed by a simple data-flow analysis, we assume without loss of generality that they are given as inputs to our algorithm. For a vertex v or edge e of G, we denote the set of variables that are alive at this vertex/edge by $L(v)$ or $L(e)$. An *assignment* is a function $f : \mathbb{V} \to [r] \cup \{\perp\}$ which maps each variable either to a register or to $\perp$. The latter models the variable being spilled. An assignment is valid if it does not map two variables with intersecting lifetimes to the same register. We denote the set of all valid assignments by F. . Cost is introduced when we need to switch the value of a register, and the goal is to find the assignment with minimum cost.

In this case, the "value" assigned to each node is the allocation of an alive variable. Suppose there are at most V alive variables at one node and there are r registers, then we can create a completed inference graph with V nodes and try to color them with r colors. Then the domain size is

$$\binom{V}{r} \cdot r! + \binom{V}{r-1} \cdot (r-1)! + \cdots + \binom{V}{0} \cdot 0! \in O(r \cdot V^r).$$

Hence with our algorithm, the time complexity is $O(|G| \cdot r^6 \cdot V^{6 \cdot r})$.

LOSPRE. LOSPRE [6] is another example of the PCSP. It is a modern redundancy elimination technique that calculates repeated expressions only once and stores the results in a template variable. Each time we need to use that expression, we can directly utilize the template variable instead of recalculating it. With the control flow graph $G = \{V, E\}$, we can define this problem as follows:

- *Use set:* Consider an expression e. We define the use set U of e as the set of all nodes of the CFG in which the expression e is computed.
- *Life set:* Our goal is to precompute the expression e at a few points, save the result in a temporary variable `temp`, and then use `temp` in place of e in every node of U. We denote the lifetime of the variable `temp` by L and call it our life set.
- *Invalidating set:* We say a node v of the CFG invalidates e if the statement at v changes the value of e. For example, if $e =$ `a+b`, then the statement `a = 0` invalidates e. We denote the set of all invalidating nodes by I. These nodes play a crucial role in LOSPRE since they force us to update the value saved in `temp` by recomputing e. We assume that the entry and exit nodes are invalidating since LOSPRE is an intraprocedural analysis that has no information about the program's execution before or after the current function.

- *Calculating set:* Given the sets U, L and I above, we have to make sure the value of our temporary variable `temp` is correct at every node in $U \cup L$. Thus, for every edge $(x, y) \in E$ of the CFG where $x \notin L$ and $y \in U \cup L$, we have to insert a computation `temp` $= e$ between x and y. Similarly, if $x \in I$, then the value stored at `temp` becomes invalid after the execution of x, requiring us to inject the same computation between x and y. Formally, the computation `temp` $= e$ has to be injected into the following set of edges of the CFG:

$$C(U, L, I) = \{(x, y) \in E \mid x \notin L \setminus I \ \wedge \ y \in U \cup L\}.$$

This time, there are two types of costs associated with the process above: (i) injecting calculations into the edges in $C(U, L, I)$ and (ii) keeping an extra variable `temp` at every node in L. These costs are dependent on the goals pursued by the compiler. For example, a compiler aiming to minimize code size will focus on (i). On the other hand, if our goal is to ease register pressure, we would want to minimize (ii). LOSPRE is an expressive framework in which these costs are modeled by two functions

$$c : E \to K$$

and

$$l : V \to K.$$

where K is a totally-ordered set with an addition operator, c is a function that maps each edge to the cost of adding a computation of e in that edge and l is similarly a function that maps each vertex of the CFG to the cost of keeping the temporary variable `temp` alive at that vertex. Our goal is to find a life set L that minimizes the total cost

$$\textsc{Cost}(G, U, I, L, c, l) = \sum_{e \in C(U,L,I)} c(e) + \sum_{v \in L} l(v).$$

To consider this problem as PCSP, we only need to have a little modification, as the edge cost is the same as the definition in PCSP, and the node cost can be easily added to the total cost. In this case, the "value" assigned to each node if it is belong to Use set, Life set, and Invalidating set, as for each set, there are 2 different case, hence the domain size is $2^3 = 8$, and hence, applying to our PCSP algorithm, this can be down in $O(|G| \cdot 8^6) = O(|G|)$, in this case, thanks to the constant domain size, we can develop a linear algorithm without taken any parameter.

4 Optimal Placement of Bank Selection Instructions

As mentioned in the previous section, register allocation and LOSPRE, which were both previously solved using tree decompositions and SPL decompositions are special cases of PCSP. In this section, we cover another classical use-case of PCSP over control-flow graphs, i.e. that of optimal placement of bank selection instructions. To the best of our knowledge, there are no previous solutions to this problem that exploit SPL decompositions.

Motivation. Partitioned memory architectures are prevalent in 8-bit and 16-bit microcontrollers. In these systems, a portion of the logical address space serves as a window into a larger physical address space. The segments of the physical address space that can be mapped into this window are referred to as memory banks. A mechanism exists to determine which part of the physical address space is visible within the window, typically achieved through bank selection instructions.

The assignment of variables to specific memory banks is generally performed by the programmer, for instance, through named address spaces in Embedded C, or by the compiler, using techniques such as bin-packing heuristics to minimize RAM usage. Some approaches integrate the placement of variables in memory banks with the insertion of bank selection instructions. However, in embedded systems, there is often more available space for code than for data. As a result, variables stored in banked memory tend to be larger, making it advantageous to prioritize the efficient packing of variables into the banks before addressing other factors such as code size and execution speed. Consequently, the placement of variables in memory typically occurs at an earlier stage of the compilation process than the insertion of bank-switching instructions.

Domain. The following formal definition of the bank selection problem is adapted from [32]. Let D be the memory bank domain, including a special symbol $\perp \in D$ that indicates that the currently selected bank is unknown. A program can be modeled as a control-flow graph $G = (V, E)$, where $E \subseteq V^2$, and each node $v \in V$ can be assigned a memory bank from D. Some of the nodes are pre-assigned since a specific bank must be active at that node.

Example. Figure 7 shows an example of a program with bank selection instructions. The program has two pre-assigned vertices and the bank b should be active at these vertices. When the program is at other locations, there is no restriction on the selected bank since there is no memory access to any bank. As a simple ad-hoc approach, we can add the bank selection instruction just before we need the bank to be active. This is shown in Fig. 7 (b) and would need the insertion of three bank selection instructions. Suppose we aim to minimize the number of bank selection instructions. Then, we can insert them at the beginning of the program, as shown in Fig. 7 (c). This only requires two instructions and is the optimal solution.

Cost Function. In the classical formulation of the optimal bank selection problem, a cost function is defined over the CFG $G = (V, E)$. This is a function $c : E \times D \times D \to \mathbb{R}$ that assigns a cost to each edge $e \in E$ based on the memory banks assigned to its two endpoints. In other words, we incur the cost $c(e, b_0, b_1)$ if b_0 is active right before the edge e and b_1 becomes active after the edge. Such cost functions may be designed based on different optimization criteria. A typical cost function for optimizing code size is as follows:

- $c(e, b, b) = c(e, b, \perp) = 0$ since no instructions need to be inserted;

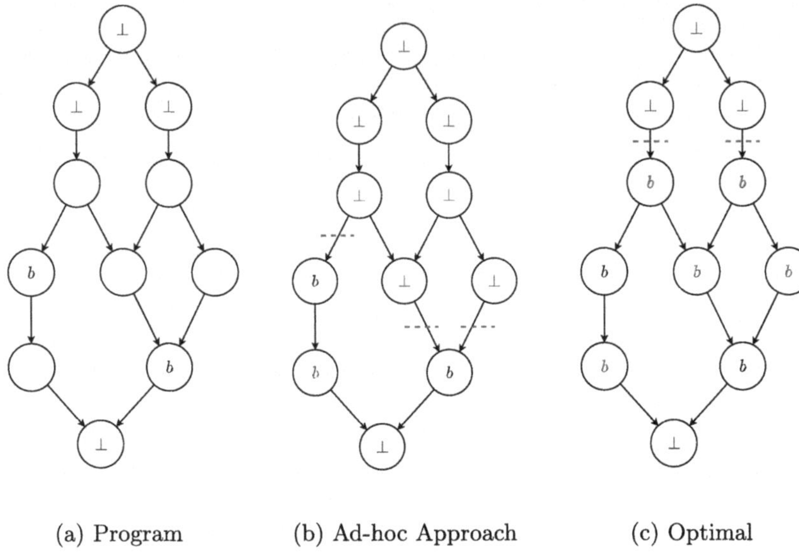

Fig. 7. Example Instance.

- $c(e, b_0, b_1) = c_1 > 0$ for $b_0 \neq b_1 \neq \perp$ when e is an edge from a taken conditional branch, as splitting such an edge generates an additional unconditional jump instruction.
- For all other cases, $c(e, b_0, b_1) = c_0 > 0$ for $b_0 \neq b_1 \neq \perp$, with the condition that $c_0 < c_1$.

Objective. The goal in optimal bank selection is to find an assignment of memory banks to the vertices of the control-flow graph that minimizes the total cost of the edges. In other words, we aim to compute

$$\min_{A} \sum_{e \in E} c(e, A(v_0), A(v_1))$$

where $A : V \to D$ maps each node to a domain. We note that this problem is NP-hard, even when the cost function is simplified to $c(e, b_0, b_1) = 0$ for $b_0 = b_1$ or $b_1 = \perp$, and $c(e, b_0, b_1) = 1$ in all other cases [32].
Our Algorithm. It is easy to verify that optimal insertion of bank selection instructions is an instance of the PCSP graph problem. Thus, we can simply apply the general solution developed in Sect. 3 and have it solved in $O(|G| \cdot |D|^6)$ time, where $|D|$ is the number of possible banks.

5 Experimental Results

As mentioned in Sect. 3, both register allocation and LOSPRE have previously been solved using SPL decompositions [6,7]. Indeed, the algorithms provided by [6,7] can be seen as instances of our general algorithm, when the domain and cost function are fixed as in Sect. 3. Therefore, we inherit their experimental results exactly. In this section, we provide further experimental results over the optimal bank selection problem of Sect. 4, which, to the best of our knowledge, has not been considered in the context of SPL decompositions before. In addition to that, we also compare our approach with the classical algorithms for NP-hard problems, including SAT and ILP.

Implementation. We implemented our bank selection algorithm in `C++` and integrated it with the Small Device `C` Compiler (SDCC) [20,21]. We will publish the implementation as free and open-source software dedicated to the public domain and link it in the final version of this article. The link was removed in the review phase to preserve anonymity.

Baseline. We compared our algorithm's runtime with the treewidth-based parameterized approach of [32], which is the current state-of-the-art in bank selection. That approach has an asymptotic runtime of $O(|G| \cdot \mathtt{tw}(G) \cdot |D|^{\mathtt{tw}(G)+1})$ where $\mathtt{tw}(G)$ is the treewidth of G, which can theoretically be up to 7 [40]. We did not consider other previous methods since they either have exponential runtime dependence on the program size [38,39] or no guarantee on the quality or optimality of the results [34].

Machine. All experiments were performed on a virtual machine with Oracle Linux (ARM 64-bit), equipped with 1 core of an Apple M2 processor and 4GB of RAM.

Benchmarks. We exactly followed the setup of [32], utilizing the SDCC regression test suite as our benchmark set. This suite comprises a total of 13,463 instances for HC08, 179,611 instances for Z80, and 84,700 instances for MCS51. These benchmarks are embedded programs expected to operate in resource-constrained environments. Therefore, there is a strong focus is on code size optimization. Thus, we used the following standard cost function:

- $c(e, b, b) = c(e, b, \perp) = 0$;
- $c(e, b_0, b_1) = 1$ when e is an edge from a taken conditional branch;
- For all other cases, $c(e, b_0, b_1) = 1$.

We only compare the runtimes. There is no output comparison since both our approach and [32] find an optimal solution for bank selection and the outputs coincide.

Runtimes. Fig. 8 provides a comparison of the runtimes of our algorithm and that of [32] over the three different architectures. For HC08, our algorithm took an average of 1,998.3 nanoseconds, while the treewidth-based approach took an average of 8,558.8 nanoseconds. For Z80, our algorithm took an average of 2,402.1 nanoseconds, while the treewidth-based approach took an average of 8,209.3 nanoseconds. For MCS51, our algorithm took an average of 1,834.3 nanoseconds, while the treewidth-based approach took an average of 6,268.3 nanoseconds.

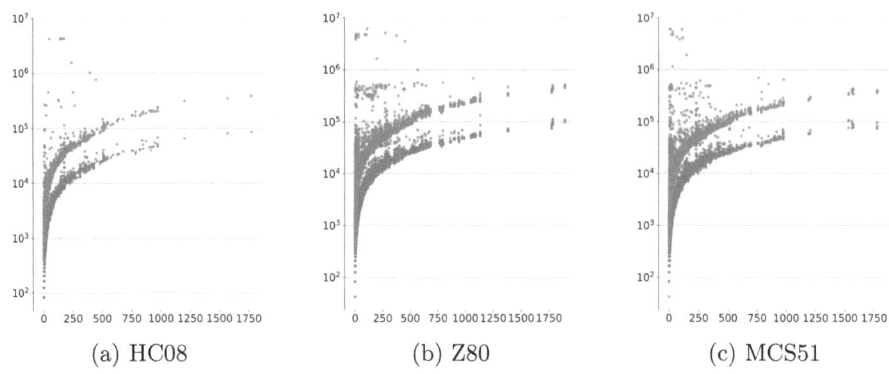

(a) HC08 (b) Z80 (c) MCS51

Fig. 8. Runtime comparison of the treewidth-based algorithm of [32] (orange) and our approach (green). The x axis is the number of vertices in the CFG and the y axis is the time in nanoseconds. The y axis is in logarithmic scale.

Comparison with SAT and ILP Solvers. Since Optimal Bank Selection is NP-complete, we compare our runtimes with state-of-the-art approaches for NP-complete problems via SAT and ILP solving. We encoded the problem in the natural way in both SAT and ILP. We then used the state-of-the-art SAT solver, Kissat [23], and the industrial ILP solver Gurobi [28] over the benchmarks. The results, as shown in Fig. 9, illustrate that our method is nearly 10 times faster than the ILP approach, which is itself approximately 100 times faster than the SAT solver.

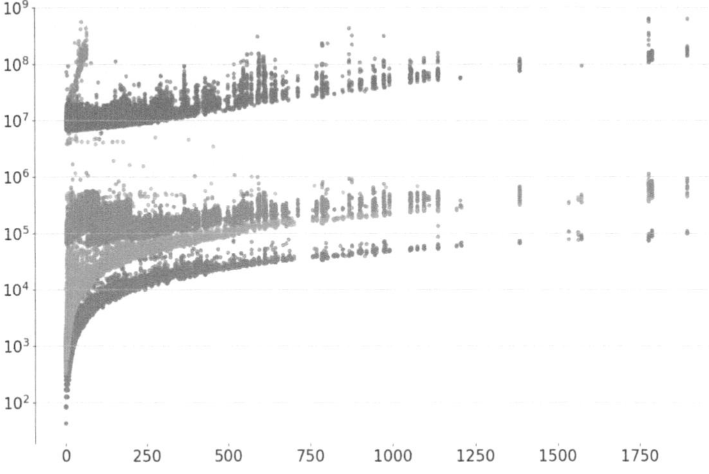

Fig. 9. Runtime comparison of the treewidth-based algorithm of [32] (orange) and our approach (green) compared to SAT-based (brown) and ILP-based (purple) methods. The x axis is the number of vertices in the CFG and the y axis is the time in nanoseconds. The y axis is in logarithmic scale.

Discussion. In summary, our approach is approximately four times faster than the previous state-of-the-art for bank selection. This is a notable improvement, particularly given that the treewidth-based approach of [32] is already highly optimized and included in the well-established SDCC compiler. We believe the speed-up is mainly because our algorithm's runtime does not depend on parameters such as treewidth and the constant factor hidden in our $O(n)$ asymptotic runtime analysis is small in practice.

6 Conclusion

In this work, we present an efficient linear-time algorithm for graph PCSPs over control-flow graphs, leveraging SPL decompositions [7]. Our solution applies to various compiler optimization tasks, including register allocation [7], Lifetime-optimal Speculative Partial Redundancy Elimination (LOSPRE) [6], and Optimal Bank Selection. The main contribution is a dynamic programming algorithm that addresses all graph PCSP problems, eliminating the need for separate algorithms for different optimization tasks. Our solution demonstrates significant theoretical performance improvements for bank selection, and experiments show it is approximately four times faster than the treewidth-based approach of [32] in practice.

Acknowledgments. This work was partially supported by the ERC Starting Grant 101222524 (SPES) and the Ethereum Foundation Research Grant FY24-1793.

References

1. Ahmadi, A., Chatterjee, K., Goharshady, A.K., Meggendorfer, T., Safavi, R., Zikelic, Đ.: Algorithms and hardness results for computing cores of markov chains. In: FSTTCS, pp. 29:1–29:20 (2022)
2. Ahmadi, A., Daliri, M., Goharshady, A.K., Pavlogiannis, A.: Efficient approximations for cache-conscious data placement. In: PLDI, pp. 857–871 (2022)
3. Asadi, A., Chatterjee, K., Goharshady, A.K., Mohammadi, K., Pavlogiannis, A.: Faster algorithms for quantitative analysis of MCs and MDPs with small treewidth. In: Hung, D.V., Sokolsky, O. (eds.) ATVA 2020. LNCS, vol. 12302, pp. 253–270. Springer, Cham (2020). https://doi.org/10.1007/978-3-030-59152-6_14
4. Bodlaender, H.L., Gustedt, J., Telle, J.A.: Linear-time register allocation for a fixed number of registers. In: SODA, pp. 574–583 (1998)
5. Burgstaller, B., Blieberger, J., Scholz, B.: On the tree width of ada programs. In: Ada-Europe, pp. 78–90 (2004)
6. Cai, X., Goharshady, A.: Faster lifetime-optimal speculative partial redundancy elimination for goto-free programs. In: SETTA, pp. 382–398. Springer (2024)
7. Cai, X., Goharshady, A.K., Hitarth, S., Lam, C.K.: Faster chaitin-like register allocation via grammatical decompositions of control-flow graphs. In: ASPLOS, pp. 463–477. ACM (2025). https://doi.org/10.1145/3669940.3707286
8. Chatterjee, K., Goharshady, A.K., Goharshady, E.K.: The treewidth of smart contracts. In: SAC, pp. 400–408. ACM (2019)

9. Chatterjee, K., Goharshady, A.K., Goyal, P., Ibsen-Jensen, R., Pavlogiannis, A.: Faster algorithms for dynamic algebraic queries in basic rsms with constant treewidth. ACM Trans. Program. Lang. Syst. **41**(4), 23:1–23:46 (2019)
10. Chatterjee, K., Goharshady, A.K., Ibsen-Jensen, R., Pavlogiannis, A.: Algorithms for algebraic path properties in concurrent systems of constant treewidth components. In: POPL, pp. 733–747 (2016)
11. Chatterjee, K., Goharshady, A.K., Ibsen-Jensen, R., Pavlogiannis, A.: Optimal and perfectly parallel algorithms for on-demand data-flow analysis. In: ESOP, pp. 112–140 (2020)
12. Chatterjee, K., Goharshady, A.K., Okati, N., Pavlogiannis, A.: Efficient parameterized algorithms for data packing. Proc. ACM Program. Lang. **3**(POPL), 53:1–53:28 (2019)
13. Chatterjee, K., Goharshady, A.K., Pavlogiannis, A.: JTDec: a tool for tree decompositions in soot. In: D'Souza, D., Narayan Kumar, K. (eds.) ATVA 2017. LNCS, vol. 10482, pp. 59–66. Springer, Cham (2017). https://doi.org/10.1007/978-3-319-68167-2_4
14. Chatterjee, K., Ibsen-Jensen, R., Goharshady, A.K., Pavlogiannis, A.: Algorithms for algebraic path properties in concurrent systems of constant treewidth components. ACM Trans. Program. Lang. Syst. **40**(3), 9:1–9:43 (2018)
15. Chatterjee, K., Lacki, J.: Faster algorithms for markov decision processes with low treewidth. In: CAV, pp. 543–558 (2013)
16. Conrado, G.K., Goharshady, A.K., Kochekov, K., Tsai, Y.C., Zaher, A.K.: Exploiting the sparseness of control-flow and call graphs for efficient and on-demand algebraic program analysis. Proc. ACM Program. Lang. **7**(OOPSLA2), 1993–2022 (2023)
17. Conrado, G.K., Goharshady, A.K., Lam, C.K.: The bounded pathwidth of control-flow graphs. Proc. ACM Program. Lang. **7**(OOPSLA2), 292–317 (2023)
18. Dechter, R., Pearl, J.: Network-based heuristics for constraint-satisfaction problems. Artif. Intell. **34**(1), 1–38 (1987). https://doi.org/10.1016/0004-3702(87)90002-6
19. Dechter, R., Pearl, J.: Tree-clustering schemes for constraint-processing. In: AAAI, pp. 150–154 (1988)
20. Dutta, S.: Anatomy of a compiler: a retargetable ansi-c compiler. Circuit Cellar **121**(5) (2000)
21. Dutta, S., Drotos, D., Vigor, K., et al.: Small device c compiler (2003), http://sdcc.sourceforge.net/
22. Ferrara, A., Pan, G., Vardi, M.Y.: Treewidth in verification: local vs. global. In: Sutcliffe, G., Voronkov, A. (eds.) LPAR 2005. LNCS (LNAI), vol. 3835, pp. 489–503. Springer, Heidelberg (2005). https://doi.org/10.1007/11591191_34
23. for Formal Models, I., Verification: Kissat-public (2025), https://fmv.jku.at/kissat/
24. Freuder, E.C.: Complexity of k-tree structured constraint satisfaction problems. In: AAAI, pp. 4–9 (1990)
25. Freuder, E.C., Wallacex, R.J.: Partial constraint satisfaction **58**, 21–70 (1992). https://doi.org/10.1016/0004-3702(92)90004-H
26. Goharshady, A.K., Lam, C.K., Parreaux, L.: Fast and optimal extraction for sparse equality graphs. In: OOPSLA (2024)
27. Goharshady, A.K., Zaher, A.K.: Efficient interprocedural data-flow analysis using treedepth and treewidth. In: VMCAI, vol. 13881, pp. 177–202 (2023)
28. Gurobi Optimization, L.: Gurobi (2008), https://www.gurobi.com/

29. Gustedt, J., Mæhle, O.A., Telle, J.A.: The treewidth of java programs. In: Mount, D.M., Stein, C. (eds.) ALENEX 2002. LNCS, vol. 2409, pp. 86–97. Springer, Heidelberg (2002). https://doi.org/10.1007/3-540-45643-0_7
30. Koster, A.M.C.A., van Hoesel, S.P.M., Kolen, A.W.J.: Solving partial constraint satisfaction problems with tree-decomposition **40**, 170–180 (2002). https://doi.org/10.1002/net.10046
31. Koster, A.M., Hoesel, S.P., Kolen, A.W.: The partial constraint satisfaction problem: facets and lifting theorems. Oper. Res. Lett. **23**(3), 89–97 (1998). https://doi.org/10.1016/S0167-6377(98)00043-1
32. Krause, P.K.: Optimal placement of bank selection instructions in polynomial time (2013). https://doi.org/10.1145/2463596.2463598
33. Krause, P.K.: Optimal register allocation in polynomial time. In: Jhala, R., De Bosschere, K. (eds.) CC 2013. LNCS, vol. 7791, pp. 1–20. Springer, Heidelberg (2013b). https://doi.org/10.1007/978-3-642-37051-9_1
34. Liu, T., Xue, C.J., Li, M.: Joint variable partitioning and bank selection instruction optimization for partitioned memory architectures. ACM Trans. Embed. Comput. Syst. **12** (2013). https://doi.org/10.1145/2442116.2442126
35. Mackworth, A.K., Freuder, E.C.: The complexity of some polynomial network consistency algorithms for constraint satisfaction problems. Artif. Intell. **25**, 65–74 (1985). https://doi.org/10.1016/0004-3702(85)90041-4
36. Obdrzálek, J.: Fast mu-calculus model checking when tree-width is bounded. In: CAV, pp. 80–92 (2003)
37. Sankaranarayanan, S.: Reachability analysis using message passing over tree decompositions. In: CAV, pp. 604–628 (2020)
38. Scholz, B., Burgstaller, B., Xue, J.: Minimizing bank selection instructions for partitioned memory architecture. In: CASES, pp. 201–211. ACM (2006). https://doi.org/10.1145/1176760.1176786
39. Scholz, B., Burgstaller, B., Xue, J.: Minimal placement of bank selection instructions for partitioned memory architectures. ACM Trans. Embed. Comput. Syst. **7** (2008). https://doi.org/10.1145/1331331.1331336
40. Thorup, M.: All structured programs have small tree width and good register allocation. Inf. Comput. **142**, 159–181 (1998). https://doi.org/10.1006/inco.1997.2697

Neural Networks and Large Language Models

Risk-Averse Certification of Bayesian Neural Networks

Xiyue Zhang[1,5(✉)], Zifan Wang[2], Yulong Gao[3], Licio Romao[4], Alessandro Abate[1], and Marta Kwiatkowska[1]

[1] Department of Computer Science, University of Oxford, Oxford, UK
{alessandro.abate,marta.kwiatkowska}@cs.ox.ac.uk
[2] Division of Decision and Control Systems, KTH Royal Institute of Technology, Stockholm, Sweden
zifanw@kth.se
[3] Department of Electrical and Electronic Engineering, Imperial College London, London, UK
yulong.gao@imperial.ac.uk
[4] Department of Wind and Energy Systems, Technical University of Denmark, Kongens Lyngby, Denmark
licro@dtu.dk
[5] School of Computer Science, University of Bristol, Bristol, UK
xiyue.zhang@bristol.ac.uk

Abstract. In light of the inherently complex and dynamic nature of real-world environments, incorporating risk measures is crucial for the robustness evaluation of deep learning models. In this work, we propose a **R**isk-**A**verse **C**ertification framework for Bayesian neural networks called RAC-BNN. Our method leverages sampling and optimisation to compute a probabilistically sound approximation of the output set of a BNN, represented using a set of template polytopes. To enhance risk-aware robustness evaluation, we integrate a coherent distortion risk measure–Conditional Value at Risk (CVaR)–into the certification framework, providing probabilistic guarantees based on empirical distributions obtained through sampling. We validate RAC-BNN on a range of regression and classification benchmarks and compare its performance with a state-of-the-art method. The results show that RAC-BNN effectively quantifies robustness under worst-performing risky scenarios, and achieves tighter certified bounds and higher efficiency in complex tasks.

Keywords: Uncertainty · Bayesian neural networks · Risk measure · Probabilistic certification

1 Introduction

There has been growing interest in formal verification of neural networks [16,18,29,31,38,40], in particular when deploying deep neural models to safety- and security-critical systems, such as autonomous vehicles [7,12], healthcare systems [3], and cyber security [14,28]. Different from deterministic neural networks,

A. Goharshady and C. Haase (Eds.): SETTA 2025, LNCS 16458, pp. 299–317, 2026.
https://doi.org/10.1007/978-981-95-7826-9_16

which learn a fixed set of weights and biases from a set of training data, Bayesian neural networks (BNNs) provide a principled approach to modelling uncertainty [23] and learn a posterior distribution over these network parameters. During inference, BNNs quantify uncertainty and assign high uncertainty values to out-of-distribution inputs instead of being overconfident in wrong predictions [17]. At the same time, the stochastic nature of BNNs complicates certification, as both the model parameters and, as a result, the predictive outputs are probability distributions rather than point estimates. Even when applying relaxation-based certification techniques to BNNs, the computational complexity can increase drastically.

In order to reliably deploy BNN solutions and reason about their safety in the presence of uncertainty, techniques have been developed to handle stochastic constraints within BNNs and compute certified bounds on their reachable outputs. These approaches typically fall into two categories: sampling-based techniques, which provide probabilistic guarantees [9,22,34], and approximation-based techniques, which evaluate the robustness of BNNs by computing the expectation of the output distributions over an input set [1,37]. While approximation techniques significantly increase the scalability of evaluating larger-size BNNs, they often introduce relaxation losses to the certified output range. Such relaxation can lead to conservative output bounds, limiting the precision of robustness evaluations. Furthermore, existing works adopt a risk-neutral perspective towards BNN certification by applying an expectation operator, focusing solely on bounding the expected value of the entire output distribution. However, in real-world decision-making scenarios, considering the average performance over the full distribution may not suffice. Instead, it is important to account for challenging scenarios by adopting a *risk-averse* perspective; that is, to evaluate robustness under adverse conditions (e.g., the most adversarially unstable 25% cases).

In this work, we consider a risk-averse perspective for BNN certification by employing a risk measure in place of the simple expectation operator. Specifically, we propose a principled approach to BNN certification that incorporates a coherent distortion risk measure – Conditional Value at Risk (CVaR) [25] – which enables flexible and targeted evaluation of BNN performance. The key idea of our method is to sample the input points and the parameters of the BNN weights, obtaining the empirical output distribution, to compute a sound approximation of the output set (using template polytopes) and certified CVaR bounds with probabilistic guarantees. We implement our method as a prototype tool, RAC-BNN, and demonstrate that it achieves tighter certification bounds with better efficiency than the state-of-the-art technique on a range of regression and classification benchmarks. To the best of our knowledge, RAC-BNN is the *first* method capable of computing certified bounds under different risk levels (denoted by α), enabling the flexibility between analysing average robustness over the entire output distribution ($\alpha = 1$) and evaluating robustness against worst-performing outcomes ($\alpha < 1$).

The main contributions of this work are summarised as follows:

❶ ***New Perspective***. We present the first systematic study of *risk-aware certification* for Bayesian neural networks, integrating CVaR to flexibly support risk measures under different levels of risk sensitivity.
❷ ***Novel Methodology***. We propose RAC-BNN, a framework that combines template polytopes with probabilistic sampling to approximate output sets and provide certified lower and upper bound guarantees.
❸ ***Empirical Validation***. Through extensive experiments on both regression and classification benchmarks, we demonstrate that RAC-BNN consistently produces tighter certified bounds than the state-of-the-art baseline. Moreover, it uniquely delivers certified guarantees across a spectrum of risk levels, with visualisations confirming the precision of template polytope-based approximations.

2 Related Work

In the following, we discuss closely related works in robustness certification of BNNs and risk-averse learning.

Robustness Certification of BNNs. The last decade has witnessed a growing interest in formal certification of neural networks, including complete verification methods based on constraint solving [16,18,31] and incomplete verifiers based on convex relaxation [29,38,40]. However, these methods all assume deterministic neural networks with fixed weights and thus cannot be directly applied to certify BNNs. To address this limitation, a series of certification techniques have been proposed for the certification of BNNs [1,9,34,37]. In [9], the authors proposed a statistical approach to estimate the probability of the existence of adversarial examples with *a priori* guarantees by viewing the robustness of a BNN as a Bernoulli random variable. The approach in [34] focused on the probabilistic robustness of BNNs, i.e., the probability that weights sampled from the posterior yield a deterministic neural network satisfying a safety property. This method computes a certified lower bound for probabilistic safety based on relaxation techniques of interval and linear bound propagation. These bounds are later generalised in [35], where they are applied to bound sequential decisions for BNN-based models, and specifically in [36] for reach-avoid (bounded-until) specifications. The study in [37] further investigated decision robustness, which focuses on the decision step aligned with Bayesian decision theory, as also used in this work, and proposed a unified approach to compute certified lower and upper bounds for both probabilistic robustness and decision robustness. In related efforts, the method proposed in [4] generalised the Lagrangian duality and provided a functional Lagrangian framework for verifying BNNs on probabilistic specifications, while BNN-DP [1] leveraged dynamic programming to bound the output range of BNNs over an input region.

Certification methods have also been extended to reason about the robustness of closed-loop systems where BNNs are applied for decision-making. For example, the work of [22] introduced a statistical framework to evaluate the safety of end-to-end BNN controllers in autonomous driving, whereas the method in [21] focused on computing safe weight sets in BNN policies and ensuring the safety of the closed-loop systems by recalibrating BNN policies via rejection sampling.

While existing certification methods for BNNs provide probabilistic or decision-level robustness guarantees, they do not capture tail-risk behaviour or evaluate robustness through coherent risk measures. Our proposed RAC-BNN framework complements this line of work by introducing a risk-aware certification perspective where tail-risk robustness can be formally assessed using distortion risk measures. In doing so, RAC-BNN extends the scope of BNN certification beyond average-case or probabilistic robustness guarantees and enables a principled evaluation of risk-sensitive behaviour under uncertainty.

Risk-Averse Learning. Risk-averse learning has emerged as a critical area in machine learning, particularly for applications where decisions have significant consequences under uncertainty. Traditional machine learning models typically focus on minimising expected loss, which may not adequately capture the risk of rare but severely adverse outcomes. To address this, researchers have proposed risk-averse approaches that consider not only the expected performance but also the tail risks [20,24,30,32]. For example, the work of [32] introduced a risk-averse classification framework leveraging coherent risk measures to handle class-specific misclassification risks, while the authors of [20] proposed a risk-adjusted cost-effectiveness framework in healthcare, integrating risk aversion and diminishing returns into health technology assessments.

In reinforcement learning, early works established gradient-based and actor-critic algorithms for optimising CVaR and other coherent risk measures in Markov decision processes [11,19,30]. In supervised learning, risk measures such as CVaR have been incorporated directly into training objectives to enhance worst-case (tail) performance. For instance, a boosting procedure was proposed for classification that minimises the CVaR objective to improve worst-case accuracy in [39], while adaptive sampling and optimisation strategies were developed in [13] for efficient CVaR estimation and minimisation during training. From a theoretical perspective, recent results have established concentration bounds for CVaR and broader risk measures using Wasserstein stability arguments [5].

Although existing risk-averse methods employ coherent risk measures to improve worst-case or minority group performance, they primarily do so by incorporating it into optimisation objectives and offer point estimates without formal probabilistic guarantees. Moreover, these approaches do not address predictive uncertainty arising in BNNs. Our approach RAC-BNN bridges this gap by integrating CVaR analysis into the certification framework for BNNs. Specifically, we derive probabilistically sound bounds on CVaR across a spectrum of risk levels and on the approximation of output sets. This certification perspective complements existing optimisation-based risk-averse learning by providing formal guarantees for risk assessment in BNN decisions.

3 Preliminaries and Problem Formulation

In this section, we present the necessary background and notations used throughout the paper, followed by the formal problem formulation.

3.1 Preliminaries

Notation. We denote the input space by $\mathcal{X} \subseteq \mathbb{R}^m$, the output space by $\mathcal{Y} \subseteq \mathbb{R}^n$, and the parameter space by $\mathcal{W} \subseteq \mathbb{R}^p$. We use $\mathcal{P}(\mathcal{X})$ to denote the set of probability distributions over $\mathcal{X}$, that is, $\mathcal{P}(\mathcal{X}) = \{\mu : \int_{\mathcal{X}} \mu(d\xi) = 1, \mu \geq 0\}$, and similarly for $\mathcal{Y}$ and $\mathcal{W}$. For a finite collection of points $\{x_1, \ldots, x_N\}$ in $\mathcal{X}$, we denote the corresponding empirical distribution as $\hat{\mu}_N(x) = \frac{1}{N}\sum_{i=1}^N \delta_{x_i}(x)$, where $\delta_{x_i}(x)$ is the Dirac measure centered at x_i. Similarly, for points in the output space $\mathcal{Y}$ and parameter space $\mathcal{W}$, we denote the empirical distribution by $\hat{\nu}_N$ and $\hat{\lambda}_N$, respectively. Given two probability distributions μ and μ' defined on the input space, i.e., $\mu, \mu' \in \mathcal{P}(\mathcal{X})$, we denote by $W_1(\mu, \mu')$ the *type-1 Wasserstein distance* between these measures, defined as

$$W_1(\mu, \mu') = \inf_{\pi \in \Pi(\mu, \mu')} \int_{\mathcal{X} \times \mathcal{X}} \|\xi_1 - \xi_2\| d\pi(\xi_1, \xi_2), \tag{1}$$

where $\Pi(\mu, \mu')$ is the set of couplings (or joint distributions) with marginals given by μ and μ'.

Risk Measure. Conditional Value at Risk (CVaR) is a coherent risk measure, meaning it satisfies the properties of monotonicity, sub-additivity, homogeneity, and translational invariance, which enables a mathematically sound quantification of risk [27]. CVaR measures the expected loss occurring beyond the Value at Risk (VaR) threshold, where VaR represents the maximum potential loss at a given confidence level. Formally, for a random variable X with the cumulative distribution function (CDF) denoted by F_X and a specified risk level $\alpha \in (0, 1]$, the CVaR value of X at level α is defined as:

$$\mathrm{CVaR}_\alpha[X] := \mathbb{E}[X \mid X \geq \mathrm{VaR}_\alpha[X]],$$

where $\mathrm{VaR}_\alpha[X] = \inf\{y \mid F_X(y) \geq 1 - \alpha\}$ represents the $(1 - \alpha)$-quantile of the distribution, referred to as the Value at Risk (VaR). Intuitively, CVaR quantifies the expected loss within the worst α-fraction of outcomes, making it a widely employed measure of tail risk in risk-sensitive optimisation and decision making.

Bayesian Neural Networks. We next define Bayesian neural networks (BNNs) and review related concepts, building on the notation introduced in the previous section.

Definition 1 (Bayesian Neural Network). *Given a distribution $\lambda \in \mathcal{P}(\mathcal{W})$ over the parameter space $\mathcal{W}$, a Bayesian Neural Network (BNN) is defined as a continuous stochastic function $f : \mathcal{X} \times \mathcal{W} \mapsto \mathcal{Y}$, where the weight w is sampled from the distribution λ, i.e., $w \sim \lambda$.*

In the training of BNNs, we start with a prior distribution $p(w)$ over the parameters w and then compute the posterior distribution $p(w|\mathcal{D})$ conditioned on the dataset $\mathcal{D} = \{(x_i, y_i) \in \mathcal{X} \times \mathcal{Y} : i = 1, \ldots, N\}$. Note that the measure $\lambda \in \mathcal{P}(\mathcal{W})$ introduced in Definition 1 refers to the posterior distribution $p(w|\mathcal{D})$. With dataset $\mathcal{D}$ observed, the prior distribution of a BNN is updated according to the likelihood, $p(\mathcal{D}|w) = \prod_{i=1}^{N} p(y_i|x_i, w)$, which models how likely the outputs are observed under the stochasticity of model parameters and the inputs. The posterior distribution, given the dataset, is then computed by virtue of the Bayes formula, i.e., $p(w|\mathcal{D}) \propto p(\mathcal{D}|w)p(w)$. In practice, the posterior distribution $p(w|\mathcal{D})$ can be obtained by different inference techniques, e.g., Hamiltonian Monte Carlo (HMC) [23], Variational Inference (VI) [6], and Monte Carlo Dropout (MCD) [15].

The posterior $p(w|\mathcal{D})$ then induces the distribution over outputs called the posterior predictive distribution for an input point x^*, which is defined as $p(y^*|x^*, \mathcal{D}) = \int p(y^*|x^*, w)p(w|\mathcal{D})dw$. The final decision is obtained using Bayesian decision theory for regression and classification, which selects the value $\hat{y}$ that minimises the corresponding loss function $\mathcal{L}$ averaged over the predictive distribution:

$$\hat{y} = \arg\min_{y} \int_{\mathbb{R}^n} \mathcal{L}(y, y^*)p(y^*|x^*, \mathcal{D})dy^*$$

Motivating Example. We present a motivating example to demonstrate why investigating the expectation of the entire distribution alone is insufficient to evaluate the performance of BNNs. In high-stakes applications, outputs that deviate significantly from the safe region and lead to catastrophic consequences are unacceptable [20,24], even if their probability of occurrence is low. In such cases, relying solely on the expectation of the outputs fails to account for the risks, as illustrated in the following example.

We consider the MNIST classification task (handwritten digits from 0 to 9) and visualise the empirical output distribution of a BNN under three types of perturbations: Gaussian noise applied to all image pixels, rotation that alters image orientation, and changes in brightness contrast. To evaluate the robustness performance, we define the function $h(y) = \max_{t \in [10] \setminus c} y_t - y_c$, where y_t denotes the random variable of the BNN output for the largest probability among the 10 classes except the ground truth, and y_c denotes the BNN output for the ground-truth class c. The value of $h(y)$ ranges from -1 to 1, with -1 indicating the BNN is robust and correctly classifies the input, while 1 indicates the BNN makes a confident incorrect decision. A value $h(y) > 0$ indicates that the BNN is not robust to the perturbations.

As shown in Fig. 1, we observe tail distribution bumps under different types of perturbations: around $[-0.1, 0.1]$ for Gaussian noise, $[0.1, 0.3]$ for contrast perturbations, and $[0.25, 0.75]$ for rotation perturbations. These tails correspond to instances where the BNN assigns high confidence to incorrect predictions. In risk-sensitive or safety-critical applications, such tail risks can lead to severe consequences [3,10,14,26]. Standard expected-value metrics, which are negative across all three cases, fail to capture the vulnerability, highlighting the need for risk-averse certification techniques that explicitly account for low-probability yet high-impact failures.

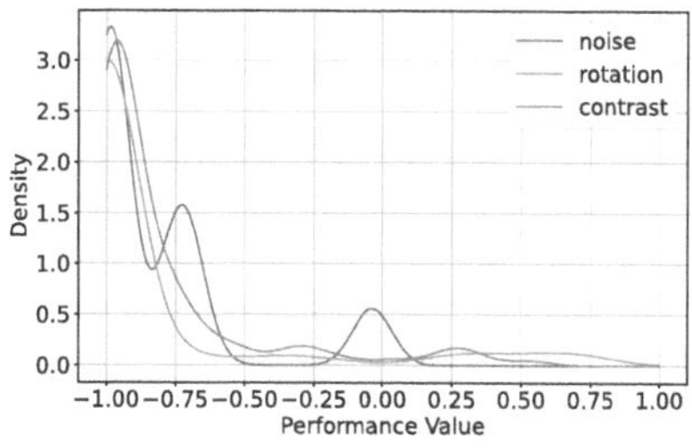

Fig. 1. Tail distributions exist in Bayesian neural networks when recognising images with different types of perturbations.

3.2 Problem Statement

In contrast to the original risk-neutral problem that focuses on bounding the expected value of the output distribution, our risk-averse framework provides robustness guarantees with regard to worst-case adversaries.

Consider a BNN f, with the input $x \sim \mu$ and the parameters $w \sim \lambda$, and the output given by $y = f(x, w)$. Let ν denote the distribution of y. We assume that the output set $\mathcal{Y}$ is compact. This assumption holds for many BNN tasks. For instance, in classification tasks, the outputs of a BNN are typically normalised using the *softmax* function, which ensures that the output set $\mathcal{Y}$ is compact. Moreover, outputs can always be mapped to a prescribed compact set if needed. For a given risk level α and an evaluation function $h : \mathcal{Y} \to \mathbb{R}$, we define the risk-averse evaluation as $\phi_\nu^{\texttt{Perf}} = \text{CVaR}_{\alpha, y\sim\nu}[h(y)]$. In this work, we evaluate a BNN through the following problems.

1. Output support set computation: approximate the output set of the BNN, $\mathcal{Y} = \{f(x, w) \mid x \in \mathcal{X}, w \in \mathcal{W}\}$, over the input region $\mathcal{X}$.
2. Risk-averse evaluation: compute certified (lower and upper) bounds, $\text{CVaR}_{\alpha,\texttt{LB}}$ and $\text{CVaR}_{\alpha,\texttt{UB}}$, on the CVaR of the BNN output evaluated through the performance function h, such that $\text{CVaR}_{\alpha,\texttt{LB}} \leq \text{CVaR}_{\alpha,y\sim\nu}[h(y)] \leq \text{CVaR}_{\alpha,\texttt{UB}}$.

Using the motivating example for illustration, evaluating the robustness of the BNN involves addressing two interrelated tasks: approximating the output set of y_t and y_c, and computing the CVaR bounds of the performance function $h(y) = \max_{t\in[10]\setminus c} y_t - y_c$. Approximating the output set enables a geometric representation and visually interpretable assessment of the BNN's outputs, allowing us to determine whether the outputs remain within a specified safe region. However, the set approximation alone cannot capture the probabilistic information about the likelihood of outputs lying in the safe region. The second task, i.e., computing the CVaR value, addresses this drawback, as it quantifies the tail risks by focusing on the most extreme and potentially hazardous outcomes. Together, these tasks provide a comprehensive framework for assessing the robustness of the BNN in high-stakes applications, where both the nature of the outputs and their risk profiles are crucial considerations.

4 Methodology

4.1 Output Set Approximation

In this section, we present our sampling-based method to approximate the output support set. Given the posterior distribution of BNN parameters λ and the input distribution μ, we first collect a group of independent and identically distributed (i.i.d.) sampled inputs $x_i \in \mathcal{X}$ and a group of i.i.d. sampled parameters $w_j \in \mathcal{W}$. For each pair (x_i, w_j), we compute the corresponding output samples $y_{ij} = f(x_i, w_j)$. For notation simplicity, we rewrite the output samples as y_k and use N to denote the total number of samples.

For the output set approximation, we aim to compute a convex approximation of $\mathcal{Y}$. Leveraging the output samples, we build the approximation by taking the intersection of all half-spaces that contain $\{y_k\}_{k=1}^N$. This convex hull for the output samples serves as an approximation of the true output set, which can be conveniently represented as a template polytope.

Example. To provide an illustration of the proposed output-set approximation, Fig. 2 shows the convex hull of the output pair (y_c, y_t) from a BNN trained on the MNIST dataset, where y_c is the output for the ground-truth class c and y_t represents the *maximum* value among the remaining classes. Each output point corresponds to an input sample under rotation or noise perturbations. The shaded regions represent the approximated output sets constructed using a hexadecagon template.

We provide high-confidence guarantees for the approximation gap by applying the scenario optimisation theory to our problem. Consider a convex template polytope $\mathbb{V} = \{z \in \mathbb{R}^n \mid Vz \leq \mathbf{1}\}$ where $V \in \mathbb{R}^{L \times n}$, $\mathbf{1} \in \mathbb{R}^L$, and L is the number of half spaces or inequalities. Given the set $\mathbb{V}$, we introduce a parameterised set in the form of $\mathcal{H}(\boldsymbol{\theta}) := \{z \in \mathbb{R}^n \mid Vz \leq \boldsymbol{\theta}\}$, where $\boldsymbol{\theta} \in \mathbb{R}^L$. We now approximate the output set $\mathcal{Y}$ by computing the optimal parameterised set $\mathcal{H}(\boldsymbol{\theta}_N^\star)$ with respect to the output samples, where $\boldsymbol{\theta}_N^\star$ is the

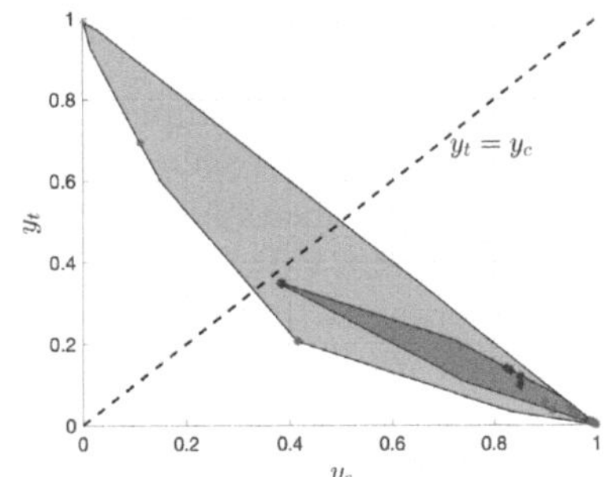

Fig. 2. Output set approximation for Bayesian neural networks under rotation (red) and noise (blue) perturbations. (Color figure online)

optimal solution to the following optimisation problem.

$$\begin{cases} \min_{\theta \in \mathbb{R}^L} & \mathbf{1}^T \boldsymbol{\theta} \\ \text{s.t} & V y_k \leq \boldsymbol{\theta}, k = 1, \cdots, N. \end{cases} \tag{2}$$

The optimisation result is presented in the following proposition.

Proposition 1. *The optimal solution $\boldsymbol{\theta}_N^\star$ to the optimisation problem in Eq.* (2) *is*

$$[\boldsymbol{\theta}_N^\star]_i = \max_{k=1,\cdots,N} [V]_i y_k, \tag{3}$$

where $[V]_i$ denotes the i-th row of V. Let $\hat{\mathcal{Y}}_N = \mathcal{H}(\boldsymbol{\theta}_N^\star)$. Given $\epsilon_1 \in (0,1)$, $\beta_1 \in (0,1)$, and the Euler's constant e, if $N \geq \frac{1}{\epsilon_1}\frac{e}{e-1}\left(\ln\frac{1}{\beta_1} + n + L\right)$, then with probability no less than $1 - \beta_1$, $\mathbb{P}[y \in \mathcal{Y} : y \notin \hat{\mathcal{Y}}_N] = \int_{\mathcal{Y}\setminus\hat{\mathcal{Y}}_N} \nu(d\xi) \leq \epsilon_1$.

Proof. Given the optimisation problem in Eq. (2), it follows that the constraint $V y_k \leq \boldsymbol{\theta}$, for $k = 1, \cdots, N$, should be active with the optimal solution $\boldsymbol{\theta}_N^\star$, where $[\boldsymbol{\theta}_N^\star]_i = \max_{k=1,\cdots,N}[V]_i y_k$. If we enforce constraints for all $y \in \mathcal{Y}$, not just the observed samples, the corresponding optimisation problem becomes

$$\begin{cases} \min_{\theta \in \mathbb{R}^L} & \mathbf{1}^T \boldsymbol{\theta} \\ \text{s.t} & V y \leq \boldsymbol{\theta}, \forall y \in \mathcal{Y} \end{cases} \tag{4}$$

where Equation (2) represents its corresponding scenario-based linear programming formulation. Since the set $\mathcal{Y}$ is compact, the conditions of [2, Theorem 4] hold. Applying that result yields the sample complexity bound and the confidence guarantee stated in Proposition 1.

Proposition 1 provides a statistical bound on the discrepancy between the estimated output set $\hat{\mathcal{Y}}_N$ and the true output set $\mathcal{Y}$. The error bound ϵ_1 has an inverse relationship with N, indicating that achieving tighter error bounds requires a substantially larger sample size. The dimensionality of the sample space n and of the structured polytope L contributes linearly to the sample size, reflecting the increased effort needed to address higher-dimensional or structurally complex problems. Besides, the term $\ln\frac{1}{\beta_1}$ introduces a logarithmic dependence on the confidence level. These results indicate that tighter precision and higher confidence come at the cost of increased computational and data collection demands.

4.2 Risk-Averse Evaluation

Given the output samples $\{y_k\}_{k=1}^N$, we define the empirical distribution of ν as $\hat{\nu}_N(y) = \frac{1}{N}\sum_{i=1}^N \delta_{y_i}(y)$, which approximates the true output distribution ν based on the observed samples. Our goal is to estimate the value of

$\text{CVaR}_{\alpha,y\sim\nu}[h(y)]$, which represents the CVaR value of the performance function h at level α under the distribution ν. Specifically, we seek to compute certified lower and upper bounds on the CVaR across a range of risk levels, accompanied by probabilistic confidence guarantees, as presented in Proposition 2. To facilitate the construction of these confidence bounds, we first introduce the following lemmas.

Lemma 1. *[8] Let $\hat{\nu}_N(y) = \frac{1}{N}\sum_{i=1}^{N}\delta_{y_i}(y)$ be the empirical distribution of ν, where $y_i \in \mathbb{R}^n$. Given $\beta \in (0,1)$, we have*

$$\mathbb{P}(W_1(\nu, \hat{\nu}_N) \geq \epsilon_2) \leq \beta \tag{5}$$

where $\epsilon_2 = \rho(\mathcal{Y})(C^* N^{-\frac{1}{n}} + \sqrt{n}(2\ln\beta^{-1})^{\frac{1}{2}}N^{-\frac{1}{2}})$, $C^* = \sqrt{n}2^{(n-2)/(2)}\Big(\frac{1}{1-2^{1-n/2}} + 2\Big)$, and $\rho(\mathcal{Y})$ is the diameter of the support of $\mathcal{Y}$.

Lemma 2. *[33] Suppose $h(y)$ is L_0-Lipschitz in y. For any two probability distributions $\mathcal{D}_1$ and $\mathcal{D}_2$, we have $|CVaR_{\alpha,y\sim\mathcal{D}_1}[h(y)] - CVaR_{\alpha,y\sim\mathcal{D}_2}[h(y)]| \leq \frac{L_0}{\alpha}W_1(\mathcal{D}_1, \mathcal{D}_2)$.*

The Lipschitz assumption on $h(y)$ is relatively mild in many applications. Robustness properties for classification are typically formalised in a canonical margin form comparing the ground-truth output with the largest competing output. Accordingly, the performance function h maps the original BNN output vector to a scalar quantity corresponding to the robustness property of interest, as illustrated by the performance function h in our motivating example. Since h consists of simple linear comparisons of normalised outputs, its Lipschitz constant L_0 is easy to compute and typically takes a small value in robustness certification scenarios. Building on Lemmas 1 and 2, we derive certified bounds on BNN robustness under different risk levels, as stated in the following proposition. The proof follows from the above two lemmas and is therefore omitted.

Proposition 2. *Suppose that $h(y)$ is L_0-Lipschitz continuous in y. We have*

$$|CVaR_{\alpha,y\sim\hat{\nu}_N}[h(y)] - CVaR_{\alpha,y\sim\nu}[h(y)]| \leq \frac{L_0}{\alpha}\epsilon_2(\beta) \tag{6}$$

with probability at least $1-\beta$, where $\epsilon_2(\beta) = \rho(\mathcal{Y})(C^* N^{-\frac{1}{n}} + \sqrt{n}(2\ln\beta^{-1})^{\frac{1}{2}}N^{-\frac{1}{2}})$, $C^* = \sqrt{n}2^{(n-2)/2}\Big(\frac{1}{1-2^{1-n/2}} + 2\Big)$, $\rho(\mathcal{Y})$ is the diameter of the support of $\mathcal{Y}$.

Proposition 2 states that the gap between the empirical CVaR and the true CVaR depends critically on the sample size N. For a given confidence level β and a target *certification tightness* $H := \frac{L_0}{\alpha}\epsilon_2(\beta)$, i.e., the difference between the upper and lower bounds ($\text{CVaR}_{\alpha,\text{UB}}$-$\text{CVaR}_{\alpha,\text{LB}}$), the required sample size is

$$N = \Big(\frac{L_0\rho(\mathcal{Y})(C^* + \sqrt{n}(2\ln\beta^{-1})^{\frac{1}{2}})}{\alpha H}\Big)^n,$$

where n denotes the output dimension of the BNN. This sample complexity exhibits the following key dependencies: (1) *Exponential sensitivity to certification tightness*: The sample size N scales inversely with H^n, indicating that, as the certification interval tightens ($H \downarrow$), N increases exponentially with an exponent determined by the output dimension n. In practice, neural network certification often introduces an additional layer that maps the robustness specification from the original output player to a single scalar output, reducing the effective output dimension n to 1, thus eliminating the exponential dependence on the original output dimension. (2) *Impact of the CVaR parameter* α: A smaller α (focusing on the worst α-fraction of the outcome distribution) demands a larger number of samples to accurately estimate the tail expectation. (3) *Logarithmic dependence on confidence level*: N increases logarithmically with the confidence level β^{-1}, which means that achieving a higher confidence (smaller β) requires an increase in sample size, but at a slower rate compared to tightening H or reducing α.

5 Experiments

In this section, we present the experimental setup and evaluate the proposed method for output set approximation and risk-averse robustness certification.

5.1 Experimental Setup

Benchmark and Baseline. Following recent work [1], we evaluate our method on three regression tasks: (i) a 1D Noisy Sine dataset, where the BNN is trained on samples from a sine function with additive noise, (2) a 2D extension of the Noisy Sine dataset, and (iii) the Kin8nm dataset, which consists of state-space readings for the dynamics of an eight-link robot arm. We further investigate the performance of our method on two classification tasks using BNNs trained on the MNIST and Fashion-MNIST datasets. For each experiment, we evaluate the risk-averse robustness of BNN models under various noise and attack scenarios by computing certified CVaR values across a range of risk levels. Specifically, at risk level 1, we compare our approach with the state-of-the-art method BNN-DP in [1] by evaluating their performance in terms of the *tightness* of the certified bounds and the computation overhead. All experiments are conducted on a cluster with Intel Xeon Gold 6252 2.1GHz CPU, and NVIDIA 2080Ti GPU.

Evaluation Metric. To evaluate the certification performance of our approach, we use γ-robustness [1], defined below in its generalised form for CVaR.

Definition 2 (γ-robustness). *Let $CVaR_{\alpha,y\sim\nu}[h(y)]$ be the exact CVaR value of the performance function h at risk level α under the output distribution ν. Given a pair of certified lower and upper bounds for the target CVaR value, denoted as $CVaR_{\alpha,\mathtt{LB}}$ and $CVaR_{\alpha,\mathtt{UB}}$, which satisfy that $CVaR_{\alpha,\mathtt{LB}} \leq CVaR_{\alpha,y\sim\nu}[h(y)] \leq CVaR_{\alpha,\mathtt{UB}}$, γ-*`robustness` *is computed by*

$$\gamma\text{-}\mathtt{robustness} = CVaR_{\alpha,\mathtt{UB}} - CVaR_{\alpha,\mathtt{LB}}$$

Intuitively, γ-`robustness` computes the difference between the upper and lower bounds on the expectation outputs of a BNN with regard to a property formulated by the performance function. Proposition 2 allows us to bound $\text{CVaR}_{\alpha,y\sim\nu}[h(y)]$ systematically through the certification tightness, defined as $H := \frac{L_\Omega}{\alpha}\epsilon_2(\beta)$. A smaller γ-`robustness` value implies a tighter certified bound computation.

In the following experimental results, we *(i)* characterise the output set of a BNN over an input region using a set of template polytopes in RQ1, *(ii)* present the certified CVaR values under different confidence and risk levels for both regression and classification tasks in RQ2, *(iii)* compare the tightness of certified γ-`robustness` achieved by our approach and the SOTA technique [1] in RQ3, and *(iv)* investigate the sampling feasibility with regard to the bound tightness, confidence and risk parameters in RQ4.

5.2 Evaluation Results

RQ1: Is Our Approach Effective in Characterising the Output Set? We consider the MNIST dataset under two perturbation scenarios: *(i)* rotation perturbation that alters the image orientation to a certain angle, and *(ii)* noise perturbation where Gaussian noises are applied to all image pixels. We set the maximum rotation angle for the geometric (rotation) perturbation to 45° and sample Gaussian noise from a distribution with a mean of 0 and a standard deviation of 0.5.

Table 1. Comparison of template polytope with different number of sides.

Number of sides L	4	8	16	32	64
Sample count	285	412	665	1171	2184
Volume (rotation)	0.986	0.306	0.236	0.223	0.218
Volume (noise)	0.216	0.095	0.043	0.031	0.021

We have shown in Fig. 2 the relationship between two output variables of the BNN, where y_c (x-axis) represents the output for the ground-truth class c, and y_t (y-axis) represents the maximum output among the remaining nine classes. The black dashed line $y_t = y_c$ serves as a decision boundary: samples lying below this line are classified correctly by the BNN, since the ground-truth output y_c exceeds all others. Points marked in red and blue correspond to samples perturbed by rotation and noise, respectively. To approximate the output support set, we select the template set $\mathbb{V}$ as a regular 2D polytope with L sides. For each choice of L, Proposition 1 provides the required sample size to achieve an approximation error of at most 0.05 with 95% confidence. Approximation quality is measured by the volume of the approximated set. Table 1 summarises the results for different L. We find that the hexadecagon ($L = 16$) offers a sufficient number of support directions and good approximation quality, while larger values of L yield diminishing returns. In Fig. 2, the red and blue shaded regions show the approximated output sets for rotation and noise perturbations, respectively, obtained with a hexadecagon template ($L = 16$) and a sample size of 1000.

To systematically evaluate the robustness of the BNN under these perturbations, we compute the output support set as the convex hull of all possible output pairs (y_t, y_c) for each perturbation type. The output support set provides a geometric and quantitative characterisation of BNN behaviour. If the support set lies predominantly below the decision boundary, the BNN demonstrates robustness against the perturbation. Conversely, if substantial portions extend above the boundary, it indicates vulnerability. As shown in Fig. 2, the BNN exhibits robustness to noise perturbations but is susceptible to rotations. This geometric perspective provides an intuitive way to evaluate BNN's performance under different perturbation scenarios.

RQ2: Is Our Approach Effective in Characterising Risk-Averse Robustness of BNNs? To answer this question, we evaluate the effectiveness of our approach in characterising certified CVaR bounds under a range of risk levels. A comparison of certification performance for the entire output distribution ($\alpha = 1$) with the baseline method BNN-DP is deferred to RQ3.

Table 2. Certified CVaR bounds under different confidence and risk levels for regression tasks.

Tasks	$\beta = 0.05$			$\beta = 0.01$		
	$\alpha = 1$	$\alpha = 0.5$	$\alpha = 0.25$	$\alpha = 1$	$\alpha = 0.5$	$\alpha = 0.25$
1D Noisy Sine	0.074 ± 0.1	0.146 ± 0.1	0.147 ± 0.1	0.058 ± 0.1	0.148 ± 0.1	0.165 ± 0.1
2D Noisy Sine	0.081 ± 0.1	0.173 ± 0.1	0.268 ± 0.1	0.077 ± 0.1	0.203 ± 0.1	0.272 ± 0.1
Kin8nm	0.080 ± 0.1	0.088 ± 0.1	0.097 ± 0.1	0.079 ± 0.1	0.088 ± 0.1	0.103 ± 0.1

Regression Benchmarks. We first evaluate the proposed method on BNNs trained with three regression datasets: 1D Noisy Sine, its 2D equivalent, and Kin8nm. To assess the effectiveness of our method, we compute certified CVaR bounds under different levels of risk ($\alpha = 0.25, 0.5, 1$) and confidence guarantees ($\beta = 0.05, 0.1$).

Table 2 summarises the evaluation results for the regression tasks. For each configuration, the CVaR value represents the estimated expectation of the subset of the distribution for the performance function. The upper and lower bounds from the true CVaR value are constrained by a pre-defined limit of $H = 0.1$. As a result, the γ-`robustness`, which measures the tightness of the computed upper and lower bounds, is therefore 0.2. For the 1D Noisy Sine task, we apply noise up to 0.01 around the input point $\pi/2$ and the property of interest is the deviation from the ground truth output, with the performance function defined as $h(y) = 1 - y$. As expected, when we focus on the worst-case outcomes, the CVaR values, which indicate the average deviation in the subset scenarios, show an increase. For the 2D Noisy Sine task, we use the same perturbation noise (up to 0.01), except that the perturbations are applied to two input features rather than one. The same performance function, $h(y) = 1 - y$, is used for evaluation. In this case, CVaR values show slight increases across all settings compared to the 1D dataset, largely due to the added noises to the 2D input space.

For the Kin8nm dataset, we simulate input perturbation noise up to 0.01 for eight input features and evaluate the output deviation from the ground truth, formulated using the performance function $h(y) = |y^* - y|$, where y^* indicates the ground-truth value. Notably, the estimated CVaR values demonstrate small variance across different risk levels ($\alpha = 1, 0.5, 0.25$). As previously discussed, a consistent performance under varying risk levels is the ideal *risk-averse robustness* we aim to achieve for BNN certification.

Table 3. Certified CVaR bounds for different attacks on classification tasks.

Tasks	CVaR Level	L_∞ noise	Rotation	Contrast
MNIST	$\alpha = 1$	-0.999 ± 0.1	-0.998 ± 0.1	-0.997 ± 0.1
	$\alpha = 0.5$	-0.999 ± 0.1	-0.998 ± 0.1	-0.993 ± 0.1
	$\alpha = 0.25$	-0.999 ± 0.1	-0.997 ± 0.1	-0.986 ± 0.1
FASHION	$\alpha = 1$	-0.191 ± 0.1	-0.119 ± 0.1	-0.152 ± 0.1
	$\alpha = 0.5$	0.443 ± 0.1	0.525 ± 0.1	0.562 ± 0.1
	$\alpha = 0.25$	0.885 ± 0.1	0.964 ± 0.1	0.849 ± 0.1

Classification Benchmarks. Table 3 summarises the certified bounds for image classification tasks under different levels of risk α. We evaluate the risk-averse robustness of BNNs against three types of attacks: L_∞ attack, where perturbation noise up to a specific limit is applied to all image pixels, and two geometric attacks, rotation (altering the image's orientation) and contrast (changing its brightness and contrast). For each configuration, the CVaR value represents the estimated expected value of the performance function, w.r.t. a property of interest, over (the subset of) the distribution.

For the MNIST dataset, the perturbation limit for the L_∞ attack is set to 0.1, the rotation range to $[-45°, 45°]$, and the contrast factor to 0.5. Robustness is evaluated by checking whether the predicted labels remain consistent with the ground truth label, denoted as c among the 10 classes. The corresponding performance function is defined as $h(y) = \max_{i \in [10] \setminus c} y_i - y_c$, where c is the ground-truth label. The BNN is robust to perturbations if $h(y) < 0$. For both L_∞ and *rotation* attacks, our approach reveals that the trained BNN achieves strong certified risk-averse robustness, with very low variance in performance across the entire output distribution and the worst 25% outcomes. Under the *contrast* attack, the BNN shows small variance when evaluating the overall expectation and the worst-performing 25% subset. Nonetheless, the expected values for the most challenging cases remain far below 0, demonstrating the BNN's risk-averse robustness across all attack types.

For the FASHION dataset, we set the perturbation limit for the L_∞ attack to 0.1, the rotation range to $[-15°, 15°]$, and the contrast factor to 0.9. As with the MNIST dataset, We investigate output label consistency, formulated by the performance function $h(y) = \max_{i \in [10] \setminus c} y_i - y_c$. Note that the expectation values over the full output distribution for all three attack types are negative, indicating overall certified robustness. However, when focusing on the worst-performing 50% and 25% subset of the output distribution, the expectation values are all positive, highlighting the necessity of risk-averse evaluation for BNNs. Compared with the BNN for the MNIST dataset, this BNN demonstrates a lack of robustness, especially in risk-sensitive scenarios.

Table 4. Comparison with SOTA in certified bound tightness and computation time.

Method	1D Noisy Sine		Kin8nm		MNIST	
	γ-robustness	Time (s)	γ-robustness	Time (s)	γ-robustness	Time (s)
BNN-DP	**0.065**	6.148	0.137	7.886	1.572	24.956
RAC-BNN (0.1)	0.2	**0.815**	0.2	**0.984**	0.2	**1.064**
RAC-BNN (0.05)	0.1	1.640	**0.1**	1.893	**0.1**	4.099

RQ3: What Is the Certification Performance of Our Approach in Tightness and Efficiency? We perform comparison experiments with BNN-DP in computing certified bounds for the entire output distribution (corresponding to $\alpha = 1$). The evaluation focuses on two metrics: the tightness of the certified bounds (γ-`robustness`) and the computation time of the certification procedure.

Table 4 summarises the results for both regression and classification tasks. In the evaluation, we assess the performance of our method (RAC-BNN) under two certification range settings: $H = 0.1$ and $H = 0.05$. The corresponding γ-robustness is given by $\gamma = 2H$, enabling a direct comparison with the baseline method for the performance evaluation of the entire output distribution, i.e., $\alpha = 1$. Note that our approach systematically bounds the tightness of the expectation of the target performance function through the certification range, defined as $H := \frac{L_0}{\alpha}\epsilon_2(\beta)$ (see Proposition 2). By the definition of γ-`robustness`, which measures the difference between the upper and lower bounds of the expected value of the performance function, it follows that the corresponding γ-`robustness` is $2H$.

The evaluation results in Table 4 demonstrate that our method improves both the tightness and efficiency of computing certified bounds. For the 1D Noisy Sine dataset, while BNN-DP demonstrates competitive performance in certification tightness, to achieve comparable tightness with our method requires further tightening of the certification range H. On the other hand, our method significantly reduces the computational overhead for certification. As the input dimension increases and the task gets more complex, the advantages of our method in certification performance become more significant than the baseline method. Specifically, when $H = 0.05$, our method surpasses the baseline in tightness for all the remaining tasks. Particularly, for the MNIST dataset, our method improves the tightness of the certified bounds by 87.3% and 93.6% for $H = 0.1$ and $H = 0.05$, respectively. In terms of computation time, our method achieves a reduction of 76.0% and 83.6% for Kin8nm and MNIST under the $H = 0.05$ setting.

Table 5. Sample complexity for different hyper-parameters.

Task	γ-robustness	$\beta = 0.05$			$\beta = 0.01$		
		$\alpha = 1$	$\alpha = 0.5$	$\alpha = 0.25$	$\alpha = 1$	$\alpha = 0.5$	$\alpha = 0.25$
Kin8nm	$H = 0.1$	17648	69923	278354	26950	107129	427177
	$H = 0.05$	69923	278354	1110733	107129	427177	1706025
MNIST	$H = 0.1$	2520	9835	38844	3808	14986	59445
	$H = 0.05$	9835	38844	154379	14986	59445	236783

RQ4: What Is the Sample Complexity of Our Approach? In Sect. 4.2, Proposition 2 provides a theoretical relation between the sampling complexity and key hyper-parameters, including certified bound tightness H, risk parameters α and confidence errors β. For benchmark tasks, the performance function $h(y)$, which measures the output difference to the ground-truth value for regression tasks or label consistency for classification tasks, is a scalar random variable. With the dimension n reduced to 1, according to Proposition 2, the required sample size N is inversely proportional to H and the risk level α, while depending logarithmically on the confidence level β.

To demonstrate the practical sampling feasibility of our approach, we compute the required sample size under different configurations to evaluate the impact of individual parameters on sampling complexity. The results are summarised in Table 5. Across all configurations, the sampling complexity is manageable, with the largest required sample size reaching 10^6. This is the case when evaluating a narrow 25% worst-performing region of the distribution with a tightness bound of 0.05 and a 99% confidence guarantee.

6 Conclusion

We introduce a novel risk-averse robustness evaluation method for computing certified bounds of Bayesian neural networks using the coherent risk measure

CVaR. By leveraging sampling and optimisation, our approach approximates the output distribution and bounds the CVaR values with probabilistic guarantees. We implement this method in a tool, RAC-BNN, and demonstrate its ability to compute probabilistically sound approximations of output sets and quantify robustness under worst-performing conditions. The results show that RAC-BNN achieves improved certification tightness and better efficiency compared to the state-of-the-art baseline. An interesting future direction is to extend our approach to the safety evaluation of closed-loop dynamical systems with BNN controllers.

Acknowledgments. MK and XZ received partial support from ELSA: European Lighthouse on Secure and Safe AI project (Grant No. 101070617 under UK guarantee) and the ERC under the European Union's Horizon 2020 research and innovation program (FUN2MODEL, Grant No. 834115).

References

1. Adams, S., Patane, A., Lahijanian, M., Laurenti, L.: BNN-DP: robustness certification of bayesian neural networks via dynamic programming. In: International Conference on Machine Learning, ICML 2023. Proceedings of Machine Learning Research, vol. 202, pp. 133–151. PMLR (2023)
2. Alamo, T., Tempo, R., Luque, A.: On the sample complexity of randomized approaches to the analysis and design under uncertainty. In: Proceedings of American Control Conference, pp. 4671–4676 (2010)
3. Babak, A., Delong, A., Weirauch, M.T., Frey, B.J.: Predicting the sequence specificities of dna- and rna-binding proteins by deep learning. Nat. Biotechnol. **33**(8), 831–838 (2015). https://doi.org/10.1038/nbt.3300
4. Berrada, L., et al.: Make sure you're unsure: a framework for verifying probabilistic specifications. In: Proceedings of Annual Conference on Advances in Neural Information Processing Systems, pp. 11136–11147 (2021)
5. Bhat, S.P., LA, P.: Concentration of risk measures: a wasserstein distance approach. In: Advances in Neural Information Processing Systems, vol. 32 (2019)
6. Blundell, C., Cornebise, J., Kavukcuoglu, K., Wierstra, D.: Weight uncertainty in neural network. In: International Conference on Machine Learning, pp. 1613–1622. PMLR (2015)
7. Bojarski, M., et al.: End to end learning for self-driving cars. arXiv preprint arXiv:1604.07316 (2016)
8. Boskos, D., Cortés, J., Martínez, S.: High-confidence data-driven ambiguity sets for time-varying linear systems. IEEE Trans. Autom. Control (2023)
9. Cardelli, L., Kwiatkowska, M., Laurenti, L., Paoletti, N., Patane, A., Wicker, M.: Statistical guarantees for the robustness of Bayesian neural networks. In: Proceedings of International Joint Conferences on Artificial Intelligence (2019)
10. Chen, Z., Huang, X.: End-to-end learning for lane keeping of self-driving cars. In: IEEE Intelligent Vehicles Symposium (IV), pp. 1856–1860 (2017). https://doi.org/10.1109/IVS.2017.7995975
11. Chow, Y., Ghavamzadeh, M.: Algorithms for cvar optimization in mdps. In: Advances in Neural Information Processing Systems 27: Annual Conference on Neural Information Processing Systems 2014, pp. 3509–3517 (2014)

12. Codevilla, F., Müller, M., López, A.M., Koltun, V., Dosovitskiy, A.: End-to-end driving via conditional imitation learning. In: Proceedings of the 2018 IEEE International Conference on Robotics and Automation, pp. 1–9. IEEE (2018). https://doi.org/10.1109/ICRA.2018.8460487
13. Curi, S., Levy, K.Y., Jegelka, S., Krause, A.: Adaptive sampling for stochastic risk-averse learning. Adv. Neural. Inf. Process. Syst. **33**, 1036–1047 (2020)
14. Dahl, G.E., Stokes, J.W., Deng, L., Yu, D.: Large-scale malware classification using random projections and neural networks. In: Proceedings of the 38th IEEE International Conference on Acoustics, Speech and Signal Processing, pp. 3422–3426. IEEE (2013). https://doi.org/10.1109/ICASSP.2013.6638293
15. Gal, Y., Ghahramani, Z.: Dropout as a bayesian approximation: representing model uncertainty in deep learning. In: Proceedings of International Conference on Machine Learning, pp. 1050–1059. PMLR (2016)
16. Huang, X., Kwiatkowska, M., Wang, S., Wu, M.: Safety verification of deep neural networks. In: Majumdar, R., Kunčak, V. (eds.) CAV 2017. LNCS, vol. 10426, pp. 3–29. Springer, Cham (2017). https://doi.org/10.1007/978-3-319-63387-9_1
17. Kahn, G., Villaflor, A., Pong, V., Abbeel, P., Levine, S.: Uncertainty-aware reinforcement learning for collision avoidance. arXiv preprint arXiv:1702.01182 (2017)
18. Katz, G., Barrett, C., Dill, D.L., Julian, K., Kochenderfer, M.J.: Reluplex: an efficient smt solver for verifying deep neural networks. In: Proceedings of International Conference on Computer Aided Verification, pp. 97–117. Springer (2017)
19. La, P., Ghavamzadeh, M.: Actor-critic algorithms for risk-sensitive mdps. In: Advances in Neural Information Processing Systems, vol. 26 (2013)
20. Lakdawalla, D.N., Phelps, C.E.: Health technology assessment with diminishing returns to health: the generalized risk-adjusted cost-effectiveness (grace) approach. Value Health **24**(2), 244–249 (2021)
21. Lechner, M., Zikelic, D., Chatterjee, K., Henzinger, T.A.: Infinite time horizon safety of bayesian neural networks. Proc. Adv. Neural Inf. Process. Syst. **34**, 10171–10185 (2021)
22. Michelmore, R., Wicker, M., Laurenti, L., Cardelli, L., Gal, Y., Kwiatkowska, M.: Uncertainty quantification with statistical guarantees in end-to-end autonomous driving control. In: Proceedings of IEEE International Conference on Robotics and Automation (ICRA), pp. 7344–7350. IEEE (2020)
23. Neal, R.M.: Bayesian Learning for Neural Networks, vol. 118. Springer Science & Business Media (2012)
24. O'Donoghue, T., Somerville, J.: Modeling risk aversion in economics. J. Econ. Perspect. **32**(2), 91–114 (2018)
25. Rockafellar, R.T., Uryasev, S., et al.: Optimization of conditional value-at-risk. J. Risk **2**, 21–42 (2000)
26. Rushe, D.: Tesla's autopilot faces us investigation after crashes with emergency vehicles (2021), https://www.theguardian.com/technology/2021/aug/16/teslas-autopilot-us-investigation-crashes-emergency-vehicles
27. Shapiro, A., Dentcheva, D., Ruszczynski, A.: Lectures on stochastic programming: modeling and theory. In: SIAM (2021)
28. Shin, E.C.R., Song, D., Moazzezi, R.: Recognizing functions in binaries with neural networks. In: Proceedings of the 24th USENIX Security Symposium, pp. 611–626. USENIX Association (2015)
29. Singh, G., Gehr, T., Püschel, M., Vechev, M.: An abstract domain for certifying neural networks. In: Proceedings of the ACM on Programming Languages, pp. 1–30 (2019)

30. Tamar, A., Chow, Y., Ghavamzadeh, M., Mannor, S.: Policy gradient for coherent risk measures. In: Proceedings of Annual Conference on Advances in Neural Information Processing Systems, vol. 28 (2015)
31. Tjeng, V., Xiao, K.Y., Tedrake, R.: Evaluating robustness of neural networks with mixed integer programming. In: Proceedings of International Conference on Learning Representations. OpenReview.net (2019)
32. Vitt, C.A., Dentcheva, D., Xiong, H.: Risk-averse classification. Ann. Oper. Res. 1–35 (2019)
33. Wang, S., Wang, Z., Yi, X., Zavlanos, M.M., Johansson, K.H., Hirche, S.: Risk-averse learning with non-stationary distributions. arXiv preprint arXiv:2404.02988 (2024)
34. Wicker, M., Laurenti, L., Patane, A., Kwiatkowska, M.: Probabilistic safety for bayesian neural networks. In: Proceedings of Conference on Uncertainty in Artificial Intelligence, pp. 1198–1207. PMLR (2020)
35. Wicker, M., Laurenti, L., Patane, A., Paoletti, N., Abate, A., Kwiatkowska, M.: Certification of iterative predictions in Bayesian neural networks. In: de Campos, C., Maathuis, M.H. (eds.) Proceedings of the Thirty-Seventh Conference on Uncertainty in Artificial Intelligence. Proceedings of Machine Learning Research, vol. 161, pp. 1713–1723. PMLR, 27–30 July 2021, https://proceedings.mlr.press/v161/wicker21a.html
36. Wicker, M., Laurenti, L., Patane, A., Paoletti, N., Abate, A., Kwiatkowska, M.: Probabilistic reach-avoid for bayesian neural networks. Artif. Intell. **334**, 104–132 (2024). https://doi.org/10.1016/j.artint.2024.104132
37. Wicker, M., Patane, A., Laurenti, L., Kwiatkowska, M.: Adversarial robustness certification for bayesian neural networks. In: Proceedings of International Symposium on Formal Methods, pp. 3–28. Springer (2024)
38. Xu, K., et al.: Automatic perturbation analysis for scalable certified robustness and beyond. In: Proceedings of Annual Conference on Advances in Neural Information Processing Systems (2020)
39. Zhai, R., Dan, C., Suggala, A., Kolter, J.Z., Ravikumar, P.: Boosted cvar classification. Adv. Neural. Inf. Process. Syst. **34**, 21860–21871 (2021)
40. Zhang, H., Weng, T., Chen, P., Hsieh, C., Daniel, L.: Efficient neural network robustness certification with general activation functions. In: Proceedings of Annual Conference on Advances in Neural Information Processing Systems, pp. 4944–4953 (2018)

EM-Merge: Consolidating Fragmented Templates in LLM Log Parsing

Qiyue Zhu, Jinyuan Wang, Yani Yang, and Tong Li(✉)

Beijing University of Technology, Beijing, China
{qiyue.zhu,yani.yang}@ucdconnect.ie, wangjinyuan@emails.bjut.edu.cn,
litong@bjut.edu.cn

Abstract. Log parsing is a critical step for log analysis, responsible for converting raw, semi-structured log messages into structured templates. Despite using semantic knowledge to enhance template extraction, LLM-based log parsers frequently generate fragmented templates, generating several marginally distinct templates for semantically identical events. This fragmentation generates duplicate downstream processing, reduces cache hit rates, and inflates the template pool. We introduce EM-Merge, a lightweight, model-independent postprocessing layer that directly mitigates fragmentation without requiring further LLM calls. EM-Merge employs a two-stage strategy: (1) semantic screening, where newly generated and cached templates are encoded with Sentence-BERT and nearest-neighbor search selects semantically plausible candidates; (2) confidence-weighted structural merging, where candidate pairs are scored by a normalized longest-common-subsequence measure modulated by LLM generation confidences, then clustered and merged into generalized templates (non-common tokens replaced by wildcards). This design preserves semantic distinctions while preventing misleading splits driven by punctuation or surface variation. We evaluate EM-Merge on 14 public log datasets and find that, with no runtime overhead, it reliably reduces template redundancy, improves grouping and parsing accuracy, and lowers end-to-end processing cost when compared to strong baselines.

Keywords: Log Parsing · Large Language Models · Postprocessing

1 Introduction

Large-scale software systems, such as cloud services, distributed storage clusters, and internet-scale applications, produce massive volumes of semi-structured log data that record every system event, performance statistic, and error condition. Critical processes including capacity planning, failure prediction, anomaly detection, and root-cause analysis are supported by these logs [1–3]. However, raw log messages are a combination of fixed text and variable fields, making direct analysis both inefficient and error-prone. Log parsing addresses this by extracting a template (the invariant scaffold of a message) and its parameters (the dynamic elements). For example, "`User Alice logged in from`

A. Goharshady and C. Haase (Eds.): SETTA 2025, LNCS 16458, pp. 318–338, 2026.
https://doi.org/10.1007/978-981-95-7826-9_17

`192.168.0.1`" is parsed into the template ``` ``User <*> logged in from <*>'' ```, with ``` ``Alice'' ``` and ``` ``192.168.0.1'' ``` identified as parameters. Such structured output is essential for reliable downstream processing by ML and rule-based systems.

Recent advances have applied large language models (LLMs) such as GPT-3 [4] and its offspring to log parsing via prompt-based, zero-, and few-shot learning [5]. These methods excel at handling novel formats and capturing subtle semantics. Yet, two core challenges remain unaddressed in existing LLM parsers:

1. Template Fragmentation. A single event type, meaning log messages that describe the same underlying system action, often produces multiple slightly different templates due to minor token order shifts, synonym choices, or wildcard insertions. This "fragmentation" bloats the template set, reduces cache reuse, and complicates clustering for anomaly grouping.
2. Lack of Lightweight Consolidation. While some approaches attempt offline merge or split operations [6], they typically require repeated calls to the LLM or manual intervention, incurring high latency and resource costs that make real-time deployment impractical.

To overcome these limitations, we introduce EM-Merge, a lightweight, model-independent postprocessing framework that can be retrofitted onto any cache-based LLM parser without additional LLM inference. Our design rationale is as follows: (1) Semantic Screening. Recognizing that LLMs can misinterpret punctuation and domain cues, we first embed each newly generated and cached template into a dense vector space using SentenceBERT [7]. By performing a fast nearest-neighbor search, we select only the most semantically similar template candidates, dramatically reducing downstream computational cost. (2) Confidence-Weighted Structural Merging. Within this candidate set, we compute a merge score that blends normalized Longest Common Subsequence (LCS) overlap with the LLM's own confidence estimates. Templates that exceed a tunable threshold are then grouped via density-based clustering and merged into a single generalized template by preserving common tokens and masking divergent ones. By explicitly combining semantic embeddings with structural and confidence signals, EM-Merge unifies fragmented templates into coherent representations, improving cache hit rates and simplifying downstream analysis, all with minimal performance overhead.

We validate EM-Merge on fourteen public datasets from the LogPAI Loghub-2.0 collection [3,8], demonstrating substantial reductions in template redundancy and notable gains in end-to-end accuracy and throughput compared to state-of-the-art parsers.

To summarize, this paper makes the following contributions:

- We propose EM-Merge, a novel postprocessing pipeline that consolidates semantically equivalent log templates without requiring additional calls to large language models.
- We develop a semantic screening mechanism based on Sentence-BERT to efficiently preselect candidates for merging.

- We introduce a confidence-weighted structural similarity metric combined with a clustering strategy to achieve precise fusion of log templates.
- We perform comprehensive evaluations on fourteen real-world datasets, demonstrating consistent improvements in template coherence and parsing efficiency.
- The source code of EM-Merge is publicly available at https://github.com/VictoriaZQY/EM-Merge to benefit both practitioners and researchers in the field of log analysis.

2 Background

In this section, we review the two foundational pillars of our work. First, we present the evolution of log parsing techniques in software systems, then demonstrate the emergence and capabilities of large language models (LLMs) in natural language processing. Together, these perspectives motivate the design of EM-Merge, a lightweight, embedding-aware postprocessing framework for log template consolidation.

2.1 Log Parsing

Modern software systems continuously generate large volumes of semi-structured logs that record runtime behaviors such as system events, errors, and user interactions [9,10]. To support downstream tasks like anomaly detection or root cause analysis, these logs must first be converted into structured formats. This process is known as log parsing, which separates constant patterns (templates) from variable content (parameters) [11,12].

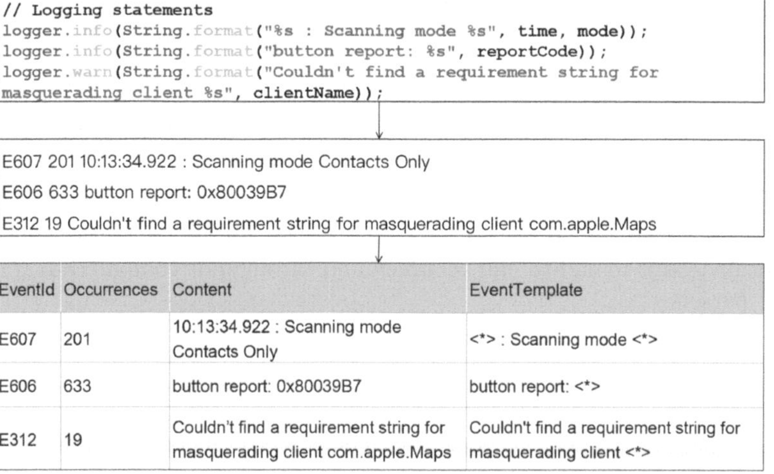

Fig. 1. An example of log parsing.

For example, in Fig. 1, the message: "`10:13:34.922 : Scanning mode Contacts Only`" can be parsed into the template "`<*> : Scanning mode <*>`" where "`10:13:34.922`" and "`Contacts Only`" become dynamic fields. Once structured, these templates enable downstream machine learning and rule-based analytics to be applied more reliably.

Traditional log parsers often rely on manually crafted regular expressions, which lack scalability and generalizability across evolving systems [13]. To address this, a variety of automated, data-driven methods have emerged:

- Frequent pattern mining methods (e.g., Logram [14]) assume that static tokens occur more frequently and extract templates accordingly.
- Clustering-based approaches (e.g., LenMa [15]) group similar log lines using token-based distances but often require sensitive threshold tuning.
- Heuristic parsers (e.g., Drain [9]) build parse trees based on token positions and delimiters, offering a balance between efficiency and flexibility.

More recently, semantic-based methods have introduced neural models to capture contextual meaning within logs, enabling improved discrimination between static and dynamic parts. For example, sentence-level embeddings (e.g., SentenceBERT variants) have been used to represent log events for downstream tasks such as anomaly detection and semantic grouping, demonstrating that semantic representations help identify paraphrased or semantically equivalent events that token-only methods miss [7,16]. These methods typically rely on labeled data for supervised learning and show promise in handling complex log structures, though their practical deployment is often limited by annotation costs and sensitivity to domain shift [17,18].

2.2 Large Language Models for Log Parsing

Transformer-based LLMs have transformed many NLP tasks by providing strong contextual representations and by enabling few-shot or in-context learning: large pretrained models can often perform new tasks with only a handful of examples or simple prompts, reducing dependence on large hand-labeled corpora [4]. These capabilities translate naturally to log parsing: LLMs and LLM-derived encoders capture semantic relations that allow them to recognize when differently worded log messages share the same underlying template, and they can be prompted or few-shot tuned to locate variable fields with much less annotation than conventional supervised methods. Recent works demonstrate several concrete benefits from this shift. First, LLM-based parsers produce rich, reusable artifacts, such as line- or token-level embeddings, token confidences, and alternative candidate parses that enable powerful downstream operations (e.g., embedding-based clustering, confidence-weighted selection, and caching) beyond a single template output. Second, LLM-centric systems (e.g., LogPPT [19], LILAC [17] and subsequent LLM-parsing studies) combine prompt or few-shot strategies with caching or selective invocation to achieve high parsing accuracy while mitigating labeling cost and improving robustness across datasets [20].

At the same time, practical deployment of LLM-based parsing faces clear constraints: repeated LLM calls over high-volume streams incur latency and monetary cost, and models can produce inconsistent templates across repeated or slightly different prompts, which harms cache hit rates and downstream stability. These trade-offs have motivated hybrid designs that treat the LLM as a semantic signal generator rather than an end-to-end oracle, i.e., systems extract embeddings and confidences from a limited set of LLM inferences and then apply lightweight, efficient postprocessing (caching, embedding pre-screening, and confidence-weighted merging) to consolidate templates and avoid further expensive model calls [17,19,21]. EM-Merge follows this hybrid philosophy: by reusing embeddings and token-confidence information emitted by LLM-based parsers and by applying an efficient, confidence-aware merging strategy, EM-Merge aims to improve cross-call consistency and cache effectiveness without invoking additional LLM inference for consolidation.

3 Approach

Based on our preliminary evaluation using ChatGPT (gpt-3.5-turbo-0613) in zero-shot parsing over the Loghub-2.0 datasets, we found that LLMs often misinterpret domain cues (e.g., splitting hexadecimal fields after colons), fail to generalize recurring structural patterns, and produce fragmented templates for semantically identical events. These issues inflate the template inventory and reduce grouping accuracy. ChatGPT's excessive sensitivity to punctuation signals and irregular structural anchoring, which were also observed in earlier LLM-based parsing studies [22], were responsible for almost all of these errors.

As illustrated in Fig. 1, the raw message `10:13:34.922 : Scanning mode Contacts Only` is correctly abstracted into `<*> : Scanning mode <*>`, where the timestamp and mode vary while the rest remains stable. This parameterization is acceptable because it preserves the invariant event structure. However, excessive sensitivity to punctuation can lead to incorrect variants such as `10:13:34.<*> : Scanning mode Contacts Only` or `<*> : Scanning mode Contacts Only`, which either break a token boundary or remove a useful anchor. Such cases fragment the event pattern and lower parsing consistency.

A model that understands sentence structure and semantics could easily avoid such issues and produce the correct segmentation shown in Fig. 1. This observation motivates the design of EM-Merge, which was designed to (a) use SentenceBERT embeddings to capture semantic similarity beyond token-level signals [7], (b) apply a confidence-modulated structural similarity metric to merge only templates that align both semantically and structurally, and (c) cluster and merge similar templates. Together, these stages form a lightweight postprocessing layer that repairs fragmented templates before they are cached, improving consistency and reducing redundant LLM invocations.

3.1 Overview and Motivation

Figure 2 presents the overall design of the EM-Merge workflow.

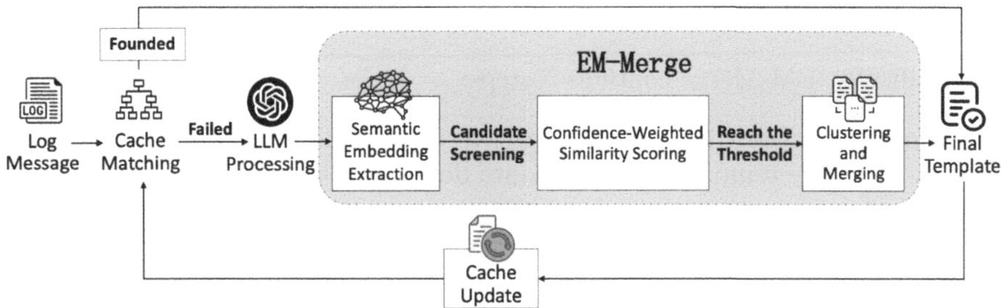

Fig. 2. Overview of the Workflow.

When a log message arrives, it first enters the parser and is checked against the parsing cache. If a confident cache hit is found, the cached template is returned immediately, and the system moves on to the next message. If no adequate match exists, the system retrieves a small set of relevant cached templates and uses them as candidate demonstrations for the in-context learning enhanced parser, which queries the LLM and obtains a proposed template together with any available token-level confidence signals. However, this raw LLM output is not always correct. For example, in Fig. 3, the model may produce a fragmented form such as "`10:13:34.<*> : Starting AirDrop server for user <*> on wake`" or even an over-abstracted "`<*> : Starting AirDrop server for user <*>`", both of which mishandle punctuation and token boundaries. Instead of committing that raw output to the cache, EM-Merge takes over and encodes the generated template and the retrieved candidates into dense semantic vectors so that meaning, not just surface tokens, guides subsequent decisions. These embeddings are used to pre-screen plausible merge candidates, then a confidence-weighted structural similarity test compares token alignments with greater emphasis on high-confidence elements and downweights uncertain or model-generated parts. Candidates that pass this combined semantic and structural scrutiny are grouped by clustering, and clusters that meet consolidation thresholds are merged into a single canonical template. The parsing cache is then updated transactionally so that fragmented duplicates are replaced by the consolidated template, and future messages benefit from higher cache hit rates. After EM-Merge's screening, scoring, clustering, and merging steps, the erroneous or fragmented candidate is repaired to the correct canonical form shown in Fig. 3 (for example, "`<*> : Starting AirDrop server for user <*> on wake`"), so subsequent cache matches return a consistent template.

This whole sequence, including cache match, selective LLM invocation, embedding screening, confidence-aware comparison, clustering, and cache update, repeats for every incoming message, forming a continuous processing loop. Each iteration both produces parsed output and yields signals such as new templates, confidence scores, and merge decisions that adapt the cache over time. When enough new evidence accumulates, the loop will drive more substantial consolidation decisions so the cache remains compact and consistent as log distributions evolve, and then the system returns to handling the next incoming log.

Specifically, EM-Merge contains 5 steps:

- **Semantic Embedding Extraction** overcomes LLMs' punctuation sensitivity by encoding template semantics into dense vector representations, capturing contextual meaning beyond surface tokens.
- **Candidate Screening** eliminates exhaustive $O(n^2)$ comparisons through approximate nearest-neighbor search, reducing computational overhead by 2–3 orders of magnitude while preserving recall.
- **Confidence-Weighted Similarity Scoring** fuses structural alignment with the LLM's intrinsic confidence signals, creating a noise-resistant similarity metric that prioritizes high-quality merges.
- **Clustering and Merging** discovers natural template groupings using DBSCAN, accommodating arbitrary cluster shapes while filtering outlier templates.
- **Cache Update** ensure transactional replacement of fragmented templates with consolidated versions, maintaining parsing consistency.

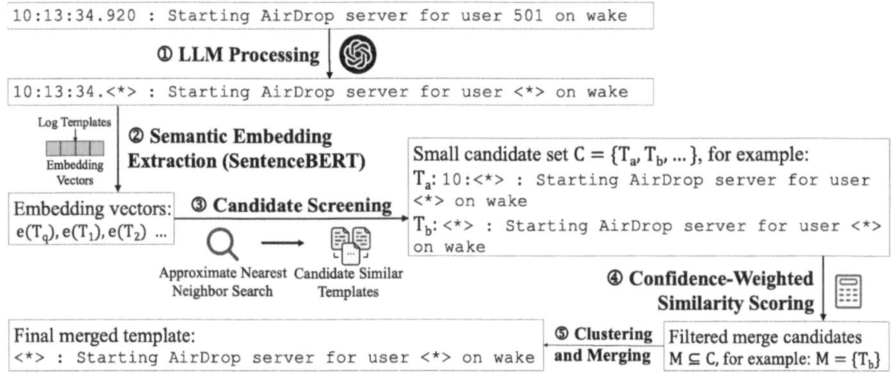

Fig. 3. Overview of EM-Merge.

Figure 3 shows the EM-Merge pipeline for a single parsed result. When the LLM returns a new candidate template T_q, the system first converts every template into a fixed-length numeric representation commonly called a dense vector. By "dense vector", we mean an embedding produced by a pretrained sentence encoder like SentenceBERT, a compact array of real numbers (often hundreds of dimensions) that places semantically similar templates near one another in

Euclidean or cosine space. These embeddings make it efficient to retrieve a small set of semantically related cache entries via an approximate nearest-neighbor search (for example, using an ANN index such as Faiss). The retrieved set C is the pool of candidates that will be examined more carefully.

For each candidate T_i in the retrieved set C, we evaluate two complementary signals: semantic proximity (which is already implied by the neighbor search) and structural agreement. Structural agreement is measured by a normalized longest common subsequence (LCS) computed over tokenized templates. Concretely, templates are tokenized with a consistent rule so that punctuation, timestamps, and placeholders are handled predictably. We then compute the LCS length between the token sequences of T_q and T_i. To make this comparable across templates of different lengths, we divide the LCS length by the length of the longer template, yielding a score between zero and one that captures how much ordered token sequence material the two templates share. For example, given the raw message ``10:13:34.920 : Starting AirDrop server for user 501 on wake'', the LLM might produce slightly different templates that nonetheless share the backbone ``: Starting AirDrop server for user on wake'', and the normalized LCS highlights that shared backbone even when numeric or timestamp tokens differ.

EM-Merge combines this structural measure with the LLM's confidence signals to form a confidence-weighted similarity score. We first reduce token-level confidences to a template-level confidence (for instance, by averaging per-token confidences after ignoring wildcard placeholders). Pairs where the model expresses very different certainty should be merged more cautiously, since high agreement in confidence increases merge propensity, and large differences decrease it. For a candidate T_i, we compute the absolute difference between its template confidence and the confidence of T_q, and a large difference indicates disagreement in certainty and should reduce the propensity to merge. In practice, we combine the two signals with a simple convex mixture. The score increases with normalized LCS and with close agreement in confidences, and candidates whose combined score exceeds a chosen threshold form the merge set M.

The merge set is then clustered to find groups of mutually compatible templates using a density-based clustering such as DBSCAN on the filtered candidates. Within each cluster, we create a consolidated template by keeping the longest common subsequence as the stable backbone and replacing tokens that differ across cluster members with a wildcard token (for readability, we show the wildcard as <*>) so that variable fields are abstracted while shared structure is preserved. These consolidated templates replace the originals in the cache in a transactional update, ensuring that the cache remains consistent and that subsequent logs benefit from higher hit rates.

3.2 Semantic Embedding Extraction

Our preliminary analysis revealed that LLM-generated templates often misinterpret punctuation and word semantics (e.g., colons and parentheses) and produce fragmentary templates as a result. In contrast, humans leverage semantic awareness to identify variables as single units. To overcome this, we incorporate a semantic embedding stage to capture the global meaning of each template. We chose Sentence-BERT [7] for this task because it transforms templates into fixed-length vector representations using a Siamese/Triplet architecture built upon BERT. Sentence-BERT is an enhanced version of the pre-trained BERT model that uses Siamese and triplet network architectures to produce semantically meaningful sentence embeddings. This approach greatly improves the efficiency of semantic similarity computations, reducing the computational cost from over 65 h with naive BERT to just a few seconds for thousands of templates while preserving semantic fidelity [7]. SentenceBERT complementarily fills the gap left by ChatGPT's sequence generation, as the former encodes semantic content holistically, whereas the latter focuses on token-by-token generation [23]. Formally, each template T is mapped to an embedding vector:

$$\mathbf{e}(T) = \text{SentenceBERT}(T) \in \mathbb{R}^d,$$

These embeddings serve as the foundation for downstream similarity evaluation.

3.3 Embedding-Based Candidate Screening

Although SentenceBERT embeddings capture semantics, comparing every new template T_q against thousands of cached ones would be prohibitively expensive. We therefore perform semantic filtering via an approximate nearest-neighbor (ANN) index to retrieve only those candidates likely to merge, thus focusing subsequent expensive operations on a small set. All cached embeddings $\{\mathbf{e}(T_i)\}$ are indexed in Faiss [24]. This allows us to retrieve only those templates whose embeddings lie within a Euclidean distance threshold ϵ:

$$\|\mathbf{e}(T_q) - \mathbf{e}(T_i)\|_2 < \epsilon.$$

By tuning ϵ, we reduce the candidate set from $O(n)$ to a manageable size $k \ll n$, balancing recall and efficiency. In practice, we selected $\epsilon = 0.3$ as the operating point by grid search on a development split and validated it on the HPC benchmark. As shown in Sect. 5.3 RQ2: Efficiency (Table 3), $\epsilon = 0.3$ gave the best practical trade-off in our experiments since it produced the lowest end-to-end parse time while preserving parsing and grouping accuracy, and thus was used across the reported evaluations.

3.4 Confidence-Weighted Structural Similarity

Semantic closeness alone may admit false positives (e.g., semantically related but structurally distinct templates), while structural overlap alone may ignore high-quality semantic matches. To refine, we blend structure with the parser's own confidence signals. For each candidate pair $(T_q, T_i) \in \{T_q\} \times \mathcal{C}$, we compute:

- $\text{LCS}(T_q, T_i)$: length of the longest common subsequence over tokenized templates.

- $|T_q|$, $|T_i|$: token counts of the two templates.
- $c_q, c_i \in [0, 1]$: average per-token confidence scores returned by the original LLM when generating each template.

To ensure high-quality merging, we define the *confidence-weighted similarity*:

$$\mathrm{sim}_{\mathrm{cw}}(T_q, T_i) = \frac{\mathrm{LCS}(T_q, T_i)}{\max(|T_q|, |T_i|)} \cdot \Big(1 - \alpha\,|c_q - c_i|\Big),$$

where $\alpha \in [0, 1]$ modulates the influence of confidence differences. Note that the parameter α encodes our belief in the LLM's confidence scores. An α=0.0 degenerates the similarity to pure structural overlap, while a large α (e.g., ¿0.5) amplifies confidence effects. Through ablation studies, we found that α=0.3 best preserves high-quality matches while suppressing spurious low-confidence ones. Pairs with $\mathrm{sim}_{\mathrm{cw}} \geq s_{\mathrm{cw}}$ are promoted to the merge candidate set $\mathcal{M}$. This threshold determines merging strictness: A high threshold (e.g., 0.9) ensures near-identity before merging, while a lower threshold (e.g., 0.7) admits more variation. We select $s_{\mathrm{cw}} = 0.8$ based on maximizing cluster cohesion (Silhouette Score) and parsing accuracy improvements across multiple datasets.

Longest Common Subsequence (LCS) is a well-established measure for identifying structural overlap, and by weighting with confidence differences, we mitigate errors where one template may be under-confident. A higher confidence agreement boosts similarity; if $\mathrm{sim}_{\mathrm{cw}} \geq s_{\mathrm{cw}}$ (e.g., 0.8), the pair enters merge consideration.

The choice of ϵ determines the balance between recall and efficiency. In our experiments, values between 0.6 and 0.8 yielded the best balance: smaller ϵ led to high precision but missed potential matches; larger ϵ captured more matches but increased false positives. We default to ϵ=0.75 based on development set performance.

3.5 Clustering and Merging

Multiple candidate pairs may collectively describe a single event type. A clustering step groups interconnected templates into merge clusters, ensuring each event category yields exactly one consolidated template. Instead of pairwise merging, we apply DBSCAN [25], a density-based clustering algorithm well-suited for discovering arbitrarily shaped clusters and ignoring noise, to group semantically and structurally similar templates. Using $\mathrm{sim}_{\mathrm{cw}}$ as the similarity metric, each cluster $\mathcal{G}$ must satisfy $\mathrm{sim}_{\mathrm{cw}} \geq s_{\mathrm{cw}}$ for at least a minimal number of points (minPts=2). For each cluster, we compute a multi-sequence LCS across all member templates to extract the shared structural skeleton:

$$L = \mathrm{LCS}\big(T_j \mid T_j \in \mathcal{G}\big).$$

Non-overlapping tokens are replaced with the wildcard symbol `<*>` to produce a generalized merged template T_{merged}. This step directly addresses template fragmentation by unifying semantic variants into a single representation. For example, fragmented templates from OpenStack logs such as:

```
"Connected to <*> port <*>"
"Connection to <*> port <*> established"
"Connected <*>:<*>"
```

will yield a shared skeleton L corresponding to the backbone phrase `"Connected to <*> port <*>"`, and the consolidated template becomes

```
"Connected to <*> port <*>"
```

The merged template is therefore the canonical form that best captures the invariant structure present across the cluster members.

3.6 Cache Update

After a cluster produces a consolidated template, the system must make the merged representation the operative template in the parsing cache. To maintain historical continuity, for each clustered set $\mathcal{G}$ we perform an atomic replacement transaction in three steps. First, we create the merged template T_{merged} as described above. Second, we delete the constituent templates $T_j \in \mathcal{G}$ from the active cache and insert T_{merged} in their place. Third, we reassign all historical and in-flight log records that had previously been mapped to any T_j so that they now point to T_{merged}. These reassigned mappings include any metadata used by downstream consumers, such as counts, timestamps, and provenance pointers, which we aggregate or carry over to preserve historical continuity.

Using the OpenStack example above, the cache update replaces the three fragmented entries with the single canonical entry `‘‘Connected to <*> port <*>’’` and remaps prior matches of `‘‘Connected <*>:<*>’’`, `‘‘Connection to <*> port <*> established’’` and similar variants to the new canonical template. This ensures that subsequent cache matching returns the unified representation and that analytics consuming template identifiers observe a consistent template id rather than multiple near-duplicates.

To support correctness and traceability, the replacement is atomic: consumers never observe an intermediate state in which some records point to old templates while others point to the merged template. We also maintain optional backward pointers (aliases) from removed template identifiers to the new canonical identifier for a configurable retention period. These aliases facilitate debugging and allow consumers that have cached template IDs to transition gracefully. If no candidate exceeds the similarity threshold, the new template T_q is simply inserted into the cache as is. Together, these measures keep the template database compact, semantically coherent, and operationally efficient without further LLM interaction.

4 Experimental Design

4.1 Research Questions

We evaluate our approach by answering the following research questions (RQs):

- **RQ1: How effective is EM-Merge compared to existing log parsers?**
- **RQ2: How efficient is EM-Merge in processing large-scale log data?**
- **RQ3: How much do different modules contribute?**

4.2 Datasets

All experiments utilize the large-scale log parsing dataset Loghub-2.0 benchmark [8] from [3], comprising 14 real-world datasets totaling approximately 50 million logs with 3,489 manually verified templates. This collection spans distributed systems (HDFS, Spark), OS kernels (Linux, Windows), server applications (Apache, Zookeeper), and embedded systems (HealthApp), presenting various challenges. Standard preprocessing includes timestamp removal, case normalization, and special character handling following the LogPAI [3,8] pipeline.

4.3 Baselines

To demonstrate our work, we have chosen four open-source, cutting-edge log parsers for comparison with our approach. More specifically, considering their exceptional efficacy relative to all syntax-based log parsers, we select AEL and Drain; regarding the superior parsing accuracy among recent semantic-based log parsers, we choose UniParser [12], LogPPT [19], and LILAC [17] as baselines to implement dynamic demonstration through semantic similarity search. All baselines use official implementations with default parameters, with stochastic methods executing seven runs for statistical reliability.

4.4 Evaluation Metrics

We use four standard metrics from log parsing literature [12,17,26] with refined definitions:

Grouping Accuracy (GA): Measures if each log message's template matches exactly the same log group as ground-truth.

Parsing Accuracy (PA): Assesses if templates and parameters are correctly extracted, requiring exact static token match and perfect variable identification.

F1 of Grouping (FGA): Addresses GA's cluster-size bias by computing the harmonic mean of the Precision of Grouping Accuracy (PGA) and the Recall of Grouping Accuracy (RGA) at the template level.

F1 of Template Accuracy (FTA): Emphasizes correctly recognized templates, defined as those whose tokens fully match the ground-truth and whose assigned logs share the same template. FTA can be calculated as the template accuracy's precision and recall harmonic mean.

4.5 Implementation and Environment

Experiments were performed on a Lenovo Legion Y7000 laptop with an 8-core Intel i7 CPU (2.6 GHz max turbo), NVIDIA RTX 30-series GPU (8GB VRAM), and 24GB DDR4 RAM. The environment utilized Python 3.10 with NumPy/Pandas for core processing, CUDA 11.8 and cuDNN 8.6 for GPU acceleration in baseline models. Experimental constraints included API dependency limiting reproducibility and GPU memory restricting batch sizes. For the large language model component, we used the OpenAI API v1.3 with gpt-3.5-turbo-0613, which provides a 4K token context window and temperature set to 0. We selected GPT-3.5 to align with prior baseline settings and ensure comparability of results, while future work will examine the applicability of more recent models.

5 Experimental Results and Analysis

5.1 RQ1: Effectiveness

Tables 1 and 2 report Grouping Accuracy (GA), Parsing Accuracy (PA), F1 of Grouping (FGA) and F1 of Template Accuracy (FTA) for six parsers over fourteen benchmarks. EM-Merge consistently outperforms both traditional methods (Drain, AEL) and recent LLM? based parsers (UniParser, LogPPT, LILAC). On average, EM-Merge achieves GA = 0.92, PA = 0.82, FGA = 0.93, and FTA = 0.76, representing relative improvements over the strongest baseline (LILAC). Notably, on challenging datasets such as OpenSSH and HealthApp, EM-Merge raises FTA by over 10 points, indicating its superior ability to unify fragmented templates without overgeneralizing.

Table 1. Metric comparison with existing log parsers (Part 1)

	Drain				AEL				UniParser			
	GA	PA	FGA	FTA	GA	PA	FGA	FTA	GA	PA	FGA	FTA
Proxifier	0.69	0.69	0.21	0.18	0.97	0.68	0.67	0.42	0.51	0.63	0.39	0.52
Apache	**1.00**	0.73	**1.00**	0.52	**1.00**	0.73	**1.00**	0.52	0.99	0.96	0.84	0.25
OpenSSH	0.71	0.59	0.87	0.49	0.70	0.36	0.69	0.33	0.22	0.55	0.06	0.04
HDFS	**1.00**	0.62	0.94	0.61	**1.00**	0.62	0.76	0.56	0.52	0.95	0.01	0.01
OpenStack	0.75	0.03	0.01	0.00	0.74	0.03	0.68	0.17	0.99	0.52	0.86	0.26
HPC	0.79	0.72	0.31	0.15	0.75	0.74	0.20	0.14	0.78	0.95	0.60	0.33
Zookeeper	0.99	0.84	0.90	0.61	**1.00**	0.84	0.79	0.47	**1.00**	**0.99**	0.67	0.48
HealthApp	0.86	0.31	0.01	0.00	0.73	0.31	0.01	0.00	0.46	0.79	0.72	0.35
Hadoop	0.92	0.54	0.79	0.38	0.82	0.54	0.12	0.06	0.75	**0.85**	0.79	0.55
Spark	0.89	0.39	0.86	0.41	–	–	–	–	0.83	0.72	0.00	0.00
BGL	**0.92**	0.41	0.62	0.19	**0.92**	0.41	0.59	0.17	0.91	**0.95**	0.61	0.21
Linux	0.69	0.11	0.78	0.26	**0.92**	0.08	0.81	0.22	0.29	0.16	0.44	0.21
Mac	0.76	0.36	0.23	0.07	0.80	0.25	0.79	0.21	0.76	0.58	0.69	0.27
Thunderbird	**0.83**	0.22	0.24	0.07	0.79	0.16	0.12	0.04	0.49	0.41	0.10	0.05
Average	0.84	0.47	0.55	0.28	0.86	0.44	0.56	0.25	0.68	0.72	0.48	0.25

5.2 RQ2: Efficiency

To assess the runtime efficiency of EM-Merge in a realistic setting, we measured end-to-end parsing time on all 14 Loghub-2.0 datasets using our reference platform. Considering the average total parsing time (in seconds) for the base LILAC parser versus LILAC augmented with EM-Merge, LILAC alone required on average 1,686.50 s to parse all messages, whereas EM-Merge reduced this to 1,313.80 s. This is a 22.1% decrease in overall processing time.

The runtime improvement stems largely from the embedding-based candidate screening. By tuning the semantic distance threshold ϵ used in the ANN retrieval, we can sharply reduce the number of expensive structural comparisons per template. Table 3 shows a focused sensitivity study on the HPC dataset that demonstrates this effect. All other EM-Merge modules were kept enabled for these runs so that the timing reflects realistic, postprocessing-enabled parsing.

From this experiment, we draw two practical conclusions relevant to RQ2. First, the choice of ϵ has a large impact on end-to-end parse time: in our HPC runs $\epsilon = 0.3$ produced the smallest parse time (164.62 s), substantially faster than both tighter ($\epsilon = 0.2$) and looser ($\epsilon \geq 0.4$) thresholds. Second, core accuracy metrics (GA, PA, FGA, FTA) remain broadly stable across the tested ϵ range, indicating that $\epsilon = 0.3$ offers a favorable trade-off–substantial efficiency gains with no meaningful drop in parsing quality. Intuitively, too-small ϵ can harm downstream stability by missing true candidates and increasing downstream corrective

Table 2. Metric comparison with existing log parsers (Part 2)

	LogPPT				LILAC				EM-Merge			
	GA	PA	FGA	FTA	GA	PA	FGA	FTA	GA	PA	FGA	FTA
Proxifier	0.99	**1.00**	0.87	**0.96**	0.52	0.52	0.86	0.86	**1.00**	0.99	**1.00**	0.82
Apache	0.87	0.95	0.56	0.35	**1.00**	**1.00**	**1.00**	**0.86**	**1.00**	**1.00**	**1.00**	**0.86**
OpenSSH	0.28	0.65	0.07	0.09	**0.75**	**0.97**	0.80	0.71	**0.75**	**0.97**	**0.88**	**0.85**
HDFS	0.41	0.90	0.52	0.31	**1.00**	0.95	**0.97**	**0.93**	**1.00**	**1.00**	**0.97**	0.90
OpenStack	0.56	0.41	0.89	0.75	**1.00**	**0.98**	**1.00**	**0.94**	**1.00**	0.97	**1.00**	0.90
HPC	0.83	**1.00**	0.71	0.70	**0.87**	0.71	**0.86**	**0.74**	**0.87**	0.71	0.82	0.66
Zookeeper	0.98	0.85	0.92	0.78	**1.00**	0.66	**0.96**	0.80	**1.00**	0.63	**0.96**	**0.82**
HealthApp	0.71	**0.98**	0.90	0.81	**0.99**	0.61	0.97	0.81	**0.99**	0.62	**0.97**	**0.84**
Hadoop	0.73	0.69	0.38	0.33	**0.93**	0.79	**0.96**	**0.72**	0.92	0.82	0.94	**0.72**
Spark	0.45	0.95	0.41	0.34	**1.00**	**1.00**	0.88	**0.74**	**1.00**	**1.00**	**0.89**	0.71
BGL	0.28	0.94	0.43	0.42	0.90	**0.95**	0.89	**0.77**	0.90	**0.95**	**0.91**	**0.77**
Linux	0.20	0.23	0.66	0.40	0.81	0.70	0.87	0.48	0.82	**0.72**	**0.93**	**0.70**
Mac	0.55	0.44	0.48	0.28	0.78	0.53	0.84	**0.54**	**0.87**	**0.63**	**0.85**	**0.54**
Thunderbird	0.51	0.40	0.18	0.10	**0.83**	**0.58**	0.79	0.47	0.79	0.53	**0.84**	**0.54**
Average	0.60	0.74	0.57	0.47	0.88	0.78	0.90	0.74	**0.92**	**0.82**	**0.93**	**0.76**

Table 3. Effect of semantic distance threshold ϵ on HPC

ϵ	parse_time	GA	PA	FGA	FTA
0.2	477.04	0.85	0.691	0.78	0.61
0.3	**164.62**	0.845	0.692	0.777	0.619
0.4	777.32	0.845	0.691	0.777	0.619
0.5	780.47	0.845	0.691	0.777	0.604

work, while too-large ϵ increases candidate counts and similarity-comparison cost without improving merges.

In short, integrating EM-Merge improves end-to-end throughput while preserving or improving parsing quality, provided hyperparameters such as ϵ are selected via the described tuning procedure.

5.3 RQ3: Module Contribution

To evaluate the contribution of individual components within the EM-Merge framework, we conducted a series of ablation studies using the HPC dataset. This dataset was chosen due to its high structural and semantic complexity, broad coverage of message types, and strong representativeness of mission-critical computing environments. Its logs combine technical and human-readable messages, display significant lexical variation, use specialized jargon, and include both strictly formatted and free-form content, making it an ideal benchmark for evaluating system components.

In particular, HPC logs are generated by large-scale high-performance computing systems that interleave technical messages (e.g., MPI operations, node failures, GPU management) with human-readable status and error reports. These logs exhibit a high degree of lexical variation, frequent use of domain-specific jargon, and a mixture of rigidly structured and free-form messages. Table 4 summarizes the observed performance changes when semantic embedding, longest common subsequence (LCS) filtering, and the merging stage were selectively removed.

Table 4. Ablation Study Results on HPC Dataset with Relative Changes

Configuration	GA	PA	FGA	FTA
Full EM-Merge	0.871	0.714	0.823	0.658
w/o Semantic	0.845 (−2.99%)	0.646 (−9.53%)	0.780 (−5.22%)	0.596 (−9.42%)
w/o LCS Filtering	0.845 (−2.99%)	0.685 (−4.06%)	0.777 (−5.59%)	0.590 (−10.33%)
w/o Merging	0.845 (−2.99%)	0.692 (−3.08%)	0.783 (−4.86%)	0.623 (−5.32%)

Note: Relative percentages in parentheses indicate performance drops with respect to the full EM-Merge configuration. GA = Grouping Accuracy, PA = Parsing Accuracy, FGA = F1-Grouping Accuracy, FTA = F1-Template Accuracy.

When the semantic embedding module was excluded, the FTA score dropped from 0.658 to 0.596, representing a 9.42% relative decrease. Parsing accuracy (PA) also declined by 9.53%, indicating that semantic information plays a central role in resolving lexical variability and enabling the alignment of functionally equivalent logs, such as `"Node <*> failure"` and `"Compute node <*> crashed"`. The FGA score also dropped by over 5%, confirming that many semantically similar instances failed to cluster properly without embedding-based screening.

Removing the LCS filtering stage led to an even larger decline in FTA, dropping to 0.590 (a 10.33% decrease). This suggests that while semantic embedding enables high-recall candidate generation, structural alignment through LCS is critical to improving precision during merge decisions. The FGA drop of 5.59% further supports the view that LCS filtering reduces structural fragmentation and over-grouping errors.

Disabling the merging stage resulted in the smallest performance degradation, with FTA falling by 5.32% and PA by just 3.08%. Nevertheless, merging remains essential for consolidating structurally redundant templates and compressing the output space for downstream tasks. Its absence still introduced measurable fragmentation, as evidenced by a 4.86% drop in FGA.

Across all metrics, the complete EM-Merge pipeline outperformed any ablated variant. These results reaffirm the complementary roles of semantic embedding, structural refinement, and hierarchical merging. Embedding identifies high-recall candidates; LCS filtering aligns them structurally; and merging consolidates clusters into concise, meaningful templates. Together, they form a robust and generalizable approach for parsing log data in semantically rich and structurally diverse systems such as HPC platforms.

Across diverse datasets and evaluation criteria, EM-Merge demonstrates significant gains in both accuracy and efficiency. Its modular design proves robust to parameter variations, and ablation studies confirm the necessity of each component. These results validate EM-Merge as a practical, high?performance post-processing enhancement for LLM?based log parsing systems.

6 Discussion

6.1 Efficiency and Practicality

To assess the practical viability and architectural soundness of EM-Merge, we conducted targeted ablation studies on the HPC dataset, a challenging benchmark characterized by its high semantic diversity, structural variability, and operational significance. The results in Table 4 highlight that each module in EM-Merge contributes non-trivially to both parsing accuracy and output coherence.

6.2 Deployment and Practical Implications

Without the need for further LLM inference, model retraining, or supervision, EM-Merge is implemented as a modular postprocessing layer that enhances current log parsers. Its compatibility with both traditional parsing algorithms and LLM-generated outputs allows seamless integration into existing infrastructure. In production settings, EM-Merge has proven effective in consolidating near-duplicate templates, especially in large-scale environments like HPC systems, where template redundancy can hinder performance monitoring and anomaly detection. Moreover, the method's semantic sensitivity and structure-aware design improve both human interpretability and downstream indexing efficiency, providing operational value beyond raw parsing accuracy.

6.3 Limitations and Future Work

Several limitations are worth discussing. First, EM-Merge's evaluation depends on the quality of ground-truth template labels, which may be incomplete or inconsistent in real-world datasets. Second, the semantic screening part, which is based on Sentence-BERT embeddings that have already been trained, may have trouble with extremely domain-specific jargon and may overlook equivalencies that general-purpose language models miss. Third, the current implementation of DBSCAN clustering uses fixed hyperparameters that may not generalize optimally across all log domains. We note that we were unable to test EM-Merge built directly on the very latest large models (for example, GPT-5) due to resource and access constraints; doing so could plausibly reduce fragmentation and improve confidence signals, but those potential gains remain to be empirically validated.

Future work could address these challenges by incorporating adaptive semantic models trained on domain-specific corpora, exploring active learning techniques for robust template labeling, and designing dynamic clustering algorithms that adjust sensitivity based on log structure and entropy. In particular, a natural next step is to evaluate EM-Merge in conjunction with state-of-the-art LLMs, either via few-shot prompting, lightweight fine-tuning, or adapter layers, to study how stronger contextual understanding and calibrated confidences affect consolidation quality. Additionally, extending EM-Merge to support multilingual log streams and integrating it into end-to-end observability pipelines are promising directions for scaling its practical impact.

7 Related Work

Prior research on log parsing can be grouped into three broad families. Early rule-based and heuristic parsers (e.g., Drain) rely on token positions, delimiters and handcrafted regular expressions to generate templates but struggle to adapt to evolving formats and noisy logs [9,13]. Frequency- and pattern-mining approaches (e.g., Logram) detect common substrings or n-grams as candidate templates, while clustering-based methods group similar lines using token-level distances; these methods reduce manual effort but are sensitive to thresholds and often miss semantic equivalence across syntactic variants [11,14]. More recently, semantic and learning-based parsers (for example, UniParser and other neural approaches) use learned representations to distinguish constants from parameters, improving generalization at the cost of requiring labeled data or expensive training and being brittle under domain shift [10,12]. Concurrently, large language models have been applied to template abstraction via zero- and few-shot prompting, demonstrating strong per-instance understanding but introducing new issues such as template fragmentation and high inference cost when used naively [5,19]. EM-Merge differs from these lines of work by acting as a lightweight, model-independent postprocessing layer: it leverages semantic embeddings (Sentence-BERT) and LLM-derived confidence signals to identify and reliably merge semantically equivalent templates without issuing extra LLM calls, thereby addressing fragmentation and improving cache efficiency while remaining compatible with both traditional and LLM-based parsers [7,17].

8 Conclusion

In this paper, we introduced EM-Merge, a novel embedding-aware and confidence-guided framework designed to enhance the quality and coherence of log templates generated by LLM-based parsers. EM-Merge uses a five-stage process that combines semantic embedding, efficient retrieval, confidence-weighted similarity scoring, clustering, and historical consolidation to systematically address key challenges, including LLM's misinterpretation of punctuation and semantic cues and the fragmentation of semantically similar logs into overlapping templates. Experimental results on 14 Loghub-2.0 datasets demonstrate that EM-Merge consistently outperforms both traditional and state-of-the-art LLM-augmented log parsers. Its modular, LLM-independent architecture enables seamless integration with existing frameworks without extra language model calls or retraining, effectively unifying semantic and structural information to produce more compact, coherent log representations suitable for real-time, high-throughput environments.

Acknowledgments. This work was supported by the National Innovation and Entrepreneurship Training Program for College Students, the Beijing University of Technology Education and Teaching Research Project (No. ER2024KCA01), the open project of the IoT Standards and Application Key Laboratory of the Ministry of Industry and Information Technology (No. 202407), and the Spark Plan Key Project of Beijing University of Technology. The authors would like to express their sincere gratitude to these programs for their financial support. We also thank the faculty and staff at Beijing University of Technology for their guidance and assistance throughout the research.

References

1. Xu, W., Huang, L., Fox, A., Patterson, D., Jordan, M.I.: Detecting large-scale system problems by mining console logs. In: Proceedings of the ACM SIGOPS 22nd Symposium on Operating Systems Principles, pp. 117–132 (2009)
2. Du, M., Li, F., Zheng, G., Srikumar, V.: DeepLog: anomaly detection and diagnosis from system logs through deep learning. In: Proceedings of the 2017 ACM SIGSAC Conference on Computer and Communications Security, pp. 1285–1298 (2017)
3. Zhang, X., et al.: Robust log-based anomaly detection on unstable log data. In: Proceedings of the 2019 27th ACM Joint Meeting on European Software Engineering Conference and Symposium on the Foundations of Software Engineering, pp. 807–817 (2019)
4. Brown, T., et al.: Language models are few-shot learners. In: Advances in Neural Information Processing Systems, vol. 33, pp. 1877–1901. Curran Associates, Inc. (2020). https://proceedings.neurips.cc/paper_files/paper/2020/file/1457c0d6bfcb4967418bfb8ac142f64a-Paper.pdf
5. Zhi, C., Cheng, L., Liu, M., Zhao, X., Xu, Y., Deng, S.: LLM-powered zero-shot online log parsing. In: 2024 IEEE International Conference on Web Services (ICWS), pp. 877–887. IEEE (2024)

6. Xiao, T., Quan, Z., Wang, Z.-J., Zhao, K., Liao, X.: LPV: a log parser based on vectorization for offline and online log parsing. In: Proceedings of the 2020 IEEE International Conference on Data Mining (ICDM), pp. 1346–1351 (2020). https://doi.org/10.1109/ICDM50108.2020.00175
7. Reimers, N., Gurevych, I.: Sentence-BERT: sentence embeddings using Siamese BERT-networks. In: Proceedings of the 2019 Conference on Empirical Methods in Natural Language Processing and the 9th International Joint Conference on Natural Language Processing (EMNLP-IJCNLP), pp. 3982–3992. Association for Computational Linguistics, Hong Kong, China (2019). https://doi.org/10.18653/v1/D19-1410
8. Jiang, Z., et al.: A large-scale evaluation for log parsing techniques: how far are we? In: Proceedings of the 33rd ACM SIGSOFT International Symposium on Software Testing and Analysis, pp. 223–234 (2024)
9. He, P., Zhu, J., Zheng, Z., Lyu, M.R.: Drain: an online log parsing approach with fixed depth tree. In: 2017 IEEE International Conference on Web Services (ICWS), pp. 33–40. IEEE (2017)
10. Ma, J., Liu, Y., Wan, H., Sun, G.: Automatic parsing and utilization of system log features in log analysis: a survey. Appl. Sci. **13**(8), 4930 (2023). https://doi.org/10.3390/app13084930
11. Jiang, Z.M., Hassan, A.E., Flora, P., Hamann, G.: Abstracting execution logs to execution events for enterprise applications (short paper). In: 2008 The Eighth International Conference on Quality Software, pp. 181–186. IEEE (2008)
12. Liu, Y., et al.: UniParser: a unified log parser for heterogeneous log data. In: Proceedings of the ACM Web Conference 2022, pp. 1893–1901 (2022)
13. Zhu, J., He, S., Liu, J., He, P., Xie, Q., Zheng, Z., Lyu, M.R.: Tools and benchmarks for automated log parsing. In: Proceedings of the 2019 IEEE/ACM 41st International Conference on Software Engineering: Software Engineering in Practice (ICSE-SEIP), pp. 121–130 (2019). https://doi.org/10.1109/ICSE-SEIP.2019.00021
14. Dai, H., Li, H., Chen, C.-S., Shang, W., Chen, T.-H.: Logram: efficient log parsing using n-gram dictionaries. IEEE Trans. Software Eng. **48**(3), 879–892 (2020)
15. Guo, W., Mu, D., Xu, J., Su, P., Wang, G., Xing, X.: LEMNA: explaining deep learning based security applications. In: Proceedings of the 2018 ACM SIGSAC Conference on Computer and Communications Security (CCS '18), pp. 364–379. Association for Computing Machinery, Toronto, Canada (2018). https://doi.org/10.1145/3243734.3243792
16. Hu, C., Sun, X., Dai, H., Zhang, H., Liu, H.: Research on log anomaly detection based on sentence-BERT. Electronics **12**(17), 3580 (2023). https://doi.org/10.3390/electronics12173580
17. Jiang, Z., et al.: LILAC: log parsing using LLMs with adaptive parsing cache. Proc. ACM Softw. Eng. **1**(FSE), 137–160 (2024). Article 7, https://doi.org/10.1145/3643733
18. Wu, X., Li, H., Khomh, F.: On the effectiveness of log representation for log-based anomaly detection. Empirical Softw. Eng. **28**, 137 (2023). https://doi.org/10.1007/s10664-023-10364-1
19. Le, V.H., Zhang, H.: Log parsing with prompt-based few-shot learning. In: 2023 IEEE/ACM 45th International Conference on Software Engineering (ICSE), pp. 2438–2449. IEEE (2023)
20. Ma, Z., Chen, A.R., Kim, D.J., Chen, T.P., Wang, S.: LLMParser: an exploratory study on using large language models for log parsing. In: Proceedings of the 2024

IEEE/ACM 46th International Conference on Software Engineering (ICSE), Lisbon, Portugal, pp. 1209–1221 (2024). https://doi.org/10.1145/3597503.3639150
21. Zhong, A., et al.: LogParser-LLM: advancing efficient log parsing with large language models. In: Proceedings of the 30th ACM SIGKDD Conference on Knowledge Discovery and Data Mining (KDD '24), pp. 4559–4570. Association for Computing Machinery, New York, NY, USA (2024). https://doi.org/10.1145/3637528.3671810
22. Le, V.-H., Zhang, H.: Log parsing: how far can ChatGPT go? In: Proceedings of the 2023 38th IEEE/ACM International Conference on Automated Software Engineering (ASE), pp. 1699–1704 (2023). https://doi.org/10.1109/ASE56229.2023.00206
23. Zhou, Y., Chen, Y., Rao, X., Zhou, Y., Li, Y., Hu, C.: Leveraging large language models and BERT for log parsing and anomaly detection. Mathematics **12**, 2758 (2024). https://doi.org/10.3390/math12172758
24. Johnson, J., Douze, M., Jégou, H.: Billion-scale similarity search with GPUs. In: IEEE Transactions on Big Data, vol. 7(3), pp. 535–547 (2019)
25. Son, M.: Density-based Algorithms for Active and Anytime Clustering. Master's thesis, Ludwig-Maximilians-Universität München, Munich (2014). https://edoc.ub.uni-muenchen.de/17533/1/Mai_Son_T.pdf
26. Khan, Z.A., Shin, D., Bianculli, D., Briand, L.: Guidelines for assessing the accuracy of log message template identification techniques. In: Proceedings of the 2022 IEEE/ACM 44th International Conference on Software Engineering (ICSE), pp. 1095–1106 (2022). https://doi.org/10.1145/3510003.3510101

Blockchains and Distributed Protocols

Strategy-Aware Liquidity for Account-Based Blockchains

Ximeng Li[1,2], Sensen Chen[1], Yong Guan[1,3], Qianying Zhang[2], Guohui Wang[2], and Zhiping Shi[2,4(✉)]

[1] College of Information Engineering, Capital Normal University, Beijing, China
{lixm,guanyong}@cnu.edu.cn
[2] Beijing Key Laboratory of Electronic System Reliability and Prognostics, Capital Normal University, Beijing, China
{qyzhang,ghwang,shizp}@cnu.edu.cn
[3] Beijing Advanced Innovation Center for Imaging Theory and Technology, Capital Normal University, Beijing, China
[4] Beijing Academy of Science and Technology, Beijing, China

Abstract. A prominent functionality of smart contracts is regulating financial transactions on the blockchain. Flaws in a smart contract could cause funds to be frozen in the contract, resulting in financial losses of honest users. This issue of frozen funds is often considered a violation of liquidity requirements. In this work, we propose a liquidity property for account-based blockchain platforms such as Ethereum. The property captures the situation where the process of claiming funds by the honest users can be disrupted by the strategy of the environment. We formally establish the connection between this property and a strategy-less notion of liquidity under particular conditions, devise sound proof methods for the property, mechanize the theories and proof methods in the Rocq prover, and apply the proof methods to verify or refute the property for example smart contracts. Informative verification and refutation results are obtained for the examples—strategies help reveal how a user may act to ensure the transfer of funds out of a contract or how an attacker may exploit the inherent vulnerabilities of a contract to freeze funds.

1 Introduction

Blockchain technology has seen a growing range of applications since the introduction of Bitcoin [26]. A major type of applications is related to finance [38]. The realization of financial contracts on blockchains is facilitated with the advent of Ethereum [39]—an account-based blockchain platform that greatly eased the programming of smart contracts [31].

As smart contracts have become increasingly widespread, their security vulnerabilities have led to significant economic losses [11]. One major type of security vulnerability is that programming errors in a smart contract could cause digital assets to become locked within the contract. In 2017, digital assets worth

A. Goharshady and C. Haase (Eds.): SETTA 2025, LNCS 16458, pp. 341–362, 2026.
https://doi.org/10.1007/978-981-95-7826-9_18

over 150 million USD were locked in the Parity wallet [8]. More recently, approximately 34 million USD was frozen in the Akutar NFT contract [6]. Many similar incidents with severe consequences have been observed.

Research in formal methods addresses the critical issue of locked funds in smart contracts via the development of *liquidity properties* and techniques for analysis and verification [12,13,15,18,19,33,37]. A clearly defined liquidity property articulates the target requirement of formal verification. A general liquidity requirement is: a group of users should be able to transfer an amount of funds out of a smart contract, despite the potential interference of the environment.

The potential behaviors of the protected users and their environment can be captured by strategies. A strategy of the environment that prevents the desired transfer of funds by the users provides a witness that a smart contract could suffer from the problem of locked funds. A strategy of the protected users that enables the desired transfer elucidates how this problem can be avoided. Hence, strategies offer deeper insights into the liquidity characteristics of a smart contract beyond a simple yes-or-no determination. However, existing definitions of liquidity properties for smart contracts are either strategy-agnostic (e.g., [12,19,23,37]) or tailored to UTxO-based blockchain models such as Bitcoin (e.g., [13,15]). A foundational criterion for the formal analysis and verification of strategy-aware liquidity requirements in account-based blockchain models is still lacking.

A potential definition of a strategy-aware liquidity property for account-based blockchains would characterize the joint effects of the users and the environment on the amount of funds in an account. It would be possible to verify or refute such a property for a smart contract by directly constructing a proof that the defined property or its negation holds. However, such a direct proof would involve intertwined reasoning about the behaviors of the user and the environment. Moreover, the application-independent part of the direct proof must be replicated for different smart contracts to be examined. Hence, the proposal of a strategy-aware liquidity property for account-based blockchains should be accompanied by proof methods to simplify the verification and refutation of the property.

In this work, we provide a formal foundation for expressing and verifying strategy-aware liquidity requirements for smart contracts in account-based blockchains. Our main technical contributions include:

- the definition of a strategy-aware liquidity property (Sect. 4),
- a formal result on the relationship between the strength of the property and the strength of the environmental strategy (Sect. 5),
- a formal result on the relationship between the property and a strategy-less notion of liquidity under particular conditions (Sect. 5),
- sound proof methods relying on well-founded orders and invariants, for the verification and refutation of the property (Sect. 6),
- mechanization of the theory and proof methods for the property in the Rocq prover[1] [9,16],
- proofs and refutations of liquidity for example smart contracts (Sect. 7).

[1] formerly known as the Coq proof assistant.

Compared with the existing definitions of liquidity properties, a distinguishing feature of our property is in allowing the environment to exert influence on the users not only before the process as they attempt to transfer funds out of the smart contract, but also during this process. This feature reflects the potential ability of a realistic attacker. Our mechanization of theories and liquidity proofs are based on the ConCert framework [10,28] for modeling and reasoning about smart contracts. Our newly developed definitions total approximately 3.2k LOC and newly constructed proofs approximately 6.2k LOC. The mechanization [5] contains all the proofs in our development. An extended version of this article also contains most of the proofs for the theoretical results [5].

2 Background and Motivation

In an account-based blockchain (e.g., Ethereum [39]), an account is an entity at an address that contains a certain amount of funds. An account may optionally contain a smart contract. The smart contract is an object that maintains data and offers methods that implement the logic of a business contract (e.g., starting shipment of goods upon receipt of digital money). A user with an account may execute transactions. A transaction could transfer funds to some account, deploy a smart contract at some address, or invoke a method in an existing contract.

Consider a smart contract c_{fm} where a user (whose account is at the address *usr*) attempting to withdraw funds has to request for the withdrawal and wait for approval by the administrator (whose account is at the address *adm*). This administrator role is common in lending protocols, insurance contracts, multi-signature wallets, etc. (e.g., [20]). The allowed changes of the user's status are illustrated in Fig. 1. Here, a transition arrow represents a transaction. Below each arrow, the action that triggers the transaction is annotated. Above the arrow, the business logic for the transaction is expressed via pseudo-code. In the pseudo-code, *from* refers to the address of the account that performs the action.

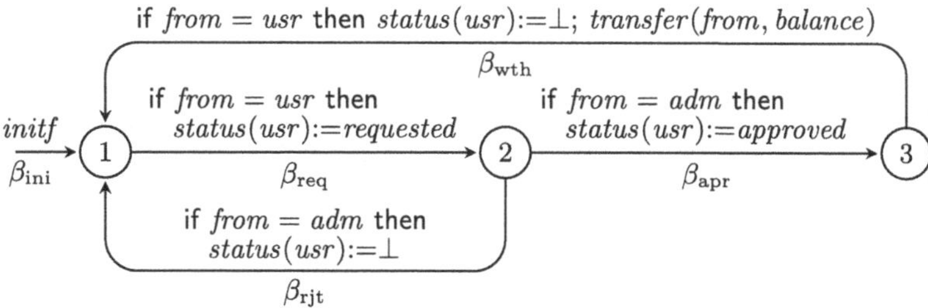

Fig. 1. Illustration of the user's status changes in c_{fm}.

Intuitively, the smart contract c_{fm} fulfills the liquidity requirements that are sensible in this funds management scenario as long as the administrator is honest. This is because a benign user is able to achieve their intended withdrawal of funds under the approval of the collaborative administrator.

Consider a smart contract $c_{\mathrm{fm}}^{\times}$ that is like c_{fm}, except that the function *initf* used to initialize the contract $c_{\mathrm{fm}}^{\times}$ can be invoked at any time (as opposed to contract creation only) to set the caller as the administrator. This flawed mechanism has been located in real-world financial contracts like Rubixi [4] and 88mph [1]. It enables a malicious user to become the administrator and reject all requests for the withdrawal of funds by the benign user. If Fig. 1 is re-used to help understand how $c_{\mathrm{fm}}^{\times}$ differs from c_{fm}, what the malicious user could do in $c_{\mathrm{fm}}^{\times}$ is the execution of the transition $2 \to 1$ in the administrator role. Intuitively, the flawed contract $c_{\mathrm{fm}}^{\times}$ violates liquidity requirements because the adversary is able to freeze funds in the contract.

In the literature, a basic notion of liquidity requires the existence of an execution trace that decreases the balance of the given smart contract [19,37]. A more fine-grained notion of liquidity requires that in any state resulting from the execution of a smart contract potentially driven by a group of users and an adversary, the users should have a way of withdrawing the funds in the contract in a sequence of moves [15,23]. Since the adversary is non-collaborative, this fine-grained liquidity notion can be employed to express stronger liquidity concerns than expressible by the basic notion. If strategies are used for the adversary [15], then the fine-grained notion also enables the reasoning about the liquidity guarantees of a smart contract under assumptions on what the adversary could do.

The smart contract c_{fm} fulfills the requirements of both liquidity notions mentioned above. At any state, the balance of the contract can be reduced to zero by following the suffix of the trace $1 \to 2 \to 3 \to 1$ starting from that state. Moreover, each transition in this trace is taken by a member in the group of honest users (consisting of the benign user and the honest administrator). The state of these honest users cannot be influenced by the adversary. The discussion above supports the conformance of the existing liquidity notions with the informal liquidity requirements for the contract c_{fm}.

However, the requirements of both liquidity notions are also fulfilled by the flawed contract $c_{\mathrm{fm}}^{\times}$. Firstly, the trace $1 \to 2 \to 3 \to 1$ is also permitted by this flawed contract, reducing the balance of the contract to zero. Secondly, although the adversary may trigger the transition $2 \to 1$ in the administrator role, the honest administrator can re-gain the administrator role via the function *initf* afterward. Then, the group of honest users can again achieve the intended decrease of $c_{\mathrm{fm}}^{\times}$'s balance through the trace $1 \to 2 \to 3 \to 1$. This discussion reveals the discrepancies between the existing liquidity notions and the informal liquidity requirements for the contract $c_{\mathrm{fm}}^{\times}$.

The discussion above is based on an informal understanding of the liquidity property of [15] in our setting of an account-based blockchain. This liquidity property was formulated in the model of Bitcoin, which is a UTxO-based blockchain platform. To our knowledge, none of the existing liquidity properties for account-based blockchain models distinguishes between the strategies of honest and malicious users. In this article, we propose such a liquidity property. The proposed property captures the fulfillment of the intuitive liquidity requirements by the smart contract c_{fm}, as well as the violation of the intuitive liquidity requirements by the smart contract $c^{\times}_{\text{fm}}$. Furthermore, we devise methods for the sound verification and refutation of the proposed liquidity property, and demonstrate the use of these methods on example smart contracts.

3 Model of Smart Contract Execution

We introduce formal concepts concerning the execution of blockchain transactions according to strategies. These formal concepts provide the basis for our definition of the strategy-aware liquidity property.

3.1 Blockchain States and Transaction Execution

We denote the set of all account addresses as Adr. An account that does not contain a smart contract is called an *externally owned account*. We denote the set of account addresses for externally owned accounts by Adr_{eoa}.

We model the status of the blockchain at a specific point in the execution of transactions by a *blockchain state* $\sigma \in \Sigma$. This blockchain state reflects the status of each existing account—including the balance of the account, as well as the code and the storage state of the smart contract (if any) in the account.

We represent the balance of the account at the address a in the blockchain state σ as $balance(\sigma, a)$. We represent the state of the smart contract at address a in the blockchain state σ as $ctr\text{-}st(\sigma, a)$. If there is no smart contract at a, then $ctr\text{-}st(\sigma, a) = \bot$. We use $s.v$ to represent the value of the variable v in the smart contract state s (where $s \neq \bot$).

We capture the *execution of a transaction* by $\sigma \xrightarrow{\beta} \sigma'$. Here, σ and σ' are the blockchain states before and after the transaction, respectively. In addition, β is the *action* triggering the transaction. This action could be the deployment of a contract, a call to a contract, or the transfer of funds to an account. We write $orig(\beta)$ for the address of the account that originally initiated the transaction. We assume that transactions are always initiated by externally owned accounts, as is the case in Ethereum [39]. Hence, we have $orig(\beta) \in Adr_{\text{eoa}}$.

The blockchain users send transactions in a parallel fashion. However, the transactions are uniquely ordered when recorded in the blocks, and are executed in this order. We write $\sigma \rightarrow^* \sigma'$ to express that σ and σ' are related by the reflexive, transitive closure of the binary relation induced by $\exists\beta : \sigma \xrightarrow{\beta} \sigma'$. Hence, $\sigma \rightarrow^* \sigma'$ captures the effects of executing a sequence of blockchain transactions.

We capture the history of transaction execution at a specific point in the evolvement of the blockchain state by a *trace* π. It is an alternating sequence of blockchain states and actions, starting and ending with blockchain states. We denote the set of all traces by $Trace$. We use $last(\pi)$ to represent the last blockchain state of the trace π.

We say that the smart contract c is *initial* in the blockchain state σ, as denoted by $init\text{-}ctr(a, c, \sigma)$, if the blockchain state σ is reachable from the initial state of the blockchain, and the contract has just been deployed at a and has not received any transfers or invocations in the blockchain state σ.

3.2 Strategy-Driven Transaction Execution

We use strategies to capture the intended ways in which the users attempt to interact with the blockchain.

Definition 1 (Strategies). *A* strategy *for the set as of addresses is a function* $\delta^{as} \in \mathit{Trace} \to 2^{\{\beta \in Act | orig(\beta) \in as\}}$.

Intuitively, after each possible history $\pi \in \mathit{Trace}$, the strategy gives the set of possible actions that could be performed by the accounts at the addresses in as. The strategies we consider are non-deterministic. A strategy could suggest no action to be performed, or multiple candidate actions to be picked from for execution, after an execution history of the blockchain. This kind of strategies has been employed in the security literature [25,30,40].

Example 1. Based on the understanding of the business logic of the smart contract c_{fm} (Sect. 2), the following strategy $\delta_{\text{fm-u}}^{\{usr,adm\}}$ captures a way in which the honest users may ensure the withdrawal of funds from the contract.

$$\delta_{\text{fm-u}}^{\{usr,adm\}}(\pi) := \begin{cases} \{\beta_{\text{req}}\} & \text{if } \mathit{ctr\text{-}st}(\mathit{last}(\pi), a).\mathit{status}(usr) = \bot \\ \{\beta_{\text{apr}}\} & \text{if } \mathit{ctr\text{-}st}(\mathit{last}(\pi), a).\mathit{status}(usr) = \mathit{requested} \\ \{\beta_{\text{wth}}\} & \text{if } \mathit{ctr\text{-}st}(\mathit{last}(\pi), a).\mathit{status}(usr) = \mathit{approved} \\ \emptyset & \text{otherwise} \end{cases}$$

Following this strategy, the benign user executes the action β_{req} if the status of this user is $\bot$ in the last blockchain state of the history. Furthermore, the administrator executes the action β_{apr} if the status of the benign user is *requested* in the last blockchain state of the history. Moreover, the benign user executes the action β_{wth} if the status of this user is *approved* in the last blockchain state of the history. Finally, if none of the above conditions holds for the current history, then the benign user and the administrator do not perform any action. □

We capture the execution of a transaction according to the strategy δ^{as} with $\delta^{as} \vdash \pi \to \pi'$, which is given by

$$\delta^{as} \vdash \pi \to \pi' := \exists \beta \in \delta^{as}(\pi) : \exists \sigma' : \mathit{last}(\pi) \xrightarrow{\beta} \sigma' \wedge \pi' = \pi \,\hat{}\, [\beta] \,\hat{}\, [\sigma']$$

That is, the execution of a transaction according to the strategy δ^{as} extends the trace π to the trace π', if and only if there is an action β allowed by δ^{as} for the history π, such that the execution of β from the last blockchain state of π results in the blockchain state σ', and the trace π' is obtained by appending β and σ' to the trace π in order. In the definition, an expression of the form $[\triangledown]$ represents a singleton sequence containing the element $\triangledown$. The operator $\hat{}$ gives the concatenation of two sequences. Moreover, we write $\delta^{as} \vdash \pi \to^* \pi'$ to express that π and π' are related by the reflexive, transitive closure of the binary relation induced by $\delta^{as} \vdash \cdot \to \cdot$.

4 Definition of Strategy-Aware Liquidity

In this section, we define the strategy-aware liquidity property. The basic requirement of this property is: from an arbitrary blockchain state reached after the target smart contract is initialized, the honest users may interact with the contract to decrease the balance of the contract. However, the interaction of the honest users with the smart contract is expected to be performed under potential interference by other users in the environment. This interference has potentially adversarial effects on the honest users. Hence, we model these other users collectively as an adversary. We suppose the honest users and the adversary always interact with the smart contract following their strategies. Taking strategies of both sides into consideration, we illustrate the actual requirement imposed by our liquidity property in Fig. 2.

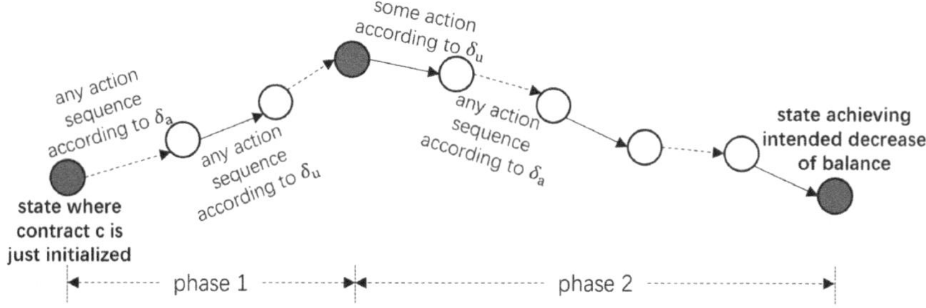

Fig. 2. Illustration of the requirements of strategy-aware liquidity.

The part annotated with "phase 1" in Fig. 2 reflects the process where the adversary and the honest users alternatingly perform actions to update the blockchain state. This process is captured with the help of the judgment

$$(\delta_{\mathrm{u}}^{as_1}, \delta_{\mathrm{a}}^{as_2}) \vdash \pi \rightsquigarrow \pi' : nxt$$

Here, π and π' are the traces before and after the alternating execution of the actions by the honest users (following the strategy $\delta_{\mathrm{u}}^{as_1}$) and the adversary (following the strategy $\delta_{\mathrm{a}}^{as_2}$). Moreover, $nxt \in \{\mathrm{u\_nxt}, \mathrm{a\_nxt}\}$ indicates whether the honest user or the adversary will execute next. The instances of this judgment are established inductively, according to the rules in Fig. 3.

$$[\text{REFL}] \quad \frac{}{(\delta_{\mathrm{u}}^{as_1}, \delta_{\mathrm{a}}^{as_2}) \vdash \pi \rightsquigarrow \pi : nxt} \quad \text{if } nxt \in \{\text{u\_nxt}, \text{a\_nxt}\}$$

$$[\text{U-EXE}] \quad \frac{(\delta_{\mathrm{u}}^{as_1}, \delta_{\mathrm{a}}^{as_2}) \vdash \pi \rightsquigarrow \pi'' : \text{u\_nxt} \quad \delta_{\mathrm{u}}^{as_1} \vdash \pi'' \rightarrow \pi'}{(\delta_{\mathrm{u}}^{as_1}, \delta_{\mathrm{a}}^{as_2}) \vdash \pi \rightsquigarrow \pi' : \text{a\_nxt}}$$

$$[\text{A-EXE}] \quad \frac{(\delta_{\mathrm{u}}^{as_1}, \delta_{\mathrm{a}}^{as_2}) \vdash \pi \rightsquigarrow \pi'' : \text{a\_nxt} \quad \delta_{\mathrm{a}}^{as_2} \vdash \pi'' \rightarrow^* \pi'}{(\delta_{\mathrm{u}}^{as_1}, \delta_{\mathrm{a}}^{as_2}) \vdash \pi \rightsquigarrow \pi' : \text{u\_nxt}}$$

Fig. 3. Alternating execution of actions from honest users and adversary.

The rule [REFL] captures the effect of zero execution step. The rule [A-EXE] expresses that if the adversary should execute next, and they take zero or more steps, then the alternating execution is extended by these steps, switching the next turn back to the honest users. The rule $[textrmU - EXE]$ expresses that if the honest users should execute next, and they take a further step, then the alternating execution is extended by this step, switching the next turn to the adversary. Multiple consecutive steps by honest users are derived by jointly using the rules $[textrmU - EXE]$ and [A-EXE], since [A-EXE] allows the adversary to take zero step.

The part annotated with "phase 2" in Fig. 2 reflects that the honest users are able to decrease the balance of the smart contract c at address a, even though the adversary may interfere with the process after each transaction executed by the honest users. We capture this requirement with the predicates *usl* and *asl*. These two predicates are defined in a mutual inductive fashion, as shown in Fig. 4. In the definition, we use the predicate ϕ_{bal} to express that the intended decrease of balance for the target contract is achieved by the honest users.

$$[\text{U-BASE}] \quad \frac{}{usl(\delta_{\mathrm{u}}^{as_1}, \delta_{\mathrm{a}}^{as_2}, \pi, \sigma, a, c)} \quad \text{if } \phi_{\mathrm{bal}}(\sigma, last(\pi), a, c)$$

$$[\text{U-TRAN}] \quad \frac{\delta_{\mathrm{u}}^{as_1} \vdash \pi \rightarrow \pi' \quad asl(\delta_{\mathrm{u}}^{as_1}, \delta_{\mathrm{a}}^{as_2}, \pi', \sigma, a, c)}{usl(\delta_{\mathrm{u}}^{as_1}, \delta_{\mathrm{a}}^{as_2}, \pi, \sigma, a, c)}$$

$$[\text{A-BASE}] \quad \frac{}{asl(\delta_{\mathrm{u}}^{as_1}, \delta_{\mathrm{a}}^{as_2}, \pi, \sigma, a, c)} \quad \text{if } \phi_{\mathrm{bal}}(\sigma, last(\pi), a, c)$$

$$[\text{A-INTF}] \quad \frac{\forall \pi' : \delta_{\mathrm{a}}^{as_2} \vdash \pi \rightarrow^* \pi' \Rightarrow usl(\delta_{\mathrm{u}}^{as_1}, \delta_{\mathrm{a}}^{as_2}, \pi', \sigma, a, c)}{asl(\delta_{\mathrm{u}}^{as_1}, \delta_{\mathrm{a}}^{as_2}, \pi, \sigma, a, c)} \quad \text{if } \neg\phi_{\mathrm{bal}}(\sigma, last(\pi), a, c)$$

Fig. 4. The rules defining the predicates *usl* and *asl*.

In Fig. 4, the rules [U-BASE] and [A-BASE] express that if $\phi_{\mathrm{bal}}(\sigma, last(\pi), a, c)$ holds, then both $usl(\delta_{\mathrm{u}}^{as_1}, \delta_{\mathrm{a}}^{as_2}, \pi, \sigma, a, c)$ and $asl(\delta_{\mathrm{u}}^{as_1}, \delta_{\mathrm{u}}^{as_2}, \pi, \sigma, a, c)$ can be derived. The rule [U-TRAN] expresses that if the honest users execute a transaction to extend the trace π to the trace π', and $asl(\delta_{\mathrm{u}}^{as_1}, \delta_{\mathrm{u}}^{as_2}, \pi', \sigma, a, c)$ can be derived, then $usl(\delta_{\mathrm{u}}^{as_1}, \delta_{\mathrm{a}}^{as_2}, \pi, \sigma, a, c)$ can be derived. The rule [A-INTF] expresses that if $\phi_{\text{bal}}(\sigma, \mathit{last}(\pi), a, c)$ does not hold, but for any trace π' resulting from zero or more transactions by the adversary starting from the trace π, $\mathit{usl}(\delta_{\text{u}}^{as_1}, \delta_{\text{a}}^{as_2}, \pi', \sigma, a, c)$ can be derived, then $\mathit{asl}(\delta_{\text{u}}^{as_1}, \delta_{\text{a}}^{as_2}, \pi, \sigma, a, c)$ can be derived.

Hence, the expression $\mathit{usl}(\delta_{\text{u}}^{as_1}, \delta_{\text{a}}^{as_2}, \pi, \sigma, a, c)$ can be interpreted as: if the honest users transact next (when the current trace is π), then there exists a way to achieve the intended decrease of balance for the target contract, relative to the blockchain state σ. The expression $\mathit{asl}(\delta_{\text{u}}^{as_1}, \delta_{\text{u}}^{as_2}, \pi, \sigma, a, c)$ can be interpreted as: if the adversary may transact next (when the current trace is π), then no matter how it behaves (in accordance to its strategy), there exists a way for the honest users to achieve the intended decrease of balance for the target contract, relative to the blockchain state σ.

We give the definition of our strategy-aware liquidity property below.

Definition 2 (Strategy-aware liquidity). *The smart contract c at address a satisfies* strategy-aware liquidity *with user strategy* $\delta_{\text{u}}^{as_1}$ *and adversary strategy* $\delta_{\text{a}}^{as_2}$, *denoted by* $SL(\delta_{\text{u}}^{as_1}, \delta_{\text{a}}^{as_2}, a, c)$, *if and only if*

$$\forall \sigma, \pi : \mathit{init\text{-}ctr}(a, c, \sigma) \wedge (\delta_{\text{u}}^{as_1}, \delta_{\text{a}}^{as_2}) \vdash [\sigma] \rightsquigarrow \pi : \text{u\_nxt} \Rightarrow \mathit{usl}(\delta_{\text{u}}^{as_1}, \delta_{\text{a}}^{as_2}, \pi, \mathit{last}(\pi), a, c)$$

Hence, the formal requirement of strategy-aware liquidity is: for any blockchain state σ that is reachable from the initial state of the blockchain and where the contract c is in its initial state, if trace π results from arbitrary execution of transactions driven jointly by the adversary and the honest users, then the honest users must be able to decrease the balance of the contract c through further transactions (following $\delta_{\text{u}}^{as_1}$) that extend π, no matter how the adversary continues to interfere with the process following $\delta_{\text{a}}^{as_2}$.

Compared with existing notions of liquidity [12,13,15,19,23,37], a salient feature of strategy-aware liquidity is that the adversary may keep interfering with the honest users' process of withdrawing funds. Intuitively, this feature is illustrated in Fig. 2 where any finite sequence of actions from the adversary may be inserted between two actions of the honest users in phase 2. Technically, the admittance of the interfering actions is captured by the rule [A-INTF] in Fig. 4.

The aforementioned feature of strategy-aware liquidity captures strengthened ability of the adversary. This feature reflects that in reality, it can be difficult to guarantee that all the transactions the honest users should execute to achieve the intended decrease in the balance of a smart contract are packaged consecutively in a block. Hence, the adversary can exert influence between two consecutive transactions executed by the honest users.

Remark 1. It may seem that the second phase in the interacting process of the honest users and the adversary as described by strategy-aware liquidity (more precisely, by *usl*) does not permit any interfering actions of the adversary before the honest users' first transaction. This is not a problem because the first phase ends with arbitrary interference according to the adversary strategy.

Remark 2. The strategy-aware liquidity property (Definition 2) can potentially be understood in the setting of two-player games (e.g., [32]). However, game theory does not directly offer tools that help with the design of the proof and refutation methods for our liquidity property (see Sect. 6). Hence, we present our concepts and results without relying on game-theoretic notions.

5 Theoretical Aspects of Strategy-Aware Liquidity

We formally establish the relationship between the strength of the adversary strategy and the strength of strategy-aware liquidity. Moreover, we establish the connection between strategy-aware liquidity and a strategy-less notion of liquidity, under specific strategies for the adversary and the honest users.

5.1 Monotonicity

Our adversary strategies specify the set of actions that can be performed by the adversary after it observes each history. Intuitively, given the same history, the more actions allowed by the adversary strategy, the stronger liquidity requirement that is imposed by the strategy-aware liquidity property. Below, we establish this result formally.

We start by defining the relative strength of strategies.

Definition 3 (Relative strength of strategies). *For two strategies δ_1^{as} and δ_2^{as} over the same set of addresses, δ_2^{as} is* at least as strong as *δ_1^{as}, as denoted by $\delta_1^{as} \preceq_{\mathrm{stg}} \delta_2^{as}$, if and only if for each trace π, it holds that $\delta_1^{as}(\pi) \subseteq \delta_2^{as}(\pi)$.*

The relation $\preceq_{\mathrm{stg}}$ is a partial order on the set of strategies for each *as*.

We establish the following result about how the relative strength of strategies affects the strength of the predicate *usl*.

Lemma 1. *If $\delta_1^{as} \preceq_{\mathrm{stg}} \delta_2^{as}$ holds, and $usl(\delta_{\mathrm{u}}^{as'}, \delta_2^{as}, \pi, \sigma, a, c)$ can be established, then $usl(\delta_{\mathrm{u}}^{as'}, \delta_1^{as}, \pi, \sigma, a, c)$ can be established.*

This lemma expresses that if $\delta_1^{as} \preceq_{\mathrm{stg}} \delta_2^{as}$, and the honest users can achieve the intended decrease of balance for the target contract under the interference from the adversary following the strategy δ_2^{as}, then the honest users can achieve the same goal under the interference from the adversary following the strategy δ_1^{as}.

We establish the following monotonicity result of strategy-aware liquidity based on Lemma 1.

Proposition 1 (Monotonicity). *If $\delta_1^{as} \preceq_{\mathrm{stg}} \delta_2^{as}$ holds, and $SL(\delta_{\mathrm{u}}^{as'}, \delta_2^{as}, a, c)$ can be established, then $SL(\delta_{\mathrm{u}}^{as'}, \delta_1^{as}, a, c)$ can be established.*

Firstly, this monotonicity result is a sanity check on the definition of strategy-aware liquidity. The result reflects the intuition that the more actions can be attempted by the attacker, the more easily a system could violate liquidity requirements. Secondly, it supports the refutation of a smart contract's liquidity property – if the contract is shown to violate strategy-aware liquidity once the adversary is permitted to perform particular actions, the contract must also violate strategy-aware liquidity if further actions could be performed by the adversary.

There are usable smart contracts that do not satisfy liquidity requirements if the adversary may act arbitrarily. However, if an action by the adversary is unlikely to occur in reality, we can consider a weakened strategy of the adversary that does not permit the performance of this action. It can be sensible to examine the satisfaction of strategy-aware liquidity under this weakened strategy. An example is with an insurance smart contract (e.g., Nexus Mutual [7]), where the adversary may in principle vote to reject a legitimate insurance claim, but it will not actually do so for fear of losing its staked crypto-assets.

5.2 Connection with Strategy-Less Liquidity

In the literature, there are notions of liquidity (e.g., considered in [19,23,37]) that disregard the distinction between the honest users and the adversary, as well as their strategies. We define strategy-less liquidity in our technical setting. We show that strategy-aware liquidity and strategy-less liquidity express the same requirements under specific strategies for the adversary and the honest users.

We refer to our strategy-less notion of liquidity as basic liquidity.

Definition 4 (Basic liquidity). *The smart contract c at address a satisfies* basic liquidity*, denoted by $BL(a, c)$, if and only if*

$$\forall \sigma, \sigma' : \mathit{init\text{-}ctr}(a, c, \sigma) \wedge \sigma \rightarrow^{*} \sigma' \Rightarrow \exists \sigma'' : \sigma' \rightarrow^{*} \sigma'' \wedge \phi_{\mathrm{bal}}(\sigma', \sigma'', a, c)$$

Hence, the requirement of basic liquidity is: for any blockchain state σ that is reachable from the initial state of the blockchain and where the contract c is in its initial state, if an arbitrary blockchain state σ' can be reached from σ through the execution of zero or multiple transactions, then there should exist a further series of transactions that update the blockchain state to σ'', where the intended decrease of the balance for the smart contract c is achieved.

We introduce the notion of a *complete strategy*. A strategy δ^{as} is complete, denoted by $\mathit{is\text{-}complete}(\delta^{as})$, if and only if

$$\forall \beta, \pi : \ (\exists \sigma' : \mathit{last}(\pi) \xrightarrow{\beta} \sigma') \wedge \mathit{orig}(\beta) \in \mathit{as} \ \Rightarrow \ \beta \in \delta^{as}(\pi)$$

We establish the following result about the connection between strategy-aware liquidity and basic liquidity.

Proposition 2 (Connection between liquidity notions). *If is-complete* $(\delta_{\text{u}}^{Adr_{\text{eoa}}})$ *holds, then for all addresses a and contracts c, we have* $SL(\delta_{\text{u}}^{Adr_{\text{eoa}}}, \delta_{\text{a}}^{\emptyset}, a, c) \iff BL(a, c)$.

This proposition expresses that if the strategy of the honest users is complete and there are no adversarial users (i.e., all users are corporative), then strategy-aware liquidity is equivalent to basic liquidity. If there exist adversarial users, however, then $usl(\delta_{\text{u}}^{as_1}, \delta_{\text{a}}^{as_2}, \pi, last(\pi), a, c)$ in the definition of strategy-aware liquidity is typically stronger than $\exists\sigma'' : \sigma' \to^* \sigma'' \wedge \phi_{\text{bal}}(\sigma', \sigma'', a, c)$ in the definition of basic liquidity, assuming $last(\pi)$ is the blockchain state σ'.

6 Proof Methods for Strategy-Aware Liquidity

We devise two proof methods that facilitate the verification and refutation of strategy-aware liquidity, respectively. We establish the soundness of both proof methods. The application of the proof methods will be demonstrated in Sect. 7.

6.1 Method for Verification

The verification of strategy-aware liquidity can be performed by a direct proof of $SL(\delta_{\text{u}}^{as_1}, \delta_{\text{a}}^{as_2}, a, c)$. However, this will involve intertwined reasoning about the behaviors of the honest users and the behaviors of the adversary. We propose sound verification conditions for strategy-aware liquidity. These verification conditions disentangle the reasoning about the behaviors of the honest users and the reasoning about the behaviors of the adversary, thereby reducing the conceptual complexity in the verification of strategy-aware liquidity.

For the design of the verification conditions, we use an *invariant condition* $\mathcal{I} \in \Sigma \times \Sigma \to Prop$. For two blockchain states σ and σ', $\mathcal{I}(\sigma, \sigma')$ captures the condition that is satisfied by σ' relative to σ. Intuitively, the invariant condition describes the condition that the current state σ' keeps satisfying relative to some state σ as transactions execute on the blockchain. In addition, we consider a *transitive, well-founded order* $\prec_{\text{vc}}$ on a set X. Recall that in a well-founded order, all the descending chains are finite. We also use a *variant function* [17] $\mathcal{V} \in \Sigma \times \Sigma \to X \cup \{\bot\}$. For two blockchain states σ and σ', if $\mathcal{V}(\sigma, \sigma') = x \in X$, then x captures the changes from σ to σ'. Intuitively, such changes should contribute to the satisfaction of the target condition $\phi_{\text{bal}}(\sigma, \sigma', a, c)$. The variant function $\mathcal{V}$ need not be defined for all pairs of blockchain states. This feature increases the level of flexibility in providing the formal definition of $\mathcal{V}$ in verification tasks.

In Fig. 5, we present the verification conditions for the strategy-aware liquidity of the smart contract c at the address a. The parameters c and a are implicit in these verification conditions. The condition *VC_B* says that for two blockchain states σ and σ', if the invariant holds and the variant gives a minimal element in the well-founded order, then the predicate ϕ_{bal} should hold on σ and σ'. Intuitively, this means if the result of the variant cannot decrease any further, then

$$
\begin{aligned}
VC\_B &:= \forall \sigma, \sigma', x \in X : \mathcal{I}(\sigma, \sigma') \wedge \mathcal{V}(\sigma, \sigma') = x \wedge \mathit{min}(x) \;\Rightarrow\; \phi_{\mathrm{bal}}(\sigma, \sigma', a, c) \\
VC\_R &:= \forall \sigma_0, \sigma : \mathit{init\text{-}ctr}(a, c, \sigma_0) \wedge \sigma_0 \to^* \sigma \;\Rightarrow\; \mathcal{I}(\sigma, \sigma) \wedge \mathcal{V}(\sigma, \sigma) \neq \bot \\
VC\_A(\delta_{\mathrm{a}}^{as}) &:= \forall \sigma, \pi, \pi', x \in X : \\
&\qquad \mathcal{I}(\sigma, \mathit{last}(\pi)) \wedge \mathcal{V}(\sigma, \mathit{last}(\pi)) = x \wedge \delta_{\mathrm{a}}^{as} \vdash \pi \to^* \pi' \;\Rightarrow \\
&\qquad\quad \mathcal{I}(\sigma, \mathit{last}(\pi')) \wedge \\
&\qquad\quad \exists x' \in X : \mathcal{V}(\sigma, \mathit{last}(\pi')) = x' \wedge (\neg \mathit{min}(x) \Rightarrow x' \preceq_{\mathrm{vc}} x) \\
VC\_U(\delta_{\mathrm{u}}^{as}) &:= \forall \sigma, \pi, x \in X : \\
&\qquad \mathcal{I}(\sigma, \mathit{last}(\pi)) \wedge \mathcal{V}(\sigma, \mathit{last}(\pi)) = x \wedge \neg \mathit{min}(x) \;\Rightarrow \\
&\qquad\quad \exists \pi' : \delta_{\mathrm{u}}^{as} \vdash \pi \to \pi' \wedge \mathcal{I}(\sigma, \mathit{last}(\pi')) \wedge \\
&\qquad\qquad \exists x' \in X : \mathcal{V}(\sigma, \mathit{last}(\pi')) = x' \wedge x' \prec_{\mathrm{vc}} x
\end{aligned}
$$

Fig. 5. The verification conditions for strategy-aware liquidity.

the honest users have achieved the intended decrease of balance for the target contract. The condition *VC_R* says that for any blockchain state that is reachable from a blockchain state σ_0 where the contract c has just been created, the invariant holds and the variant is defined. This condition provides a basis for reasoning about the strategy-driven transitions of the adversary and the honest users, as long as these transitions take place from reachable blockchain states. The condition $VC\_A(\delta_{\mathrm{a}}^{as})$ says that if the adversary executes a series of transitions according to the strategy δ_{a}^{as}, then the invariant and the well-definedness of the variant are preserved under these transitions, and the value of the variant does not increase, unless the value x of the variant before these transitions is minimal. If x is already minimal, then the condition *VC_B* helps ensure that the intended decrease of balance for the target contract is already achieved. Hence, no further reasoning is required for the verification. The condition $VC\_U(\delta_{\mathrm{u}}^{as})$ says that if the invariant is satisfied and the variant is defined and not minimal in the blockchain state σ, then the honest users can take a further transition from σ. This transition will preserve the invariant and decrease the variant.

The soundness of the verification conditions in Fig. 5 is supported by the following theorem.

Theorem 1 (Soundness of verification). *The following statement holds.*

$$
\forall \delta_{\mathrm{u}}^{as_1}, \delta_{\mathrm{a}}^{as_2} : VC\_B \wedge VC\_R \wedge VC\_U(\delta_{\mathrm{u}}^{as_1}) \wedge VC\_A(\delta_{\mathrm{a}}^{as_2}) \;\Rightarrow\; SL(\delta_{\mathrm{u}}^{as_1}, \delta_{\mathrm{a}}^{as_2}, a, c)
$$

The theorem can be used to show the satisfaction of strategy-aware liquidity for all adversary strategies or for a class C of adversary strategies. To achieve this, we define a user strategy $\delta_{\mathrm{u}}^{as_1}$ that could potentially depend on an arbitrary adversary strategy $\delta_{\mathrm{a}}^{as_2}$ (potentially restricted in the class C) and then establish the verification conditions *VC_B*, *VC_R*, *VC_U*, and *VC_A*. The validity of these verification conditions implies the satisfaction of strategy-aware liquidity by the smart contract c. Furthermore, the strategy $\delta_{\mathrm{u}}^{as_1}$ reveals how the honest users can act to ensure the intended transfer of funds out of the contract.

We sketch the proof of Theorem 1 below. For this proof, the following lemma is a key intermediate result.

Lemma 2. *The following statement holds.*

$$\forall \sigma_{\text{ref}}, \pi, \delta_{\text{u}}^{as_1}, \delta_{\text{a}}^{as_2} : \\ \begin{pmatrix} \mathcal{I}(\sigma_{\text{ref}}, \mathit{last}(\pi)) \wedge \mathcal{V}(\sigma_{\text{ref}}, \mathit{last}(\pi)) \in X \\ \wedge\ \mathit{VC\_B} \wedge \mathit{VC\_U}(\delta_{\text{u}}^{as_1}) \wedge \mathit{VC\_A}(\delta_{\text{a}}^{as_2}) \end{pmatrix} \Rightarrow \mathit{usl}(\delta_{\text{u}}^{as_1}, \delta_{\text{a}}^{as_2}, \pi, \sigma_{\text{ref}}, a, c)$$

Proof (proof of sketch). The proof of this lemma is by well-founded induction on the value x of $\mathcal{V}(\sigma_{\text{ref}}, \mathit{last}(\pi))$. If $\mathit{min}(x)$ holds, then we can derive $\phi_{\text{bal}}(\sigma_{\text{ref}}, \mathit{last}(\pi), a, c)$ using $\mathit{VC\_B}$. Hence, we derive $\mathit{usl}(\delta_{\text{u}}^{as_1}, \delta_{\text{a}}^{as_2}, \pi, \sigma_{\text{ref}}, a, c)$ using the rule [U-BASE]. Suppose $\neg \mathit{min}(x)$ holds. Then, using the condition $\mathit{VC\_U}(\delta_{\text{u}}^{as_1})$, we derive $\delta_{\text{u}}^{as} \vdash \pi \rightarrow \pi'$, $\mathcal{I}(\sigma_{\text{ref}}, \mathit{last}(\pi'))$, $\mathcal{V}(\sigma_{\text{ref}}, \mathit{last}(\pi')) = x'$, and $x' \prec_{\text{vc}} x$ for some π' and x'. Suppose $\phi_{\text{bal}}(\sigma_{\text{ref}}, \mathit{last}(\pi'), a, c)$ holds. Then, using the rule [A-BASE] and then the rule [U-TRAN], we derive $\mathit{usl}(\delta_{\text{u}}^{as_1}, \delta_{\text{a}}^{as_2}, \pi, \sigma_{\text{ref}}, a, c)$. On the other hand, suppose $\neg\phi_{\text{bal}}(\sigma_{\text{ref}}, \mathit{last}(\pi'), a, c)$ holds. Then, we have $\neg \mathit{min}(x')$ using $\mathit{VC\_B}$. Using the condition $\mathit{VC\_A}(\delta_{\text{a}}^{as_2})$, we have that for all π'', if $\delta_{\text{a}}^{as} \vdash \pi' \rightarrow^* \pi''$, then $\mathcal{I}(\sigma_{\text{ref}}, \mathit{last}(\pi''))$, $\mathcal{V}(\sigma_{\text{ref}}, \mathit{last}(\pi'')) = x''$ and $x'' \preceq_{\text{vc}} x'$ for some x''. Using the transitivity of $\prec_{\text{vc}}$, we have $x'' \prec_{\text{vc}} x$. Hence, using the induction hypothesis, we have $\mathit{usl}(\delta_{\text{u}}^{as_1}, \delta_{\text{a}}^{as_2}, \pi'', \sigma_{\text{ref}}, a, c)$. Using the rule [A-INTF] and then the rule [U-TRAN], we derive $\mathit{usl}(\delta_{\text{u}}^{as_1}, \delta_{\text{a}}^{as_2}, \pi, \sigma_{\text{ref}}, a, c)$.

To establish Theorem 1, we assume $\mathit{init\text{-}ctr}(a, c, \sigma)$ and $(\delta_{\text{u}}^{as_1}, \delta_{\text{a}}^{as_2}) \vdash [\sigma] \rightsquigarrow \pi : \text{u\_nxt}$. From the latter, we are able to derive $\sigma \rightarrow^* \mathit{last}(\pi)$. Hence, using the condition $\mathit{VC\_R}$, we have $\mathcal{I}(\mathit{last}(\pi), \mathit{last}(\pi))$ and $\mathcal{V}(\mathit{last}(\pi), \mathit{last}(\pi)) \in X$. Then, using Lemma 2, we derive $\mathit{usl}(\delta_{\text{u}}^{as_1}, \delta_{\text{a}}^{as_2}, \pi, \mathit{last}(\pi), a, c)$. This reasoning shows $\mathit{SL}(\delta_{\text{u}}^{as_1}, \delta_{\text{a}}^{as_2}, a, c)$ and establishes Theorem 1.

6.2 Method for Refutation

The refutation of strategy-aware liquidity for the smart contract c at address a can be performed by a direct proof of $\neg \mathit{SL}(\delta_{\text{u}}^{as_1}, \delta_{\text{a}}^{as_2}, a, c)$. This would involve establishing the negation of the predicate *usl* that supports the definition of strategy-aware liquidity. The predicate *usl* is defined by mutual induction with the predicate *asl*, but it would be cumbersome to set up an inductive proof to establish the negation of *usl* for each new smart contract. We propose sound refutation conditions to simplify the refutation proof for strategy-aware liquidity.

The refutation conditions are based on two invariants, $\mathcal{I}_1 \in \Sigma \times \Sigma \rightarrow \mathit{Prop}$ and $\mathcal{I}_2 \in \Sigma \times \Sigma \rightarrow \mathit{Prop}$. These conditions are presented in Fig. 6. The condition $\mathit{RC\_B}$ says for two arbitrary world states σ and σ', if either invariant holds, then the condition $\phi_{\text{bal}}(\sigma, \sigma', a, c)$ does not hold. Hence, in any blockchain state σ' satisfying $\mathcal{I}_1$ or $\mathcal{I}_2$ with a reference state σ, the intended decrease of balance for the target contract is not achieved by the honest users. The condition $\mathit{RC\_R}(\delta_{\text{u}}^{as_1}, \delta_{\text{a}}^{as_2})$ says that there exists a trace consisting of alternating execution by the adversary and the honest users such that the last state of the trace satisfies the invariant $\mathcal{I}_1$. The condition $\mathit{RC\_U}(\delta_{\text{u}}^{as})$ says that starting from a blockchain state satisfying $\mathcal{I}_1$, no matter how the honest users act according to their strategy δ_{u}^{as}, the resulting blockchain state satisfies $\mathcal{I}_2$. The condition $RC\_A(\delta_{\mathrm{a}}^{as})$ says that starting from a blockchain state satisfying $\mathcal{I}_2$, the adversary is able to update the blockchain state such that $\mathcal{I}_1$ is again satisfied.

$$
\begin{aligned}
RC\_B &:= \forall \sigma, \sigma' : (\mathcal{I}_1(\sigma, \sigma') \vee \mathcal{I}_2(\sigma, \sigma')) \Rightarrow \neg \phi_{\mathrm{bal}}(\sigma, \sigma', a, c) \\
RC\_R(\delta_{\mathrm{u}}^{as_1}, \delta_{\mathrm{a}}^{as_2}) &:= \forall \sigma_0 : \mathit{init\text{-}ctr}(a, c, \sigma_0) \Rightarrow \\
&\qquad \exists \pi : (\delta_{\mathrm{u}}^{as_1}, \delta_{\mathrm{a}}^{as_2}) \vdash [\sigma_0] \rightsquigarrow \pi : \mathrm{u\_nxt} \wedge \mathcal{I}_1(\mathit{last}(\pi), \mathit{last}(\pi)) \\
RC\_U(\delta_{\mathrm{u}}^{as}) &:= \forall \sigma, \pi, \pi' : \mathcal{I}_1(\sigma, \mathit{last}(\pi)) \wedge \delta_{\mathrm{u}}^{as} \vdash \pi \rightarrow \pi' \Rightarrow \mathcal{I}_2(\sigma, \mathit{last}(\pi')) \\
RC\_A(\delta_{\mathrm{a}}^{as}) &:= \forall \sigma, \pi : \mathcal{I}_2(\sigma, \mathit{last}(\pi)) \Rightarrow \exists \pi' : \delta_{\mathrm{a}}^{as} \vdash \pi \rightarrow^* \pi' \wedge \mathcal{I}_1(\sigma, \mathit{last}(\pi'))
\end{aligned}
$$

Fig. 6. The refutation conditions for strategy-aware liquidity.

The soundness of the refutation conditions in Fig. 6 is supported by the following theorem.

Theorem 2 (Soundness of refutation). *The following statement holds.*

$$
\begin{aligned}
&\forall \delta_{\mathrm{u}}^{as_1}, \delta_{\mathrm{a}}^{as_2} : RC\_B \wedge RC\_R(\delta_{\mathrm{u}}^{as_1}, \delta_{\mathrm{a}}^{as_2}) \wedge RC\_U(\delta_{\mathrm{u}}^{as_1}) \wedge RC\_A(\delta_{\mathrm{a}}^{as_2}) \Rightarrow \\
&\qquad \neg SL(\delta_{\mathrm{u}}^{as_1}, \delta_{\mathrm{a}}^{as_2}, a, c)
\end{aligned}
$$

This theorem can be used to show that strategy-aware liquidity is violated by a smart contract irrespective of the honest users' strategy. To achieve this, we define an attacker strategy $\delta_{\mathrm{a}}^{as_2}$ that could potentially depend on an arbitrary strategy $\delta_{\mathrm{u}}^{as_1}$ of the honest users, and then establish the refutation conditions RC_B, RC_R, RC_U, and RC_A. The validity of these refutation conditions implies the violation of strategy-aware liquidity. Furthermore, the definition of the strategy $\delta_{\mathrm{a}}^{as_2}$ explains the liquidity vulnerability of the target smart contract.

For the proof of Theorem 2, the lemma below is a key intermediate result.

Lemma 3. *The following statement holds.*

$$
\begin{aligned}
&\forall \delta_{\mathrm{u}}^{as_1}, \delta_{\mathrm{a}}^{as_2}, \pi, \sigma_{\mathrm{ref}}, a, c : \\
&\quad \left(\begin{array}{l} usl(\delta_{\mathrm{u}}^{as_1}, \delta_{\mathrm{a}}^{as_2}, \pi, \sigma_{\mathrm{ref}}, a, c) \Rightarrow \\ (RC\_B \wedge RC\_U(\delta_{\mathrm{u}}^{as_1}) \wedge RC\_A(\delta_{\mathrm{a}}^{as_2}) \wedge \mathcal{I}_1(\sigma_{\mathrm{ref}}, \mathit{last}(\pi)) \Rightarrow \mathsf{false}) \end{array} \right) \wedge \\
&\quad \left(\begin{array}{l} asl(\delta_{\mathrm{u}}^{as_1}, \delta_{\mathrm{a}}^{as_2}, \pi, \sigma_{\mathrm{ref}}, a, c) \Rightarrow \\ (RC\_B \wedge RC\_U(\delta_{\mathrm{u}}^{as_1}) \wedge RC\_A(\delta_{\mathrm{a}}^{as_2}) \wedge \mathcal{I}_2(\sigma_{\mathrm{ref}}, \mathit{last}(\pi)) \Rightarrow \mathsf{false}) \end{array} \right)
\end{aligned}
$$

This lemma can be proven by mutual induction on *usl* and *asl*. We omit the details about this proof.

To establish Theorem 2, we show that under the assumption of $\mathit{init\text{-}ctr}(a, c, \sigma)$, there exists a trace π, such that $(\delta_{\mathrm{u}}^{as_1}, \delta_{\mathrm{a}}^{as_2}) \vdash [\sigma] \rightsquigarrow \pi : \mathrm{u\_nxt}$ but not $usl(\delta_{\mathrm{u}}^{as_1}, \delta_{\mathrm{a}}^{as_2}, \pi, \mathit{last}(\pi), a, c)$. Using $RC\_R(\delta_{\mathrm{u}}^{as_1}, \delta_{\mathrm{a}}^{as_2})$, there exists π such that $(\delta_{\mathrm{u}}^{as_1}, \delta_{\mathrm{a}}^{as_2}) \vdash [\sigma] \rightsquigarrow \pi : \mathrm{u\_nxt}$ and $\mathcal{I}_1(\mathit{last}(\pi), \mathit{last}(\pi))$. Hence, using Lemma 3, we deduce that the condition $usl(\delta_{\mathrm{u}}^{as_1}, \delta_{\mathrm{a}}^{as_2}, \pi, \mathit{last}(\pi), a, c)$ does not hold.

7 Evaluation of the Proof Methods

We mechanize the proof methods proposed in Sect. 6 based on the ConCert framework [16] in the Rocq prover. We apply the mechanized proof methods in verifying or refuting strategy-aware liquidity for four example smart contracts.

7.1 The Motivating Examples

Using the proof method in Sect. 6.1, we verify that the smart contract c_{fm} in Sect. 2 satisfies strategy-aware liquidity under any adversary strategy, as long as the honest users follow the strategy $\delta_{\text{fm-u}}^{\{usr,adm\}}$ in Example 1.

The contract c_{fm} goes through several status changes for the benign user, until the benign user is able to withdraw funds from the contract. We reflect these status changes by the decrease of the variant. Since the relevant statuses for c_{fm} are simple, we define the variant to give optional natural numbers, and define the well-founded order $\prec_{\text{vc}}$ between the results to be the "less than" order of natural numbers. The definition of the variant is given below.

$$\mathcal{V}_{\text{fm}}(\sigma,\sigma') := \begin{cases} 3 & \text{if } \mathit{ctr\text{-}st}(\sigma',a).\mathit{status}(\mathit{usr}) = \bot \wedge \mathit{balance}(\sigma',a) > 0 \\ 2 & \text{if } \mathit{ctr\text{-}st}(\sigma',a).\mathit{status}(\mathit{usr}) = \mathit{requested} \\ 1 & \text{if } \mathit{ctr\text{-}st}(\sigma',a).\mathit{status}(\mathit{usr}) = \mathit{approved} \\ 0 & \text{if } \mathit{ctr\text{-}st}(\sigma',a).\mathit{status}(\mathit{usr}) = \bot \wedge \mathit{balance}(\sigma',a) \le 0 \\ \bot & \text{otherwise} \end{cases}.$$

We define the invariant $\mathcal{I}_{\text{fm}}$ to say that the administrator recorded in the state of the contract c_{fm} is the user designated as the administrator upon the initialization of c_{fm}. This reflects that the adversary cannot usurp the authority of the administrator and cause state changes that increase the variant (e.g., rejecting the benign user's withdrawal request by changing its status from *requested* to $\bot$). A special case of this definition is that $\mathcal{V}_{\text{fm}}(\sigma,\sigma') = \bot$ if $\mathit{ctr\text{-}st}(\sigma',a) = \bot$—if no smart contract exists yet at the address a in the blockchain state σ'.

The verification result for the smart contract c_{fm} is the following theorem.

Theorem 3. (Verification result for c_{fm}) *For any adversary strategy δ_{a}^{as}, it holds that $SL(\delta_{\text{fm}}^{\{usr,adm\}}, \delta_{\text{a}}^{as}, a, c_{\text{fm}})$, where a is the address of c_{fm}.*

Hence, it is ascertained that the smart contract c_{fm} satisfies liquidity requirements under the potential influence of an arbitrary adversary. Furthermore, the strategy $\delta_{\text{fm}}^{\{usr,adm\}}$ provides guidance for the honest users on how to achieve their intended withdrawal of funds from the contract.

We also show that the flawed contract $c_{\text{fm}}^{\times}$ in Sect. 2 violates strategy-aware liquidity if the adversary follows the strategy $\delta_{\text{fm-a}}^{as}$ given below, irrespective of how the honest users behave.

$$\delta^{as}_{\text{fm-a}}(\pi) := \begin{cases} \{\beta_{\text{ini}}\} & \text{if } \mathit{ctr\text{-}st}(\mathit{last}(\pi), a).\mathit{status}(\mathit{usr}) = \mathit{requested} \vee \\ & \quad \mathit{ctr\text{-}st}(\mathit{last}(\pi), a).\mathit{status}(\mathit{adm}) = \mathit{requested} \\ \emptyset & \text{otherwise} \end{cases}$$

An adversary following this strategy will re-initialize the smart contract $c^{\times}_{\text{fm}}$ if an honest user has just requested for withdrawal of funds. This will clear the recorded status *requested* for the honest users, essentially rejecting their requests.

The refutation of strategy-aware liquidity for $c^{\times}_{\text{fm}}$ is performed using the refutation method of Sect. 6.2. We instantiate the invariant $\mathcal{I}_1$ to express that the status of any user is $\perp$, and the contract $c^{\times}_{\text{fm}}$ has positive balance. We instantiate the invariant $\mathcal{I}_2$ to express that the status of the benign user and the initially designated administrator could be either $\perp$ or *requested*, the status for any other user is $\perp$, and the contract $c^{\times}_{\text{fm}}$ has positive balance. The refutation result for the smart contract $c^{\times}_{\text{fm}}$ is the following theorem.

Theorem 4. (Refutation result for $c^{\times}_{\text{fm}}$) *For any strategy $\delta_{\text{u}}^{\{usr,adm\}}$ of the honest users, $\neg SL(\delta_{\text{u}}^{\{usr,adm\}}, \delta^{as}_{\text{fm-a}}, a, c^{\times}_{\text{fm}})$ holds, where a is the address of $c^{\times}_{\text{fm}}$.*

The adversary strategy $\delta^{as}_{\text{fm-a}}$ explains the reason that $c^{\times}_{\text{fm}}$ suffers from liquidity problems. According to Theorem 1, $c^{\times}_{\text{fm}}$ also violates strategy-aware liquidity for any adversary strategy that suggests more candidate actions than $\delta^{as}_{\text{fm-a}}$ does for some of the histories. However, attacks following these alternative strategies would be more expensive than attacks following $\delta^{as}_{\text{fm-a}}$ are.

7.2 Further Verification and Refutation Examples

We consider two further smart contracts that handle financial transactions. The first is an escrow contract and the second is a honeypot contract.

Escrow Contract. We consider an escrow contract that is similar in spirit to [2]. The escrow contract holds an agreed-upon amount of digital currency for the purchase of a product. If the seller ships the product and the buyer accepts it, the digital currency in the contract will be transfered to the seller. Either the buyer or the seller may trigger a dispute in case of disagreement. The dispute can be resolved by an arbitrator, either completing the payment to the seller, or refunding the cryptocurrency to the buyer.

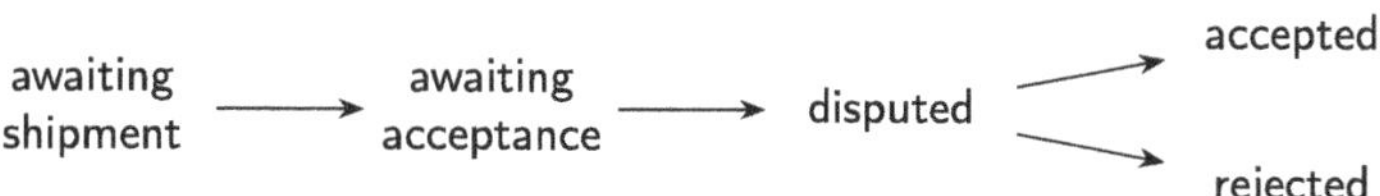

Fig. 7. The well-founded order based on the statuses of the escrow contract.

We prove the satisfaction of strategy-aware liquidity by the escrow contract under any adversarial strategy, in case the adversary is the seller or the buyer. In doing so, we also identify the strategy of the honest users that ensures the transfer of digital currency out of the contract. In applying the proof method of Sect. 6.1, we directly define the well-founded order $\prec_{\text{vc}}$ on the statuses of the escrow contract instead of mapping the blockchain states to natural numbers first. This definition is illustrated in Fig. 7. In this figure, each node is labeled with a status of the escrow contract. A path from x to x' represents $x' \preceq_{\text{vc}} x$. Hence, the use of a non-linear order as enabled by our verification method provides convenience for the liquidity verification of the escrow contract.

Honeypot Contract. We consider a honeypot contract [3,36]. The contract allows a user to set a password for manipulating the funds in the contract, under the condition that the password is not locked and the user transfers at least 1 unit of funds in the action to set the password. If the password is not locked, and a user provides the hash of the current password, then the user may lock the password. If a user is able to provide the current password, then the user may withdraw all the funds stored in the contract.

A user could attempt to profit from the honeypot contract by setting the password to their own, and withdraw all the funds using this password. However, the owner of the contract can freeze the funds of all users by updating the password and then locking it. We prove that the honeypot contract violates strategy-aware liquidity under an adversary strategy that updates the password and then locks it. In applying our refutation method, we instantiate both invariants, $\mathcal{I}_1$ and $\mathcal{I}_2$, with the condition that the balance of the contract is positive, and the password is the one provided by the adversary and is already locked.

7.3 Common Aspects, and Summary of the Proof Efforts

The verification condition *VC_R* for strategy-aware liquidity asserts the condition that should be satisfied by all blockchain states reachable from a blockchain state where a smart contract has just been initialized. The proof of such a condition is supported by the proof tactic of *contract induction* in the ConCert framework [10]. The application of this proof tactic improves the level of automation in establishing *VC_R* in our verification examples.

Both the verification condition *VC_A* and the refutation condition *RC_U* concern the effects of arbitrary transactions. Although our smart contract examples feature relatively simple business logics, the reasoning required to establish *VC_A* and *RC_U* can be non-trivial. This is because each transaction may amount to a series of actions. For instance, the execution of the action β_{wth} on the smart contract c_{fm} generates the action β_{trf}, which transfers the amount withdrawn to the account performing β_{wth}. Moreover, each call to a smart contract may be re-entrant. We identify intermediate invariants preserved by the execution of a single action to support the formal proof of *VC_A* and *RC_U*.

For the verification or refutation of strategy-aware liquidity for the smart contracts c_{fm}, $c_{\text{fm}}^{\times}$, the escrow contract, and the honeypot contract, the ratio between the LOC for contract formalization and the LOC for proof code is approximately 1 : 8.6. The proof methods provide clear guidance on how to approach and organize these verification and refutation tasks.

8 Related Work

Since liquidity issues heavily undermine the security of smart contracts, substantial recent research efforts in formal and semi-formal analysis and verification [34] have been dedicated to addressing liquidity concerns.

The Securify tool [37] is capable of verifying liquidity properties by statically checking compliance patterns in internal representations of smart contract code. The Solvent tool [12] verifies a class of liquidity properties through bounded model checking and predicate abstraction. In the target property, the maximal number of transactions that are needed to implement the desired transfer of assets can be specified. Neither work considers strategies as we do.

Bartoletti and Zunino [15] propose a liquidity property that is aware of the strategies of users and an adversary for UTxO-based Bitcoin contracts written in their BitML language [14]. They develop model checking techniques for the verification of the proposed property. They also extend their development to support recursion in BitML [13]. Compared with our present work, their property design does not address situations where an adversary could interfere with the process as honest users attempt to transfer funds out of the target smart contract.

The MAIAN tool [29] detects the bugs in smart contracts with symbolic execution. The range of detectable bugs covers locked funds. There are alternative tools that detect the same kind of bugs through static and dynamic analysis [18,21,24,33] or fuzzing [27,35]. These developments do not consider formal notions of liquidity or offer approaches to formal verification.

Other developments help obtain liquidity guarantees through built-in mechanisms of programming languages. The semantics of the Marlowe language ensures that the unspent money is returned to users by the end of any smart contract's execution [22]. This mechanism helps provide liquidity guarantees for the Cardano blockchain, which is UTxO-based. The Stipula language is equipped with types that support algorithms to verify a notion of liquidity and a weaker notion of k-separate liquidity [23]. These two developments do not consider user strategies in the liquidity requirement.

Our work differs from existing work in defining a strategy-aware liquidity property for the account-based blockchain model. A second difference is that we formally establish meta-theoretical properties of the proposed liquidity property, including monotonicity and connection with strategy-less liquidity. A third difference is that we support a deductive approach to the verification and refutation of the proposed liquidity property via sound proof methods with mechanization.

9 Conclusion

We consider the problem of verifying that a group of users is not exposed to the risk of locked funds when using a smart contract in an adversarial environment. We address this problem by formulating and enforcing liquidity properties. Technically, we define a liquidity property that is aware of the strategies followed by the users and the environment for account-based blockchains like the Ethereum.

We establish theoretical properties of the proposed liquidity property, including its relationship with strategy-less liquidity, and the relationship between its strength and the strength of the environmental strategy. We devise sound proof methods for the verification and refutation of the property. We mechanize the theories and proof methods in the Rocq prover, and apply the proof methods to smart contract examples. Our work addresses a more powerful adversary model than existing work on liquidity analysis and verification does, allowing the adversary to interrupt the honest users' process of transferring funds out of a smart contract. Our deductive approach to liquidity verification complements existing formal approaches based on model checking and static analysis.

Currently, the strategy for the honest users (resp. the adversary) needs to be manually specified in a verification (resp. refutation) of strategy-aware liquidity. A potential direction for future work is the synthesis of these strategies. Another future direction is the further improvement of proof automation to facilitate the verification or refutation of strategy-aware liquidity for complex smart contracts.

Acknowledgment. This work was partially supported by the National Natural Science Foundation of China (62272322, 62272323, 62372312, 62372311, 62002246).

Disclosure of Interests. The authors have no competing interests to declare that are relevant to the content of this article.

References

1. Critical bug identified in 88 mph awarded with $42,069 bounty. https://iosiro.com/blog/88mph-bug-bounty-post-mortem. Accessed 31 May 2025
2. Decentralized escrow. https://github.com/ShivamKumar2002/30days-of-solidity-web3compass/blob/main/day-24-decentralized-escrow/DecentralizedEscrow.sol. Accessed 31 Oct 2025
3. Etherscan – Gift_1_ETH contract. https://etherscan.io/address/0xd8993f49f372bb014fb088eabec95cfdc795cbf6. Accessed 5 June 2025
4. Etherscan – Rubixi contract. https://etherscan.io/address/0xe82719202e5965Cf5D9B6673B7503a3b92DE20be. Accessed 31 May 2025
5. Extended version of the article and mechanization of the development. https://github.com/lixm/liquidity
6. How Akutar NFT loses 34M USD. https://blocksecteam.medium.com/how-akutar-nft-loses-34m-usd-60d6cb053dff. Accessed 10 June 2025
7. Nexus Mutual – claim assessment. https://docs.nexusmutual.io/protocol/claims-assessment. Accessed 27 May 2025
8. Parity wallet hack: What, when and how? https://medium.com/@web3author/parity-wallet-hack-demystified-all-you-need-to-know-91b8dcb5b81. Accessed 10 June 2025
9. ROCQ. https://rocq-prover.org/. Accessed 25 Aug 2025
10. Annenkov, D., Nielsen, J.B., Spitters, B.: ConCert: a smart contract certification framework in COQ. In: the 9th ACM SIGPLAN International Conference on Certified Programs and Proofs (CPP), pp. 215–228 (2020)

11. Atzei, N., Bartoletti, M., Cimoli, T.: A survey of attacks on Ethereum smart contracts (SoK). In: the 6th International Conference on Principles of Security and Trust (POST), Held as Part of ETAPS, pp. 164–186 (2017)
12. Bartoletti, M., Ferrando, A., Lipparini, E., Malvone, V.: Solvent: liquidity verification of smart contracts. In: International Conference on Integrated Formal Methods (IFM), pp. 256–266 (2024)
13. Bartoletti, M., Lande, S., Murgia, M., Zunino, R.: Verifying liquidity of recursive Bitcoin contracts. Log. Methods Comput. Sci. **18** (2022)
14. Bartoletti, M., Zunino, R.: BitML: a calculus for Bitcoin smart contracts. In: the 2018 ACM SIGSAC Conference on Computer and Communications Security (CCS), pp. 83–100 (2018)
15. Bartoletti, M., Zunino, R.: Verifying liquidity of Bitcoin contracts. In: International Conference on Principles of Security and Trust (POST), Held as Part of ETAPS, pp. 222–247 (2019)
16. Bertot, Y., Castéran, P.: Interactive theorem proving and program development: COQ'Art: the calculus of inductive constructions. Springer Science & Business Media (2013). https://doi.org/10.1007/978-3-662-07964-5
17. Dijkstra, E.W.: A Discipline of Programming. Prentice-Hall (1976)
18. Feist, J., Grieco, G., Groce, A.: Slither: a static analysis framework for smart contracts. In: IEEE/ACM 2nd International Workshop on Emerging Trends in Software Engineering for Blockchain (WETSEB), pp. 8–15 (2019)
19. Ferariu, T., Wadler, P., Melkonian, O.: Validity, liquidity, and fidelity: formal verification for smart contracts in Cardano. In: The 6th International Workshop on Formal Methods for Blockchains (FMBC), pp. 1–21 (2025)
20. Kao, H.T., Chitra, T., Chiang, R., Morrow, J.: An analysis of the market risk to participants in the compound protocol. In: the Third International Symposium on Foundations and Applications of Blockchain (FAB), pp. 1–10 (2020)
21. Khan, Z.A., Namin, A.S.: Dynamic analysis for the detection of locked ether smart contracts. In: IEEE International Conference on Big Data (BigData), pp. 2466–2472 (2023)
22. Lamela Seijas, P., Nemish, A., Smith, D., Thompson, S.: Marlowe: implementing and analysing financial contracts on blockchain. In: Financial Cryptography and Data Security: FC International Workshops, AsiaUSEC, CoDeFi, VOTING, and WTSC, pp. 496–511 (2020)
23. Laneve, C.: Liquidity analysis in resource-aware programming. J. Logical Algebr. Methods Programm. **135**, 100889 (2023)
24. Li, X., Chen, T., Luo, X., Wang, C.: CLUE: towards discovering locked cryptocurrencies in Ethereum. In: The 36th Annual ACM Symposium on Applied Computing (SAC), pp. 1584–1587 (2021)
25. Li, X., Nielson, F., Nielson, H.R.: Factorization of behavioral integrity. In: The 20th European Symposium on Research in Computer Security (ESORICS), pp. 500–519 (2015)
26. Nakamoto, S.: Bitcoin: a peer-to-peer electronic cash system (2008). https://bitcoin.org/bitcoin.pdf
27. Nguyen, T.D., Pham, L.H., Sun, J., Lin, Y., Minh, Q.T.: sFuzz: an efficient adaptive fuzzer for solidity smart contracts. In: The ACM/IEEE 42nd International Conference on Software Engineering (ICSE), pp. 778–788 (2020)
28. Nielsen, J.B., Spitters, B.: Smart contract interactions in Coq. In: International Symposium on Formal Methods (FM), pp. 380–391. Springer (2019). https://doi.org/10.1007/978-3-030-54994-7_29

29. Nikolić, I., Kolluri, A., Sergey, I., Saxena, P., Hobor, A.: Finding the greedy, prodigal, and suicidal contracts at scale. In: The 34th Annual Computer Security Applications Conference, pp. 653–663 (2018)
30. Rafnsson, W., Hedin, D., Sabelfeld, A.: Securing interactive programs. In: the 25th IEEE Computer Security Foundations Symposium (CSF), pp. 293–307 (2012)
31. Szabo, N.: Smart contracts: building blocks for digital markets. https://www.fon.hum.uva.nl/rob/Courses/InformationInSpeech/CDROM/Literature/LOTwinterschool2006/szabo.best.vwh.net/smart_contracts_2.html (1996)
32. Tadelis, S.: Game Theory: An Introduction. Princeton University Press (2013)
33. Tikhomirov, S., Voskresenskaya, E., Ivanitskiy, I., Takhaviev, R., Marchenko, E., Alexandrov, Y.: SmartCheck: static analysis of ethereum smart contracts. In: the 1st International Workshop on Emerging Trends in Software Engineering for Blockchain, pp. 9–16 (2018)
34. Tolmach, P., Li, Y., Lin, S., Liu, Y., Li, Z.: A survey of smart contract formal specification and verification. ACM Comput. Surv. **54**(7), 148:1–148:38 (2022)
35. Torres, C.F., Iannillo, A.K., Gervais, A., State, R.: Confuzzius: a data dependency-aware hybrid fuzzer for smart contracts. In: IEEE European Symposium on Security and Privacy (EuroS&P), pp. 103–119 (2021)
36. Torres, C.F., Steichen, M., State, R.: The art of the scam: demystifying honeypots in Ethereum smart contracts. In: 28th USENIX Security Symposium, pp. 1591–1607 (2019)
37. Tsankov, P., Dan, A., Drachsler-Cohen, D., Gervais, A., Buenzli, F., Vechev, M.: Securify: practical security analysis of smart contracts. In: ACM SIGSAC Conference on Computer and Communications Security (CCS), pp. 67–82 (2018)
38. Werner, S., Perez, D., Gudgeon, L., Klages-Mundt, A., Harz, D., Knottenbelt, W.J.: SoK: Decentralized finance (DeFi). In: The 4th ACM Conference on Advances in Financial Technologies (AFT), pp. 30–46 (2022)
39. Wood, G.: Ethereum: a secure decentralised generalised transaction ledger. https://ethereum.github.io/yellowpaper/paper.pdf
40. Yao, J., Li, S., Yin, X.: Sensor deception attacks against security in supervisory control systems. Automatica **159**, 111330 (2024)

A Program Logic for Byzantine-Fault-Tolerant Protocols

Yuwen Kuang, Hongjin Liang, and Xinyu Feng(✉)

State Key Laboratory for Novel Software Technology, Nanjing University, Nanjing, Jiangsu, China
kyw@smail.nju.edu.cn, {hongjin,xyfeng}@mail.nju.edu.cn

Abstract. Byzantine-fault-tolerant (BFT) protocols allow distributed systems to function correctly even when some of the nodes act maliciously. Byzantine linearizability, as an extension of linearizability in the presence of faulty nodes, is often used as the correctness criterion for BFT protocols. In this paper, we propose a program logic for verifying Byzantine linearizability. We reason about the effects of faulty nodes using a helping mechanism that instruments the protocol code with abstract operations that model the faulty nodes' behaviors in the views of correct nodes. We prove the soundness of our logic by establishing a contextual refinement that is equivalent to Byzantine linearizability. We apply our logic to verify two typical BFT protocols.

1 Introduction

Byzantine-fault-tolerant (BFT) protocols are distributed protocols that can keep functioning correctly in the presence of faulty nodes which may exhibit arbitrary behaviors (i.e., Byzantine faults). BFT protocols are increasingly important, but are notoriously complex and error-prone. They usually contain multiple asynchronous rounds of message passing, with sophisticated mechanisms to handle the possibly malicious messages sent from faulty nodes.

It is even unclear what it means for a BFT protocol to be correct. On the one hand, protocol designers often create their own definitions of correctness, which are tied to specific functionality and not generally applicable. On the other hand, linearizability [9] is commonly accepted as a standard correctness criterion for concurrent objects. It relates the concurrent execution of object implementations (i.e. the *concrete* level) to the execution of their sequential specifications (i.e. the *abstract* level), but the executions assume the absence of faulty clients (that is, all clients access the shared object through the object methods only).

As a result, people propose correctness criteria [8,16,19] that extend linearizability to take faulty nodes into account. At the core of their definitions is the safety requirement, which we will call "*Byzantine linearizability*" in this paper. It says that 1) linearizability holds in the absence of faulty nodes; and 2) the abstract effects of operations from faulty nodes are *harmless* from the view of correct nodes. Harmlessness means that what correct nodes observe can

A. Goharshady and C. Haase (Eds.): SETTA 2025, LNCS 16458, pp. 363–382, 2026.
https://doi.org/10.1007/978-981-95-7826-9_19

be explained as if all nodes were correct. It requires that the abstract effects of operations from faulty nodes appear to follow the sequential specification.

The main challenge in verifying Byzantine linearizability is to reason about the effects of faulty nodes. On the one hand, the abstract effects of faulty nodes cannot be generated out of thin air. Instead, they must be traceable back to some concrete actions of the faulty nodes. On the other hand, not all the concrete actions of faulty nodes correspond to abstract effects. Even if there is correspondence, this correspondence may be indirect, in the sense that the abstract operations may take place much later and in a different order than the concrete actions. The reason is that, the messages sent from faulty nodes must be received and processed by correct nodes before they can take effect, but the network may lose messages or transmit them out of order.

In this paper, we propose the first program logic for modular verification of Byzantine linearizability. To address the above challenge, our key idea is to let the correct nodes *help* the faulty nodes. When the correct nodes see the concrete effects of the faulty nodes, they can decide what abstract operations should be used to capture the faulty nodes' effects, and when the abstract operations should be completed. We formalize the idea by introducing new auxiliary commands called **flin**, which are instrumented in the protocol code, allowing the correct nodes to help execute specific abstract operations for faulty nodes.

Our work is inspired by earlier program logics for verifying linearizability with helping mechanisms, but makes the following new contributions:

- We develop a rely-guarantee-based program logic to verify Byzantine linearizability of BFT protocols. The key novelty is the helping mechanism for reasoning about the effects of faulty nodes. We introduce auxiliary commands called **flin**, which can be instrumented in the protocol code, so that the correct nodes executing the protocol can help simulate the effects of the faulty nodes. We provide new logic rules for the auxiliary commands.
- We propose a contextual refinement that takes into account faulty clients and show it is equivalent to Byzantine linearizability. Then we prove our logic is sound by establishing the refinement via simulations. This means our logic allows reasoning about refinement in the presence of Byzantine nodes.
- We apply our logic to verify the no-duplicity broadcast algorithm [22] and the single-writer multiple-reader register algorithm (SWMR) [19].

Outline. We informally explain our ideas in Sect. 2 and then formally introduce the definition of Byzantine linearizability in Sect. 3, where we prove its equivalence to contextual refinement. We present our program logic in Sect. 4 and use it to verify the broadcast protocol and the SWMR protocol in Sect. 5. We discuss related work in Sect. 6. Full formal details are provided in the technical report (TR) [14], including semantic rules, logic rules, equivalence proofs, soundness proofs, and two example proofs.

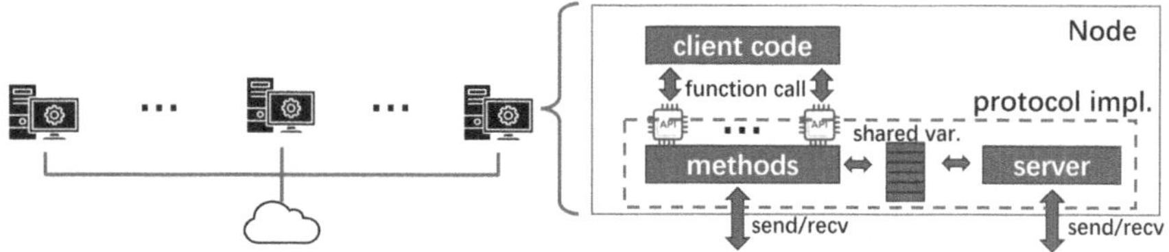

Fig. 1. System model.

2 Informal Development

2.1 System Model

We study a distributed system in which some nodes may exhibit Byzantine behavior. As shown in Fig. 1, there is a set of nodes in the network, some of which are faulty. The nodes communicate through message passing, where messages may be lost or duplicated, and no ordering is assumed.

BFT protocols run on each correct node (we do not care their execution on faulty nodes because faulty nodes can behave arbitrarily anyway). We view a BFT protocol as a concurrent object. The client on each correct node can only call the APIs of the object methods to access the functionality.

Implementation of a protocol mainly consists of two parts, a set of methods and a server. The methods can be called by the client code. On each node, there is only one client thread, which runs in parallel with the server. The server is a background thread that keeps monitoring the network, receiving incoming messages, and sending protocol messages. The methods (running in the client thread) and the server threads may share variables on the local node. They can also send messages to other nodes through the send and recv primitives.

2.2 The Motivating Example: The Broadcast Protocol

We use the broadcast protocol [22] as an example to explain the effects of faulty nodes and how we reason about them. The protocol provides a no-duplicity broadcast abstraction, which supports two operations: (1) $\mathsf{broadcast}(ts, v)$ that allows the current node t to broadcast the message v with timestamp ts, (2) $\mathsf{deliver}(t', ts)$ that allows the current node to deliver the message broadcast by node t' with timestamp ts. The no-duplicity property ensures that two correct nodes cannot deliver different messages v_1 and v_2 by calling the same $\mathsf{deliver}(t', ts)$, even if t' is a Byzantine client.

Figure 2 shows the concrete implementation of the broadcast protocol. Following our system model in Fig. 1, the implementation consists of the library code implementing the two methods (line 1 to 18), and code of the server (line 19 to 36). Each node t maintains a local MailBox which maps each message (t_{d}, ts, v) to a pair $(\mathsf{votes}, \mathsf{flag})$. Here votes is a set of nodes that agree on the message v broadcast by node t_{d} with timestamp ts, and flag is boolean and indicates whether the current node t has already delivered (t_{d}, ts, v), so as to prevent t from delivering the same message more than once. Initially MailBox is empty.

```
1: var MailBox := ∅, SentTs := ∅, Inited
   := ∅;
2: operation broadcast(ts, v) {
3:     if (ts ∉ SentTs) then
4:         SentTs := SentTs ∪ {ts};
5:         send(Nodes, (INIT, (tid, ts,
   v)));
6:         return ok;
7:     else
8:         return bad;
9:     end if
10: }
11: operation deliver(td, ts) {
12:     res := None;
13:     while (res = None) do
14:         res := getEnough(MailBox,
   td, ts, TH);
15:     end while
16:     MailBox := setFlag(MailBox,
   (td, ts, res));
17:     return res;
18: }
19: process server {
20:     while (true) do
21:         msg := recv();
22:         if (msg.tag = INIT) then
23:             (_, (t', ts', v')) := msg;
24:             if ((t', ts') ∉ Inited) then
25:                 Inited := Inited ∪ {(t',ts')};
26:                 send(Nodes, (ECHO, (t', ts',
   v'), tid));
27:             end if
28:         else if (msg.tag = ECHO) then
29:             (_, cont, t') := msg;
30:             if (cont ∉ dom(MailBox)) then
31:                 MailBox := MailBox{cont
   ⇝ (∅, false)};
32:             end if
33:             MailBox := addVote(MailBox,
   cont, t');
34:         end if
35:     end while
36: }
```

Fig. 2. The broadcast protocol.

The implementation in Fig. 2 proceeds as follows:

- When a node t calls broadcast(ts, v), it sends a protocol-level message (INIT, (t, ts, v)) to all nodes (line 5). Here Nodes denotes the set of all node IDs in the system, and tid denotes the current node ID. They are two built-in constants in every node. Note that the INIT message is at the protocol level and sent directly over the network (by **send**), while the message v in broadcast(ts, v) is at the application level and is broadcast using the protocol. The protocol also uses the local variable SentTs to record all the timestamps of sent messages to avoid duplicated timestamps (lines 3 and 4).
- When a node receives an INIT message for the first time, it sends an ECHO message to all nodes (line 26). The (ECHO, $(t', ts', v'), t$) message indicates that the current node t votes for the broadcast of v' with timestamp ts' by t'. Any subsequent (INIT, $(t', ts', \_)$) messages received by t are discarded, with the help of the local variable Inited (lines 24 and 25). This means a correct node can only vote for at most one value for each (t', ts') pair.
- When a node receives an (ECHO, cont, t') message, it records the content cont in MailBox (line 31), and adds t' into the set MailBox(cont).votes (line 33), indicating that t' votes for cont.
- When a node t calls deliver(t_d, ts), it waits until its MailBox contains enough votes for (t_d, ts, v) for a specific v (line 14). Here res is a local variable for storing the result of the deliver method, and getEnough is defined as follows:

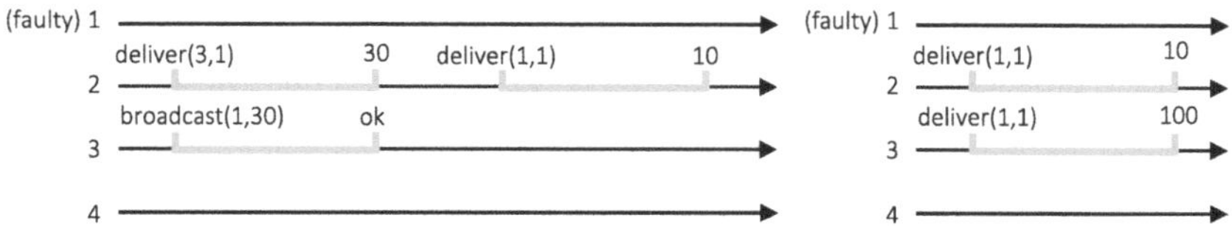

Fig. 3. Example executions on cooperating through broadcast object.

$$\text{getEnough}(\text{MailBox}, t', ts, \text{TH}) \stackrel{\text{def}}{=} \begin{cases} v & \text{if } \exists N.\ \text{MailBox}(t', ts, v) = (N, \mathbf{false}) \\ & \wedge |N| > \text{TH} \\ \text{None otherwise} \end{cases}$$

The threshold TH is a predefined real number, $(|\text{Nodes}| + F)/2$, where F is the total number of faulty nodes in the system. The protocol assumes $F \leq (|\text{Nodes}| - 1)/3$. Note that although the domain of MailBox may contain multiple distinct v values, such as both (t, ts, v_1) and (t, ts, v_2) where $v_1 \neq v_2$, the protocol ensures that there can be only one of them that obtain more than TH votes. Hence, a single evaluation of getEnough yields at most one non-None value. Finally, the current node sets the flag bit of $\text{MailBox}(t_\text{d}, ts, v)$ (line 16) to indicate that (t_d, ts, v) is delivered, and returns v.

2.3 Byzantine Linearizability

As an extension to linearizability, Byzantine linearizability requires that every method call of *correct* clients should take effect instantaneously at the linearization point (LP) between the method invocation and return. That is, correct clients' method calls should correspond to abstract atomic operations which take place at their LPs. But the sequential execution of these abstract atomic operations may not satisfy the sequential specification of the object, due to the interference from faulty nodes. Byzantine linearizability requires that such a sequential execution should be able to be made to satisfy the specification, by inserting additional abstract atomic operations. These additional operations can be viewed as the abstract effects of faulty clients.

To facilitate understanding, we present execution examples in Fig. 3. In these examples, clients are cooperating through objects that claim to implement the broadcast abstraction we introduced in Sect. 2.2. We use light yellow line segments to represent the execution of methods. The starting point is labeled with the method invocation, and the endpoint with the return value.

The left side scenario in Fig. 3 aligns with our intuitive notion of how a broadcast object should behave in the presence of Byzantine clients. Client 2 first delivers message from client 3, whose return value 30 corresponds to the first broadcast made by client 3. Then it initiates another deliver on client 1 and returns 10. Though we do not exactly know what Byzantine client 1 does (unlike client 3 performing broadcast(1,30)), its behavior can be explained by inserting an abstract broadcast(1,10) before deliver(1, 1) returns. Thus the first example is Byzantine linearizable. However, the right side scenario is not. In the right side execution, correct clients observe inconsistent values from client 1's first broadcast. Since it violates the no-duplicity property, the execution cannot be made to satisfy the specification by inserting abstract effect of the faulty client.

Why the Broadcast Protocol is (Byzantine) Linearizable, in the Absence of Faulty Nodes. When there are no faulty nodes, we can show that the broadcast protocol is linearizable by finding the LPs. For the successful call of broadcast(ts, v), the LP occurs no later than the current node sending the INIT message (line 5). For the unsuccessful call, it occurs before the return (line 8). For deliver(t_d, ts), the LP occurs after the current node receives the first ECHO message. By then, the broadcast(ts, _) method of node t_d must have been linearized, so it is guaranteed that the message being delivered must be the one being broadcast by t_d.

However, the reasoning for deliver(t_d, ts) does not apply when there are faulty nodes. If t_d is faulty, it might never have called broadcast, thus it seems unclear what message is supposed to be delivered. Even if t_d is correct, locating the LP just after receiving the first ECHO is wrong, because this message might be sent by faulty nodes with made-up content in order to mislead the current node.

2.4 What Can Faulty Nodes Do, Concretely and Abstractly?

To understand why the broadcast protocol is Byzantine linearizable in the presence of faulty nodes, we analyze what faulty nodes can do, and how the protocol tolerates their interference.

It might be natural to think that faulty nodes can send arbitrary messages. However, this is often *not* true, because BFT protocols are often accompanied by model assumptions, saying that faulty nodes cannot send messages in the identity of correct nodes. For instance, many protocols assume that messages are authenticated by digital signatures and the signatures cannot be forged, thus faulty nodes cannot send messages with correct nodes' signatures. For the broadcast protocol in Fig. 2, we can simply assume that a faulty node t cannot send an (INIT, (t', _, _)) or (ECHO, _, t') message with some correct node ID t'.

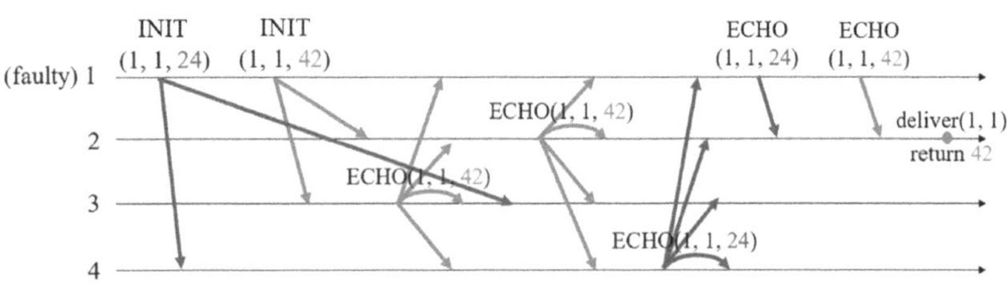

Fig. 4. An execution of the broadcast protocol. Node 2's deliver(1, 1) returns 42.

Faulty nodes may send messages without complying with the protocol. For instance, they may send ECHO messages without receiving INIT before, and they may send different messages to different nodes. Figure 4 shows an execution of the broadcast protocol, where the system contains 4 nodes, and only node 1 is faulty. We draw arrows for messages from sending to receiving, and use different colors to distinguish the values contained in the messages. At first, node 1 sends different $(\mathtt{INIT}, (1, 1, \_))$ messages to different nodes. Then, the three correct nodes send ECHO messages according to the protocol, among which node 3 echoes 42, the first INIT message it receives. Afterwards, node 1 sends two different ECHO messages to node 2. Finally, when node 2 calls $\mathsf{deliver}(1, 1)$, it would get 42, because it receives three ECHO votes for 42, exceeding the threshold $\mathsf{TH} = 2.5$.

The concrete execution in Fig. 4 seems reasonable because it can correspond to the following execution at the *abstract* level: node 1 performs $\mathsf{broadcast}(1, 42)$, and then node 2 calls $\mathsf{deliver}(1, 1)$ and returns 42. However, it is unclear why the faulty node's concrete behaviors can be abstracted as $\mathsf{broadcast}(1, 42)$ rather than $\mathsf{broadcast}(1, 24)$, since the faulty node sends both 24 and 42 concretely.

2.5 Our Idea: Helping

To determine the abstract operations of faulty nodes, we take inspiration from the helping mechanism [15,23] in linearizability verification, allowing correct nodes to determine and complete abstract operations on faulty nodes' behalf.

Specifically, faulty nodes' concrete behaviors do not immediately correspond to abstract operations. Only after they are observed by correct nodes can the faulty nodes' behaviors take effect and correspond to abstract operations. In other words, the correct nodes determine when the faulty nodes perform abstract operations and what abstract operations they perform. For the execution in Fig. 4, node 2 observes three ECHO votes for 42, so it determines that 42 is the value broadcast by node 1 at the abstract level. This determination also captures the essence of a broadcast, that it must have reached a majority of votes (ECHO messages) from correct nodes (in this execution, node 2 and 3).

To formulate this idea, we adapt the instrumentation approach in [15]. Its core is a simulation that establishes a correspondence between the execution of the algorithm code and the abstract operations. The simulation is modeled through an instrumentation semantics with certain auxiliary commands. The semantics tracks both concrete and abstract states, allowing the auxiliary commands to update abstract state so that both sides can proceed. For example, the auxiliary **linself** command is inserted at the LP. When executing **linself**, the current client's abstract operation is executed atomically.

Following the instrumentation approach, we introduce an auxiliary command $\mathbf{flin}(t, \gamma, v)$ to be inserted into the protocol code. It allows the current correct node to determine the abstract operation of the faulty node t is $\gamma(v)$ and helps complete it. For the broadcast protocol in Fig. 2, we instrument the following code just before the deliver method returns (between line 16 and 17):

if ($\mathsf{t_d} \in \mathsf{Nbad}$) **then flin**($\mathsf{t_d}$, broadcast, (ts, res));

Here, Nbad is a global auxiliary variable that records the set of faulty nodes in the system. Note that introducing Nbad here does *not* mean the correct client needs to know the set of faulty nodes, because Nbad is used only in the auxiliary code, and the auxiliary code is actually *parameterized over* Nbad. That is, Nbad is used symbolically, whose value is universally quantified in the soundness theorem of our proof method. The proof does not need to know the concrete value of Nbad. The key point of this segment of instrumented code is that only after the current node has obtained the result res can it determine and help complete the faulty nodes abstract operation by executing **flin**.

Comparison with the Helping Mechanism in Linearizability Verification. In linearizable algorithms based on helping (e.g. the elimination stack [7]), threads *cooperate*: one thread t_1 records a descriptor of its intended operation in the shared memory, and then another thread t_2 helps complete the operation when seeing t_1's descriptor. By contrast, in BFT protocols, faulty nodes *interfere* with correct nodes. That is, faulty nodes may intentionally violate the protocol, and even in this case, correct nodes should be able to interpret the faulty nodes' behaviors as some valid abstract operations. As a result, our helping mechanism requires correct nodes to determine the abstract operations of faulty nodes, as well as to help complete the operations.

3 Byzantine Linearizability and Contextual Refinement

We give a formal definition of Byzantine linearizability in this section, and show it is equivalent to a contextual refinement. The equivalence allows us to prove Byzantine linearizability via the contextual refinement.

3.1 Byzantine Linearizability

We model a distributed protocol as a concurrent object Π. The corresponding abstract atomic specification is Γ, as defined in Fig. 5. Then we write $\Pi \preceq_{\varphi,\eta} \Gamma$ to mean Π is Byzantine linearizable w.r.t. the specification Γ. Its definition is similar to standard linearizability, except that we need to insert additional abstract operations to reflect the behaviors of the faulty nodes, as explained in Sect. 2. The extra arguments φ and η are explained below.

Object Π. As shown in Fig. 5, Π consists of method implementations L (e.g. the left column of Fig. 2), server code C_s (e.g. the right column of Fig. 2) and the assumption ζ on faulty nodes' behaviors. In L, each method is defined as a pair (x, C), where x is the formal argument and C is the method body.

In the code C, the command **send**(E_1, E_2) sends the message E_2 to all nodes in the set E_1, and $x :=$ **recv**() receives a message sent to the current node and stores the message in x. Besides, a node can do local computation (e.g. $x := E$).

$$
\begin{array}{rll}
(\mathit{ODecl})\ \Pi & ::= (L, C_s, \zeta) & \\
(\mathit{MImpl})\ L & ::= \{f_1 \rightsquigarrow (x_1, C_1), \ldots, f_k \rightsquigarrow (x_k, C_k)\} & f \in \mathit{MName} \\
(\mathit{Stmt})\ C & ::= \mathbf{skip} \mid \mathbf{send}(E, E) \mid x := \mathbf{recv}() \mid x := E \mid x := f(E) & \\
 & \mid \mathbf{return}\ E \mid \ldots & \\
(\mathit{Assum})\ \zeta & \in \mathit{NodeSet} \times \mathit{MsgPool} \rightharpoonup \mathscr{P}(\mathit{Val}) & (\mathit{NodeSet})\ \mathcal{N} ::= \{t_1, ..., t_n\} \\
(\mathit{MsgPool})\ M & ::= \{(\mathcal{N}_1, v_1), ..., (\mathcal{N}_n, v_n)\} & t \in \mathit{NodeID} \\
(\mathit{OSpec})\ \Gamma & ::= \{f_1 \rightsquigarrow \gamma_1, ..., f_n \rightsquigarrow \gamma_n\} & \\
(\mathit{MSpec})\ \gamma & \in \mathit{NodeID} \to \mathit{Val} \times \mathit{AbsObj} \rightharpoonup \mathit{Val} \times \mathit{AbsObj} & (\mathit{AbsObj})\ \theta \in \mathit{Var} \rightharpoonup \mathit{Val}
\end{array}
$$

Fig. 5. Object and specification

In BFT protocols, people usually use cryptographic mechanisms (e.g. signatures) to prevent faulty nodes from doing certain bad behaviors. Instead of modeling them directly, we use ζ to specify what messages *cannot* be sent by faulty nodes. It takes the set of faulty nodes and the current message pool as input. For the broadcast protocol in Fig. 2, faulty nodes cannot send an $(\mathtt{INIT}, (t', \_, \_))$ or $(\mathtt{ECHO}, \_, t')$ message with some correct node ID t', so its ζ is defined as follows:

$$\zeta \stackrel{\text{def}}{=} \lambda \mathcal{N}_{\mathsf{bad}}, M.\ \{(\mathtt{INIT}, (t', \_, \_)) \mid t' \notin \mathcal{N}_{\mathsf{bad}}\} \cup \{(\mathtt{ECHO}, \_, t') \mid t' \notin \mathcal{N}_{\mathsf{bad}}\}$$

We let ζ take the current message pool M as input, in order to model the protocols that allow faulty nodes to forward existing messages. For instance, ζ_{ok} is defined as $\lambda \mathcal{N}_{\mathsf{bad}}, M.\ \{(\mathtt{OK}, t') \mid t' \notin \mathcal{N}_{\mathsf{bad}} \wedge \neg\exists \mathcal{N}.\ (\mathcal{N}, (\mathtt{OK}, t')) \in M\}$, saying that faulty nodes cannot send an $(\mathtt{OK}, t')$ message with t' being correct, *unless* the $(\mathtt{OK}, t')$ message has already been sent. The message pool M is a set of $(\mathcal{N}, v)$ pairs, where $\mathcal{N}$ specifies the set of nodes that v is intended to be sent to. That is, every $\mathbf{send}(\mathcal{N}, v)$ command adds a new pair $(\mathcal{N}, v)$ to the current M.

Specification Γ. Γ maps method names to their abstract operations γ, which takes the node ID, an argument value and the abstract object as arguments, and returns a value and a resulting new abstract object. The abstract object θ is shared among the nodes, and maps program variables to abstract values.

For instance, for the broadcast protocol in Fig. 2, we can define the abstract object as a mapping from a shared variable $\mathtt{POOL}$ to a finite set of abstract messages $\{(t_1, ts_1) \rightsquigarrow (v_1, \mathcal{N}_1), \ldots, (t_n, ts_n) \rightsquigarrow (v_n, \mathcal{N}_1)\}$. Here for each (t_i, ts_i), v_i is the broadcast message, and $\mathcal{N}_i$ is the set of nodes where the message has already been delivered. Γ_{B} maps $\mathsf{broadcast}$ and $\mathsf{deliver}$ to their corresponding method specification. Here we present the formal definition of $\Gamma_{\mathsf{B}}(\mathsf{deliver})$:

$$\Gamma_{\mathsf{B}}(\mathsf{deliver}) \stackrel{\text{def}}{=} \lambda t.\ \lambda((t', ts), \theta).\ \begin{cases} (v, \theta\{\mathtt{POOL} \rightsquigarrow \theta(\mathtt{POOL})\{(t', ts) \rightsquigarrow (v, \mathcal{N} \uplus \{t\})\}\}) & \text{if } \theta(\mathtt{POOL})(t', ts) = (v, \mathcal{N}) \wedge t \notin \mathcal{N} \\ \mathit{undefined} & \text{otherwise} \end{cases}$$

In detail, when the node t does the abstract operation of $\mathsf{deliver}(t', ts)$, it queries $\mathtt{POOL}$, returns the message recorded at (t', ts), and updates $\mathtt{POOL}$ to record that the message is delivered at t. If (t', ts) is not in $\mathtt{POOL}$, or if the message has previously been delivered at t, then the operation is blocked. This example illustrates why γ needs to take the current node ID as a parameter.

The Arguments φ and η. The Byzantine linearizability $\Pi \preceq_{\varphi,\eta} \Gamma$ needs to take two extra arguments φ and η. The refinement mapping $\varphi \in Mem \rightharpoonup AbsObj$ relates the initial concrete object state σ_o (with the type of Mem) to the abstract object θ. The argument $\eta \subseteq Nat \times Nat$ describes the ratio between the number of correct nodes and faulty nodes. Usually the correctness of a BFT protocol assumes an upper bound on the fraction of faulty nodes. For instance, the broadcast protocol assumes that the number of faulty nodes $F \leq (|\mathsf{Nodes}|-1)/3$. Then we can define η as $\{(n, n') \mid n > 2n'\}$.

Byzantine Linearizability of Objects. Finally we define $\Pi \preceq_{\varphi,\eta} \Gamma$ in Definition 1. It requires that every completed concurrent history H_c of Π should be Byzantine linearizable w.r.t. some abstract sequential history H' produced by Γ, i.e., $H_c \preceq^{\mathcal{N}_{\mathsf{ok}}} H'$. Here we write $\mathcal{H}_\Pi[\![t_1.C_1 \parallel ... \parallel t_n.C_n, \mathcal{N}_{\mathsf{bad}}, (\sigma_c, \sigma_o)]\!]$ for the set of histories produced by the program $t_1.C_1 \parallel ... \parallel t_n.C_n$ that uses Π, where σ_c and σ_o denote the initial client and object memory for each node respectively. $\mathcal{H}_\Gamma[\![t_1.C_1 \parallel ... \parallel t_n.C_n, \mathcal{N}_{\mathsf{bad}}, (\sigma_c, \theta)]\!]$ is the abstract counterpart, where θ denotes the initial abstract object. The program consists of correct clients $t_1.C_1 \parallel ... \parallel t_n.C_n$, where t_i is the node ID and C_i the client code. A history H is a simplified view of a program execution, formalized as a list of invocation and return events. For the concrete execution, only correct clients generate events. For the abstract execution with the abstract object Γ, both correct and faulty clients may invoke methods. Correct clients invoke methods as specified by their client code, while faulty clients may non-deterministically call methods in Γ. Each call executes atomically, producing an invocation-return event pair. Allowing the abstract history to contain events from faulty nodes is the key difference between Byzantine linearizability and the standard linearizability as in [9].

We *complete* a history H following [9] by non-deterministically appending zero or more return events to H, and then dropping the remaining pending invocations. This gives a set of complete histories, denoted $\mathsf{completions}(H)$.

Definition 1 (Byzantine linearizability of objects). *$\Pi \preceq_{\varphi,\eta} \Gamma$ iff, for all $n, t_1, \ldots, t_n, \mathcal{N}_{ok}, \mathcal{N}_{bad}, C_1, \ldots, C_n, \sigma_c, \sigma_o, \theta$, if $\mathcal{N}_{ok} = \{t_1, ..., t_n\}$, $(n, |\mathcal{N}_{bad}|) \in \eta$ and $\mathcal{N}_{ok} \cap \mathcal{N}_{bad} = \emptyset$, then*

$$\begin{aligned} &\forall H.\ H \in \mathcal{H}_\Pi[\![t_1.C_1 \parallel \ldots \parallel t_n.C_n, \mathcal{N}_{bad}, (\sigma_c, \sigma_o)]\!] \wedge \varphi(\sigma_o) = \theta \\ &\quad \Longrightarrow \exists H_c, H'.\ H_c \in \mathit{completions}(H) \wedge (H_c \preceq^{\mathcal{N}_{ok}} H') \\ &\qquad \wedge \exists C_1', ..., C_n', \sigma_c'.\ H' \in \mathcal{H}_\Gamma[\![t_1.C_1' \parallel \ldots \parallel t_n.C_n', \mathcal{N}_{bad}, (\sigma_c', \theta)]\!] \end{aligned}$$

At the core of Definition 1 is the concept of Byzantine linearizability of histories, $H \preceq^{\mathcal{N}_{\mathsf{ok}}} H'$, which is defined in Definition 2. Here $\mathcal{N}_{\mathsf{ok}}$ is the set of correct node IDs. For the program $t_1.C_1 \parallel ... \parallel t_n.C_n$, the set $\mathcal{N}_{\mathsf{ok}}$ is $\{t_1, ..., t_n\}$. The concrete history H contains events from $\mathcal{N}_{\mathsf{ok}}$ only, whereas the abstract history H' may contain events from both $\mathcal{N}_{\mathsf{ok}}$ and the faulty clients in $\mathcal{N}_{\mathsf{bad}}$.

Definition 2 (Byzantine linearizability of histories). *$H \preceq^{\mathcal{N}_{ok}} H'$ iff*

1. *$\forall t \in \mathcal{N}_{ok}.\ H|_t = H'|_t$;*

2. *there exists an injective function* π *such that* $\forall i.\ H(i) = H'(\pi(i))$ *and* $\forall i, j.\ i < j \wedge \textsf{is-ret}(H(i)) \wedge \textsf{is-inv}(H(j)) \implies \pi(i) < \pi(j)$.

Here we write $H(i)$ for the i-th event of H, and $H|_t$ for the sub-history consisting of all the events whose node ID is t. The predicates $\textsf{is-inv}(e)$ and $\textsf{is-ret}(e)$ mean that the event e is a method invocation and a return respectively. Then, Definition 2 says, when projecting to the correct nodes $\mathcal{N}_{\textsf{ok}}$, H' is a permutation of H, preserving the order of events in the same nodes and the order of non-overlapping method calls.

3.2 Contextual Refinement and the Equivalence Theorem

Below we formulate contextual refinement, another widely accepted correctness for object. Informally, the contextual refinement says, for any correct clients, the program using Π has no more observable behaviors than the corresponding program using Γ, when executing with the same set of faulty nodes $\mathcal{N}_{\textsf{bad}}$. An observable event $(t, \textbf{out}, v)$ is generated when some client executes $\textbf{print}(E)$, where t is the node ID and v the evaluation of E. We write $\mathcal{O}_\Pi[\![t_1.C_1 \parallel ... \parallel t_n.C_n, \mathcal{N}_{\textsf{bad}}, (\sigma_c, \sigma_o)]\!]$ for the set of observable event traces produced by program using Π, $\mathcal{O}_\Gamma[\![t_1.C_1 \parallel ... \parallel t_n.C_n, \mathcal{N}_{\textsf{bad}}, (\sigma_c, \theta)]\!]$ for the abstract counterpart.

Definition 3 (Contextual refinement). $\Pi \sqsubseteq_{\varphi,\eta} \Gamma$ *iff, for all* n, $t_1, \ldots, t_n$, $\mathcal{N}_{\textsf{ok}}$, $\mathcal{N}_{\textsf{bad}}$, $C_1, \ldots, C_n$, σ_c, σ_o, θ, *if* $\mathcal{N}_{\textsf{ok}} = \{t_1, \ldots, t_n\}$, $(n, |\mathcal{N}_{\textsf{bad}}|) \in \eta$, $\mathcal{N}_{\textsf{ok}} \cap \mathcal{N}_{\textsf{bad}} = \emptyset$ *and* $\varphi(\sigma_o) = \theta$, *then*

$$\mathcal{O}_\Pi[\![t_1.C_1 \parallel \ldots \parallel t_n.C_n, \mathcal{N}_{\textsf{bad}}, (\sigma_c, \sigma_o)]\!] \subseteq \mathcal{O}_\Gamma[\![t_1.C_1 \parallel \ldots \parallel t_n.C_n, \mathcal{N}_{\textsf{bad}}, (\sigma_c, \theta)]\!].$$

We can prove that Byzantine linearizability is equivalent to contextual refinemnt, i.e. Theorem 1. This is directly inspired by the classic result that linearizability is equivalent to contextual refinement [6,15]. The full proof is in TR [14].

Theorem 1 (Equivalence). $\forall \Pi, \Gamma, \varphi, \eta.\ \Pi \preceq_{\varphi,\eta} \Gamma \iff \Pi \sqsubseteq_{\varphi,\eta} \Gamma$.

4 Verifying Byzantine Linearizability

4.1 Overview of the Logic and Instrumentation

We propose a program logic to prove the contextual refinement $\Pi \sqsubseteq_{\varphi,\eta} \Gamma$, which implies the Byzantine linearizability based on the Equivalence Theorem. Following [15], the key idea is that the program logic establishes a simulation relation between the concrete implementation Π and the abstract specification Γ. In this simulation, execution of the concrete code in Π corresponds to stuttering steps that have no effects over the abstract state. When the linearization point (LP) is reached, the atomic abstract operation in Γ is executed over the abstract state correspondingly in our simulation. The execution at the concrete and the abstract levels always preserves some invariant that relates the concrete state to the abstract one.

To mark the LP in the concrete code, we introduce an auxiliary statement $\textbf{lin}(E)$ and insert it at the proper program point. Whenever it is executed, the corresponding abstract operation at the thread with ID E is executed. For faulty nodes, as explained in Sect. 2.5, we introduce an auxiliary command $\textbf{flin}(t, \gamma, v)$. It is inserted into the protocol code, which reflects the interpretation of the faulty node's behavior as an abstract operation $\gamma(v)$ by the current correct node. Crucially, these auxiliary commands do not change the concrete states nor affect the original program's control flow, unless they are inserted into the wrong places or executed with wrong arguments, which may cause the instrumented program to abort. But these incorrect uses will be prevented by our program logic.

Our program logic is based on Rely-Guarantee (RG) reasoning [11]. It ensures the overall simulation relation in a *modular* way. Specifically, users verify the protocol by proving a rely-guarantee judgment for each instrumented method and the server code. Each judgement ensures a thread-local simulation parameterized with rely and guarantee conditions. Such a simulation is compositional, in that composing these thread-local simulations gives the overall simulation.

4.2 Assertions

$$\begin{array}{rl} (Assn)\ p, q ::= & B \mid \textbf{msgPool}(E) \mid x \Rrightarrow E \mid E \rightarrowtail (\gamma, E) \mid E \rightarrowtail (\mathsf{end}, E) \\ & \mid\ p \wedge q \mid \mathsf{emp} \mid p * q \mid \ldots \\ (Action)\ R, G ::= & p \ltimes q \mid [p] \mid \mathsf{nonLocal}(R) \mid \ldots \end{array}$$

Fig. 6. Syntax of assertions.

The rely-guarantee judgments are built from assertions about relational states Σ (i.e. pairs of concrete and abstract states). We give the syntax of assertions in Fig. 6. The state assertions p and q specify the relational states Σ, consisting of states at the concrete and the abstract levels. The rely and guarantee conditions R and G specify transitions over Σs.

Our assertion language includes bool expression B, asserting B is true. We use $\textbf{msgPool}(E)$ to describe the message pool, which must be the same as E. The assertion $x \Rrightarrow E$ describes the abstract object, which contains only x with value E. As in separation logic, state assertions can be composed using separating conjunctions ($p * q$), and emp represents empty state. We describe the abstract operations of *correct* nodes using $E_1 \rightarrowtail (\gamma, E_2)$ and $E_1 \rightarrowtail (\mathsf{end}, E_2)$. For instance, we can write $(\mathsf{tid} \rightarrowtail (\mathsf{broadcast}, (ts, v))) * (\mathsf{POOL} \Rrightarrow \emptyset)$ to mean that tid needs to finish its abstract operation broadcast at an empty abstract POOL.

For rely and guarantee conditions, we use $p \ltimes q$ to mean that the initial state of the transition satisfies p and the resulting state satisfies q, and $[p]$ describes an identity transition at the state satisfying p. $\mathsf{nonLocal}(R)$ transforms the actions R of other nodes to the rely condition of the current node by ignoring the update of node-local states specified in R. More forms are presented in TR [14].

4.3 Inference Rules

Figure 7 shows the key logic rules. In addition to the top judgment $\vdash \{p, \eta\}(\Pi, \Gamma)$, we also introduce $R, G \vdash \{p\}\widetilde{C}\{q\}$ and $\vdash \{p\}\widetilde{C}\{q\}$, for reasoning about the instrumented method implementations and the instrumented server code.

Informally, the rely-guarantee judgment $R, G \vdash \{p\}\widetilde{C}\{q\}$ requires that, starting from initial states satisfying p and under the environment interference satisfying R, the transitions of $\widetilde{C}$ should satisfy G, and the final states should satisfy q when $\widetilde{C}$ terminates. Here the environment includes both the other nodes (whether correct or faulty) and the other thread within the same node.

The sequential judgment $\vdash \{p\}\widetilde{C}\{q\}$ is used to reason about atomic statements without interference with the environment.

The OBJ *Rule.* As shown in Fig. 7, the OBJ rule allows us to verify $\vdash \{p, \eta\}(\Pi, \Gamma)$ by verifying the instrumented code. The first premise $\mathsf{Er}(\widetilde{L}, \widetilde{C}_s, \zeta) = \Pi$ says that erasing the auxiliary statements of $(\widetilde{L}, \widetilde{C}_s, \zeta)$ gives us exactly Π.

Then we prepare the rely and guarantee conditions for verifying the instrumented server code $\widetilde{C}_s$ and every instrumented method's code $\widetilde{L}(f)$. We write G^{m} and G^{s} for the guarantee conditions for the method code and for the server code respectively, and write R^{m} and R^{s} for their rely conditions. As the method code and server code are replicated on every node, we assume that G^{m}, G^{s}, R^{m}, R^{s}, and state assertions p are implicitly parametrized over node IDs.

To ensure the threads of all nodes can collaborate, we check the *interference constraint*: the rely condition of each thread must permit the guarantee conditions of its environment. As we said, the environment of thread $\widetilde{C}$ on node t includes the other thread on t and all the other nodes (including both correct and faulty nodes). The guarantee condition for the faulty nodes is generated from the faulty nodes' assumption ζ in Π, using the generator GF defined below.

$$\begin{aligned}\mathsf{GF}(\zeta) \stackrel{\text{def}}{=}\ & \mathsf{Id} \vee (\mathsf{IdV} \wedge \mathsf{IdSpec} \wedge \exists M, msg. \\ & \mathbf{msgPool}(M) \wedge msg \notin \zeta(\mathsf{Nbad}, M) \wedge \mathsf{Nbad} \neq \emptyset \ltimes \mathbf{msgPool}(M \cup \{(\_, msg)\}))\end{aligned}$$

It says faulty nodes can do identity transitions (Id), or send a message allowed by ζ. Clearly, $\mathsf{GF}(\zeta)$ precisely captures the concrete behaviors of faulty nodes.

Besides this, we also check some side conditions on p, G^{m} and G^{s}. For instance, we require p_t to state that the constant variable tid is set to t, and $\mathsf{readOnlyVarProp}(\eta)$ holds. The latter says the predefined constant variables tid, Nok, Nbad and Nodes have consistent values while satisfying the node proportional relation η, formally $\mathsf{tid} \in \mathsf{Nok} \wedge \mathsf{Nodes} = \mathsf{Nok} \uplus \mathsf{Nbad} \wedge (|\mathsf{Nok}|, |\mathsf{Nbad}|) \in \eta$. Since p encodes the $\mathsf{readOnlyVarProp}(\eta)$ condition, when reasoning about the protocol code, we are able to make use of the assumption of the node proportional relation η that the correctness of the protocol relies on.

Finally, and most importantly, we reason about the instrumented server code $\widetilde{C}_s$ and every instrumented method's code $\widetilde{L}(f)$, using the rely and guarantee conditions we have just explained. The precondition p is an object invariant that should be preserved by every method call, so we use it in both the precondition and the postcondition of the method code. In addition, the precondition of the method code $\widetilde{L}(f)$ also requires that the remaining abstract operation of the current node should be $\Gamma(f)$, and the postcondition requires that this abstract operation should have been finished. For the server code $\widetilde{C}_s$, the precondition is p, and the postcondition is **true** because we do not care about its final states. In fact, the server code often does not terminate, as in the broadcast example in Fig. 2. In this work we do not care whether the code terminates or not, since our goal is to verify Byzantine linearizability, which is a partial correctness property.

$$\frac{\begin{array}{c}\mathsf{Er}(\widetilde{L}, \widetilde{C}_s, \zeta) = \Pi \qquad \textit{(interference constraint and side conditions)} \\ \text{for all } t, f: \quad R^{\mathsf{s}}_t, G^{\mathsf{s}}_t \vdash \{p_t\}\widetilde{C}_s\{\mathbf{true}\} \qquad \widetilde{L}(f) = (x, \widetilde{C}) \\ R^{\mathsf{m}}_t, G^{\mathsf{m}}_t \vdash \{p_t \wedge (\mathsf{tid} \rightarrowtail (\Gamma(f), x) * \mathbf{true})\}\widetilde{C}\{p_t \wedge (\exists v.\ \mathsf{tid} \rightarrowtail (\mathsf{end}, v) * \mathbf{true})\}\end{array}}{\vdash \{p, \eta\}(\Pi, \Gamma)} \text{ OBJ}$$

$$\frac{\vdash \{p\}\widetilde{C}\{q\} \qquad p \ltimes q \Rightarrow G}{\mathsf{Id}, G \vdash \{p\}\langle\widetilde{C}\rangle\{q\}} \text{ ATOM} \qquad \frac{\mathsf{Id}, G \vdash \{p\}\langle\widetilde{C}\rangle\{q\} \qquad \mathsf{stable}(\{p, q\}, R)}{R, G \vdash \{p\}\langle\widetilde{C}\rangle\{q\}} \text{ ATOM-R}$$

$$\text{LIN}\ \frac{[p]\gamma(E, E_1)[q, E_2]}{\vdash \{E \rightarrowtail (\gamma, E_1) * p\}\mathbf{lin}(E)\{E \rightarrowtail (\mathsf{end}, E_2) * q\}} \qquad \text{FLIN}\ \frac{p \Rightarrow (E \in \mathsf{Nbad}) \qquad [p]\gamma(E, E_1)[q]}{\vdash \{p\}\mathbf{flin}(E, \gamma, E_1)\{q\}}$$

$$\frac{}{\vdash \{E \rightarrowtail (\mathsf{end}, E')\}\mathbf{lin}(E)\{E \rightarrowtail (\mathsf{end}, E')\}} \text{ LIN-END}$$

$$\frac{}{\vdash \{\mathbf{msgPool}(E_{\mathsf{M}})\}\mathbf{send}(E_{\mathsf{N}}, E)\{\mathbf{msgPool}(E_{\mathsf{M}} \cup \{(E_{\mathsf{N}}, E)\})\}} \text{ SEND}$$

$$\frac{x \notin \mathsf{FV}(E_{\mathsf{M}})}{\vdash \{\mathbf{msgPool}(E_{\mathsf{M}})\}x := \mathbf{recv}()\{\mathbf{msgPool}(E_{\mathsf{M}}) \wedge \exists x_{\mathsf{N}}.\ (x_{\mathsf{N}}, x) \in E_{\mathsf{M}} \wedge \mathsf{tid} \in x_{\mathsf{N}}\}} \text{ RECV}$$

Fig. 7. Selected logic rules

Rules for Atomic Statements. Following RGSep [24], we have two rules for verifying atomic blocks. The ATOM rule allows us to reduce the rely-guarantee reasoning to sequential reasoning, as long as the overall transitions satisfy the guarantee condition G, and the environment consists of identity transitions Id only. To allow a more general environment R, we can apply the ATOM-R rule later, which requires that both the precondition and the postcondition be stable with respect to R. The stability is defined in the standard way:

$$\mathsf{stable}(p, R) \text{ iff } \forall \Sigma, \Sigma'.\ \Sigma \models p \wedge (\Sigma, \Sigma') \models R \implies \Sigma' \models p$$

When verifying the primitive commands, such as the concrete commands $\mathbf{send}(E_1, E_2)$, and the auxiliary commands $\mathbf{lin}(E)$, we always assume that they are wrapped in atomic blocks, and apply the ATOM and ATOM-R rules to reduce the concurrency verification to sequential reasoning. We also have other concurrency rules, which are mostly standard and omitted here.

*Sequential Rules for the **lin** and **flin** Statements.* The two rules LIN and LIN-END allow us to reason about $\mathbf{lin}(E)$. If the abstract operation γ of node E is pending, then $\mathbf{lin}(E)$ will finish it (see the LIN rule); otherwise, $\mathbf{lin}(E)$ has no effects (see the LIN-END rule). The condition $[p]\gamma(E, E_1)[q, E_2]$ in the LIN rule describes the effect of γ executed by node E with argument being E_1. It transforms the abstract objects satisfying p to new ones satisfying q, and returns E_2.

The FLIN rule allows us to reason about $\mathbf{flin}(E, \gamma, E_1)$. It requires E to be a faulty node (see the first premise $p \Rightarrow (E \in \mathsf{Nbad})$). The second premise $[p]\gamma(E, E_1)[q]$ has similar meanings as $[p]\gamma(E, E_1)[q, E_2]$, except that E is a faulty node, reflecting that executing γ is to *help a faulty node.*

*Sequential Rules for the **send** and **recv** Statements.* The SEND rule captures the atomic effect of $\mathbf{send}(E_\mathsf{N}, E)$. It puts the pair (E_N, E) into the message pool E_M.

The RECV rule says that, when the $x := \mathbf{recv}()$ command completes, x is assigned the message sent to tid in the message pool E_M. Recall that the execution of $x := \mathbf{recv}()$ would get stuck if the message pool does not contain a message sent to tid. This is fine because we care about partial correctness only. We know that *if* $x := \mathbf{recv}()$ terminates, the postcondition must hold.

Logic Soundness. Theorem 2 says $\vdash \{p, \eta\}(\Pi, \Gamma)$ implies the contextual refinement $\Pi \sqsubseteq_{\varphi,\eta} \Gamma$. As contextual refinement is equivalent to Byzantine linearizability (Theorem 1), our logic therefore ensures Byzantine linearizaibility.

Theorem 2 (Logic soundness). $\forall p, \eta, \varphi, \Pi, \Gamma.\ \vdash \{p, \eta\}(\Pi, \Gamma) \wedge \mathit{refMap}_\eta(\varphi, p) \implies \Pi \sqsubseteq_{\varphi,\eta} \Gamma$.

Here $\mathsf{refMap}_\eta(\varphi, p)$ relates the refinement mapping φ with the object invariant p. It requires that p should hold over any initial relational state Σ where the concrete and abstract objects σ_o and θ are related by φ and the number of correct and faulty nodes satisfies η.

We prove Theorem 2 by first prove our logic ensures a compositional simulation between the instrumented code $\widetilde{\Pi}$ and the specification Γ. Then, we erase the auxiliary code, and show another compositional simulation between Π and Γ. Finally, we prove adequacy of the simulation, i.e. it ensures contextual refinement.

Extensions for Supporting Future-Dependent LPs. We also introduce another two auxiliary statements to support LPs whose locations depend on future executions. Our full logic (see TR [14]) contains rules for reasoning about them. The soundness proof of the full logic is more involved, where we construct forward-backward simulations [18] to handle the future-dependent LPs.

5 Examples

5.1 Broadcast Example Revisited

In this section we give an overview of the verification of the broadcast protocol [22]. We have explained the protocol code in Sect. 2. Our goal is to prove Byzantine linearizability, $\Pi_{\mathsf{B}} \preceq_{\varphi_{\mathsf{B}},\eta_{\mathsf{B}}} \Gamma_{\mathsf{B}}$. Here the specification Γ_{B}, the refinement mapping φ_{B} and the node proportional relation η_{B} are defined in Sect. 3.1.

Code Instrumentation. We first instrument the protocol code with auxiliary commands. For the successful call of $\mathsf{broadcast(ts, v)}$, we instrument line 4 of Fig. 2 with **lin**(tid) using an atomic block, so that the current node tid's abstract broadcast operation is executed simultaneously with the concrete update of SentTs. For the unsuccessful call, we insert **lin**(tid) just before the return statement. In this case, both the concrete and abstract operations simply return bad without changing the object states.

For the call of $\mathsf{deliver(t, ts)}$, we first insert **flin**(t, broadcast, (ts, res)) if t is a faulty node just before the method returns. At this point, the current node tid has obtained sufficiently many votes for the message (t, ts, res) and set the corresponding flag bit in MailBox, so it knows that the behaviors of the faulty node t have the same effects as the abstract operation broadcast(ts, res). Afterwards, we insert **lin**(tid), which executes the current node tid's abstract deliver operation.

The Object Invariant. To verify Byzantine linearizability, $\Pi_{\mathsf{B}} \preceq_{\varphi_{\mathsf{B}},\eta_{\mathsf{B}}} \Gamma_{\mathsf{B}}$, by Theorem 1 and Theorem 2, we need to find an object invariant p which satisfies $\mathsf{refMap}_{\eta_{\mathsf{B}}}(\varphi_{\mathsf{B}}, p)$, and prove $\vdash \{p, \eta_{\mathsf{B}}\}(\Pi_{\mathsf{B}}, \Gamma_{\mathsf{B}})$ using our logic rules.

We show the definition of p below. At the core of the definition is the assertion inv, which specifies the invariant relationship between the concrete and abstract objects (defined as goodAbsPOOL) and the invariant property of the concrete message pool (defined as goodMsgPool). In addition, p_t also ensures $\mathsf{tid} = t \wedge \mathsf{readOnlyVarProp}(\eta_{\mathsf{B}})$, as required by the OBJ rule in Fig. 7.

$$
\begin{aligned}
p_t &\stackrel{\text{def}}{=} \mathsf{inv} * \mathbf{true} \wedge \mathsf{tid} = t \wedge \mathsf{readOnlyVarProp}(\eta_{\mathsf{B}}) \\
\mathsf{inv} &\stackrel{\text{def}}{=} \exists A.\ \mathtt{POOL} \Rrightarrow A \wedge \mathsf{goodAbsPOOL}(A) \wedge \mathsf{goodMsgPool} \\
\mathsf{goodAbsPool}(A) &\stackrel{\text{def}}{=} \mathsf{broadcastRelated}(A) \wedge \mathsf{InitHasLinearized}(A) \\
&\qquad \wedge \mathsf{deliverRelated}(A) \wedge \mathsf{faultyRelated}(A) \\
\mathsf{goodMsgPool} &\stackrel{\text{def}}{=} \mathsf{echoHasInited} \wedge \mathsf{uniqueECHO} \wedge \mathsf{mailboxHasECHO} \wedge \mathsf{msgFlow}
\end{aligned}
$$

The assertion goodAbsPOOL is a conjunction of the following properties. The first three properties mainly characterize the LPs of the broadcast and deliver methods. The last property faultyRelated characterizes the helping mechanism for faulty nodes. It says that if an abstract broadcast operation of a faulty node t is completed, then there must be a quorum set of nodes which have sent the corresponding ECHO messages in the concrete side.

The second key part of inv is the assertion goodMsgPool encoding the temporal ordering of concrete actions. It is a conjunction of the following properties.

First, echoHasInited says that every ECHO message sent by the current node must have been recorded in its local variable Inited. It can help us prove the preservation of uniqueECHO, which says that a correct node t' never sends multiple ECHO messages with the same (t, ts) but different values v and v'. The property uniqueECHO is quite important, because it allows us to prove that, if two correct nodes help the same faulty node t by doing $\mathbf{flin}(t, \text{broadcast}, (ts, v))$ and $\mathbf{flin}(t, \text{broadcast}, (ts, v'))$ respectively, then v and v' must be the same value. The next property mailboxHasECHO says that every vote recorded in MailBox can be traced back to an ECHO message. Then msgFlow further says that a correct node sends an ECHO message only in response to an existing INIT message.

The Proofs. By applying our logic rules, we can prove $\vdash \{p, \eta_{\mathsf{B}}\}(\Pi_{\mathsf{B}}, \Gamma_{\mathsf{B}})$. We give the detailed proofs in TR [14].

5.2 The SWMR Protocol

We verify the SWMR protocol [19], demonstrating our logic's ability to handle future-dependent LPs. The protocol implements an array REG where node t writes to REG$[t]$ via write(v) and any node reads REG$[i]$ via read(i).

In the implementation, each node maintains a local copy of the register array mReg. Writers broadcast signed, timestamped values and wait for acknowledgments from a quorum of nodes. Upon receiving a write request (ts, v) from node t, a node updates mReg$[t]$ if ts is higher than the stored timestamp. Readers execute two rounds: first gather signed timestamped values from a quorum and choose the one with the highest timestamp, then *rewrites* the selected value.

Our Verification. To apply our logic for verification, we need to first find the LPs of the methods, and also determine what abstract operation corresponds to the effects of faulty nodes and when it is completed.

For the write(v) method call, the LP is fixed and occurs when more than half of the correct nodes have acknowledged the write request.

For a read(i) call where i is correct, the LP is future-dependent, because which write the node t finally reads cannot be known statically. We handle this using a try-commit mechanism: auxiliary **trylin** statements are inserted after all concurrent writes on i to speculate possible read results, keeping both the result and the original state, and insert a **commit** statement just before read return, which commits to the correct result and discard the other speculations. When i is faulty, for whatever value v returned by read(i), we can view that the faulty node i's effect is an abstract write(v) operation. So we insert $\mathbf{flin}(\mathtt{i}, \text{write}, v)$ and also **lin**(tid) just before read(i) returns v.

We give the object invariant and the full proof in TR [14].

6 Related Work and Conclusion

Correctness Criteria for BFT Protocols. Byzantine linearizability has been used as the correctness criterion in many works about BFT protocol design (e.g. [5, 12]). It also serves as the basis for many stronger variants. Prior work [8,16,19] extends Byzantine linearizability with various recovery conditions, which basically ensure that the effects of faulty clients will disappear after their removal. Recently proposed Byzantine register linearizability [13] strengthens Byzantine linearizability with conditions designed specifically for registers. Our work focuses on verifying Byzantine linearizability. It may serve as the starting point for us to support these stronger correctness criteria in the future.

Verification of BFT Protocols. Castro and Liskov [3] prove the correctness of the PBFT algorithm by modeling the concrete implementation and the abstract specification as automata and constructing simulations between them. In a sense, our program logic can be viewed as a proof method with higher-level abstraction where the details of constructing simulation are hidden by the logic soundness proofs. We are interested in applying our logic to verify PBFT in the future.

There are works that build proper abstractions for BFT protocols. The abstract model AdoB [10] can represent both benign-fault and Byzantine-fault-tolerant protocols. Later LiDO [20] further refines AdoB and provides better support for liveness refinement. They both prove useful properties of the model, and establish refinement between concrete protocols and the model. Their refinement is largely similar to Byzantine linearizability, but against a more concrete abstraction – one expressive enough to capture behaviors for both benign-fault and Byzantine-fault-tolerance. Unlike these works, our work focus on proposing a syntax-directed program logic for verifying Byzantine linearizability (equivalent to a contextual refinement) of the protocols w.r.t. atomic specifications. When the parameter η restricts the number of faulty nodes to zero, Byzantine linearizability reduces to linearizability for benign-fault-tolerant protocols. We do not support liveness reasoning as done in their works. To reason about liveness, we need to extend our work to support infinite traces, which is left as future work.

Cirisci et al. [4] share the same goal with them and present QTree. They prove the refinement between protocol executions and QTree executions by instrumenting the protocols with LPs, as in the linearizability proofs for concurrent objects with *fixed* LPs. Our work also relies on code instrumentation for proving refinement, but our full logic supports both fixed and non-fixed LPs.

Many works have verified BFT protocols but focus on ad-hoc protocol properties [1,2,17,21,25], without proving (Byzantine) linearizability or refinement w.r.t. abstract specifications. Our program logic supports syntax-directed verification of refinement, but we have not automated or mechanized the proofs.

Conclusion. We propose a program logic for verifying Byzantine linearizability of BFT protocols. We reason about the effects of faulty nodes by introducing a helping mechanism. We prove that Byzantine linearizability is equivalent to a contextual refinement, making our logic a sound proof method for refinement under Byzantine faults. We use our logic to verify two typical BFT protocols.

Acknowledgments. We thank anonymous referees for their suggestions and comments on earlier versions of this paper. This work is supported in part by National Natural Science Foundation of China (NSFC) under Grant No. 62232015.

References

1. Bertrand, N., Gramoli, V., Konnov, I., Lazić, M., Tholoniat, P., Widder, J.: Holistic verification of blockchain consensus. In: Scheideler, C. (ed.) 36th International Symposium on Distributed Computing (DISC 2022), vol. 246, pp. 10:1–10:24. Schloss Dagstuhl - Leibniz-Zentrum für Informatik, Dagstuhl, Germany (2022). https://drops.dagstuhl.de/entities/document/10.4230/LIPIcs.DISC.2022.10
2. Carr, H., Jenkins, C., Moir, M., Miraldo, V.C., Silva, L.: Towards formal verification of hotstuff-based byzantine fault tolerant consensus in agda. In: NASA Formal Methods: 14th International Symposium. NFM 2022, Pasadena, CA, USA, May 24–27, 2022, Proceedings, pp. 616–635. Springer, Heidelberg (2022)
3. Castro, M., Liskov, B.H.: A correctness proof for a practical byzantine-fault-tolerant replication algorithm. Tech. rep., USA (1999). https://publications.csail.mit.edu/lcs/pubs/pdf/MIT-LCS-TM-597.pdf
4. Cirisci, B., Enea, C., Mutluergil, S.O.: Quorum tree abstractions of consensus protocols. In: Proceedings of 32nd European Symposium on Programming (ESOP 2023), pp. 337–362. Springer, Heidelberg (2023)
5. Cohen, S., Keidar, I.: Tame the wild with byzantine linearizability: reliable broadcast, snapshots, and asset transfer. In: Gilbert, S. (ed.) 35th International Symposium on Distributed Computing (DISC 2021), vol. 209, pp. 18:1–18:18. Schloss Dagstuhl - Leibniz-Zentrum für Informatik, Dagstuhl, Germany (2021)
6. Filipović, I., O'Hearn, P., Rinetzky, N., Yang, H.: Abstraction for concurrent objects. Theoret. Comput. Sci. **411**(51–52), 4379–4398 (2010)
7. Hendler, D., Shavit, N., Yerushalmi, L.: A scalable lock-free stack algorithm. In: SPAA'04, pp. 206–215 (2004)
8. Hendricks, J.: Efficient Byzantine Fault Tolerance for Scalable Storage and Services. Ph.D. thesis, Carnegie Mellon University, July 2009
9. Herlihy, M.P., Wing, J.M.: Linearizability: A correctness condition for concurrent objects. ACM Trans. Program. Lang. Syst. **12**(3), 463–492 (1990)
10. Honoré, W., Qiu, L., Kim, Y., Shin, J., Kim, J., Shao, Z.: Adob: bridging benign and byzantine consensus with atomic distributed objects. Proc. ACM Program. Lang. **8**(OOPSLA1), 419–448 (2024)
11. Jones, C.B.: Tentative steps toward a development method for interfering programs. ACM Trans. Program. Lang. Syst. **5**(4), 596–619 (1983)
12. Kowalski, V., Mostéfaoui, A., Perrin, M.: Atomic register abstractions for byzantine-prone distributed systems. In: Bessani, A., Défago, X., Nakamura, J., Wada, K., Yamauchi, Y. (eds.) 27th International Conference on Principles of Distributed Systems (OPODIS 2023), vol. 286, pp. 35:1–35:20. Schloss Dagstuhl - Leibniz-Zentrum für Informatik, Dagstuhl, Germany (2024)

13. Kshemkalyani, A.D., Piduguralla, M., Peri, S., Misra, A.: On constructing a byzantine linearizable swmr atomic register from swsr atomic registers. In: Proceedings of the 26th International Conference on Distributed Computing and Networking, pp. 239–243. ICDCN '25. Association for Computing Machinery, New York (2025)
14. Kuang, Y., Liang, H., Feng, X.: A program logic for byzantine-fault-tolerant protocols. Tech. rep. (2025). https://plax-lab.github.io/publications/byzlin/setta25-tr.pdf
15. Liang, H., Feng, X.: Modular verification of linearizability with non-fixed linearization points. In: Proceedings of the 34th ACM SIGPLAN Conference on Programming Language Design and Implementation, PLDI '13, pp. 459–470. Association for Computing Machinery, New York (2013)
16. Liskov, B., Rodrigues, R.: Tolerating byzantine faulty clients in a quorum system. In: Proceedings of the 26th IEEE International Conference on Distributed Computing Systems (ICDCS 2006). IEEE Computer Society (2006)
17. Losa, G., Dodds, M.: On the formal verification of the stellar consensus protocol. In: Bernardo, B., Marmsoler, D. (eds.) 2nd Workshop on Formal Methods for Blockchains (FMBC 2020), vol. 84, pp. 9:1–9:9. Schloss Dagstuhl - Leibniz-Zentrum für Informatik, Dagstuhl, Germany (2020)
18. Lynch, N.A., Vaandrager, F.W.: Forward and backward simulations: I. untimed systems. Inf. Comput. **121**(2), 214–233 (1995)
19. Malkhi, D., Reiter, M., Lynch, N.: A correctness condition for memory shared by byzantine processes. Unpublished manuscript, Sept 98 (1998)
20. Qiu, L., Kim, Y., Shin, J., Kim, J., Honoré, W., Shao, Z.: Lido: linearizable byzantine distributed objects with refinement-based liveness proofs. Proc. ACM Program. Lang. **8**(PLDI), 1140–1164 (2024)
21. Rahli, V., Vukotic, I., Völp, M., Esteves-Verissimo, P.: Velisarios: byzantine fault-tolerant protocols powered by coq. In: Ahmed, A. (ed.) ESOP 2018. LNCS, vol. 10801, pp. 619–650. Springer, Cham (2018). https://doi.org/10.1007/978-3-319-89884-1_22
22. Toueg, S.: Randomized byzantine agreements. In: Proceedings of the Third Annual ACM Symposium on Principles of Distributed Computing, PODC '84, pp. 163–178. Association for Computing Machinery, New York (1984)
23. Turon, A.J., Thamsborg, J., Ahmed, A., Birkedal, L., Dreyer, D.: Logical relations for fine-grained concurrency. In: POPL, pp. 343–356. ACM (2013)
24. Vafeiadis, V.: Modular fine-grained concurrency verification. Ph.D. thesis, University of Cambridge, Computer Laboratory, July 2008. http://www.cl.cam.ac.uk/techreports/UCAM-CL-TR-726.pdf
25. Zhao, Q., Pîrlea, G., Grzeszkiewicz, K., Gilbert, S., Sergey, I.: Compositional verification of composite byzantine protocols. In: Proceedings of the 2024 on ACM SIGSAC Conference on Computer and Communications Security, CCS'24, pp. 34–48. Association for Computing Machinery, New York (2024)

Author Index

A. Goharshady and C. Haase (Eds.): SETTA 2025, LNCS 16458, pp. 383–384, 2026.
https://doi.org/10.1007/978-981-95-7826-9

The manufacturer's authorised representative in the EU is Springer Nature Customer Service Centre GmbH, Europaplatz 3, 69115 Heidelberg, Germany. If you have any concerns regarding our products, please contact ProductSafety@springernature.com

Printed and bound by CPI Group (UK) Ltd, Croydon, CR0 4YY

07/07/2026

02160913-0011